Airlines
of Asia

Since 1920

In 1919 China ordered a considerable number of Vickers Vimy Commercials and one is seen here at Shanghai. Cecil Lewis was one of the Vimy pilots and he describes their operation in his superb book *Sagittarius Rising*.

Airlines
of Asia

since 1920

R E G Davies

PUTNAM

OTHER BOOKS BY R E G DAVIES

A History of the World's Airlines
Airlines of the United States since 1914
Airlines of Latin America since 1919
Continental Airlines — The First Fifty Years
Rebels and Reformers of the Airways
Pan Am: An Airline and Its Aircraft
Lufthansa: An Airline and Its Aircraft
Delta: An Airline and Its Aircraft
Aeroflot: An Airline and Its Aircraft
Fallacies and Fantasies of Air Transport History
Commuter Airlines of the United States
Saudia: An Airline and Its Aircraft
Transbrasil: An Airline and Its Aircraft
Charles Lindbergh: An Airman, His Aircraft, and His Great Flights

First published in Great Britain in 1997 by
Putnam Aeronautical Books,
an imprint of Brassey's (UK) Ltd., 33 John Street,
London WC1N 2AT

R E G Davies has asserted his moral right to be identified as
the author of this work.

British Library Cataloguing in Publication Data
A catalogue record for this book is available from the British Library

ISBN 0 85177 855 0

Typeset by Action Typesetting Limited, Gloucester
Printed in Great Britain by The Amadeus Press, Huddersfield, West Yorkshire

CONTENTS

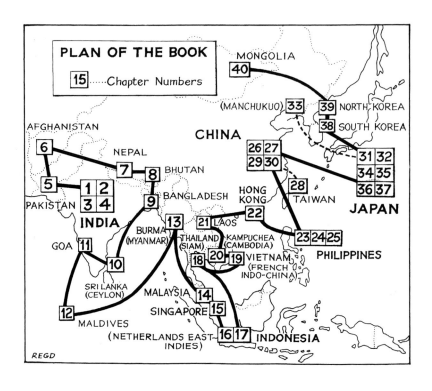

PLAN OF THE BOOK

15 ······ Chapter Numbers

MONGOLIA 40

(MANCHUKUO) 33   39 NORTH KOREA
                 38 SOUTH KOREA

AFGHANISTAN   CHINA

6   NEPAL
           7   8 BHUTAN   31 32
5   1 2   34 35
     3 4   9 BANGLADESH HONG   28 36 37
PAKISTAN   KONG TAIWAN
  INDIA   BURMA 13 21 LAOS 22   JAPAN
          (MYANMAR)
GOA 11   THAILAND KAMPUCHEA   23 24 25
         10 (SIAM) (CAMBODIA)
                  18 20 19 VIETNAM   PHILIPPINES
  SRI LANKA   (FRENCH
  (CEYLON)   MALAYSIA 14   INDO-CHINA)
12   SINGAPORE 15
  MALDIVES
     (NETHERLANDS EAST 16 17 INDONESIA
         INDIES)
REGD

26 27
29 30

Foreword

After a more than 12-hour overnight flight from London, I was *ready* to land ... despite what I'd heard about Hong Kong's Kai Tak airport. Its single runway stretching into Victoria Harbour is usually approached on a glide path over the high-rise blocks of Kowloon, sometimes so low you can almost read the labels on the laundry hanging on lines stretched between buildings over the crowded narrow streets. It takes a steady and experienced airline pilot to handle the Kai Tak approach – and even experienced passengers are slightly apprehensive despite the dramatic skyline of one of the world's most fascinating cities.

Our Boeing 747-400 had already dipped in a curve out over the South China Sea to come back and line up for Kai Tak, and I had seen something quite different – an exciting glimpse of aviation's future in the making. The aeroplane window filled with a view of the hectic activity at one of the world's largest construction projects – the huge new Chek Lap Kok airport. Its two 12,500-foot runways and ample terminal space (created partly by carving off the top of an island to reclaim a large land area a few feet above sea level) are due to replace overcrowded Kai Tak in 1998. To serve its new airport, Hong Kong is also building what is claimed to be the world's longest suspension bridge to carry a new highway and rapid transit service to make airport-to-city travel more efficient. This hugely expensive infrastructure effort – the Hong Kong Airport Core Programme – underlines the central importance of civil aviation links to the island finance and trading center. It also symbolizes the critical role that air transport has played in the economic growth of the countries of Asia.

Asian dependence on air transport is demonstrated by other new international airports, including those at Seoul, Macau, Kuala Lumpur, and Bangkok – and one on a huge man-made island near Osaka, Japan, plus increasing talk about a floating airport in Tokyo Bay. Further, massive new aircraft orders from airlines all over Asia, especially China, are needed to cope with the continued dramatic growth of air travel to, from, and within the huge region. Indeed, some of the most heavily-travelled air links in the world are found in Asia. Yet despite all this activity, the available literature on Asian air transport – especially that in English – is still remarkably skimpy. As I discovered while compiling *Commercial Air Transport Books: An Annotated Bibliography,* remarkably few books explore the often fascinating history of individual Asian airlines or airports, and many of these are often very difficult to find. This lack of material seems especially odd, considering the size, population, and importance of the region. Several countries – India, China, and Japan come to mind, with Indonesia, the Philippines, Korea, and others not far behind – should be subject to intensive study as air transport grows increasingly more central to the success of their huge economies. Yet until now, no one has attempted to tell the full and varied story of airlines in all of these and other Asian countries.

This book, the product of well over a decade's work, admirably fills that gap, relating the fascinating story of air transport development across a major part of the world, in countries large and small. And Ron Davies, doyen of air transport historians, is well equipped to write such a benchmark, given his half century of working with and writing about airlines, his travel experience (to more than 130 countries including most of those discussed here), and his extensive research files and world-wide contacts. As with his still-definitive earlier histories of the airlines of the world (1964), the United States (1972) and Latin America (1983) – each one a collector's item today – this latest 'Davies survey' of a major world region is an invaluable and readable historical resource – a record of amazing achievement. Combining an intriguing narrative which incorporates a host of specifics on first flights and aircraft particulars, descriptions of key individuals and major trends, and a unique feel for the countries discussed, Davies's new regional history is every bit as definitive as its distinguished forebears. (Given their basic research – including use of original time-tables, interviews, and other primary documentation, fact-checking, map-drawing, photo-finding, and the writing time required, little wonder that one of these definitive tomes appears only once every decade.)

Davies conducts a comprehensive trip through time and across the geography of this widely varied continent. And arranged in a logical sequence from west to east, what a journey its 40 chapters carry us on ... beginning on the warm and humid plains of India; moving out to the contrasting landscapes and aviation hinterlands of the Sub-continent, from Afghanistan and Pakistan to Burma and the Maldives; working down through southeast Asia to the thousands of islands that make up Indonesia (a country requiring air transport if ever there was one); travelling up through Thailand and the countries of Indochina, over to island Hong Kong, out to the Philippines (where airlines are like bus routes); back to vast China and concentrated Japan; finally moving on to Korea; and ending up on the dry and windy Mongolian plains bordering Siberia.

Along the way, Davies introduces us to a host of fascinating people as varied as the countries in which they operated – pioneer pilots and navigators, managers, government officials, and countless unsung heroes – along with a few shadier characters as well. We learn of Asia's first air transport efforts both in Siam (today's Thailand) and Japan in the early 1920s. Some chapters trace the development of long-range colonial flying from European capitals out to distant Asian colonies – flights by Imperial Airways to India, Singapore, and Hong Kong; KNILM to the Netherlands East Indies; and Air Orient and Air France out to French Indo-China – many of them made with flying-boat fleets of a bygone era.

The first generation of Asian air travel pioneering concluded with the amazing but now little-remembered saga of airline operations during the Second World War. Under sometimes appalling conditions, the Chinese CNAC persisted in flying – in one case with the infamous DC-2½, and in another with a bullet-riddled DC-3 called Whistling Willie. Davies demonstrates how the line between commercial and military transport flying blurred as the Japanese Army developed links to occupied areas of southeast Asia, while the Imperial Navy, often flying long-range Emily flying-boats, reached distant island bases in the South Pacific. Maps illustrate the amazing reach of these extensive Japanese scheduled air links from 1941 to 1945.

Most of this history concentrates, however, on events since 1945 as Davies follows the often complex tale of start-up air carriers, using war surplus aircraft amid crude ground conditions in the 1940s, to the introduction of improved service with longer-range propeller airliners in the 1950s, the inception of jet services in the 1960s and 1970s – reducing huge distances with shorter times – and the more recent adoption of wide-bodied jet equipment. And deregulation is evident here, too, with the rise of dozens of new companies, the takeover or demise of others, and increasing competitive pressures. Tiny countries such as Bhutan, Nepal, and Sri Lanka are given attention, while the more complex air transport stories of India, China and Japan are told in several chapters each. Given Asia's complex geography and terrain that defies easy solutions for surface transport – the driving reason for establishment of air transport in the first place – maps are crucial to understanding air routes in a region little known to most Western readers. More than seventy of Ron Davies's clear hand-drawn maps depict airline progress from pioneering short flights between little-known cities to today's globe-circling routes of giant air corporations that connect world capitals.

To absorb everything offered here will take time, but each chapter can be conveniently – and enjoyably – digested as a self-contained episode. So fasten your seatbelts, relax, and settle back for another Ron Davies-conducted journey across the miles and through the years. It is a fascinating trip.

Washington, D.C.
February 1997

Christopher H. Sterling
Associate Dean, Arts and Sciences
The George Washington University

Airlines of Asia since 1920

Author's Preface

I have to admit that, when I originally proposed to follow up *Airlines of the United States since 1914* and *Airlines of Latin America since 1919* with a third volume about Asia, I did not fully appreciate the magnitude of the task I was undertaking. I had not realized, for example, that with few exceptions, records of the past, even the recent past, are not as readily available as, for instance, in Europe or the Americas, and there are good reasons for this. Hardly a single country, with the possible exception of the Maldives, has escaped the disruption – often the destruction – of such records because of social, political, or military strife of one kind or another. Wars of liberation from colonial rule, even events of peaceful transition towards independence; internal revolutions; and a destructive world war: all these have combined to wreck havoc in those government agencies that would normally have retained precise accounts.

Secondly, when about ten years ago, I started to collect material, much of it from personal contacts that I had made during a couple of decades or so of business travelling throughout Asia, I could not have predicted the intensity of vigorous growth that would characterize air transport throughout this vast continent. Part of my task, therefore, has been to keep up-to-date with current events while striving to recapture the past. When I started this book, for example, Royal Air Nepal hardly ventured beyond its borders, and then only to Delhi and Calcutta; now it reaches into the heart of Europe and the Far East. A bare ten years ago, measured by traffic statistics, only Japan Air Lines ranked among the world's leaders, today the Asian representation in the higher echelons of world air transport matches that from Europe.

For the purposes of this book, the geographical definition of Asia has given way to a more selective one which, simply expressed, is from Afghanistan eastwards to the Pacific Rim. The structure is illustrated in the map on page vi. Middle Eastern countries, from Turkey to Iran and Saudi Arabia, have been far more closely linked with Europe; and their airlines can be categorized as a defined group in their own right. As for Siberia, accounting for half the continent, this is omitted because it is politically part of Russia; and only recently have the central Asian republics become totally independent – too late for inclusion in this book.

Throughout my researches – some of which began 40 years ago – I have been impressed by the spirit of enterprise, creativity, determination, even adventure, which has motivated the Asian countries towards the objective of providing a public transport service where little or none existed before. These ranged from the mountain villages of Nepal, where tiny airstrips challenge the best efforts of Twin Otters to find a foothold; to the alpine meadows of North Borneo (now Sabah) where Twin Pioneers used to land in pastures hardly big enough to lay down a cricket pitch; and the Merpati Nusantara flight into Wamena, in Indonesian New Guinea, which was totally inaccessible to the outside world until the advent of air transport.

I hope that I have adequately recognized the leaders whose perception and imagination laid firm foundations; the gracious J R D Tata, to whom the Indian airline industry owes so much; the genial Enver Jamall, whose steady hand guided PIA through many troubles; Wiweko Soepono, whose mercurial direction elevated Garuda to a higher plane; and not forgetting William Langhorn Bond, who steered CNAC along the path of progress, in peacetime and in war.

During the course of my researches, as with all airlines the world over, I found everywhere that spirit of dedication to the cause of air transport that drives the industry at every level. I found it among it among the pilots of Pakistan who threaded their way through the precipitous passes of the western Himalayas to reach such isolated communities as Gilgit; at Biak, where Merpati Nusantara maintained a complete DC-3 overhaul and restoration 'production line' to serve the local routes in West Irian where no aircraft, excepting that venerable Douglas machine, feared to fly; and I found it, too, among the veteran Japanese pilots whose task it once was to keep vital supply routes open throughout the short-lived Greater East Asia Prosperity Sphere, dodging United States fighters in the process.

I remember the pride with which IAC's Captain Samant related how, during the India-China skirmishes on the Tibetan frontier in the Sixties, IAC worked night and day to create instant military airlift support; and the pride of the Xi'an base staff of CAAC in being responsible for a special Ilyushin Il–18, the one that was always used by the great statesman Chou En-lai as his personal aircraft.

Altogether, I shall look back on this book as the most formidable writing assignment that I ever undertook. Yet I have no regrets whatsoever; for without the stimulation to compile the collective record of achievement, I would never have visited so many wonderful places to conduct my researches and interviews; and I would never have met so many wonderful airline people, from the truly great J R D Tata himself, to the veteran Chinese mechanic who modestly explained how he managed to keep the DC-2s on schedule, even when the Yangtse River flooded the island airport at Chingking.

Writing this book was a labour of love; researching for it was a joy; meeting the people who made the history, gave their countries a transport system, and put aeroplanes to peaceful uses was a privilege.

R E G Davies
1996

Acknowledgements

During the past decade of writing, derived from many years of research, hundreds of people, over the years, have helped, advised, and contributed to *Airlines of Asia since 1920*. They have ranged from senior executives to junior clerks, from veteran pioneers to fresh young new hires, from four-ring pilots to ramp agents. I thank them all, rank and file.

But in particular, I must select certain individuals for special mention, if only because they could have written sections of this book, at least those applicable to their own specialized experience and knowledge; but who generously shared their considerable reference resources with me.

Eiichiro Sekigawa, for example, possibly the most distinguished aviation historian and commentator in Japan, supplied material of meticulous precision, including priceless data on the activities of Japanese air transport during the Second World War. Without his generous help, Chapter 34 would have contained no more than a few bare bones of generalized observation.

For thirty years and more, through the thick and thin of the convoluted progress of Philippine Air Lines, and in his role of public relations guru, Enrique Santos kept a detailed diary. He made this available to me almost as a statutory beneficiary. I hope that my account will meet with his approval.

Bill Leary has made exhaustive and truly scholarly studies of the complex history of aviation in China, from the adventurous years of CNAC to the dangerous days of Air America and CAT. His authoritative documentation, together with that of Bodo Wiethoff (*see* bibliography) have been invaluable.

Other names to be recognized are J R D Tata, the great Indian pioneer and promoter, who, during his distinguished career as pilot, promoter, president, and elder statesman, placed on record the history of Tata and Air-India. On a personal note, I remember with considerable pride the occasion when, over an elegant tea in his suite at New Delhi's Ashoka Hotel, he shared with me some vignettes of his career.

Across the border, I was also privileged to meet Enver Jamall, who worked with J R D in the old days, before Indian Independence and before Partition. Enver rose 'from grease monkey' – as he describes his apprenticeship – to lead Pakistan's national airline. He also wrote a book that is refreshingly free from rancour, to remind us all that airline people invariably set an example of dedicated service, regardless of race, colour, creed, or political affiliation.

Vital Ferry, from Paris, provided the hitherto little-recorded early history of commercial aviation pioneering in French Indo-China, and Ian Quinn, of the Hong Kong Historical Association supplied detailed material on the first attempts to link Hong Kong and Macao by air, which, if successful, would have been the first airline operation in Asia. I would also like to thank the many staff members of the airlines in Indonesia, from Garuda, Bouraq, and Merpati Nusantara, especially.

In Asia, books of reference are few, and official airline annual reports are published on a regular basis by only a few of the leading companies. Those in the English language from which I have drawn are listed in the bibliography. But I must also give praise to the splendid volumes in the Japanese language, of encyclopaedic scope, that have been produced by Japan Air Lines and All Nippon Airways. These have been valuable sources.

I must also acknowledge the generous assistance of members of the public relations departments of the Japanese airlines, especially Geoffrey Tudor, of Japan Airlines, Tetsuo Fukuda, of All Nippon Airways; and also the veteran pilots of the various transport divisions of the Japanese military operations during the Second World War, especially the late Captain Nagano, who was so respected that a small museum has been founded to preserve his memorabilia.

Closer to home, I thank John Wegg, editor of *Airways* magazine, who has frequently supplied facts and photographs from his voluminous collection and reference system. In addition to books, many magazines have been consulted, notably *Flight International*, the *Aeroplane*, *Aviation Week*, and *Air Transport World*. And the now defunct *Exxon Air World* was for many years an authentic source.

And not least, I must thank Putnam's indefatigable technical editor, John Stroud, whose strict standards I have endeavoured to meet. As many of my fellow writers will no doubt confirm, he has been a polite but firm critic of the slightest deviation from absolute accuracy, down to the last accented vowel; but he has always provided welcome assistance and encouragement when needed. In this particular book, he has also been a great source of photographs, drawn from his own extensive collection.

Over the years, I may not have kept a strict record of all those who advised me; but I hope that they will realize that, however obscured in these pages, they have helped, for the first time, to assemble, within the covers of one book, a fascinating story of how the airlines have changed the entire history of a whole continent.

CHAPTER ONE

Airlines of Imperial India

A Decade of Apathy

In the annals of aviation history, India can lay a legitimate claim to an important achievement and a place in the record books. On 18 February 1911, the first official (as opposed to speculative attempts) air mail was carried at Allahabad. As a dramatic adjunct to the United Provinces Exhibition held at the time, Henri Piquet, flying a Humber biplane, carried mails from the Exhibition grounds to Naini Junction, a distance of six miles, taking 13 minutes for the journey, and thus, theoretically at least, and albeit by a small margin, proving that carriage by air was faster than by land. The operation, incidentally, was organized by Captain Walter Windham, who was later to organize the Coronation Post from London to Windsor.

Such pioneering was not followed up. After this brief episode, transport services in India reverted to the daily round of train timetables over one of the world's largest railway networks, and the Viceregal Government in New Delhi showed virtually no interest in aviation whatsoever, except for the use of aeroplanes in support of military movements on the Northwest Frontier, where the natives were inclined to be restless.

Throughout the 1920s, India seemed, in fact, to be regarded by Great Britain as a mere staging point on the route to the Far East and to Australia, the latter of which inspired a great deal of interest during an era when long-distance flights were the objective of many an intrepid aviator, partly because it was almost halfway round the world. Thus, many of the rare flights in southern Asia tended to go *through*, rather than *to* India. True, Major Wilfred Blake and Norman Macmillan flew from Croydon to Calcutta in 1922, but almost all the others aimed for Sydney, Melbourne, Tokyo or Shanghai, or even around the world. India was just a place to refuel and take a rest on the way.

This was especially true of the systematic survey and proving flights made by the Dutch, whose overseas territories during the Colonial Empire era were whole continents or oceans distant from the homeland. Richest of these by far were the Netherlands East Indies, the source of much agricultural and mineral wealth for the Netherlands, whose airline, KLM, quickly moved to fulfil its aspirations to link the East Indies capital, Batavia (now Jakarta, Indonesia) with Amsterdam. In pursuance of this ambitious goal, A N G Thomassen piloted a Fokker F.VII to Batavia from 1 October to 24 November 1924 (he was delayed in Bulgaria for a month after a forced landing); a KLM Fokker F.VIIa charter flight, hired by an American, Van Lear Black, made the trip in 15 days from 15–30 June 1927; and the F.VIIa/3m *Postduif* did it in ten days from 1–10 October 1927. All this work by KLM was to culminate in an impressive scheduled service operation. As a matter of interest, Allahabad, locale of the world's first air mail flight, was one of the refuelling stops for KLM, and, along with stops at other Indian cities, was to remain so throughout the pre-Second World War period.

Against this commendable Dutch enterprise, the British effort, at least in the furtherance of commercial air service, was relatively modest. Sir Alan Cobham, with the Director of Civil Aviation, Sir Sefton Brancker, did, however, make an extensive survey, setting off in a de Havilland D.H.50 biplane on 20 November 1924 and arriving in Rangoon, the furthest point eastwards of the then Indian Empire, on 17 March 1925. This was no record-breaking flight, but a painstaking survey, to prepare for ultimate airline service; but the British authorities seemed to be in no hurry to reach India.

De Havilland 66 Hercules three-engined biplanes were used east of Egypt when Imperial Airways opened its United Kingdom—India service in 1929. The illustration shows a Hercules at Delhi in January 1927 at the end of the first Imperial Airways survey flight. This Hercules was named *City of Delhi* by Lady Irwin, wife of the Viceroy. (*Courtesy John Stroud*)

The Imperial Link with Britain

Eventually, after considerable efforts in laying down the infrastructure to support the route in crossing the Arabian Desert, traversing the Persian Gulf, and negotiating the harsh coastline of Baluchistan, Britain's Imperial Airways started a service from London's Croydon Airport to Karachi, starting on 30 March 1929 and arriving on 6 April. Passengers on the de Havilland D.H.66 Hercules biplane that opened this first scheduled air route to India had been quite busy en route. Starting their journey in an Armstrong Whitworth Argosy to Basle, Switzerland – the extent of Imperial Airways' European ambitions at the time – they had taken the train to Genoa. Thence, a Short Calcutta flying-boat took them to Alexandria, Egypt, via Suda Bay, in Crete, and Tobruk. Another train was necessary for the transfer from the Alexandria flying-boat base to Cairo's landplane airport, and thence the D.H.66 valiantly braved the desert sands and the possible rifle fire of the nomadic peoples of eastern Arabia, not to mention the negotiation of the stretch from Sharjah to Karachi, with only the Cathedral Rock as a navigational signpost along the way.

2

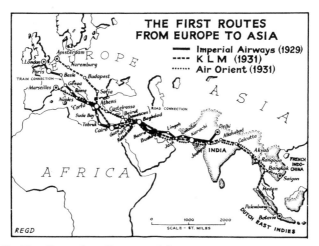

Map 1a. The First Routes from Europe to Asia
Although Britain's Imperial Airways was the first European airline to reach India, it did so rather ponderously, with different aircraft types over different sections of the route; and with surface transport interruptions. Pride of place must go to the Dutch KLM, which forged a much faster through route, with the same aircraft – and the same crews! – all the way to the East Indies, making 1931 a banner year for long-distance air transport.

Lighter-Than-Air Interlude

British shortcomings – compared with the Dutch enterprises – could perhaps be forgiven, in the light of a fundamental conflict within both Government and technical aviation circles as to the preferred course to take in the development of long-distance air services. Throughout the 1920s, and in the case of Germany, well into the 1930s, there existed considerable support, leading to large investment and construction programmes, for lighter-than-air, i.e. dirigible airships, as the answer to all the problems of long-distance air travel. Certainly, in the early, and even in the late 1920s, heavier-than-air craft had suffered from the inability to be able to fly with any kind of reasonable payload for more than a few hundred miles. Engines were notoriously unreliable, and one of the airship's advantages was that its power units were needed only to maintain forward flight, not to achieve lift by speed. They could thus be used at economical power settings, and could enable airships to fly thousands rather than hundreds of miles. Also, if an engine failed on the flight, it could often be repaired in the air.

With these factors in mind, and encouraged by the knowledge that both German and American aviation authorities also sought to exploit the capabilities of the airship, Britain built two large dirigibles which, in spite of construction delays and changes of Government that altered the administrative control of the projects, both made first flights towards the end of 1929, the R101 on 14 October and the R100 on 16 December. Both airships were giants, twice the size (measured by lifting capacity) of Germany's great flagship the *Graf Zeppelin*. The R101, selected to make an historic first flight to India, was, after it was lengthened during the autumn of 1930, 730 feet (223 metres) long.

To accommodate this bulk, a big airship shed was built at Karachi, which was rapidly gaining prominence, because it was the nearest port to the European ship-

3

ping routes. Construction began in 1926 and it was completed in time to prepare for the coming of the R101. This great building was 850 ft long, 180 ft wide and 170 ft high. Unfortunately, the R101 never came.

During its construction, the airship had fallen short of expectations and alterations had to be made to save weight and increase gas capacity. An extra section was inserted to accommodate an extra gasbag, and the lengthened ship first flew on 1 October 1930, making a nonstop circuit of 16 hr 51 min. Such was the obsessive enthusiasm of the Air Minister, Lord Thomson, who had thoughts about becoming Viceroy of India, that, together with Sir Sefton Brancker and fifty-two other notables and crew, they set off for India, leaving Cardington only three days later, on 4 October. If the airship was lighter than air, then its directives were positively light-headed, to embark on such a gruelling and uncharted (for airships) journey days after it had completed its one and only test flight in its new configuration. On 5 October, next day, the R101 crashed and burned at Beauvais, north of Paris, killing 48 of its occupants.

The airship mooring mast and large shed erected at Karachi when United Kingdom—India airship services were envisaged. (*Courtesy John Stroud*)

The airship hangar at Karachi was never used, at least not for airships. But it survived as a landmark for half a century, and was demolished only in 1961.

The First Indian Airlines

Compared to the initiative undertaken by the Dutch and the French, who had colonies in eastern Asia, British efforts in India were sluggish. KLM undertook a series of experimental proving flights in 1929, began permanent mail service to Batavia (now Jakarta) in 1930, passenger service in 1931, and opened a branch line to Singapore in 1933. The Dutch merchants of the East Indies had started their own airline,

4

KNILM, in 1929, to link outlying cities and islands of the archipelago. The French Lignes d'Orient began service to Indo-China in 1929, where it linked up with the local Air Asie, formed as early as 1926. Foreign flags of aeroplanes flying through India in the early 1930s were more common than the Union Jack.

Ponderously, the British and Indian Governments, which could have shown as much enterprise in developing air services within India as in debating traffic rights for the foreign airlines, finally began to take action. Why this should have taken so long is a mystery, for all the elements to encourage airline development were present, especially the demographic parameters. The two biggest cities, Bombay and Calcutta, and the third port, Karachi, were about 700 or 800 miles distant from the capital, Delhi. Madras was 1,000 miles from Delhi; and several major cities were also hundreds of miles from each other.

The train services were adequate and the route map seemed to cover every need. But the Indian railways of the 1930s were not of the best. To quote a contemporary observer, J Parker van Zandt, a prominent American writer and analyst: 'When you go by train, you have to take your own bedding with you, and preferably a bearer as well, to look after your bedding roll and guard your luggage from theft when you leave your compartment for meals. Travel by train in India, particularly in the summer heat, is an adventure which has to be experienced to be appreciated.' All the more reason, it would seem, to accelerate the development of air service.

When Imperial Airways finally reached Karachi in April 1929, no connecting service existed, even to the capital, Delhi. During 1928, Indian Airways Ltd had been formed, and tendered for permission to operate from Karachi to Delhi and Calcutta; and Eastern Airways, backed by capital amounting to £375,000, had planned services to Bombay and Delhi. But nothing came of these.

At last the connection to the capital was made. On 20 December 1929 the Indian

In 1932 Handley Page H.P.42 *Hannibal*-class aircraft took over operation of the Egypt—Karachi section of the UK—India services. (*Courtesy John Stroud*)

5

State Air Service began operations from Karachi over the 715-mile route, via Jodhpur, but the aircraft and crews were from Imperial Airways. Plans to provide the State Air Service with Avro aircraft fell through, even though a direct subsidy of £26,250 had been voted to provide the service. On 31 December, the contract with Imperial expired, and the next day, the Delhi Flying Club, one of several flourishing in India at the time, and for which financial support had also been given from the Government, took over the task. It operated a Gipsy Moth (mostly flown by P D Sharma) on loan from the Indian air authorities, to maintain the Karachi—Delhi connection, and managed to do this until July 1933, when Imperial Airways extended full service onwards over the route.

For the Delhi Flying Club to be operating Gipsy Moths with two open seats in parallel with KLM's Fokker F.XIIs, fitted with four luxury reclining seats and other amenities, was, to say the least, undignified. Such an aspect of affairs must have stirred the consciences of some of India's leaders of industry, as well as those in Government (although, to be fair, the latter were controlled by London's representatives). Necessity is, they say, the Mother of Invention; and perhaps this was the situation in India in 1932. For out of this inertia rose a small, independent airline that was to become one of the world's best, and the man who founded, built, and inspired it was to take his place in the international Hall of Fame as one of air transport's greatest leaders.

J R D Tata and Tata Sons Limited

The conventional image of India, seen through British eyes during the early part of the 20th Century, and as an inheritance from the prejudices of the 19th, was of a benevolent rule by a Colonial civil service, working in harmony with a privi-

J R D Tata was the first Indian to hold a pilot's licence. He flew the first Tata service, from Karachi to Bombay, on 15 October 1932 and also the 50th anniversary special flight. He is seen here at Hatfield in 1948 when he flew a de Havilland Vampire jet fighter. (*de Havilland*)

6

Juhu, the first Bombay airport, with Tata hangar, Puss Moths and a Fox Moth. VT-ADN, partly in the hangar, operated the first Tata service. (*Courtesy John Stroud*)

A Tata Sons de Havilland Fox Moth about to leave Juhu (Bombay) with mail for Hyderabad, Deccan. (*Courtesy John Stroud*)

leged Indian aristocracy – the princes and maharajahs, with 99 per cent of the population consisting of illiterate peasants. The problems were certainly enormous: scores of different racial divisions; scores of religious sects, in addition to the mainstream of Hindus, with large Moslem, Buddhist, and Sikh minorities; and underlying everything, a rigid caste system that condemned, for example, the Untouchables to the most menial of occupations, and banishment from society.

Often forgotten, however, is that one of the castes was the merchant class, and they were great survivors during the revolutionary process that the Sub-continent underwent after the British conquest. The merchants of India – and some of them adopted that occupation as the family name – are among the smartest businessmen in the world, and a little thing like foreign domination was only a temporary interruption of their way of life. Little known among the average readers of the newspaper dailies in Britain, much of the huge trading machinery on which the prosperity of the British Empire depended was in the hands of Indian merchants and big industrial conglomerates. Many of these were owned by distinguished Parsi families from Bombay, and prominent among these was the House of Tata.

Tata Sons Limited, in fact, is one of the largest industrial companies in Asia, outside Japan, and even in the 1930s, its capital approached £50 million, and it employed 60,000 workers. Its various branches included large iron and steel

A Tata de Havilland 89 Dragon Rapide at Juhu with a somewhat earlier form of transport.

Tata Air Lines began operating de Havilland 86s in October 1938. (*Courtesy John Stroud*)

works, hydro-electric plants, textile mills and a wide variety of associated factories engaged in manufacturing.

One of the scions of the dynasty was J R D Tata, already a director of all the Tata enterprises although, in 1932, still in his late twenties. During the earlier years, he had observed the impasse that had resulted from the Indian Government's insistence that aspirant airlines should be prepared to shoulder the entire financial risk, and should expect no subsidy from New Delhi. Now, with a growing interest in aviation, and encouraged by his friend Nevill Vintcent, J R D decided to enter the airline field.

In July 1932 he established an aviation department in Tata Sons Limited, and under that company name, began service, as an entirely private enterprise, without subsidy, on 15 October 1932. He had successfully applied for a licence to operate a connecting service to Imperial Airways' base at Karachi, linking the southern Indian city of Madras by a route through Bombay and the textile city of

8

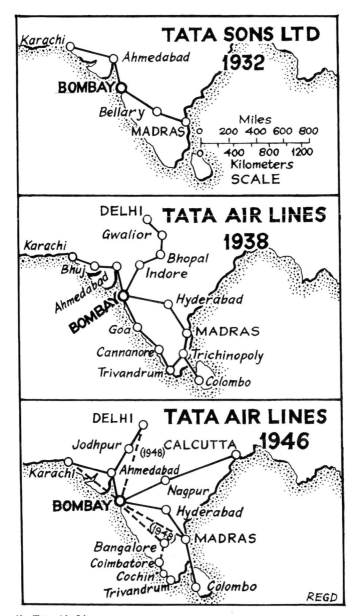

Map 1b. Tata Air Lines
One of the truly visionary giants of prewar commercial air transport was J R D Tata, scion
of the Indian manufacturing conglomerate Tata Sons Ltd. Identifying a need for an inter-city
airline within the country (rather than depending on the improbable extensions of the
Imperial route from Britain) he founded the airline that was to be the nucleus of all Indian
airline activity today.

9

Ahmedabad, and with a technical stop at Bellary. In effect this was an air service to cover the whole of southern India. The initial fleet was two Puss Moths and such was the success of the operation that a Fox Moth was added to the fleet within a year. J R D Tata himself was no desk-bound executive. His enthusiasm for aviation had prompted him to obtain his flying licence and he piloted the inaugural Tata Sons Limited schedule.

This was a true pioneering effort, for the Government was no more anxious to provide landing fields or navigation aids than it was to provide financial help; but the ten-year contract did include air mail payments on a sliding scale on a pound-mileage basis.

Although the Tata organization had to make a considerable investment in the airline, it was successful beyond expectations, revealing perhaps that the Indian Government, with direction from London, had been dilatory in realizing the airline potential of the Sub-continent. On 1 January 1935 the night stop at Bellary was abandoned when the airfield at Hyderabad, a more important city, became operational; and the weekly service was doubled. On 26 November of the same year, a new route was opened, from Bombay to Trivandrum via Goa and Cannanore, using a Miles Merlin. In 1936, Bhuj, an isolated town in the Kathiawar peninsula, was included on the Karachi—Ahmedabad segment, and larger aircraft, de Havilland D.H.89 and American Waco types were ordered.

On 8 November 1937 the important trunk route from Bombay to Delhi opened, via Indore, Bhopal and Gwalior; and soon afterwards, on 22 January 1938, the southern route was extended from Madras to Colombo, Ceylon (Sri Lanka), via Trichinopoly. This step was stimulated by the airline, now renamed Tata Air Lines, befitting its growing stature and status, being admitted to the enterprising British Empire Air Mail Scheme, under which all first class letters to the British Empire were carried at ordinary postage rates, even though speeded up by air carriage. Tata was granted a ten-year contract under the Scheme to carry all the mails from Karachi to Colombo.

The network now embraced the whole of southern India, serving every major city. On 2 March 1938 the two main routes extending southwards from Bombay were linked by a new segment from Trivandrum to Trichinopoly; and in 1939, reflecting a further increase in traffic and momentum, two four-engined de Havilland D.H.86 Express airliners were purchased from Mac.Robertson-Miller Airlines of Australia. But for the time being, J R D Tata was unable to progress to greater heights; for the outbreak of the Second World War put an end to greater ambitions.

A Marriage of Convenience

With the Dutch and French flags displayed on their aircraft as they flew through India and with Tata showing its flag throughout southern India, consciences were at last stirred in the most populous and industrial north, the region stretching from the Punjab in the northwest, through the United Provinces, to Bengal. The progress towards airline operation was, however, slow, as the consciences were differently stirred, on the one hand by the British, represented by Imperial Airways, and on the other hand by the Indian authorities in Delhi, now beginning to flex quasi-Dominion status muscles, and demanding fair representation in the matter of the British flag carrier making its way across some 2,500 miles (4,000 km) of Indian territory. A compromise was arrived at, and in the early summer of 1933, two airlines were formed, to provide service from Karachi to Rangoon, via Delhi, Calcutta, and intermediate points.

10

Indian National Airways' de Havilland 84 Dragon *Sapphire*. (*Courtesy John Stroud*)

In May 1933, Indian National Airways Ltd (INA) was registered in New Delhi, with a capital of 3,000,000 rupees. The controlling interest was held by Govan Brothers Ltd, whose ownership was 60 per cent non-Indian. On 21 June, Indian Trans-Continental Airways Ltd (ITCA) was formed with the specific responsibility to operate the trans-India service, in association with Imperial Airways which held 51 per cent of the capital. The arrangement was that INA should be the principal agents for both Imperial and ITCA, selling tickets at eleven of its offices throughout India, and handling the travel agencies; while ITCA should operate the services with two Armstrong Whitworth Atalantas leased from Imperial Airways. Every alternate service across India was flown by the ITCA aircraft, under the Indian flag, but with Imperial Airways crews, management, and technical support. On 7 July 1933 INA took a 25 per cent interest in ITCA, while the Indian Government picked up the balance of 24 per cent.

Honour having been satisfied on both sides of this interlocking relationship, services began, on the same day, 7 July, from Karachi to Calcutta, via Delhi, Cawnpore and Allahabad. The Bengal city, at that time still the most important commercial centre in India, was now only seven days flying time from London. On 23 September the service was extended to Rangoon, and on 9 December 1933, further extended to Singapore, where the Dutch KLM had already established a branch line from its East Indian trunk service.

Other new Indian routes were opened in 1934. On 10 February 1934, an attempt was made to link Madras, India's third largest city in the 1930s, directly with Calcutta. The Madras Air Taxi Service began passenger and mail service over the Bay of Bengal route on 10 February 1934; but it was short-lived, and ended on 31 March of the same year. On 4 December 1934, under Government contract, INA opened its own service, independently from ITCA and Imperial Airways, with its own aircraft – mainly de Havilland types – from Karachi to Lahore, in the Punjab, via Jacobabad and Multan. INA had also supplemented ITCA's service east of Calcutta, starting local flights to Dacca and Chittagong, and onwards via coastal points to Rangoon, on 1 December 1933; but these were suspended in the summer of 1935.

During this period, a substantial stimulus to aviation in India was provided by the excitement of the England—Australia Mac.Robertson Race, held on 20–24 October 1934. Once again the Dutch were a thorn in the British side. Although a

11

Indian Trans-Continental Airways' Armstrong Whitworth XV *Arethusa* at Willingdon Airport, New Delhi. (*Courtesy John Stroud*)

specially-built de Havilland D.H.88 Comet won the race, a KLM Douglas DC-2, following the airline's normal route to Batavia, and with a load of passengers and freight, came in second. The event sent shock-waves through an incredulous British industry and air administration, which reacted by announcing two measures that changed the history and momentum of Imperial Airways' hitherto somewhat pedestrian progress. On 20 December 1934 the British Government announced the Empire Air Mail Scheme, and simultaneously Imperial Airways ordered twenty-eight Short S.23 Empire Flying-boats.

Flying-boats Through India

After its outstanding success in the Mac.Robertson Race, KLM consolidated its acceptance of American all-metal landplanes and set a cracking pace in establishing a truly magnificent airline service to the East Indies. Such problems that had arisen for KLM traffic and operating rights through British India evaporated as the British Imperial Airways now required similar rights across the Indonesian archipelago to complete its route to Australia.

On 18 February 1937 Imperial Airways began to show signs of shaking itself out of the apparent lethargy that had restrained it for so long. At long last, the British flag-carrier had an aircraft that could match KLM's DC-3s in speed, and more than match them in comfort. The Short S.23 Empire Flying-boats, however, did have the disadvantage of having to alight on water that was less stable than land, and at times could be treacherous.

Nevertheless, Imperial Airways put on a brave face. On that February day, the *Caledonia* left Southampton Water, in the south of England, on a test flight, nonstop to Alexandria, Egypt, covering the distance in 14 hr 23 min. Reporters noted that the aircraft 'was in constant touch with London by short-wave radio' – an amenity taken for granted today but considered a luxury for the aircrew in the late Thirties, even in Europe.

On 5 March Imperial opened its flying-boat base at Hythe, near Southampton, and introduced the Empire Flying-boats on a route as far as Alexandria, with stops at Macon and Marseilles, Rome, Brindisi and Athens. A year later, the second stage of the 'all-up' Empire Air Mail service was opened as far as Singapore (the first stage had been the route to South Africa). In India, the flying-boats took a different route from that of the landplanes; from Karachi, they proceeded eastward via the Raj Samand Reservoir, at Udaipur, and Gwalior. The stretches of water looked beautiful and romantic in the publicity pictures, but the provision of duplicate stations along the route was doubly expensive because of the need to provide launches for both passenger service and for maintenance and refuelling duties.

Undoubtedly, however, the Imperial Airways service to Australia, fully accomplished with the elegant S.23s on 28 July 1938, reaching Sydney in $9\frac{1}{2}$ days, was a great pioneering achievement; and Indian Trans-Continental Airways played its part by providing supplementary and parallel service from Karachi to Calcutta with the Atalantas via Jodhpur, Delhi and Allahabad.

Imperial Airways Short S.30 C class Empire Flying-boat *Champion* taking-off from Gwalior.
(*BOAC*)

An Indian Local Service

In 1936 Air Services of India Ltd (ASI) was founded to operate to the Indian States in the Kathiawar district, to the north of Bombay. This was a new departure for air service in India, as it did not aim to provide inter-city service, not was it supported or subsidized directly from the Indian Government in New Delhi. The area served from Bombay was a peninsula that was separated from the main Indian land mass by the Gulf of Cambay; and to reach the small cities and communities by land from Bombay required a circuitous rail journey via Ahmadabad, taking at least two days to cover a straight-line distance of about 200 miles.

ASI put an end to this inconvenience, beginning operations in November 1937 as a private company, subsidized by several of the Indian States which it served. With a fleet of small de Havilland and Percival cabin aircraft, it operated to Bhavnagar, Rajkot, Jamnagar and Porbandar, in Kathiawar; and also started a route to Poona and Kolhapur, to the south. As with many air services in India during the 1930s, operations had to be suspended during the monsoon season from June to September, when the rainfall was extremely heavy; but the low fare levels – little more than 2nd Class rail fares – compensated for the variable nature of the service.

During the wartime years ASI had to suspend operations, in February 1941, because it was losing money, in spite of its valiant efforts to provide a good transport service to a relatively neglected area. But in 1943, the Scindia Steamship

13

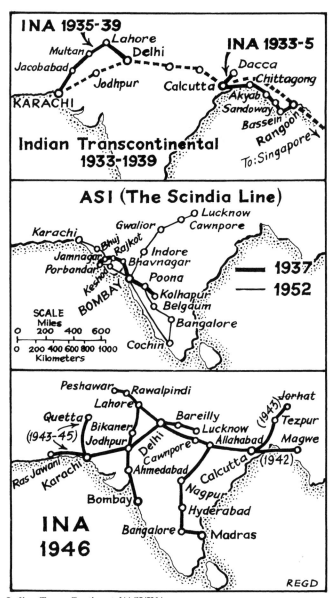

Map 1c. Indian Trans-Continental/ASI/INA

After the Tata enterprise (see map 1b) other companies sought to develop air transport in India during the 1930s. Indian National Airways (INA) established connections with Indian Trans-Continental Airways, which was the nominal extension of Britain's Imperial route to India; while in Bombay, the Scindia shipping line began local services in western India. After the Second World War, INA became a nationwide airline force before the nationalization process that formed IAC. (*see* map 3).

14

Air Services of India D.H.89 Dragon Rapide *City of Bhavnagar* at Jamnagar on 21 November 1937 on the inaugural Bombay—Porbandar service. (*Courtesy John Stroud*)

Company bought the company, and it became familiarly known as the Scindia Line when it resumed service, with a more ambitious programme of routes, after the war ended.

India's Rise to Nationhood after the Second World War

When Great Britain declared war on Germany on 3 September 1939, the self-governing Dominions quickly followed, in a display of Commonwealth loyalty to the Crown. India's position was different; for although it enjoyed a status far more elevated than that of a Colony, much of its affairs were still ordained from London. Landmarks towards freedom from what was little more than serfdom had been modest in their effect during the 19th and early part of the 20th Century. The Indian Mutiny of 1857–8 was succeeded by the dissolution of the East India Company in 1858, when India became a Viceroyalty; and Queen Victoria assumed the title of Empress of India in 1877. Development of India's considerable wealth in such products as cotton, jute, tea, and other products of the land were mostly in British hands; and the supporting infrastructure of roads, railways, ports, and irrigation were undertaken, as were the industries, almost entirely by British management and control and with Indian labour.

Political consciousness among Indians was almost dormant until the founding of the Indian National Congress in 1885, and this at least played a part in expanding the opportunities for Indian nationals to participate in the administrative, if not the legislative workings of government. The Moslem League was founded in 1906 – to find expression in a vehement form forty years later – and the capital of India was moved from Calcutta to Delhi with great pomp in 1911. Indian pride found expression during the Great War of 1914–18 when the Indian Army, which included Gurkha troops from Nepal, distinguished itself on the field of battle.

The nadir of modern Indian-British relations was reached in December 1919, when, at Amritsar, British troops fired indiscriminately at a crowd of demonstrators, killing or wounding more than a thousand people. This accelerated further

15

diversion of governmental powers to Indians, although police, defence, and financial power still remained firmly British. Then, in the 1920s, Mohandas Gandhi, hailed as a saint by Indians but as a political agitator by the British, began a campaign for independence, based entirely on a policy of non-violence. Spending his time in and out of prison and engaging the British in interminable dialogue, Gandhi's efforts led first to round-table conferences in London from 1932 to 1934, and to the Government of India Act of 1935. In 1937, the Congress Party won six of eleven provincial elections.

During the Second World War, Indian feelings ran high, for they felt that a European conflict, in which they had no interest whatsoever, was serving to delay the momentum towards independence. The most extreme political movement, under Subhas Chandra Bose, actually supported Nazi Germany, but the dominant Congress Party, now led by Jawaharlal Nehru, and strongly supported by Gandhi, went no further than a declared policy of pacifism. The Indian Army, however, was anything but pacific, again performing great deeds, and gaining considerable respect from the British people in all walks of life, whose previous knowledge of the 400 million inhabitants of the Sub-continent had been confined to lurid reports of Gandhi's fasting and the fortunes of the All-India test match teams on the cricket field.

When the war ended in 1945, Sir Stafford Cripps had already offered Dominion status to India, as early as 1942; but the independence movement was not to be denied, and Gandhi himself campaigned vigorously with what amounted almost to a battle-cry: 'Quit India.'

And so India became a Sovereign State. Prime Minister Clement Attlee, head of the victorious Labour Government of postwar Britain, honoured the Cripps commitment and the Sub-continent prepared itself for the long sought independence. Lord Mountbatten presided over the complex discussions that led to the Indian Independence Act of 1947, which was followed, tragically, by massive, religion-inspired unrest, especially in the Punjab, where Moslem and Hindu communities overlapped and who, until the issue of Pakistan reached its height, had managed to live together in relative peace. Sadly, Mahatma (the noble-hearted) Gandhi was assassinated in 1948, and did not live to witness the emergence of a proud Indian nation, under the leadership of Nehru.

The Horseshoe Route

Politics notwithstanding, India was irrevocably embroiled as part of the Allied effort in the war against Hitler's Germany. And both Britain's Imperial Airways and India's domestic airlines were part of the effort. Imperial's role was clearly to maintain the swift air links with the Commonwealth, and this was not easy, with Germany controlling airspace in western Europe, and after Italy joined Germany on 11 June 1941, with Mussolini's forces making life hazardous in the Mediterranean. By this time, Imperial Airways had merged with British Airways to form British Overseas Airways Corporation (BOAC) on 1 April 1940.

BOAC, in fact, had to go the long way round, via the west coast of Africa and across that continent to the Arabian peninsula, as a safe alternative route to India, east Asia, and Australia. The last S.23 flying-boat crossed Europe on 11 June 1940, larger Boeing 314 flying-boats joined the West African service as far as Lagos on 26 May 1941 (to be supplemented on 18 July, by the Short S.26 G Class), to connect with trans-African services with Khartoum as a hub for both flying-boats and landplanes.

On 10 June 1941 a full engineering base was established at Durban, South Africa, and this became both the southern terminus of the North-South African route and the new emergency service to connect all the British Dominions and territories in the eastern hemisphere. The Horseshoe Route, as it became known because of its shape on the map, was inaugurated on 19 June 1941. A fleet of S.23 Empire Flying-boats completed the journey from Durban to Sydney in about two weeks, on average, calling at points along the eastern coast of Africa to Mombasa, then to Khartoum, via Lake Victoria, on to Cairo and through the Middle East to the Persian Gulf and Karachi, across India, and down through Singapore and the Netherlands East Indies to Australia.

It was a magnificent effort, demanding considerable discipline under wartime conditions, with inevitable shortages of supplies of spare parts and a draining of essential services and manpower into the armed forces. India comprised a vital segment of the whole enterprise, and Karachi became a halfway-house for the pilots and passengers of the Horseshoe Route, just as it had become for the Europe—Australia services before the war, and where, in fact, KLM had built a hotel of that name. Karachi's geographical position as the gateway to India from the west was never more emphasized than during the Second World War. The eastern half of the route, incidentally, became the responsibility of the Australian airline, Qantas, which extended its stewardship westwards from Singapore as far as Karachi on 16 October 1941.

The strategically important air link was broken at the beginning of 1942. The Japanese had entered the war with its dramatic attack on Pearl Harbor on 7 December 1941. The last S.23 called at Singapore on 3 February 1942, less than two weeks before that outpost of Empire surrendered to the invading army. As a precaution against the possibility of Axis forces occupying Egypt, a reserve route was added to the Horseshoe on 11 May 1942, when Lockheed Lodestars opened landplane service from Khartoum to Karachi, via points on the southern Arabian coast. Meanwhile, the Japanese-occupied areas of southeast Asia, with troops almost within striking distance of Calcutta, was bypassed in remarkable fashion, by the introduction of a Qantas Consolidated PBY-5 Catalina flying-boat service, from Colombo to Perth, on 10–11 July 1943. It was the world's longest air route, 3,513 miles, and the journey usually took 27 hours, sometimes longer, and became known as the Double Sunrise service. On 30 October 1943, Qantas extended this service to Karachi, and introduced Consolidated Liberator landplanes on 17 June 1945.

An even further refinement, and additional fall-back position in case the worst happened – although by this time the Allies were in the ascendant – was the supplementary route directly across the Indian Ocean from Mombasa to Colombo, via Mahé, in the Seychelles, and Attu Island, in the Maldives, using one of the G Class Short flying-boats. This started on 28 November 1944, but was not used extensively and, with the silver lining appearing from behind the clouds of war, all trans-Indian Ocean services terminated on 8 April 1946.

The Indian Airlines During the Second World war

For the Indian airlines during the war against Hitler, the mood was inclined to lean towards the philosophy of 'business as usual', a philosophy that has characterized the Hindu people especially through hard times, when they have displayed a remarkable resilience to overcoming hardships and tribulations. Compared, for example, with the religious strife occasioned by the postwar creation of Pakistan,

A Tata Dragon Rapide in wartime camouflage. (*Courtesy John Stroud*)

the Second World War did not cause too much alarm on the Sub-continent.

Tata Air Lines seized the opportunity to upgrade its fleets and its installations. It acquired three Model A Stinson tri-motors from Marquette Airlines in the United States, and on 1 November 1941 began non-scheduled flights from Bombay to Baghdad, with Douglas DC-2s, leased from the Indian Government. By 1942 the 14-seat DC-2s were plying the Bombay—Karachi route, as an important branch line from the Horseshoe Route, and although the southern route to Trichinopoly was suspended in January 1943, Tata strengthened its network to the larger Indian cities. Jodhpur was added to the Delhi route in April 1944, Bangalore to the Madras route on 24 June 1945, and an important new route, Bombay–Nagpur–Calcutta had added further stature to the Tata map on 16 April of the same year.

During 1941 Tata Air Lines introduced some Stinson Model A aircraft. VT-AQX is seen on the approach to Mauripur, Karachi. (*BOAC*)

18

As for Indian National Airways (INA) it too made considerable strides during the wartime years, mainly with its Waco aircraft. It provided supplementary services across northern India, extending its Karachi—Delhi route to Calcutta on 27 June 1940, to link up with its route to Rangoon. Also, in addition to these inter-city routes, INA provided valuable feeder services to outposts such as Magwe, on the Burma Front, in 1942; to Peshawar, on the Northwest Frontier, in 1943; to Tezpur and Jorhat, in Assam (and at the eastern end of the vital supply routes to China) also in 1943; and from Karachi to Ras Jiwani and Quetta in 1944. All these wartime routes were operated with Government co-operation and assistance.

Largely in support of the Allied war effort, the airlines of India gained much strength from the experiences during the Second World War. They had entered the conflict very much as supplementary services to a Commonwealth world-wide air network of Imperial design. During the war, they won their spurs by demonstrating that they could match BOAC, KLM, and Qantas in almost all aspects of airline operations. In J R D Tata, India had a leader who would steer it into the international arena, in a political environment in which the airlines were now their own masters, and no longer dependent upon what they wished to do coinciding with what Imperial Airways wanted. When the war ended, the Indian airlines were up and running, and there were exciting times ahead.

19

CHAPTER TWO

Postwar Emergence of Airlines in India

Every Man For Himself

In Chapter 1 of this book, the closing words, as the narrative of the wartime years ended, were 'exciting times ahead'. The excitement had both positive and negative aspects: positive in that the new British Labour Government, under the astute leadership of Clement Attlee, was determined to end the bitter strife that had characterized Anglo-Indian affairs since the British conquest of the 18th Century; negative in the realization that the peoples of the Sub-continent were to undergo all the 'blood and toil, tears and sweat' that Winston Churchill had promised the British people in the worst days of the Second World War.

The airlines that had been founded before the war picked themselves up by their bootstraps and, with much ingenuity and improvization, managed to resume reasonably normal services within a few months of the end of hostilities. In these efforts, they had to use the miscellaneous aircraft that had been left behind by the Allied Forces when they departed back to Europe and America. There were various de Havillands, Fox Moths, Puss Moths, Leopard Moths and Dragons, Dragon Rapides and D.H.86 Expresses; there were Avro and Percival types; and from the United States, there were Beech, Wacos and Stinsons; but above all, there were Dakotas.

Like manna from heaven, these last, the ubiquitous Douglas twin-engined airliner that had shown its paces in India in 1937 when KLM put it on the route from Amsterdam to Batavia, were to be found at every major airfield, and even at quite a few of the up-country strips, abandoned by the military operators, their existence acknowledged only in a distant register in Delhi, London or Washington. They were, of course, military versions of the Douglas DC-3, most of them C-47s, but some C-49s and C-53s here and there. Now, surplus to requirements and of no use back home, where more modern types were being put into service, and where there was also a surplus of the same veteran Gooney Birds, the armed forces left in India were as pleased to dispose of them as the local Indian airline entrepreneurs were to obtain them. Some were bought or leased at knock-down prices from the United States Foreign Liquidation Commissioner, some came from the Royal Air Force and some were no doubt assembled from collections of written-off spare parts. From all these sources, the postwar Indian airlines quickly turned the wartime aircraft into civil airliners and collectively, though not necessarily in harmony, resumed the momentum of building an airline system for India that the start of war in 1939 had interrupted.

The Old Pioneers

The first companies to get under way were, predictably, the airlines that had been operating already and which, therefore, still possessed a skeleton force of experienced personnel, a knowledge of airline operations and an infrastructure, however

20

One of Air-India's war-surplus Douglas C-47s at Santacruz Airport, Bombay, in 1948.
(*Courtesy John Stroud*)

flimsy, to go into business. These veterans comprised Tata Air Lines, Indian National Airways (INA) and Air Services of India (ASI).

Tata had maintained an inter-city network, headquartered in Bombay, throughout the Second World War, providing essential air communication to Delhi, Calcutta and Madras as well as to Colombo. With the clouds of war lifting, Tata received temporary route certificates, to replace the ones covering the wartime emergency restrictions, for the Calcutta route via Nagpur on 16 April 1945, for Bangalore and Coimbatore on 25 April and for Madras via Bangalore on 24 June. The route to Delhi via Ahmadabad was confirmed in September by which time the airline had acquired, either by Government allocation of war-surplus or by purchase or lease, a dozen DC-3s, and these were put into service immediately to replace the Beech 18s. To mark its return to the competitive world of commercial aviation J R D Tata converted the Tata-owned company into a public corporation on 29 July 1946. The name was changed to Air-India Ltd, the capital was a handsome £3,750,000 and J R D himself took the helm.

By this time, the powerful US airline, Transcontinental & Western Air (TWA), under the inspirational (if at times unpredictable) leadership of Howard Hughes, had obtained valuable international operating and traffic rights from the US Civil Aeronautics Board, and, under the cloak of authority from the bilateral agreements empowered by the Bermuda Agreement, had inaugurated through-service from New York to Bombay on 5 January 1947. Within the month, Air-India was appointed as general agents for TWA, simultaneously to provide TWA with a marketing base throughout India and providing Air-India with a link to the United

An Air-India Vickers-Armstrongs Viking on a test flight before delivery (*Vickers*)

States. On 13 April of the same year, Air-India received its first postwar commercial aircraft, the first of four Vickers Vikings, to supplement its fleet of DC-3s on Indian domestic routes.

Such a relationship was only a stepping stone to greater ambition in the international field. Every newly independent country has to have an overseas airline, just as it has to have a flag. India's independence of 1947 was followed quickly by the desire to have a flag-carrying airline of 'chosen instrument' status. J R D Tata had the status, the stature, and the influence to ensure that his Air-India would be a major player in the negotiation and legislation necessary to provide India with an airline of which it could be proud. Accordingly, on 8 March 1948, Air-India International (AII) was organized as a joint corporation with a capital of £5,250,000. Fifty-one per cent of the shares were owned by Air-India Ltd, which was to manage the airline and the remaining 49 per cent by the Indian Government. The new corporation received its first Lockheed Constellation on 16 March 1948, only a week after its foundation. This aircraft was the *Rajput Princess* and its sister aircraft *Malabar Princess* inaugurated service to London on 8 June of that year.

Air-India's early terminal on the south side of Bombay Airport (Santacruz).
(*Courtesy John Stroud*)

22

POST-WAR AIRLINES IN INDIA
(before merger into I A C)

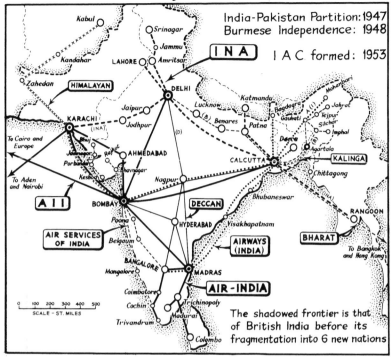

India-Pakistan Partition: 1947
Burmese Independence: 1948

I N A

I A C formed: 1953

The shadowed frontier is that of British India before its fragmentation into 6 new nations

Map 2a. Post-War Airlines in India (before merger into IAC)
Wartime aerial activity had intensified the airmindedness that had already been established by Tata, INA, and ASI during the 1930s (*see* maps in Chapter 1). These companies resumed operations in the mid-1940s (Tata became Air-India) and were joined by other aspiring enterprises. Much of the competition was counter-productive, and the formation of Indian Airlines Corporation (IAC) in 1953 was an inevitable consequence.

Such is the importance of the Indian international airline that it merits a separate chapter in this book – Chapter 4.

Challenging the Tata organization for pride of place on the Indian domestic postwar airline scene was Indian National Airways Ltd (INA). It, too, had the background necessary to maintain and expand air service on the return of peacetime conditions. All its wartime routes were continued in 1945 under new certificates of authority. Its network spread from Karachi in the west to Calcutta in the east, through Delhi, the Punjab and the United Provinces, and it added new routes to Bombay and to Madras. Its network was as extensive as Tata's, and its initiative to expand was no less. Like every other airline enterprise, the mainstay of the fleet was the trusty old DC-3 but it matched Tata's order for postwar airliners by ordering six Vickers Vikings from Britain in April 1946. While Tata was to have TWA as a partner, INA had links with the independent British aviation enterprise Airwork which, however, was restricted in its scope by the British Labour Government's decision to confine all scheduled service airline operations

23

One of Indian National Airways Bristol 170 Wayfarers. (*Bristol*)

in Britain to three State-owned corporations; any ambitions that Airwork might have had to form strong links to India through an airline network (it had helped to found Misrair in Egypt in the early 1930s) were stillborn.

Indian National developed its postwar services with a flair. On 7 February 1946, its new service from Delhi to Rampur/Bareilly and Lucknow, capital of the United Provinces (later renamed Uttar Pradesh), was named the *UP Indiaman*. On 1 June the new Delhi–Lahore–Bikaner–Jodhpur–Ahmadabad service was called the *Rajputana Indiaman*; its other routes were given somewhat less splendid but nevertheless appropriate names *East* and *West Indiaman* titles. But best of all was the *Khyber Indiaman* from Delhi to Peshawar via Lahore and Rawalpindi. Its southern route to Madras via Allahabad, Nagpur, Hyderabad and Bangalore was operated only for a few weeks in July 1946 and INA withdrew in favour of Deccan Airways.

The airline continued to progress during the late 1940s. It introduced the Vikings but then suffered a setback with the partitioning of the country and the creation of Pakistan; for perhaps 40 per cent of its traffic was in the eastern parts of India which formed the western wing of the new nation, and where Orient Airlines, later Pakistan International, held sway; and where, in fact, INA was quite definitely *persona non grata*.

Abandoning the routes in the east, INA transferred its emphasis and some of its aircraft to the west, and opened a route from Calcutta to Rangoon in November 1947. During the summer of 1949, for three weeks in June, it joined up with Deccan Airways to operate the Night Air Mail service, and then it turned its atten-

Indian National Airways took delivery of the Viking *Jumna* on 8 August 1947. (*Vickers*)

24

tion to the north. This was, specifically, the former Indian Province of Kashmir, and now the subject of considerable dispute over demarcation lines and sovereignty in general. Even today the problem has not been completely resolved, but a tacit truce, succeeding an often uneasy, sometimes confrontational, manoeuvring by armed forces of India, Pakistan and, in the Aksai Chin district, China, has superseded conflict.

In July 1949 INA started a service from Delhi to Amritsar, Jammu, and Srinagar, capital of Kashmir. Situated 5,250 ft above sea level, Srinagar was a popular destination for tourists and vacationing Government officers alike. It now became the focal point of India's claim for Kashmir rule and INA was the main communications link.

But in the context of Kashmir, Srinagar was in the lowlands. Kashmir is bordered in the north by the Karakoram range of mountains, in which is found the world's second highest mountain, K2 (Mount Godwin Austin) and there are several ranges in between. The Indus River, which empties into the Arabian Sea south of Karachi, and flows for most of its course through Pakistan, also flows through northern Kashmir, in the Ladakh region, having its source to the east, in Tibet. The chief town of Ladakh is Leh, on the Indus, and 11,000 ft above sea level. In 1950, INA pioneered – and the term is used without reservation – a civil air route to support the garrison which protected Indian claims against incursions from Pakistan to the west and China to the east. To reach Leh, the aircraft – DC-3s, of course – had to cross mountains rising to 23,000 ft, negotiating passes that were themselves at 17,000 ft, without pressurization, although oxygen was carried.

Compared to this effort, the new service to Nepal opened the following year was quite simple. For the first time, Kathmandu became accessible from India by airline service, when INA began flights from Calcutta via Patna. Hitherto, the Himalayan kingdom had seemed as remote as Lhasa and Tibet, or Spitzbergen or Franz Josef Land. Today, Kathmandu is a major tourist destination, and INA can claim, through its descendant, IAC, to have been the first to touch down there with a paying passenger.

The third prewar airline, Air Services of India (ASI), not so well capitalized, but ready to regain its former participation in airline affairs, resumed service from Bombay in 1946, still under the stewardship of the Scindia Steamship Line. Possibly rewarded for its previous efforts to provide transport into an area poorly served by the railways, it was given routes by the Indian air authorities that only partially conflicted with Tata's Air-India or INA. On 11 July 1946 it signalled its growing strength by opening a route to Lucknow, capital of the United Provinces, via Indore, Gwalior, and the big industrial city of Cawnpore (Kanpur). Later, it added a route to the north, to Karachi – as relations between India and Pakistan became, at least temporarily, less strained; and also a route to the south, to Cochin via Poona, Belgaum, and Bangalore, paralleling Air-India, but with only Bangalore as a common station.

The three prewar Indian airlines thus quickly asserted themselves in the postwar period, and collectively covered the territory very well. Every main city was receiving airline service from at least one of the old-timers, and most of the middle-level cities could also boast an airport and an airline schedule to Bombay, Calcutta or Delhi. This would possibly have seemed adequate; but with a surplus of DC-3s waiting to be used, and with the spirit of independence stimulated by the new political and commercial freedoms, Air-India, INA and ASI soon found that they had some competition to face.

An Airways (India) Douglas C-47.

The New Pioneers

With the British Government preoccupied with the complex negotiations that would lead to independence, Partition, and strife, the attitude towards commercial developments in India immediately after the complete cessation of hostilities was very much one of laissez faire. Aspiring airlines were tolerated and given the freedom to act, although they were neither encouraged nor supported. Thus, several companies ventured into the uncertain arena of Indian air transport to join the three incumbents.

First off the mark was Airways (India) Ltd (AIL), registered in Calcutta in September 1945. It began non-scheduled services to Gauhati and Bagdogra, two airfields in Assam that had been important staging points in the India-China airlift operations – 'The Hump' – during the War, and whose wartime activities were winding down during the months following the termination of that perilous operation. It also operated into Burma, the first western airline to do so after the departure of the Japanese.

On 15 April 1947 AIL began scheduled services down the west coast of the Bay of Bengal, on a route from Calcutta to Bangalore via Visakhapatnam and Madras. Calcutta—Dacca followed on 15 June 1948, and the Assam routes were promoted to scheduled status in February 1949. The obligatory DC-3 fleet was supplemented by a couple of de Havilland Doves, as well as other small Cessna and Piper types. In 1950 a trans-Indian route was added, from Calcutta to Bombay, with a midway staging point at Nagpur. By December 1951 AIL had a respectable network which included a route to Delhi, stopping at Patna, Cawnpore and Agra, neatly avoiding the points served by INA.

Two more airlines entered the fray in 1946, both beginning service in the autumn and both opening up a new line of development: that of providing direct service to link the major cities across India rather than in a roughly diamond-shaped network around the perimeter. Deccan Airways Ltd was based in Hyderabad, and controlled by the Government of Hyderabad State. The city and State were predominantly Moslem, ruled over by the Nizam, whose predecessors had maintained such local authority under British rule, a relationship that perhaps owed something to Hyderabad's loyalty to Britain during the Indian Mutiny of

26

1857. This spirit manifested itself at the time of India's independence in 1947, and Hyderabad was not incorporated into the Indian Union (Bharat) until 1948, after disputes that came close to a minor civil war, with religious undertones.

Thus, although Deccan had started scheduled DC-3 services on a network of routes in a perfect spoke system from Hyderabad: to Delhi in the north, Calcutta to the northeast, Bangalore and Madras to the south, and Bombay to the west, these had to be suspended from 3 July until 14 October 1948, while the dust settled during the political wrangling. The following year, Deccan took over the Night Air Mail services and in July 1952, in compliance with the Indian Companies Act, the State of Hyderabad, which had ceased to exist as a political unit (the territory having been partitioned into the boundary alignments of the new India) transferred its 78 per cent shareholding to the Government in Delhi.

One of Airways (India) de Havilland Doves, with port engine shut down (*de Havilland*)

Simultaneously with Deccan's Hyderabad-based operation, another company seems to have had the same idea of fashioning an air network around a central hub. Also in the autumn of 1946, Mistri Airways Ltd started scheduled service between Bombay and Calcutta, stopping only at Nagpur. Geographically, this was a shorter itinerary than a route through Hyderabad; so that when the Indian Night Air Mail was launched in 1949, this could have been a factor in the Post Office's choice in letting the contract. By this time, Mistri had, late in 1947, changed its name to a more impressive Indian Overseas Airlines Ltd (although there is no record of it having ventured beyond India's shores) and had opened a second route from Nagpur, north to Allahabad and Lucknow. Uniquely among the postwar independent airlines, incidentally, Mistri had inherited a fleet of seventeen Noorduyn Norseman single-engined aircraft, the sturdy Canadian craft that must have been as ideally suited to Indian unprepared strips as was the DC-3. But Mistri/Indian Overseas did not live up to its ambitions, and ceased operations altogether in 1950.

One of Bharat Airways' Douglas DC-4s.

Another short-lived company was Ambica Airlines Ltd which began local services to points north of Bombay on 10 March 1947. Operating the inevitable DC-3s, with a few Beech 18s and other types, it was associated with the Shri Ambica Steam Navigation Company; but the latter did not feel inclined to provide continued support for an airline whose revenue base was flimsy, and which faced competition in the Kathiawar Peninsula from the long-established Air Services of India. Ambica Airlines was liquidated on 7 February 1949.

Far more impressive was Bharat Airways Ltd incorporated on 11 August 1945 with a capital of £3,750,000, and controlled by the Birla industrial group. It began scheduled services – with Douglas DC-3s, what else? – from Calcutta to Delhi via Gaya and Lucknow, on 30 June 1947. In October of that year, a second service linking the same two termini was routed via Allahabad and Cawnpore and extended beyond Delhi to Amritsar. This latter extension had to be suspended on 10 March 1949, because of problems arising from the continued friction between India and Pakistan. Bharat also opened services in 1948 and 1949 to Chittagong, in East Pakistan, to Agartala in Tripura, and to Gauhati, in Assam; but these local operations were outshone by the airline's ambitious programme of international extension to east Asia.

On 28 May 1949 Bharat Airways – proudly carrying the Hindi name for the Indian Union – began international services to Bangkok using Douglas DC-4s, unpressurized aircraft but with comforting four-engined safety that was of para-mount interest among travellers at that time. Bharat's original plan was to open a route to Tokyo, but this was frustrated because of the revolutionary war in China that prevented a practical route via Shanghai. The service was, however, extended to Singapore in 1950, and had the complete reorganization of the Indian airline industry not occurred in 1953 the world may have heard much more of the Bharat name. J R D Tata's and Air-India's eyes were set on Europe and beyond to the United States, so that a division of the international spoils (but for the creation of the two State corporations in 1953), may have seen Bharat as the chosen instrument for India's airline involvement in east Asia.

Three other airlines operated scheduled services in India before the creation of the Indian Airlines Corporation. Himalayan Aviation Ltd was founded in 1948 and became one of the participants in the Night Air Mail; but as its name suggests, it was also identified with operations farther north. During 1952 and 1953, it provided air links between Kathmandu and domestic points in Nepal, under an arrangement with the Nepal Government: operations which were taken over by the Indian Airlines Corporation in 1953 and continued until such time as Nepal could start up its own airline.

Himalayan also operated air services as far west as Karachi and even to Zahedan in Iran, the terminus of the rail line from Quetta; and also to Kandahar and Kabul in Afghanistan; but these services were intermittent, because of the fluctuating nature – to put it mildly – of the political climate in that region.

Kalinga Air Lines started service in 1949, linking Calcutta with Agartala, the chief city of the State of Tripura, fiercely independent of its neighbours, and for which a direct link to the big city, Calcutta, was essential for its well-being, especially after the creation of Pakistan separated it completely, except by a completely impractical circuitous route, from the rest of India.

One other airline left only a minor imprint on the pre-nationalization scene. Jupiter Airways Ltd was founded in Madras, and operated DC-3s for a short time in 1949–1950 to Bombay. Its motto was 'By Jupiter, that's quick'. In spite of its declared capital of about £400,000, which might have suggested stability, the quickness was marked mainly by the speed of its demise.

The Indian Night Air Mail

Somewhere, some time during the late 1940s, someone in the Indian Post Office came up with an idea. His name is probably lost in the sands of time, but his idea is far from lost. For this anonymous innovator devised a scheme that for a few years was a model for others to copy; and was eventually copied in a far wider arena than India. The Indian Night Air Mail depended for its success on the successful operation of a central hub in a spoke-shaped air network, in which aircraft would arrive from the extremities of each spoke, exchange their mail payloads with each other, and return to their origin points. This was exactly the same idea that was put into practice with such spectacular effect by Fred Smith in 1973, when he launched the now famous Federal Express package service from a hub in Memphis, Tennessee, and which operated in the same manner as the Indian Night Air Mail of a quarter of a century earlier.

As has already been mentioned in this chapter, the four main cities of India, Bombay, Delhi, Calcutta and Madras, are situated at the four corners of a roughly-shaped diamond. Two diagonals drawn to join the opposite points of the diamond, i.e., Bombay–Calcutta and Delhi–Madras, cross almost precisely at Nagpur, in what used to be the Central Provinces and which is now the eastern part of Maharashtra. Although the distance from Nagpur to Bombay is a little shorter, that to the other three points is about 600 miles, or about 1,000 kilometres, and about the range of a DC-3, fully loaded with mail, and a four-hour flight time.

The Night Air Mail scheme was simple. Aircraft would depart from the four corner points of the system mid-way through the evening, arrive at Nagpur soon after midnight, exchange their loads during the wee small hours of the night, and return to arrive at about daybreak. Letters posted for air mail delivery by early evening would be delivered to any of the other three cities by the late morning

29

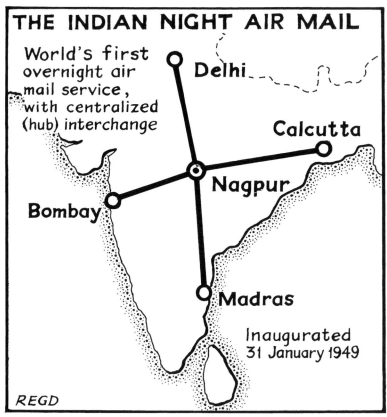

THE INDIAN NIGHT AIR MAIL

World's first overnight air mail service, with centralized (hub) interchange

Delhi

Calcutta

Nagpur

Bombay

Madras

Inaugurated 31 January 1949

REGD

Map 2b. The Indian Night Air Mail
The inauguration of the night-time air mail system on 31 January 1949 was a remarkable example of applied ingenuity. Letters and packages posted in the four main cities of India during the evening would be delivered in each of the three other destinations the next morning, thanks to a system in which the aircraft from each originating point would meet at Nagpur, which served as an interchange clearing-house for the mail. Such an innovative system pre-dated the famous Federal Express and other dedicated air express services by a quarter of a century.

post next day. Nagpur was the clearing house, and it quickly developed as a busy air mail sorting office for the Indian postal authorities.

First of the independent airlines to bid successfully for the contract to carry this mail was Indian Overseas Airlines, which may have won the privilege through a low bid. It had the honour of opening the service on 31 January 1949, but unfortunately could not last the pace, even though it had already established itself in Nagpur. From 10 to 30 June of that year, the veteran Indian National Airways was obliged to take over as a temporary measure, until Himalayan Aviation, an apparent jack-of-all-trades, took over the responsibility on 15 October. Two years later, on 1 June 1951, Deccan Airways, based at Hyderabad adjusted its map to include Nagpur, and continued to carry the night mail until the formation of the Indian Airlines Corporation which took over in 1953.

Two of Indian Airlines Corporation's Douglas DC-4s at Nagpur during the night mail exchange which normally involved four aircraft.

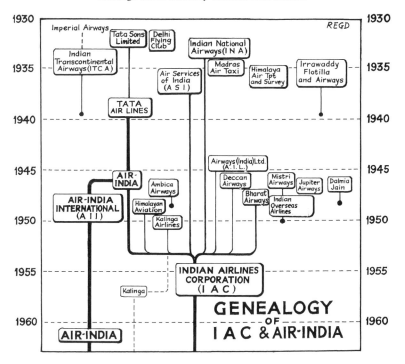

Genealogy of IAC and Air-India

This chart shows the shape of the corporate development of the two leading Indian airlines, formed, it is believed, on the British pattern of BOAC and BEA – dividing the long-haul and short/medium responsibilities into two managements. The IAC merger was a formidable challenge, as Indian law prevented any layoffs, and for many years, the airline suffered from a surplus of staff, at all levels.

31

The early independent airlines of India, operating as they did almost entirely with a fleet of ex-military DC-3s, and mostly with inadequate capital resources or cadre of experienced personnel, were no great torch-bearers of aviation progress, viewed in a worldwide context. But the Indian Night Air Mail was evidence that the spirit of enterprise was not completely absent; it was a great credit to all concerned, and a shining example for others to follow.

For much of the time after it took over the Night Mail, IAC used DC-4s, carrying passengers at low fares as well as mail. During transit at Nagpur the passengers could refresh themselves in the terminal and even watch a film. Before the aircraft were airborne many of the passengers were already asleep with their feet up on the seats in front.

The whole exchange progress at Nagpur worked with military precision. When a DC-4 was in maintenance a segment would be served by a DC-3 with mail and a Viscount with passengers – thus up to ten movements could be handled during the brief Nagpur transit.

CHAPTER THREE

Indian Airlines Corporation

New Delhi Takes a Hand

The postwar years had witnessed the emergence of several independent airlines in India to join the three prewar incumbents. As narrated in the previous chapter there had been a few casualties, but the early 1950s found eight airlines competing for domestic air traffic. Some were well organized, operated according to conventional administrative and organizational practices, and had a good chance of survival in a competitive world. But others lacked such professionalism, and the prospect was looming of a bitter battle for survival in which the fittest would emerge eventually, but only after much harm to Indian air transport as a whole. The Indian Government in New Delhi could also observe that, with the possible exception of Air-India, backed by the Tata industrial group, and presided over by J R D Tata, none of the airlines had sufficient capital to ensure controlled growth, expansion, and modernization. Specifically, over the entire Indian domestic scene, of the more than 100 aircraft in service, three quarters of the total were DC-3s of prewar design, and the dozen or so Vikings and DC-4s used on domestic routes were, at best, obsolescent by the standards of Europe and America. Not a single aircraft used on domestic routes was pressurized.

Foreseeing approaching chaos, the Government took firm steps. On 28 May 1953, the Air Corporations Act was approved by the President. This drew inspiration, as did a great deal of India's newly-independent administration activities, from British practice. Just as the British had rationalized its airline industry into three, later reduced to two, State corporations – one to take care of long-haul traffic, the other to specialize in the short- and medium-haul – India did the same, creating the long-haul company simply by nationalizing the overseas operations of Air-India International and the short- and medium-haul element by amalgamating all the others, together with Air-India's domestic routes. On 15 June 1953, the two new airlines peremptorily took over and the independents effectively ceased to exist.

The domestic airline, the Indian Airlines Corporation (IAC) absorbed the undertakings of eight privately-owned companies, including Deccan Airways, in which the State already held a 70 per cent interest, resulting from the political action in dissolving the former State of Hyderabad. The total compensation amounted to 47 million rupees (about £3,500,000), of which 10 per cent was in cash and the remainder in $3\frac{1}{2}$ per cent interest-carrying government bonds.

The former airline names disappeared, to be replaced, during an interim period of reorganization, by seven Lines, as follows:

Air-India Ltd (domestic routes only) . . . Line 6
Air Services of India Ltd . . . . Line 7
Airways (India) Ltd . . . . Line 1
Bharat Airways Ltd . . . . Line 2
Deccan Airways Ltd. . . . . Line 5

Indian Airlines Corporation took over 74 Dakotas (mostly Douglas C-47s) from the airlines
it absorbed. This one is seen at Safdarjang Airport, New Delhi, in 1958. *(John Stroud)*

Himalayan Aviation Ltd. . . . . Line 3
Indian National Airways Ltd . . . . Line 4
Kalinga Airlines Ltd . . . . Line 3
Himalayan and Kalinga were amalgamated into one operating Line.

An Arduous Beginning

The new corporation did start with one advantage: the network was already in
place, with station staff everywhere to deal with the commercial, operational, and
engineering/maintenance requirements that face any airline. The big problem was
that there were far too many staff, both at the stations, and at the new headquarters of IAC in Delhi. One of the main advantages of an amalgamation is that
economies can be identified by eliminating duplicated functions, and typically this
is dealt with either by arbitrary dismissal of superfluous staff; by a slightly more
tolerable lay-off programme, with compensations; or by a combination of these,
aided by natural attrition, involving retirements, deaths and infirmities, or resignations. Unfortunately for Indian Airlines, dismissal, even laying-off, was not
permitted by law, as such practices had been viewed as one of the less commendable aspects of the former colonialism that had to be stopped.

Thus, India's domestic airline was burdened with two or three employees for
every job, from vice-presidential and director level right down to the most menial
stratum of floor-sweepers and messenger boys. The process of attrition took many
years, as in India, the job security that employment with a State airline bestowed
was almost priceless.

If the rate of attrition was slow with the staff, it was all too swift with the fleet.
As had been the case from the first months of peacetime operations in 1945, Indian
Airlines depended almost entirely on the Douglas DC-3, conversions of which
amounted to an impressive number – IAC took over 74 of them – and their age
was not excessive as most were C-47s built in the mid-1940s. But the standard of
maintenance was not, the repair shops scattered around the network often resorting to practices that would not have met with the approval of headquarters in
Delhi, and would have been met with shock, if not disbelief, by an FAA inspector. To be fair, the maintenance crews too often had to try to keep the aircraft

34

IAC Dakotas, one being refuelled, at Hyderabad, Deccan. (*John Stroud*)

Air Chief Marshal P C Lal, one time chairman of IAC. (*Courtesy John Stroud*)

An IAC Dakota at Trivandrum in South India. (*John Stroud*)

One of IAC's regional bases is at Bombay Airport (Santacruz). (*Courtesy John Stroud*)

flying with inadequate tools and equipment, a chronic shortage of spare parts, and working conditions that would have been unacceptable elsewhere – and in fact would become unacceptable in India too. The aircraft also had to operate into a large number of aerodromes that are sometimes described euphemistically as unprepared. In some areas of India, this was an exaggeration; neglected would be a closer description. IAC protested to the Government continuously, and pleaded for aerodrome and airport improvements, but to no avail, for many years.

The net result of these shortcomings was an unhappy record of accidents during the early stages of IAC's existence. During the first three years, there were seventeen accidents; and although the number of passengers killed was mercifully small, the situation was clearly unsatisfactory. The DC-3s, wartime veterans, and the unpressurized Vikings, had to be supplemented, if not replaced, by more modern types.

IAC Modernizes Its Fleet

Barely a year after its formation, the Indian Airlines Corporation moved to keep up with the times. Impressed by the success of the launching customer, British

IAC's Dakotas did outstanding work in Assam. (*IAC*)

European Airways, in July 1954 it ordered five Vickers Viscount 768 propeller-turbine airliners for its main trunk lines. Delivery was still three years off, and meanwhile, to reinforce the fleet for the feeder routes of lower traffic density, IAC also ordered eight de Havilland 114 Herons, which were delivered within a year of the October 1954 contract.

During the mid-1950s, the Vikings operated on the main inter-city routes of the 'diamond' while the DC-3s backed them up and took care of all the secondary routes. The Herons filled in on the short segments, but although their four engines was seen as an advantage, they had problems, including two accidents, and were retired after only a few years of service. The Douglas DC-4s, inherited from Bharat, were put on to the Night Air Mail on 5 November 1955, and their capacity not only met the growing demand for the air mail, but made room for passenger service also.

An IAC Vickers-Armstrongs Viscount 768 before delivery. (*Vickers*)

37

The Viscounts came into service on 10 October 1957. Their 44 seats, large windows, and pressurized modernity, suddenly elevated Indian Airlines to a new level of higher standards of passenger comfort. The first route for the new type was Delhi–Calcutta, and on to Rangoon, followed, a month later, by Delhi–Bombay, then, on 10 December, Bombay–Karachi, and Bombay–Madras–Colombo two weeks later. On 9 April 1958, the Viscount took over part of the Night Air Mail, so that India now had a network of the world's best short-medium haul airliners deployed to all its main cities.

At this time, much attention was being paid by the world's airliner manufacturers to the problem of what became known as the 'DC-3 Replacement'. While the term was misleading, in that no aircraft has replaced that ubiquitous and apparently ageless Douglas product, but only supplemented its many and varied talents, several new types came close. These were 40–44 seater twins, all powered by Rolls-Royce Dart propeller turbines, the same that powered the four-engined Viscount. The trio included the Dutch Fokker F.27 Friendship, a high-wing design that was to achieve great success – more than 800 were eventually built, in the Netherlands and in the USA (as the F-27) over a period of a quarter of a century.

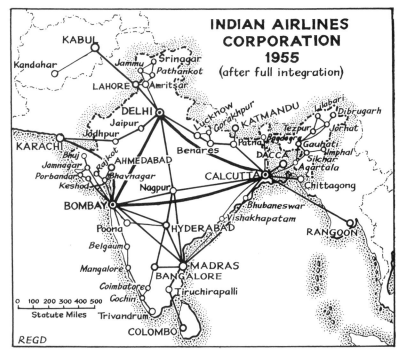

Map 3. The Indian Airlines Corporation, 1955 (after full integration)
The eight airlines that amalgamated in 1953, to form an integrated domestic system, gave India a truly national airline network within its own frontiers as a partner to Air-India International. Although it served the main cities of neighbouring countries in the Sub-Continent, the range of its operations was limited by the terms of the Corporations Act; so that IAC was comparatively little known overseas. Nevertheless, it has always been in the vanguard of progress, and has served India's 800 million people well.

In the mid-1950s IAC ordered de Havilland Herons for feeder routes with low traffic density. (*de Havilland*)

Another similar design was the British Handley Page Herald, and a third contestant for this market category was another British effort, the Avro 748, differing from the other two in that it was a low-wing design, and with claims to be of sturdier construction, enabling it to cope with the same kind of unprepared strips that the DC-3 could take in its stride.

After much negotiation and discussions between the rival manufacturers and the Indian authorities – with Indian Airlines only one element of the customer side of the hard bargaining – the Avro 748 (soon to be the Hawker Siddeley 748 after a British industry re-structuring) won the battle. But the Indians drove a hard bargain. To win the contract, Avro had to agree to help India set up its own production line, building the 748 at a new factory in Cawnpore.

This process necessarily took time. New aircraft factories cannot be set up overnight; and Cawnpore was a long way from Avro's home base in Manchester. Indian Airlines was not prepared to wait – almost interminably, it seemed – for home production to deliver the goods, and it therefore ordered a fleet of Fokker Friendships, out of sheer necessity, and these were delivered a full six years before the 748s were ready.

These latter went into service early in May 1961, at first on all the routes to the north, northeast, and east of Calcutta, mainly into the small strips in Assam. The need for good air service to this region was imperative. The peculiarities of the Partition that formed Pakistan had turned the former province of Assam into a political island, so isolated was it from Indian West Bengal by the Bengali East Pakistan. Only a narrow strip of land in the far north of Bengal linked Assam with the rest of India; and to reach Agartala, in the newly-formed State of Tripura, for example, the railway line had to traverse a meandering route of about 800 miles (1,300 km) even to get close to the border, or four times the distance in a straight line from Calcutta. There were times of stress when even the DC-3s and Friendships were not allowed to fly in a straight line, i.e. across Pakistan, but the aerial diversion that was sometimes necessary was comparatively slight.

The geographical alienation was compounded by an extreme example of ethnic diversity. In what used to be the province of Assam are to be found one hundred distinct languages, of which more than half are native to the province. In an effort to recognize such ethnic diversity, with its attendant demands for autonomy, the old Assam was severely fragmented – and cut down to less than half its original size – so as to provide autonomous status to six new diminutive states: Meghalaya, Nagaland, Mizoram, Manipur, Tripura, and Arunachal Pradesh. If India was to retain its unity and the integrity of its former frontiers to the east and northeast, air communication, for legislative, commercial, logistics, and quasi-military purposes, was absolutely essential. The Friendships became the workhorses of the Assam routes, and later on they provided also the stopping services between Delhi and Calcutta, via cities in Uttar Pradesh (the former United Provinces), and from Delhi to Kashmir.

Confrontation

During the years of British colonialism, and expansionist incursions made into territory on the fringes of the sub-continental land mass, the British Army had never been able to conquer the mountain fastnesses and tribal areas in the mountainous regions to the northwest and the north. The Afghan Wars had resulted in a stalemate, with the tribesmen able to deal in their own way with technically superior but strategically and tactically outmanoeuvred forces. In Nepal, the local fighters, the Gurkhas, defended their land with such effect that a truce resulted to ensure Nepal's independence, while the Gurkha troops became eligible for the British and Indian Armies, whom they served with great honour and distinction. Further east, Bhutan was a mountainous kingdom that served as a buffer state with Tibet; and further east still was an area that was claimed by the British and delineated by a line drawn on the map, and known as the MacMahon Line, after the British statesman who had negotiated the peace treaty with China and Tibet in 1914.

During the years of British domination that followed, the boundary lines to the north were never seriously disputed. Tibet was so isolated that a single visit by an individual was enough to provide the subject for a travel adventure book. China was still dormant, presided over by an oligarchy of foreign commercial exploitation. But after the Second World War, and the emergence of China as a fiercely independent, even belligerent nation, under the communist government that came into power in 1949, things changed. China began to question the conditions under which its lands had been encroached upon, and, as it asserted its sovereignty over Tibet, and as modern technology eased the transport and logistics problems, the former somnolent frontiers with India were shaken out of their inertia.

Along the MacMahon Line, which, for India, comprised the northern border of Assam, the soldiers guarding the frontier posts on both sides became involved in skirmishes and sporadic fighting broke out. In December 1962, these actions were exacerbated to the stage where a state of emergency was declared, and the Confrontation, as it was called, created a minor crisis in India.

The Indian Airlines Corporation rose to the occasion. All its aircraft were requisitioned, to provide logistics support for the Indian armed forces. IAC transported troops, arms, and supplies of all kinds to the northeast frontier. Happily, the hostilities did not multiply or develop into a full-scale war; but there had been anxious moments, and the role of the national airline in times of military preparedness had been demonstrated. But sadly, this role was to be called upon only too often in the years that followed. Wars with Pakistan in 1965 and again in 1971–72, when Bangladesh was created, placed great demands on IAC, completely disrupt-

40

ing services and testing the calibre of the personnel.

In September 1967, another face-to-face episode in the north, where the Indian state of Sikkim had a common frontier with Chinese Tibet through a narrow corridor between Nepal and Bhutan, erupted into a minor military clash. Once again, IAC reacted immediately to the emergency, with aircrews and maintenance men alike throwing away all the labour rule-books, and rushing to the north, from bases in Bombay, Delhi and Madras, as well as nearby Calcutta, at a minute's notice on receiving the cry for help from the troops. As a matter of interest, the Chinese soldiers actually occupied some Indian territory, advancing about 40 miles; but after negotiation, pulled back to their original line of demarcation, possibly the only occasion in history when a victorious force has voluntarily done so.

Short-Haul Jets for India

In the summer of 1962, Indian Airlines decided that it had to move into the jet age. It still turned to Europe for its choice, because the Caravelle had put France into contention for world markets when Air France successfully introduced it in 1959. It was the world's first short-haul jet, and the first to make the bold, and at the time, revolutionary, step of placing the two engines at the rear of the fuselage, thereby producing a very clean wing. The only other contender was the British Trident, and in spite of a presentation by de Havilland that visualized a succession of variants to keep pace with IAC's growing traffic, it was not yet in service; and furthermore, the manufacturer had surrendered to an ill-judged insistence of the launching customer, BEA, to reduce it in size. The three-engined Trident, in fact, could carry only a few more passengers than the Caravelle twin; and so, in due course, the French airliner entered service, equipped with 89 all-economy seats, on India's domestic trunk routes early in February 1964.

Even though the Caravelle did well, there were problems. While IAC's intensive use of its new jet placed it at the top of the charts in terms of annual utilization (revenue hours flown per year) – its 3,000 hours was the best in the world – this was not without penalties. During 1966, two Caravelles were lost in accidents, and although they were replaced, the paradox was that, such was their success, bigger aircraft were needed on the trunk routes (just as de Havilland had predicted in its long-term plan, involving Trident 3s). Some relief came in 1967, when, at last, the first HS 748 went into service at the end of the year, after a Boeing 707 had been leased from Air-India for the trunk services. Incidentally, in this year, the official name underwent a slight change, to become Indian Airlines.

The search for a larger short-haul jet resulted in Government approval to buy seven Boeing 737-200 twins early in January 1970, and within days, a letter of intent was signed on 15 January. The first one, fitted with 126 seats, entered service on 1 January 1971. The deal had not been without controversy – deals in India seldom are. In this case, the Douglas company, with the DC-9, and the British Aircraft Corporation, with the One-Eleven, were strong contenders. The long-drawn out negotiations included a second evaluation because it was alleged that the Douglas agent had offered a 'commission' to the head of the evaluation committee. The case dragged on until 1977, when it was discovered that Exhibit A, an incriminating letter, was found to be a forgery, and all people concerned were acquitted by the Indian High Court.

IAC's first pure-jet transports were Sud-Aviation Caravelle VINs. The aircraft illustrated was named *Gagandoot (Heavenley Messenger)*. (*Sud-Aviation*)

Problems of the Seventies

Indian Airlines entered the decade of the Seventies laden with difficulties, some of which were special for India, but all of which combined to make life hard for both management and employees, not to mention the customers. Any one of the individual problems would have put some strain on most airlines; but Indian Airlines had quite a number, and collectively they imposed a severe handicap to unencumbered progress. Not necessarily unique, but certainly unusual, they are worth listing, not to excuse but perhaps to explain what to some foreign observers appeared to be neglect or inefficiency.

In the 1960s IAC acquired a fleet of Hawker Siddeley 748s built by Hindustan Aviation at Kanpur (Cawnpore) from British-built components.

42

1. Local wars, or the threat of them, seemed ever-present, with the Pakistan–India recurrent confrontations and conflicts a constant deterrent to stabilized operations. The logistics efforts to support the armed forces in the Chinese incidents interrupted regular services; and making aircraft available for refugee airlifts was a common occurrence.
2. The East Wing of Pakistan customarily acted as a barrier between the main part of India to its far eastern states. The diversions necessary were operationally and financially costly.
3. Indian airlines have always paid highly for fuel. Its basic price was high because it had to be imported. There was a high excise tax and a sales tax. Fuel costs alone amounted to a quarter of the airline costs, a level probably unmatched anywhere in the world among major airlines.
4. The airline was obliged to provide social services to underdeveloped and, by definition, poor areas, and required to charge low fares, sometimes lower than rail fares. These routes were seldom subsidized by the central or the state governments, with the result that Indian Airlines had to cross-subsidize the unprofitable lines itself.
5. As an inheritance from the manner of its foundation – the merger of eight private airlines – and in an effort to share the benefits of the new organization, Indian Airlines refrained from concentrating all its maintenance and overhaul in one place. Four bases spread the load, but were less economical than one.
6. Labour rates in India at the time of independence were abysmally low. Even with the Government's best efforts, and with a conscious awareness of the deficiency by the airline, progress in raising wages was slow; and this led to many strikes, as the staff became aware of corresponding rates elsewhere.
7. There were special deterrents to travel and to operations that were peculiar to India. In 1971, a cholera epidemic did not encourage visitors. No airline in the world of comparable size has had to include bird strikes (with vultures, not sparrows) as a common cause of aircraft damage.
8. One of Indian Airlines' biggest traffic-generating cities suffered a decline in importance. Calcutta had been a great commercial centre for local heavy industry, which was stagnating. Large British trading companies were transferred to Indian ownership. Many foreign airlines bypassed Calcutta, in favour of the capital Delhi, and Bombay. New bridges over the Ganges and Brahmaputra depleted the formerly heavy freight traffic to Assam.

If a US or European airline had to face compounded problems like these, it would not last very long. But Indian Airlines has demonstrated a resilience to misfortune that has sustained it through troublesome times, and even enabled it to benefit the Indian community as a whole beyond expectations.

The year 1973 was a bad one. It started off with the January announcement of a 45 million rupee loss for the previous fiscal year, with the blame placed squarely on the 1971–72 Pakistan War and strict hijacking measures. On 31 May, one of the 737s crashed in poor weather at Delhi, and major damage was sustained by a Caravelle and two HS 748s; and later on a Friendship also had to be taken out of service. On 12 September, the Night Air Mail Service ended as a separate operation after 24 years and all except two of the Viscounts were retired. All this was against a background of labour unrest which led to a crisis, in which some staff, including air crew, were locked out, and only a skeleton service was maintained with non-union staff. Eventually, a 'new deal' was negotiated between the management and the unions. Wasteful work practices were eliminated, pay scales

Boeing 737-200s entered IAC service in 1971. (*IAC*)

reviewed, and the union recognized management's 'right to manage'.

This led to a 25 per cent tariff increase, coming into effect on 1 February 1974; and on 18 March, an historic day, although there were no great fanfares, no dignitary-attended ceremonies, the Douglas DC-3s – about 30 of them – were retired. They had been the ever-present jack-of-all-trades to provide passenger service into any dirt strip or field that could be prepared with minimum labour or equipment, they had airlifted supplies, carried refugees, and substituted for other aircraft a thousand times. Some measure of the DC-3's sheer versatility can be judged from the fact that, when they were retired, sixteen stations were also closed down, officially 'for economic reasons' – and this was the case in many areas – but mainly because not even the Friendships could operate from the small strips.

Indian Airlines soldiered on, re-grouped, and recharged its batteries during the next few years. Such was the growing demand for domestic air service, as the country began to develop its industries and strengthen its economy that, in spite of the accidents, the diminution of the fleet, and reduction in the points served, the need for a larger aircraft for the trunk routes became critical. In April 1975, the corporation took the bold step of ordering three wide-bodied Airbuses. Once again, there were exciting times ahead.

Into the Wide-Bodied Era

In the sub-continent of strife, Indian Airlines served as a bonding agent, as quick to help restore normality after a conflict as it was to provide support in defence of its realm when the storms erupted. After each of the bitter struggles with Pakistan, service was restored to Karachi, Lahore and Dacca, as soon as reasonable precautions against terrorism or sabotage could be assured and political sensitivities reassured. When the British formerly held sway over what it liked to call the Indian Empire, three countries of the sub-continent, on its periphery, had

44

successfully defended their independence: Afghanistan, Nepal and Bhutan. Ceylon (Sri Lanka) had been separated from India as a Crown Colony almost since the British arrived, and became a Dominion in 1948. Subsequently, Pakistan was created in 1947, Burma seceded from the Commonwealth in 1948, the Maldives gained their independence in 1965, and finally Pakistan split in two, and Bangladesh gained nationhood in 1972.

During the 1970s, therefore, while enduring its different crises from within, Indian Airlines gradually restored order to the fragmented air transport system of the Sub-continent, resuming service to Kabul, with overflying rights across Pakistan, in April 1976, having, in the south, begun a service from Trivandrum to Malé, the capital of the sun-drenched and pacific Maldive Islands.

With the exception of Bhutan, which remained comparatively isolated and aloof from international entanglements, even commercial relations, Indian Airlines served seven neighbouring countries. By the time the decade drew to a close, it had also begun services to the Persian Gulf, serving Dubai and Muscat, on charter to Air-India, and these were later promoted to full schedules; and with growing confidence and official recognition, it extended its route network to Bangkok and Singapore in the mid-1980s. For a long time, Indian Airlines had lived in the shadow of the prestigious Air-India and had been conscious of a perceived inferior status. No longer: for in 1976, it moved into the premier division of the airline leagues by introducing the latest and best of the wide-bodied Airbuses.

In April 1975, Indian Airlines ordered three Airbuses, plus three on option, Series A300B-2, in a 278-seat, 33-inch pitch, all-economy layout. Austere, perhaps, by European or American standards, the demand in India was for volume rather than high standards of luxury or a five-star cuisine up front. In fact, the traffic on the main inter-city routes of India was booming.

Large wide-bodied commercial aircraft are expensive; and even though Airbus's price was right by international financial criteria (to the extent that Airbus was accused frequently by its competitors as being subsidized by the French and German Governments) the bill was a stiff one for India. It was reduced slightly by a domestic manufacturing programme, under which $2.4 million's worth of ground support equipment was produced by Indian factories.

The Airbuses were delivered earlier than originally planned. In October 1976, a Caravelle had crashed, and such was the concern that the entire fleet was grounded, creating a severe capacity shortage. Consequently, the first Airbus

In 1975 IAC ordered three 278-passenger Airbus A300B-2 wide-bodied aircraft. (*Airbus*)

45

A300B-2 went into service on 1 December of the same year, and by 14 January 1977, all three were plying the Bombay–Delhi–Calcutta–Madras 'diamond' and also to Bangalore, and thus achieving, right from the start, a high level of annual utilization. The on-board service, already good on the main-line routes, was improved still further, with gracious sari-clad flight attendants, and excellent Indian cuisine, with a selection for all tastes, including fine vegetarian dishes.

Wide-Bodied Indigestion

As Indian Airlines entered the decade of the Eighties, it began to see itself as India's domestic trunk airline, rather than an air transport service that was all things to all people; and in 1981, an important decision was made to form a third airline to serve the nation. Jointly sponsored and owned, half each, by Indian Airlines and Air-India, a third national airline, Vayudoot, took over the responsibilities of serving the small communities. It leased some of Indian Airlines' Fokker Friendships and HS 748s so as to get under way quickly, and later, under the part-time chairmanship of Gerry Pais, IA's managing director, it purchased them. Relieved of the irritation of trying to do too many different things at once, the national domestic airline thereupon took steps to strengthen its main-line fleet.

On 22 August 1984, it ordered twelve Boeing 757s, the twin-engined development of the 727 that was so different from the earliest model that only the fuselage cross-section was common to both. A letter of intent was signed, with a $900,000 refundable deposit, and the aircraft were to be delivered in 1988. Three days later, seven Sikh dissidents hijacked a Boeing 737 at Dubai, and although this incident did not affect Boeing's fortunes in India, the rise to power as Prime Minister of India by Rajiv Gandhi, son of Indira Gandhi, formerly Prime Minister herself, most certainly did. Rajiv was sworn into office on 31 October 1984, when his mother was shot down by her own Sikh bodyguard, four months after the storming of the Sikh Golden Temple at Amritsar.

At the end of August 1985, one year after the 757 order, and shortly after Rajiv Gandhi's visit to the Paris Air Show, Indian Airlines switched its choice of aircraft to complement the A300s from the Boeing 757 to the Airbus A320. By 20 September, a letter of intent had been signed for nineteen aircraft, plus twelve on option. While there was some justification for the larger order, because of the chronic shortage of capacity, this was clearly a political decision, not a technical one, as there was nothing wrong with the 757, except that it was not a wide-bodied type; but neither is the A320.

The option for the additional twelve A320s was exercised in 1988. By this time, Indian's fleet consisted of ten A300s, including two A300B-4s; twenty-seven Boeing 737s, six HS 748s, and two F.27s. The last two types were employed on feeder routes that had not yet been taken over by Vayudoot. The mainline fleet was flying intensely at 3,000 hours a year per aircraft. In 1988, Indian Airlines carried, for the first time, more than ten million passengers in a year, a figure exceeded only by five US and two Japanese domestic airlines. The airline shopped around for additional capacity and leased both A300s and 737s from Transavia, Netherlands, until the situation was relieved on 1 July 1989, when the first 'fly-by-wire' A320 went into service.

Such was IA's eagerness to supplement its fleet numbers that it looked carefully at the Soviet Union's new generation types, the Ilyushin Il-96 and the Tupolev Tu-204, the first with Pratt & Whitney engines, the second with Rolls-Royce. But the historic transition of political power and the termination of the Soviet state at the end of 1991 interrupted these discussions.

The A320 had come under critical scrutiny in 1989 when one of them crashed in France, near Mulhouse, under circumstances that cast some doubt on the reliability of the new revolutionary fly-by-wire and glass cockpit systems; and the exact causes of that accident have never been categorically explained. When, therefore, an Indian Airlines A320 crashed at Bangalore on 14 February 1990 – the second major disaster to the type within two years – Indian official eyebrows were raised so high that the A320 fleet was grounded. Then followed a debate on a grand scale. Inspection and enquiry revealed substantial evidence that the cause had been a clearcut case of pilot error, in which the crew had not 'followed the book'. The pilots' union refused to accept the verdict of the Indian Inspector of Accidents, and a royal free-for-all ensued, in which the propriety of the circumstances of the original order for A320s, suggestions of bribery and kickbacks, and corruption on a grand scale, were resurrected.

As such emotional eruptions seem to do in India, rather as terrifying volcanoes subside after having exploded on to the community with great force, everyone woke up one morning to find the whole affair a matter of history, with everyone agreeing to disagree, but getting on with the job of running an airline. For Indian Airlines, the creation of Vayudoot had been a great relief. After only two years from its foundation in 1981, the new airline entered a spectacular period of growth. In addition to the Friendships and HS 748s transferred from Indian Airlines, it acquired a fleet of ten Dornier 228-200 light transports, signing a contract with Germany on 29 November 1983 that allowed for half of the order to be assembled in India from sub-components delivered from Dornier, with the objective of licensed production at a later date. Vayudoot would be a valuable customer. By 1990, it was serving no less than 110 communities in India, many of which had never had scheduled air service before, even in the halcyon days of the versatile Douglas DC-3.

The Incredible Accident

The term incredible has to be used with caution, and can apply only to very rare occurrences. One that springs to mind is when a Jugoslav flight attendant fell out of an aircraft at 20,000 feet over the Tatra Mountains of Czechoslovakia – and lived to tell the tale. Another recent incident, involving Indian Airlines, should go into the history books as another almost unbelievable survival story.

To state the case in simple, factual terms: on 9 January 1993, a Tupolev Tu-154 trijet, leased from Uzbekistan (one of the newly independent republics that emerged after the collapse of the Soviet Union in December 1991), was trying to land at Delhi at 4 a.m. in fog, without instruments – or at least without instruments that were compatible with the airport's. The aircraft flipped over after a wingtip snared the ground, broke into three pieces, and later caught fire. Not a single occupant of the aircraft, 152 passengers and 13 crew, was killed, although, on extricating themselves from an upside down position, half a dozen sustained injuries, the worst of which, however, was a broken leg or two.

While there was much praise for the integrity of the aircraft's structure and its reluctance to burst into flames immediately on impact, the repercussions on Indian Airlines and on the Indian civil air authorities were considerable. For the accident, or one similar to it, had been predicted by many, in a worsening situation that seemed to repeat the history of many an industrial dispute in the past, when the pilots had gone on strike. In this case, they had walked out on 10 December 1992 in protest at low pay scales, compared with those that were being paid by a new domestic feeder airline, East-West Airlines. Indian Airlines had attempted to circumvent the crisis and improve its bargaining position by hiring renegade crews and wet-leasing aircraft. These latter included four from Uzbekistan and three from Bulgaria, all Tupolev Tu-154s.

The Indian civil aviation minister, Madhavrao Scindia, resigned. The Indian pilots union threatened to institute legal proceedings. Undoubtedly, the disputes will continue and drag on, while India attempts to find a formula that can reconcile management problems with staff sensitivities so as to ensure some operational equilibrium that is essential to carry Indian air transport into the 21st Century. The need is paramount. India's population is already in excess of 850 million, and still growing. Like every other industrialized country, the urban population growth has expanded at an uncontrolled rate. At least fifteen cities have populations of more than a million – Bombay and Calcutta have more than 10 million each.

Indian Airlines' passenger count of more than 10 million in 1988 has already been noted. If this seems a large number, it is nothing compared with the estimated 11 million passengers *per day* carried by Indian Railways. While not all of the latter are travelling over inter-city routes that would qualify as competitive with air travel, the statistic does offer some indication of the magnitude of the problem that faces the airline element of India's transport industry as a whole. For Indian Airlines, there are still exciting times ahead.

Diversity by Deregulation

During the 1970s, throughout the commercial aviation world, the sustained growth of traffic had led to pressures for more competition on the more heavily-travelled routes. This trend was evident both in the USA, where all airlines were privately owned, and also in Europe, where state-owned or state-sponsored flag carriers were customary. In India, the state-owned Indian Airlines Corporation had been subjected to criticisms of excessive bureaucracy, and of operational shortcomings, exacerbated by a spotty accident record. While the Indian Government was in no hurry to introduce legislation that would open up the Indian skies to free competition, it did allow the thin end of a free enterprise wedge.

During the 1970s, a few aviation companies were formed to exercise limited rights. Air Works India, for example, operated freight services with a DC-3, DC-4, even a Britannia; while Huns Air and Goldensun Aviation operated charter services to the Gulf and on short feeder routes (*see* table). As narrated above, the state airlines countered the independent pressures on their domain by forming Vayudoot, so as to concentrate all the secondary and third level airlines into one subsidiary organization; and to meet the specialized aircraft need, an agreement was made on 29 November 1983 with the German Dornier Company for the licensed production of the Dornier 228 feeder-liner by Hindustan Aeronautics in Bangalore.

In the 1980s, possibly echoing the past history of this category of air transport in America, about fifteen licences to operate air taxi services were issued by the Minister of Tourism and Civil Aviation. Ostensibly intended only to encourage tourism, this thin end of the wedge was pushed further through the scheduled airline door. The taxi services often developed into regular or quasi-scheduled operations, although there were other restrictions. Then, in 1990, the new Minister eased the restrictions and encouraged the small companies to expand, thereby relieving the capacity shortage on many inter-city routes.

Initially, the lack of experience led to the early demise of those airlines that tried

Independent Indian Airlines

Date of First Service	Airline (and Base)	Fleet	Routes	Remarks
The Early Trailblazers				
(1970s)	Air Works India (Bombay)	DC-3, DC-4, Britannia	(Charter services)	Ceased operations
Nov. 1974	Huns Air (Bombay)	Vickers Viscount Boeing 707	Services to Sharjah (Gulf)	Cargo outbound, guest workers in-bound. Ceased operations
20 Dec 1977	Goldensun Aviation (Bombay)	Beech 18	Local routes from Bombay	ceased operations
The First Deregulated Wave				
Late 1990	Air Asiatic (Madras)	Boeing 737	Routes in Southern India	ceased operations, July 1991
Early 1990	UB Air (Bangalore)	Dornier 228	Routes in Southern India	operated only for a few months
1991	Continental Air (Bombay)	Boeing 720 Fokker F.27	Routes to Delhi, Hyderabad, etc.	Operations short-lived
1991	City Link (New Delhi)	Rombac One-Eleven	Routes to Bombay and Calcutta	Operations short-lived
Jet Airlines from 1992				
28 Feb 1992	East-West Airlines (Bombay)	Boeing 737-200	Serves all main Indian cities	Founded by East-West Travel and Trade Links (Wahid family)
March 1993	Skyline NEPC (Bombay)	Boeing 737-200	Routes to all main Indian cities	Founded by Pervez Dalmania as Dalmania Airways. Purchased by NEPC (*see* below) and renamed 1 Jan 1996
2 May 1993	Modiluft (New Delhi)	Boeing 737-200 and -400	Routes to all main Indian cities	Founded by MG Express, of the R K Modi Group, in cooperation with Lufthansa
5 May 1993	Jet Airways (Bombay)	Boeing 737-400 and -300	Routes in southern India	Subsidiary of Tailwinds. Gulf Air and Kuwait Air each hold 20% shares. Link with KLM
3 Dec 1993	Sahara India Airlines (New Delhi)	Boeing 737-400 and -200	Routes mainly in northern India	Founded 20 Sept. 1991

Regional Airlines from 1993

Date of First Service	Airline (and Base)	Fleet	Routes	Remarks
April 1993	VIF Airways (Hyderabad)	Dornier 328	Local Services in southern India	
May 1993	Archana Airways (New Delhi)	DHC Dash 8 Let L-410	Local routes, mainly in western India	Founded by Bhartiya Vehicles & Engineering. Madhaya Pradesh provincial government holds some shares
5 Dec 1993	Rajair (Bombay)	Dornier 328 Fokker 50	Local routes, mainly in western India	
30 March 1994	NEPC Airlines (Madras)	Fokker F.27	Local services in Tamil Nadu and southern India	Purchased Dalmania Airways and renamed it as Skyline NEPC, 1 Jan, 1996 (*see* above)
1994	UP Air (New Delhi)	DHC Dash 8 Fokker F.27	Local and charter services, mainly in Uttar Pradesh	Owned by NCM (Singapore) and provincial government of Uttar Predesh
1994	Continental Aviation (Bhopal)	Fokker F.27	Local services in Madhya Pradesh	
1994	Jagson (New Delhi)	Dornier 228	Local routes north of Delhi	

Cargo and Charter Airlines

Date of First Service	Airline (and Base)	Fleet	Routes	Remarks
June 1995	Elbee Airlines (Bombay)	Fokker F.27	Cargo charters	Majority owner-Elbee services
	Goa Way (Bombay)	HS 748	Charters	'India's Holiday Airline'

to emulate IAC, but in 1993, another new Minister opened the door further to the private section by relaxing particularly the restrictions on currency exchange and aircraft financing. A new wave of airlines, more soundly capitalized, had learned by the mistakes of their predecessors, and also benefited from the sudden demise of Vayudoot, which had outgrown itself and collapsed in 1993, leaving behind a residue of aircraft that were quickly given new paint schemes.

No doubt, in a country where entrepreneurship is endemic and spontaneous, the surge of new airlines will gradually evolve into an oligopoly of a few independent or provincially-owned airlines, competing vigorously with IAC and Air-India, which are themselves in the process of privatization. But it is to be hoped that Goa Way will survive, if only to preserve the spirit of cheerful free enterprise in its unashamed name.

Air-India International began operations in 1948 with three Lockheed L-749 Constellations. One of these, *Mogul Princess,* is seen near Burbank before delivery. *(Lockheed)*

CHAPTER FOUR

Air-India Carries the Flag

A World Airline for India

When India gained its independence in 1947, Air-India International (AII) wasted no time in establishing an international airline, with world-wide aspirations with which to carry India's flag and to demonstrate that it represented a country with great traditions, pride in its heritage, and by no means dependent upon technical or commercial guidance from Europe. From the time when the Lockheed Constellation *Malabar Princess* inaugurated service from Bombay to London via Cairo and Geneva, on 8 June 1948, to travel by Air-India was a refreshing and new oriental experience, even for seasoned and sophisticated air travellers.

Still heading a private company, and conscious of the hazards of entering into the challenging international arena, J R D Tata limited his initial goals to two primary spheres of overseas interest to India: the European market, especially London, home of thousands of Indian overseas people; and the East African market, where Indian merchants occupied a special place in the commercial community, especially in Nairobi.

The weekly London service was increased to three a fortnight on 24 September and increased to twice weekly frequency on 1 November 1948. A third weekly service began on 16 October 1949. Budgetary restraints prevented a further increase until the summer of 1955, after nationalization and delivery of additional aircraft. Air-India International, for all its proud flag-carrying role, had to face the harsh realities of stiff competition from European and United States operators of long standing and great experience, not to mention a proved reputation for good service. In particular, BOAC's Comets introduced jet service to the Asian routes in 1952 and 1953, and – like those of other competitors – Air-India's piston-engined flagships could not match the Comet speed to London, the most important overseas destination.

51

Nevertheless, AII did what it had to do. It added European points to the London routes: Rome on 12 March 1950, to supplement Geneva; Paris on 7 April 1951; and Düsseldorf on 21 February 1953. On 2 July 1955, adding a touch of class to a prestige-conscious route, one of the six weekly services was made all first class, romantically called the *Flying Ranee* service, by a Super Constellation from Bombay to London, stopping only at Cairo.

The flair with which Air-India International promoted its on-board service was directly attributable to a genius of the art of public relations promotion. Bobby Kooka will long be remembered for his introduction of the Little Maharajah symbol of on-board graciousness, and for the little booklets distributed to the clientele. These contained useful hints such as to transfer your wife and wallet to a non-aisle seat when the captain approached, and to ensure that nothing was left on the seat, such as a watch, similar to that worn by the crew. There were humorous warnings not to stuff pockets with cutlery or conceal the real age of children, and a comforting reminder that an alarm bell would be sounded just before dawn so that everyone could return to their correct seats. There is no record of passengers transferring from another airline to Air-India, because of the booklets, but they are certainly collector's items today.

Beirut – then a peaceful and attractive resort and business city – and Zürich were added to the London route on 4 July 1955, and Frankfurt, growing hub of central Europe, replaced Düsseldorf on 10 April 1960.

Simultaneously with the London-centred European services, good money-makers right from the start, and aimed at least as much to attract European travellers to visit India as to provide Indians with their own airline to go to Europe, Air-India International also sought to serve the important Indian overseas community in East Africa. This was one of the first times – and may have been the first time – when an airline gave such a priority to this type of market. Service to Nairobi, Kenya, began, via Aden, on 21 January 1950, and on 7 December 1952, a special tourist service, at cheaper fares, was introduced, using non-pressurized Douglas DC-4s, leased from Airways (India) Ltd.

A New Start

The nationalization of Air-India International, along with the amalgamation of the many domestic airlines to form Indian Airlines Corporation, led to a realignment of goals, ambitions and directions of development. Though there were some losses, these were of minor consequence, compared with the confirmation of 'chosen instrument' status, and the injection of and guaranteed availability of fresh capital needed for vital investment in new equipment.

Air-India International became a State corporation on 1 August 1953, six weeks after the creation of Indian Airlines. Air India's domestic routes were transferred, except for key trunk services that were extensions of the main intercontinental artery to Europe. These were from Bombay to Calcutta, extended as a through service on 17 October 1950, and to Delhi on 1 December 1952. These routes were operated under joint co-operative arrangements with IAC that were satisfactory and entirely advantageous to both sides. Sadly, although Karachi had been added on 26 July 1950, during a rare period of armistice between India and Pakistan as both nations fought intermittently over disputed territories and minority persecutions, the former gateway city to the Sub-continent was never to become a permanent point on Air-India's route map.

Little more than a week after acquiring its new status, the Indian state-owned, and state-financed corporation ordered five new Lockheed Model 1049s, on 10 August 1953. This addition to the fleet was absolutely vital if the airline was to expand its horizons, which, as India's flag carrier, it had to do to maintain the country's parity with growing international competitors, not only from the west, but from the east as well. To show its mettle, in a move that has almost been erased from historical aviation memory, Air-India International also ordered two Comet 3 jet airliners, long-range variants of the Comet 1 and Comet 2 – this was before the tragic and fateful crashes in the Mediterranean – and obviously intended to help India to set a cracking pace on the southern Asian route. Air-India was the second airline to order the Comet 3, after Pan American, which had ordered it for the trans-Atlantic route, and six months before Britain's own airline, BOAC, did so. The Comet 3, of course, was never built except as a prototype, although the Comet 4 was aerodynamically similar, and meanwhile, AII put the Super Constellations on to the London route on 19 June 1954. This signalled a quickening of pace and an expansion of the route map.

Air-India Looks Eastward

Rudyard Kipling's famous quotation of 'East is east, and west is west, and never the twain shall meet', was helped on its way to the realms of mythology by Air-

S K (Bobby) Kooka, traffic manager, and Capt K Vishvanath, senior captain, at Heathrow on 11 May 1948. Bobby Kooka was the man who set such high standards, not to mention a welcome touch of humour, in AII's publicity and premises. (*Flight*)

53

Air-India International's Constellation *Rajput Princess* on 15 April 1948 at London Airport – Heathrow after completing the first proving flight from Bombay.

India International during the 1950s. Within little more than three years of nationalization, the route mileage was almost doubled, entirely by new routes that were to eastern destinations. First came a route to Singapore on 16 July 1954 – another city with an element of Indian merchants among its citizenry; then Bangkok and Hong Kong on 14 August 1954, and finally extended to the Japanese capital, Tokyo, on 7 May 1955.

The Singapore route was extended to Australia on 5 October 1956, with a technical stop at Darwin; and in due course, this traffic flow was augmented by en route traffic stops at Jakarta on 4 January 1958, and Kuala Lumpur in March 1959. Continuity of political stability has never been, as yet, a feature of Indian life, with upheaval on religious grounds, even to assassinations all too frequently in the news. Yet if this was not enough, Air-India was struck by political events beyond India's frontiers but which effectively produced almost a blockade of its main trunk services, just as it was asserting itself and offering through flights throughout Asia.

Air-India's first Lockheed L-1049C Super Constellation service on arrival at London Heathrow on 20 June 1954. The aircraft is *Empress Nurjehan*, later *Rani of Jhansi*. The statue on the right depicts Alcock and Brown, the first to fly an aeroplane nonstop across the North Atlantic.

The Suez Crisis, when Britain and France landed troops in Egypt, ostensibly to protect what were seen to be vital interests in the operation of the Suez Canal, under threat of seizure by the Egyptian Government, shocked the world on 4 November 1956 – just a month after AII had opened its route to Australia. All flights to the United Kingdom had to be diverted from their stopping points at Cairo and Beirut, temporarily to Basra, and then, on 10 November, to Abadan and Istanbul. Fortunately, the crisis was over almost as soon as it began, with the withdrawal of the foreign troops and the resignation of Britain's prime minister, Anthony Eden. Air-India resumed service to Beirut (and Damascus) on 25 December, and resumed full frequencies through Cairo on 3 April 1957.

During the frantic situation, Air-India had to resort to considerable flexibility in its scheduling arrangements, amounting almost to improvised sleight-of-hand. While the emergency was short, it may have taught a lesson. For the next year, in co-operation with Aeroflot, the State airline of the Soviet Union, with which India was becoming on increasingly friendly commercial terms, a route was opened to Moscow, on 15 August 1958, with a stop at Tashkent, with the Super Constellation *Rani of Bijapur*. Should there be a new outbreak of violence of any kind in the brittle Middle East, then Air-India was laying the foundation of an alternative route to western Europe.

India's political manoeuvring in the commercial air transport world was not always defensive. Its geographical position, athwart the trunk route between West and East, provided a trump card at the international bilateral agreement bargaining tables. Years previously, the British, when in control of India, had used this same bargaining chip to drag out negotiations with the Dutch airline KLM. Now, with the old 1930s collaboration between Imperial Airways (and later BOAC) and the Australian Qantas still very much alive, with pooled services and tariffs from London to Sydney, the former Colony took a leaf out of its former master's book.

The original pooling compromise between BOAC and Qantas, known as the 'Kangaroo' agreement, was modified to include Air-India International. The main clause of the revised version, signed on 4 December 1959, was that revenues would in future be shared on the basis of 51 per cent for BOAC, 28 per cent for Qantas, and 21 per cent for Air-India. Scheduling was adjusted to conform with approximate capacity offered to match these revenues; but the most important aspect was the tacit recognition of Air-India's Sixth Freedom rights, that is, the coveted Fifth Freedom rights, bestowed upon any country that (like Iceland on the trans-Atlantic route) was fortunate enough to be strategically situated to take advantage of its geographical position. The new pooling agreement went into effect on 1 April 1960.

By Air-India Jet to America

The agreement was well timed. On 19 April AII began Boeing 707 jet service to London, following this with an extension across the Atlantic on 14 May to New York. With the sure promotional touch of Bobby Kooka's talents, the Indian intercontinental jets attracted much favourable comment. Later *Interavia*, the cosmopolitan Swiss-published aviation news bureau, for example, declared 'The Air-India B-747s are, without doubt, amongst the most exotic and luxurious in service today. An embarking passenger steps straight into India, be he in New York, London, Geneva, or Rome' – praise indeed from a totally impartial source. Air-India, in fact, was the world's first airline to operate the 707-430 series, powered by Rolls-Royce Conway bypass engines; and it was also the first Asian airline to provide through service to New York.

55

GROWTH OF AIR-INDIA INTERNATIONAL

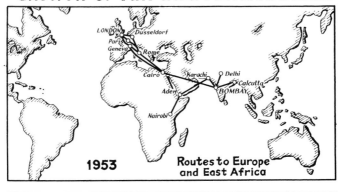

1953 — Routes to Europe and East Africa

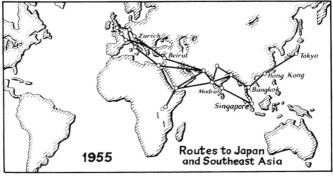

1955 — Routes to Japan and Southeast Asia

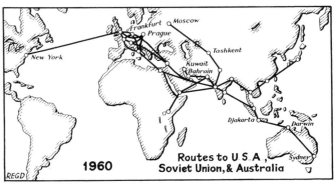

1960 — Routes to U.S.A., Soviet Union, & Australia

Map 4. Growth of Air-India International
From its very first venture into the highly competitive intercontinental airline arena, Air-India International quickly established a good reputation for an excellent on-board cuisine and gracious hostess service. Benefitting from the foresight of J R D Tata, who had ordered Constellations for his Air-India, the nationalized AII was able to match the airlines of Europe and the United States, not only in reciprocal services, but also by pioneering a route to Moscow, thus creating an interesting itinerary to the East for air travellers who wished for a change from the time-honoured route via the Middle East.

56

VT-DJI *Nanda Devi*, a Boeing 707-437, made Air-India International's first North Atlantic proving flight, on 7 April 1960. (*Boeing*)

The airline wasted little time in deploying its Boeing 707s throughout the network: to Tokyo on 16 January 1961, to Nairobi on 4 May, and to Moscow on 6 April 1962. The superseded Super Constellations were converted to cargo carriers and on 14 November 1960 replaced the Douglas DC-4s that had been wet-leased for the purpose since 15 November 1958 on the London route. Various modifications of the agreements with Indian Airlines Corporation maintained connections throughout India from Bombay; and the community of interest between southern India and southeast Asia was recognized by a service from Madras to Singapore, opened on 5 April 1962 with Comet 4s chartered from BOAC.

Change of Name and Claim to Fame

Sensing perhaps that the appendage 'International' was superfluous – as well as being a bit of a mouthful – AII became simply Air-India (which is how it was in the immediate postwar years) on 8 June 1962. The Super Constellation fleet had been retired a month before, and was handed over to the Indian Air Force on 11 June. Air-India was thus able to claim that it was the first major international flag carrier to have an all-jet fleet.

The next few years were ones of consolidation, with some interesting additions and changes to the route pattern. On 1 October 1962, the Western Australian capital, Perth, hitherto somewhat ignored as an international calling point, but rapidly growing in importance, size and wealth, because of the considerable development of mineral deposits in the region, replaced Darwin on the route to Sydney. This latter outpost of Northern Australia had outlived its usefulness. Once viewed with relief by trans-Timor flyers, as it came in sight, it was now ignored as its technical services became superfluous with long-range aircraft.

Air-India welcomed pool agreements for many years. It signed one with East African Airways on 1 April 1964, with Japan Air Lines on 1 October 1965, and participated in an expanded Australia–Asia pool on 1 April 1967 that added Malaysian Airlines System (MAS) and Air New Zealand (ANZ) to the existing tripartite partners, BOAC and Qantas.

Continuing its policies of serving Indian communities overseas, Air-India added

57

some interesting new points to its system during the 1960s. On 3 August 1964 it extended some of its Australian flights onwards to Nadi, the international airport of the Fiji Islands, where half of the 600,000 population were either Indian or of Indian ancestry. Three years later, on 15 August 1967, it gave additional credence to the name Indian Ocean by a service to Mauritius, another haven for overseas Indians, who comprise a substantial percentage of the million inhabitants. While the Mauritius service was only operated twice monthly, an expansion of the East African service on 27 October 1968, to include Addis Ababa and Entebbe, further consolidated Air-India's influence throughout the ocean with which it shared its name.

The mainline services to the West underwent a change of emphasis as the decade drew to its close. Although Amsterdam came on line on 1 April 1969, the Little Maharajah's stay was short-lived, as the Dutch city was deleted from the Air-India map on 17 July 1971, along with Zürich and Prague. Such withdrawal of service was the result of hard commercial realities. Amsterdam was reinstated on 1 April 1976, but in general the traffic volume to and from Europe was beginning to be eclipsed by the traffic volume to the new cities of the Persian Gulf. Oil-rich, the small Sheikhdoms and Emirates were growing at an astounding pace, and the growth was made possible only by the employment of hundreds of thousands of immigrant workers from southern Asia, employed to build – in a climate that they could physically tolerate – offices, apartment blocks, palaces, factories, refineries, water purification plants, and ... airports.

By 1968 Air-India had settled down permanently in Kuwait, where it had, unusually, been serving with Vickers VC10s, chartered from BOAC. New names appeared in quick succession on the Gulf map: Dubai on 2 July 1969, Abu Dhabi on 1 October 1970, and Dhahran on 4 November of the same year.

The Wide-Bodies Era Begins

The then dominant world airline, Pan American Airways, began a new era in air transport when it introduced the wide-bodied Boeing 747 on the New York—London route on 22 January 1970. Most of the industry leaders in Europe, the USA and the Pacific Rim rushed to keep pace, and Air-India was one of those that attained a respectable position in the queue for orders and deliveries of the very large airliner. The 747 proclaimed the now not-so-little Maharajah's presence in London on 24 May 1971, and in New York two days later. To show India's flag at New York's Kennedy Airport was a great triumph for J R D Tata, still at the helm after almost 40 years of leadership, and who had had to fight a stiff battle in the boardroom at Bombay to persuade the airline's management to take this bold step.

By the summer of 1977, when J R D was withdrawing from the scene – some say he was pushed out – Air-India was operating a daily 747 service to New York, and a predominantly 747 service on the twice-daily London service. It was carrying about 60,000 Fifth Freedom passengers (those who did not originate in India) across the Atlantic every year; and 30,000 on the Tokyo route, which welcomed the 747 in 1978. During this period of transition into the wide-bodied era, Air-India wisely made no dramatic route additions, although a Boeing 707 connection was made directly from Bombay to Dacca on 4 February 1972. Air-India was second only to Thai International in bringing international air service to the Bangladesh capital. During the mid-1970s Muscat and Doha were added to the growing list of Gulf destinations, and Osaka was added as a second Japanese city on the network, on 2 November 1972.

One of Air-India International's first Boeing 747s. (*Boeing*)

Changing of the Guard

J R D's stewardship of India's international flag-carrier was one of the finest records of unbroken leadership in the history of air transport. Whether as a pioneer in the 1930s, or in support of the war effort in the 1940s; as representing the private owner or, after nationalization in 1953, as the State's guiding hand, Tata had never wavered, neither flinching from making bold decisions (such as the 747 order) nor plunging into ill-advised speculative ventures of doubtful commercial value. Until 1980, after he had stepped down, all except three of the airline's nationalized years had been profitable. One, 1974/75, had been attributed to the fuel crisis, a tribulation shared by all the world's carriers; and such was the assumed financial stability of Air-India that when it lost money in 1979/80, many found it hard to believe.

They could hardly blame J R D, for, early in 1978, the rumours were confirmed that he was to step down from the chairmanship, to be succeeded by Air Marshal P C Lal. K G Appuswamy had already taken over as managing director, in the summer of 1977.

Just before his retirement, J R D had delivered a notable speech at the 27th Annual Conference of the Pacific Area Travel Association in Delhi, on 23 January 1978. It was a tour de force from a great man. The wisdom and vision so articulately expressed are as germane today as they were then. After analysing with precision the main trends in cost and revenue structures of the world's airlines, he made several predictions that showed uncanny foresight – for though many others shared his views, few were prepared to stand up and be counted for them.

For example, he looked forward – even then – to a twin-deck 750-seat mainline aircraft. He predicted a long-term growth rate of about six per cent, a forecast that has stood the test of time, and which was closer to the mark than most wilder predictions by self-serving economists. He praised Freddie Laker for introducing to the world a third-class service, and was convinced that the time had come for formal recognition of such a level of fares. Unhappily this did not happen, as Skytrain was eliminated for reasons that had nothing to do with J R D's or the general public's wishes. He made forceful remarks about the shortage of hotels, especially in India, asked pointedly whether the banks would lend the enormous sums of money needed to buy the big fleets of big aircraft, and cast devastating doubts about the Concorde's influence on air transport trends as a whole.

Having thus left his intellectual mark on those of the commercial aviation world

59

who were prepared to listen and learn from one of its great leaders, he then proceeded to demonstrate that, like Old Soldiers, some airline people never die, they fade away, but in his case, the fading was accompanied by a flourish. On 15 October 1982, at the age of 78, he re-enacted his Karachi—Bombay flight of 1932 by flying solo in an old Leopard Moth, over the same route. Such a repetition, over a 50-year span, is unique in the annals of air transport history.

J R D Tata, at Kidlington, Oxford, with de Havilland Leopard Moth VT-AKH which he flew from Bombay to Karachi in October 1982 to mark the 50th anniversary of Tata's first service, which he also flew. (*Air-India*)

Belt-Tightening

J R D Tata's was a hard act to follow, although he would be the last to claim that even he was indispensable. His successors faced fundamental problems. Air-India had already achieved many of its long-term objectives: to serve all the Indian overseas communities, estimated to total 13 million; and to provide intercontinental service at the highest standards in a competitive world market. It served every continent except South America, where the demand was too low for efficient operation; and it had adapted with conspicuous success to the unprecedented demands of the contract workers in the Gulf, who also generated a substantial contribution to the VFR (Visiting Friends and Relatives) traffic which constituted one of Air-India's most important sources of revenue.

Geographically, therefore, there was little scope for expansion and Air-India moved cautiously and selectively. During the latter 1970s, it extended its East African route from Nairobi to Lagos and Accra, and included Seychelles as a stop on some of its services to Mauritius on 25 June 1976. Dar-es-Salaam, Lusaka and Harare (formerly Salisbury) were added to the African network in the spring of 1981.

For the intensive services to the Persian Gulf, Jeddah and Ras-al-Khaymah were added in the late 1970s, and in March 1981 Sharjah became the ninth point in this mini-network. A large proportion of the contract workers originated from southern India and Air-India shrewdly recognized this situation by providing direct services to the Gulf, without change of aircraft or routeing through Bombay. The first of such direct routes linked Trivandrum with Dubai in February 1978, and the Kerala city became the hub for further deployment to other Gulf destinations. Madras also received direct service to the Gulf.

One enterprising route was inaugurated in January 1982. This originated in Delhi, and called at Amritsar and Moscow en route direct to Birmingham. It thus provided a link for the overseas Sikh community in the British Midlands to fly directly to Amritsar, the Sikh capital of the Indian Punjab.

But such ventures were the exception during the 1980s. In April 1980 the 64-year-old Raghu Raj took over the chairmanship of an airline that was in the unaccustomed position of having to watch its finances extremely carefully. There had even been rumours of a merger with Indian Airlines as a means of co-ordinating efforts and streamlining overlapping administrations; but memories of the problems that arose in 1953, with the previous amalgamation, were perhaps a severe deterrent to this idea.

Under Raghu Raj's direction, the route network was trimmed, to eliminate those service points where the traffic was clearly below economical levels, however impressive they may have appeared on the map. Thus, Montreal (which had been added in 1982, Addis Ababa, San'a (Yemen), Aden and Perth, lost Air-India service during the mid-1980s. The practice of deep discounting was severely discouraged, though not entirely eliminated; for although Air-India had been forced to share with its travel agencies the necessity to match the low fares offered by all and sundry, the point had been reached in which revenues fell below operating costs, which were not eligible for discounting.

Like all other world airlines, Air-India recognized that it was in a tough, almost ruthless, competitive environment. It had, long ago, on 9 September 1971, taken care of the challenges from non-scheduled operators by setting up Air-India Charters, an autonomous subsidiary under the initial direction of Bobby Kooka.

An Air-India Airbus A300B-4 taking-off on a test flight at Toulouse. (*Airbus*)

But in the harsh new world, the Little Maharajah, symbol of Indian oriental charm and hospitality, and the creation of Kooka, was seen as old-fashioned. The tripartite agreement of former days, between Air-India, BOAC and Qantas, had been terminated on 1 April 1972, to be replaced the following year by a normal bilateral agreement with the United Kingdom.

So, by the mid-1980s, Air-India was on its own feet, without much assistance, technical or commercial, from any source. Its maintenance bases were first-class, its commercial policies finely tuned to contemporary needs, its management alert and disciplined. Yet it had to operate under the overcast of international apprehension that the unrest and often violence in India that too often hit the world's newspaper headlines were characteristics not only of India's religious and social tensions, but typical of all its activities. The effects of the disaster that overcame Air-India on the fateful morning of 23 June 1985, therefore, were quite shattering. With 304 passengers and 22 crew members on board, Air-India Flight 182 had left Montreal en route to London, and was being tracked normally by Shannon air traffic control. At 08.15 a.m. it abruptly vanished from the radar screen, 90 miles southwest of the Irish coast. Although the precise cause of the instantaneous event has not been proved, the perception has always been that it was caused by a bomb having been placed on board at Montreal. Such perception of a real or imagined cause always reflects on the airline, and Air-India's public relations department had a rough few months after the disaster.

For whatever reason, Air-India's statistics have revealed a plateau of traffic production during the latter 1980s. Revenue ton-miles in 1991 were almost exactly the same as in 1987. Yet the stability of the figures did not necessarily reflect stagnation; for during the same period, both revenues and expenditures went up by more than half, and Air-India was consistently profitable throughout.

By some standards, Air-India is not a large airline. Among its Asian neighbours, for example, its fleet is only half that of Singapore Airlines or of Hong Kong's Cathay Pacific; and far smaller than those of the Japanese giants, JAL and All Nippon Airways. But the traffic base is permanent, its finances are sound, and it serves India impeccably as its flag carrier. As it moved into the 1990s, there was much talk about privatization – another trend in which India often seems to follow the example of the British – and if Air-India falls into private hands, the new investors should find themselves in charge of an excellent property.

CHAPTER FIVE

Airlines of Pakistan

A Nation Divided

One of the most important developments in world political history after the end of the Second World War in 1945 was – in spite of Mr Winston Churchill's protests to the contrary – the dissolution of the British Empire. In some areas the process was swift and emphatic. Burma seceded from the loose Commonwealth in 1948. Various Colonies, Protectorates, and formerly Mandated Territories gained different forms of independence, most of them to remain, at least nominally, as members with Dominion or other self-governing status. Easily the biggest problem area was what had been termed, in vice-regal times, the Indian Empire, stretching from close to the Persian Gulf in the west to Thailand and the Malay Peninsula in the east. And within this region, also termed the Sub-continent, lived about 450 million people, constituting about two-thirds of the population of the whole Empire. (Incidentally, the population today is more than a thousand million.)

The problems within this macrocosm of the human race were vast. There were scores of languages and dialects; complex administrative variations ranging from direct rule from London to almost dictatorial rule by local princes; many different races and ethnic divisions; and just as many religious groups and sects. For one reason or another, this great melting pot of conflicting ideas, attitudes and customs inspired strife, sometimes expressed peacefully, but all too often in belligerence, fighting, and alas, massacre and mayhem.

Of all the rivalries in this great human permutation, easily the greatest was the schism between the Moslems and the Hindus. The former comprised mainly Urdu-speaking people in the west and Bengali people in the east, and unfortunately they were geographically divided by the mainly Hindi-speaking Indians of mainly Hindu religion in the centre. When, during the postwar wave of nationalism, the Moslems campaigned for independence, the independent nation that was created to satisfy these aspirations was unlike any other in the world. Pakistan, as it was called, was divided into two parts, the West Wing and the East Wing, with the West having most of the area and the East having most of the population.

The Partition of the old India in 1947 was accompanied by some of the bloodiest internecine fighting and wholesale destruction and mass murder, ruthlessly conducted by both sides, within living memory. When the agony finally subsided, Pakistan's divided State was separated by a nation that was not even friendly, at least for many years; so that communication between the two halves was difficult, to say the least. The sea journey between Karachi, the chief port of the western half, and Bengal, the eastern half, was a circuitous route via Ceylon (Sri Lanka), taking a week or so; and the overland route was a long and indirect rail journey through sometimes hostile territory. An air route was the obvious solution to passenger travel, and even this required delicate negotiation for overflying rights.

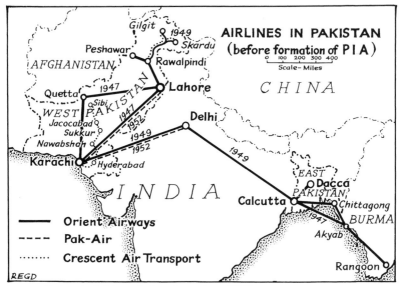

Map 5a. Airlines in Pakistan (before formation of PIA)
After the painful partition of the old Indian Empire, leading to the creation of Pakistan, airline activity was fragmented and uncertain. From being an on-line station, Karachi suddenly became a hub, and several small companies, led by Orient Airways, started new services. Flying across India was sometimes beset by political problems, but Orient's service to East Pakistan was the testing ground for what became known as the Inter-Wing route, linking the two halves of Pakistan, before the East became Bangladesh.

Orient Airways

Because of its overwhelming population majority, most of the businesses in British India, those that were not controlled by the British themselves, were predominantly Hindu, and Moslem participation was usually at best nominal and of token significance only. The British Government had promised Dominion status to India in 1942, and the Moslem community began to think about setting up businesses that were of their own religious calling. One of these was an airline, and its origins date back to February 1944, when the idea was put forward at a meeting between Habib Rahimtoola and the Quaid-e-Azam, spiritual leader and head of the Muslim League. By the end of the year the idea had become a plan of action, and the objective was to form an airline that would operate commercially, but at the same time act as a reserve for pilot training for a Pakistan Air Force, as and when this might be required.

And so, on 23 October 1946, Orient Airways was formed in Calcutta by two brothers, Merza Ahmad and Merza Abol Hassan Ispahani. The Ispahani family was one of the most prominent and wealthy of the textile industrialists of Bengal, and they were sympathetic to the objectives of the Moslem League, at the same time joining in the movement in postwar India to make use of hundreds of redundant Douglas Dakotas (C-47s/DC-3s) left over from the war. Staffed at first by foreign pilots and technicians (but progressively replaced thereafter) Orient began regular service between Calcutta and Rangoon, via Akyab, on 30 June 1947, and quickly gained a reputation for maintaining that service, regardless of weather –

64

and that was quite an achievement in itself, in a region that can have as much rain in a day or two as England has in a whole year.

As a precautionary measure, as the terrible war erupted with the Partition of India during that summer, Orient moved its headquarters from Calcutta to Chittagong on 1 August, and soon after Pakistan was created as an independent nation and as a member of the Commonwealth on 14 August 1947, it moved again to Karachi. With its small fleet of C-47s and a couple of Beech 18s, it undertook many missions of mercy in relief work during the mass migration of peoples that was one of the unhappy consequences of Partition. Orient Airways may have been short in equipment but it was long in spirit. Rafi Ispahani, its managing director, used to work late, and having settled on the passenger count for the next day's flights, would prepare the box lunches. Such enthusiasm and dedication was to see the future Pakistani national airline through many a crisis in the years to come.

In contrast to much confusion and disorganization elsewhere, Orient Airways managed to pick up the pieces of its operation quite quickly. On 1 October 1947 it began the vital air service between East and West Pakistan, and the next day started flights on the trunk routes of West Pakistan, from Karachi to Lahore and Rawalpindi, and thence to Peshawar, and also to Quetta from both Karachi and Lahore. A few months later, on 2 February 1949, by which time it had a fleet of twenty C-47/DC-3s, it started regular flights to Gilgit and Skardu, high up in the upper reaches of the Indus River and its tributary, the Gilgit, on behalf of the Ministry of States and Defence. For most European or American civil airline pilots, this operation would have been quite an adventure, demanding as it did the threading through a meandering river valley, flanked by precipitous mountains, and too narrow to turn round in a DC-3, and with no possible place to land in the event of engine failure. Orient Airways, and subsequently PIA (Pakistan International Airlines), took it in their stride. This remarkable operation was more than simply a social service to a remote community; it was a tactical expression of Pakistan's determination to retain sovereignty over northwestern Kashmir, in the face of similar, and warlike claims by India.

Establishing itself more firmly, Orient Airways acquired a small fleet of three pressurized Convair 240 twin-engined airliners and put them into service on a Karachi–Delhi–Calcutta–Dacca route on 1 May 1949. While making two stops in India, this aircraft had the capability of flying directly between Karachi or Lahore

One of the Convair 240s introduced by Orient Airways in May 1949. (*Consolidated Vultee*)

65

and Dacca, should nonstop inter-Wing flights ever become necessary. To Orient went the honour of putting into service the first Convair-Liners in Asia. Sadly, such satisfaction that might have been derived from this achievement was clouded by a crash in March 1953, curtailing operations, which had already suffered as a result of foreign flag competition, including that from the new BOAC Comet jet airliners.

By this time Orient Airways was in decline. Some minor competition had arisen in September 1948, when Pak-Air was formed to operate DC-3 services from Karachi to Lahore and Delhi; and it even obtained permission to fly international routes to the Middle East and Ceylon, even to the United Kingdom. But after two accidents, the Pakistan Government ordered its suspension in November 1949.

But this was of little consequence, compared with the growing movement within the Government to form a national airline, although Orient Airways maintained its identity for no less than nine years after its official formation. Mostly long forgotten today, it played its part in the foundation of the airline industry of Pakistan.

Pakistan International Airlines

Early in 1951 the Pakistan Ministry of Defence first organized Pakistan International Airlines (PIA) as a department within the administration. It operated no air services, but its first act was to order, on 25 May, three Lockheed Model 1049C Super Constellations. Following Orient Airways' troubles it was officially amalgamated with PIA on 1 October 1953. Orient was taken over by the Government, but retained its identity. Less than a year later, on 7 June 1954, the first PIA service began from Karachi to Dacca, with the first Super Constellation replacing Orient's CV-240. This latter type began Karachi—Bombay service on 13

One of PIA's first acts was to order three Lockheed L-1049C Super Constellations. Later L-1049H mixed passenger/cargo aircraft were added to the fleet. One of these is seen at Dacca in January 1959 before operating the night service to Karachi. (*John Stroud*)

December 1954. The Constellations, resplendent in PIA's handsome green colours, inaugurated service to London, via Cairo, on 1 February 1955. At the time, it was the fastest flight on a highly competitive route.

On 11 March 1955 Pakistan International Airlines was formed into a State corporation. All the assets and routes of Orient Airways were absorbed (it had continued to operate domestic services during the interim period), and its shareholders received 40 per cent of PIA stock. It also inherited a local service route in southern West Pakistan, which had been operated by Crescent Air Transport. Crescent had been formed in early 1952, and flew de Havilland D.H.89A Dragon Rapides from Karachi to Sibi, an important railway junction near Quetta, Baluchistan, via Hyderabad and Sukkur. It also undertook supply runs to Gilgit and Skardu, but ceased operations at the end of 1954.

One of PIA's Convair 240s taken over from Orient Airways, at Karachi. (*PIA*)

One of the first acts of the new corporation was to link the commercial capital of Pakistan, Karachi, with the capital of India, Delhi, on 15 March 1955; and it also gave notice that it intended to maintain technical parity with the airlines of the world. In the summer of that year, it recruited Pan American Airways for technical assistance, and a year later, ordered three of the latest Vickers Viscount 815 short-haul propeller-turbine airliners, at the same time bringing its CV-240 fleet up to four.

During the late 1950s PIA continued to show the flag in London, and on 18 July 1956, opened an additional weekly service via Geneva as well as via Cairo. But with its fleet of Convair-Liners, backed up by the trusty old DC-3s, it concentrated on providing Pakistan with a good domestic air route network. By October 1956 frequency on the inter-Wing route from Karachi to Dacca was on a daily basis, as was the route between West Pakistan's two biggest cities, Karachi and Lahore. Twice weekly flights were made from Dacca to Lahore (completing a traffic triangle) and from Karachi to Bombay. Super Constellations appeared on the Karachi—Dacca route on 6 March 1958; but – as happens to all airlines struggling to establish new standards, and working from an inexperienced technical foundation – it suffered setbacks, in the form of two crashes, a DC-3 in 1957 and a CV-240 on 15 May 1958, in which 38 people were killed on take-off from Delhi. To replace these PIA increased its Viscount order to five, and began its first propeller-turbine service with that aircraft on 31 January 1959, from Karachi to Delhi.

The Douglas Dakota remained the backbone of PIA's domestic fleet for many years. This one is arriving at Rawalpindi from Peshawar. (*John Stroud*)

A PIA Dakota at Chitral in the far northwest after making the first proving flight from Rawalpindi on 18 February 1962. The terrain behind the camera is a mirror image of that seen here. (*John Stroud*)

First Jets in Asia

The progress made during PIA's formative years stemmed in no small measure from the guiding hand of Zafarul Ahsan, a seasoned civil servant who pulled things together after a shaky start. But after a lengthy investigation into the

Early in 1959 PIA introduced its first turbine-powered aircraft, a fleet of three Vickers-Armstrong Viscount 815s. (*Vickers*)

airline's affairs, and after the institution of martial law under Ayub Khan, who came to power in October 1958, he was made a scapegoat and forced to resign from the airline he had helped to mature and from the work that he loved. He was not on hand to witness one of PIA's greatest triumphs, Air Commodore Malik Nur Khan having taken over as managing director in March 1959,

The year 1960 was a great one for PIA. Only five years after its official foundation, it became the first jet operator in Asia, beginning Boeing 707 service once a week to London on 7 March. True, the Pakistan identity was revealed only by a sticker on the fin, the -321 series aircraft having been leased from Pan

The first Friendship for PIA was accepted by the airline's then managing director, Air Commodore Nur Khan.

69

American; but by 20 June it was being flown by Pakistani crews and on 4 October it was repainted in PIA colours. The Super Constellation that it replaced was transferred to the Karachi—Dacca Inter-Wing 'Airlift'.

A year later, on 5 May 1961, PIA trumped its own ace by extending the London service to New York, but this was suspended in 1963 because the traffic volume did not justify its continuance. Nevertheless, Western trans-Atlantic travellers who took advantage of the Fifth Freedom rights enjoyed by PIA (in exchange for BOAC privileges for onward flights east of Karachi) were given an opportunity to enjoy the gracious service provided by the Pakistani flight attendants. The 707s were replaced in 1961 by the smaller Boeing 720Bs, which for a short while, happened to be the longest-ranged airliners in the world.

Nur Khan did not neglect the domestic routes. In fact, in addition to introducing twin-engined Fokker Friendships in East Pakistan in February 1961, he started a DC-3 'Airbus' service in the East Wing on 25 March 1961. This service – unlike some which claim the use of the metaphor – was a genuine bus service, offering fares that were competitive with, and even less than those of the railways. PIA did not claim a government subsidy for the service, preferring to transfer funds from the profits that it made quite comfortably from its other operations. Not unexpectedly, the amenities on board were austere, as were the ground arrangements. Passengers had to make their own way to the 'bus-stops', there were no reservations, no meals, and no reading material. But there were seats, and a generous baggage allowance, that allowed the clientèle to bring their own bedding, if necessary.

Topping this admirable experiment, and judging them to be a cheaper solution than building airfields in inhospitable terrain, PIA replaced the DC-3s with helicopter services on 5 November 1963. Ten points were served by Sikorsky S-61N helicopters; and although the service shared the fate of other ambitious scheduled helicopter networks in Europe and the United States, and closed down in 1966, it was a noble effort.

Fokker F.27 Friendships were added to PIA's fleet early in 1961, and operated in both Wings of Pakistan. (*Fokker*)

PIA's first owned jet transport, the Boeing 720B AP-AMG on arrival at Karachi on 2 January 1962 after its record-breaking nonstop flight from London – 3,900 nautical miles in 6 hr 43 min 51 sec.

The Chinese Connection

In 1964 PIA established a Viscount service over (but not through) the Khyber Pass from Peshawar to Kabul, Afghanistan; and a Friendship link – in both senses of the term – was made from Lahore to Delhi. But the most important event of that year was to begin the first non-communist route from the West to the People's Republic of China which, for fifteen years, had been isolated from the rest of the world, almost as if the Great Wall had been extended around the whole of China, like the counterpart in Berlin. China did not have diplomatic relations with Japan; it did not recognize Taiwan; it had just been at war with India; and did not wish to lose face by approaching Hong Kong; and China's flirtation with the Soviet Union had soured. Pakistan was therefore a logical choice, and PIA seized the opportunity. Accordingly, on 29 April 1964, it began Boeing 720B service from Dacca to Shanghai, via Canton (now Guangzhou). At the latter city, Chinese construction workers, with characteristic unorthodox methods and energy, constructed a new runway in record time.

Simultaneously, PIA played some international bargaining chips with the USSR. On 10 May 1964 it began flights to Europe via Moscow, operating rights for which had been traded with Aeroflot, which wished to strengthen its base in southern Asia on its route to Jakarta. Early in 1965 Teheran was added to the European service, but further expansion was halted as tensions grew in the Sub-continent.

Seeking to improve its Inter-Wing services, PIA had sought to find a jet successor to its Viscounts. The PIA technical and commercial departments all selected the Boeing 727 tri-jet, but were over-ruled by Nur Khan, who selected the British Trident 1E. The Trident's range was barely adequate for the vital Inter-Wing flights, mainly because of the tropical temperatures, but in due course, it was introduced on main domestic services in the spring of 1966, and later did good service to the Gulf. Whether through accident or design – and Nur Khan was a far-sighted and shrewd individual – the Trident purchase had long-term indirect consequences that were beneficial to Pakistan. The Chinese airline, CAAC, badly

71

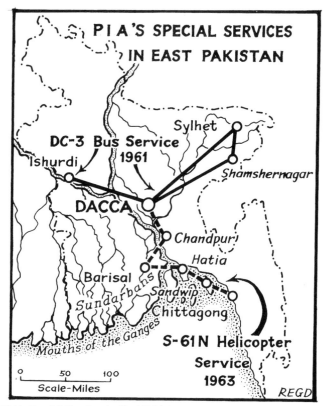

Map 5b. PIA's Special Services in East Pakistan
Eastern Bengal had never had a coherent transport system, even on land. The region was divided into two halves by the main course of the Brahmaputra-Ganges estuary; and the great delta area, the Sunderbans, subject to flooding at frequent and unpredictable intervals, defied efforts to develop through roads and railways. Commendably, PIA stepped into this arena of deprivation, and began DC-3 Bus Services in the north, and later Sikorsky S-61N helicopter services (one of the few ever to be operated on a scheduled basis outside the United States and Europe) in the south.

needed a modern airliner for its domestic routes. Supplies from the USSR were out of the question, and relations with the United States were still cool, even frigid. China did not even have an embassy in Great Britain. Through its service to Shanghai, therefore, PIA had established a 'China Connection' that was to act as a neutral channel through which commercial contact could be made between Peking (Beijing) and the British manufacturer of the Trident, Hawker Siddeley Aviation, which had acquired the original designer, de Havilland.

Not only that, but PIA sold its four Tridents to China in 1970, after deploying them on main domestic routes and to new routes to the Gulf states. CAAC purchased an additional thirty-five Tridents, and so the Pakistan airline had been the catalyst for a transaction that benefited everybody. Hawker Siddeley's Chinese customer was its second biggest (and almost its only other) customer, after British European Airways; the Tridents did well under less stringent climatic conditions;

72

THE AIR ROUTE TO SHANGRI LA

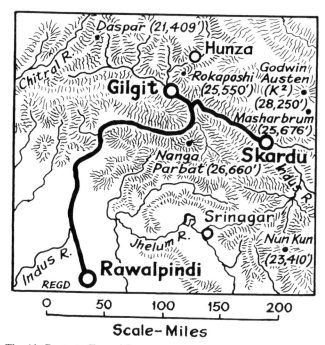

Map 5c. The Air Route to Shangri La
Reminiscent of the legendary and mythical mountain paradise of the fictional *Lost Horizon*, some communities in the extreme north of Pakistan are almost cut off from the outside world, such are the formidable barriers of the mountainous terrain. Pakistan International, preceded by Crescent Air Transport (*see* map 5a), pioneered a unique air service to remote Gilgit and Skardu, surface access to which demanded the stamina of accomplished mountaineers. The redoubtable Douglas DC-3s that first ventured into these unique destinations were, at one point, obliged either to turn right or to turn left, as they could not go straight on (into the face of a mountain) and could not go back (because there was no room to turn round in the pass).

and, as things turned out, political events of far-reaching import rendered the need for Inter-Wing services a redundant requirement.

War With India

Following its diplomatic success in starting service to China and the USSR, the year 1965 was a dismal one for both Pakistan and PIA. First, a Boeing 720B crashed at Cairo, killing 123 passengers and crew, with only six survivors, on 19 May 1965. Nur Khan, now promoted to the rank of Air Marshal, stepped down from his managing directorship, in favour of Asghar Khan. The former became the C-in-C of the Pakistan Air Force, a position of considerable importance and responsibility, in the light of subsequent events.

With growing religious and nationalistic fervour throughout the Sub-continent, the flames of violence were fanned by fanatical elements on both sides, and in September 1965, armed conflict – there was never a formal declaration of war –

73

For a time PIA used Hawker Siddeley Trident IEs.

broke out between Pakistan and India, concentrated, as usual, in the Punjab, a Province that had always been a cauldron of conflicting factions, compounded by its being the traditional home of the Sikhs, who owed allegiance neither to Moslem nor Hindu. PIA's aircraft were temporarily based in Teheran and Istanbul, and one Boeing was stationed in Peshawar; but in this instance, the disruption was fortunately of relatively short duration, and services were resumed by the end of the year.

In 1963 PIA inaugurated a helicopter network in East Pakistan, this was closed in 1966 after one of the three Sikorsky S-6INs was lost in a fatal accident and one was badly damaged in a training incident. An S-6IN is seen here at Chittagong in February 1964. (*John Stroud*)

Such was the speed of the return to normality that the Inter-Wing route from Dacca to Lahore, over-flying the Indian West Bengal and the United Provinces, was reinstated on 9 February 1966, and the Karachi—Dacca route resumed by a direct route over southern India, rather than by the circuitous diversion via Colombo.

During the mid-1960s PIA greatly expanded its international route network, after receiving two Boeing 707-340s in the summer of 1966. On 1 November of that year, new European points, Paris and Istanbul, were added; and the next day, service began to Nairobi via Aden. But the main expansion occurred in the Persian Gulf, where the profits made by the burgeoning oil industry were being channelled into vast public works projects, demanding an influx of skilled and semi-skilled labour. Much of the skilled and technical, including managerial inputs, came from Europe; but much of the semi-skilled came from southern and southeastern Asia, where the workers were already acclimatized to the severe conditions of intense heat. Of all the Asian sources of labour, Pakistan was the nearest, and of the same religious persuasion; and PIA was alert in exploiting these advantages.

Baghdad and Kuwait (whose national airlines also had Tridents, suggesting that the aircraft may not have been as bad as PIA painted them) came on line on 1 November, and Jeddah the next day. A week later, on 10 November, service began to Bahrain, Doha and Dubai. Suddenly, the Pakistan airline had become a major airline force in the Middle East.

Elsewhere PIA expanded its route network to the Far East and, at the other end of the operational spectrum, in the outback of East Pakistan. On 1 April 1967, Boeing 707 service started from Dacca to Bangkok, and this was extended to Manila and Tokyo in November 1969. PIA was beginning to make good use of its Sixth Freedom privileges. Such a freedom was not on the list of the Five Freedoms of the Air, as recognized by the International Civil Aviation Organization (ICAO); but it was applied, nevertheless, by those countries which could take advantage of their fortuitous geographical positions. Iceland was a well-known example, where the airline could combine bilateral agreements, employing the acknowledged Third and Fourth Freedoms, with, on the one hand, countries to the east, in Europe, and, on the other hand, to the west, in America, and thus conduct services that were close to being direct, simply by changing the flight numbers, and not necessarily by changing the aircraft itineraries, to gain the coveted Fifth Freedom rights. In the same manner, PIA was able to offer through service from European points to Bangkok, Manila and Tokyo.

Back home, a new service in West Pakistan in November 1967, included Dera Ismail Khan as an alternative stop between Karachi and Rawalpindi; and DC-3s gave way to Friendships on East Pakistan local routes in June 1968, the fleet of the Dutch aircraft having been increased to ten. Late in 1970, Boeing 707 freighter service opened to London; and the establishment of the air cargo market to Britain was to prove of immense value to the airline during the next decade.

Broken Wings

Only half a decade after the explosive conflict of 1965, the Indian Sub-continent began to witness increasing violence, but this time, the issues were more complex. Not only did the traditional suspicion, even enmity, between Moslems and Hindus rise to the surface; this time, the two major elements of the Moslem community, the Urdu-speaking peoples of the West Wing and the Bengalis of the East, were at odds with each other. As Pakistan began to grow as a Sovereign State, it also grew to be divided among itself. The geographical cleavage which was its unfortunate birthright deteriorated into a serious handicap as East Pakistan perceived, not without some justification, that the Government, based in West Pakistan, was asserting its power unevenly and that the East was not receiving its fair share of the national budget, even though it provided the main source of the wealth, and contained the majority of the population. In March 1969 unrest in East Pakistan led to the resignation of President Ayub Khan, who was succeeded by Yahya Khan. By December 1970, a strong political movement from the East, the Awami League, had gained strength and influence, but could not attain legislative support in its bid for autonomy. Severe and bloody uprisings in East Pakistan, accompanied by the declaration of independence for East Pakistan in April 1971, campaigning to form the new independent State of Bangladesh, compounded to launch a civil war, in which millions of Bengalis fled to India, which promptly gave them full relief and support. War began on 3 December and within two hectic weeks of fighting, India convincingly defeated Pakistan, and the independent State of Bangladesh became a reality. Rudyard Kipling is credited with first voicing the axiom: East is East and West is West, and Never the Twain Shall Meet. He could never have foreseen the situation in which East did meet West and yet was torn asunder in such an abrupt and irrevocable manner.

PIA Shows Its Mettle

The war with India and the creation of Bangladesh completely destroyed the Inter-Wing operations of Pakistan International Airlines, and in so doing reduced the size of its traffic demand by about half in one blow. Many an airline would have withdrawn into its shell, curtailed its total production drastically, laid off half its staff, and appealed to its government for special dispensation, including subsidies and other privileges to help it overcome its very real problems. PIA did just the opposite.

Demonstrating tremendous qualities of resourcefulness and resilience to misfortune, it harnessed all its energies and assets in a systematic programme of action that was based not on retrenchment but on expansion. The management, in an unprecedented display of effective teamwork, altered the marketing thrust of the operations, explored other outlets for its talents, and turned disaster into triumph.

When Zulfikar Ali Bhutto became president of Pakistan after the calamitous war, he appointed a young businessman as managing director of PIA. Rafique Saigol was fortunate, during his short stay in office, to oversee the launching of new initiatives, all of which were successful, and some of which were productive beyond the dreams of their protagonists. Every department of the airline seemed to vie with the others in innovative marketing efforts. These were made against a re-orientation of the fleet and routes of the existing patterns, which involved curtailment of some, expansion of others.

As early as February 1972, only a few short weeks after Bangladesh broke away and destroyed the Inter-Wing service, PIA re-routed its flights to Shanghai from the Dacca terminus to Karachi, with Colombo as an intermediate stop. On 1 April it reinstated the trans-Atlantic route to New York. On 3 November it began the 'Batik Route' from Karachi to Jakarta, via Colombo, Kuala Lumpur and Singapore. And on 20 January 1973, the way to China was again re-routed via Islamabad, thence across the Himalayas direct to Peking, and on to Shanghai. Canton was eliminated from the network, but to serve the Chinese capital direct was a fair exchange, especially as it required no overflying rights from a foreign country. The more direct routeing cut $4\frac{1}{2}$ hours off the journey time, and PIA ran twice-weekly through services from Europe to China, both starting from London, both calling at Paris, but then alternating between Damascus–Baghdad or Rome–Cairo before reaching Karachi.

Sensible measures were taken to trim the fleet to the reduced capacity requirements. Five Twin Otters and two Friendships, used on East Pakistan domestic services, were sold or leased; and five Boeing 707s, used on the Inter-Wing routes, were leased to British Caledonian and Jugoslav Air Transport. But amazingly, before many more months were to pass, PIA's seat-mile output was back to its pre-1972 total.

Outshining even passenger sales increases, the freight department excelled. A sustained and successful selling campaign resulted in, for example, an export drive in sports equipment, turning to good use the traditional leather goods craftsmanship of Pakistan. Soon, almost every football kicked across the playing fields in Britain and most of the cricket paraphernalia, were brought in by PIA. Other items in the export drive, all air-freighted to Europe and the USA, ranged from carpets to surgical instruments.

Two fields of passenger traffic received particular attention. Many Pakistani families had emigrated to Great Britain, and PIA made special efforts to develop this overseas ethnic market. Fate also came to the rescue with an immense increase in the demand for 'guest workers' in the Gulf States and Saudi Arabia, rich in finance and resources (oil) but poor in willing muscular power. The increase in passenger loads to the Middle East, all at standard fares so that the yield was high, was unprecedented. Towards the end of the year the annual Haj pilgrimage to Mecca provided extra traffic, so that, contrary to all expectations, the airline needed more total capacity, both for passengers and freight.

The concerted effort by all Pakistan International personnel reached into every department and at every level, and extended to some areas of airline practice not normally considered to be relevant. PIA operated its own nursery to produce its own flowers for on-board use – adding a gracious touch at minimum expense; and it ran its own chicken farm, supplying eggs and chickens to its catering department, which was growing by leaps and bounds to supply not only PIA but also many other airlines for whom Karachi was a halfway house to the East and where reinforcements of catering supplies were in demand.

Wide Bodies

Emphasizing that PIA was back on its feet again, negotiations were initiated during the closing months of 1972 that culminated in the order for three Douglas DC-10-30 wide-bodied tri-jets in April 1973. The fuel crisis of that period may have played its part in the choice of a long-range tri-jet against the four-engined Boeing 747; but unfortunately later revelations pointed to illegal payments of commissions; and ultimately PIA received $2.1 million damages, awarded by a US criminal court.

By the time the DC-10s arrived, to enter service on the Karachi—London route on 4 April 1974, a new top management had taken over. Air Marshal Nur Khan returned from the Air Force as chairman, and Enver Jamall, a popular and efficient administrator who had first learned his trade under the great Indian pioneer, J R D Tata, back in the 1930s, returned as managing director. Together, they added new impetus to the momentum that was already under way. During the first months of their tenure, capacity was increased by 60 per cent, mainly because of the arrival of the DC-10s, which, in addition to the London route operated into New York, and carried PIA's flag to all the main destinations. Jamall used his long experience to negotiate terms with the British authorities, which wished to curtail Pakistan's operating rights at London, and refused to play second fiddle to a much larger airline. Early in 1974 the New York service was re-routed through Paris and Jamall threatened to stop London services altogether and concentrate on Amsterdam; and Copenhagen also came into the picture, as the Dutch and the Scandinavians alike knew the strategic value of Karachi. The outcome was that an amicable agreement was reached that was entirely satisfactory to PIA.

In the month of November 1975, no less than 20,000 pilgrims were carried to Jeddah for the obligatory Hajj ceremony, more than three times the number five years previously. The pilgrims came not only from Pakistan itself, but from other Moslem countries, from Indonesia to Kenya, on charter flights. Ever ingenious, and making allowance for the untutored ways of many of the unsophisticated pilgrims, PIA engineers devised a special plastic base for the toilets to allow for an excess of what was euphemistically described as 'spillage'.

Pakistan International Airlines was moving quickly into larger aircraft, such was the success of its entire operation. Even in the Himalayan mountains, the former DC-3 adventure became almost routine after Lockheed C-130s were leased from the Air Force in August 1974. But such local events were outshone by the introduction, on 5 May 1976, of Boeing 747-200 service, with two aircraft leased from Portugal's airline, TAP. The big Boeings began their operations with nonstop flights to London from both Karachi and Rawalpindi.

Such participation in the big leagues of world air transport were backed by political activity that made it all possible. Reference has already been made to the confrontation with London. Closer to home, normal relations were gradually resumed with India, and once again, Enver Jamall was the man to head the PIA team, which successfully signed a new Air Agreement with the Indians in July 1976. For Jamall, the meetings were hardly the kind of adversarial struggles that too often characterize such affairs. Little wonder: among the Indian delegates were Messrs Mehta and Appuswamy, managing directors of Indian Airlines and Air-India, respectively. Along with Jamall, all three had worked together (as 'grease-monkeys' according to Jamall) in junior capacities in pre-Partition days.

PIA introduced its first Boeing 747s in May 1976. (*Boeing*)

Enver Jamall who began his long career in air transport by sweeping the Tata hangar at Juhu and eventually became chairman of PIA. (*John Stroud*)

In addition to the resumption of service to India, Bangladesh was also linked again in 1977. PIA had demonstrated commendable initiative during its darkest days after losing East Pakistan (aside from all the other initiatives already reviewed) by using the high standards of its technical staff, especially in engineering and maintenance, to sell its expertise to other, younger and smaller, airlines. On 1 April, for example, it actually acquired a 20 per cent interest in Air Malta, and supplied hundreds of technical staff, seconded to the airline, and including M M Salim, one of its leading executives, as a senior guiding hand. PIA subsequently assisted other airlines in Africa and the Middle East, where ex-colonial territories regarded PIA in a more co-operative light than would perhaps have been the case with a former European colonial power.

Enver Jamall became chairman of Pakistan International Airlines in 1978, and oversaw further increases in the fleet of large aircraft, ordering more 747s and four more Airbus A300Bs, the latter for $167 million. In 1980 M M Salim returned as managing director, to maintain a continuity of managerial expertise that dated back to the formation of the airline.

Moments of Truth

Pakistan was in a state of political upheaval during the latter 1970s and into the next decade, with dictatorial practices alternating with attempts to establish democratic principles. There were imprisonments and executions, and all this was complicated by the role that the country played in the power groups of the area; while the Soviet occupation of Afghanistan in 1979 accentuated the strategic importance of the country, bordering as it did Iran, India, and even China – all nations which the world's super-powers wished to keep under control, if not to dominate.

All this did not help Pakistan International Airlines, which, after its great years of the 1970s, when everything seemed to go right, now faced many problems. For almost the first time in its existence, it faced red ink on the balance sheet, and, again for the first time, belts had to be severely tightened.

In 1981 Major General Rahim Khan was appointed chairman and Air Marshal Wigar Azim managing director. They were given wide powers. Union activities were banned, and during the next four years, staff numbers were drastically reduced by several thousands; on the other hand, salaries were increased in some areas. To meet the severe cash flow crisis, the Government injected $60 million into the airline in the form of loans and direct cash in exchange for an equity shareholding. Gradually, PIA pulled itself together.

The decade of the 1980s was one of holding the line and making sound decisions in aircraft procurement and route development, nothing spectacular, but effective in maintaining the stability of the airline. There was considerable scope on the domestic front. Even after the loss of the East Wing, Pakistan was still a large country, with more than 100 million people; and though the majority of them were peasant farmers, there was also much industry. Three cities (other than the capital, Islamabad and nearby Rawalpindi), had populations well in excess of a million each. Two routes, Karachi—Lahore and Karachi—Rawalpindi, each generated more than half a million passengers a year. Additionally, the secondary and feeder routes were growing, to the extent that the Fokker Friendship 44-seaters needed to be augmented by aircraft with more capacity, but not necessarily as big as the 250-seat Airbuses.

PIA's choice was the Boeing 737-300, powered by CFM-56 engines. Put into service in July 1985, the airline provided an echo of earlier initiatives, when it became the first airline in Asia to operate this superior version of the short-haul twin-jet, which could even fly into Skardu and Gilgit. The six aircraft had cost $157 million in August 1984. Further down the line, to fill out the domestic route network which, by 1988, was serving 30 cities, and still growing, PIA bought four F.27s from Brazil, to bring the Fokker Friendship fleet, still going strong after 28 years, to fourteen. Two Twin Otters helped out where the Friendships had airfield limitations.

Already serving a worldwide network from New York to Tokyo (the long way round), expansion in the international sector was steady but not spectacular. In the summer of 1985, taking advantage of its bilateral rights with the USSR, a short-cut route via Moscow linked the Pakistan capital, Islamabad (sharing its airport with Rawalpindi) with London. In 1989 Toronto brought Canada into the network as an additional North American destination. In 1990 Lahore became the third Pakistan city to have direct Boeing 747 service to London, and in the same year Manchester was added as a second British terminal, thus providing a convenient direct connection between the substantial ex-patriate Pakistani community in the north of England with their ancestral home.

GROWTH OF PAKISTAN INTERNATIONAL

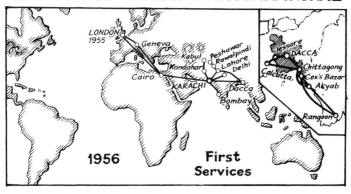

1956   **First Services**

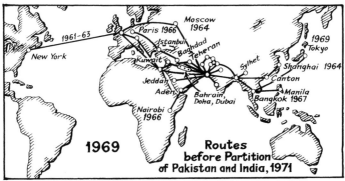

1969   **Routes before Partition of Pakistan and India, 1971**

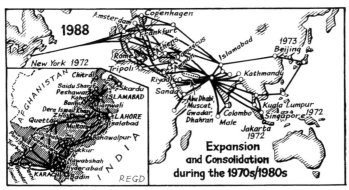

1988   **Expansion and Consolidation during the 1970s/1980s**

Map 5d. Growth of Pakistan International

Pakistan entered into the 'big league' of international airlines in 1956, when it opened its first services to Britain, where many Pakistani families had taken up residence, and who wished to maintain contacts with relatives in the homeland. In 1964, PIA became the first western airline to provide a direct service to China, hitherto accessible by air only via the Soviet Union. Since then, a route pattern has been consolidated throughout Southern Asia, the Middle East, and across the Atlantic to the United States.

A New Opportunity

The momentous events of the closing days of 1991, when the Soviet Union ceased to exist, to be succeeded by the Commonwealth of Independent States (CIS), suddenly provided PIA with the kind of opportunity which it had seized in the past, often through adversity which spurred it into greater innovative efforts. The spirit still seems to be alive and well. Five of the Central Asian republics, and one of the Caucasian republics of the former USSR were Moslem states, sharing a common religious heritage, and therefore many of the customs and habits, with Pakistan. The countries in between, Iran and Afghanistan, were also Moslem, so that the community of interest over a large contiguous area, almost as large as the Sub-continent itself, seemed to offer possibilities for new initiatives.

Accordingly, and acting promptly, in March 1992 PIA became the first foreign airline to provide service to Tashkent, Uzbekistan, with a once weekly Boeing 737 flight direct from Islamabad, marking, incidentally, the 43rd international destination. Maintaining the contact with the newly independent Republic, PIA leased two Ilyushin Il-86 four-engined wide-bodied airliners from the Uzbek airline (once a sub-division of the mighty Aeroflot) and used them on the Haj pilgrimage flights from 7 May to 15 July 1992.

On 3 August of the same year, the Pakistan Government approved a new commercial aviation policy that may have far-reaching consequences for Pakistan International Airlines. For the first time since the embryo stage of the nation itself, private airlines would be permitted to start operations. They would be permitted to compete with PIA on domestic routes, but internationally, a policy of one airline only for each route would be allowed. For the first time PIA's monopoly 'chosen instrument' status was challenged. But erstwhile domestic challengers should be warned: they will face an airline with a great tradition of providing excellent service, with good catering even on short feeder routes, and at low fares (albeit supported in many instances by subsidies), and in the international arena PIA already flies to almost every city where an air service is financially or operationally viable. Whatever the outcome, the spirit and creativeness that have sustained Pakistan International Airlines through many crises in the past will not be found wanting in the future.

Challenge to PIA

Although neighbouring India had put the deregulatory process into motion in 1990, Pakistan did not do so until three years later. Several airlines began service in 1993, offering competitive services on the main inter-city domestic routes, at fare levels lower than Pakistani air travellers had been accustomed to under the PIA monopoly.

As is usually the case, only the fittest of the newcomers survived, and of those listed in the accompanying table, two at least appear to have established themselves as permanent segments of the air transport system. Aero-Asia was first off the mark, apparently well capitalized by the Tabani group of companies. Of the others, Shaheen Air was backed by the Shaheen Foundation, an investment arm of the Pakistan Air Force, in association with Akbar Aviation. The latter then sold its interest, leaving the Foundation as the sole owner.

The independent airlines now provide an alternative to PIA on all the major domestic routes, especially the trunk lines from Karachi to Lahore and Rawalpindi/Islamabad. PIA, meanwhile, is still responsible for operating social services to the more remote corners of the country, especially to the far north, in precipitous mountain terrain, where, it is said, even eagles fear to fly.

Independent Airlines in Pakistan

Date of First Service	Airline (and Base)	Fleet	Routes	Remarks
6 May 1993	Aero-Asia (Karachi)	Boeing 707 Rombac One-Eleven	Serves all main cities in Pakistan,	Owned by the Tabani Group
(Summer) 1993	Hajvairy Arlines			Operated for a few months only
(Summer (1993)	Raji Aviation			Operated for a few months only
7 Nov 1993	Bhoja Air (Karachi)	Boeing 737-200	Serves some main cities	Suspended service earlly 1994 but resumed in summer. Lease agreement with Lithuanian Airlines
1 Dec 1993	Shaheen Air (Karachi)	Boeing 737-200 MD-83 Tupolev Tu-154M	Serves all main cities in Pakistan, also to the Gulf (Peshawar-Dubai)	Founded by Pakistan Air Force (through the Shaheen Foundation) and Akbar Aviation. Had operated a cargo Boeing 747 in 1991. Akbar sold interest in 1994 to the Foundation, now sole owner

CHAPTER SIX

Afghanistan Enters the Air Age

While most of the preliminary sorties that eventually led to the establishment of air services in southern Asia originated in Europe and were routed through the Mediterranean and the Persian Gulf, those to Afghanistan (which has no coastline) came from a different direction. The first airline to reach Kabul was the Russian Dobrolet, which extended its pioneering routes in Central Asia to Kabul, the Afghan capital, on 14 September 1926, almost certainly with Junkers-F 13s that were probably built at the Fili factory in Moscow, under contractual agreements with the German manufacturer. Except for occasional interruptions through technical reasons or climatic problems, the connection to the Soviet Union was maintained until the latter's involvement in the Second World War.

The second airline to venture into Afghanistan – and venture is the operative word, because the terrain was, to be charitable, inhospitable; and the inhabitants were actually neither charitable nor hospitable – was Deutsche Luft Hansa. Barred from traditional directions of route development because of difficulties arising from sustained repercussions from the bitterness of the First World War, DLH was unable to join in the traditional route to the east until a month before the start of the Second. Meanwhile, in 1937, it tried to take a short cut to China by an audacious route through the Wakhan Pass, in northeastern Afghanistan, where, by a peculiarity of the whims of international boundary commissions, there was a common frontier with China, thus allowing the German airline to bypass British India. An encounter with Chinese bandits put an end to this kind of audacity.

DLH extended its European route from Istanbul to Baghdad on 29 October 1937, reached Teheran in Persia on 1 April 1938, and two weeks later extended this even further to Herat and Kabul. At the time, it was the longest route on the

Ariana (Aryana) began operations, like so many others, with Douglas C-47s.
(*Courtesy John Stroud*)

German airline system. But it also ceased abruptly just before the start of the war, in August 1939, and many years were to pass before regular air services were resumed.

Eventually, on 27 January 1955, Aryana Afghan Airlines Co Ltd was founded in Kabul, with the assistance of Indamer Co Ltd, an Indian concern started by Peter Baldwin, an American, who held 49 per cent of the shares, with the Afghan Government holding the controlling 51 per cent balance. Aryana, incidentally, was the name given to the area in the first century BC by the Greek geographer, Strabo.

By the end of the year, Aryana began its first service, from Kabul to Mazari-i-Sharif, via Kunduz, with a modest fleet of three Douglas ex-C-47s (DC-3s). The route was to a town near the Soviet frontier station of Termez, and the DC-3 completed in three hours a journey which previously took a week on poor roads.

On 27 June 1956, in a key political–commercial move, the Air Transport Development Project Agreement was signed with the United States, as a consequence of which Pan American Airways bought Indamer's share, becoming responsible for all technical and operational matters, and changing the spelling of the name to Ariana. A Douglas DC-4 had already left New York, on 3 June, with an Afghan crew, to be on hand for the Haj pilgrimage traffic to Mecca, from Kandahar. While regional services were introduced, from Kabul to Amritsar and

Map 6. Ariana, 1958
During the 1950s, with the assistance of Pan American Airways, the Afghan national airline was able to establish direct links with neighbouring countries. Air transport in this land-locked country is especially important, as there are no railways and the roads are not very good. The link with India's capital is essential, avoiding the Khyber Pass, still hazardous because of the terrain, if not the threat of tribal raids. (Into the latter part of 1996 a desperate struggle continues for control.)

Delhi, and to Karachi, with the DC-3s, Ariana prepared to show the Afghan flag in Europe; and on 11 September 1959, the DC-4 did just that, with a weekly service, proudly named *The Marco Polo Route*, to Frankfurt, via Teheran, Beirut, Ankara and Prague.

Although the unpressurized DC-4 was replaced in May 1960 by the better, and pressurized, DC-6B, the potential attraction of Afghanistan as a tourist destination was such that few Europeans were anxious to follow in Marco Polo's footsteps, even by air, partly because the tourism infrastructure had not been developed in parallel with the demand generally for the Near and Middle East and the Subcontinent. For adventurous souls who sought a hand-made Lee-Enfield rifle, then Ariana was the way to go, in keeping with the novelty; but without a swimming-pool-equipped Kabul Hilton, Kabul was by-passed in favour of Delhi. Service had to be reduced to twice monthly, Karachi flights were discontinued in August 1961, when diplomatic relations between Afghanistan and Pakistan were suspended, and early in 1962, the European route had to be curtailed to Beirut.

The airline was almost dormant when a lifeline was thrown out in March 1963 by the United States Agency for International Development, which granted a $2,625,000 loan to the Government of Afghanistan to assist Ariana to expand service by the addition of another DC-6 and two Convair-Liner twin-engined aircraft. The terms of the loan were almost synonymous with the word gift. The loan was to be repaid over 40 years (it will be repayable by AD 2003) with an annual credit fee of 0.75 per cent. The government was, in turn, to lend the money to the airline for ten years at $3\frac{1}{2}$ per cent. The aircraft arrived in September 1963, the DC-6A passenger/cargo version from AAXICO, the Convair-Liners from Pan American. Paradoxically, this reinforcement came just as road communications to the railheads in Pakistan were improved, and Ariana was deprived of much of its charter traffic.

In 1964, the Afghan shareholding was re-distributed between various government agencies: the Monopoly Department 16 per cent, the Civil Aviation Department 15 per cent, the Da Afghanistan Bank 10 per cent, and others. On 24 March, a new Convair-Liner 340 was purchased from Allegheny Airlines, and introduced on the main domestic line to Herat in the west, to Kunduz in the north, and Kandahar in the south; and also onwards to Karachi, now back in favour diplomatically. In July 1965 the DC-6A opened service to Tashkent in Uzbekistan under a pooling agreement with the Soviet airline Aeroflot. And on 13 August, to open a new era, a DC-6B resumed service to Europe, linking Kabul and Kandahar with London, stopping only at Beirut and Frankfurt.

Ariana Afghan Airlines entered the jet age early in April 1968, when a Boeing 727 entered service on the route to London, by now re-routed via Teheran, Istanbul, and Frankfurt. No Fifth Freedom traffic was allowed, so that flights from London's Gatwick Airport could accept passengers bound only to Kabul. If this was not sufficient as a limitation, the 727 crashed in dense fog near London on 5 January 1969. The airline did well to lease another 727 from World Airways and bought the aircraft outright on 25 January 1970; and then added a second 727, bought from Executive Jet Aviation in May 1971.

The early Seventies witnessed an undercurrent of political rivalry in Afghanistan, with pro-Soviet groups vying for national leadership. Some of the influence from the north was possibly reflected in the purchase, in June 1973, of three Yakovlev Yak-40s from the USSR. Afghanistan was one of the few international customers for this unique Yakovlev aircraft, the only tri-jet feeder airliner – it had 28 seats – in the world. These aircraft were operated on domestic services

Boeing 727s began work with Ariana in 1968. (*Boeing*)

by Bakhtar Afghan Airlines, which had been established in 1967 by the Government to take over Ariana's domestic route network, with the objective of applying special emphasis to the problems of operating to remote communities – although there may have been a political motive, aimed to ensure that the Pan American aided Ariana did not inadvertently permit US political agencies to filter into the northern areas of the country. Meanwhile, Ariana benefited by Pan Am's presence, when it was able to acquire, on generous terms, a Boeing 720B from the airline in May 1973.

This was the year of the first military coup, which established Afghanistan as a republic, to replace a monarchy whose history had been one of continuous feuding by rival tribes and families, and which only after the Great War had shown any indication of co-operation with neighbouring countries, except when the latter were inclined to assist in the internecine disputes. Over the past century, relations with the British in India had been particularly unpredictable, leading to the occasional demonstration of force by British Army contingents to revenge the massacre of resident agents and diplomats. But the last king, or Amir, surrendered his throne in 1973.

In 1978, a Soviet-backed group mounted another coup, and assumed power. On

Bakhtar Afghan Airlines was established in 1967 and used 28-passenger Yakovlev Yak-40s on domestic services.

87

Christmas Eve 1979, the USSR initiated a massive airlift of armed forces that began the Soviet occupation of Afghanistan, which established a puppet regime on 27 December, under Babrak Kamal, usurping Hafizullah Amin, who had ruled as president for only three months. The Soviets soon found that they had bitten into something that, if they could not chew, was decidedly unpalatable. Just as the British Army had discovered during the Afghan Wars of the later years of the 19th Century, the tribesmen were masters of the art of guerilla warfare, and modern equipment, even the latest tanks, and rocket-firing aircraft, could be absorbed and even repulsed by courageous freedom fighters who knew every inch of the mountainous terrain that they defended to the last man.

This was hardly the environment for airline operations; and effectively, there was little activity that could be described as scheduled airline service – or any other. For nine years, no aircraft could venture into the Afghan skies unless it was well-armed, and many an Ilyushin or Antonov troop-carrier or military freighter, some in Soviet Air Force colours, some in Aeroflot's, were shot down by accurate sniper fire from weapons that made up in accuracy and determination for what they lacked in modernity.

With the Communists firmly in control, its designated puppet operator, Bakhtar, now assumed the ascendancy. On 23 October 1985, it took over Ariana Afghan, and became the new national airline, as Bakhtar Afghan Airlines. Predictably, the direction of international operations changed, with services to Moscow and Prague, and to nearby Tashkent, in Uzbekistan. It also took over Ariana's domestic services, adding some Tupolev Tu-154s and Antonov An-26s to the Boeing 727s and Yak-40s left over from the previous two airlines.

Eventually, after an agonizing period in which two million Afghans were estimated to have been killed, no less than six million civilians to have fled the country, and 15,000 well-armed Soviet soldiers killed, a United Nations mediated truce was signed, to create a peaceful, neutral State. On 15 February 1989 the evacuation of Soviet troops was completed; on 16 April, the Communist President Najibullah resigned; rebel forces achieved power on 28 April, and the fundamentalist Burhanuddin Rabbani became president on 28 June 1989. Prospects for the re-establishment of both the necessary infrastructure and the operational, commercial, and technical organization for the rebirth of Ariana were, to say the least, not encouraging.

CHAPTER SEVEN

Nepal's Airlines of the Himalayas

Like Afghanistan, the sovereign State of Nepal was never conquered by the British during the most ambitious years of Asian expansionism, which, at one time, even led to covetous colonial eyes as far into the continental heartland as Tibet. Again, like Afghanistan, Nepal owed its independence to the bravery of its soldiers, who defended their land with as much determination as it had been ruthlessly ruled by a succession of autocratic regents, for whom the hereditary dynasty was of figurehead status. In 1857, Jung Bahadur, the de facto ruler, who had visited Britain, despatched several thousand troops in support of the British Army during the Indian Mutiny. The Gurkhas (the name is derived from the region of Nepal where most of them live), won their spurs – partly with their kukris, their broad-bladed knives – and became a highly-respected segment of the British Army in India. In the Great War of 1914–18, the 20 Gurkha battalions were increased to 40, and served with great distinction. And Nepalese Gurkhas still serve today.

Such a display of military cordiality would normally have led to much greater Anglo-Nepalese interchange of social and commercial activity; but, yet again like Afghanistan, the frontiers were almost closed, and no railway has ever been seen in Nepal. To visit Kathmandu was quite an adventure, demanding a certain stamina to reach the Nepalese capital from the Indian railhead, in much the same way that a journey through the Khyber Pass from the Indian railhead was a victory of endurance. But halfway through the 20th Century, the old order changed. In 1951, King Tribhubana Bir Bikran ended the system of rule by hereditary premiers of the Rana family, who had kept the kings virtually as prisoners in their own kingdom. He established a cabinet system of government, and set in motion a programme of modern-style administration which included the decision to open up the frontiers, to welcome visitors, and to help his citizens to enjoy a better life.

One of the immediate actions was to permit Indian National Airways (INA) to open services to Kathmandu, from Patna, the nearest major Indian city. Two years later, Himalayan Aviation, another Indian airline, began domestic services from Kathmandu to Pokhara, Bhairawa, Simra and Biratnagar. Inevitably, these latter were operated by the versatile but venerable Douglas C-47/DC-3, but the 45-minute flight to Pokhara was infinitely more preferable to the tortuous route formerly taken via Nepal's roads and tracks that took eight days. Himalayan's service was taken over soon afterwards by the Indian Airlines Corporation (IAC) when the many Indian airlines were amalgamated into a nationalized corporation on 15 June 1953.

Five years later, on 1 July 1958, the Royal Nepal Airline Corporation (RNAC) was formed, with mixed government and private backing, to take over the contracted IAC services. Two days later, RNAC began domestic service with DC-3s. On 12 October 1959, the Government of Nepal assumed complete ownership of the airline, and in mid-January 1960, took over the international route to Patna, and added additional connections to Delhi and Calcutta. RNAC was formally incorporated in 1962.

Royal Nepal Airline Douglas C-47s await the day's work at Kathmandu Airport (elevation 4,386 ft). (*Courtesy John Stroud*)

The first upgrading of equipment came in April 1966, when a 40-passenger propeller-turbine Fokker Friendship entered service. The single Fokker crashed at Delhi on 25 January 1970, and although its tenure was short-lived, it had the honour of opening the unique Mountain Flights, one-hour round trips which, weather permitting, take off every morning (sometimes with extra sections later in the day) from Kathmandu to the vicinity of Everest, or Sagarmatha, as it is called in Nepal. Tourists are offered the opportunity to observe the breathtaking panorama of the eastern Himalayas, and to view, in this one single short flight, five of the eight highest mountain peaks in the world. Another unique feature of the flight is that the passengers are issued with the only airline tickets in which the origin and destination points (Kathmandu) are the same.

On 26 January 1970, a day after the Friendship crash, two Avro 748s (in the Sub-continent, they were always Avros, not HS748s) took over the main routes, while RNAC began to expand air services, on the one hand to open up its mountainous land to the luxury of air service to every community, however remote and isolated, and on the other hand, to improve and expand its international network.

For the local routes, RNAC bought a small fleet of DHC-6 Twin Otters, for which small strips were built in more than a dozen communities throughout the length (there was not much breadth) of the land. Most of these were in valleys and in the foothills of the Himalayan mountain chain; but here and there, the strip was precariously situated on slopes that were more suited to mountain goats. At Lukla, for example, twenty miles south of the peak of Everest, the 2,500 ft strip is at an altitude of 8,900 ft at the bottom end (the 'ski-jump' off the precipice) but 9,200 ft at the top, where it abuts on to the mountainside. Taking off down the 12 deg slope is quite sporty.

Yet there were places where even the generally versatile STOL-performance Twin Otter could not go, and for further challenges to the ultimate air transport equivalent of mountaineering, two single-engine Pilatus Porters exercised one of the world's more remarkable change-of-gauge schedules, taking over from the Twin Otters, at Lukla for example, to seek higher altitudes such as Syangboche, at 12,300 ft. Both aircraft went into service in 1971, the Twin Otter in August, and the Porter in November.

A Royal Nepal Airline Twin Otter at Lukla near Everest. The landing strip is about 1,200 ft long with a gradient of 12–15 percent. It is at an elevation of 8,900 ft at one end and 9,200 ft at the other. The remains of a Twin Pioneer are in the background.
(R E G Davies)

The Swiss STOL Pilatus Porter has proved remarkably successful in meeting RNAC's special needs such as operating from landing grounds at elevations above 12,000 ft.

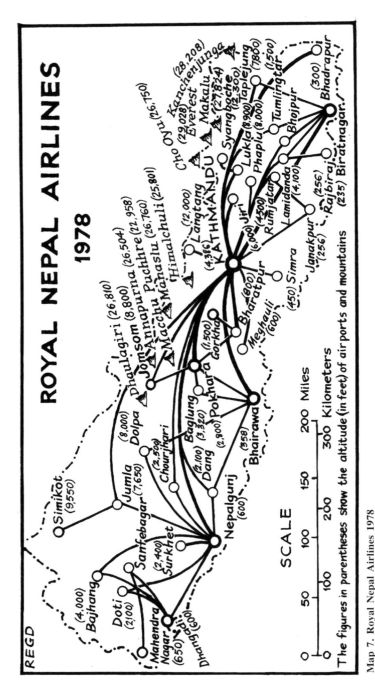

Map 7. Royal Nepal Airlines 1978

RNAC faces the formidable task of providing the only practical mode of transport along the Himalayan cordillera. Ten of the communities served regularly, some on a daily schedule, are more than 6,000 ft above sea level. Two of them are even more than 12,000 ft, yet the Twin Otters and the Pilatus Porters take them in their stride.

RNAC introduced the Boeing 727 in 1972. (*Boeing*)

To move into the realms of international jet operations, a substantial technical step for any airline, but especially so for an airline that had introduced airline service to its country with DC-3s little more than a decade earlier, a co-operative agreement was made with Air France, on 13 July 1970; and this resulted in the acquisition of a Boeing 727-100, fitted with 120 seats, in June 1972. Three months later, a proud day for RNAC, it opened service to Delhi on 15 September, and soon added Bangkok and Calcutta to its jet destinations. As if to celebrate its elevation to a new stratum of sophistication, the last DC-3 was sold. Such was the Nepalese spirit of independence and resolve that it was able to dispense with Air France's help on 31 October 1973.

RNAC Forges Links with the World

While the direct link with a European airline had been loosened, the association with Europe had not; and the Nepalese airline had, with its injection of European airline co-operation, no doubt acquired a taste for carrying its flag further afield. By the 1970s, Nepal was becoming far more accessible to visitors and was growing as an international tourist attraction. No longer was it identified with the spirit of adventure, even danger, as the destination only of intrepid mountain-climbers. Kathmandu was becoming one of the features of tourism literature, seeking the custom of a clientèle ranging from the jet set to the hippie community, and offering attractions such as exotic trekking itineraries in the Himalayas or fabulous shopping tours of the city's crowded streets.

For these sources of tourism revenue, RNAC introduced a Pilatus Porter service on a few of its more inaccessible domestic routes on 31 October 1975. Passengers who, only the previous day, had taken off from a two-mile-long runway in Europe, now had the chance to alight on a strip no longer than the width of a standard 747

93

runway. Then, on 31 January 1977, the airline began a helicopter service, with newly-acquired Aérospatiale Alouettes and Pumas, to the Tiger Tops National Park, south of Kathmandu, on the Indian frontier.

To cater for this burgeoning business, RNAC started to expand into the international, even intercontinental arena. On 16 March 1977, direct service opened from Kathmandu to Colombo in Sri Lanka, whence connections could be made to Singapore and other southern Asian points. Later in the year, it opened a route to Frankfurt, in pool with Lufthansa, and using the latter's aircraft, with on-board catering provided by the Oberoi Hotel. Soon, Nepal had its own 757s, fitted out with 174 economy-class and 16 'Shangri-la' business-class seats. A maintenance agreement was signed with HAECO in Hong Kong.

In September 1989, a new route extension from Frankfurt put London on the RNAC map, and thereafter the network in Asia and the Middle East was strengthened by the addition of Dubai, Dhaka, Karachi, and Bombay. As the airline entered the last decade of the century, it had become the largest single employer in the predominantly agrarian country. Three quarters of its passengers were foreign tourists, and it had become the country's largest earner of foreign exchange.

Success breeds success, not necessarily always to the innovator. In 1992, the Nepalese Government decided to liberalize its domestic airline policy, and allow the formation of new airlines.

Necon Air and Nepal Airways each operate a couple of Avro 748s on scheduled routes and on the enormously popular sightseeing flights. Nepal Airways also has three Chinese Yun-12s. Everest Air is a strong competitor, with three Dornier 228s, which have impressive performance to cope with the precarious airstrips in the high Himalayas. Everest also has four Mil Mi-8 helicopters, which can take-off with 24 passengers aboard at 12,000 ft altitude. Himalayan Helicopters, with a Bell 206L3, completes a list of four independent Nepalese airlines which now account for 70 per cent of the domestic traffic. Royal Air Nepal, meanwhile, continues to expand its international network, serving Bangkok, Hong Kong, and Singapore, to bring ever more tourists to a country which, only half a century ago, was considered to be inacecessible to all but the adventurous, or even the foolhardy who wished to challenge the mountain fastnesses of the mighty Himalayas.

CHAPTER EIGHT

Bhutan Becomes Airborne

Land of the Thunder Dragon

Situated squarely in the Eastern Himalayan mountain chain, Bhutan, or Druk-Yul, is a small independent country with a population of 1.6 million, and an area only a little larger than that of Switzerland. Its geography is rather similar to Switzerland's, except that the different climate and vegetation zones are reversed from north to south. The fertile valleys of the central area are separated by the high Himalayas in the north and the tropical forests of the south. In a way, Bhutan's topography and geography are like a slice of Nepal, from which it is separated by the Indian State of Sikkim.

Many centuries ago, it was part of Tibet, but British influence during the 19th Century led to the establishment of a monarchy in 1907, which, three years later, acquired the status of a British Protectorate. After the Second World War, and the withdrawal of Britain from the Sub-continent, Bhutan became fully independent in 1949, by which time such slender contacts with the outside world that existed, political, commercial, or social, were towards India. The capital of the country, Druk-Yul (Land of the Thunder Dragon), is Thimphu, but the main centre for commerce, and a slowly growing destination for adventurous tourists, seeking the unusual attractions of this heavily Buddhist land, is Paro Daong.

Until recently, Bhutan was as accessible for normal international travel as Antarctica or Spitzbergen. Paro could be reached by taking Indian Airlines to the northern Bengal town, Bagdogra, and then by road for many hours by a precipitous track, a journey that could take all day, just to the border town of Phuntsholing. A visit to the Land of the Thunder Dragon was quite an adventure, with no hot and cold running water, and the number of foreign visitors, of whom few were tourists, numbered only a few hundred annually.

Druk-Air

All this changed early in the 1980s, on 12 February to be exact. On that day, the first flight of the Bhutanese airline, Druk-Air, took off from Paro en route to Calcutta, the Indian metropolis and entrepot of trade in southern Bengal. The airline had been founded officially on the previous day. It is wholly owned by the Government, with four directors, and the chairman is HRH Princess Ashi Sonam Wangchuk. The equipment consisted of two Dornier 228s, fitted with 18 seats each, ample for the volume of traffic until Bhutan builds up a reputation as a tourist destination. This is not going to happen quickly, for this little country, steeped in tradition and religious protocol, is in no hurry to welcome the construction of a Paro Hilton or a Thimphu Oberoi. Nevertheless, for those who seek something different, there is now an easier way to go to the Land of the Thunder Dragon than by dangerous roads.

The Dornier 228 is a STOL (Short Take-Off and Landing) aircraft, and fuel

95

A Druk-Air Dornier 228 STOL aircraft with a background typical of the area in which it operates.

efficient. While the airstrip at Paro is paved, it is less than a mile long, and there is an unpaved overshoot. The field elevation is 7,400 ft. The local flying rule is that the pilot must be able to see the mountain-fringed airstrip before trying to land, which must be comforting for the passengers. Traffic control, under contract to the Indian Air Force, does not yet run to ILS approaches or anything fancy; and in the monsoon season, delays can be measured not in hours, but in days. But the 1 hr 45 min flight from Calcutta is operated, under normal weather conditions, three times a week; and the passengers can, on clear days, see both Everest and Kanchenjunga to the left as they approach Paro.

Druk-Air was one of the last airlines to join the ranks of the international air transport fraternity; but, with its unique operating environment, it is arguably not by any means the least. Because of its efforts, annual visitors to Bhutan can no longer be measured in hundreds, as the flying representative of the Thunder Dragon has raised these numbers to several thousand every year.

DRUK-AIR

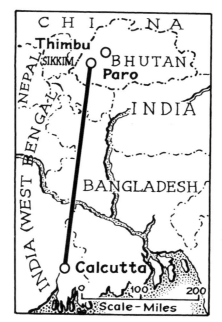

Map 8. Druk-Air
For centuries Bhutan was possibly the most inaccessible of all the lands of Asia, even Tibet; but it has now come to terms with the modern world and boasts its own air service, linking it with India's eastern metropolis, Calcutta.

CHAPTER NINE

An Airline for Bengal

A Country Sub-divided

In 1947, Pakistan had become an independent State, breaking away from the old British India, and forming its frontiers with that nation almost entirely on the basis of major population distribution by religious faith. Those areas where Muslims predominated (though this did not necessarily include all Muslims, as several millions remained scattered throughout Hindu and Buddhist India) became Pakistan, but by the fate of history and heritage, this created a divided State, as the eastern, Muslim, part of the province of Bengal was completely separated from the larger, western part of Pakistan. For more than two decades, these were known as the East and West Wings of Pakistan.

Gradually, however, dissatisfaction began to smoulder and rivalry increased between the two Wings. The birth of Pakistan had been precipitated mainly from politicians in the West. Karachi became, almost overnight, the commercial (and until the construction of Islamabad, the political) capital, instantly elevating its status from that of an Indian port city to a rapidly-expanding cosmopolitan metropolis. A glance at the map suggested that this was the natural outcome. But the map was deceptive. The majority of the population, about 55 per cent, lived in the East; yet the area of the East was only about one-sixth that of the West Wing, or slightly less than the area of the State of Wisconsin. Today, in this area of about 55,000 square miles, live more than 120 million people, mostly poor farmers. Over the years, little was done from Karachi to provide some sense of equality between the two Wings. Dacca (now Dhaka) was regarded as a distant provincial town, rather than the focal point of half the nation. And eventually, the smouldering embers of frustration burst into flames. In a bitter civil war, Pakistani troops attacked local mercenaries in East Pakistan on 25 March 1971. East Pakistan declared its independence, as the new State of Bangladesh, on the next day. In a tragic episode only too reminiscent of the mass migration and genocide of the Punjab refugee marches of the Partition period, homeless people sought asylum in nearby India's West Bengal. In an almost inevitable confrontation, bearing in mind the recent history of adversarial attitudes on both sides, war began between India and Pakistan on 3 December. Thankfully, it was soon over, Pakistan surrendering ten days later. But Bangladesh was now on its own. With a history of having been controlled in politics, commerce, and almost every aspect of life, from Karachi and Islamabad, it had to start from scratch in almost every activity of industrial and social endeavour.

Showing the Airline Flag

It has often been said, with quite a few examples to prove the point, that no sooner has a newly-independent country raised its flag for the first time, than the first flight with its own airline takes to the skies. While this might be criticized as being over-nationalistic or the display of some illusions of grandeur, there is a certain logic to such a level of priority. For in today's world, and especially in Asia, Africa, and Latin America, air transport is the almost exclusive means of travel, for politicians, businessmen, tourists, or simply people wishing to visit friends and relatives. Without its own airline, any country would have to use those of foreign countries, and this is a drain on precious reserves of foreign exchange. Just as every coin spent by a visiting tourist is strictly defined as an export; equally every one spent in the reverse direction is an import: a luxury that a poor new country cannot afford. Thus, to create its own airline is a long-term investment, the full value of which cannot always be measured just by the accountants' balance sheet.

With this in mind, and almost before a name had been decided for it, the new airline that was to become Bangladesh Biman was established, on 4 January 1972, as a semi-autonomous agency of an administration that was itself still learning the ropes of full responsibility. Of the former staff of Pakistan International Airlines who were based in the East Wing, about 80 per cent of the 2,600 Bengalis still remained. The others had either gone to the West, or to India, or had been killed during the strife. But all the aircraft had gone back to base, in the West; and that too was where all the maintenance was done, in the fine shops, well equipped and skilfully operated, in Karachi.

Nevertheless, the embryo airline tried to overcome the difficulties. A Douglas DC-3 (the aircraft that always seems to be available when any emergency arises) was allocated from the armed forces – Bangladesh hardly had an air force, in the generally understood definition, but it found an aeroplane somewhere. On 4 February 1972, it made the first flight of a Bangladesh airline, with ten passengers, from Dhaka to Chittagong. This city had suddenly become the new country's chief port, as it was directly on the Indian Ocean, rather than up a river estuary. Only 200 miles from the new capital, Dhaka, it was, however, an arduous, even adventurous rail or road journey therefrom; and an air service was more than simply a business venture; it was a national priority.

Two new short domestic routes were quickly added, to Sylhet, in the northeast, and to Jessore, halfway to Calcutta, across the Indian border, and serving Bangladesh's third largest community, the sprawling Khulna. Sadly, this brave gesture, to try to demonstrate normality in the face of desperation, was short-lived. On 10 February 1972, less than a week after starting, the DC-3 crashed and all flights were stopped. A month later, however, on 9 March, domestic services were resumed, with two Fokker F.27 Friendships donated by the Indian Government, and since then, Bangladesh has always had a domestic airline service to provide for its needs.

Even before this, on 4 March, a long-haul service started from Dhaka to London, destination for a constant flow of emigrants from a recently war-torn country, and now destined to suffer from some of the worst typhoons and floods that the peoples of the Ganges Delta had ever experienced throughout history. The service was operated under contract by a Boeing 707 of British Caledonian Airways, under exempt charter rules, the strict provisions and conditions of which were waived by the British authorities on humanitarian grounds. Also, the following month, a twice-daily service started to Calcutta, operated with a Douglas DC-6B leased for a few weeks from Troll Air, a Norwegian charter carrier. This was Bangladesh Biman's first scheduled international service.

Bangladesh Biman was officially founded, as a fully government-owned agency, on 27 October 1972, by Presidential Order No. 126. Its first chairman was Musleh Uddin Ahmed, though his term of office was not of long duration. During the next

A Bangladesh Biman Fokker F.27 Friendship at Dhaka (Dacca). (*R E G Davies*)

dozen years, the airline was to have, on average, a new chairman once a year.

With its priorities correctly directed, the airline concentrated on building up the domestic network. One of the inherited problems of this new sovereign state, for which no plans had ever been made and whose destiny had always been linked with and dependent upon distant economies, was that there was no systematic surface transport system, road, rail, or inland waterway, designed to revolve around Dhaka. The mighty Brahmaputra and Ganges Rivers split the country into three parts and Dhaka was not on either waterway. One railway meandered to Chittagong, but Dhaka had no rail link with the north, the east, or the west. Bangladesh Biman stepped into the breach. Between May 1972 and June 1973, eight Fokker F.27s, four -200s and four -600s, were acquired from donations by the Netherlands and Australian Governments; and these were deployed on new routes to Comilla, Cox's Bazar, and Ishurdi, in addition to Chittagong, Sylhet and Jessore, already on the map. Later, in 1977, Thakurgaon, in the northwest, would be added to complete the spoke network from Dacca.

Long-Haul Expansion

Only a year and a half after the gruelling transition into independence, Bangladesh Biman showed the new green and red flag of its country at London's Gatwick Airport. It began regular service with a Boeing 707-321, leased from Pan American Airways, on 18 June 1973. Six months later, it acquired its first Boeing 707-320C from Northwest Airlines, and on 31 December, put it into service, with a stop at Dubai. The second Boeing 707, from no less a source than Pakistan International (revealing, perhaps, the eternal brotherhood of airline people), arrived on 6 November 1975, and a third, from Transair, Canada, on 8 February

A Bangladesh Biman Boeing 707 at London Airport – Heathrow in July 1973. (*John Wegg*)

1976. Major maintenance and overhaul for this small fleet was contracted with HAECO of Hong Kong. Now with some flexibility, the international network was steadily expanded, to points in southern Asia: Bangkok, Bombay, Karachi and Singapore; and to Abu Dhabi and Jeddah in the Middle East. By the end of the 1970s, further points were added, to Khatmandu, Kuala Lumpur and Rangoon; and to a number of cities in the Gulf states; while Rome, Athens, Paris and Amsterdam were added as European destinations.

All these services were well patronized, with high load factors, and the Boeing 707 fleet grew to five. They were all fitted out in an all-economy layout, to match the popular demand, which was predominantly of Bangladesh nationals. These comprised emigrants to Europe, mainly to the United Kingdom, where the immigrant population grew to half a million; contract workers to the oil-rich sheikhdoms of the Gulf; and Haj pilgrims to Jeddah. It had been a struggle, but the little country that had emerged by political caesarian section, was now firmly in business, and had taken its place on the world airline map.

Coming of Age

Bangladesh Biman was able to put on a brave show in the highly competitive airline world, even with a fleet of aircraft that, by some standards, might have been regarded as a little long in the tooth. Not a single one had been bought new; some had been gifts, and some had been acquired with funds voted by the United Nations Development Programme (UNDP), in association with the recommendations of ICAO. But the airline benefited largely from enjoying captive markets in its domestic, its medium-haul, and in its long-haul routes. The only competition domestically was the mostly unconnected strips of railway line that, in any case, did not radiate from the capital city and poor roads, subject to attack by atrocious weather; the medium-haul routes were mostly to points in the Gulf, and therefore with a predominantly guest-worker clientèle of Bangladesh citizens; and the long-haul routes, especially to London, were the links to home for the emigrants to Europe. Nevertheless, as the 1970s drew to a close, by which time most of the aircraft it flew were showing signs of old age, bold steps had to be taken to upgrade the fleet.

Bangladesh Biman's Fokker F.28 S2-ACI at Amsterdam in December 1981. (*Bob Neumeier via John Wegg*)

On 13 June 1980, the airline ordered two 85-seat Fokker F.28-400 Fellowship jets, for use on the main domestic route, Dhaka—Chittagong, which had now reached almost shuttle-service frequency, and to Calcutta, Kathmandu and Rangoon. The aircraft were delivered early in 1982, to provide a much-needed level of capacity to supplement the 44-seat F.27s and the 165-seat Boeing 707s.

Moving right along, in 1983, negotiations were completed to introduce three Douglas DC-10-30s, purchased from Singapore Airlines, whose policy of maintaining a superior fleet of low average life meant that even its discarded aircraft were close to being in new condition, rather like a one-owner, low-mileage second-hand car. The wide-bodied aircraft came 'as is' and consequently produced a minor revolution in Bangladesh Biman's service standards. For the first time, it began to cater for passengers other than those whose pockets demanded the lowest fares possible in ultra-economy class. Singapore Airlines DC-10s had an excellent first-class section – the kind that had helped the airline to win votes as the world's best airline – and Biman had no reason to change it, except at unnecessary cost. It simply introduced the *Royal Bengal* service. Major maintenance was provided by KLM at one of its European termini.

One of Bangladesh Biman's McDonnell Douglas DC-10-30s on the approach to Amsterdam-Schiphol in January 1984. (*Bob Neumeier via John Wegg*)

102

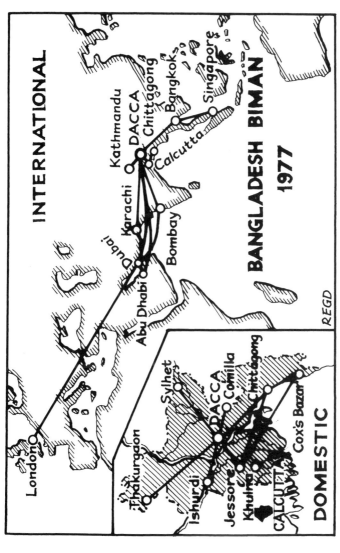

Map 9. Bangladesh Biman 1977
After breaking away from Pakistan, of which it formerly constituted the 'East Wing', to become a separate nation, Bangladesh had to form its own airline, particularly to establish a good communications link with its overseas ex-patriates, settled mostly in London. It has also established a domestic network to connect Dacca (Dhaka) with provincial cities, supplementing surface routes that are circuitous and subject to the ravages of floods and typhoons, of which the country is a regular victim.

As a matter of interest, when a fourth DC-10 was added to the fleet, in 1989, and delivered directly from the manufacturers at Long Beach, this was the last one built. Also, during the same year, Bangladesh Biman carried more than a million passengers in a year for the first time. The following year, in 1990, the last of the veteran Fokker F.27s was retired, the type having served faithfully for close to two decades, to be replaced by the new British feeder airliner, the British Aerospace ATP.

CHAPTER TEN

Ceylon/Sri Lanka's Opportunities

The island of Ceylon, a British Crown Colony off the southern end of the Indian peninsula, was granted Dominion status in 1948. But even before this, the colonial Civil Aviation Department had established an Air Transport Branch as a separate division. This was, in effect, Ceylon's first airline, and – predictably – its first fleet consisted of the ubiquitous Douglas twin, the DC-3, in this case war-surplus C-47s.

The Air Transport Branch began domestic service from Colombo to Jaffna, via the port city of Trincomalee, on 3 December; and a week later, started the first international route as an extension from Jaffna to Madras. The flagship DC-3 was named *Vihara Maha Devi*, and technical support was provided by Air-India.

Following its elevation to Dominion status, the name Air Ceylon was adopted, and almost simultaneously, in August 1948, an agreement was made with Australian National Airways (ANA), not only for technical assistance, but also for the provision of larger, transocean four-engined airliners. This fitted in with ANA owner Ivan Holyman's plan to extend his influence overseas. Proscribed by Australian law from competing with Qantas directly, he infiltrated in the latter's catchment area by the device of obtaining substantial shareholdings in the strategically placed Hong Kong (with a 40 per cent shareholding of Cathay Pacific) and Ceylon, where he was later to acquire an interest. Incidentally, ANA also supplied aircraft for the short-lived British Commonwealth and Pacific Airlines (BCPA) in 1946–47, so that Holyman's aircraft could be observed all the way from Karachi to Vancouver.

The Douglas DC-4 *Laxapana* was one of the two DC-4s which enabled Air Ceylon to become a long-haul airline, with a route system stretching from London to Sydney. (*Courtesy John Stroud*)

105

ANA Douglas DC-4s, named *Ratmalana* and *Laxapana*, extended Air Ceylon's routes onwards from Jaffna and directly from Colombo to Trichinopoly, and direct service from Colombo to Bombay and Karachi, in 1949. Then, in what must at the time have been a great day for the young dominion, 28 January 1950, these two aircraft inaugurated service from London to Sydney, via Rome, Tel Aviv (Lydda), Karachi, Bombay, Colombo, Singapore and Jakarta. Ceylon's geographical position was revealing itself to be as important to the airways of southern Asia as a refuelling stop as it had been for the sea routes as a vital coaling station.

When Air Ceylon was constituted as a corporation on 1 May 1951, the Government had the controlling 51 per cent interest, but ANA had the other 49 per cent. At first, this arrangement continued to strengthen, with the Australians training Singalese aircrew, and, by the end of the year, with an improvement of domestic services, as de Havilland D.H.89A Dragon Rapides started flights to Trincomalee via Minneriya and Amparai.

Unfortunately for both Air Ceylon and ANA, this apparent consolidation of mutual interest occurred only a year before the British airline BOAC changed the world of air transport by introducing the Comet jet airliner, first on its African route, and quickly followed by expansion throughout Asia, including a route to Colombo. The American airline TWA also extended its Super Constellation trans-Atlantic route, already established as far as the Middle East, into southern Asia, as it sought to fashion a round-the-world service (which was never fulfilled). Such was the force of the competition, from two of the world's leading airlines, with considerable sources of traffic in Europe, that Air Ceylon had to suspend its DC-4, unpressurized, service in the summer of 1953. ANA's own position was weakening at home, and it was absorbed by Ansett Airways four years later.

Colombo Airport's terminal building in the early post-war years. (*BOAC*)

During the next two decades, Air Ceylon entered into a series of partnerships with, successively, four different airlines, the longest of which lasted half that time. No doubt Air Ceylon tried to do the best that it could, in a fiercely competitive situation, in which the strong airlines of Europe were under no illusions about the strategic value of Colombo as a staging point to southeast Asia; but at the same time, displayed little charity in the interests of the indigenous carrier, which had to be satisfied with what it could bargain for, always in the position of the disadvantaged. In retrospect, perhaps the Singalese Government should have bitten the bullet and tried to stand on its own feet right from the start; but, as a small country, its resources were limited; and long-range pressurized aircraft, jet, propeller-turbine, even piston-engined, were still expensive; and sources of financing were slim.

On 1 February 1956, Air Ceylon was able to re-open European services, when the Dutch airline KLM bought ANA's shares and, on 17 February, operated into Colombo, from both Amsterdam and London, with one of its own Lockheed Model 049 Constellations, via Rome, Cairo, Bahrain, Karachi and Bombay. The BOAC jet threat had subsided, after the dramatic and tragic Comet crashes of early 1954; and so the Constellations were not outclassed. Service was re-opened to Bangkok on 26 April 1956, but this destination was suspended in favour of Singapore on 18 April 1957. KLM upgraded the equipment to Super-Constellations (Model 1049G) in 1958, and although reducing its shareholding in Air Ceylon to 24 per cent in January 1959, it continued to provide better aircraft, the Lockheed Electra introducing Air Ceylon's 'Sapphire' service to Europe on 1 November 1960, by which time, however, the Jet Age had permanently reached the whole of Asia.

International service was once again suspended on 1 November 1961, when KLM terminated its agreement with Air Ceylon. As before, equipment competition was a strong factor, as BOAC was back again with the improved Comet 4, and KLM's Douglas DC-8 could not land at or take off from Colombo with full payload, and runway extensions were not yet in sight. Even though the Air Ceylon operation had been consistently profitable, the Electras were withdrawn as KLM had to compete with DC-8s on its eastern routes, where Pan American Airways' Boeing 707s were now deployed to all the major Asian cities.

If you can't beat 'em, join 'em. Air Ceylon transferred its affections to BOAC, and on 30 March 1962, was able to enter the jet age by starting Comet 4 service

Propeller-turbine Lockheed Electras operated Air Ceylon's 'Sapphire' services to Europe from November 1960. (*Courtesy John Stroud*)

107

Air Ceylon was one of the few operators of the Hawker Siddeley Trident. This Trident 1E was delivered to the airline in July 1969. (*Hawker Siddeley*)

to London. The Comets were operated by BOAC, in Air Ceylon's colours, and with Singalese cabin crews. In August 1962, a pool agreement was signed with Indian Airlines Corporation for regional routes, services, and maintenance. Various experiments were then conducted in an attempt to find a solution of the 'DC-3' problem – the ideal aircraft to replace it. In a sharply contested rivalry – Fokker claimed that it was the low bidder with its Friendship – Hawker Siddeley emerged with an order for an HS 748 and the British propeller-turbine twin began local services as far north as Madras on 7 November 1964. Air Ceylon then ordered a French Nord 262 in 1965, put it into service the following year, but had so many problems that it was sold in 1970. As if trying to have one of every aircraft available, Air Ceylon took delivery of a Trident 1E from Hawker Siddeley on 19 July 1969. This was not quite so rash as it appeared, as Pakistan International (PIA) was operating the Tridents and at first undertook the maintenance for Air Ceylon's as well, at its base in relatively nearby Karachi.

For a time BOAC operated Air Ceylon trunk routes with Vickers-Armstrongs VC10s.

After about eight years, the understanding with BOAC seems to have fallen apart, as in November 1970, Air Ceylon announced a similar one with the French independent airline UTA which had its country's official 'sphere of influence' authority to serve French territories in the Pacific Ocean, through southern Asia. The BOAC association ended on 31 March 1971 and the agreement with UTA was officially signed on 27 September of the same year.

To airline observers, the double negotiations, under the direction of Air Ceylon's chairman, Sunil de Silva, under which Air Ceylon changed its technical and commercial partners, was somewhat confusing. BOAC continued to operate on Ceylon's behalf, upgrading the equipment to the fine Vickers VC10s, which operated in Air Ceylon's colours as the 'Golden Falcon' service. The Singalese airline thus had the unusual distinction of having flown all the British jet airliners except the BAC One-Eleven, and the HS 748 as well.

UTA began its own DC-8 service to Jakarta, via Colombo, on 1 November 1971, and co-opted Air Ceylon into this route on 6 April 1972. Although the aircraft flew in UTA colours, the decor was Air Ceylon's, and the cabin crew was Singalese throughout, whereas the BOAC VC10s had had British cabin crew in the first-class section.

Transition towards Airline Independence

Ceylon became the Republic of Sri Lanka on 22 May 1972, a change of name that signified a growing sense of nationalism which, in the field of aviation, was translated into a move towards complete sovereignty from dependence, financially or otherwise, on a foreign partner. Arguably, this should have been the policy from the time of Air Ceylon's foundation in 1947; and now followed a period of confusion, some the result of political rivalries and intrigue, and some the result of bad luck – if the choice of an uncertain new partner, in spite of the desire for independence, can be so described.

Sri Lanka's Government was itself undergoing repeated personnel changes, and Air Ceylon echoed the progress, so that a lack of managerial continuity did not help. However, in February 1976, the agreement by which the UTA DC-8 would eventually become the sole property of Air Ceylon seemed to be an important step in the right direction. The winding down of what became generally known as a lease-purchase, under which regular lease payments would be credited as if for a purchase, if the decision was made by an agreed date, was the subject of dispute between Air Ceylon and UTA. The affair was finally settled on 30 September 1976, by which time, one of the regular charter flights to the Gulf, to Sharjah, had been converted into a scheduled route on 20 March, operated by the Trident.

By this time, all the world seemed to be operating wide-bodied jets, and Air Ceylon did its best to join the ranks. It was negotiating with Lockheed for L-1011 TriStars, when the Japanese scandal broke and the talks ended. At the end of October – all this was happening in one year, 1976 – an agreement was signed, retroactive to 1 October, for the operation of Air Siam's McDonnell Douglas DC-10 to Europe. But by this time, Air Siam was itself in a desperate position and was about to go out of business. In Air Ceylon's defence, therefore, some of its trials and tribulations in a difficult year could be attributed to circumstances beyond its control.

To plug the dyke, the Government appointed Padwan 'Paddy' Mendis as chairman. He had been an Air Vice Marshal of the Air Force, and his declared policy was that Air Ceylon was 'on its own'. He took over on 15 December 1976, and

Air Ceylon Boeing 720 with shady passenger stairs. (*R E G Davies*)

two months later, wet-leased a Boeing 720 (for $1,800 per hour) from an American company, and a DC-8-41 (Conway engines) from Templewood Aviation in Britain. But, because of the lack of confidence by the public – the TriStar and DC-10 fiascos had left many passengers holding booked tickets that they could not use – Air Ceylon's foundations were on shifting sands. An extra European service, terminating in Paris, started in July 1977, but did not last long. The DC-8-41 lease (with Air Canada) was terminated, and all European services stopped on 7 December 1977.

If this was not bad enough, in the following year, domestic air service ended, because one of the two HS 748s was blown up by a hijacker. The last remaining 748 continued to fly to Malé, in the Maldives, now rising in popularity as a vacation resort, while the Trident maintained services to India, to Bombay and Madras. The situation was desperate, and the mood of the Government was shown by its critical decision to form a new airline.

Airlanka

On 11 January 1979, Air Lanka, or Airlanka – the English language treatment of the name was undecided at first – was formed as a public corporation, with the Sri Lanka Government injecting 60 per cent of the US $33 million authorized capital. The remainder was offered for public subscription. Rather than continuing to bail out Air Ceylon from one crisis to another, and recognizing that the lack of adequate capital was at least partly responsible for the problem, this was a bold step.

Curiously, Air Ceylon still continued to operate for a short time, with its single

HS 748 and its single Trident, to the Maldives and to India. It even made a small operating profit, and although most of the staff joined Airlanka or other airlines, those who stayed, even those who had no work to do, were paid their full salaries until all activity ceased towards the end of 1979.

Captain Rakkhita Wikramanayake ('Capt Wik') was appointed as chairman and managing director. Formerly a pilot with Singapore Airlines, he immediately signed an agreement with his former employer, to indicate that, in spite of the new capitalization, Airlanka's finances were not yet strong enough to permit it to buy its own aircraft. The difference was that the operational, commercial, and engineering services provided by Singapore were to be paid in cash, and SIA was also to train local crews.

Airlanka began regional operations with a Boeing 707, leased from SIA, on 1 September 1979, to Bangkok and to Singapore. Additional services were quickly added, to resume the European network after a lapse of almost two years, serving all the important points: London, Paris, Frankfurt and Zürich. The lucrative routes to the Gulf were reopened, to Dubai, Doha, Dhahran and Kuwait. Then, in November 1979, regional services were expanded with a Boeing 737, to Madras, Tiruchirapali, Trivandrum, Bombay, Malé and Karachi.

The picture began to look brighter. In 1980, two Lockheed L-1011-1s were leased from Air Canada, and the following year, the bold step was taken to purchase – a term seldom rising to the surface in the former Air Ceylon's history – another of the same type from All Nippon Airways. Coinciding with a maintenance agreement with HAECO, a new route was opened to Hong Kong. The Boeing 707 was retired.

In 1982, the Airlanka capital was raised from $15 to $30 million, from additional government funds, as financial support from the public was not forthcoming. The airline thus became almost entirely government-owned. The new funds were used to purchase two new Lockheed L-1011-500 TriStars – the long-range version. Such was the new confidence that thoughts were directed towards larger aircraft and negotiations were put in hand to buy two Boeing 747s from Qantas.

Unfortunately, this activity coincided with an outbreak of civil war, involving what amounted to a minor revolution by the Tamil minority of northern Sri Lanka. It was a bitter conflict that dragged on for many years, and about 25,000 people are estimated to have been killed. As it invariably does, such a period of internal

4R-ALF, the first Lockheed L-1011 TriStar, operated by Airlanka, formerly Air Ceylon.

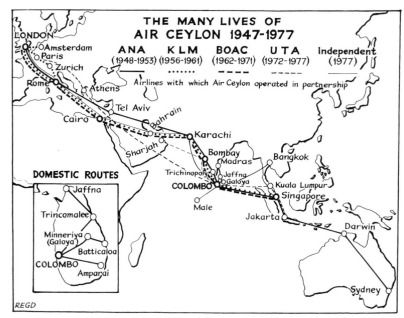

Map 10. The Many Lives of Air Ceylon 1947–1977
Vigorously independent, Ceylon, now Sri Lanka, has never been an affluent country, even though it produces some of the world's best tea and some rare precious stones. But its geographical position, athwart the main route between Europe and southeast Asia and Australia, offered opportunities for airline enterprise. This was achieved by setting up partnerships, first with the Australian ANA, then with the Dutch KLM, the British BOAC, and finally the French UTA, all of whom found it convenient to stop at Colombo, especially when neighbouring countries were at war or otherwise obstructive.

strife severely affected Airlanka's traffic, especially its tourist business, which suffered a sharp downturn; and the situation was worsening just as the Boeing 747s arrived. First, the new TriStars had to be leased out, to British Airways, in April 1985, and then the 747s had to be taken out of service in March 1986, and also leased out, one to Egyptair and one to Qantas. Airlanka's fleet was thus reduced to three TriStars and a single Boeing 737.

It never rains but it pours, goes the old saying. As if the tribulations brought on indirectly by the domestic violence were not enough, Airlanka then suffered a blow that was only too direct. On 3 May 1986, one of its TriStars was destroyed on the ramp at Colombo Airport by a bomb that had been loaded on to the aeroplane in a container of spares. Seventeen passengers and one crew member were killed, and more than forty people were injured both on the aircraft and on the ground. This was a bitter blow because, for all its problems, Airlanka had had a perfect safety record hitherto.

Belt-tightening was again the order of the day. Fortunately one of the 747s had not yet actually left Colombo for its lease, and was promptly put back into service. Nevertheless, some European destination points had to be taken off line. When it was formed Airlanka had been supported by the Government by the grant of tax-free status, for seven years. This expired on 1 September 1986, just a few months after the Colombo tragedy and during the worst effects of the bad publicity arising from the civil war.

There had to be a scapegoat. On 21 November 1986, Captain Wik was forced to resign, along with four other board members, and the next year, a commission of enquiry made a scathing indictment of his administration. Dunstan Jayawardena replaced him, made some economies, and increased the salaries of key personnel to stop the attrition rate of employees seeking better paid jobs elsewhere. In 1987 the two Boeing 747s were sold, and two L-1011-1s leased from GPA Leasing in Ireland. The two L-1011-500s that had been leased out were put back into service.

The terrorist activity continued to flare up sporadically, to the extent that, in 1988, the British and other European governments actually advised tourists not to visit Sri Lanka, for personal safety reasons. Yet, in spite of this, and with vigorous promotion of low-fare package tours and other incentives, Air Lanka managed to stay afloat and even to win back lost traffic. In the spring of 1990, service started again, after a long interval, to Australia, and in August 1991, with the addition of two L-1011-200s leased from British Airways, Air Lanka was back on its feet, with a fleet of six TriStars, and the arrival of the first Airbus A320 heralding the retirement of the Boeing 737s on its regional routes.

The history of air transport in Ceylon/Sri Lanka has been a chequered one. Name any kind of problem that could beset an airline, and Air Ceylon/Airlanka has had it: inefficient management, even corruption, hijacking, aircraft destruction by terrorism, aircraft acquisition difficulty because of a manufacturing scandal or the demise of a lessor, and the effects of civil war at home as well as of the Gulf War in one of the most lucrative areas of traffic and revenue generation. One writer described Airlanka as 'a vainglorious nationalistic exercise'. This was unfair, as Sri Lanka's attractions as a tourist destination, and its strategic position as a staging point en route to the Pacific entitle it to a fair share of the airline cake. Surely it has now paid its dues and responded to the notorious Murphy's Law in good measure. Fate should be kinder to Airlanka in the future.

CHAPTER ELEVEN

Portuguese Colonial Postscript

The last vestiges of a once extensive Empire disappeared in India in 1961. Close to half a millennium had passed since the Portuguese explorer Vasco da Gama first sighted land on the western coast of the Deccan peninsula, now southern India, in AD 1498. His voyage was the first of a series of voyages of discovery between two European rival nations, Portugal and Spain, which, between them, established colonies or trading posts around the world, later to be challenged by Dutch, British, and French commercial and political enterprises for domination of inter-continental trade.

In Asia, Portuguese influence survived in tiny enclaves of territory, whose continued existence depended upon the benevolence of the adjacent dominant power. Across the Pearl River from Hong Kong, Portuguese trade flourished from Macao; in Timor, one of the larger Sunda Islands, now part of Indonesia, the Portuguese flag still flew, even after the Dutch had established the East Indies as their almost exclusive domain. And in India, the city of Goa and the surrounding area, together with two small pieces of territory to the north, Diu and Daman, remained defiantly Portuguese throughout the period of British dominance of the Sub-continent.

In a faint echo of the manner in which their great navigators had pioneered and established ocean sea routes, a Portuguese airline started operations from Goa on 15 August 1955. Its name, long forgotten, was Transportes Aéreos da India Portuguesa (TAIP). At first its mission was simply to provide air links with Diu and Daman, with de Havilland D.H.114 Herons, then a route to Karachi, with Vickers Vikings. In 1957, it ambitiously bought two Douglas DC-4s and began a twice-monthly service to the homeland, to Lisbon, via Karachi and Bahrain. The next year, almost in defiance of the Winds of Change that, in the words of a British Prime Minister, were sweeping through Africa, it had the colonial effrontery to start a route from Goa to Portuguese East Africa, now Mozambique, reaching Lourenço Marques (now Maputo) via Aden, Dar-es-Salaam and Beira. Vasco da Gama would surely have approved of this aerial retracing of his trans-Indian Ocean conquest 460 years earlier. But in 1961, India ejected the last remnant of Portuguese rule, and TAIP ceased to exist.

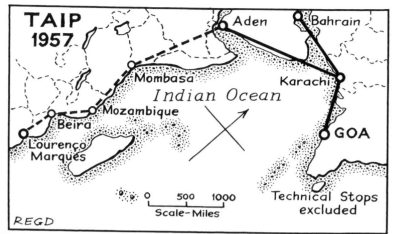

Map 11. TAIP 1957
Almost forgotten as an outpost of the once far-ranging vestiges of a Portuguese colonial and commercial presence, Goa is now part of India, having been occupied by its former neighbour in 1961. But as a last, almost defiant gesture, the Goanese had a little airline during the waning years of the European political connection; and offered services to points acros the Indian Ocean, with the objective of reaching Lourenço Marques – although this route was not maintained on a regular basis.

CHAPTER TWELVE

Indian Ocean Airline Outpost

An Isolated Domain

About 400 miles (650 km) to the southwest of the southern tip of India, or of Sri Lanka, are the Maldive Islands, a group of small atolls whose total area is equivalent to that of an average-sized city of Europe or America, and whose total population comprises about 250,000, of whom one-fifth live in the capital, Malé. For the past 800 years, it has been a Moslem Sultanate, relatively isolated from the world until the 17th Century, when Portuguese explorers and traders imposed their rule for a period. Eventually, in 1887, it became a British Protectorate, and in due course, served the Empire because of its strategic location on the high seas of the Indian Ocean. It was used as a coaling station for the Royal Navy, and during the Second World War, it was an important staging point for the Royal Air Force, specifically at the tiny island of Gan, at the southern end of the chain that extended in a lace-like pattern for about 800 miles (1,300 km) from north to south.

The Royal Air Force abandoned the base at Gan in 1976, and the Maldives was deprived of one of its main sources of income. However, the fishing folk quickly adapted themselves to the 20th Century, and grasped the opportunity to develop their tourist industry for the kind of clientèle, particularly from northern Europe, who 'wanted to get away from it all', the all being the stresses of commercial and industrial life in the Western world. The Maldives offered the sun, the sand, and the palm-fringed lagoons, beloved of the tourism sales brochures, added to which were the serenity and calm that is quite unusual, together with an almost clinical cleanliness that, in tropical lands, is often difficult to achieve.

The Republic of the Maldives acquired that status in 1968, but the tiny country had, as a sultanate, gained its independence from Great Britain's protection on 26 July 1965. Soon afterwards, it began to join the list of the more ambitious European tourist destinations, in company with Colombo, the Seychelles and Bali, as one of the places to go for those fortunate few who had been everywhere else.

Air Maldives

At first, the air link to the Asian mainland (or near enough to it) was provided, in 1967, by Air Ceylon, forerunner of the present-day Air Lanka. But this was short-lived, as the tourist traffic was still in its infancy, and the service from Colombo was uneconomic. Then, in November 1971, the Sri Lanka Air Force (SLAF) provided a twice-monthly service, before Air Ceylon returned to the scene in 1971. With the assistance of the SLAF, the Maldives Government selected and acquired two Convair 440s, so as to provide its own service and to fly its own flag over the aerial connection with the Sub-continent. The aircraft were named *Flying Fish I* and *Flying Fish II*, to symbolize the special attractions of the island group.

With these aircraft, Air Maldives was formed on 1 October 1974, and eight days later, made its first scheduled flight from Malé to Colombo. Frequency was daily,

An Air Maldives Convair CV-440 Metropolitan. (*R E G Davies*)

from the neighbouring island airport of Hulule, whose airstrip base is of crushed coral, and from which the connection to Malé is made by motor launch, itself a charming departure from the typical airport-connecting bus trip or rail connection that can often be far from welcoming at many a much-advertised tourism haven.

Incidentally, Air Maldives was flying the 400-mile trip with a twin-engined aircraft that, at the time, would not have been permitted in most parts of the world, because of the absence of any alternate airport; but with no practical alternative, the risk of a wet 'landing' was preferable to having no service at all. Assisted in its operations by the SLAF, this arrangement came to an end, however, on 31 May 1976; and the next day, Air Maldives Ltd was formed as a holding company by a US-owned Singapore company, TRI-9. The problem had been, at least partly, caused by the shortage of pilots. There was only one in the Maldives, and the SLAF could not spare theirs indefinitely.

Another problem was the potential corrosion caused by the salt-laden air of Hulule, where the aircraft always had to land, take off, and park for the night or when not in use. This sustained exposure made them especially dependent upon frequent inspection and maintenance; and this was a heavy drain upon any organization. And so this partnership too was short-lived, and Air Maldives ceased operations in May 1977. By this time, Indian Airlines had started a connecting service to Malé from Trivandrum, in the southern State of Kerala, and an agreement was made on 2 November 1977, with Indian assistance, to form Maldives International Airlines (MIA). Service began immediately with Boeing 737s, leased from IAL.

Once again, the Maldives Government cherished ambitions of complete independence; and on 30 September 1984, in co-operation with business interests from the Gulf, established Maldives Airways Limited as the official designated flag carrier of the Republic. Ambitiously, it ordered three Douglas DC-8-51 four-engined jets, with which to reach further afield than the coastal cities of southern India and Sri Lanka. After some delay, the inaugural flight, to Madras, took place on 3 March 1985; but the new airline's resources were quite insufficient to maintain services, which were suspended in the summer of 1986. Of the three DC-8s and three Fokker F.27s originally intended to form a well-balanced long-haul and short-haul fleet, only two of the Douglases and one F.27 were ever delivered.

117

The Air Maldives name was revived by a local travel bureau, which provided a regular thrice-weekly service from Malé to Gan, using a Shorts Skyvan, fitted with 18 seats, which had been used initially by the Maldives Government as early as 3 August 1981. Also, another small airline, Inter Atoll Air, began using a de Havilland Canada DHC-6 Twin Otter floatplane between Kadhdhoo Island and resorts in the southern atolls; but an accident, fortunately not a fatal one, to the aircraft on 7 February 1987, put an end to that enterprise.

Currently, the Maldive islands depend on various intercontinental airlines for air connections to foreign parts. Other than Indian Airlines and Air Lanka, Singapore Airlines and Royal Nepal Airlines provide neighbouring links, and farther afield Emirates, from the Gulf, and several airlines such as Alitalia, Condor, LTU, and Balair, continue to bring sun-worshipping tourists to this island paradise in the Indian Ocean.

Such was the growing popularity of the Maldives that arrangements had to be made to transfer passengers arriving at Hulule Airport to other islands – if tiny atolls can be dignified by the name. Indeed, most of them, quintessentially idyllic as tropical island paradises, are too small to permit the construction of an airstrip, even for a Twin Otter. Accordingly, in May 1988, the enterprising Mr and Mrs Chris Chambers founded Hummingbird Helicopters (Maldives) Ltd, initially equipped with two Sikorsky S-61Ns. When serious operations began, however, in December 1991, the Sikorskys had been replaced by a small fleet of Russian Mil Mi-8 22-seat helicopters, leased from various sources, including Bulgaria, which also supplied the experienced pilots, who, doubtlessly, enjoyed the assignment. The Mi-8, incidentally, has been the most successful helicopter, in terms of production numbers (more than 8,000) ever built. Hummingbird operates them to ten destinations throughout the Maldive chain of breathlessly beautiful specks of land in the Indian Ocean.

An unusual combination, a Maldives Air Transport Cessna Caravan on twin floats. (*Christian Laugier*)

Hummingbird's Mil Mi-8 LZ-CAM at Malé in November 1994. (*Christian Laugier*)

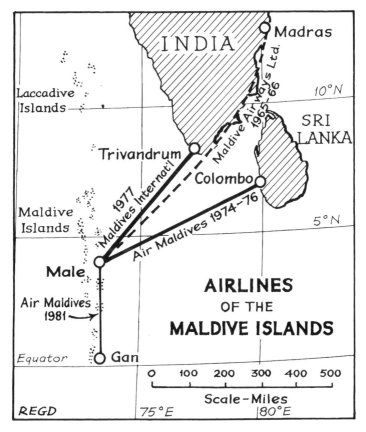

Map 12. Airlines of the Maldive Islands
Once a British Protectorate, the Maldive Islands became independent in 1965 and the Sultanate gave way to a republican administration three years later. With few resources, this island paradise has become a tourist haven for sun-worshippers and this has generated a thriving airline business. Early attempts to have an airline of its own were sporadic, as shown on this map, but with tourism its biggest industry, this island group is now firmly on the world airline map.

CHAPTER THIRTEEN

The Air Road to Mandalay

In his famous work that conjured up a word-picture of the romantic east, as seen through the eyes of a Victorian colonialist, Rudyard Kipling referred to Mandalay 'where the flying fishes play'. No doubt this added to the romance, and helped with a convenient rhyme, but it was not zoologically correct. The nearest likeness to a flying fish that the good citizens of Mandalay were to witness over the Irrawaddy River was probably a de Havilland Fox Moth floatplane of the Irrawaddy Flotilla and Airways Ltd, a small airline on the fringes of the then Indian Empire in the 1930s.

This enterprising pioneer began a service from Rangoon to Mandalay in November 1934, following the course of the Irrawaddy, with air stations for the Fox Moths at Prome and Yenangyuang. This served as a connecting link, once a week, with the Imperial Airways route through Rangoon to Singapore, so that adventurous passengers could take a side trip, perhaps, to the glorious pagodas, not to mention the imaginary flying fishes, up-country; and they could also fly to Moulmein and Tavoy, to the southwest of Rangoon, the latter point added as a real outpost of Empire, on 1 January 1935.

The demand must have quickly outstripped the capacity of the Fox Moths, for the company ordered two four-engined Short Scion Senior floatplanes, each able to carry passengers in a relatively comfortable cabin. Conditions could not have been easy, even with technical assistance from Imperial Airways. During the summer of 1936, the Irrawaddy Flotilla was reduced by the loss of one Scion and one Fox Moth, and although a third Scion was delivered early in 1937, the

One of the Short Scion Senior floatplanes used by the Irrawaddy Flotilla and Airways. It is seen on test at Rochester before delivery.

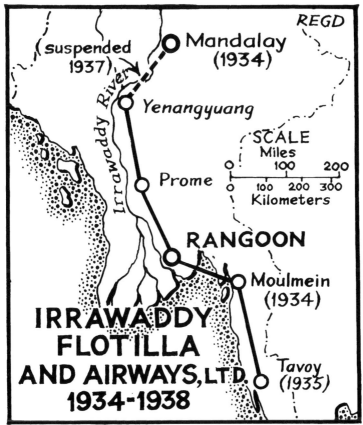

Map 13a. Irrawaddy Flotilla and Airways Ltd, 1934–1938
Possessing possibly the most romantic-sounding name of any airline in the world, with shades of Rudyard Kipling and the era of the British Indian Empire, this little company could indeed, in a different sense, have been a little Jewel in the Crown of air transport development in that regime. For Burma was still part of India in those days, and the seaplanes of the Flotilla opened local eyes to a faster mode of travel than the slow-moving Burma Railways.

Mandalay service had to be curtailed to Yenangyuang. Kipling would have had more rhyming problems with this operational terminus.

The 'flotilla across the bay' – to quote Rudyard once again – was unable to maintain service, even though, for example, the one-hour flight – saving a whole day by train – to Moulmein, and the $2\frac{1}{2}$-hour flight to Tavoy – saving about a week by land or by sea – were good bargains at 25 and 60 rupees respectively. Sadly, the wonderfully-named Irrawaddy Flotilla and Airways Ltd had to cease operations late in 1938.

121

Union of Burma Airways

The first slice to be cut away from the perimeter of the Indian Empire of British colonial days was Burma, which invoked the Statute of Westminster, authorizing any part of the British Commonwealth to secede of its own free will. Much anti-British sentiment had been built up by the Japanese, during their Second World War occupation from 1942 to 1945, and the Buddhist Burmese had already been granted a fair degree of autonomy, independent of rule from New Delhi, but still under direct rule from London as a Crown Colony. After internal political strife, an independence treaty was signed in London in 1947 and the Socialist Union Republic of Burma came into being on 4 January 1948. Almost immediately the new government became embroiled with dissidents on all sides: Christian Karens to the east, on the Thai border; and both communist and former Kuomintang Chinese forces in the north, who found it easier to fight the Burmese than to fight each other.

One of the fleet of de Havilland Doves operated by Union of Burma Airways from 1949.
(*de Havilland*)

The circumstances were not auspicious for the operation of a commercial airline, but nevertheless, the new republic made a promising start. Early in 1948, the Air Transport Board was founded with a capital of 5 million kyats, six de Havilland D.H.104 Doves were purchased, and services started in October of the same year from Rangoon to Mandalay, and later to Akyab in the northwest and to Moulmein. It was, in effect, picking up where the Irrawaddy Flotilla had left off ten years previously, but with landplanes, making use of airstrips that had been constructed during the Second World War, mainly by the Japanese. In 1949 the name was changed to Union of Burma Airways (UBA) and by the end of the year the eight-seat Doves were flying to 19 communities throughout the country where there was only one north–south railway and where all-weather roads were the exception rather than the rule.

In 1950, UBA fell into line with most other airlines throughout Asia and acquired some war-surplus Douglas DC-3s, with which it started international services to Chittagong (then in East Pakistan), Calcutta and Bangkok. Quite apart from the inadequacy of poor roads, all surface transport was under fire – literally – far too often to encourage travel, and UBA was in great demand. Recognizing the importance of air transport to the nation, the Government reconstituted UBA

In 1950 Union of Burma Airways began operating Douglas DC-3s to Chittagong where this one is seen. (*John Stroud*)

on 1 October 1952, giving it a full-time chairman and board membership, with wider autonomy to replace departmental status within the Ministry.

The new administration's first major decision was unfortunate. It ordered from Britain three Handley Page (formerly Miles) Marathons, a 14-seat feeder airliner. Taking delivery in the summer of 1953, the Marathons opened service to Singapore, via Mergui and Penang, but shortly afterwards, one was destroyed by fire on the ground. Recurring mechanical troubles forced their early retirement in 1954, and so UBA was back to the Old Faithful DC-3s. It could not be blamed for its initial choice of a so-called 'DC-3 Replacement', for British European Airways and the Japanese Far East Air Lines, later to become All Nippon Airways, had also chosen the Marathon.

UBA's next choice was a happier one. In May 1955, it ordered three Vickers Viscount 761s and these went into service early in 1958, permitting the Burmese flag-carrier to extend its Bangkok service to Hong Kong and its Singapore service to Jakarta. Unfortunately, the severely introspective policies of the Burmese Government not only prevented Burmese citizens travelling abroad, but placed unacceptable restrictions on foreigners wishing to visit Burma. There was just not enough traffic to sustain the Viscount services, and the route to Hong Kong was suspended in 1959, although operations to Bangkok were resumed the following year.

On 2 March 1962, the restrictions suddenly became much worse, when, in a coup d'état, the Burmese Army, under General U Ne Win, seized power. Ostensibly, this was because the chronic fighting with all the different rebel tribesmen had reached crisis proportions, and the military took things into its own hands, out of desperation. But, as the main channel of communication throughout Burma, UBA soldiered on, learning from its experience, and tailoring its cost to the cloth.

In 1962, it made a wise choice of equipment to serve the Burmese homeland. Between 1963 and 1964, some, but not all, of the DC-3 flights were replaced by Fokker Friendship services, the first one in November 1963. The 40-seat Dutch airliner was ideal for the main domestic routes, but the DC-3 had to be retained because of airfield restrictions in some places. By 1966, seven Friendships were

Union of Burma Airways introduced Vickers-Armstrongs Viscount 761s early in 1958.
(*Vickers*)

in domestic service, while the Viscounts flew internationally, including an additional station at Siem Reap, Cambodia, area of the archaeological site of Angkor Wat, one of the architectural wonders of the ancient world.

Recognizing that, to compete at all with foreign carriers which were fully equipped with jet airliners, UBA leased a Boeing 727-100 from Northwest Airlines in 1969 and resumed service to Hong Kong, via Bangkok and Phnom Penh, the Cambodian capital; and the following year purchased another 727 (from Hughes Air West) to replace the lease. But the service to Hong Kong had to be suspended again early in 1975, because of flying restrictions over Vietnam. In November 1976, the 727 was sold, along with the last Viscount; for the crippling travel restrictions, both for Burmese and for visitors, prevented UBA from building up a traffic base that was sufficient to maintain adequate load factors and a reasonable financial balance between income and expenditure. For tourists, eager to visit the shrines and temples of Burma (the Shwe Dagon pagoda in Rangoon is higher than St Paul's Cathedral, and covered in pure gold), the visa handicaps were bad enough; the accommodation was unacceptable: only three hotels in Rangoon, one of these built in 1901 and unchanged since, and the largest built by the Russians, on the edge of a beautiful lake, but a hazardous taxi-ride from the city.

The name of the airline had been changed in December 1972 to Burma Airways Corporation (BAC), with the managing director reporting directly to the Government. Once again, vital decisions had to be made regarding the right equipment for the Burmese airline's special requirements of jet modernity but modest aircraft size. A good selection was made, in fact two good selections: the 65-seat Fokker F.28 (-1000 series) began service on the main domestic route from Mandalay in the north to Tavoy in the south on 1 April 1976, and the 19-seat de Havilland Canada DHC-6 Twin Otter began to replace the veteran DC-3 on 19 September of the same year. Later, the 85-seat Fokker F.28-4000 supplemented the earlier version, and was able to show the flag in Jakarta, where the Indonesian national airline Garuda was a big F.28 operator. The earlier F.28s had already established themselves on the routes to Bangkok and Singapore, on 2 May 1976, and had extended the Calcutta route to Khatmandu in Nepal on the same date.

Unlike almost every other Asian nation, Burma has shown little inclination to modernize in line with the onrush of westernized development that has swept through the continent since the Second World War. The streets of Rangoon have

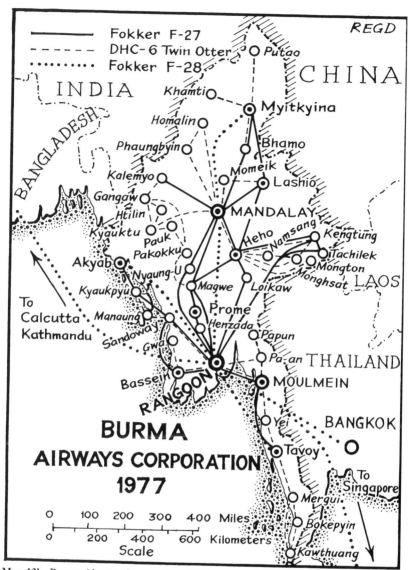

Map 13b. Burma Airways Corporation, 1977
When Burma seceded from the British Empire in 1948, the new nation clearly had to supplement its railway system, which was narrow-gauged, and served only a single north–south route, terminating at Myitkyina and Lashio, and providing the only link between the two main cities, Rangoon and Mandalay. Even though the Burmese Government remained somewhat aloof from international trading, it promoted the establishment of a comprehensive airline system, reaching every corner of the land, from the mountains of the north to the beaches of the Malay Peninsula.

Sixty-five passenger Fokker F.28-1000s began service on main domestic routes in April 1976.

changed little from their appearance before the First. Outside the capital, there are few motorized vehicles, and most of these would be classified as vintage elsewhere. The Strand Hotel looks exactly the same as when it was built, almost a century ago, and many of the staff could have been at the opening. In line with this developmental inertia, Burma Airways has shown no desire to increase either the range of its route network or the size of its fleet.

During the mid-1980s, it standardized the latter to become almost an all-Fokker airline, as problems arose with the Twin Otters, and three were lost in a period of only a year. The remaining six were grounded in August 1984, and the network adjusted so that the Friendships covered most of the feeder services, with the F.28s serving all the main cities. Burma Airways has also operated three Aérospatiale Puma helicopters since 1977, and these are used mainly on contract work for off-shore oil-drilling.

CHAPTER FOURTEEN

Airlines of Malaysia and Brunei

Outpost of Empire

As early as 1824, the British had established trading bridgeheads in what was then the remote Malayan Peninsula. Sir Stamford Raffles, representing the East India Company, had purchased the island of Singapore in 1819. Penang and the Province Wellesley (with the Dindings), and Malacca were annexed in 1824, and the four areas became the Straits Settlements, administered from India until 1867 when they became a Crown Colony. From 1874 several sultanates became British Protectorates as the Federated Malay States, and to these were added other unfederated states, coming under British rule by peaceful agreement with Siam, with which country good political relations have been maintained, except during the Second World War.

The area did not exploit resources until late in the 19th Century, when rich deposits of tin were discovered, and early in the 20th Century, when rubber became important for the motor car industry. By the 1920s Malaya was the world's chief source of both tin and rubber. Yet the colony-protectorates received little incentive from Britain for local development, except at the booming port of Singapore, which grew to become one of the world's great shipping centres, situated as it was in a key strategic position for both commercial and naval sea routes. In general, Malaya's administration was undertaken by career British civil servants, and most of the general commerce by emigrant Chinese. Seven thousand miles away from the homeland, Malaya was a truly remote outpost of empire. The only trunk railway linked it with Siam, not India. Only the P & O shipping line kept the British population from being isolated.

Bearing in mind the importance of Singapore, not only as a focal point for trade, but as a vital base if Britain was to retain any military or naval power in southeast Asia, the neglect of the area by Imperial Airways, the British flag airline, was a curious defect in air transport policy. True, the main objective was to provide a good air service to India, and this was not easy, as bases had to be established along a tortuous route, across countries that would not grant overflying rights, across others where hostile tribesmen would shoot at the aircraft, and, whether on land or on sea, where airfields or harbours had to be laboriously constructed. So much was concentrated on the Indian goal, and possibly because the pioneering of a route beyond Calcutta was even more difficult, the British rested on their laurels when the adventurous air route to Karachi (then in the British Indian Empire) was opened on 30 March 1929. The journey from London took $7\frac{1}{2}$ days, and involved three different aircraft on different segments of the trip, interspersed with rides on European and Egyptian trains.

By comparison, in the same way that the subject of Indian communications was all-consuming to the British, the need for fast and efficient links with the Netherlands East Indies (as it was then) was all-consuming to the Netherlands in the years between the two World Wars. The NEI accounted for about ninety per cent of the European country's overseas possessions and wealth. Because of this factor, the persevering Dutch were able to build an air route that, until after the Second World War, was second to none. Charged with the one single objective of a route to Batavia (now Jakarta) the great Dutch airline KLM forged an aerial artery to the Far East that was a model of efficiency. After some years of survey and proving flights, it opened a regular passenger service, with Fokker F.XIIs, on 1 October 1931. The journey from Amsterdam to Batavia was accomplished in ten days. Singapore still had no air service.

Links with Europe

To those British administrators charged with the responsibility of establishing air communications throughout the British Empire – and elaborate plans were made with correspondingly elaborate maps – the determined efforts of the Dutch was a constant challenge. This culminated on 3 May 1933 when KLM opened a branch line to Singapore, seven months before Imperial Airways provided a British link with India. This occurred on 9 December, at least in time for the Christmas mails, and Armstrong Whitworth Atalantas at last showed the flag and brought British colonial civil servants for a triumphant tiffin at the Raffles Hotel.

The following year, the Dutch achieved a master-stroke. In the famous England–Australia Mac.Robertson Air Race, one of the entrants that took off from Mildenhall aerodrome, in England's East Anglia, on 20 October 1934, was – to the astonishment and incredulity of many – a commercial airliner, a Douglas DC-2 no less, entered by KLM. Carrying four passengers and a load of mail, it had the temerity to come in second overall (and first in the handicapped placings) against a small armada of sports and racing aircraft, some of them especially built for the race. Such was the fame of the achievement that much of the commercial airline world of the day beat a hasty path to Douglas's door; KLM ordered a quantity of DC-2s and became pre-eminent on the Europe–Far East trunk route; and the British had to take some urgent steps to regain some semblance of pride and performance.

To Britain's credit, it did well with limited resources, and without resorting to the indignity of going to the United States for its aircraft. But it was a struggle, with KLM setting a hot pace, and Imperial always coming in a gallant second. But, as the car rental advertisement proclaims, those who are second have to try harder, and Imperial was not entirely disgraced. On 8 December 1934, the first Atalanta carried the Christmas mails to Brisbane, for after political wrangling, the Australian airline had joined with Imperial on 18 January of that year to form Qantas Empire Airways to perform the Singapore–Australia segment of the 12,722-mile journey from London. Even if the local administration at Singapore was consulted, there was no Malayan participation in the grand scheme of things, even when, on 13 April 1935, a branch line was opened from Penang to Hong Kong, via Saïgon, with de Havilland D.H.86s. Malaya's geographical location should have suggested, perhaps, some more wide-reaching recognition.

The next few years witnessed competition between KLM and Imperial Airways on a grand scale. The Dutch airline did all the front running at first, introducing the DC-2 on 12 June 1935, to replace the slow and ageing Fokkers, then trumped its own ace on 2 October 1937 by bringing in the improved

Douglas DC-3. The British reply was to introduce the larger, faster, and more comfortable Short S.23 C class Empire Flying-boats, and at long last, Imperial Airways was able to hold its head up high and achieve parity with the Dutch and their Douglases. The first S.23 to operate without change from London to Singapore inaugurated the Empire Air Mail Scheme on 23 February 1938. In this novel and unprecedented programme, by which all first class letters to anywhere in the British Empire (except trans-Atlantic Canada) could be sent with only an ordinary stamp, Imperial received such a boost that there were times when passengers had to give way to the mails, such was the volume. On 26 June 1938, passengers could fly all the way to Australia on the S.23s without change of aircraft.

Compared with the Dutch, the British could now claim that they were in the van of progress in the operation of intercontinental air routes. The same could not, however, be said for its development of air services within parts of the Empire itself, where aviation seemed still to be regarded with suspicion, if not with apathy. The Dutch had developed a fine system of air routes throughout the East Indies. By comparison, activity in India was sluggish, at best; and in Malaya there were no local air services until 1936, and these were created without Imperial Airways lifting a finger.

Wearne's Air Services

On 18 December 1936, Messrs C & T Wearne, a prominent motor car dealer and importer, formed an airline, Wearne's Air Services Ltd (Singapore). It opened discussions with the de Havilland company in England, with the result that, on 28

Wearne's Air Services' de Havilland 86 *Governor Murchison* was purchased from Jersey Airways. It is seen at Jersey Airport before delivery.

129

June 1937, it started a thrice weekly service to Kuala Lampur and Penang. The aircraft was a de Havilland D.H.89 Rapide *Governor Raffles*, and with the arrival of a second Rapide, *Governor Fullerton*, on 4 September, the frequency was increased to a daily flight. The following year, with the addition of other de Havillands, a

Map 14a. Wearne's Air Services
One of the richest outposts of the British Empire during the inter-war years was the Federated States of Malaya. But it was not a large country, and its railway seemed to serve adequately the main cities, which were less than 200 miles apart. Nevertheless, this was before the widespread use of air-conditioning; and this prompted a local bus operator, Messrs C and T Wearne, to establish an air service. This was the ancestor of what became the Malaysia Airlines of today.

130

The Airspeed Consul was the first type operated by Malayan Airways.

smaller D.H.60 and two larger D.H.86s, Ipoh was added to the modest network, and on 3 April 1940, an extension was made from Penang to the east coast town of Kota Bharu. This latter, however, was suspended shortly thereafter.

Early in 1939, with commendable initiative, Wearne's used one of its four-engined D.H.86 Express airliners (*Governor Ibbotson*) to make a survey flight across the South China Sea to the British protectorate Sarawak. The D.H.86 demonstrated the feasibility of an air service to the British-administered territories in northern Borneo, but this objective was not to materialize until after the Second World War, as Malaya was overwhelmed by the Japanese attack in December 1941. Wearne's had, as a defensive measure, become B Flight of the Malayan Volunteer Air Force; but regrettably, the de Havilland aircraft could not stave off the Japanese attack.

Malayan Airways

Many war-ravaged countries took quite a while to recover from the commercial and administrative disruption caused by the Japanese occupation; and Malaya was no exception. But on 1 May 1947 there were signs of renewed confidence and initiative when Malayan Airways Ltd started operations over the same route that had been pioneered by Wearne's. The company had originally been registered in 1937 by the Ocean Steamship Company, of Liverpool, England, and the Straits Steamship Company, of Singapore, with some help from Imperial Airways. But it had never emerged from the status of a paper project backed by legal documents.

Malayan Airways quickly made up for lost time. The first operations were under the management of Mansfield and Company, a shipping and trading organization, and the first aircraft were modest enough, Airspeed Consuls, with only five seats. On-board service was also correspondingly modest: refreshments consisted of a flask of iced water, refilled at each stop. But the Consuls opened up Malayan air communications again, to supplement the good rail services, and prepared the way for the introduction of the ubiquitous Douglas DC-3. By 1950, the fleet of these versatile 28-seaters had grown to seven. Even by the end of 1947, frequency of service between Singapore and Kuala Lumpur was thrice daily; to Ipoh once daily, and to Kota Bharu four times a week, split equally between west and east coast routes. Additionally, international connections were made to Medan, Sumatra, across the Strait of Malacca; Batavia, soon to become Jakarta; Palembang, in southern Sumatra; and to Saïgon. In April 1948, service began to Bangkok; in June 1949, to Kuching, Labuan and Jesselton (now Kota Kinabalu); and in

A Malayan Airways Douglas DC-3 at Ipoh.

September 1949, to Rangoon, via Mergui – although this last destination was deleted when Burma, which in 1948 had become the first country to take advantage of the Statute of Westminster and secede from the British Empire, plunged into civil war with the tribes along its frontiers.

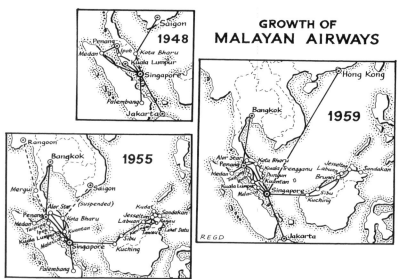

Map 14b. Growth of Malayan Airways

This map series shows the development of a new post-war airline in Southeast Asia. Originally formed to serve Malaya and neighbouring countries, it gradually expanded to the British Protectorate and Colonies in northern Borneo (the majority of which became part of Malaysia in later years) and then linked Singapore with Hong Kong, to provide an essential line of rapid communication between the two largest business centres of the western Pacific Rim.

Better late than never, therefore, Singapore was at last assuming its role as a communications hub of the southeastern countries of Asia. Paradoxically, this was occurring about two decades after Imperial Airways should have grasped the opportunity and taken steps to lay the foundation of an aviation equivalent of the great seaport and key strategic base that Sir Stamford Raffles' mangrove swamp had become. In the 1930s, this could have served to embellish the influence of the British Empire, when colonial rule throughout the region (except in Thailand) was internationally recognized and accepted. Now, Malayan Airways was laying the foundations for a remarkable development in air transport that, in turn, was only two decades away in the future, but which was to revolutionize the industry within the region, and have a profound influence world-wide.

Imperial Airways' successor, British Overseas Airways Corporation (BOAC) at least moved fairly briskly to show the flag in southeast Asia, using Malayan Airways as a springboard. It acquired a 10 per cent shareholding in 1948, and when the Federation of Malaysia replaced the collection of federated and unfederated states in 1957, the British airline strengthened its position, sharing a 64.5 per cent shareholding with Qantas (recalling distant memories of the prewar association, Qantas Empire Airways). The governments of Brunei, North Borneo, and Sarawak each held 6.25 per cent, as did the Straits Steamship and Ocean Steamship Companies. The remaining 4.25 per cent was privately owned. Malayan became publicly owned on 6 February 1958.

On 1 March 1958, Malayan took over the Federation Air Service, which had been formed in Kuala Lumpur in November 1951. Radiating from the Malayan capital, it had operated a fleet of five de Havilland Canada DHC-2 Beavers, at first for government officials, but becoming successful as a common carrier. By this time, Malayan Airways, with its injection of fresh additional capital, technical support and advice, and the awareness of the new Federation that it must keep abreast of aviation progress in the region that was ready to undergo an economic explosion, moved out of its subordinate status as an operator of prewar DC-3s.

Bayan Lepas airport at Penang was a stop on Imperial Airways United Kingdom—Australia route and junction for services to Hong Kong. (*Courtesy John Stroud*)

133

In 1959 Malayan Airways leased two Vickers-Armstrongs Viscounts.

Early in 1959, through its shareholders' connections, Malayan was able to charter a Douglas DC-4 longer range aircraft from Qantas, specifically to introduce service direct to Hong Kong, in pool with the Hong Kong airline, also with BOAC connections. Later in the year, Malayan also leased two Vickers Viscount medium-range propeller-turbine airliners to operate the more important of its regional routes, and to remove the prewar image of the trusty but ageing DC-3s. For a short while, it also operated a Super Constellation on the Hong Kong service, as Cathay's new Lockheed Electras were also emphasizing the obsolescence of the unpressurized DC-4.

The early 1960s witnessed a further upgrading of equipment when Malayan reinstated (the Super Constellation service had been suspended in October 1960, after operating for only six months) the Hong Kong service on 2 September 1961. Fitted with 82 seats, a Bristol Britannia was leased from BOAC on 2 September 1961, to match Cathay Pacific's standard of service on the route. Cathay had experienced some embarrassment when its Electras were grounded, and had also leased a Britannia from BOAC. Little more than a year later, Malayan went one better: it leased a de Havilland Comet 4, which launched Malayan's *Silver Kris* service from Singapore and Kuala Lumpur to Bangkok on 4 December 1962.

On the home front, the DC-3s had had their day too. On 31 May 1963, the first of five Fokker Friendships added some sophistication to the Singapore–Kuala Lumpur route, which was beginning to acquire the character of an air shuttle service, although it was not operated on a no-reservations basis. In September 1963, *Silver Kris* service was added to Kuching, when BOAC's Viscounts were transferred to Aden Airways.

Malayan Airways had undergone an amazing transformation. Until late in 1959 it was a local DC-3 operator. By the end of 1962, it was a fully-fledged jet airline, able to hold its own against all competition. Thus, when, on 9 January 1963, three airlines in southeast Asia decided to form a pool partnership, instead of indulging in a cut-throat competitive conflict, the basis of the revenue pool was Thai Airways International 30 per cent, Cathay Pacific Airways 32 per cent, and Malayan Airways 28 per cent.

Fokker F.27 Friendships began working Malayan Airways' Kuala Lumpur—Singapore services on 31 May 1963. (*Fokker*)

Much of this progress had been made because of the rising sense of nationalism, and the certain knowledge that independence would replace the colonial status. The Federation of Malaya, formed in 1948 as a member of the British Commonwealth, attained complete autonomy in 1963 with the declaration of the Federated States of Malaysia, with the complete political merger of Malaya, Singapore, Sarawak and North Borneo, the last territory renamed Sabah, after its historic heritage. Brunei remained independent from Malaya as a sultanate, and Singapore was to secede shortly afterwards; but the Malayan peoples had achieved a sense of national pride and dignity, in charge of their own affairs. In line with this new-found freedom, Malayan left the International Air Transport Association (IATA), known for its price-fixing policies, thus easing problems with non-IATA Thai and Cathay.

In November 1963, the name was changed to Malaysian Airways Ltd to reflect the changing alliances that the new political association had brought about. But while, from afar, this appeared to be a logical step forward, there were many obstacles ahead. Relations with the big neighbour to the south, Indonesia, itself flush with the joys of independence from the Dutch, were not good, especially as the Indonesian Government followed an aggressive policy with ambitions of taking over the whole of the island of Borneo, including Sarawak, Brunei and Sabah. The predominantly Chinese-oriented Singapore could not see eye-to-eye with the Malay authorities in Kuala Lumpur. Nevertheless, against a background of widespread political differences, and even military confrontation, a new era for air transport in the Malayan peninsula had begun.

Borneo Airways

The new Federation broke new ground in its creation; for it offered a common destiny to the peoples of Malayan ancestry who lived not only in Malaya itself, but also on the islands of the East Indies; so that a union with the British territories along the northern coast of Borneo was a logical development; and this area became known by the general term East Malaysia. Apart from the political problems of the threat of invasion from Kalimantan, the Indonesian southern part of the island of Borneo, there was the matter of the existence of a small local airline

135

that had to be cleared up. In its role as the Malaysian flag carrier of the air, Malaysian Airways had reinforced the link across the South China Sea by flying the Comet 4 to Jesselton, British North Borneo, on 1 April 1964. Soon to be renamed Kota Kinabalu, in a former colony soon to be renamed Sabah, Jesselton was just beginning to transform itself from a sleepy outpost of empire, where time seemed often to stand still, to a brisk new provincial capital of a progressive new nation. Sleepy though it may have been, there was wealth everywhere, especially the oil, which, however, was located almost entirely in Brunei; but also tea and coffee plantations, and rich resources of hardwood timber in the forests. With no land transport except in the immediate vicinity of the small towns, Sarawak, Brunei and North Borneo shared in a small airline.

Back in 1949, Sabah Airways had been formed by Mansfield & Company Ltd, the shipping agents who had also been instrumental in forming Malayan Airways. In 1953, Malayan acquired two old de Havilland D.H.89A Dragon Rapides, and began to operate feeder services, first in North Borneo (Sabah), then in Sarawak. Early in 1957, this local operation, stretching from Kuching in the west to Tawau in the east, became a Malayan operating subsidiary under the name of Sabah Airways. No doubt reacting to protests from Sarawak and Brunei, the name was changed in October 1957 to Borneo Airways.

Refuelling one of Borneo Airways' Scottish Aviation Twin Pioneer STOL aircraft. (*BOAC*)

For a while, this diminutive airline, based on the island of Labuan, still then under direct British sovereignty, and not yet part of Malaysia, operated like a latter-day survival of a prewar operator. The three separate territories each held 17 per cent of the shares, while BOAC held 49 per cent; but the latter's presence was hardly felt. The routes were flown by the Rapides, aided by two Scottish Aviation Twin Pioneers which dealt with the flights to airfields up in the highlands where the Rapide, not exactly a mainliner itself, was too fastidious for the meadowlands that served as landing grounds for the rugged Pioneers. While Douglas DC-3s took care of Borneo Airways' 'trunk' routes, and the Rapides coped with the 'feeders'; the Twin Pioneers wandered out into the bush, carrying hardy passengers over the high pass next to 14,000-ft Mount Kinabalu, with no pressurization; and into the jungles of Sarawak.

The charming anachronism that was Borneo Airways came to an end on 1 April 1965, when Malaysian Airways absorbed it, and replaced the Twin Pioneers with three brand new Cessna 310s. The disappearance of Borneo Airways was symbolic of the end of an era, when everything still stopped for tea at 3.30 in the afternoon, and cocktails were always served at 6 p.m. and you dressed for dinner.

Malaysia-Singapore Airlines

Malaysian Airways Limited did not last long. The fates were against it from the start. In June 1964, the respected chairman, Loke Wan Tho, was killed in an air crash in Taiwan. Then, no sooner had Malaysian bought four Comets from BOAC in May 1965, when in the August of the same year, under the dynamic leadership of Lee Kuan Yew, Singapore forced its political separation from Malaysia. Easily the largest and most prosperous city in the whole Federation, Singapore's secession was, in relative terms, like London separating itself from England. Suddenly, Kuala Lumpur ceased to be secondary to Singapore as an aviation centre, and prepared itself for a central role.

On 14 May 1968, the two governments – at odds on most issues – signed an agreement by which Malaysian Airways should be renamed Malaysia-Singapore Airlines (MSA), and this change came into effect on 1 January 1967. Initially, the shareholdings were: Singapore and Malaysian Governments 38 per cent each, BOAC and Qantas 11.6 per cent each, and Brunei 13.2 per cent. The first managing director was an experienced BOAC veteran of the Far East, David Craig.

For a precarious few years, MSA continued to build, expanding its route network and upgrading its fleet. Even as Malaysian Airways, Comets had started service to Manila, direct from Singapore, on 1 July 1966. On 13 April 1967 MSA elevated its status by sharing in an extensive pooling arrangement with BOAC, Qantas, Air-India, and Air New Zealand, by starting Comet services to Perth and to Sydney, Australia. For the first time, the Malaysian and Singapore flags were flown to a country outside the Asian continent. On 1 April 1968, Boeing 707s, chartered from Qantas, replaced the Comets on the Australian route, and on

Britten-Norman BN.2 Islanders replaced Twin Pioneers in East Malaysia in 1968.

137

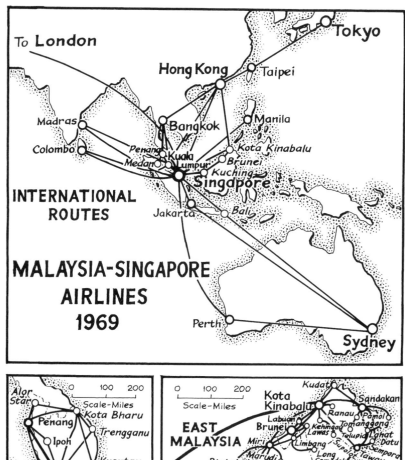

Map 14c. Malaysia-Singapore Airlines, 1969
In 1965, the prosperous city of Singapore, no longer a mere communications centre on the map of the British Empire, but a thriving business centre in its own right, broke away from the newly-formed Malaysia; and the airline adopted a joint nomenclature for what was to be a short-lived consortium. During the seven years of its existence, however, MSA consolidated its position as an intercontinental airline, and forged an efficient transport link between the two halves of the new nation, separated by the South China Sea.

138

One of the Twin Pioneers that was replaced by the Islanders.

1 August of the same year, 707s inaugurated service to Tokyo. Regional services began to Taipei and Pnom Penh, and were resumed to Medan and Jakarta. At the lowest stratum of MSA's operations, Britten-Norman BN.2 Islanders replaced the Twin Pioneers in East Malaysia in 1968, and in the following year, on 21 August 1969, Boeing 737 short-haul jets started to replace the Comets on the main regional routes, and opened service to Bali on 19 October. To proclaim its growing stature, MSA opened a new headquarters in its own 16-storey building in Singapore. Both the Malaysian and the Singapore Governments increased their shareholdings to 42.7 per cent each, at the expense of the minority participants.

But the partnership was showing signs of severe strain. Each country, both of them tasting the privileges of independence for the first time, jealously fought for what it felt was an equitable share of the benefits accruing from MSA's success. And this was not inconsiderable – the profit for the financial year 1970/71 was announced as more than S$42 million, more than twice as much as in the previous year. In January 1971, to the surprise of no-one in the aviation world of southeast Asia – though to the regret of many who admired the achievements of the united MSA – the impending dissolution was announced.

The road towards amicable, or even any, agreement was not easy. Talks began on 27 April 1971 to discuss details of the agreed split of assets and goodwill, but broke down the next day over frequency disputes on the Singapore—Kuala Lumpur service and the routes to Kota Kinabalu. Malaysian Airways Ltd was created, but the name was later changed to Malaysian Airline System. The Malaysian Prime Minister, Tun Abdul Razak, felt that the abbreviation MAL could have unfortunate implications if used as an acronym, MAL; whereas the word for gold in Malaysian was MAS.

Such semantic considerations apart, the dissolution process ran into heavy weather. On 20 July 1971, David Craig, the ex-BOAC managing director, was summarily dismissed over a reported personality conflict, as the euphemism has it for a stand-up nose-to-nose shouting match. During the interim period that followed, three joint chairmen were appointed, one from Malaysia, one from Singapore and Kuok Hock Nien in a neutral corner.

From then, the step-by-step, if apparently unequal, division of MAS proceeded smoothly. In remarkable contrast with the plush new edifice in Singapore that was to become Singapore Airlines' new headquarters, the infant MAS opened for business in a tiny office in the Police Co-operative Building in Kuala Lumpur. Malaysian also seemed to have had the worst of the deal in the share-out of flying equipment. Singapore kept five Boeing 707s and five Boeing 737s, while Malaysia kept eleven Fokker Friendships, and three Britten-Norman Islanders. Seven Boeing 737s on order would go to Malaysian. While Singapore clearly had the advantage in long-haul aircraft, it could support such a claim with convincing statistics that showed the city as a concentrated hub of air traffic, not only to and from the region, but also as a stop-over point for traffic between Europe and Australia, where tourists and returning residents were apt to spend a few days in Singapore, just for the duty-free and the bargain-price shopping. On the other hand, the island nation – and a tiny island, moreover – had no use for all the feeder aircraft essential for Malaysia's internal air network.

Before the break-up, MSA was able to show its colours in London, by opening a service on 2 June 1971, from Singapore, via Bombay, Bahrain and Rome, thrice weekly, with Boeing 707s leased from BOAC. By the end of the year, the airline was also operating affinity charters, with BOAC 707s and VC10s; and on 1 August 1972, Athens, Zürich and Frankfurt were added as three new European destinations on the London route. MAS local domestic routes were actually started on 1 June 1972, with F.27s, and on regional routes, especially Kuala Lumpur–Singapore, with Boeing 737s. The first of the new 737s arrived on 23 August and were welcomed by Prime Minister Tun Abdul Razak himself. When, finally, on 1 October 1972, the two new airlines acquired their separate identities, the winged tiger emblem of the old MSA retired with honour, and gave way to the new Wau Bulan, the traditional kite of Kelantan, which was to gain further distinction as the emblem of the new MAS.

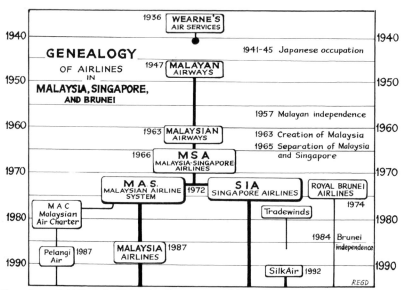

Genealogy of Airlines in Malaysia, Singapore, and Brunei
As the change in sovereignty went its course in the post-war developing world of Southeast Asia, the airline industry based in the former British segment of the region mirrored the changes. As shown in this chart, the most important event was the division of the single airline into two completely separate entities in 1972. Both have prospered mightily since, reflecting the inherent wealth and prosperity of the region as a whole.

Malaysian Airline System

The first president of the Malaysian Airline System, Saw Huat Lye, under the chairmanship of G K Rama Iyer, set about the task of creating a new base, a new international hub, and a new independent image for a country that the world at large had imagined to be centred only in Singapore. MAS patiently tried to put Kuala Lumpur on the airline map and gradually introduced intercontinental and regional services direct from the Malaysian capital. Starting with Bandar Seri Bagawan (formerly Brunei city) on 12 January 1973, Hong Kong and Jakarta were added on 1 April, Taipei on 1 October, then in 1974, Tokyo on 1 April, Madras on 1 August, and Manila on 2 October. More important, service to London, with only one stop, at Dubai, started on 1 July 1974, with a journey time of only 16 hours; and direct service to Sydney from 2 October of that year permitted England–Australia services with only two stops.

During 1974, MAS consolidated its position as one of the leading carriers for the annual Hajj pilgrimage traffic to Mecca, with an extensive programme of charter flights, organized through the Lembaga Urusan & Tabung Haji (LUTH), or the Pilgrims Management Board. Like Indonesia, the large Moslem population in Malaysia provided a ready and almost captive market for MAS's aircraft.

But the main thrust was to exploit Malaysia's as well as Singapore's geographical position athwart the trunk intercontinental route from Britain to Australia, traditionally a lucrative air travel market linking the Commonwealth nation with the home country, but now augmented by the addition of much traffic from Europe, as Australia welcomed new immigrants from southern Europe, notably from Greece and Yugoslavia. The city of Melbourne was said to have become the second largest Greek city in the world, and MAS's opening of a service to the Victorian metropolis on 1 October 1975 may have been no coincidence.

All these services were aimed to put MAS firmly on the world airline map – and this had to be undertaken against formidable competition from Singapore Airlines, as will be described later in this book. They were flown by that workhorse of long-distance routes of the first jet age, the Boeing 707; but by the mid-1970s, an airline had to have wide-bodied comfort if it was to survive in the world dominated by the giant flag carriers of Europe, Japan, and the United States. Sensing that the Boeing 747, with its 360–400 seats, was too large for most of its route segments, MAS opted for the tri-jet Douglas DC-10-30, with a 252-seat layout. MAS introduced it on the route to Tokyo on 2 October 1976, but most important, on the same day added Perth, Western Australia, as a third Australian destination, with one of the Boeing 707s released by the addition of the DC-10s. Not only did this provide extra convenience for the passengers drawn from Europe, but it also offered a convenient connection for the Japanese, who now had business interests in the western State, with its iron-mountain-rich economy.

Such headlong expansion was not achieved without cost. Indeed, MAS's balance sheets suffered, and economies were made in the domestic services, as the airline did not wish to pull back from the penetration into overseas markets that it had successfully made. In keeping with other airlines in the region, it launched an attractive tour programme, with *Golden Holiday* vacations to Bangkok and its nearby beach resort, Pattaya, on 24 July 1976, and followed this with a second tour to Manila, Taiwan and Hong Kong. The Malaysian Government, too, was conscious of its own potential as a tourist destination, and on 19 June 1977, the opening of a new runway at Penang permitted flights by aircraft as large as the Boeing 747.

Boeing 737s were used by Malaysian Airline System on regional routes. (*Boeing*)

Such was Malaysian Airline System's impact on the trans-Asian and Europe–Australia trunk route as a whole that by the summer of 1977 it was called to task by the British aviation authorities. MAS wanted to introduce the DC-10 on the London route, but the British (which still controlled Hong Kong) claimed that this would divert revenue from Cathay Pacific, which was not yet operating to the United Kingdom. MAS threatened to change its European terminus to Frankfurt or Amsterdam, but after discussions, a compromise was agreed, in which MAS had to agree to surrender a fixed percentage of the revenue earned on the London–Australia route through its 'Sixth Freedom' privileges arising from its convenient geographical position.

MAS introduced the DC-10 on the London route on 30 October 1977, and on the route to Sydney two days later. On 30 November it did add Frankfurt as an en route stop, thus tapping the European market at its busiest hub; and three years later, on 4 January 1980, service was added to Amsterdam. The Malaysian airline must have derived some satisfaction from the knowledge that it had been the cause of concern to London. Less than twenty years earlier, as a local DC-3 operator, London was hardly aware of its existence. Now, it could fly with confidence on an equal basis with airlines such as British Airways and Qantas, and demonstrated its resourcefulness by offering, from December 1977, a service from Australia to Britain, with only one stop, at Kuwait, besides Kuala Lumpur.

On the regional front, steps were taken to maintain parity of equipment with the host of aggressive rivals, and on 16 November 1979 it began Airbus A300B-4 services, first to Jakarta, Hong Kong, Madras and Perth, then, on 1 January 1980, to Taipei, Tokyo and Seoul, the last city having been added to the network on 3 April 1979. On 24 July 1980, an important New Air Services agreement was signed between Malaysia and Singapore, with liberal concessions made on both sides, particularly in the matter of wide-bodied aircraft utilization. MAS was allowed to provide direct service from Singapore to East Malaysia, while Singapore Airlines was allowed to fly direct to Penang. Such was the volume of traffic by now on the Kuala Lumpur–Singapore route that 246-seat Airbuses became the standard equipment by both airlines, operating in pool; and on 1 November 1982, this shuttle service boasted fifteen daily flights each way, most of them with Airbuses.

In the winter of 1979–80 MAS introduced Airbus A300B-4s on numerous routes.

During the 1980s, MAS maintained its momentum in upgrading its fleet, and this applied not only to its prestigious long-distance intercontinental services, but also to its domestic and rural services, both in West and East Malaysia. The DC-10s had done well, in spite of their grounding after the notorious Chicago crash of 6 June 1979; but – in contrast with its past record of developing its thoroughbred airliners – Douglas (now McDonnell Douglas, by official name as well as by parent ownership) was reluctant to stretch the airliner's fuselage to accommodate the increased demand that it had itself generated. In company with many other otherwise satisfied customers, MAS had to buy larger aircraft and turned to Boeing, ordering the Boeing 747, and putting it into service on 11 April 1982 on the Europe–Malaysia–Australia route.

But MAS did not neglect its responsibilities on the home front. By 1982, its fleet of aircraft employed on domestic mainline services and trans-border routes to neighbouring countries had grown to 24, a dozen each of 106-seat Boeing 737s and 40-seat Fokker Friendships. This was in addition to a balanced fleet of nine wide-bodied aircraft – two four-engined 747s, three DC-10 tri-jets, and four Airbus twins. At the other end of the scale, the Britten-Norman Islanders, while performing well in the jungles of Sarawak and the alpine meadows of Sabah, needed reinforcements, as their nine-seat capacity was inadequate. Help came from the introduction of the ubiquitous maid-of-all-bush-work, the de Havilland Canada DHC-6 Twin Otter, which joined the Rural Air Service on 1 April 1982.

All Is Not Gold . . . .

In 1982, Abdul Aziz Rahman took over the management of MAS when Saw Huat Lye retired. His title was managing director, rather than general manager, and he was to be in control of his airline's fortunes during a challenging period. He had to face a situation in which almost every airline in the east Asia region – or the Pacific Rim as it was beginning to be called – was vying for position as the world's most popular, judged by the standards of punctuality, regularity, and – all-important – standards of cabin service. Companies such as Japan Air Lines had introduced the element of oriental charm as well as oriental customs and courtesy, and Cathay Pacific, Thai Airways International, China Air Lines, and others, had

143

been quick to emulate the Japanese. Singapore Airlines, in fact, rapidly established a reputation as being second to none, and was regularly voted to offer the finest standards of service in the whole world.

The initials MAS, as an acronym, spelled the Malay word for gold; and, as already mentioned, this theme was used for such promotions as the *Golden Holidays*. Comfort standards in its *Golden Club* business class sections were as good as those in first class on some other airlines. Responding to the kimonos of the Japanese and the chong sams of the Chinese, MAS flight attendants wore traditional Malay costumes that accented the 'gentle Malaysian charm that comes naturally'. On the ground, first-class passengers enjoyed Golden Lounges, as well as a No Baggage Check-in Counter, where only twenty minutes check-in time was required if the lightly loaded passenger confirmed the reservation by telephone.

MAS's Boeing 747 fleet included -100, -200 and -400 models. (*Boeing*)

All this was of vital importance when MAS joined the trans-Pacific airline fraternity by starting a twice-weekly service to Los Angeles, via Tokyo, in 1986. And in the following year, when it opened a magnificent 34-storey building as its headquarters in Kuala Lampur, Malaysia's flag carrier would have seemed to be on top of its own world. Such was its self-sufficiency, because of its continued profitability, that the transition from a wholly-owned State enterprise to a private one, in which the Malaysian Government retained a minority 42 per cent share, presented no difficulty.

Yet a slight kink in the otherwise smooth curve of progress and prosperity came from an unusual source. All over the world of airlines, customers and commentators alike have enjoyed inventing special interpretations of airline acronyms. In some quarters, much to the airline's disgust and disapproval, the initials MAS were alleged to mean not gold, but 'mano ada system' which was Malay for 'where is the system?' The allegation may have been justified in isolated instances – for what airline does not have its share of late arrivals or technical malfunctions? – but this seemed especially unfair at a time when MAS had received the Boeing Company's *Pride In Excellence* award for Boeing 737 despatch reliability in 1988, the only airline to have been a three-time winner. The outcome of this uneasiness with its image was that the operating name of the airline was changed to Malaysia Airlines, although the corporate identity remained the same. MA stands for Master of Arts, and this was perhaps appropriate for an airline that had built itself up from very humble beginnings and had taken its place among the best as one of equals. Further progress was made in the late 1980s, as new points were added to the network: to Delhi and Karachi on 1 January 1989, and to Guangzhou, Zürich and Fukuoka in June of that year. Business was so good on the Haj flights, whose timing had now advanced through the year into the summer months, that three DC-10s were chartered from World Airways. In 1989 also, Malaysia Airways joined with Singapore Airlines, Cathay Pacific, China Airlines and Philippine Air Lines in setting up the Abacus computerized reservation system (CRS) rather than subscribe to either of the European or the American systems that threatened to invade the Pacific Rim.

Moving on, in the autumn of 1989, Malaysia took delivery of two new aircraft types, one to keep pace with the challenges of the intercontinental arena, the other to raise the standards of its domestic feeder system. The first Boeing 747-400 was delivered in October to complement the existing fleet of -100 and -200 series; and the first of nine propeller-turbine Fokker 50s began to replace the faithful Friendships. Orders were placed for eight new 311-seat Airbus A330-300s and sixteen 146/106-seat Boeing 737 Series 400s and 500s.

Twenty-six years previously, in 1963, the former Malayan Airways had left IATA, so as to join with Thai Airways International and Cathay Pacific in the freedom of non-IATA fare structures, that were then manipulated and dictated by the dominant airlines of Europe and America. On 1 July 1989, Malaysia Airlines, along with Cathay, Singapore, and Royal Brunei, rejoined IATA. It no longer needed to fear dominance from anyone.

Beginning of the Rainbow

The emergence of small feeder airlines in the wake of inevitable growth by their larger brethren is a process that has become axiomatic in the history of air transport. It happens in every kind of operating environment, from the bastions of determined private enterprise to the most dogmatic of centralized and state-controlled nations. And Malaysia was no exception.

Early in 1962, an ex-RAF pilot who had come to fly for Malaysian Airways, founded a small air charter company, making his first revenue flight with a Cessna 310 four-seater on 14 May. Like all energetic operators of his kind, F J Bussell and his wife, in what the Americans call a 'mom-and-pop outfit', took on every kind of aerial work activity, including survey and mapping, crop-spraying, and cloud-seeding – though Malaysia would seem to be an unlikely place to need a rain-maker. One of the most lucrative contracts was to carry newspaper matrices for the *Straits Times* in both directions between Kuala Lumpur and Singapore.

This little company was named Malaysian Air Charter, and was familiarly known as Macair or MAC. As Bussell prospered, his fleet grew to match the increased business, from small Cessnas and Pipers to Aero Commander 600s, then on to Britten-Norman Islanders, that strictly utility transport that made no pretensions to speed or comfort, but did get into small strips, and was cheap to buy and to operate. The Islander had nine seats, and when Macair was given permission to operate a small network of feeder services, mainly to points on the east coast of the Malayan Peninsula, this was too small for the traffic to an area that boasted new-style vacation resorts on palm-fringed strands, together with a growing oil centre at Kerteh, in the State of Trengganu.

During the 1970s, Macair thrived well enough, to such an extent that it bought a Shorts SD3-60, with 36 seats, and it became known as the rainbow airline,

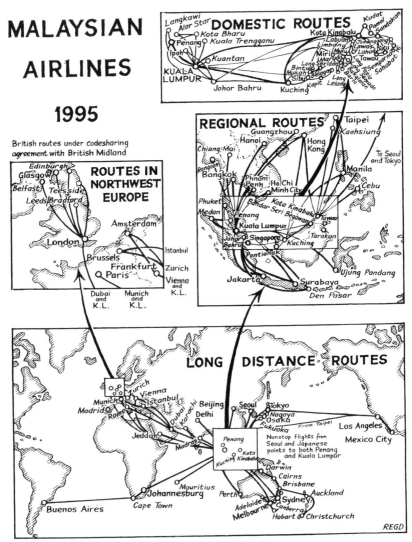

Map 14d. Malaysian Airlines, 1995
After the break-up of Malaysia-Singapore Airlines in 1972, the new Malaysian Airline System (MAS) operated almost in the shadow of Singapore Airlines for many years. The latter had the advantage of inheriting the lion's share of the fleet and the routes from the old airline; and Singapore was an entrepot of trade – not to mention a duty-free stopover for travellers between Britain and Australasia. To the eternal credit of those in Kuala Lumpur, Malaysia itself can match Singapore by any criterion of comparison, save actual volume of traffic.

146

because of its colourful paint scheme. But like so many aspiring small airlines, the earlier prosperity was not sustained, partly because the oil boom subsided, and partly because competitive services, including good roads from Kuala Lumpur, cut into the passenger demand. Late in 1986, Macair went bankrupt, and Malaysia Airline System took over the routes as a temporary measure.

Following many a precedent, the big airline discovered that the feeder routes operated by Macair could not easily be integrated with the fleets of Friendships and Boeings 737s; and there may well have been an element of provincial pressure from the State of Trengganu. At all events, in September 1987, Pelangi Air was formed to take over the operations of Macair (Pelangi means Rainbow in Malay), as an affiliate of Malaysia Airlines, and with the experienced Captain Ismail A Bakar as its general manager. The State of Trengganu was the majority shareholder, with 44 per cent, Perak held 33 per cent, Malaysian Helicopters 11 per cent and Malaysia Airlines 9 per cent.

On 1 January 1988, operations began on substantially the same network as that operated by Macair, but with de Havilland Twin Otters which, with 19 seats, were much better matched to the traffic volumes on the small feeder routes. In 1990, services were expanded to serve some nearby Indonesian points in Sumatra: Padang and Pekanbaru; and to the island of Pulau Batam, to the south of Singapore. Because of the obvious interlining advantages accruing from its relationship with the national airline, the airline revived. Captain Ismail replaced the Twin Otters with three Dornier 228s, noted for their good field performance, and although of the same size as the Canadian workhorse, were faster and more economic.

Pelangi Air has established itself as the domestic feeder line of Malaysia. It provides direct service from Singapore to the resort island of Tioman, on behalf of Singapore's Tradewinds. With Malaysia Airlines backing, it is here to stay, evidenced by its introduction, on 1 November 1991 of a new 50-seat Fokker 50.

An Airline Fit for a Sultan

Time was when the Sultanate of Brunei's empire extended over the whole of Borneo and over many of the southern islands of the Philippines. But in 1888 Brunei became a protectorate of Great Britain, and effectively fell under the economic influence of what became an extension of Malaya, together with Sarawak and British North Borneo. But Brunei never became part of Malaysia when that country was created in 1983, and it became a sovereign state on 1 January 1984. That such a tiny country, about the size of Delaware, and with a population of only 400,000, should achieve such independence was because it was immensely wealthy in oil and natural gas; and as a result, the Sultan of Brunei is one of the richest men in the world.

By this time, as full political authority gradually passed from London to Bandar Seri Begawan (formerly Brunei City), the Sultanate had already formed its own airline. Royal Brunei Airlines was founded on 18 November 1974, wholly government-owned, but operated strictly as a commercial enterprise. It began service, with a single Boeing 737-200, on 14 May 1975, from Bandar Seri Begawan to Kota Kinabalu (formerly Jesselton) in nearby Sabah (formerly British North Borneo) and to Singapore. The next day, Kuching and Hong Kong were added, and soon afterwards a second 737 provided the necessary basis for full scheduled service. In 1977, extensions were made, on 3 April, to Manila, and, on 9 December, to Bangkok. With the delivery of more 737s, the year 1983 saw

One of Royal Brunei's smartly painted Boeing 737s. (*Boeing*)

further growth, to Kuala Lumpur in May, Darwin, Australia, in June, and Jakarta in December.

In 1987, Royal Brunei spread its wings much further than to the neighbouring southeast Asia countries. It acquired three Boeing 757-200ERs and began service to Frankfurt, via Bangkok and Dubai; and this was followed by one to London, via Singapore and Dubai. The airline also bought a Boeing 767-200ER, and proclaimed its background of oil-fuelled affluence by the luxurious standards of its first-class cabin, complete with gold-plated fittings. In the summer of 1993, a third service to Europe, to Zürich, via Bahrain and Cairo, established the tiny sultanate as a worthy member of the international, indeed intercontinental, club of world airlines.

CHAPTER FIFTEEN

Singapore Airlines

A Flying Start

Seldom has any newly-founded or -created airline had such a beginning. Without diminishing any credit due to Singapore Airlines for its magnificent achievements, its dowry was, to say the least, substantial. Dowry is perhaps not quite apt. Marriage settlement as a divorce took place is a closer analogy. And Singapore's share of the former assets of the failed experiment of Malaysia-Singapore Airlines (MSA) could be described, by any standards, as generous. The acronym for the new Malaysian Airline System, MAS, may have been the Malay word for gold; but Singapore Airlines was the one born with a silver spoon in its mouth.

The embryo airline could hardly wait, and at first it advertised its determination to succeed with an announcement that, to many neutral observers, seemed like impudence, and in the eyes of Malayan peoples across the causeway at Johore as an insult. On 3 February 1972, eight months before the official dissolution of

When it was opened on 12 June 1937 the Singapore Marine and Land Airport at Kallang was one of the finest on the Empire routes.

The marine section of Kallang with three Imperial Airways Short C class flying-boats at moorings.

Malaysia-Singapore Airlines (MSA), the Singapore faction incorporated Mercury Singapore Airlines, which by deliberate coincidence also had the same initials, MSA. This was a not-too-subtle assertion that the city-state of Singapore – by any measure a commercial metropolis several orders of magnitude larger than any other in the region – was synonymous with the old airline. To some extent it was. It inherited all the overseas points on the previous MSA network, with the exception of Medan and the points in the new eastern portion of Malaysia; all the long-range aircraft and most of the medium-range ones; and the MSA head office and engineering base in Singapore. Of the $245 million of assets, Singapore

Singapore Airlines was quick in acquiring Boeing 747s. (*Boeing*)

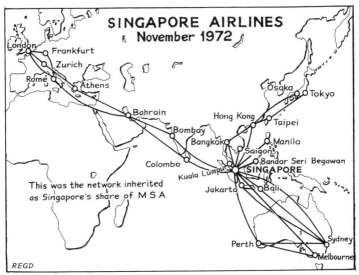

Map 15a. Singapore Airlines, November 1972
When the Malaysia-Singapore Airlines split occurred in 1972, the new republic, founded only in 1965, inherited not only a ready-made airline network, but also a geographically streategic location as – along with Bangkok and Hong Kong – a fulcrum of travel patterns in the western Pacific region. Singapore Government and business officials alike grasped a golden opportunity, offered almost by Fate, to link the major cities of Europe with major destinations in East Asia and Australia.

received $203 million, or 83 per cent.

Fortunately for all concerned, Singapore withdrew from its hasty and thoughtless action and on 30 June, after what was politely referred to as a dispute with Malaysia, agreed to call the new airline Singapore Airlines (SIA) and it adopted this identity, with modern and striking aircraft markings and insignia. Making a bold beginning in the manner in which it clearly wished to go on, SIA ordered two new 349-seat Boeing 747s on 26 July and three Boeing 707-312s from Continental Airlines in August. By the end of the year SIA has almost doubled its long-haul fleet of 707s to a total of nine; had started a 737 service to Bandar Seri Begawan (Brunei); and had retired its two Friendships. Clearly, the new airline was going to lose no time in making its presence felt on the Pacific Rim.

Self Sufficiency

The population of Singapore when it became independent was about two million, of whom only about one in a hundred lived in the limited areas of countryside around Singapore City. In like proportion, only about 2 per cent of the population of the 280-square miles island worked on the land. Three-quarters of the remainder were highly industrious Chinese immigrants who worked in factories, workshops, and in trading, from dawn to dusk and sometimes through the night, in an effort to emulate Hong Kong as the most productive commercial centre in east Asia, with the possible exception of Tokyo or Osaka. Hitherto the majority of these had worked for foreign-owned concerns, mostly British, including the port

151

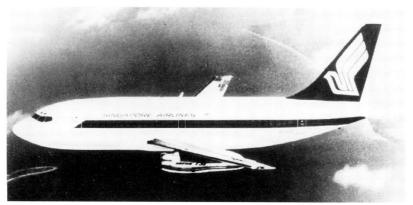

Before the end of its first year Singapore Airlines had begun Boeing 737 services to Brunei.

and dockyards. Now, this enormous resource of energy and talent was harnessed to the furtherance of an independent Singapore, freed from the inhibiting restraints – shackles is too strong a word – of colonialism. Cottage industries and sweat shops were replaced by small business enterprises; concrete and steel structures replaced the wooden shacks and warehouses of a bygone age; and a new managerial society, determined to win its place in the industrialized world, superseded the honest and fair-minded, but ultimately colonial bureaucracy, for whom Singapore did not symbolize nationhood, but only an outpost of Empire.

One of the instruments of the new industrial society was Singapore Airlines. Much in the same way as, in colonial times, the Royal Navy or the British merchant marine carried the flag as a symbol of power, so now did the national airline take its natural place in the new world of rapid communications by air, rather than by sea. All over the world, airports were replacing seaports as the visible gateways of trade, commerce and travel. And the new city state of Singapore made itself evident, in an amazingly short time, through the agency of its ambitious and aggressive airline.

Typically, new airlines, as the modern equivalent of the former gunboat in 'showing the flag', have to lease aircraft, or borrow them, and usually have to contract with outside companies for maintenance, marketing, and often management. Singapore, as has been observed, inherited aircraft, marketing, and management but only part of this was completely under its own control. It soon made it clear that it intended to be its own master, beholden to no-one.

In addition to ensuring that all its aircraft were its own property, rather than of some other leasing corporation or associated airline, Singapore Airlines took steps to provide the essential installations and services that are the apparatus of a modern international airline. On 11 August 1972, even before the ink was dry on the official separation with Malaysian Airline System, Singapore purchased a Boeing 707-312B simulator from the Redifon company in England, and on 7 August 1973, mock-up layouts and structures of both the 707 and 747 were completed. Clearly, Singapore was going to do its own pilot training.

For maintenance, and to keep pace with the onrush of computer technology in all aspects of airline operations, including reservations, a $23 million Kriscom IBM complex was opened in February 1973, and soon afterwards Singapore Airport Terminal Services (SATS) was established at Paya Lebar Airport. On 15

152

August 1975, the $11.5 million Engine Overhaul Building, including a $1.5 million Engine Test Cell, was completed at the airport. Technically, Singapore Airlines was not only able to take care of itself, but was also able to provide maintenance, overhaul, and pilot training for other airlines.

The commercial side of the airline business was not neglected as Singapore Airlines forged ahead on all fronts. From the start, recognizing that, for the vast majority of the air travelling public, the closest contact with the airline in personal terms is through the service by the flight attendants, Singapore Airlines introduced striking new uniforms for the stewardesses, a most attractive oriental style of the batik sarong kebaya, worn by their owners with dignity, charm and elegance, to add to the oriental standards of service and courtesy. The Singapore ground crews shared in the new elegance; their new uniforms were designed by Pierre Balmain.

Breaking Out

With such an infrastructure and with a fleet of aircraft that matched its competition, Singapore Airlines was prepared to challenge the world, if necessary; and the world of airlines watched with wonder and respect as it proceeded to do so with an unerring touch. The airline was in tune with its people, who were energetically showing their determination to create a new City-State that would be an example for all, and a residual element of this process was the emergence of a prosperous society in which there were material rewards, partly in the form of discretionary income, and a source of funds for travel. SIA began to cater for this demand, starting a holiday programme on 3 April 1973 – only a few months after splitting up with Malaysia – to Medan, in northern Sumatra, Indonesia, with excursions to the breathtakingly beautiful Lake Toba. In May 1974, the Fiesta Filipinas Holiday programme was launched, and – an idea that would have been unthinkable less than a decade earlier – SIA European Holidays took care of those who wished to take a tour in the reverse direction to the normal flow.

This flow itself had been growing apace, with many non-scheduled airlines in Europe competing for the burgeoning traffic between Europe and southeast Asia, where Singapore was, geographically and commercially, the natural hub. To offset this erosion of its traffic base, Singapore Airlines joined with BOAC on 1 July 1973 in introducing special low fares, at £225 for the round-trip to or from London, compared with the normal £512. This was just in time to complement the opening of SIA's Boeing 747 services, the first with the giant airliner in southeast Asia, on the Singapore–Hong Kong–Tokyo and London–Singapore–Sydney routes on 1 October of the same year.

During the 1970s Singapore completed its initial stage of modest expansion of the international and intercontinental route system it had inherited from MSA. Little needed to be done in Asia, as all the major cities were already on-line; but service was resumed to Madras in January 1973, after more than a year's suspension; Boeing 707 flights began to Seoul, via Bangkok, Hong Kong and Taipei, on 18 August 1975. Consolidating its position as a recognized Europe–Australia trunk airline (albeit with a stop at Singapore to observe the so-called Sixth Freedom legal requirements, and – making a virtue out of necessity – providing passengers with extensive duty-free shopping opportunities) Amsterdam was added on 1 April 1973 and the next day the frequency to London was upgraded to a daily service. On 1 May 1976, additions were made at both ends of the route, to Paris and to Auckland, New Zealand. The latter point was at first served as an extension through Melbourne; but such was the popularity that on 3 November 1977, nonstop service began, with, in this instance, McDonnell Douglas DC-10s, leased from both Malaysian and Air New Zealand. Copenhagen became Singapore Airlines' eighth European station on 1 July 1977.

The pace of progress was fast and furious. On 2 May 1976, the daily service to London became an all-Boeing 747 schedule. In August of the same year SIA set up Tradewinds Charters as an air charter subsidiary of its hotel management subsidiary already established in February 1975. In November 1976, Singapore Aviation and General Insurance Group was founded, so that the airline was self-insured. The new engine maintenance base became Singapore Aero-Engine Overhaul (Private) Ltd on 1 April 1977, and a $14 million Air Freight Terminal was opened on 28 July of the same year.

All this concerted effort paid off. Singapore Airlines was the talk of the airline industry everywhere except in the United States, operating rights to which were the subject of some hard bargaining with the US authorities. But in its major market, Europe, in a competition conducted by the *Travel News* magazine of Great Britain, SIA was voted 'Airline of the Year'. This was in January 1978, only six years after the airline began its independent existence, only twelve years after the creation of Malaysia-Singapore Airlines (MSA), and less than thirty years since its ancestor, Malayan Airways, had chartered its first four-engined (and unpressurized) Douglas DC-4.

Flirtation with Fantasy

In April 1975 Singapore Airlines' dynamic chairman, J Y M Pillay, had coupled an announcement of an $800 million aircraft purchasing programme with an expressed desire to start a trans-Pacific air route. This was to take four years before becoming a reality but meanwhile, if only to ensure continuing momentum of its market penetration by spectacular advertising, SIA entered the élite fraternity of supersonic airlines.

In 1976 British Airways and Air France, to the delight of romantic and patriotic flagwavers, to the satisfaction of engineers and technicians who had performed a miracle, but to the despair of economists who correctly predicted financial disaster, launched the world's first – and so far the only – supersonic passenger services. The dreamers foresaw Concorde routes all over the globe, and both of the launching customers had high hopes of making a commercial scoop. This did not happen. The high fares that had to be charged to match the astronomical operating costs appealed only to a very small percentage – a fraction of one per cent – of the air travelling public; and after a spate of new Concorde routes opened in the late 1970s, these were gradually reduced to only two across the Atlantic, the only trunk route system that could generate adequate loads.

But this did not stop the British and French flag carriers – and what better way to show the flag? – from trying. One of British Airways' original ideas was to fly the Concorde to Australia, in less than a day; but this was before the operational and financial realities were finally accepted by minds that were otherwise hypnotized by the promises and undertakings made by the manufacturers. The Australian ambitions were curtailed to that of a service to Singapore, in tacit recognition perhaps of the value of the city as an entrepôt and traffic hub of a burgeoning region.

Another reality was the political one. Traffic rights in Singapore were no longer controlled from London, as they still were in Hong Kong, Singapore being now a Sovereign State. The outcome of negotiations was that, on 21 October 1977, an agreement was signed in London for a joint Concorde service by British Airways and Singapore Airlines, three times a week, via Bahrain (British Airways' first Concorde route), with the aircraft painted with BA's colours on one side, and Singapore's on the other. The flight time would be cut from the 16 hours of the subsonic airliners to the Concorde's nine. The fare was set at fifteen per cent above the existing first-class fare. Thus, for the sum of 4,298 Singapore dollars, a passenger could leave Singapore at 11.30 a.m. and arrive in London at 1.15 in the early afternoon.

This prestigious service was planned to begin on 9 December 1977, the outward-bound trip to depart from London at 1 p.m. and arrive in Singapore at 6 a.m. the next day. The London–Bahrain segment was to be flown under a British Airways flight number, the Bahrain–Singapore under Singapore's. The service did not start with a flourish, as expected. In fact, it hardly started at all. The Malaysian Government, possibly feeling that Singapore was, in the euphoria of its brilliant success, riding rough-shod over its less well-endowed neighbours, refused overflying rights. The inaugural flight had to be cancelled at the last minute, and only six flights were completed, not exactly as scheduled.

For a short period in 1979–80 Singapore Airlines had a joint Singapore—London Concorde service with British Airways. Singapore Airlines' markings appeared on one side of the aircraft and British Airways' on the other.

After considerable diplomacy, the Malaysian authorities, on a rare occasion in which it held a trump card in the game, permitted the use of its airspace, and Concorde services were resumed on 24 January 1979. The service lasted for about eighteen months, ending on 30 October 1980, because of what were described officially as 'rising costs' (as though they had never been high) and 'route difficulties' (although, with Middle East tensions, these had never been easy). The real reason was the impossibility of persuading enough passengers to pay the almost extortionate price of the Concorde fares so that the technical miracle could pay its way.

The Concorde experience was possibly the only time when Singapore Airlines did not carefully measure the financial advantage, both in the short-term and the long, of a decision in aircraft selection and deployment. The peripheral effect of the powerful advertising is difficult to assess. To claim membership of the élite club of supersonic airlines was a big feather in Singapore Airlines' cap. It gave the airline a place in history, one shared by few. Other than the State-persuaded indigenous operators of the two countries that built the Concorde, only three other airlines ever operated supersonic airliners: Braniff Airways, a US airline that leased British Airways Concordes as an extension of the latter's New York service

155

on to Dallas; Aeroflot, which was the short-lived and reluctant operator of the Soviet Tupolev Tu-144, and then only on cargo flights from Moscow to Alma Ata; and Singapore Airlines, which was probably the only one that did not lose its supersonic shirt.

Singapore World-wide

Chairman Pillay's efforts to gain access to the United States market were finally successful. On 23 September 1977, Singapore Airlines was granted landing rights enabling it to fly to San Francisco, via Hong Kong, Guam and Honolulu. In exchange Singapore had to grant generous rights to US airlines for access to its southeast Asia hub; but this did not concern the airline too much, as it was confident of its own ability to compete with anybody.

The airline started cautiously, however. Its first trans-Pacific service, started on 1 April 1978, was only for cargo. A few months later, plans for the passenger service hit a snag when the British quibbled over traffic rights through Hong Kong. But in resolving these, Singapore decided to omit Guam as a stop, and would thus become the first airline to operate nonstop from Hong Kong to Honolulu.

In preparation for additional service patterns, including trans-Pacific, SIA had ordered four McDonnell Douglas DC-10-30s on 6 July 1977. With 268 seats and capacity for 13 tons of cargo, they were about a quarter of the size of the Boeing 747s, which gave the airline the flexibility of deployment of wide-bodied equipment, according to the level of traffic demand. The versatile DC-10 was also used extensively on the regional services but its debut was made in fine style, as the aircraft of choice for the trans-Pacific service, started on 4 April 1979, with only two stops, at Hong Kong and Honolulu. Singapore then suffered the consequences of an event that was quite beyond its control. An American Airlines DC-10 literally dropped one of its engines, in full view of thousands of people, as it took off from Chicago's O'Hare Airport on 25 May, less than two months after SIA had started DC-10 service. The US Federal Aviation Administration grounded all DC-10s world-wide.

Such was Singapore Airlines' power of resilience, made possible by the sheer

In July 1977 SIA ordered four 268-passenger McDonnell Douglas DC-10-30s.

156

efficiency of its operations and management, and the foresightedness of its planners, that it was able to take this setback almost without breaking stride. It was already building its modern fleet, having ordered eight Airbus A300B-4s simultaneously with the opening of its Pacific service. Now, it proceeded to intensify this latter major extension of its world-wide route network. Boeing 747s had been substituted for the DC-10s, and a second route was added on 2 July 1980, to Los Angeles, via Taipei and Honolulu. A third route, a one-stop Singapore–Tokyo–Los Angeles $16\frac{1}{2}$-hour service, was the fastest between Singapore and the United States. SIA now offered nine weekly flights across the Pacific, between four major gateways in the Orient and three major destinations in the USA.

The European services were also augmented during the latter 1970s. These had been steadily increased, in frequency, in capacity, and in routeing, with Brussels added as a ninth destination on 1 April 1979. One year later, Singapore Airlines was operating 17 services a week to Europe, of which seven terminated in London, five in Amsterdam, three in Frankfurt, and two in Copenhagen; and all were operated with Boeing 747s.

Singapore Airlines was the first Far East operator of the Airbus A310. (*Airbus*)

The first Airbus, fitted with 246 all-economy seating, entered service on the Singapore–Kuala Lumpur route on 2 February 1981. By this time, the Malaysian capital had grown in stature, from being only the third city of British Malaya (Penang ranked second in the postwar years) to a thriving city which, while not as spectacular as Singapore, was nevertheless becoming a big generator of local traffic. On the same day, Singapore's 'Superbus' also started service to the Indonesian capital, Jakarta.

The Australasian route group was also prospering. By 1 April 1981, there were eight flights per week to Australia (six to Sydney and Melbourne, two to Perth), and two to Auckland, New Zealand. Again, all were with Boeing 747s. By this time, Singapore Airlines' fleet had grown to sixteen Boeing 747s, five DC-10s, three Airbuses (with more to come), and four Boeing 727-200s. The 747 became the standard aircraft for long-haul routes, such was the continued demand, with load factors customarily in the high seventies; some DC-10s were first leased, then sold to the Brazilian airline, VARIG, as the Airbus deliveries permitted wider use throughout the east Asia region.

All these expansionist moves were made against a background of unprecedented prosperity and profitability, which envious rivals alleged were the direct result of

Four Boeing 727-200s were part of Singapore Airlines always modern fleet.

low wages and salaries. This was certainly part of the reason, but by no means the only one. Like its parent city, whose skyline had come to resemble New York's Manhattan, Singapore Airlines was efficient. Its standards of service had, in the eyes of the travelling public, become the best in the world, even eclipsing that of Japan Air Lines, which for many years until the late 1970s, itself set an unparalleled standard. Singapore Airlines' smallest aircraft was the 168-seat Boeing 727; and one of these had the honour of being the first airliner to land at Singapore's magnificent new airport at Changi (on a site where the Royal Air Force had once held sway), which opened on 1 July 1981, replacing Paya Lebar, which had served for 26 years.

On To Greatness

During the history of air transport, many airlines have surprised their contemporaries by some remarkable efforts in pioneering new routes or in launching new aircraft types, even in developing new market strategies. But none has made such an impact on the airline industry and on the travelling public as a whole as Singapore Airlines. Its sustained and complete success has been amazing. Within only a few years of the first appearance of its handsome insignia at some of the world's busiest airports, its fame had spread far and wide. Possibly no airline has enjoyed such expansion of its traffic base simply by the best form of advertising of all: word of mouth. Seldom has any passenger had cause for complaint, and such consistency and reputation for quality paid high dividends.

Undoubtedly, the superb cabin service was a major contributor to SIA's awesome reputation, which was the envy of the airline world. The exquisitely-clad 'Singapore Girls' were attractive to behold, but their attraction has not rested solely upon their feminine charm. They are always young. Contracts are for only three years, and are renewed only three times; and the competition is intense. There are more of them, 19 in a Boeing 747, compared with the customary 15. All of them speak at least one, and often two foreign languages, at least more than adequately for ministering unto the needs of the most fastidious passenger. They are trained to learn the names of every passenger, even in economy class. Such standards are the epitome of service, without servility. And, contrary to the general impression, half of the cabin staff on Singapore Airlines is male.

Many satisfied customers claimed that no airline could match the *Raffles* non-smoking upper deck lounge on SIA's Boeing 747s, with its fine crystal, selection of 23 international wines, and the usual sleeper-reclining seats. One innovation was to offer freshly-laundered blankets, a luxury that will be extended to all passengers in due course. Chinese laundries used to be the subject of humour; but no-one complains at Singapore Airlines' laundries.

The same kind of impressionable service is evident on the ground. The Silver Kris Lounge at Singapore is possibly the most well-appointed in the world, with its business centre, equipped with computers and fax machines, television rooms, massage chairs, conference facilities, even the opportunity to take a shower. Changi Airport is the kind of transit point where passengers would even want to miss their flight.

Such flair is in the tradition of Emerson's famous dictum, and the world of knowledgeable air travellers beat a pathway to the doors of the Singapore airline offices. By 1981 SIA ranked 15th among world airlines in annual revenue passenger-kilometres flown, and sixth in the international rankings. A decade later, it was in the top dozen, an almost incredible achievement for an airline with no domestic network, and whose own people in Singapore accounted for only one fifth of its clientèle. Singapore Airlines boards twice as many passengers every year than the population of Singapore itself.

After the opening of the trans-Pacific service the airline rested on its laurels, at least in terms of route expansion. No new stations were added between 1980 and 1984, although it did resume direct service to nearby Penang, Malaysia's smart vacation resort. It concentrated instead on ensuring that its fleet was not comprised merely of the best that money could buy, but also of the youngest. Singapore Airlines' 747s, DC-10s, Airbuses, and 727s have an *average* age of less than five years. Since becoming independent under its own name in 1972, it has never failed to make a profit, and they are normally big ones – the kind that most world airlines have not experienced for many years, if ever. When SIA orders aircraft, it does so in style, for example, on 15 December 1981, when it ordered eight Boeing 747 SUD (Stretched Upper Deck)s and four Airbuses, for US $1.6 billion. On 31 May 1983 it repeated the performance, with an order for six more 747 SUDs, six Airbus A310s, and four Boeing 757s. On 5 May 1983, Singapore Airlines made the world's first trans-Pacific flight with the 'Big Top' 747 SUD, on its Singapore–Tokyo–Los Angeles route. Earlier in the year, in February, to match the operational intensity in the air with maintenance support on the ground, it opened, at Changi Airport, the world's largest column-free hangar, next door to its new headquarters which had been completed as an annex to the hangar in September 1982, and which opened officially on 23 September 1983.

At this time, Singapore Airlines began to add more lines on its map. With the world's highest load factor, averaging about 75 per cent consistently, it could indulge itself a little. On 1 November 1982, it had agreed with Malaysian Airline System to turn the Singapore–Kuala Lumpur route into a non-reservations Shuttle Service, every hour, on the hour, to be maintained mainly with Airbuses by both airlines, thus eradicating uneconomic competition from high frequencies and from duplication of low-productivity ground staff. On 15 November 1983, a service to Kuantan, on Malaysia's east coast, opened jointly with MAS, for tourists tempted by Club Mediterranée's delights and the famous turtles. In Australasia, Brisbane and Adelaide were added on 30 March 1984, Christchurch on 7 October 1986, and Darwin on 1 February 1988; in India, Delhi on 1 April 1986 and Calcutta on 29 October of that year, stopping at Dhaka (Dacca), Bangladesh; and in the Indian Ocean, Malé (Maldives) on 28 March 1984, and Mauritius on 1 June 1985. Direct services to Bali, bypassing Jakarta, and in co-operation with Garuda, began on 10 May 1986.

A World-wide Airline Force

The 1980s was the decade in which the airline deregulation process, fired off by the United States in 1978, began to infiltrate around the world, affecting the policies and prospects of all airlines, large and small, private and state-owned. But deregulation did not affect Singapore Airlines very much, for it had been born in an unregulated airline climate, in which very few of its main competitors were interested in European or American-style regulatory processes of route allocations or fare-fixing. And very few of its neighbour airlines were members of IATA, the international agency which, in spite of continual protests to the contrary, was essentially a price-fixing organization. Eventually, on 1 July 1990, SIA, along with Malaysian, Cathay Pacific and Royal Brunei, joined that august body; but by this time, IATA no longer ruled the airwaves with an iron hand; and it had more to learn from the southeast Asian airlines than they could learn from it.

In 1986 SIA ordered fourteen Boeing 747-400s but before the -400 became available the airline operated the interim stretched-upper-deck -300. The words 'Big Top' appeared just aft of the flight deck windows. (*Boeing*)

Throughout the 1980s Singapore Airlines continued its headlong pace. In March 1986, keeping in the forefront of equipment superiority, it ordered fourteen of the newest wide-bodied jets, the Boeing 747-400, which had 8,000 miles range, and sure enough, when service with the type began, it was a nonstop Singapore–London link, added to the comprehensive web of routes to Europe on 29 March 1989. The same aircraft also augmented the Pacific services, on the biggest traffic-generator, Singapore–Los Angeles, with only one stop, at Tokyo. Trying to keep pace, the contracts department prepared the documentation for another massive order that included fifteen Boeing 747-400s and five McDonnell Douglas MD-11s, on 15 January 1990. By this time, the fleet consisted of thirty 747s of various kinds and fourteen Airbuses. Its entire fleet was wide-bodied, the responsibility for smaller and shorter routes having been handed over to a subsidiary, Tradewinds.

As Singapore Airlines entered the last decade of the 20th Century, its strength and its prospects, even in spite of a previous decade of astonishing growth and success, had never been better. Its net cash balance was more than a billion Singapore dollars, or more than half a billion US dollars. It had made profits at an average of more than a billion for the past three years. Its long-term forecasts suggested that it would need a fleet of fifty 747s alone by the year 2000. Its world-wide network was secure, and its geographical position at the hub of the Pacific Rim, stretching from Sapporo to Christchurch, guaranteed its security against erosion of the traffic base. Announcements of new routes were seldom in the news, because the airline already went almost everywhere. On 28 October 1990, however, the changing political scene in Europe permitted a service into Berlin for the first time by any airline in Asia; and in June 1991 SIA made its first appearance in Canada, with service to Toronto.

This latter addition to the world-wide network had an interesting feature. The routeing was not by the traditional trans-Pacific access from east Asia to the North American continent; it was through Europe – a logical step, as the distance was about the same, eastbound or westbound from Singapore. The next month, alarm bells should have sounded in quite a few intercontinental airline corridors when Singapore announced plans to open a route to New York, via Frankfurt, in 1993. Like the Toronto pathfinder, the distance to New York via Europe is, if anything, marginally shorter than via the Pacific, even by the Great Circle; yet the existing fare structure is in inverse proportion, and considerably so at the first-class level. Singapore Airlines has never lowered itself to participate in an undignified fare war; but if it adjusts its tariffs to equalize the eastbound/westbound fares to the biggest city in North America and far and away the biggest revenue generator, then it may unconsciously have a profound influence on the tariff structure of the world's biggest intercontinental air route, the North Atlantic.

Regional and Other Involvement

The status of Singapore as a highly successful example of a modern City-State has never been challenged or questioned; and the State has ruled supreme in matters of commercial aviation policy. Before the dissolution of Malaysia-Singapore Airlines in 1972 and soon after the creation of Singapore as a nation in 1965, Air-Taxi Ltd had been founded in 1966, to operate small aircraft (the biggest was a DC-3) on a non-scheduled basis. In 1968, it was re-organized as Singapore Air Services, adding a DHC-6 Twin Otter to its assortment of Pipers and Cessnas; and in 1969 the Singapore Government acquired an 80 per cent interest, changing the name once again to Saber Air.

The character and role of the airline also changed, becoming a long-range charter airline, and providing support for oil exploration in south-east Asia, with a Douglas DC-6A. Then, in February 1971, Overseas National Airways (ONA) a United States Supplemental airline, took over a minor shareholding, and provided a DC-8-61, to operate special charter flights to London. Saber Air then changed its affiliation to British Caledonian Airways, which supplied a Boeing 707 for the London link; but the company ceased operations when the Singapore Government decided that

Saber Air's Douglas DC-3 9V-BAN.

161

Saber Air's de Havilland Canada Twin Otter 9V-BCE.

Singapore Airlines was to be the 'chosen instrument' of Singapore's airline industry.

Chairman Pillay apparently had ideas of his own, for in 1975 he established Tradewinds, as a tour and charter subsidiary of Singapore Airlines. By 1984, responding to popular demand, a daily shuttle service began on 25 May of that year to Malacca and Kuala Lumpur, using an 18-seat Dornier 228; and on 8 June, a second route started to the new Malaysian resort island, Tioman, using a 16-seat Shorts Skyvan.

In February 1989, Tradewinds expanded its horizons, with routes to provincial points in Thailand and Malaysia not served by the parent company, using a leased 122-seat McDonnell Douglas MD-87. Continuing healthy regional growth, the airline was renamed SilkAir in 1992, and added a fleet of Fokker 70s and Boeing 737-300s, even a couple of Airbus A310-300s, but these last were withdrawn in March 1995. Singapore now has a regional airline of stature to supplement its prestigious intercontinental flag carrier.

The Phenomenon

Despite all its many outstanding achievements and successes, Singapore Airlines has never been complacent. It has been aware of the old business axiom that the time to be on the alert is when you are on top. Keeping its fingers sensitively on the pulse of world airline activity and trends, it realized that, with deregulation spreading around the whole world, many of the small airlines were engulfed by larger ones, or simply driven out of business by them; that the medium-sized airlines were having difficulty in surviving and were seeking mergers; and that, with the creation of a united Europe, with all the international barriers in that continent due to fall in 1993, the age of the so-called mega-carriers had arrived. Already, in the United States, the oligopoly of a once many-tiered airline industry had become more concentrated, with three large airlines, United, American and Delta, dominating the field. In Europe, alliances were being formed across national frontiers, as a precautionary measure against feared dominance by giants such as British Airways, Air France and Lufthansa. Yet even the mega-carriers themselves, aware of the dangers of over-confidence and guarding against other challenges, were involved in forming alliances.

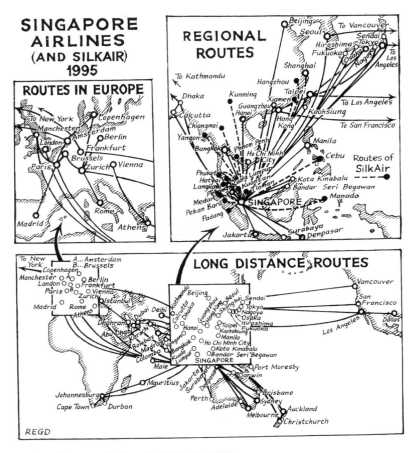

Map 15b. Singapore Airlines (and Silkair), 1995
The rise of Singapore Airlines as one of the world's leading airlines has been truly a phenomenon. Blessed with a generous inheritance and a geographical advantage, the airline exploited these assets to the full by dynamic policies of aircraft procurement, route development, and marketing. The national airline of this tiny country, with a population of fewer than 3,000,000, now ranks among the top dozen in the world.

On 1 September 1989, therefore, Singapore Airlines entered into an agreement with Delta Air Lines of the United States and Swissair of Europe, in which an alliance was forged, with each member holding a small percentage of the stock of the others. Schedules, routes, reservations, and tariffs would be integrated, with the three working together to draw upon the resources of the world's three major economic regions to comprise a global airline force of unprecedented potential. Each one of the trio holds an enviable reputation for service and quality within its own sphere of influence. That an airline of east Asia, formed only in 1972, and tracing its ancestry back only to 1947, should be a key player in world airline politics in the 1990s, is a triumph for the little City-State that is Singapore. Singapore Airlines has truly been a phenomenon.

163

CHAPTER SIXTEEN

KNILM

A Great Airline Tradition

For all empires, whether ancient, mediaeval, or modern, the ability of the conquering nation to retain its territories and to profit by their occupation has rested upon the efficiency of the communications system. This was true over land masses, as with the Romans who built an astonishing network of roads, the Chinese who built the Grand Canal; over sea routes, as with the trading nations of Europe during past centuries, when merchant venturers served to establish new colonies in distant lands; and in recent times in the air, with pioneering airlines staking their claims for far-flung route networks.

The Dutch were no laggards in such enterprise. As with their seafaring predecessors, Koninklijke Luchtvaart Maatschappij voor Nederland an Kolonien (KLM), one of the great names in the annals of air transport, was one of the first off the mark as Europe recovered from the devastation of the First World War. Turning to the aeroplane as a means of carrying passengers and mail (freight was impracticable in the early 1920s) seemed to be an obvious solution for the Netherlands; for all its colonies were thousands of miles from the homeland; in the Caribbean and northern South America or in the East Indies, now the republic of Indonesia. Even its Dutch-speaking (Afrikaans) cousins in South Africa were six thousand miles away. KLM, therefore, quickly tried to establish itself as a long-distance airline.

It did this with remarkable speed and skill. The Netherlands East Indies were one of the most valuable colonies of any nation in the world, rich in agricultural

The Rolls-Royce Eagle engined prototype Fokker F.VII which in 1924 made the first Amsterdam—Batavia proving flight. (*KLM*)

and mineral wealth; and under the leadership of Albert Plesman, KLM's managing director, a route from Amsterdam to Batavia (now Jakarta), the eastern capital, was given top priority. As early as 1924 – the year when Britain's Imperial Airways was founded – a Fokker F.VII made a proving flight over the 8,300-miles (13,350 km) route. Under the command of A N J Thomassen, H-NACC arrived in Batavia on 24 November 1924, having left Amsterdam on 1 October, and delayed for a month by a forced landing in Bulgaria. The single-engined Fokker made twenty-one stops, seven of them through British India.

The cabin of a KLM Fokker F.VIIb/3m used initially on the Amsterdam—Batavia service. Reclining seats are fitted and the bag marked 'Bagdad' presumably held mail. (*KLM*)

KLM's subsequent progress was methodical and effective. With successive improvements in the Fokker line of aircraft, and after a series of fortnightly proving flights from 12 September to 12 December 1929, the great Dutch airline began a regular mail service – also fortnightly – on 25 September 1930. These pioneering flights, which also carried some passengers, were made with the well-tried Fokker F.VIIb tri-motor, and KLM agreed with the Netherlands East Indies postal authorities to be paid for 500 kg of mail on each flight, regardless of the amount actually carried.

The F.VIIb/3m was not quite big enough for long passenger flights such as Amsterdam–Batavia, and Fokker produced an improved version, the F.XII, fitted with four luxury seats (instead of three) that could be folded back to provide a measure of comfort, permitting the clientèle to snatch some moments, perhaps even hours, of sleep. The F.XII was also slightly faster. The bi-weekly service opened on 1 October 1931, a date that must be listed among the great watersheds in airline history. The end-to-end journey took ten days and made twenty stops, and six aircraft were needed to provide the schedule.

During the early 1930s KLM was setting a pace of such demonstrable quality

Fokker F.XIIs replaced the F.VIIs on the Batavia route. Here *Uil (Owl)* is taking-off from Calcutta. (*Courtesy John Stroud*)

that all eyes of the airline world were on Amsterdam. No other company in the world matched the Dutch airline's standards of achievement in regularity or reliability, moreover on the successful operation of the world's longest air route. In 1932, the slightly faster (203 km/h v 180 km/h) Fokker F.XVIII replaced the F.XII and, in a dramatic demonstration of what aviation could offer to the world of communications, Captain Ivan Smirnoff and his crew, with considerable élan, made a round trip in the *Pelikaan* between 18 and 30 December 1933, not only delivering the Christmas mails to Batavia but arriving back in Amsterdam in time to celebrate the New Year.

Less sensationally perhaps, and with fewer headlines, Amsterdam had become a gateway of air travellers bound for the Far East, with passengers making connecting flights from other European capitals, including London. Singapore, for example, then a British Colony, could be reached by a connecting service from Batavia; and on 3 May 1933, showing much initiative – the British may have thought it effrontery – KLM provided a direct service to Singapore, without having to go all the way to Batavia first. In 1933, the airlines had not yet fashioned a garland around the earth; but Dr Plesman and the Dutch were the standard-bearers for one of the most important sections of a future round-the-world route.

Colonial Enterprise

Such outstanding performance was not achieved without some figures in the loss column – particularly in the column of fiscal reality, not in the metaphorical sense. For the challenge of operating a European air network in the Twenties, with aircraft that were not yet efficient enough to make money at the fares that had to be charged, were too great even for KLM to overcome. With each step forward in operational prowess, it took a further step into red ink on the financial balance sheet. In February 1927, it had been close to bankruptcy, and was only saved by the Netherlands Government from going out of business. After six months of solicitation, Plesman was obliged to increase private investment as a condition of support from The Hague. The Government became a major shareholder, thus safeguarding the investment of the private partners. Its representatives on the KLM board were drawn from the Ministry of Waterworks, which would have been a rather odd relationship in any other country. In the Netherlands, however, the very existence of large areas of the country is dependent upon its sea and river defences; and no public works has greater priority.

Because of the struggle for viability, KLM was obliged to abandon its ambition to establish a subsidiary company in Batavia, to serve the many islands of the East Indies. This must have been a bitter blow for Plesman, as the prospects of expansion were considerable in sheer magnitude, and exciting in the visions of a future base for air traffic. The collection of thousands of islands, big and small, was spread over an area that extended, west to east, over a distance several hundred miles longer than the width of the United States. To the far east lay the Moluccas, the so-called Spice Islands, conjuring up images of exotic products and the source of healthy trade with Europe; and the development of coffee in Java almost changed the name of the beverage. Although the prospects of a vigorous tourist trade to romantic Bali, regal Jokjakarta, or the architectural splendour of Borobudur, were still a few years in the future, the entire Colony, from Sumatra to New Guinea (now Irian) and from Borneo (Kalimantan) to Timor, held out great hopes for the future. But another airline, not KLM, was to be the instrument of aerial conquest of the many-islanded territory, and to extend by commercial aeroplane the spirit of romance and adventure that had once been the domain of the maritime fraternity.

The right to provide commercial air services throughout the Netherlands East Indies thus passed to another company, by default. KLM's loss was the gain of Koninklijke Nederlandsch-Indische Luchtvaart Maatschappij (KNILM), founded in Amsterdam by Dutch businessmen in the spring of 1927 and formally incorporated there on 16 July 1928. Aside from the opportunity offered by KLM's problems, the Dutch colonialists had become alarmed by some communist-inspired uprisings in Java and Sumatra in 1926; and the idea of an airline that could provide rapid transport for administrators and armed forces alike was an attractive prospect.

The two Dutch airlines were independent businesses, though linked by personal as well as by financial ties. Each developed its own routes and services, but sensibly did so in co-operation. In September 1927, even before KNILM was incorporated, a gentleman's agreement was concluded in Amsterdam. KLM conceded all intra-colonial routes in the East Indies to KNILM; while the latter agreed not to compete on the long-distance route to the homeland. This agreement was sustained throughout the Thirties. Each company held stock in the other to the value of 200,000 guilders. Both companies were subsidized, KLM by the Netherlands Government, which claimed 75 per cent of any profit that might be made, and KNILM was similarly subsidized by the colonial government in Batavia. KLM provided technical and operational assistance to the colonial cousin, including training, flight crews, and the delivery of aircraft. KNILM received its royal charter on 15 October 1928. It was a remarkable example of a colonial airline being able to exert a powerful influence over the authorities in the home country and to be able to make decisions with a substantial degree of independence from the dictates of the ruling power, during an era when customarily strict control was normally exerted from Europe or the United States in Far Eastern colonial affairs.

A KNILM Fokker F.VII/3m at Bandoeng. (*Courtesy John Stroud*)

KNILM Spreads Its Wings

Only two weeks after being granted its royal charter, KNILM opened its first route, from Batavia to Semarang on 1 November 1928, using a Fokker F.VII/3m eight-seat aircraft. Later on the same day, a second service opened to Bandoeng (now Bandung), which was a popular retreat in the mountain foothills, rather like the hill-stations in India. These two routes were short – Semarang was only 250 miles from Batavia, and Bandoeng half that distance – but they served as training grounds for the fledgling company, which wisely did not try to expand too soon. Both were in Java and so, as yet, no over-water risks had to be taken. But aerodromes were built, the fleet was augmented from the single F.VIIb/3m to a fleet of seven, and KLM crews were seconded from the Netherlands.

The Semarang route was extended to Surabaya, Java's (and the East Indies') second city, in 1929; and the first over-water route, albeit a short one across the Sunda Strait to the island of Sumatra, opened to Palembang early in 1930. Then, on 27 September of that year, this latter line was extended to Medan, an important city at the northern end of Sumatra. Routed also via Pakanbaroe, the Batavia–Medan journey time was reduced from the several days by surface transport (a combination of sea, rail, and primitive road) to only ten hours. Surabaya–Batavia–Palembang–Medan was an important trunk artery, as long, for example, as London to Athens or New York to Houston, and an important indication of the vigour and initiative that was to characterize Dutch airline development throughout the prewar era, helping to lay the foundations of the world's airline route network today. Furthermore a branch line opened on 4 March 1930, from Palembang to Singapore, to classify KNILM as an international flag carrier.

Such was the momentum that KNILM acquired two Fokker F.XIIs, fitted with 16 seats each, to supplement the smaller F.VIIas. But then, in a curious repetition of KLM's experience, KNILM's fortunes waned, as a general depression in trade led to a reduction of the government subsidy to only twenty per cent of the original amount, barely enough to pay the fuel tax. The connection from Medan to

Alor Star, in the northern Federated Malay States, begun in 1933, was terminated, and the service to Singapore was interrupted for a few months.

Fortunately, this was only a temporary lapse in KNILM's progress. In the mid-1930s, route expansion was resumed, with new services to Bali and to Makassar (now Ujung Padang) in Celebes (Sulawesi). The services to Sumatra, already twice weekly, were doubled, and then doubled again; and in 1936, another spoke in the pattern linked Batavia and Surabaya with Netherlands Borneo, to Banjermassim, Balikpapan and Tarakan, the centre of oil production and an outpost of Royal Dutch Shell.

True International Status

While the branch line to Singapore, operated by KNILM in conjunction with KLM, was technically an international route, it was a regional connection, and represented only a relatively minor geographical diversion from KLM's trunk line from Europe. During the latter 1930s, however, the Dutch airline authorities, working together, set their sights much higher. Recognizing the strategic advantage of the Netherlands East Indies in the matter of bargaining for traffic rights, KLM and KNILM realized that a route from Europe to Australia was within their grasp. Before the Second World War, no commercial aircraft was able to overfly such a large territorial expanse as the Netherlands East Indies, much in the same way as British India, and parts of the Middle East at that time, could have barred the way to aircraft that did not have permission from London.

The issue had been recognized back in the latter 1920s, when the British were planning an air route to India, using airships. Two massive craft were built, the R100 and the R101, but the idea ended in disaster when the R101 crashed in France on 5 October 1930. By this time, the British and Dutch were wrangling over landing rights in Baghdad (then under a League of Nations-blessed British Mandate) and through India, with the British procrastinating until Imperial Airways was ready to start its own service to Delhi. The opposition from the Indian Department of Industries and Labour – India enjoyed Dominion status within the framework of the British Empire – was intensified when Plesman requested permission to make some proving flights to Batavia. But cooler heads prevailed, and the Dutch were allowed to proceed. Unable to claim that the aerodromes were inadequate, the British Foreign Office saved its face by negotiating similar traffic rights beyond Singapore in preparation for a future extension of the Imperial Airways route to Australia. An agreement, formalized by an exchange of notes on 3 June 1930, must have been, effectively, one of the first examples of a bilateral air agreement, achieved by some old-fashioned horse-trading.

Nevertheless, there was much bickering during the decade of the Thirties, as both the British and the Dutch manoeuvred for position. The Dutch scored an impressive point when, in the England–Australia Air Race of October 1934, a KLM Douglas DC-2 completed the course in less than four days, all the way from Mildenhall to Melbourne, Plesman's flamboyant coup with the *Uiver*, however, intended to strengthen his hand, actually stiffened British resistance, and diplomatic relations were not improved between the two countries.

With British prestige at stake, the Dutch had to stand by and watch the inauguration of a British Commonwealth service to Australia, with Imperial Airways linking resources with Australia's QANTAS, on 8 December 1934. The dice then fell towards KLM/KNILM in an unpredictable way. In December 1934, in response to the embarrassment to the British aircraft industry provided by the

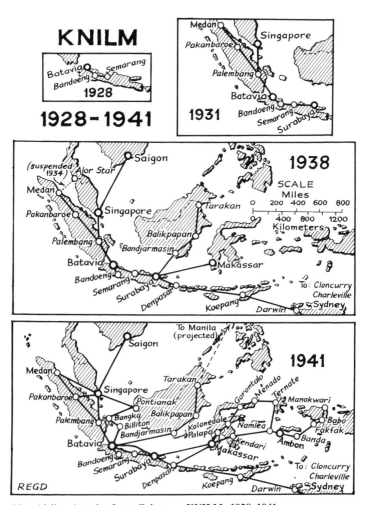

Maps 16a. Airline Arteries for a Colony — KNILM, 1928–1941

Dutch merchants in what was, until the wave of independence swept across Asia in the postwar period, the wealthy Netherlands East Indies, started their own airline. Beginning with a short route in Java in 1928, KNILM (always pronounced K'nilm) expanded throughout the extensive colony which, from west to east, covered an area — admittedly mostly water — that was wider than the continental United States. The insular nature of the colony made it ideal for airline work; and the strategic position of the NEI enabled KNILM to operate to Australia, as an extension of KLM's route from Amsterdam.

DC-2 (which had flown to Australia almost as quickly as a specially-built British de Havilland Comet racing aeroplane) the British Government announced the launching of the Empire Air Mail Scheme. It ordered a large number of four-engined Short S.23 flying-boats 'off the drawing board' so as to provide superior comfort, as well as comparable speed, to compete with the Douglases. This played into Dutch hands. The S.23s did not have sufficient range to fly from Singapore

170

to Darwin, the nearest point in Australia, without a refuelling stop. The Imperial/Qantas partnership had to have flying-boat bases in the Netherlands East Indies. The Australians did not like it, but had to comply with Dutch demands, having been forced to create, on 18 January 1934, a joint venture, Qantas Empire Airways (QEA) to overcome British versus Australian sensitivities in starting the London–Sydney service referred to. Interestingly, the eastern portion of the long intercontinental route from Europe to Australia was operated under the administrations of the Colonial/Commonwealth Governments of both the British and the Dutch empires.

In May 1931 KNILM's Fokker F.VIIb/3m *Abel Tasman* made an experimental mail flight from Batavia to Melbourne. (*Courtesy John Stroud*)

On 12 May 1932, KNILM had made an experimental mail flight when *Abel Tasman* a Fokker F.VIIb/3m flew from Batavia to Melbourne, via Timor, Wyndham and across northern Australia, to arrive on 18 May. The appropriately-named (if rather cheeky from a British viewpoint – Tasman had been the Dutch explorer who mapped out most of Australia) aircraft returned on 24 May, arriving in Batavia only four days later. But six frustrating years passed before the Australian Government finally granted, on 22 February 1938, permission for KNILM to start its service. On 3 July of that year a twice weekly service began, using Lockheed 14s, from Batavia to Sydney, as an extension of KLM's route from Amsterdam, now operated by the famous Douglas DC-3s.

The KLM/KNILM service, sharing the honour as the world's longest air route was superior to Imperial's in many respects. The Short flying-boats were undoubtedly comfortable to fly in, with ample room in a promenade deck and overnight stops in romantic places (where passengers were even known to dress for dinner); but the Douglases and Lockheeds provided a more reliable and faster service. This was not necessarily a reflection on the technical merits of the flying-boats in terms of speed or performance; but on the ponderous arrangements that had to be made for handling the waterborne craft at the stopping points, and their vulnerability to the whims of the sea and inland waterways.

The combined Dutch service was so demonstrably superior that 43 per cent of its traffic, at least as far as Batavia, were British subjects, mostly businessmen who were not so affected by patriotism as were the government officials. But within a year, the onset of the Second World War dashed all hopes of a Dutch

In July 1938 KNILM opened a Batavia—Sydney service with Lockheed 14s, thus providing a through Dutch service from the Netherlands. A KNILM Lockheed 14 is seen here at Brisbane. (*KNILM*)

challenge to the British connection to Australia. On 1 August 1939, the twice-weekly service to Sydney was reduced to one. At the European end KLM moved its terminus from Amsterdam to Naples on 16 September 1939, and then, following the Nazi invasion of the Netherlands on 10 May 1940, and with Italy entering the War in June, the Dutch route was curtailed out of Europe altogether, on 26 July, to Lydda, Palestine (now Lod-Tel Aviv, Israel). By this time, on 19 June, QEA had suspended service from Sydney to Singapore, and KNILM/KLM continued to carry the mails for the Australian Government. The Lockheed 14s were replaced by DC-3s purchased from KLM. All night flying was eliminated, as was the stop at Brisbane, and two night stops were introduced on the Batavia–Sydney segment of the now tortuous route to the United Kingdom via India and Africa.

This marriage-of-convenience lasted little more than a year, although a twice-weekly frequency was restored on 2 January 1942. No sooner had this been done when the Japanese invaded Java. All KNILM services were suspended in February as the airline rallied to provide an evacuation service for stranded Dutch people, fleeing from the invaders. Many flights were made to Australia and some aircraft were saved, including several Douglas DC-5s, recently introduced. Some were used by the United States armed forces, some were captured or destroyed, and one, at least, was shot down while carrying gold to Australia from an East Indies bank. Interestingly, the Dutch had tried to negotiate rights from Tarakan to Manila, Philippines, still a United States territory in the 1930s, but had met Pan American-inspired opposition until November 1940, when provisional and informal permission was given to KNILM to operate charter flights, carrying mail. It was a sad end to a noble enterprise of airline initiative in the great traditions of the air transport industry

A Comprehensive Colonial Air System

During all this complicated game of politics and industrial rivalry, KNILM had been going about its domestic business of fashioning a complete airline system

KNILM was an operator of Douglas DC-2s. One is seen here in company with de Havilland 86s of Imperial Airways and Qantas Empire Airways.

throughout the length and breadth of the Netherlands East Indies. Parenthetically, it also added another international air route, from Batavia to Saïgon, then in French Indo-China (now Vietnam), beginning on 1 September 1938, and operated twice weekly via Singapore with Lockheed 14s. By this time KNILM boasted a fleet of fifteen modern aircraft, mostly Douglases as well as a couple of Lockheeds, and, (in the light of past confrontations, rather surprisingly) a de Havilland D.H.89A.

Because of the difficulties of building airstrips in the tropical rain forests, where a well-rolled runway could become a sea of mud in half an hour during the monsoons, KNILM started to develop its air routes to the outer islands with flying-boats. On 21 August 1940, a new Grumman G-21A Goose amphibian, fitted with four seats, reached New Guinea by extending the Batavia–Surabaya–Makassar route via Ambon, in the Moluccas. The same aircraft type also started a circuitous route from Makassar to Ambon, via points in northern Celebes and Ternate, on 1 October of the same year. Then, in February and April of 1941 respectively, both routes were upgraded by the introduction of 16-seat Sikorsky S-43 amphibians, and this released the Grummans for service on another 'puddle-jumping' route from Batavia to Singapore, calling at a couple of small islands and at Pontianak, in western Borneo.

Meanwhile, on the main routes, within Java and to Palembang, the new 26-seat Douglas DC-5 had entered service, starting in September 1940 on the short Batavia–Bandoeng route. The DC-5 was thought to be the answer to the design problem that has eluded the best brains in the aircraft industry to this day: to produce a 'DC-3 Replacement' that was the equal of the 1936 veteran in terms of practical airline economics. The DC-5 was about the same size and was the first commercial aircraft to be equipped with a nosewheel, so that loading and unloading could be managed with the cabin on an even keel. Early in 1941, KNILM was

Douglas DC-5s entered service with KNILM in September 1940. This one is seen with a Netherlands West Indies registration.

able to introduce an evening service along the north coast of Java, to Surabaya via Semarang, thus permitting businessmen and others to make the round trip in a single day. Interestingly, these same cities were to receive similar priority service treatment some thirty or so years later, when Garuda Indonesian Airways began no-reservation shuttle services with Fokker F.28 jets and Douglas DC-9s – a latter-day heritage and an historical link with the two aircraft companies that had provided the foundations for Dutch airline ascendancy during air transport's formative years.

Thus, as the map shows, KNILM had fulfilled all the dreams, and more besides, of the Dutch merchants who needed an air service to help protect their interests in the far-flung Indoneisan archipelago. It provided trunkline service to all the big islands: Java, Sumatra, Borneo and Celebes; and to many of the small ones: to Bali and Timor in the south, and to Ternate and Ambon in the east. And its domain stretched as far as Manokwari, in distant New Guinea, which in postwar years was to be transformed into the Netherlands' last colonial foothold of the East Indies.

Among the Indonesians, the KNILM acronym for Koninklijke Nederlandsche-Indische Luchtvaart Maatschappij was humorously transcribed to mean Kalau Naik Ini Lekas Mati, which in Indonesian means 'if you use this, you die sooner'. Sadly the phrase was all too prophetic; for KNILM never flew again under its own proud name after the Japanese invasion. After the end of the Second World War air services within the Dutch East Indies were resumed by the Air Force, the Militaire Luchtvaart Dienst, and then KLM took over the former KNILM network, on behalf of the Netherlands Government, on 1 August 1947. Little remained except distant memories of an efficient airline, and the insatiable curiosity of airline historians who have been fascinated by the ultimate fate of the Douglas DC-5s, whose only operator in commercial service was KNILM. The last known example was reduced to scrap in Israel in 1974, having ended its career in Australia first with the RAAF and, from 1945 to 1947, with Australian National Airways.

174

Het Interinsulair Bedrijf (IIB)

The political situation in the Netherlands East Indies during the years immediately following the Second World War was complex, often confused, and sometimes hazardous. This was a large area for an entire administration, with extensive trading organizations, to evacuate, especially in the shadow of determined moves towards independence that were occasionally belligerent, not to mention the dangers from Indonesian warring factions themselves.

No sooner had Japan surrendered, following the dropping of the two atom bombs on 6 and 9 August 1945, to the Allies on 14 August, when the Dutch resumed air services within the liberated territory. On 15 August – the day after the surrender – air services were resumed by the 19th (Dutch) Squadron of the Royal Australian Air Force, using a fleet of thirteen Dakotas (DC-3s), four North American TB-25 Mitchell converted bombers, and five Lockheed L-12s. These were augmented in October 1945 by seventeen more DC-3s from the US Forces in Manila; and on 1 February 1946 the unit became known as the Vliegtuig Transport Group (VTG) or the Netherlands Indies Government Air Transport Group (NIGAT). Air transport services were provided to neighbouring countries, including routes to Bangkok via Singapore, and Manila via Balikpapan and Pelawan.

One of the four Consolidated PBY-5A Cansos used by IIB on routes from Batavia in 1947.
(*Joop Gerritsma*)

Meanwhile, when KLM took over the network and organization of KNILM on 1 August 1947 it immediately established a local autonomous unit, Het Interinsulair Bedrijf (IIB) (The Inter-island Service). The Dutch airline paid 243,750 florins for the acquisition, which was not much – but there was not much to acquire, as all the aircraft fleet had disappeared and the ground installations were largely destroyed. The IIB began service a month later with four 14-seat Consolidated PBY-5A Canso amphibians on routes from Batavia (Jakarta) to Pontianak, Samarinda and Tarakan; and to Singapore via Billiton, Bangka, Singkep and Tandjoeng Pinang. It also operated charter flights to the copra plantations in Celebes (Sulawesi) and to the Moluccas.

In November 1947, more as a gesture than in hope of establishing a service, the

19th Squadron made a survey flight with a Douglas DC-4 across the Pacific, via Manila, to Los Angeles; but the end was near for Dutch operations in the dying months of sovereignty in the East Indies. On 1 April 1948, the IIB took over the fleet of DC-3s and DC-4s from the 19th Squadron, and carried on also with its Canso operations to places where lakes or rivers substituted for airfields. By the time when, on 19 December 1949, Indonesian sovereignty was proclaimed to establish the new State, the IIB had carried 508,000 passengers, 14,500 tons of freight and 4,000 tons of mail. It had performed its task of helping the Dutch nationals scattered all over the East Indies to repatriate themselves back to the mother country.

THE CATALINA ROUTES
OF
K L M's INTERINSULAIR BEDRIJF (IIB)
IN 1947

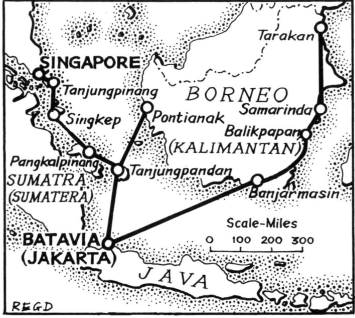

Map 16b. The Catalina Routes of KLM's Interinsulair Bedrijf (IIB)
The proud flag of KNILM never flew again after the Netherlands East Indies were abruptly occupied by the Japanese at the end of 1941. And in the post-war years, the rise of nationalism, which resulted in the creation of Indonesia, prevented the smooth resumption of air services. For a brief period, however, the Dutch flag carrier, KLM, took over a few of the former KNILM routes in 1947, and operated them for a while, under the divisional name Het Interinsulair Bedrijf (IIB). This map shows the routes operated by Consolidated PBY-5A Cansos.

CHAPTER SEVENTEEN

Airlines of Indonesia

Political Cauldron

After the defeat of Japan and the end of the Second World War in 1945, a wave of nationalism, much of it communist-inspired, swept over southeast Asia. With the possible exception of Burma, which seceded from the British Commonwealth in 1948, nowhere was this spirit more widespread and determined than in the Netherlands East Indies, where, for many years, undercurrents of an uprising against the colonial administration had been rife, but had been forced underground by the unsympathetic Japanese occupation forces, the military advance guard for the vision of the Greater East Asia Co-Prosperity Sphere, with headquarters in Tokyo.

The political situation contained all the ingredients for sustained conflict. Unlike British India, with its contiguous land mass, and with the benefit of an excellent railway system to act as a unifying element, the Netherlands East Indies was composed of four large islands, about a dozen medium-sized ones, and 13,600 small ones which, together with the western half of New Guinea, was spread over an area wider than the United States. Except in Java, which accounted for about two thirds of the population, communication between the islands was, until the 1930s, entirely by sea, until relieved in the 1930s by a fine airline, KNILM which, however, carried almost exclusively the Dutch administrators and the occasional foreign visitor.

Balancing these divisive elements, the rich Dutch colony that was to become Indonesia did possess one unifying element. Except for the island of Bali, a Buddhist enclave, all the 13,600 islands, not counting the uninhabited ones, had a common religion. Today's Indonesia is, in population, the largest Moslem country in the world. Yet even this common element held the seeds of civil unrest, for the main advocates of postwar independence for Indonesia were communists; and while these potential revolutionaries were feared by the Dutch, they were not held in great esteem either by the Moslem majority of the Indonesian people.

The leading protagonist for a free Indonesia was the charismatic Achmed Sukarno, who became a national leader, proclaiming Five Principles in the national struggle, and, in 1945, almost before the Japanese left, proclaiming the foundation of the Indonesian Republic. The situation was extremely delicate. The Dutch colonialists had given very little to the indigenous peoples in sharing the benefits of administration, commerce, and social development with them. Whereas in British India, in spite of the harsh realities of a civil war and religious strife, there was an army of Indian administrators, businessmen, and disciplined armed forces ready and able to take over the many-faceted elements of government, the Indonesians had been almost entirely deprived of them. The Netherlands East Indies had never made any pretence of being a self-governing commonwealth or dominion; it was simply a colony, whose main – almost the only – mission was to provide raw materials, including food and minerals, to the Netherlands. The

Indonesians, therefore, not only had to fight for their independence; but once achieved, they had to start from scratch.

Some internal tension was removed in 1946 by the Treaty of Linggadjati, which led to a loose union with eastern Indonesia, where the peoples of the Moluccas did not readily accept the leadership from Java. The Dutch were also doing their best to repress the spirit of independence by strong-armed police action, but this led to the United Nations persuading the Netherlands to host a round-table conference in The Hague, resulting in the announcement of the foundation on 19 December 1949, of the United States of Indonesia. Such was the extent of suspicion of the new centralized government in Jakarta (formerly Batavia) that from 1950 until 1952, the Republic of the Southern Moluccas, centred on the vigorous city of Ambon, declared itself independent.

But there was no turning back. The obvious inevitability of independence took its course. The Dutch gradually surrendered the reins of government and by 1956 the dissolution of any form of political union with the Netherlands was complete. There were rebellions everywhere throughout the archipelago, especially in Sumatra, but eventually Sukarno, as president, with Mohammed Hatta as prime minister, took over supreme power.

Indonesian Airways

While all this political strife was threatening to tear the infant country apart before it had found its first legs, an enterprising young man was earning his wings. Cometh the hour, cometh the man, and Wiweko Supono seems to have been the right man, in the right spot, at the right time. On 16 June 1948, as a goodwill gesture to the people of Banda Aceh, in northern Sumatra, and more than 1,000 miles from Jakarta, Achmed Sukarno, self-proclaimed president of the embryo republic, had presented a model of a C-47/DC-3 to the local dignitaries. This was a symbol of the future Indonesian Government's intention to provide an air service, and the response was prompt and effective. The local merchants raised a subscription – 40 kg of gold, no less – to buy an actual aircraft, and one was located, with spare parts as well, in Singapore. Wiweko Supono headed a small team of newly recruited airmen to collect the aircraft and bring it to Jakarta. Registered as RI-001 and named *Seulewah*, after a mountain in northern Sumatra, it maintained a link between Java and Sumatra, at a time when the Dutch armed forces were conducting a rearguard action against the independence movement, partly by blockading communications between Batavia (as the Dutch still called Jakarta) and the outer islands.

By now in charge of a quasi-airline, Wiweko followed the spirit of Indonesia's independence, making an historic flight in October 1948, when he flew the prime minister, Mohammed Hatta, from Jokjakarta (Java) to Sumatra, calling at Jambi and Payakumbuh before arriving triumphantly at Banda Aceh. After taking *Seulewah* to Calcutta for a necessary 50-hour overhaul, he flew the aircraft to Rangoon, because sporadic violence between the Dutch and the Indonesians prevented his return home. He might have been shot down, literally, but the risks were no less in his adopted base. Ostensibly flying ad hoc charters from Rangoon to Mandalay and Moulmein, his role was as a one-man transport command, helping the fledgling Burmese Government to combat the guerilla insurgency launched from the mountains bordering Thailand, Laos and China, particularly from the Karen tribesmen. Wiweko had arrived in the Burmese capital on 26 January 1949, and had founded Indonesian Airways two days later, to give legit-

RI-001 *Seulewah*, the Douglas C-47 presented to Indonesian Airways by merchants in Sumatra.

imacy to the operation, not to mention a source of revenue, as the airline's contract with the Burmese authorities brought in enough money to buy two more DC-3s and to hire more pilots and staff.

On 19 December 1949 Indonesia gained full independence and Indonesian Airways returned to its homeland. The team of young officers took their fleet back to Jakarta and were drafted into the Air Force. The national airline, Garuda Indonesian Airways, was founded on 31 March 1950 and the now redundant Indonesian Airways was dissolved in the following August. The little pioneering company had been both an inspiration and a training ground for Indonesia's future air transport industry. As for Wiweko himself, the spirit of innovative enterprise that had characterized his young career was to re-surface in 1968, when he took over the presidency of Garuda, to begin a new era in that airline's tempestuous history.

The Garuda Takes Wing

The new airline was named after, rather surprisingly, a Hindu mythological creature, part eagle, part man, that bore the god Vishnu through the heavens. More to the point – and hence the symbolism – the Garuda also provided a feeder service by transporting minor gods around the Indonesian archipelago. For a predominantly Moslem country to adopt a symbol of one of its minority religions is perhaps a good example of the universality of the airline world and airline people who readily cast aside political or religious intolerance or misunderstanding in the furtherance of their vocation, which is to carry everybody and everything from one place to another, in the service of Mankind as a whole.

The challenges to undertake this noble task were formidable indeed for this new airline, which actually got under way within a week of Indonesian independence on 19 December 1949. This was believed to be the date when the first Garuda Indonesian Airways aircraft made its first flight, but the company was officially

179

Garuda Indonesian Airways' first Convair CV-240, with US temporary registration, before delivery. (*Consolidated Vultee*)

registered under that name on 31 March 1950. At that time, it was jointly owned by the new Indonesian Government and the Dutch national airline, Koninklijke Luchtvaart Maatschappij (KLM), representing the former Dutch administration which was now undertaking the painful task of handing over its vast East Indian empire to its original owners, the Indonesians.

It was an uneasy alliance. The Dutch administration and the Dutch merchants, the Dutch coffee and tea planters, and the Dutch timber and oil men: the vast majority of them went back to the land of their fathers. Some families traced their ancestry back to the early days, centuries earlier, when the progressive initiative of the settlers tapped the untold wealth of the Indonesian islands. Others were of more recent origin, and some were transitory, in the Dutch armed forces. For many it was an emotional period of great stress. Some felt they were being banished from their own country; others were glad to go. Whether in the sense of fleeing from believed oppression or simply abandoning a lifetime's work, there was much bitterness.

Under the circumstances, the handing over of the KLM/KNILM assets to Garuda could have been accompanied by far more trial and tribulation than actually occurred. Airline people are airline people and seem to be a special breed whose devotion to the cause of air transport transcends petty prejudices or even major ones. Many KLM employees left in disgust; but many stayed on to oil the wheels of political transition. Garuda inherited twenty-two Douglas DC-3s and eight Consolidated Canso amphibians from KLM (which had taken over the former KNILM in 1945) and had itself acquired a fleet of transport aircraft from Allied war surplus sources. These were augmented in 1950 by eight Convair 240s, the first pressurized airliners to enter service within Indonesia; and eight de Havilland four-engined D.H.114 Heron feederliners were added in 1953. Eight more Convairs, Model 340s, and six more Herons were further added in 1954, so that, with a fleet of sixty aircraft, Garuda was in a position to fashion an airline route network that would serve the nation with a comprehensive domestic route system, modelled on that of the prewar KNILM, and to open international services to nearby foreign points, Singapore, Manila and Bangkok.

On 12 July 1954, Garuda Indonesian Airways exercised its right to acquire the KLM shareholding, but – echoing the sentiments already outlined – KLM techni-

One of Garuda's early fleet of de Havilland Heron 1s. (*de Havilland*)

cians remained as technical advisors, in maintenance, operations, and administration, as the Indonesians, mostly young in age as well as experience, learned the intricacies of running an airline. This period of collaboration lasted a little over two years. Most of the task involved unspectacular day-to-day work. The Herons were retired and, after a few years, sold as being unsatisfactory for the climate and terrain of Indonesia, and because of dissatisfaction with the unreliability of the engines. Three more Convairs, the Model 440, were ordered before the KLM people left in September 1956.

At the same time, and possibly on the advice of the KLM advisors, Garuda ordered its first turbine-powered airliners, three Lockheed L-188 Electras, and these were delivered in the first few months of 1961. On 16 May of that year, an Electra opened Garuda's first service to Hong Kong, and on 13 March 1962, extended this to Tokyo. The Garuda bird was beginning to flex its wings.

Garuda Jets World-wide

Rather like the Philippines, also with newly-acquired independence, Indonesia's need for an efficient air transport system as a public utility to unify the country with rapid access and communication was vital, simply because it was an island nation. Densely-populated Java itself had only a barely adequate railway system and a network of roads; and elsewhere, railways were rare; in fact only Sumatra had any at all, and this consisted of several isolated lines. Indonesia therefore needed a good airline service, not only to provide the obvious links between the islands; it also needed air routes within the larger islands, especially Sumatra (more than a thousand miles long), Kalimantan (formerly Borneo), and Sulawesi (formerly Celebes). During the 1950s and 1960s, such a network was built up with the veteran DC-3s, complemented by successive models of the pressurized Convair twins, the 240, 340, and 440.

181

Garuda was the fourteenth airline to receive Lockheed L-188 Electras. When delivered it completed what was then the longest Electra delivery flight – 11,052 miles from Burbank to Jakarta. (*Lockheed*)

Garuda Indonesian Airways also had the responsibility of carrying the republic's flag overseas, and this was no easy task. On all the international routes, it faced competition from well-established airlines from Europe, and from the more developed nations of east Asia. These airlines could often draw upon considerable experience from overseas partnerships with some of the world's leaders. Garuda, on the other hand, with lingering coolness in its relations with KLM, with whom it had deliberately broken off cordial co-operation in 1956, seemed to have handicapped itself by taking the spirit of independence to the extreme. For a young country, the fact that Garuda Indonesian Airways managed to elevate itself into the ranks of intercontinental jet airlines as soon as it did is to its considerable credit.

On 20 November 1963, it introduced the Convair 990A on its routes within east Asia, to Tokyo, Hong Kong, Singapore, Bangkok and Manila, supplementing th Electras. The latter propeller-turbine airliner, meanwhile, was able to inaugurate a route to mainland China, when on 6 January 1965, it opened service from Jakarta to Canton (now Guangzhou), via Phnom Penh in Cambodia. At this time Garuda was one of the few airlines to serve the People's Republic, which was then all but cut off from the rest of the world, even the Soviet Union which had abruptly severed ties and had withdrawn all its technicians in 1960. But important though they were, the regional routes in east Asia were upstaged by the opening of a major intercontinental artery to Europe.

In spite of the vicissitudes of the difficult transition from utterly dependent colony to sovereign nation, a transition that was fraught with danger and crisis from time to time, the fences between Indonesia and the Netherlands were gradually mended. Diplomatic relations improved from the frigid to the normal and when Garuda Indonesian Airways felt ready to make its intercontinental debut, the choice of Amsterdam as the European destination came as no surprise. The Dutch tradition in aviation in the East Indies had not been entirely eradicated. KLM's training programmes of the early 1950s, though terminated, had left its mark; and most educated Indonesians spoke Dutch. Accordingly, on 30 March 1965, a Convair 990A flew to the Netherlands, via Bangkok (already a Garuda station),

At the end of 1963 Garuda introduced Convair 990As on routes within East Asia including Hong Kong and Tokyo.

Bombay, Cairo, Rome, Prague and Frankfurt. The service was operated twice weekly, with Phnom Penh alternating with Bangkok on the first; and with Paris alternating with Prague and Frankfurt on the second. Jakarta was thus linked with four European destinations. The 990As were superseded by Douglas DC-8s on 12 August 1966.

But there was cause for concern with the administration of the airline, which had acquired a reputation for unreliable timekeeping and worse, unreliable maintenance and flying. In January 1966, there were two DC-3 accidents in Sumatra, and on 16 February 1967, an Electra crashed at Menado, Sulawesi. With only one DC-8 and three Convair 990s, Garuda was hard pressed to provide the frequency and capacity needed to compete with the strength and experience of its neighbour airlines.

Much of the blame was placed on the Government's control and influence over its national airline, wholly-owned since the expulsion of KLM in 1954. President Sukarno tended to regard it simply as a branch of the administration, and used Garuda as though it were an expanded Air Force One. Indonesian Government officials travelled on Garuda almost at will, for any reason and free of charge. Aircraft would be commandeered for official flights without regard to the inconvenience caused, either to the paying passengers or to Indonesian prestige abroad. The attitude to the airline, which was heavily subsidized to compensate for its inefficiency, was typical of Sukarno's approach in every field of social and political activity; and in March 1968, as pressure built up, he was replaced as president of Indonesia by Suharto. One of the new president's first moves was to call upon Wiweko Supono, now an Air Commodore in the Indonesian Air Force, to put things right in the national airline.

183

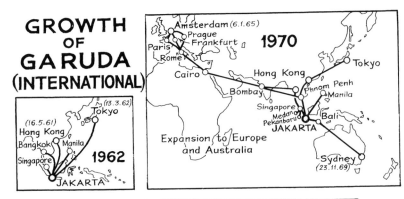

GROWTH OF GARUDA (INTERNATIONAL)

1962

(16.5.61)
(13.3.62)
Tokyo
Hong Kong
Bangkok
Manila
Singapore
JAKARTA

1970

Amsterdam (6.1.65)
Prague
Frankfurt
Paris
Rome
Cairo
Tokyo
Hong Kong
Bombay
Phnom Penh
Manila
Singapore
Medan
Pekanbaru
Bali
JAKARTA
Expansion to Europe and Australia
Sydney (23.11.69)

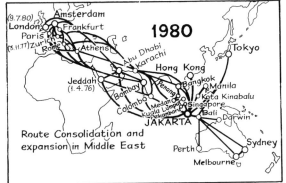

1980

(9.7.80)
Amsterdam
London
Paris
Frankfurt
Rome
Zurich
Athens
(3.11.77)
Abu Dhabi
Karachi
Tokyo
Hong Kong
Jeddah
(1.4.76)
Bombay
Penang
Bangkok
Manila
Colombo
Medan
Kota Kinabalu
Kuala Lumpur
Singapore
Pekanbaru
Bali
Darwin
JAKARTA
Route Consolidation and expansion in Middle East
Perth
Sydney
Melbourne

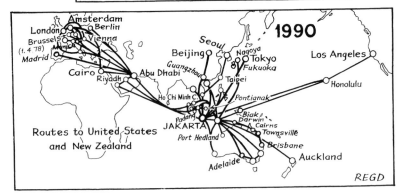

1990

Amsterdam
Berlin
London
Brussels
Vienna
Munich
(1.4.78)
Madrid
Seoul
Beijing
Nagoya
Tokyo
Los Angeles
Cairo
Guangzhou
Fukuoka
Riyadh
Abu Dhabi
Taipei
Honolulu
Ho Chi Minh C.
Pontianak
Padang
Biak
Darwin
JAKARTA
Cairns
Port Hedland
Townsville
Routes to United States and New Zealand
Brisbane
Adelaide
Auckland
REGD

Maps 17a. Growth of Garuda International

The transition from colonial status to independence was the source of much stress on both sides. The Dutch residents were more than simply usurping colonists of recent origin. Their roots went back for many generations, and the departure of most of them was a painful experience. But the airline tradition rose above the conflicts (which were less damaging than predicted) and a new airline, named after the mythological creature that bore the god Vishnu through the heavens, arose to begin a new era.

184

The New Broom

Wiweko took over Garuda Indonesian Airways on 17 February 1968. As a new broom, he did not simply sweep clean. He used harsh scouring methods and simultaneously applied actions reminiscent of a hurricane carving its way through an unprepared and complacent township. He fired the entire top management and dismissed half the staff. But he doubled the wages of those that remained, demanding only that they came to work each day and put in a good day's work. He replaced corruption with an example of personal integrity which was awe-inspiring.

Wiweko Supono can be regarded as the founder of Indonesian air transport.

During the interim period while he was out in the cold after his pioneering efforts with Indonesian Airways, he had, among other pursuits (such as improving his aeronautical knowledge by constructing light aircraft) obtained a master's degree in business administration at Berkeley, one of the finest universities in the United States. He did this in a year less than the normal requirement, and had a reputation for solving mathematical equations in his head while others were wrestling with their pocket calculators. He handled all the problems of high finance himself, and had the disconcerting habit of arriving at the office of an aircraft manufacturer's president, negotiating a price for a couple of airliners on the spot, and paying by cheque.

Such a business style was also disconcerting for his own staff, who had to get used to Wiweko making all the decisions. In his determination to balance Garuda's books, by cutting out all the administration wastage as well as all the official free flights, he became a one-man management. And he certainly succeeded. From an

185

Garuda Indonesian introduced 105-passenger Douglas DC-9s in 1969. (*McDonnell Douglas*)

inefficient and partially corrupt, subsidy-dependent collection of individuals, Wiweko turned Garuda into an airline that, whilst not perfect, was able to grow in international stature and to serve as a reliable communication agency for Indonesia's then 120 million widely-scattered people. Effectively, he introduced airline deregulation, by insisting that Garuda paid its way, by internal economies and sensible fare levels, much in the same way that the United States did on a wider scale in 1978.

Sweeping modernization plans were put into effect. For the main domestic routes, Wiweko ordered Douglas DC-9-30s and for the secondary routes, he went to Fokker, to resume an aviation connection that dated back to the earliest days of commercial aviation in the East Indies, and ordered F.27 Friendships. The former popular 105-seaters entered service in the spring of 1969, and immediately reduced the journey times from Jakarta to the more distant cities such as Medan, Makassar and Biak. The latter forty-seat Friendships began to replace the veteran DC-3s. On the long-distance routes, to overcome the temporary shortage of cash with which to buy new aircraft, Wiweko negotiated the lease of a DC-8-53 from KLM, at the same time disposing of the Convair 990s.

Fokker F.27 Friendships replaced DC-3s on domestic services of Garuda. One named *Merapi* is seen at Kemayoran International Airport, Jakarta. (*Fokker*)

Garuda operated one of the biggest fleets of Fokker F.28 Fellowships. (*Fokker*)

Through his initiative, and his own evaluation, he also ordered, in July 1971, the first small batch of 65-seat Fokker F.28 jets. These 'baby DC-9s' were to become one of the most important segments of Garuda's fleet, fitting neatly in between the DC-9s and F.27s in terms of capacity, at the same time displaying an ability to use quite small fields. Garuda was to become the world's largest operator of this versatile feeder jet, its total orders amounting to no less than 59. Carefully watching every rupiah, Wiweko's aircraft acquisition style was unspectacular. Ensuring that Garuda did not over-reach its financial resources, Wiweko never made a huge order that would attract headlines in the world's aviation press; but not a year went by in the early 1970s, without a visit to Fokker, or Douglas, to buy two more DC-9s, or three more F.28s, or to KLM (for more leases), so as to husband the airline's resources. The result was that, to replace the 1968 jet fleet of one DC-8 and three Convair 990As, by 1975, Garuda Indonesian Airways had three DC-8s, twelve DC-9s, and seventeen F.28s.

The increase of the jet fleet from four to thirty-two in seven years did not lead to a big increase in international routes, as emphasis was placed on modernizing the whole domestic system. But one important new route was inaugurated on 23 November 1969, when a DC-8 first flew to Sydney, stopping at Denpasar in Bali, en route. The Australian service was augmented to include Melbourne as a co-terminus in 1975. Also, service to Frankfurt and Singapore, suspended during the pre-Wiweko crisis, was resumed, and the addition of Taipei, Colombo and Karachi brought the number of international points served to fifteen.

Feeder Line Extraordinary

While Garuda Indonesian Airways was carrying the country's flag overseas, and linking all the main cities of the Republic, another airline emerged to take over the role as the country's major operator of secondary services to the smaller communities. And what an operation this has been! Variously described as Indonesia's second force airline, or its main feeder or regional operator, Merpati Nusantara Airlines almost defies precise definition. For this so-called regional airline's route network stretched the whole length of Indonesia, from Sabang off Sumatra's northwestern tip, to Merauke in southwestern Irian, 3,600 miles away; has operated, during its eventful life, a fleet of up to about sixty aircraft, of more than a dozen different types; and whose route network at one time included as many as 180 points.

Its beginnings were quite humble, tracing its origins to a small operation of the Indonesian Air Force in the remoter parts of Kalimantan (Borneo), founded in 1957 with four single-engined de Havilland Canada Otters (two of them float-planes) and two C-47s to provide a link with Jakarta. The Air Force started service in November 1958 and then handed over to Merpati Nusantara (the Airlines was added in 1969), when the Government decided to establish a State-owned airline to pioneer air routes in the Indonesian outback. Merpati Nusantara Airlines was officially constituted, under Government Regulation 19/1962, on 6 September 1962. It took over the small fleet from the Air Force and set about its work, under the direction of First Air Marshal Sutojo Adiputro.

Back to the Stone Age

Not long after taking over in Kalimantan, Merpati found itself charged with responsibility for providing air service to the remotest part of Indonesia, in far-off New Guinea. When the Dutch packed up their bags and said goodbye to their East Indian colony in the 1950s, the Republic of Indonesia did not immediately obtain sovereignty over the Dutch half of the island of New Guinea. Partly in recognition of the primitive state of this distant enclave – some of its peoples were discovered after the Second World War to have been so cut off from the rest of the world that they were literally living in stone age conditions – it remained as Netherlands New Guinea until 1963. The transfer of power was gradual, starting in 1961, when the name West Irian was adopted; and was finally completed by a plebiscite held in 1969. The local administrative capital, Hollandia, became Jayapura.

During this rather precarious interim period, the Dutch actually set up a local airline, named De Kroonduif, and made some progress connecting the coastal communities. They also enlarged the station and increased their presence at the offshore island of Biak, where the Japanese had first built their airstrip during the war. For a few short years, Biak became an important staging point on KLM's long route to Australia, when, because of a political stand-off, the Dutch flag carrier was unable to obtain stopping points – or even overflying rights – in India. KLM managed to fashion a route from Amsterdam to Sydney, by the Polar route, calling at Anchorage, Tokyo and Biak. This of course ended, as did De Kroonduif, when effective control passed to Indonesia.

At first, the Republic nominated Garuda Indonesian Airways, which had started a one-stop Electra route to Biak on 1 October 1962, to take over the New Guinea/West Irian routes. The Dutch personnel were repatriated, but the aircraft remained: four Douglas DC-3s, three de Havilland Canada DHC-2 Beaver float-planes; and three Prestwick Twin Pioneers, able to land in jungle clearings and in the alpine meadows of the high New Guinea mountains. A year later, however, Garuda in turn handed the West Irian problems, and the aircraft, to Merpati; and the little airline that had been born almost by accident began to grow. In 1965, Merpati acquired three Dornier Do 28 and eight Pilatus Porter aircraft, both types capable of operations from very small landing strips.

Merpati's task was not easy. Charged with serving tiny, isolated communities over hundreds of miles of featureless jungle or over mountain ranges higher than the Alps, the worst problem was in finding spare parts when anything went wrong with the aircraft. To maintain complete spares holdings was an expensive luxury that the small airline could not afford; yet the source of spare parts was on the other side of the world. Much of the airline's income was derived from a subsidy from the Dutch Government, which continued to pay the equivalent of several millions of pounds a year to maintain essential services, including an air service. But this was terminated in 1963, when the Dutch finally left. However, in addition, the Dutch had provided a large sum, equivalent to about thirty million pounds, to be used progressively for the development of New Guinea, now West Irian, and to be expended under the auspices of a United Nations fund. Most of this was to be used for developing the coastal towns, but an exception was the allocation to civil aviation, specifically to provide access to the Central Highlands, hitherto completely cut off from the world.

In 1967, under a UN aid programme, Merpati Nusantara Airlines received three de Havilland Canada Twin Otters. (*R E G Davies*)

Under this United Nations aid programme, Merpati Nusantara received, in 1967, three de Havilland Canada DHC-6 Twin Otters, ideal 20-seaters to fly the 200 miles from Jayapura up and over the lower chain of the New Guinea cordillera, only 10,000 feet high at that point: and land in the alpine meadows that doubled as airstrips. The UN also provided the necessary technical support to set up a maintenance base at Biak, specializing in DC-3s; and established a telecommunications network. Under the leadership of W C Krishnan, from India, the UN team, based at Biak, completely upgraded the operating standards of Merpati, from primitive hand-to-mouth methods suitable for bush flights to those of a modern airline.

In 1967 also, First Air Marshal Santoso took over as president and was able to witness the first service, in January 1968, of the versatile Twin Otter, an event that symbolized the turning point in Merpati's progress. During the next three years, the number of passengers carried grew six-fold, the volume of freight doubled, and the amount of mail transported grew from 35,000 kg to 335,000. This substantial growth was made possible by the acquisition of seven more DC-3s from Garuda and from Australia, and based at Biak. Merpati expanded its route structure throughout Indonesia, and even to neighbouring international points, Singapore and Kuching.

Vickers-Armstrongs Viscounts were added to Merpati's fleet in 1970. This one was named *Merauke.* (*R E G Davies*)

In 1969, Merpati Nusantara became Merpati Nusantara Airlines; and the change was more than mere window-dressing at the travel agents' premises. For in April 1970, it acquired its first modern airliners: two propeller-turbine Vickers Viscount 828s from All Nippon Airways. With these 68-seat aircraft, Merpati operated its first major route with modern equipment; and its name started to appear at the airports in the main cities of Java far more prominently than before. In December of 1970, also, it introduced the first of a fleet of 60-seat Nihon YS-11s, also from All Nippon. The following year saw the Hawker Siddeley 748s into service, each fitted with 46 seats, and then in March 1972, the first two Vickers Vanguards, with 135 seats, were added. These were the Series 952, ex-Air Canada, but these were replaced in 1974 by two ex-BEA Series 953s.

The propeller-driven turbine fleet operated in the shadow of Garuda's new jets, the DC-8s, DC-9s, and F.28s, but Merpati was not overawed, compensating for the rather longer journey times across Indonesia by offering lower fares, and often offering much better connections to some of the smaller and more remote destinations. After introducing the Vanguard, it was voted by the Jakarta Tourist Development Board as the best airline in Indonesia, an honour that could not have pleased Garuda's president, Wiweko, too much. Merpati was stepping out. In 1973, it inaugurated a Vanguard service from Jakarta to Jayapura, in Indonesia's farthest east, with only two stops, at Surabaya and Biak, making the journey (as far as the coast-to-coast trip in the United States) possible in only one day.

During the mid-1970s, Merpati Nusantara consolidated its position as Indonesia's major feeder airline. In November 1973, it acquired two Fokker F.27 Friendships, thus increasing the number of different types to seven, ranging from the Vanguard to the Twin Otter. But of these, all except the four DC-3s based at Biak were propeller-turbine powered; and of the fleet of 26, fifteen had Rolls-Royce Dart engines. The fleet was carefully deployed, each type allocated to the

In 1974 Merpati acquired two ex-British European Airways' Vickers-Armstrongs Vanguards, replacing two previously obtained from Air Canada. (*R E G Davies*)

routes best suited for its size and range; with the Twin Otters doing valiant work in the jungles and mountains. Dirgantara Air Service was established as a subsidiary company to serve the Sunda Islands, taking over the DC-3s; and to ease local administration, Merpati split into two groups in 1974, one, Merpati Operasi Barat (MOB) responsible for the main routes; and the other, Merpati Irian Barat (MIB), formerly Merpati Irian Jaya (MIJ), responsible for routes in New Guinea. These were later subdivided, in 1975, into four divisions: Jakarta/Sumatra, Sulawesi, Kalimantan, and Maluku (Moluccas)/Irian Jaya. Each operated almost autonomously.

Such expansion – this was the period when Merpati served more points than Lufthansa (albeit with a much lower traffic base) – was not without its problems. There were some heavy landings in the remote airstrips and occasionally a DC-3 was written off; but the maintenance base at Biak, possibly the last place in the world that could undertake complete DC-3 overhauls, did heroic work in keeping them flying. In 1972, a Viscount crashed near Padang, in Sumatra, and neither the aircraft nor those on board were ever seen again. The jungle simply swallowed them. Other problems were financial, as Merpati over-extended itself. With the best intentions, possibly remembering the confidence placed in it by the Tourist Board, it leased a Boeing 707 in 1977 and began charters to the United States, the Philippines and Japan, with inclusive tours to Bali. But this was not a success and had to be suspended in 1979 because of severe losses.

The Six Lives of Merpati Nusantara

Throughout its history, at least since the time when the Dutch Government withdrew its subsidy in 1967 and First Air Marshal Santoso was appointed president, Merpati Nusantara was vulnerable to repeated attempts by Wiweko Supono, head of Garuda, to reduce it to a subservient and ineffectual status in the framework of

Indonesian air transport as a whole. Wiweko, an almost puritanical man of high ethical standards, felt that Merpati was favoured by the Government and subject to abuses of many kinds, partly financial, partly operational and commercial. A D D 'Joe' Leimena, the energetic Ambonese planning director of Merpati, described the successive political sparring matches in feline terms as the six lives of Merpati.

The first was in 1967, when Wiweko tried, through his close contacts with the Government, to have Merpati formally wound up. He was unsuccessful. Quite the opposite: under First Air Marshal Santoso's leadership, Merpati expanded its domestic network and its influence in Indonesian air transport.

Next, in 1969, Wiweko tried again, this time to contain Merpati's responsibilities to the pioneer services in West Irian. Again, he was unsuccessful and to add salt to the wound, Merpati introduced the Viscount on some main routes. Far from being restricted, Merpati began to operate in parallel with Garuda. History repeated itself in 1971, and yet again the attack was repulsed, and this time, more salt was applied, by the introduction of the Vanguard.

Merpati survived its fourth life in 1974, when – not a man to give up easily – Wiweko campaigned to restrict Merpati once again to feeder routes. On this occasion, the Garuda president derived some satisfaction by persuading the civil aviation department to restrict Merpati's fleet to propeller-driven aircraft – no jets allowed. This indignity was shared by all other airlines in Indonesia, so that Garuda Indonesian Airways was confirmed as the country's only jet airline, placing it a different and higher stratum, aloof from the lower ranks.

Wiweko tried again in 1976, for the fifth time; and then, late in 1978, reinforced by reports of large financial losses by Merpati, amounting to 1.7 rupiahs (about $3,000,000) in the year, perseverance had its reward. On 26 October 1978, a Presidential decree announced by the Minister of Communications transferred the Indonesian Government shares in Merpati to Garuda. On 14 November, a further announcement reorganized Merpati as a sister company of Garuda, and effectively

A Merpati Fokker F.27 Friendship refuelling at Jayapura.

192

on 1 January 1979, the changes came into force. On scheduled services, Merpati had to withdraw from the longer trunk routes such as Jakarta–Medan and Jakarta–Ujungpandang–Biak; but it was allowed to retain short-haul international routes, such as Denpasar–Darwin, Medan–Penang, and Pontianak–Kuching. It was also allowed to fly international charters, but these would not include those to Los Angeles, which had incurred huge losses. Like other regional Indonesian airlines (Bouraq and Sempati) Merpati was allocated a minority share of charter flights to Jeddah, Saudi Arabia, during the Hajj pilgrimage period (Garuda enjoyed the lion's share of these, almost half the total); and it was charged with providing flights for the 'trans-migration' programme of population transfer, as Indonesia tried to relieve the problem of Java's high population density, one of the highest in the world, by subsidizing what amounted to constructive colonization of the more sparsely-peopled islands of Kalimantan, Sulawesi and Sumatra.

The total scope of Merpati Nusantara's operations (the airline was also becoming known by its initials, MNA) was thus not necessarily reduced in volume, only in direction and balance. On 5 January 1979, J A Lumenta, corporate secretary of Garuda, and a trusted Wiweko 'graduate', was appointed president of Merpati. Echoing the action of his chief when the latter took over Garuda in 1968, Lumenta furloughed 727 employees, including all the top management, reducing the staff to 878. A plan was evolved to retire the older aircraft types, and upgrade the fleet by adding more Fokkers and the new CASA 120 feederliner. With this, the final round of the Garuda-Merpati knock-out fight, and Merpati's sixth long count, a new life really did begin for the loser.

Wide-Bodied Long-Haul Routes for Indonesia

While Indonesia was thus painfully sorting out its domestic airline problems, Garuda was making steady progress under Wiweko's command. Although most of the world's leading airlines had quickly followed after Pan American launched the wide-bodied age in 1970, Wiweko bided his time until he felt that his airline was both technically and commercially ready to make this important leap forward. But in due course, on 1 April 1976, the first of six 270-seat McDonnell Douglas DC-10-30s entered service. PK-GIA *Irian Jaya* opened a nonstop route from Jakarta to Jeddah, and then flew on to Paris and Amsterdam. Additions to the fleet – each aircraft was named after one of Indonesia's larger islands – were not rushed, and neither were extensions to the international network. Nevertheless, Garuda gradually augmented its presence in Europe, adding DC-10 service to Zürich on 3 November 1977, to Brussels on 1 April 1978, and to London on 9 July 1980. Then, at the end of that year, on 1 December, Wiweko felt confident enough to replace the DC-10s with the larger Boeing 747s, of which four had been ordered, fitted with high-density seating layouts. Only 18 of the 425 seats were first class. With the introduction of the 747s on all the European routes, the DC-10s were used on the routes in east Asia, particularly to Tokyo and Singapore; to Australia; and on the busy domestic routes from Jakarta and Medan, Ujungpandang and Denpasar.

This last destination, on the island of Bali, was regarded by Wiweko as a valuable asset for Indonesia in negotiating bilateral agreements with other countries for routes and frequencies. He conducted a running battle with Thailand especially and with the British in Hong Kong, to the extent that traffic rights for direct service by Thai International and Cathay Pacific Airways were denied while wrangling

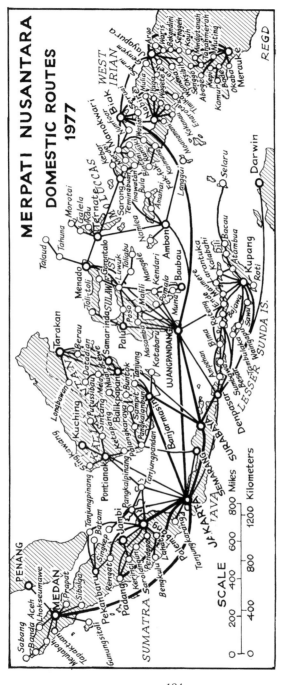

Map 17b. Merpati Nusantara Domestic Routes, 1977

Among so-called regional airlines, Merpati Nusantara was a giant. Its network reaches to the easternmost and westernmost extremities of Indonesia, from the mountain fastnesses of New Guinea to the island of Sabang, also the northernmost point of the nation. Its services included a few mainline routes between island capitals, but its feeder and bush networks are integrated with the trunk routes of Garuda. At its peak, Merpati called at no less than 128 points, of which about a third were otherwise inaccessible communities in West Irian, the Indonesian province of western New Guinea.

Garuda began operation of Douglas DC-10-30s in April 1976. (*McDonnell Douglas*)

continued. The foreign airlines were expected to fly only to Jakarta, whence Garuda would take the tourists to Bali; and for a while in the mid-Seventies, this was the procedure. Wiweko felt that these two airlines, particularly, were geographically situated whereby they could exercise the so-called Sixth Freedom rights by taking tourists from Europe or even Japan to Bali via Bangkok or Hong Kong, with no advantage to Indonesia. For several years this sparring seemed to favour first one, then the other, often reaching crisis point as, for example, in 1978, when Garuda actually stopped service to Bangkok, and initiated nonstop DC-10 services from Bali to Hong Kong.

Wiweko pursued his goals with single-minded determination. His opponents in negotiation would term his attitude as obstinate, even unreasonable; but he was acutely conscious that, in the eyes of other powerful air nations, including those of the rapidly growing industrial countries of east Asia, Indonesia was regarded as a young country, still half a lap behind the others in the technological race, and he was not to be patronized. Sometimes his impetuosity led to precipitate action, to make a point, as when, in 1977, Garuda withdrew from the Orient Airlines Association (OAA), the organization that had been set up by Filipino initiative in Manila to co-ordinate activities of mutual interest.

Garuda always seemed to be in the news. On 28 March 1981, a DC-9 en route from Palembang to Medan was hijacked by a group of Islamic extremists, and forced to fly to Bangkok. In a dramatic moment at 2.40 a.m. three days later, a 20-man assault team of Indonesian commandos freed the 42 hostages and four of the five crew, killing all five hijackers. The pilot was shot by the terrorists and the first commando to break into the aeroplane was also killed. They were both buried with full military honours in Jakarta, and the incident left an indelible mark, not only in injecting an additional sense of pride in the Garuda staff, but also in earning the respect of the airlines in general, who had been rather parsimonious in giving credit to Indonesia for anything.

By strict financial discipline, thrift, and conservatism, Wiweko had steered the Garuda ship well. The airline had always made profits for its owners, the Indonesian Government; but 1979 was a difficult year. This was when the DC-10s were grounded after the tragic crash at Chicago, and when the Indonesian rupiah was devalued by 33 per cent, depriving Garuda of a slice of its revenue. This was not allowed to interfere with Wiweko's long-term procurement plans, which included the acquistion of short-haul wide-bodied aircraft to keep pace with the traffic demands on the dense routes between Indonesia's larger cities. In

September 1977, he had visited the European Airbus production line at Toulouse, and had flown the A300. Never short of ideas and never shy about advancing them, Wiweko recommended a new cockpit layout, eliminating the flight engineer. Already operating 68 jet aircraft (four 747s, six DC-10s, 25 DC-9s, and 33 F.28s) the new type entered service in January 1982 on the Jakarta–Medan route, at a frequency of three a day, instead of four a day by the superseded DC-9s. Even so, the A300s increased the capacity offered by about fifty per cent. Shortly afterwards, on 25 February, on a special flight from Jakarta to Bali, Wiweko was able to demonstrate personally to President and Mrs Suharto the advantages of the Forward Facing Crew Cockpit that he had sponsored.

Garuda's progress from a struggling company in the immediate postwar era, with wartime DC-3s as its flagships, had, by the 1980s, been transformed into a modern airline, well-equipped with a fleet of jet aircraft, well-balanced in size and numbers for the traffic; and more important, commercially sound. Gone were the days when every Indonesian official or members of his family or his friends regarded Garuda as their private transport. There were no frills and no free rides under Wiweko. And his austere approach and policy were exonerated when, on 15 November 1982, the Government increased the exit tax, from 25,000 to 150,000 rupiahs ($222) to inhibit the flow of Indonesians travelling abroad and the drain on currency. More important, this tax was, on 18 December of the same year, imposed on all government officials, from ministers down to secretaries, and to all members of the armed forces, whether on official or on private business. For Garuda Indonesian Airways, under Wiweko's sometimes dictatorial leadership, it could face competition anywhere, on equal terms. Perhaps Wiweko himself felt that a new era had begun, and that a continuous succession of confrontations was no longer necessary to uphold his airline's position. Significantly, on 1 August 1983, casting aside all fears of dominance by a stronger competitor, Garuda launched the Tokyo Express service, in co-operation with Japan Air Lines. Garuda had won its spurs.

Garuda's Airbus A300B-4 PK-GAA, in new blue and white livery, seen at Singapore in 1992.

Indonesian Air Shuttles

Measured by area, the 13,600 islands of Indonesia constitute the world's fifteenth largest country; but measured by population, it is the world's fifth largest, exceeded only by China, India, Russia, and the United States. About two thirds of these people live in Java, one of the most densely populated areas in the world. Formerly a predominantly agricultural land, much of it existing by subsistence farming, with rice the predominant product, Java has now joined the rest of the world in an inexorable process of urbanization, as industry and commerce have supplemented agriculture as Indonesia's source of economic well-being and wealth. About the same size as the then Czechoslovakia or Greece, or the State of Louisiana, Java's 120 million people live partly in a score of cities with more than 100,000, and no less than three of these, other than Jakarta, have more than a million. Without high speed railways or fast divided highways, the airlines are vital for inter-city travel.

Garuda was equal to the task of providing this, by increasing both the frequencies and the size of the aircraft serving the main Javanese routes from Jakarta to Surabaya, Semarang and Bandung. By the early Seventies, a combination of DC-9s and F.28s were maintaining a high level of service, with the prospect of the ideal 'every hour on the hour' in sight. On 1 July 1976, Garuda took the plunge. Echoing the example first set by Brazil's *Ponte Aérea* in 1959, and popularized in the United States by the Eastern Air Shuttle two years later, it began an Air Shuttle service between Jakarta and Surabaya, Indonesia's second city. Using DC-9s, the initial frequency was eight a day. No prior reservations were needed; tickets could be purchased at the airport ticket counters. At first the average load factor was only 46 per cent, but it built up to a respectable level by mid-1977; and such was the popular acceptance that frequencies were increased to ten each way a day, and during peak periods, especially on occasions such as Ramadan or Christmas, wide-bodied even DC-10s and, later, A300s were used.

A second Air Shuttle started on 1 July 1977, with a Jakarta–Semarang service, using the smaller 65-seat Fokker F.28. Again, the load factor at first was modest and the frequency was only six a day; but as with the Surabaya route, both were increased within a few months of the initial operation. Three years later, on 1 December 1980, yet a third Air Shuttle service began, from Jakarta to Tanjungkarang in southern Sumatra, to connect with air, rail, and road termini. Garuda was undertaking its mandate in providing air transport for the nation with style and flexibility, and moreover able to set an example of efficiency to others.

The Second Level

When the Indonesian Government relaxed its regulations controlling the airlines in 1969, several enterprising companies entered the field to begin feeder and regional routes to complement those already operated by Garuda Indonesian Airways and Merpati Nusantara, already reviewed earlier in this chapter. Prominent among the early entrants was Bouraq Indonesia Airlines, based at Balikpapan, a fast-growing city in eastern Kalimantan. It was founded on 1 April 1970 by J A 'Gerry' Sumendap, as a subsidiary of Porodisa Industrial Ltd which owned extensive timber holdings in Kalimantan and Sumatra, as well as construction and other activities. Aside from being the centre of Sumendap's industrial empire, Balikpapan was chosen as the base because it was close to being the geographical centre of Indonesia, and therefore a potential crossroads for future air routes.

With a fleet of four Douglas DC-3s, Bouraq began cautiously with non-scheduled services to Jakarta and Surabaya in Java, and to Palu across the Straits of Makassar in Sulawesi; but by June it had issued its first timetable, and during that summer, fashioned a route network that extended to Ujungpandang, Banjermasin, Tarakan, and on from this last point to Tawau, in Sabah, Malaysia. During the next few years, Bouraq expanded steadily and sensibly, adding, in May 1971, Nihon YS-11s, and, in June 1972, Fokker F.27s, enabling it to operate a respectable-looking network from Jakarta to several cities of Kalimantan, to Sulawesi and to the Moluccas; and international routes from Pontianak to Singapore; from Tarakan to Tawau, Malaysia, and Zamboanga, Philippines; and Menado to Davao, also in the Philippines. The path to success, however, was not always smooth. Bouraq could carry passengers to Singapore, for example, only if they were ticketed from points east of Pontianak, but not if they originated from Pontianak: a bureaucratic restriction, with protective undertones, that was worthy of the US Civil Aeronautics Board during its most restrictive and irrational years. The route to Davao was subject to a different kind of deterrent to traffic. Opened in June 1972, it had to be suspended in 1975 when Philippine President Marcos declared martial law, and all passports for Filipinos had to be signed by Marcos himself or his deputies.

Such indignities apart, Bouraq went on its way. In 1973, Nusantara Air Service, a small charter service, was acquired by Porodisa Industrial to become a sister company of Bouraq. Named after the series of islands east of Java, Nusantara had a separate legal identity but was managed by Bouraq. At first it fulfilled charter contracts with two F.27s leased from Bouraq, but in January 1974 it changed its name to Bali International Air Services and used Britten-Norman Islanders, appropriately named and well suited to the small strips of the Nusantara archipelago.

Of wider-reaching importance was a decision made to acquire, in January 1973, the first Hawker Siddeley 748. This aircraft, PK-IHD, was fitted with 46 seats, quite high-density but matched to the demand. The British 748 was

A Hawker Siddeley 748 of Bali Air.

A Bali Air Pilatus Britten-Norman Trislander at Balikpapan. (*R E G Davies*)

one of four different twin-engined propeller-turbine types fitted with Rolls-Royce Dart engines. Though the Fokker F.27 Friendship outsold them all, the 748 was the best for operating from unprepared strips. Some of Bouraq's would have fitted the description offered by an observer in Argentina ('I've seen unprepared strips, but this one was taken by surprise') and so well did the airline and the aircraft adapt themselves that Bouraq eventually built up its fleet, by 1983, to sixteen.

Bali International had become Bali Air, and in February 1976, took delivery of the first of five Britten-Norman Trislanders, and in May 1977, added two Cessna 404s. But the casualty rate of the smaller types was high: both Cessnas and some of the Islanders and Trislanders were lost in crashes or hard landings, or just disappeared in the uncharted territories of the remoter corners of Indonesia.

On the main routes, the standards were improved with good scheduling, and on 24 January 1977, through services were consolidated from Jakarta and Surabaya to Tarakan, Menado and Ujungpandang, this last route avoiding the change of aircraft at Balikpapan, which, though the 'cross roads' was well off the direct airway to southern Sulawesi. Bouraq also invested in the Indonesian Nurtanio-CASA 212, which was beginning to come off the production lines at Bandung, licence-built from the Spanish manufacturer, and which were first deployed, on 2 November 1978, on intra-Java services. Then, in August 1980, Gerry Sumendap upgraded his mainline service by leasing two Vickers Viscount 800s from FAT Airlines of Taiwan. This was an unhappy experience. The first one was severely damaged when the undercarriage collapsed at Surabaya; and the second crashed near Jakarta when an elevator broke off. The pilot fought for sixteen minutes to prevent a crash, but his efforts were in vain and all on board were killed.

Bouraq Indonesian Airlines became an independent company in 1982, with its

A Bouraq Vickers-Armstrongs Viscount. (*R E G Davies*)

own management, without day-to-day control from Porodisa. One of the first actions of the new management was to seek some better Viscounts; for in spite of the crashes, it was still the preferred replacement for the Hawker Siddeley 748s. In September 1983, in an astute purchase, Sumendap purchased four Viscount 843s from Hong Kong. These were formerly operated by CAAC (Civil Air Administration of China), in the People's Republic, and because they had not been intensely utilized by the Chinese airline, were low-time aircraft, in spite of having gone into service on the mainland twenty years previously.

PK-IHD was one of Bouraq Indonesia Airlines' fleet of Hawker Siddeley 748s.

200

EARLY INDONESIAN INDEPENDENTS

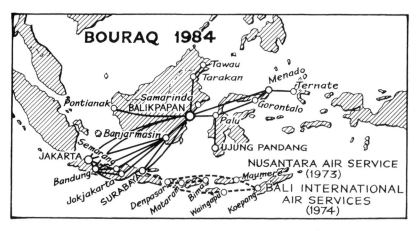

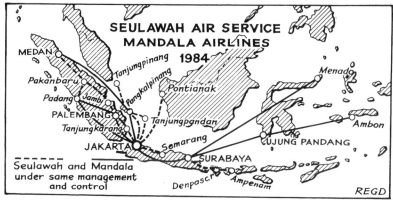

Map 17c. Early Indonesian Independents
Somewhat grudgingly, the Indonesian Government, under pressure from Garuda, on the one hand, and the spirit of independence on the other, permitted some privately-owned airlines to function as regional airlines from the late 1960s. Bouraq served mainly Kalimantan (the Indonesian part of Borneo) from its base in Balikpapan, a timber-producing centre, and close to the oilfields of Tarakan. Seulewah and Mandala served Sumatra, with other routes to the east; while Zamrud operated DC-3 services through the Lesser Sunda Islands.

Mandala Airlines' Vickers-Armstrongs Viscount 806 *Akasha* was one of those acquired from CAAC in China.

Another regional airline that got under way in 1970, starting operations even before Bouraq, was Mandala Airlines. Founded at Surabaya in February of that year, its first services were from Jakarta and Surabaya to Bali and Lombok, in the Nusantara islands, and to Ujungpandang and other points in Sulawesi as far as Menado, and onwards to Ambon. Its early equipment, except for a lone DC-3, was all Rolls-Royce Dart powered, two Viscounts, a Hawker Siddeley 748, and a Fokker Friendship.

Under the same ownership, but operating from Palembang, Sumatra, to points throughout that island, was Seulawah Air Services. The chairman of both companies was General Sofjar, but he died in 1973, to be succeeded by General Soerjo. The fleet was not integrated with that of Mandala, and its three Convair 600s appeared to operate with little attempt to take advantage of any possible commonality of equipment. By the mid-1970s, Seulewah was floundering, and trying to make ends meet – almost literally, in terms of the Seulewah-Mandala map – and eventually it was indeed merged with the latter.

Mandala managed to survive, amid much uncertainty during the early years when Indonesian entrepreneurs were allowed to enter the air transport scene. It must have had some influence with the Government, for it was able to share in the Hajj pilgrimage airlifts to Jeddah, of which it was allocated about a tenth of the total traffic. This was enough to encourage it to acquire some Lockheed L-188 Electras, with which it was also able to upgrade its domestic services.

Another airline that traces its origins from the liberalization of the air transport regulations in 1968 was Sempati Air Transport, which (like almost all aspiring airlines for several decades after the Second World War) started with the Douglas DC-3. A subsidiary of the Truba industrial group, it operated charter and other contract services before entering the scheduled field in the latter 1970s. It replaced the DC-3s with Fokker Friendships and held its own against other regional airlines.

Sempati Air Transport's black, white and red Fokker F.27 Friendship *Kurnia*. Beyond are two Bouraq HS 748s. (*R E G Davies*)

A number of other small airlines have existed sporadically throughout Indonesia, as individual entrepreneurs tried their luck with air transport. Airlines of all types have operated aircraft of all types, with the owners as determined to survive commercially as the aircraft seem determined to defy all the orthodox laws of amortization, depreciation, corrosion, and old age. Companies with intriguing names like Zamrud and Bayu have, as well as the inevitable DC-3s, flown almost every conceivable model of propeller-driven aircraft, from diminutive Cessnas, Beeches, and Pipers, to the large Canadair CL-44 swing-tail freighter. Details of this motley array of fascinating activities are summarized in the table on page 208.

All these companies put together, however, would be hard pressed to assemble such a varied fleet, both in total numbers and in different types, as that operated by Pelita Air Service. Not strictly an airline, it should be mentioned here, if only because any visitor to almost any airport or airfield in Indonesia is virtually certain to observe a Pelita aircraft parked on the apron. It might be a humble Shorts Skyvan, or a not-so-humble Grumman Gulfstream or de Havilland D.H.125 business jet; a smart Fokker F.28 or an Aérospatiale Puma helicopter. During the mid-1970s, Pelita could count a fleet of almost a hundred machines, two-thirds of them Puma and Hughes helicopters. The remaining 30 aircraft included eleven different types.

The reason why the airline could afford such prodigality – and from a scheduled airline's viewpoint – such uneconomic use of resources, was that it is a subsidiary of Pertamina, the affluent Indonesian State oil company. It is responsible for flying company employees, plus those of about fifty foreign oil contractors and a hundred sub-contractors, from Jakarta to various oil installations throughout Indonesia. It also operates into Malaysia and occasionally on special charter flights to Japan. It performs limited services to promote tourism, and carries officials on government business. It has been known to make a round-the-world flight or two for the president of Pertamina.

One of Pelita's more interesting assignments was related to the Indonesian transmigration programme. In mid-1978, a Lockheed demonstrator L-100-30, civil variant of the well-known Hercules C-130 military transport, noted for its short- and rough-field capability, made a series of twice-daily demonstration flights between Jakarta and the Sumatran cities of Padang and Jambi, about 600 miles distant. A total of 1,300 families were carried in comfort, served a lunch, and

A Pelita Air Service Fokker F.28 (*left*) and de Havilland Canada Dash 7.
(*R E G Davies*)

delivered, almost door-to-door, to their new homes in the areas designated for resettlement. Air Marshal Kardono, Indonesia's Director of Civil Aviation, signed a contract with the Government so that he could purchase three of these versatile maids-of-all-work.

One small footnote – almost an epitaph – should be added to the account of feederlines in Indonesia. As an almost anachronistic survival of a past age of colonialism, the eastern half of the island of Timor remained as a Portuguese territory until September 1976. Just as the forces of geography, if nothing else, settled its ultimate fate, as in the case of West Irian, the transfer of sovereignty was inevitable. But it was marked, sadly, by much ethnic and religious conflict. At the time of the transfer, Garuda participated in an airlift of refugees back to their homeland in Portugal; and there is still unrest and reports of oppression even today.

For a few short years in the 1960s however, the Portuguese Colony had its own little airline. Transportes Aéreos de Timor operated a service across the Timor Sea from the territory's main airport at Baucau, east of the capital, Dili, to Darwin, in Australia's Northern Territory. A de Havilland Dove made a connecting flight to the capital, but the 'trunk' route was operated by – what else? – a Douglas DC-3.

New Colours and a New Deal

After going into partnership with Japan Air Lines with the Tokyo Express in 1983, Garuda Indonesian Airways began to grow steadily, taking its place among the many airlines plying the trans-Asia route from Europe to the Pacific Rim. During the next several years, it extended its penetration of Europe and the Middle East, with additional stops en route at Riyadh and Abu Dhabi. The latter point became such a hub that it might almost have been an Indonesian domestic point, such was

One of Pelita's Nurtanio (CASA) C.212C Aviocars. Beyond is a Grumman Gulfstream.

its identity there. The various new points served, and the dates of Garuda's service inauguration, are shown on the map (page 184). In general, they represent mainly an intensification of service within Garuda's existing sphere of influence, but notably a trans-Pacific connection was added in August 1985.

Significantly, this was not from California to the capital, Jakarta, but to Bali, with a stop either at Guam or at Biak, the airfield first built by the Japanese, and then a pivotal point for KLM's vestigial route during the period of territorial transfer following Indonesia's liberation in the 1940s and 1950s. Even more significantly, the modern map of Garuda's international routes shows the tourist destination of Bali with as much emphasis as Jakarta itself. Its romantic appeal has generated so much vacation traffic that, apart from routes from Nagoya, Hong Kong, Singapore and Kuala Lumpur, no less than five points in Australia and Auckland, New Zealand, have nonstop connections to Bali.

While in the 1970s, Wiweko's recalcitrance to make deals over traffic rights to Bali may have upset many of his neighbour airlines, his instincts about Bali's potential as a tourist destination was on target. In other areas of administration, however, he was losing his ability to take direct aim at the heart of the problem. His austerity and thrift may have been successful in the early days when aircraft could be purchased from carefully husbanded savings from revenues. But as the airline world progressed into the wide-bodied jet age, old-fashioned thrift was not enough. Like it or not, Garuda had to do things the only way that was possible to raise the hundreds of millions of dollars needed to maintain a big enough modern fleet.

Eventually, Wiweko Supono stepped down. Garuda was losing money heavily and he was unable to plug the gap. He became involved in other aviation activities, including the oversight of the commissioning of Jakarta's new international airport, Sukarno-Hatta, to replace the old Kemayoran, which had become quite inadequate. He was also a prime mover in the establishment of the Nurtanio aircraft factory. Officially named the Industri Pesawat Terbang Nusantara (IPTN)

205

it first got under way in 1974, by making an agreement with the Spanish CASA manufacturer to produce, under licence, the CASA C-212 feeder aircraft, whose 20–26 seats was the right size for much of Indonesia's far-flung feeder route system. Later, in 1979, in co-operation with the Spanish firm, it developed the CASA CN-235, a 44-seater high-wing propeller-turbine type. This indigenous aircraft industry has been established at very high cost, more than a billion dollars, but there have been unseen dividends. The ability to deliver aircraft to a captive market that may in time be one of the world's biggest, is certainly a long-term investment for the future. It has created 15,000 jobs, and moreover jobs demanding technical skills. As the Indonesian-built 212s and 235s fly the skies over Indonesia, it is a source of pride and inspiration to this emerging nation. Bacharuddin Jusuf Habibie, Indonesian minister for research and technology, neatly summed up IPTN's achievement: 'When I started, Indonesia couldn't even build a bicycle.'

In 1988, Moehamed Soeparno took over the helm of the Garuda bird, foundering in rough financial turbulence. He tackled the problem on two main fronts, commercial and technical. The old name Garuda Indonesian Airways was changed to the sharper Garuda Indonesia and a brand new aircraft colour scheme was introduced to illustrate the Garuda bird symbol, in pleasing blue and aquamarine shades. Against the modern fleets of Singapore Airlines, only an hour away, or Cathay Pacific, in Hong Kong, or Japan Air Lines, the giant from the north, Garuda's fleet was beginning to look old, as indeed it was. Soeparno therefore undertook a massive re-equipment programme that included the acquisition of eight Boeing 737-300s, for the Shuttle services mainly; McDonnell Douglas MD-11s, the latest in long-range trijets; with additional Boeing 747s of the latest series and Fokker 100s on order.

Under a massive procurement plan, after Moehamed Soeparno took over at Garuda in 1988, the airline acquired Boeing 737s, McDonnell Douglas MD-11s, Fokker 100s and additional Boeing 747s. (*R E G Davies*)

The Seventh Life

Since Merpati Nusantara became a domestic branch of Garuda in 1978, after successive attempts by the Indonesian flag carrier's Wiweko to take control had finally succeeded, it had performed its role well as the primary regional airline. Garuda had continued to operate all the domestic trunk routes with a variety of jet aircraft, primarily Fokker F.28s and Douglas DC-9s; but sometimes allocating larger jets, even wide-bodied ones, especially on heavily-travelled routes such as Jakarta–Bali. The regional airlines, Merpati, Bouraq, and Mandala (which had absorbed Seulawah) were allowed only to operate propeller-turbine equipment, with the exception that Merpati was permitted to lease an F.28 from Garuda to operate international routes to Darwin and to Bandar Seri Begawan in Brunei.

In a far-reaching decision by the Indonesian Government in 1989, this situation changed dramatically. The winds of change were blowing throughout the airline world, after the United States deregulated its airline industry in 1978, and although a decade was to pass, the regional airlines of Indonesia were finally granted the flexibility of route and equipment selection in which they had been frustrated for so long. The main airlines affected were Merpati, Bouraq, and Sempati, which had replaced Mandala as one of the three companies that could be described as Indonesia's second level.

In September 1989, Merpati took over fifteen Fokker F.28s and two DC-9s from Garuda, together with the routes to the eastern provinces, with bases primarily at Surabaya, but also at Balikpapan – the centre of Bouraq's operations. In January 1991, Merpati took over eight more F.28s and six more DC-9s – making a total of 37 jets – to operate the trunk routes to Sumatra and other islands of the eastern part of Indonesia. It was an astounding transformation, suddenly elevating Merpati to the role of a major airline of east Asia, even though it strayed from its own borders only at a few points, and then only to smaller and nearby destinations.

In addition to the jets, Merpati also operates a dozen Twin Otters, continuing to perform sterling work in the still poorly-equipped remoter regions of West Irian; and twelve CASA 212s and ten CASA 235s, both of the latter built by IPTN

Merpati's CASA-Nusantara CN-235 PK-MNG, with a Fokker F.28 beyond.

in Bandung. As more of the local products are delivered, the older Fokker Friendships and the Hawker Siddeley 748s are being retired; and eventually Merpati plans to increase its fleet of 40-seat 235s to 25 and to augment these with sixty-five 50-seat CN-250s. Uniquely, Merpati also has two Lockheed L-382Gs, special conversions for passenger use of the two L-100s used by Pelita Air Services for the Transmigration flights. Fully certificated in a 97-seat layout and — unlike the basic L-100 — with windows, it is still able to use rough fields and, for its size, short runways, as did its famous Hercules parent type.

The Smaller Indonesian Domestic Independent Airlines

Company	Date Founded	Route Network	Aircraft Operated	Remarks
Zamrud Aviation Corp	1970	The Sunda Islands linking with Java, and east to Timor	DC-3	Ceased operation mid-1970s
Dirgantara Air Service	1970	Local charters	DC-3 CASA 212 B-N Islander	
Bali Air	1970	Local scheduled and charter	HS 748 B-N Islander B-N Trilander	Owned by Bouraq
Bayu Indonesia	1972	Domestic Cargo	Boeing 707 Canadair CL-44	
Airfast	1975	Domestic cargo	HS 748 DC-3, F.27, Aero Commander Bell 212	
Indonesia Air Transport	1975	Local charters, including cargo	BAC One-Eleven Beech King Air B-N Islander Piper PA-31 Short Skyvan	
Transna	1976	Local charters	F.27, DC-6A/B	
Deraya Air Taxi	1980	Local charters	IPTN 212	

CHAPTER EIGHTEEN

Airlines of Thailand (formerly Siam)

An Air-Minded Administration

The ruling family of Siam (as Thailand was known until the country's name was changed in June 1939) was concerned with aviation and its possible applications in the earliest years following the historic first powered flight of the Wright brothers in 1903. In 1911, a Belgian pilot demonstrated a Wright biplane in Bangkok, and the next year three army officers were sent for training as pilots to France, which in the first decade of the century was making the most headway with the new invention. On their return in 1913, the Siamese government ordered four Breguet and four Nieuport aircraft from France. Don Muang aerodrome was established on 17 March 1914, and the Ministry of the Interior set up an Army air support division on 27 March 1914.

Thus prepared – as much with enthusiasm as with equipment – King Rama VI declared war on the Central Powers in 1917 and sent an Army air support division to France. Four hundred men arrived on 30 July of that year, and many of them became pilots, with the remainder learning skills in maintenance. When they returned to Siam as the Royal Aeronautical Service after the war was over, they were ready to use their skills in non-military pursuits, including communication.

At that time, Siam lacked good roads, and the railway system was not extensive. Much of the country was flat, an endless panorama of rice paddies. One of the problems was that road-building materials were scarce and had to be brought long distances from the stone quarries. Much of the transport was done by waterways, which came under government control in 1903. This shortcoming, it should be observed, was little different from the situation in most countries of Asia, with the exception of British India and in Japan. Even in China, the railways were few and uncoordinated, and roads almost non-existent; and in the Dutch and French colonies, transport systems were sporadic.

Foreign influence in Siam was indirect. Alone among the countries of east Asia, it was politically independent – China's independence was simply that of a nominal ruling dynasty, with foreign powers controlling the commerce, the economy, and even the justice in spheres of influence that might well have been colonies. But even independent Siam had a powerful European trading partner in Denmark, which built up its famous furniture industry on the basis of imported timber from Siam. This commercial tradition was to emerge again in the field of air transport in the middle of the 20th Century.

As mentioned above, the railway system in Thailand was of limited scope, with only two lines leading to the north from Bangkok, and one to the south, to connect the Siamese portion of the Malay Peninsula with the capital. The Aeronautical Service was therefore charged with providing an air mail service to supplement the surface modes. It first conducted some test flights, the first successful one being to carry the mail from Bangkok to Chanthaburi, 200 km away on the southeast coast, on 17 February 1920. The distance was covered by two SPAD fighter aircraft in $1\frac{1}{2}$ hours, compared with the two days journey by ship. A second experiment was made on 23 June of the same year, with three Breguet 14s, from Bangkok to Korat (Nakhon Rachasima), to the northeast, and this had far-reaching implications. Having established an airfield at the latter town, the authorities realized how best to use the Royal Aeronautical Service of the Siamese Army.

The First Air Service

In a manner remarkably similar to the way in which the Australian airline QANTAS initiated its first routes, the Siamese Aeronautical Service set about the task of providing aerial extensions from the existing rail terminus at Nakhon Rachasima. Using Breguet XIVs, it began air mail service on 1 June 1922. This was two days before Mr Inouye founded the first airline in Japan, and five months before the latter began operations. The difference between the two pioneer airlines was that the Siamese one carried mail almost exclusively, whereas Inouye carried passengers, though not many – only 27 in the first year – and a little air freight.

When the Siamese Aeronautical Service began air mail services in 1922 it operated Breguet XIV single-engine biplanes similar to the French example illustrated. (*Courtesy John Stroud*)

The Siamese Royal Aeronautical Service chose, as its first route from Nakhon Rachasima, one that extended due eastwards, via Roi-Et, to Ubon Rachasima, close to the Laotian frontier and the Mekong River. The French-trained pilots seem to have done their job well, carrying, in the first six months, more than 47,000 letters, 33,000 newspapers and about 1,600 parcels. This encouraged the service to open another route, northwards from Nakhon Rachasima, to Udorn (Udon Thani), via Khonkaen, on 3 January 1923; and a year later, on 11 December, this was extended to Nong Khai, across the Mekong from Vientiane, then a town in the French Indo-Chinese Province of Laos and today the Laotian capital.

The Air Service operated for nine years, during which time it carried 3,700 passengers, 25,000 bags of mail, and 64,700 lb of freight. This laid the foundations for future air routes and future airline development. By 1926, the fleet of fifteen Breguets included at least six that were allocated to the mail service; spare aircraft were deployed at the outlying termini to ensure regularity in case of breakdown; weather reports were forwarded to the hub at Nakhon Rachasima; and aircraft did not leave unless these were favourable. The service provided transport for doctors and for ambulance patients, often free of charge. While all this was subsidized, the benefits to the nation as a whole were considerable.

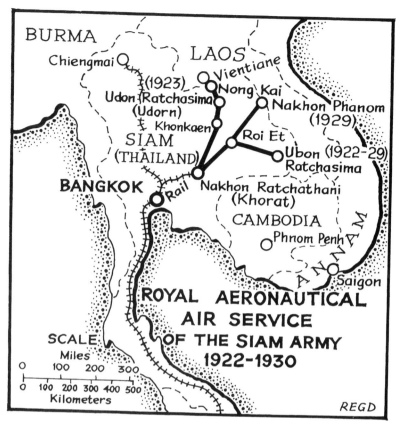

Map 18a. Royal Aeronautical Air Service of the Siamese Army, 1922–1930
Siam (as the country was called until after the Second World War) was the only nation in southern and southeast Asia to resist the inroads of European colonization. It was sympathetic to the Allied cause during the Great War of 1914–18, and the Siamese Army sent men to Europe, where they gained some flying experience. Returning home, they put this to good use, starting regular air services as extensions of the short railway line northeast of Bangkok.
This was one of the earliest air services in the entire continent.

Much of the incentive was removed as Siam developed its railways. In 1929 the eastern line was completed to Ubon Rachasani, and the one to the north was well under way. To compensate for this depletion of its traffic, the Air Service transferred the northern route to Nakhon Phanom. But it had fulfilled its role of keeping Siam abreast of the times in the field of air transport, even as the more powerful European airline countries, Britain, France and the Netherlands, were showing their flags with air services linking the homelands with distant colonies in southeast Asia. In a statement issued in January 1929, HRH Prince Purachatra, Minister

211

of Commerce and Communications, voiced an awareness of Siam's strategic and geographic position as a stopping point en route to destinations such as Singapore, Batavia, Hanoi, Hong Kong, and even further to Australia and Japan. The Siamese Government took some practical steps: opening discussions with the European airlines, which resulted in KLM making a stop at Bangkok; bringing in Otto Praeger, the former Assistant Postmaster General of the United States as a consultant; and most important, setting up a national airline to replace the Royal Aeronautical Service, which had hitherto borne the cost of developing the air mail service.

The First Siamese Airline

On 7 July 1930, the Aerial Transport Company of Siam Ltd was formed by the Ministry of Finance, which seems to have acted as a caretaker until the company could be properly organized. During this brief stewardship, one of the objectives of the new airline policy was attained when the French Air Orient opened a connecting service from Bangkok to Hanoi on its route to Saïgon. The possibility was also examined of a short-cut from Rangoon, then in British India, to Hanoi, via Pitsanulok and Udorn (Udon Thani) both points in northern Siam; but this idea never materialized.

The Aerial Transport Company was formally registered as a public company on 13 July 1931, to operate under the supervision of the Minstry of Commerce and Communication. Its initial fleet was four de Havilland D.H.80A Puss Moths. Echoing the principle laid down and proven by the previous Aeronautical Service, its services radiated from Nakhon Rachasima, the important rail junction northeast of Bangkok, on precisely the same routes. Service began on 24 August 1931, with a rail journey to Nakhon Rachasima, and thence the next morning to the outlying places. The two-passenger Puss Moths provided a twice weekly frequency, and the service was apparently good enough to draw comment from the British magazine *Flight* to the effect that 'passengers taking breakfast at Korat (Nakhon Rachasima) will be able to have tiffin in Nakhon Phanom.'

During the 1930s, the airline had its ups and downs, with the indignity and misfortune of an early accident, on 22 June 1933, and depletion of traffic when full rail service was completed to Udorn, compensated for, however, by the addition of a four-seat Fairchild F-24. By the standards of Europe, Australia, or North America, such aircraft as the Puss Moth or the Fairchild were tiny; but they were suited to the volume of traffic demand. Siam was an unusual country, in that, except for Bangkok, there were no other large cities, and in the 1930s, even the towns had populations seldom exceeding 15,000. Even today, only Chiangmai boasts more than 100,000; yet Bangkok accounts for more than a fifth of Thailand's 50 million people.

Because of its systematic appraoch in aircraft procurement, the discipline of its pilots who inherited a long aviation tradition, and the government-directed policy of working in cooperation with, rather than in competition with the railway, the Aerial Transport Company operated with complete regularity, and without direct subsidy, although (as in all countries with airlines) such infrastructure as airports and radio communications were provided by other government agencies. Such was the conviction that transport should be an integrated, not a fragmented operation, that in 1936 the airline took some of the bus services under its wing; and the name of the company was changed appropriately to the Transport Company Ltd, and its mission was to link Bangkok with other places in Siam by air, land, or inland waterway.

Towards the end of the decade, six Fairchild 24Js were delivered, enabling the company to open new services from 1939 to 1941, one from a station on the northern railway, Nakhon Sawan, to Chiangmai, via Tak, near the western frontier with Burma; one from Khon Kaen to Vientiane, in Laos; and another from Surat Thani, in the far south, to the island of Phuket, the same that was eventually to become an elite tourist destination for discerning visitors (see map on page 216).

In June 1939, the name of the country was changed from Siam to Thailand, to reflect the correct name of the majority of the indigenous people, the Thais; but before the world could get used to the new name and revise its atlases, the whole of east Asia underwent more far-reaching changes when, at the end of 1941, Japan launched its massive attacks on all the territories of the European colonial powers.

Thailand too was overrun by Japanese forces, and spent the next three years as a submissive vassal state of the new Empire of the Rising Sun, rewarded for its cooperation by the transfer of territory from Burma, Malaya, and French Indo-China. The Transport Company had carried, during its nine years, 700 passengers, 113,000 kg of mail, and 18,000 kg of freight.

Picking Up the Pieces

During the years immediately following the Second World War, Thailand was slow to recover its nationhood; and it did not receive much help from the victorious allies. The first postwar airlines contained, therefore, an element of foreign influence. One of these was Pacific Overseas Airlines (Siam) Ltd (POAS) which was formed by United States and Thai interests on 25 May 1947, to operate a weekly service to the United States. US investors held 44 per cent of the stock, the Thai Government 26 per cent, and the remaining 30 per cent went to Thai businessmen. Operations began in July, with routes to Singapore, Hong Kong, Tokyo and, somewhat intermittently, to San Francisco. Organized by a company of the same name, based in Ontario, California, POAS's long-haul fleet consisted of two Douglas DC-4s, and it also had two DC-3s and a Catalina. But its tenure was short-lived, and on 1 November 1951, it was absorbed by the Siamese Airways Company. Another airline was Trans-Asiatic Airlines (Siam) Ltd (TAAS), with 49 per cent of the shareholding held by an American, William D Davis, and the rest by Siamese Airways. It operated mainly charter flights to Hong Kong and Singapore with DC-3s. Founded on 10 April 1948, it ceased operations on 11 November 1952. But in spite of overseas connections, these two small companies were only peripheral to the main stream

Siamese Airways

On 1 March 1947, Siamese Airways Company Ltd (SAC) was formed by the Thai Government in Bangkok. Its main fleet consisted of four DC-3s and two Beech 18s, but it also seems to have inherited the two Rearwins and the Fairchild F-24 of the former Aerial Transport Company, and it also had six Consolidated L-5s. With this motley assortment, it began services only two days later, to Chiangmai, and onwards to the far north of the country at Chiang Rai. Three days later again, SAC started a route to the far south; and for the first time, Thailand had a national domestic airline, operated in its own right, and not merely as an extension of the railway system.

Of course Thai Airways used DC-3s and here are three of them at Bangkok. (*Courtesy John Stroud*)

By the end of the year, on 22 December, SAC opened its first international link, to Penang, in Malaya, as an extension from Songkhla; and on 16 January 1948, it started a route to Saïgon, via Phnom Penh. Making good headway, Singapore was added to the Penang route on 19 January 1948, Hong Kong a week later, and Calcutta, via Rangoon, in the following year. During this period of steady route expansion, SAC acquired five Beech C-35 Bonanzas on 23 January 1948, and six Noorduyn Norsemans in 1950. These aircraft were strictly for operations into small fields – the Norseman was particularly ruggedly-built – and they were small, to match the modest traffic. Nevertheless, the Thai national carrier was conscious of the strategic position held by Bangkok on the map of southeast Asia; and it began to think about more ambitious expansion. To this end, on 1 November 1951, Siamese Airways merged with Pacific Overseas Airlines (Siam) to form Thai Airways Company Ltd (TAC).

Long-Haul Aspirations

Within two years of the merger, and making use of the DC-4s from POAS, TAC extended its main route to Hong Kong on to Taipei and Tokyo. Bangkok was beginning to establish itself as one of the important commercial cities of southeast Asia, rivalling Hong Kong and Singapore, as well as Saïgon and Jakarta (the former Batavia), whose status as centres of colonial influence was no longer relevant in a postwar world. Thailand's former comparative isolation as an independent nation was no longer a handicap. Tokyo, on the other hand, was emerging as the fulcrum of commerce in the East, as Japan began to re-establish its industrial strength. Tokyo became the dominant generator of air traffic in the entire western Pacific region; and Bangkok became more important, not only as a destination for Japanese businessmen and tourists, but as a traffic hub, because of its geographical location.

Trying to upgrade the standards of its service, to keep pace with the modern equipment of its many competitors, TAC sought to replace its aging and unpressurized DC-4s. In 1953, it ordered two Super Constellations from Lockheed, but financial limitations led to these being sold to Qantas in 1955, even before they were delivered. In 1956 TAC tried again, ordering three L-1049G Super Constellations and these were delivered in 1957. The airline then discovered that

214

there was a vast difference between operating mainly DC-3s and small aircraft (which could be maintained or repaired in workshops equipped only with simple tools, and with sources of war-surplus spare parts) and the latest products of aeronautical engineering, demanding high skills and standards of technical support.

At first TAC entered into a contract with Pan American Airways, to provide management and other services, but by the end of 1958, the Thai Government became dissatisfied with the costs of the arrangement and tried to negotiate a new contract with Northwest Orient Airlines. This, however, required (as had the Pan American deal) the approval of the US Civil Aeronautics Board, which at that time exercised strict control over the allocation and certification of air routes by all US airlines. In the international arena, the CAB still believed in the idea of spheres of interest. Bangkok had been in Pan American's, in its round-the-world pattern of routes; but Northwest's was considered to reach westwards only as far as Hong Kong. The Board therefore turned down the proposal.

The next move was to find another partner, and this was an outstanding case of 'third time lucky,' for not only did TAC find a partner that could do everything it needed; but a partner which, in fact, was itself anxious to find an oriental associate, for commercial reasons that had much to do with overcoming traffic restrictions imposed on it by rival airlines in Europe which still controlled the channels of air travel because of political sovereignty. Independent Thailand offered many advantages, and Bangkok's geographical situation was ideal.

Thai International Airways

While TAC was negotiating with the two US airlines, Hans Erik Hansen, a representative of Scandinavian Airlines System (SAS) went to Bangkok to study the situation. SAS was a consortium, an airline jointly owned by three countries, Sweden, Norway and Denmark, formed in 1946 so as to create a company whose stature would at least be comparable with, if not matching completely, the large European airlines such as British Overseas Airways, Air France or KLM. Independently, the three countries were too small to compete adequately; together they could hold their own. Not only that, SAS began to demonstrate leadership in some directions, for example in pioneering the first so-called Polar routes from Europe to North America.

It also sought to extend its influence overseas – and to increase its international bargaining power by proxy – by acquiring part-ownership of airlines in distant lands. On 20 February 1959 SAS purchased a substantial shareholding in Aerovias Guest, a privately-owned Mexican airline that held Mexican traffic rights to the USA and to Europe. This was not a financial success, and SAS disposed of its interest after only two years. But the experience gained in the experiment suggested that the idea of a foreign involvement was sound, as long as the political and commercial circumstances were favourable. Hans Erik Hansen reported back to Copenhagen, Stockholm and Oslo that, in the case of TAC and Thailand, they were.

On 24 August 1959, the two airlines entered into an agreement whereby SAS would operate Thailand's main international services, especially to Hong Kong and Tokyo. This gave SAS vicarious access to Hong Kong, whose British colonial status meant that traffic rights were controlled from London; and the British had not been generous. But to refuse traffic rights to a Thai airline would invite diplomatic problems of a far-reaching nature. By buying into TAC, SAS opened the doors for its own expansion in the Far East.

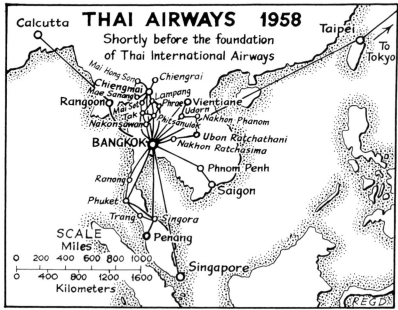

Map 18b. Thai Airways, 1958
Even before the creation of the highly successful partnership with Scandinavian Airlines System (SAS), Bangkok was emerging as an important airways hub in Southeast Asia. In pre-war years, the intercontinental trunk lines across the southern fringe of Asia had been developed by European national corporations that 'followed the flag', and thus Singapore, Hong Kong, Batavia (Jakarta), and Saïgon had been natural choices as key stations. But the proliferation of airlines world-wide after the Second World War led to Bangkok gaining favour because of its geographical position as a centralized point.

The contract was sealed on 14 December 1959 by the creation of Thai Airways International (THAI). TAC held 70 per cent of the shares and SAS 30 per cent. A clause in the contract provided for SAS to buy the three TAC Super Constellations. These were promptly transferred to Guest, already a Constellation operator, and THAI leased three Douglas DC-6Bs from SAS.

During the first week of May 1960, THAI took over from TAC all the international routes (except the short trans-border ones) and inaugurated DC-6B service. On 11 August 1960, it added service to Manila, and on 6 November to Jakarta via Singapore. On 18 May 1962, THAI began jet service, when SAS transferred one of its 99-seat Convair 990s to Bangkok, to replace one of the Douglases; but when a second DC-6B had to be retired at the beginning of 1962, the Thai international carrier's fleet was reduced to two; and although the share capital was increased, there was clearly a crisis.

In the spring of 1962 Henry Jensen arrived in Bangkok, and immediately undertook a severe cost-cutting programme, and in particular reduced the numbers of expensive ex-patriate personnel from Scandinavia. Playing the role of diplomat, he negotiated pool agreements with the two key airlines with whom THAI competed for traffic to the immediate north and to the immediate south of Thailand: Cathay Pacific Airways in Hong Kong and Malayan Airways in Singapore. This staved off the crisis and during the next year Jensen regrouped and considered its future plans and policies.

The Caravelle

At least THAI managed to retain its pride, even though it was having to face difficult problems. In 1963 it was honoured to carry the King and Queen of Thailand on royal visits to Pakistan, Malaysia, Japan, Taiwan and the Philippines; so that, in spite of restricted public service because of the shortage of aircraft, it was able to show the flag in almost imperial fashion. Meanwhile, however, far more important issues were at stake, specifically the choice of a jet aircraft to replace the Convair 990. The problem was that the standard long-range jet airliners such as the Boeing 707 or the Douglas DC–8 were not profitable on short-medium haul routes, and they were still rather on the large side for THAI's average traffic loads.

At the time, the only short-haul jet was the French Sud SE.210 Caravelle, pioneer of the design in which the two engines were mounted on the rear of the fuselage – an idea, incidentally, that was at first met with scepticism, but which was later adopted by all the leading aircraft manufacturers the world over. THAI chose the Caravelle, giving it a high standard of comfort, by reducing the normal five-abreast 89 seating to a four-abreast 72. The first of five of the French jets went into service on 1 January 1964.

Thai International chose the Sud-Aviation Caravelle as its short-haul jet and the first was put into service on the first day of 1964.

This was a bold step by THAI as hitherto all airlines operating in east Asia had considered four-engined aircraft to be essential for over-water routes such as those that linked most of the countries of the western Pacific Rim. But the Caravelle, with its Rolls-Royce Avon engines, proved to be completely satisfactory; and although one of them crashed at Hong Kong on 30 June 1967 (24 of the 79 on board were killed), THAI established itself throughout the region, and started additional services to Bali on 24 December 1967, after long negotations with a reluctant Indonesian airline and government. THAI's Caravelle was the first jet service into Bali. It also opened routes to Seoul, on 17 March 1968, to Delhi on 2 July, and to Kathmandu on 4 December of the same year.

THAI Goes Intercontinental

Gaining confidence and, more important, technical and commercial parity with its neighbour airlines in east Asia, THAI began to expand its horizons. On 1 February

In 1969 Thai International leased two Douglas DC-9s from SAS.

1969, in an upgrading of equipment paralleling the course taken by SAS, the airline became a Douglas operator, leasing two DC-9-41s from its sponsoring partner. The DC-9s had 99 seats, the same as in the Convair 990. With two engines, like the Caravelle, it was more economical for the short–medium haul routes of the region than the four-engined Convair 990. Supplementing the DC-9s, THAI leased two DC-8-33s, 146-seaters, and able to fly any long-range route throughout the world, if necessary.

Backing up the better equipment, THAI became the first airline in Asia to install the IBM 360 computer for its reservations and other duties. It began to increase the participation of Thai nationals in the management of the airline. And in 1970 it introduced the *Royal Orchid Holidays* tour programme, to launch a promotional name with which it was to establish a standard of customer and on-board service that was to become a watchword in the whole region, even challenging Japan Air Lines, hitherto the recognized standard-bearer of excellence.

During the 1970s, Thai Airways International became an airline of world renown, except in North America, which was to come later. On 1 April 1971, it started a service to Sydney via Singapore and/or Bali, the first time a Thai airline had ventured outside Asia since Pacific Overseas Airlines' short-lived trans-Pacific route in 1947. On 3 June 1972, it inaugurated the *Royal Orchid Service* from Bangkok to Copenhagen, making a technical stop only at Moscow. This long-range one-stop service, which quickly became known as the Trans-Asian Express, was made possible by the introduction of the special version of the Douglas DC-8, the -62, which was only a little larger than its predecessors, but had tankage enough

Supplementing the DC-9s, Thai International leased two Douglas DC-8-33s each with 146 seats.

for about 14 hours, or more than 6,000 miles, with reserves. Leased from SAS, as usual, they had 146 seats, the same as in the other DC-8s in the fleet. The DC-9s had by now been discarded, so that for a year or two, the THAI reservations staff knew where they stood – the entire fleet had the same seating.

On 2 November 1973, another Trans-Asian Express route was added, to London via Tashkent. Four days later, the Copenhagen service was re-routed via Frankfurt, as a traffic stop (Moscow and Tashkent had been technical stops only). Making full use of its Sixth Freedom rights – de facto rather than de jure in the eyes of the International Civil Aviation Organization (ICAO) – a through service was offered from London to Sydney, in a journey time of a little more than 20 hours, stopping only at Bangkok and Singapore. THAI was making its mark.

Not only was it making its mark in the international travelling community, it was consolidating its position in Thailand, gradually reducing its dependence on SAS. For example, as the DC-8 fleet increased in numbers, the additional aircraft were lease-purchased through the First National City Bank, rather than leased from SAS. Although the first stretched long-range DC-8-63, introduced on 27 March 1974, was brought in under the old arrangements, the second one, added a week later, was converted to full ownership on 26 October. Furthermore, although the Thai Government extended SAS's contract on 16 July of the same year, the latter's shareholding was reduced from 30 to 15 per cent.

Air Siam

While THAI was making impressive headway, especially in joining the ranks of respected airlines on the Europe–Far East trunk routes, there were political problems at home, of a most unusual nature. A member of the Siamese (he did not like the Thai name) Royal Family, His Highness Captain the Prince Varanand, had been an officer in the British Royal Air Force for many years. Aviation was in his soul, and he felt that his country was not getting a fair shake from the partnership with SAS. He resolved to create a purely Siamese airline, drawing on his own considerable wealth to back his ideas and words with deeds. Accordingly, on 15 September 1965, 'Prince Nicky', as he was always known to his many friends, founded Varanair Siam.

He assembled a team of mainly British advisers, and between them, they found serious flaws in THAI's commercial initiatives, or what they felt were examples of neglect and lost opportunities. What followed was truly astonishing. Within a period of six months in 1967, Varanair obtained no less than four vital operating authorities: from the United States on 27 April, Thai confirmation of this trans-Pacific authority on 19 August, confirmation from Japan on 26 October, and from Great Britain for Hong Kong rights on 31 October.

The scope and extent of this coup were breathtaking. Not only did these agreements constitute the legal basis for operating a route from Bangkok to the United States – in which THAI seemed to have shown no interest – but the foreign certificates also included the coveted Fifth Freedom rights, so that Varanair would be able to carry, for example, passengers between Tokyo and Los Angeles, whether or not they had started their journey in Bangkok. Not only that, but in obtaining the bilateral agreement over Hong Kong rights, Prince Nicky had managed to do what many a large intercontinental airline had failed to achieve.

But, armed though Varanair was with these precious certificates, and boldly changing its name to Air Siam, the embryo airline then found that there was more to operating air routes than possessing pieces of paper, however valuable a poten-

GROWTH OF THAI AIRWAYS INTERNATIONAL
1960 - 1990

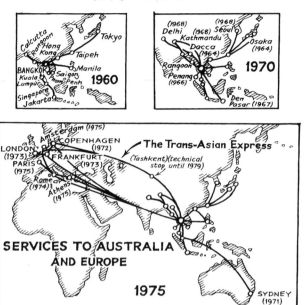

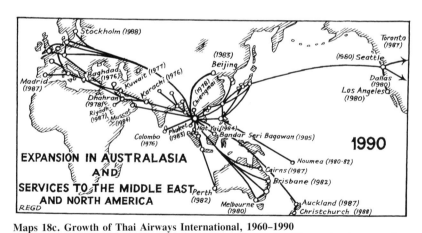

Maps 18c. Growth of Thai Airways International, 1960–1990
The association of Thai Airways and SAS was a good example of international co-operation. It brought inestimable benefits to commercial avaiation in Thailand; and it provided the Scandinavian countries with a secure aviation foothold and base in Asia. In adidition to developing Bangkok as a hub along the traditional air arteries, Thai inaugurated an unusual link with Europe, when its *Trans-Asian Express* overflew the Soviet Union from 1972. Thai now has extensive service to six cities in Australasia and four in North America.

tial for the future they might represent. Even Nicky Varanand's wealth was not enough, although he nobly sold some of his property in an effort to raise funds, and during the next three years, Air Siam desperately sought capital, and tried to find a foreign partner which was willing to underwrite the operation. Negotiations with the Flying Tiger Line fell through, as did thoughts of operating the British Vickers VC10 four-engined long-range jet. In February 1970, an old Douglas DC-4 was purchased from TAA, the Australian airline, and in March 1970 Air Siam finally began service, albeit a modest thrice weekly freighter to Hong Kong. But it did acquire another piece of paper, at little cost: it became the 105th member of the International Air Transport Association (IATA), significantly a measure that THAI had not taken.

Eventually, on 31 March 1971, Air Siam launched its trans-Pacific service, using a Douglas DC-8-63, wet-leased from a US Supplemental airline, Overseas National Airways (ONA) and configured in a mixed passenger/cargo layout. Such was the initial success of the operation, at least in the patronage, that the seating was progressively increased from the initial 57, first to 83, then to 137, and finally, on 28 July, to 152, including 12 first-class. Plans were made to add a second DC-8-63, and an agreement was signed with All Nippon Airways, the large Japanese airline that had an extensive domestic route network, but which had been frustrated in its attempts to operate overseas.

But this heady success was more apparent than real. To compete effectively on the trans-Pacific route, Air Siam needed three aircraft, and only too late did it discover that the leasing terms with ONA were such that it had to operate at a 90 per cent load factor to break even. What followed was reminiscent of Gilbert and Sullivan rather than of a member of the IATA. On 11 January 1972, the trans-Pacific service was suspended, with ONA claiming it was owed $2,000,000. In March, two defectors from THAI, Virachai Vannukul and Andreas Hansen, joined Air Siam as consultants. On 25 May, service was resumed as far as Tokyo, using a BAC One-Eleven, leased from a Singapore millionaire who had formerly been a taxi-driver. In January 1973, Vannukul leased a Boeing 707 from Germany, put it on the Tokyo route, and blatantly discounted fares in defiance of the admittedly cartel-like international fares and tariffs agreement set by IATA, but of which Air Siam was a member.

By this time Prince Varanand had had enough. On his own admission, he was not an astute businessman. He was an idealist. He had distinguished himself in the RAF as an officer and a gentleman – and indeed he was a gentleman, respected and liked by everyone who came in contact with him – and now he felt that he had been cynically used as a figurehead by his new partners, not to mention exploited as a source of funds, when he settled the ONA debt by selling off more

Air Siam leased a Boeing 707 in January 1973 and introduced it on Tokyo services.

property in downtown Bangkok. Prince Nicky resigned from Air Siam in October 1972, a poorer and wiser man.

The In-Fighting Begins

The conduct of politics in Thailand would make Machiavelli's approach look like a model of orthodoxy and straightforward dealing. And when, in October 1973, the military regime of Field Marshal Thanom Kittikachorn collapsed, the reverberations shook the Thai airline industry to the marrow. Air Siam had just begun Boeing 747 wide-bodied jet service to Honolulu, on 1 September, and was challenging Thai International not only in ruthless commercial competition but in the political arena. Air Siam was pitching low fares (and even, to use an Americanism, low-low fares) and the latest equipment against THAI's *Royal Orchid* luxury service in aging DC-8s. It was also working behind the scenes. Even members of the Government, who were supposed to support THAI as the flag carrier, were working closely with Air Siam. Niels Lumholdt, the Dane who had come to Bangkok in 1964 with the first Caravelle, had learned to speak Thai fluently within a year, and had adopted both Thailand and THAI as his home and life's vocation, described the situation: 'Thai International was being actively undermined by its own shareholders on behalf of a private company'.

For a period following the change of government, a state of near-chaos prevailed. Air Siam's wide-bodied equipment policy forced THAI to respond, and it leased the first Douglas DC-10 on 31 March 1975, from the French airline UTA. It started DC-10 service, to Amsterdam, on 3 April 1975, at the same time modernizing its image with a new corporate insignia that symbolized the orchid theme. Air Siam had already started an Airbus A300B service to Hong Kong on 21 October 1974, and had inaugurated DC-10-30 trans-Pacific service to Los Angeles via Tokyo and Honolulu. But the aircraft was forced to sit on the ground at Los Angeles, pending settlement of landing rights, as apparently Air Siam had not completed the necessary paperwork to exercise its operating certificate.

While this struggle was going on in Bangkok, THAI was going about its business. It converted the leasehold of some of its DC-8s into ownership; and it widened its foothold in Europe with new DC-10 services to Athens, on 3 November 1975, and to Paris on the next day, making a total of seven European cities with direct service to Bangkok. This success was offset, however, by the desperate rivalry nearer home, specifically on the key route to Hong Kong. In January 1976, under pressure from Cathay Pacific Airways, the Hong Kong airline, the British Government suspended all traffic rights for both Thai airlines, a crisis having been created by Air Siam which by this time was discounting fares to an absurdly low level. Meanwhile, the faction within the Thai Government reacted to a demonstration by all THAI and Thai Airways employees outside Government House on 1 August 1976, and who, two days later, called an unofficial strike, demanding the dismissal of the two pro-Air Siam ministers. The ministers ordered the arrest of Niels Lumholdt and his co-director Chatrachai Bunya-Ananta, the efficient head of commercial marketing. Chief pilot Brom and others also made themselves scarce for a few weeks.

End of Air Siam – and Withdrawal of SAS

While the state of unrest was growing, and Air Siam defiantly adding more fuel to the flames, even though it was hardly flameproof itself, there had been much

Among the wide-body types used by Air Siam were the McDonnell Douglas DC-10 (top) and the Airbus A300.

talk about a possible division of the spoils. Air Siam applied to the Thai Government for routes to Europe, and this sparked off much debate, with recriminations (and not without some foundations) about THAI's apathy towards assuring Thailand's interests across the Pacific. The possibility of a merger between all three airlines, THAI, Thai Airways, and Air Siam, was not discounted. Another idea was to divide the world into spheres of interest, with THAI concentrating on Europe and Air Siam on the United States, with both recognized as the flag carriers of Thailand.

Much to the relief of all concerned, except Air Siam, the complex situation resolved itself. For all its bombast, Air Siam was built on the flimsiest of financial foundations. And its equipment policy did little to help. In January 1975 it had four aircraft, all big, but each one different. One Boeing 747, leased from Aer Lingus, and one DC-10, ex-Atlantis, flew spasmodically across the Pacific; one Airbus, leased from Aérospatiale, flew to Hong Kong; and one Boeing 707, also leased, was awaiting disposal. This, as any airline maintenance man will assert, was no way to run an airline.

Air Siam's Virachai Vannukul had, in his efforts to invade Thai International's territory, held discussions with Air Ceylon on 10 November 1975. The idea was to use Air Ceylon's traffic rights to Europe and use Air Siam's aircraft, a case of two weak airlines in the strongly competitive intercontinental market combining to gain stature. But this idea never materialized. With debts growing, and with its Government supporters ejected by the coup d'etat of September 1976, Air Siam collapsed. Virachai Vannukul fled the country. On 12 January 1977, all Air Siam services ceased; on 4 February 1977, Air Siam's operating licence was revoked; and in September 1978 the company was liquidated by the bankruptcy court. It

AIR SIAM 1975

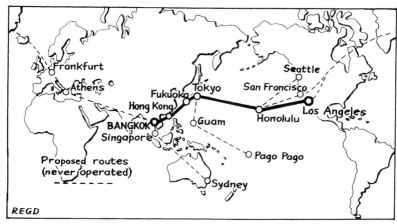

Map 18d. Air Siam, 1975
This airline was the result of a bitter-sweet story. It was the brain-child of the late Prince Varanand – 'Prince Nicky' to his former Royal Air Force friends in England – and he wished to create a purely Siamese airline (he still preferred the old designation of his country). Remarkably, he had been able to obtain operating rights, even with the coveted Fifth Freedom privileges, to Hong Kong, Japan, and to the United States. Unfortunately, the Prince was unable to overcome the established status quo in Thailand, and the ambitious airline's life was short.

was a sad end to an airline that had been founded with the best intentions, but which had been taken over by corrupt and incompetent self-seekers.

One outcome of the whole affair was, ironically, akin to Nicky Varanand's altruistic objective: to have a truly Thai airline, without foreign influence or control. Whatever else it may have achieved, or failed to achieve, Air Siam had stirred up a sense of nationalism, in a 'THAI for the Thais' approach. Niels Lumholdt, effectively running THAI, if not nominally in charge, recognized the inevitability of the trend and took steps to ward off any repetition. Although the legal agreement with SAS was not due to be reviewed until 1979, he accelerated the programme of ultimate transfer of control. Everything came together nicely. On 3 February 1977 Thai Airways International was designated as the sole international operator for Thailand, less than a month after the demise of Air Siam. On 31 March 1977 the SAS shareholding in Thai Airways International was terminated, with Thai Airways, the domestic airline, sharing the ownership with the Ministries of Finance and Communications.

THAI Consolidates

Thai Airways International was now its own master, relieved of any direct European entanglement; and the threat from within, in the shape of Air Siam, had evaporated. While the presence of SAS receded, there was a notable exception. So acclimatized was Niels Lumholdt to THAI; and so acclimatized were the Thai executives to him, that he stayed on in a senior capacity, a tribute to his integrity and his contribution to the airline's stability and survival through troubled times.

Thai Airways put its first Airbus A300B-4 into service in November 1977. (*Airbus*)

If the Thai flag carrier had been negligent or dilatory in the past, it now began to make up for lost time. On 3 March 1977 the first Thai-owned Douglas DC-10-30 (the previous ones had been leased) was delivered, just before the transfer of the SAS shareholding. On 1 November 1977 the first Airbus A300B-4 went into service. On 2 November 1979 the first Boeing 747 was delivered and promptly began to fly nonstop routes to Europe. Then, on 30 March 1980, THAI finally inaugurated trans-Pacific service, flying to Los Angeles via Tokyo and Seattle. The US terminus was soon changed from Los Angeles to Dallas.

By starting service in 1968 to Bali and to Khatmandu, together with Delhi, on the initiative of Lumholdt and Chatrachai, THAI had staked a reputation on its tendency to serve exotic destinations. In 1976 it added service to the Middle East, to Karachi on 1 April, and to Baghdad on 1 May. Kuwait was added on 3 November 1977, Bahrain on 1 November 1978, and Dhahran on 4 April 1978. Elsewhere, Seoul rounded off the east Aisan destinations on 2 November 1977, while expansion into the southwest Pacific included Melbourne on 4 April 1980, Noumea via Manila on 2 November 1980, Perth on 31 March 1982, and Brisbane on 2 April 1982. On 2 April 1981 THAI made its first connection to the People's Republic of China, with a route to Guangzhou (formerly Canton), and this was substituted by direct service to the Chinese capital, Beijing (formerly Peking) on

Thai Airways began to fly nonstop services to Europe late in 1979 using the Boeing 747. (*Boeing*)

225

29 March 1983. At the end of the 1982/83 financial year, THAI was able to report that it served 36 destinations in 28 countries. It operated 20 aircraft, 17 of them wide-bodied types; and it owned them all.

Back at the Ranch

Relieved of its responsibility to operate international trunk routes when Thai Airways International (THAI) was formed in August 1959, Thai Airways concentrated on its domestic system. This was no sinecure. Bangkok was geographically in the middle of a country that measures a thousand miles from north to south. Even though it had progressed from an almost entirely agrarian life-style in the 1920s, when Siam started the first air mail service in Asia, Thailand was still characterized by a dearth of provincial cities of a size that could generate air traffic in substantial volume, at least from the local populace. Thai Airways offset this deficiency partly by setting low fares, so that the community as a whole was able to reap the benefits of air travel, even though its domestic airline did not win any prizes for punctuality, regularity, or efficiency.

Another source of revenue emerged, however. East Asia ceased to be a distant collection of European-influenced and -directed ex-Colonies, and began to assert itself as a regional centre for industrial power and commercial activity, and in so doing created a consumer economy that was self-generated. It was able to lay the foundations of an economically prosperous base that included an element of discretionary income that found an outlet partly in air travel. Bangkok itself had become a desirable destination, for its high – or low – life-style and entertainment, as well as it architectural and cultural attactions. Chiangmai was 'discovered' as the centre of fine arts and ceramics, working elephants, and the most beautiful women in the world. In the deep south, on the Malaysian border, were the cities of Hat-Yai and Songkhla, Thai equivalents to Reno and Las Vegas; and to the southwest the resort island of Phuket, with natural scenic beauty to go with the beaches and palm trees.

Hawker Siddeley 748s served Thai Airways well in the 1960s – nine were used and HS-THC is seen here at Bangkok. (*Hawker Siddeley*)

226

Such tourism opportunities helped Thai Airways to progress steadily, first from its DC-3 status of the 1950s, to the propeller-turbines of the 1960s, and the short-haul jets of the 1970s. The airline made a wise choice for the first of these, in the Hawker Siddeley (formerly Avro) 748, a 44-seater that was reputed to be able to take off from a ploughed field. At some of the small communities in the north of Thailand, beyond Chiangmai, such performance was often close to being necessary. The first HS 748 went into service on 1 April 1964, and Thai Airways built its fleet up to a total of nine, but the DC-3 – as it has demonstrated in almost every country in the world – refused to be dispensable, and was not finally retired until 1975. By this time, the traffic on the main domestic routes, especially to Chiangmai and to Hat-Yai, had increased to such an extent that the choice of jet was the much larger 116-seat Boeing 737-200; and the first one flew to Chiangmai on 21 October 1977.

This Thai Airways Boeing 737, delivered in October 1977, was the first of the fleet in the new white, orchid and gold livery. (*Boeing*)

The HS 748s were gradually retired, but not before they had re-opened service to Hanoi, Vietnam, on 17 May 1978. Also, after negotiations with Laos, which had abruptly terminated service to Vientiane, trans-border routes were opened to that land-locked country still struglling for identity after the bitter conflicts of the Vietnam war.

If the DC-3 was the Thai Airways aeroplane of the Fifties, the HS 748 of the Sixties, and the 737 of the Seventies, then it could be said that the utilitarian Shorts 330, fitted with 30 seats, was the diminutive star of the Eighties. They were the perfect foil for the Boeing 737s, pairing with the larger airliners to match the disparity of urban populations of Thailand's cities and towns. The 737s operated on the main routes to the provincial centres, and to cities in neighbouring countries, some in co-operation with THAI, for example to Penang, Kuala Lumpur and Singapore; while the Shorts 330s provided feeder services to smaller communities. None of the Shorts was based in Bangkok; their bases were at Chiangmai, Khon-Kaen and Hat-Yai. The 737 and the 330 were a team well-matched to the traffic demand. Later, on 22 October, the larger Shorts 360 supplemented Thai Airways' sensible solution to a basic problem.

Internecine Warfare

Operationally and commercially, the 1980s represented a period of stability and prosperity for the Thai airlines. The route structures were sound, and needed little augmentation on a grand scale, the main local changes and additions being THAI'S participation in the southern Thailand markets of Phuket and Hat Yai, by interlining with Thai Airways on 1 December 1983 and 4 February 1984 respectively; and the main long-distance additions being routes to Muscat, Oman, on 6 June 1984, to Bandar Seri Bagawan, in eastern Malaysia, on 5 April 1985, and extensions to Madrid and Auckland on 5 December 1987.

Administratively, the time seemed to have come for rationalizing the peculiar situation in which the small, and relatively inconsequential domestic Thai Airways had for past decades actually been the nominal shareholder controlling Thai Airways International. Fortunately, the two airlines had always managed to get along with each other, although the peace was sometimes a little uneasy; and in recent years they had co-operated in equipment interchanges on trans-border routes. Eventually, the two airlines decided that they might as well simplify matters and on 1 April 1988 they consummated a merger, on the grounds that one could live more cheaply than two.

While such an event might have been the biggest item of aviation news in southeast Asia at the time, it was overshadowed by other goings-on. Thailand has, since the influence of the monarchy receded, been governed by a precarious balance of power-sharing by civil and military factions. The latter have always been a factor in almost every Thai walk of life, and of commerce, with senior military men invariably on the boards of large industries; and the airlines were no exception.

Late in 1988, just at a time when THAI's prosperity was at an all-time high, the airline acquired a new president, Air Chief Marshal Weera Kitchathorn. He immediately put into effect some administrative changes that the previous president had resisted, but which the chairman, Air Chief Marshal Voranart Apichari, desired. Astonishingly, the two combined to undermine the authority of the veteran airline executives who had guided THAI's fortunes, by their shrewd management decisions, to the position of eminence and respect that had been so well earned. The winter of 1988/89 was a season, not so much of discontent, but of the long knives. Several minor incidents, normally routine temporary setbacks experienced by any airline, combined to exacerbate discontent, leading to slackness in some areas. Of all people, the main victim of what could have been a disastrous purge, was Chatrachai Bunya-Ananta, possibly the most capable of all the Thai personnel who had grown up under the SAS era, and had demonstrated by his grasp of airline expertise that the Thais could run their own airline. Another victim was Captain Chusak Bhachalyud, the capable vice-president who had ensured that THAI's technical capability and maintenance shops were the equal of any airline in the east. Almost incredibly, to anyone who has even a passing knowledge of Thai affairs, charges of corruption were made against Chatrachai and Chusak – this in a country where corruption was almost a way of life.

Thankfully, this tense situation came to an end, for the good of all. On 1 October 1989, the chairman, Voranart, resigned/retired, and was succeeded by Air Chief Marshal Kaset Rojananil, who proceeded to pour some much-needed oil on sorely troubled waters. Weera ceased to be influential in policy matters, especially those affecting the upper echelons of THAI's management. And Thailand's national airline, now unified, settled down to facing the problems of the 1990s.

These concerned primarily the financing of the new fleets of wide-bodied

Thai Airways leased a number of 86-passenger British Aerospace 146s.

aircraft that were vital if THAI was to face the competition with equanimity. Because of the burgeoning traffic, the accent was on larger aircraft on all fronts: on the long-haul routes, the medium hauls, and on many of the shorter ones in the provinces. Thai Airways had leased a fleet of 86-seat British Aerospace BAe 146s to cope with the demand even to small communities. Bigger Airbuses, the A300-600R series, were needed for Asian regionals, while more Boeing 747s, including the -400s, were essential to maintain parity with the likes of Japan Air Lines and Cathay Pacific. The problem was that, under the peculiarities of Thai law, THAI's borrowing powers were limited, and some ingenious manipulation of financial arrangements were needed, with partial, if not complete privatization, viewed as the solution.

Whatever the outcome, the Thai airline will maintain its parity with its competitors, ensure that Bangkok remains as the main air traffic hub of southeast Asia, and no doubt keep a watchful eye on the dangers from within.

A de Havilland Canada Dash 8 of Bangkok Airways at Ko Samui in 1990.

Bangkok Airways

With the gradual spread of de-nationalization and deregulation throughout the world of commercial aviation, Thailand too witnessed a resurgence of the spirit of independence that had given birth to Air Siam. In 1985, Bangkok Airways was formed by Sahakol Air, an independent charter, contract, and air-taxi group. It began scheduled operations, with an Embraer EMB-110 Bandeirante, on a route from Bangkok to Samui Island, off the east coast of the southern peninsula of Thailand, now becoming a popular vacation resort.

It extended its routes, on a semi-scheduled basis, to Phuket and Hua Hin, and acquired a de Havilland Canada Dash-8, which, unfortunately, crashed at Samui on 22 November 1990, killing 38 people. This undoubtedly affected the airline's bid to achieve the status of Thailand's second designated air carrier, but fresh capital was forthcoming, and a fleet of five ATR 72s was acquired. In 1994, none other than Virachai Vannukul, who had presided over the downfall of Air Siam, took over the role of managing director, with the declared intention of creating an airline of substantial domestic and even international stature.

CHAPTER NINETEEN

Airlines of Vietnam (formerly French Indo-China)

French Airline Activity in Indo-China

During the 19th Century France gradually rebuilt its overseas empire, after ebbs and flows of territorial dominance, in conflict with other European powers, which had reached its peak during the Napoleonic era that came to an abrupt end in 1815. Retaining only fragmentary enclaves of territory in India – smaller, even, than the Portuguese possessions – the French went further east, to establish footholds in the mainland area of southeast Asia that, being neither clearly identifiable as Indian nor as Chinese, became known, with commendably neutral logic, as Indo-China.

In 1858 the French occupied Tourane (now Da Nang) on the coast of Annam (simultaneously and coincidentally with the creation of the British viceroyalty of India, with the dissolution of the East India Company). The following year, Saïgon was similarly occupied and the surrounding region, or eastern Cochin China, was added in 1862. France established a Protectorate over Cambodia in 1863, annexed the whole of Cochin China in 1867, and took over, as Protectorates, Annam in 1883 and Tonking in 1884. The Union of Indo-China was formed in 1887, and Laos became yet another Protectorate in 1893. From this territorial base France expanded its influence over the southwestern provinces of China, and built a railway from the Indo-Chinese port of Haiphong to Yunnan, as well as establishing another trading enclave at Kwang-chow (Fort Bayard) on the south coast of China, to the west of British Hong Kong and Portuguese Macao.

After the Great War of 1914–18, the colonial powers explored the potential of air transport in Asia with great caution, not least because the problems of support and maintenance of aircraft thousands of miles away from the supply source were formidable. In India, the British had taken the view that aircraft could not offer any substantial improvement over a good railway system. The Dutch, in their East Indies, had more incentives to connect the islands by air, and by the early 1930s, did so. Indo-China, comprising a narrow coastal strip with a jungle and mountain hinterland, lent itself to railway construction, and a line from Hanoi to Saïgon was built during the inter-war years.

Nevertheless, a small company, Air Asie, was formed in 1926. Its origins could be traced to the early efforts to establish aviation in French Indo-China. On 10 January 1921, a military aeroplane carried the Governor from Hanoi to Saïgon, and carried some mail on the return flight. During the next few years, about sixty airfields or strips were prepared, and by mid-1925 fairly regular flights were being made between Kratié, in Cambodia, to Savannakhet, in Laos, to avoid a long detour over land routes.

In December 1926, the Société Indochinoise d'Études d'Aviation Commerciale et Postale (SIEACP) was established, based in Saïgon, and Commandant Glaize, former head of military aviation, was appointed to plan commercial air services. But no flights were made. Then, on 1 July 1928, this organization became the Société d'Etudes et d'Entreprises Aériennes en Indochine et en Extrême Orient

An Air France Fokker F.VII/3m at Saïgon in prewar days. (*Courtesy John Stroud*)

(SEAIE), with participation by the Banque Franco-Chinoise, the Banque de l'Indochine, the Compagnie des Messageries Maritimes, the Compagnie du Canal de Suez, and the Société d'Aviation Louis Breguet.

There was an interesting diversion when the French operator Compagnie Aérienne Française (CAF) made an experimental flight from Saïgon to Hong Kong, with one of four Schreck flying-boats, on 24 May 1929; but nothing came of this international sortie.

SEAIE made two experimental flights from Nha Trang to Hanoi, via Tourane, from 8 to 18 June of the same year, and in September changed its name to the less unwieldly Air Asie, with French Government authority to carry mail between Saïgon and Bangkok, to link with the KLM service to Amsterdam. This connection got under way in December, using two Potez 32s and shortly afterwards had built its fleet to four of the Potezes and one Lioré LeO 198.

Back in the homeland, Lignes d'Orient had been formed as a subsidiary of Air Union. Much valuable survey work was performed by the famous French aviator, Maurice Noguès, and a regular air mail service began from Marseilles to Syria in June 1929. Lignes d'Orient took over Air Asie and on 17 January 1931, as Air Orient, inaugurated a ten-day mail service to Saïgon. By this time, full passenger service had been introduced as far as Baghdad, with the Mediterranean section of the route flown by CAMS 53 flying-boats, and Breguet 280Ts taking over from Damascus eastwards. The service became part of Air France when all the French airlines merged in 1933, and for several years shared service frequencies and equipment with the Dutch KLM as far east as Bangkok, until the introduction of the luxurious (by contemporary standards) Dewoitine D.338 airliners in 1939. By this time, the French route to the Orient had been extended from Hanoi to Hong Kong, via Fort Bayard, on 4 August 1938.

With the onset of the Second World War, French Indo-China fell into the Vichy Government camp, and was easily assimilated by Japanese aggressive expansion throughout the region; and Saïgon became an important base for Japanese military air support networks during the conflict. As the war drew to a close, the Japanese disarmed the Vichy forces, or the remnants thereof; the Chinese occupied northern Indo-China, or north Vietnam, while the British forces occupied southern Vietnam. The nationalist leader, Ho Chi Minh, declared the foundation of the Democratic Republic of Vietnam.

In 1946, the British transferred political authority to the French and Ho Chi Minh, the acknowledged symbol of Vietnamese independence, allowed French troops to take residence in March of that year. But reactionary French politicians and military men sabotaged any hopes of rapprochement, soured relations with the local inhabitants, and precipitated the First Indo-Chinese War.

Foundation of Air Vietnam

Although the Age of Colonialism was visibly coming to an end, French hegemony over the oriental vestige of its Empire was preserved during the late 1940s and early 1950s, and the outward appearance of French culture as well as the re-establishment of commercial links was maintained. Air France included Saïgon as a key element of its intercontinental route map, and French independent airlines also joined in this effort to retain the vital air link. Late in 1953, in fact, such was the national need that all the French airlines, together with the manufacturing company SNCASE which had produced the large piston-engined SE-2010 Armagnac, amalgamated their patriotic support efforts to form the Société Auxiliare de Gérance et de Transports Aériens (SAGETA) to ensure a regular supply line from France to Saïgon and Hanoi.

Locally, Air Vietnam was formed on 1 October 1951, to take over the domestic and regional services formerly operated by Air France, which supplied the aircraft fleet, provided managerial and maintenance support, and was effectively the parent company. Under its own name, Air Vietnam began services between all the main cities in Vietnam and to Vientiane (Laos), Phnom Penh (Cambodia) and Bangkok (Thailand), on 15 October; and soon extended service to Hong Kong. It also enjoyed the privilege of a blocked space agreement with Air France, in which one of the weekly Super Constellation flights to Paris was designated by an Air Vietnam flight number.

At this time, one of the French independent companies extended its overseas network to Vietnam. Aigle Azur began service to Saïgon and Hanoi in 1952, using ex-TWA and Pan American Boeing 307 Stratoliners, of which only a few had been built, in 1940, as the first pressurized airliners in the world, and which were to survive the vicissitudes of about thirty years of alternating peacetime commercial and military operations, under various flags and banners, during the Vietnam War.

Strange Interlude

Aigle Azur (*see* above) had set up a local branch in Indo-China, as Aigle Azur Extreme-Orient, and had equipped it with four of the sturdy Boeing 307 Stratoliners. Early in 1964, two of these passed to the Compagnie Internationale de Transports Civils Aériens (CIC) and the other two 307s followed the next year. CIC was headquartered in Paris, and its unusual role was to provide a regular airline service between two warring nations, on behalf of the International Control Commission, whose diplomats needed some way to travel between Saïgon and Hanoi, in the hope of negotiating a peace settlement between North and South Vietnam.

By 1967, the 307s were operating as many as eighteen flights a month, on the inter-capital route, and calling at Phnom Penh and Vientiane. They carried officials, business men, journalists and Red Cross staff along a precise track, with no deviation permitted outside a 20-mile-wide corridor. One aircraft disappeared, and another survived an exploding suitcase which injured seven passengers.

CIC ceased operations in the summer of 1974, after the cease-fire agreement of 23 January 1973. Two of the 307s went to a Cambodian charter airline, Cambodia Air Commercial, which, however, did not last long, as one crashed on 27 June of that year, and the other was scrapped. The third 307 had already been leased to Royal Air Lao, and written off on 27 February 1971.

Until 1954 Air Vietnam was ostensibly a French overseas airline, but in that year everything changed. Constant friction and armed conflict between French forces and Vietnamese patriots (or revolutionaries, depending on which side defined their role) culminated in a humiliating defeat of the French at Dien Bien Phu, west of Hanoi, on 8 May. Thus, the first Indo-Chinese War came to an end, and the Geneva Peace Agreement of 21 July 1954 divided the country (now no longer referred to as Indo-China but as Vietnam) into two parts. The dividing line was drawn at the 17th parallel of latitude, and Air Vietnam's northern terminus was curtailed from Hanoi to Hué. One year later, with the erosion of French influence, the Republic of (South) Vietnam was officially proclaimed, with Ngo Dinh Diem as its first president.

Air Vietnam Thrives

Hang-Khong Viet-Nam – to give the airline its full Vietnamese name – had survived all the various political and military crises, and still had a predominantly French flavour, if not absolute identity; and in fact, Air France still held, nominally, 33 per cent of the stock. In 1960 Air Vietnam leased two Vickers Viscounts from Air France, but these operated only until 1962. Seemingly immune from all the alarums and excursions that surrounded its activity – Diem was killed in a military coup in 1963, and the United States confronted Vietnamese vessels in the Gulf of Tongking in 1964 – the airline displayed commendable determination, in the true spirit of airlines everywhere, to maintain business as usual. In September 1964 it acquired an ex-VARIG Caravelle through Air France, and introduced it on the Phnom Penh–Bangkok and Hong Kong routes. This same aircraft, early in 1965, opened up a new route to Kuala Lumpur and Singapore, and was, incidentally, the first jet aircraft to land at the Malaysian capital's new airport. In December 1966 this Caravelle also exended the Hong Kong route to Taipei, a destination that, with subsequent political events, was to become an important factor in providing technical support for the airline.

In 1964 Air Vietnam acquired an ex-VARIG Sud-Aviation Caravelle and employed it on routes from Phnom Penh to Bangkok and Hong Kong.

By some criteria, Air Vietnam should have declined, in the face of threatening escalation of a bitter civil war, with massive foreign intervention. Quite the reverse happened. French influence in what used to be Indo-China was rapidly being replaced by an American presence, as the US Government perceived, rightly or wrongly, that communist penetration into South Vietnam from the North would spell the beginning of communist dominance over the whole of southeast Asia, in

Air Vietnam acquired two Boeing 727s in January 1968.

a demonstration of the 'Domino Theory', with the People's Republic of China dealing all the key pieces. Ever ready to serve US interests, Pan American Airways, the so-called 'Chosen Instrument', replaced Air France as Air Vietnam's Big Brother. In January 1968 it sold two Boeing 727 tri-jets to Air Vietnam, at a cost of $5,500,000, including spares, which was not a bad price at the time. On 1 March 1968, these entered service on all the main domestic routes and on the international connections, especially to Taipei; and the Caravelle was returned to Air France.

Now completely within the United States's sphere of influence, Air Vietnam had a fleet of almost forty aircraft, most of which, however, were old piston-engined transports, but perfectly adequate for day-to-day workhorse activities in the war-torn zone of conflict. Sixteen of its thirty-one Douglas DC-6s, 6Bs, 4s, and 3s, C-46s and Beech 18s, were leased from China Airlines, and no doubt the fleet mix was seldom the same from one month to another. The famous 'Tet Offensive' of 1968 seemed to be only a temporary interruption of Air Vietnam's operations, and the Paris Peace Talks of January 1969 then paved the way for further enterprising expansion, with the Taipei route extended to Osaka and Tokyo on 30 July 1969.

During the height of the American military presence in Vietnam, the airline's traffic, in fact, boomed, as it became part of the essential transport organization for army support, civil evacuation, and quasi-administration and communication. The route between Saïgon and Da Nang, for a short time, ranked among the busiest air routes in the world, with aircraft departing almost every hour. Encouraged by the American authorities, Air Vietnam charged very low fares, to assist the population, a large portion of which was unhappily becoming almost nomadic in its way of life. Such a flurry of activity, however, during which time load factors were seldom less than 95 per cent, began to diminish in volume when, in September 1969, President Nixon announced the beginning of a phased with-drawal of US troops from Vietnam. At the time, these numbered about 550,000, and provided quite a large market for the local airline. To reinforce the capacity, Air Vietnam leased a Boeing 707 from Northwest Airlines, from the end of 1970 until the summer of 1971.

A New Look – Pride Before the Fall

Brimming with confidence, and undoubtedly reinforced by faith in an ultimate American and United Nations cloak of imminent security, Air Vietnam moved into a wider field of ambition. Hardly had the massive North Vietnamese offensive of

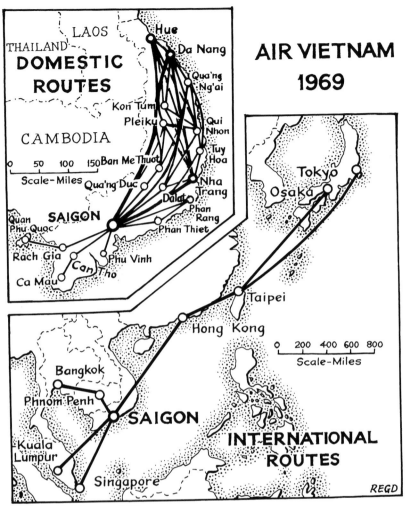

Map 19a. Air Vietnam, 1969
During the height of the Vietnamese war, when South Vietnam was surviving as an independent nation, thanks to a powerful American presence, the national airline served not only as a supporting unit for the US and Vietnamese armed forces, but also provided a low-fare air service for the community as a whole. For a short period, this was one of the most intensive airline networks in the world, and the Saïgon-Da Nang route one of the world's busiest.

1972 ended with yet another Cease-Fire Agreement, on 27 January 1973, when, in the April of the same year, Air Vietnam bought a Boeing 707-300 – i.e., a long-range aircraft – from Pan American, at a price of $2.5 million. Simultaneously, it decked itself in entirely new colours, retiring the traditional dragon of Vietnamese mythology and replacing it with a striking red and yellow new corporate identity which, had it lasted, would have been acknowledged as one of the most striking in the whole world of airlines.

The dazzling new colours epitomized the renewed hope that an innovative spirit could salvage something from the ashes of the old and create an airline that could proudly match the sophistication of its southeastern Asian neighbours. These were seen only briefly. Sadly, after a year during which the staff of Air Vietnam energetically worked towards this objective, the axe fell once more. On 30 April 1975, the South Vietnamese Government surrendered against concerted attacks on Saïgon by the Vietnamese forces from the North. On 2 July 1975 Vietnam was formally re-united; Saïgon was officially renamed Ho Chi Minh City; and Air Vietnam ceased to exist

Vietnam Airlines

The Hanoi Government began – or rather, reinstated — domestic air service in November 1976, between Hanoi and Ho Chi Minh City, and also to neighbouring Vientiane, Laos, and Phnom Penh, Cambodia (Kampuchea). The operation used whatever aircraft it could make servicable: leftover DC-3s, DC-4s, and DC-6s, even a Boeing 707; and then Antonov An-24s, Tupolev Tu-134s, and Yak-40s, with one or two Ilyushin Il-18s and Il-14s, to comprise a motley fleet of about twenty.

In February 1990, the management of the airline passed from the Defence Ministry to the Transport Ministry; the name was changed to Vietnam Airlines, and, under the new government policy of *doi mo*, or 'open-ness' it was given virtual autonomy and instructed to operate commercially.

By 1991, the new management made a code-sharing agreement with Cathay Pacific Airways, the first of many such agreements with several airlines. It tried to upgrade its fleet with western airliners but was frustrated by the United States embargo which ordained that no aircraft could go to Vietnam that had more than 10 per cent of US-manufactured components. But the following year, the siege was broken, when the airline leased two European 72-seat ATR 72s, whose construction circumvented the terms of the embargo. These were soon followed, on 15 February 1992, by two leased Boeing 737–300s, painted a neutral white, under a 'sub-service' agreement — a nice euphemism for a wet-lease. The political door was opening.

An Airbus A320 of Vietnam Airlines. (*Airbus Industrie*)

In the summer of that year, French President Mitterand made a state visit to Vietnam, along with Bernard Attali, chairman of Air France. An Airbus A310-300 was leased, but was soon grounded at Taipei and a dispute arose as to who should pay for the repairs. Vietnam Airlines was back to its Tupolev Tu-134s. But in January 1993, a wide-bodied 767-200ER was leased, and on 31 August a number of A320s wet-leased from France. The first of the latter arrived on 25 October 1993, flown in by Air France, with full technical back-up.

The US enbargo was lifted on 27 January 1994. Vietnam's economic recovery had been impressive. Airline traffic had risen from about 50,000 passengers in 1986 to 1.6 million. Service to Moscow had begun in 1993, and Berlin and Paris linked Vietnam once again to Western Europe. After the protracted exigencies of wars, in rejecting colonialism and the tragedy of civil war, few would have predicted that Hanoi-based Vietnam Airlines would, by the mid-Nineties, be making its mark and taking its place among the progressive airlines of a vibrant southwast Asia.

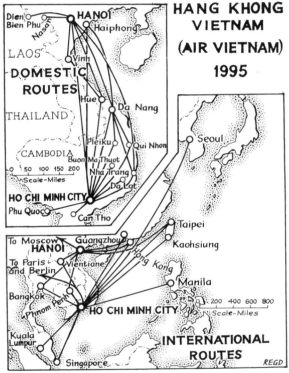

Map 19b. Hang Khong Vietnam (Air Vietnam), 1995
The Vietnamese name of the national airline was not in general use until after the unification of Vietnam in 1975. For many years, the policy was inclined to be introspective, with little outside contacts, except to communist countries. Gradually, however, relations with the West improved, and as Vietnam establishes its place in the international community, its airline echoes the trend. Ho Chi Minh City, the former French Saïgon, is beginning to emerge as a new destination for travellers in Southwest Asia.

CHAPTER TWENTY

Airlines of Cambodia

The Long Road Back to Independence

A whole millenium ago, from the 9th to the 13th Centuries, the Khmer Empire, centred on what later became known as Cambodia, extended from the present-day Thailand to Indo-China, in a civilization that produced such architectural wonders as Angkor Wat, of such structural resilience to the destructive forces of time, climate, and natural forces that, like the Roman ruins, it survives today, albeit in a delapidated state. During the Middle Ages (as European historians term the period) the Khmer Empire fell under the dominance of Siam (Thailand) until, in 1863, French colonialists assumed control and incorporated Cambodia into the Union of Indo-China, along with Tongking, Annam, Cochin China and, later, Laos.

Independence, or at least partial autonomy, was finally regained in 1953, when the wave of nationalism by the indigenous peoples of the region led to the first Indo-Chinese War that ended with the capitulation of the French forces at Dien Bien Phu in 1954. When the Japanese over-ran Cambodia in 1941, they assigned the Prince Sihanouk as the nominal head of state, and he it was who stayed in power when the French returned in 1945 and withdrew in 1953, but still retaining strong French commercial connections.

An Airline of Its Own

On 14 June 1956, a French-Khmer declaration paved the way for the formation of a national airline, and Royal Air Cambodge (RAC) was founded on 15 October of that year. The Cambodian Government held 38 per cent of the shares, 28 per cent were privately owned, and Air France had 34 per cent. Service began on 20 October with Douglas DC-3s, bequeathed by Air France, from the capital, Phnom Penh, to Siem Reap – the nearby city and airport serving Angkor Wat – and to Bangkok and Saïgon.

The following year, modest expansion took place, with the addition to the fleet of a Boeing 307 Stratoliner, one of a rare breed, of which only a few were built in 1940, but which had the merit of being the first pressurized airliners in the world. The aircraft was leased from the French independent airline Aigle Azur, and for a brief period of accelerated air activity, provided both scheduled service to Hong Kong, beginning on 2 July 1957, and on-demand service to tourists who, after a long period of denial, were once again able to re-discover the ancient glories of Angkor.

Cambodia was relatively unaffected when fighting broke out again in 1957 and the northern-based Vietcong guerilla groups began to infiltrate into southern Vietnam and crossing the borders; but though RAC airline service was intermittent and irregular, continuity was maintained, and on 11 February 1959, a Constellation leased from Air France resumed service to Hong Kong. In January

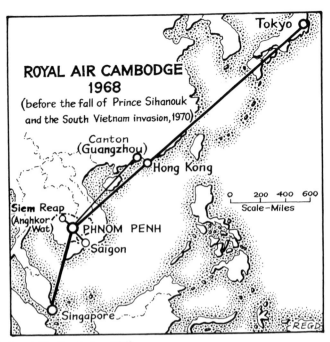

Map 20. Royal Air Cambodge, 1968

Cambodia was once a great kingdom, centre of a flourishing civilization and culture; and even in French colonial times, was a stable province of Indo-China. With the departure of the French, however, and the achievement of independence in 1953, the country was a hotbed of political intrigue. Prince Sihanouk had assumed power after the Japanese invasion in 1941, tried to maintain a neutral stand during the Vietnamese War, and for a brief period, was able to show the Cambodian flag at a few airports in East Asia.

1961 this was upgraded by the use of a blocked-space agreement on Air France's own Boeing 707 jet service.

During the 1960s, the fortunes of Royal Air Cambodge ebbed and flowed in tune with the uncertainties, the confusion, and sometimes the chaos of political conflicts, alternating with temporary and precarious alliances, that characterized the way of life in southeastern Asia. On 12 October 1961 service to Bangkok, the biggest commercial centre of the entire region, had to be suspended because of political problems between Sihanouk's government and Thailand. Displaying considerable resilience, for its resources were not great, RAC nevertheless purchased a Douglas DC-4 and began service to Vientiane, Laos, in August 1962, and to Singapore on 24 August 1963. The next year, a route to Canton (Guangzhou), via Hanoi, was added, so that, theoretically (although few followed theory into practice) airline passengers could fly from Singapore to Canton by the politically neutral Cambodian airline. For these international connections RAC purchased a Douglas DC-6 in January 1965, but had to suspend service to Vientiane and Hanoi in June of that year. Then the escalation of the war between North and South Vietnam destabilized the whole region, and Royal Air Cambodge along with it.

During the latter 1960s, while RAC actually strengthened its service to Canton –

In January 1969 Royal Air Cambodge added a Sub-Aviation Caravelle to its very mixed fleet.

such were its relations with the People's Republic of China – an interesting quasi-airline service was operated in an almost clandestine, if not secretive manner, to maintain essential communication between the disparate pieces of the former French Indo-China. The Commission Internationale de Controle (CIC) linked Saïgon with Hanoi, *i.e.* the capitals of the warring South and North Vietnam Governments, respectively, with flights that stopped at the officially neutral Cambodian capital Phnom Penh, and Laotian capital, Vientiane. The ex-Aigle Azur Stratoliners, drawn from various sources, including RAC, participated in this unusual example of air transport's vital role in the political process.

By 1967 Royal Air Cambodge's fleet consisted of a variety of aircraft, under an equal variety of leasing or trading agreements. These ranged from a Boeing 720 for the longer routes, a Convair 440 and a Fokker F.27 for regional service, and a veteran DC-3, DC-6 and DC-6B, one of each, plus a more modern Britten-Norman Islander, a diminutive but versatile aircraft which had the merit of being able to fly into and out of small fields that even the DC-3 had difficulty in using. The airline even operated a Russian Ilyushin Il-14 presented to Prince Sihanouk by a friendly Chinese Government, and made available for general – though undoubtedly privileged – use.

Changing Fortunes

The tide continued to ebb and flow at the end of the decade, with the Vietnamese War now in full swing. Royal Air Cambodge had managed to acquire a Caravelle twin-jet in January 1969, and with the fall from power and control of Prince Sihanouk in March 1970, the name of the airline was contracted to Air Cambodge. South Vietnamese forces invaded Cambodia in May 1970, and Sihanouk departed, in exile, to China, while Lon Nol seized power in Cambodia, which became known as the Khmer Republic. In January 1971, the precious Caravelle was destroyed in a guerilla attack on Phnom Penh, but, after a lapse of time, a second one was obtained and the connection with Bangkok was resumed. By this time, the

Kampuchea Airlines began services to Bangkok in November 1991 with a Tupolev Tu-134.

Kampuchea Airlines employed the Antonov An-12 on cargo services. This one still carries the Soviet registration on the fuselage ahead of the word 'Cargo' which appears in red capital letters.

political see-saw had changed direction, and the Thai capital became almost a lifeline for Cambodia as relations with Vietnam hit a new low.

Yet worse was to come. In 1973, the left-wing extremist faction, heavily backed by China, and calling itself the Khmer Rouge, began a fanatical and vicious civil war in Cambodia. Phnom Penh surrendered to the communist onslaught on 17 April 1975, and this was followed by the forcible evacuation of most of the city's

242

XU-802, a Kampuchea Airlines Mil Mi-8. The livery is white with two shades of blue.

population into the surrounding countryside, mostly rice fields, where virtually the entire land became a labour camp. At least a million people (some estimates place the figure at twice that number) were either executed or died from hunger, disease, or maltreatment in what became known as the Killing Fields. Under such circumstances of sustained privation, and during which period administration, commerce, and culture were almost non-existent, airline activity of any kind became an anachronism.

In 1978, there were – if civil carnage was not enough – further Vietnamese incursions, but on 8 January 1979, the Khmer Rouge announced the formation of a government, and changed the name of the country to Kampuchea, as a symbol of the historical heritage of the Khmer rather than the European colonial empire. With a population already reduced by perhaps 30 per cent, including almost all the educated sections of the population engaged in administration, commerce, and service industries, the country was further drained by a mass exodus of refugees into Thailand.

Eventually, a rather bedraggled phoenix arose from the blood-stained ashes. On 7 September 1982, Kampuchean Airlines announced the beginning of flights from Phnom Penh to Ho Chi Minh City (formerly Saïgon), during a short period of uneasy cessation of actual fighting. But on 10 January 1983 the Vietnamese began yet another offensive, and Kampuchea/Cambodia was reduced to a state of political and social turmoil until Vietnam withdrew its forces in 1991. As always after periods of hostilities, the airline was one of the first organizations to pull itself together again, and in November 1991 began flying to Bangkok, its Tupolev Tu-134 twin-jet revealing its political leanings and source of supply.

But things were changing, or rather a different kind of change was occurring in a country where instability was normal. The Kampuchean airline was reported to be wet-leasing its Tupolev to a company called SK Air; while Phnom Penh Airways was flying a wet-leased Fokker F-28. Time alone will tell if this unhappy land will be able to re-establish its commercial airline representative that will carry its flag into foreign parts.

CHAPTER TWENTY-ONE

Airlines of Laos

The First Air Laos

The area known as Laos was always a backwater of the region in southeast Asia that has commonly been known as Indo-China. Geographically, it has always been on the northern fringes of Siam, or Thailand, in the valley of the Mekong River; and until it became a French Protectorate in 1893, the agrarian community fell under Thai control. Little was done to develop Laos by the French, who seemed content to regard the elongated strip of territory as a kind of buffer zone, separating Annam and Tongking from Siam. The Second World War and Japanese occupation made little difference to the Laotian way of life or its destiny; so that when it gained its independence on 19 July 1949, as a constitutional monarchy under Prince Souvanna Phouma, the world took hardly any notice.

Late in 1952 Air Laos was founded by the Government, with French assistance. Laotians held 50 per cent of the shareholding, Aigle Azur 20 per cent, and Air France 30 per cent. Aigle Azur was one of the French independent airlines and it was able to provide the first Douglas DC-3 for the diminutive company. Service began in December of that year, between Vientiane and Luang Prabang, the two chief cities of Laos, and to four other Laotian towns, replacing the main form of transport, the river boats that plied along the Mekong. As more DC-3s and a de Havilland Canada DHC-2 Beaver became available, service was gradually expanded to a total of fifteen communities; and in a country that never had a railway and in which roads were sporadically located and linked provincial towns with foreign points rather than with each other, Air Laos could be said to have provided the embryo nation with its first public transport service.

In 1953 the airline ventured eastwards with DC-3 flights to the two big cities of Vietnam, Hanoi and Saïgon, so that the Laotian capital of Vientiane had connecting service with Hong Kong, gateway to the world in southeast Asia. But this did not last very long. The first Indo-Chinese War came to an end, or more correctly a pause, with the defeat of the French forces at Dien Bien Phu and with the Geneva Conference of Foreign Ministers partitioning Vietnam at the 17th Parallel on 21 July 1954. But fighting continued in Laos between the communist Pathet Lao and the pro-western General Phoumi Nosavan. The air route to Hanoi was terminated, and Air Laos all but disappeared from the scene until a modest rejuvenation occurred in 1956, when Aigle Azur deployed a couple of its Boeing 307 Stratoliners under nominal Air Laos administration to re-open the connection to Hong Kong via Tourane, now renamed Da Nang.

Routes were also started to Phnom Penh and Siem Reap in Cambodia, but the domestic network all but disappeared as guerilla forces in northern Laos regarded Air Laos's DC-3s and Beavers much in the same way as they regarded enemy aircraft. The late 1950s, in fact, was a period of severe political and military instability, with confused reports from both sides seldom revealing the true situation. By 1958, fighting in Laos was widespread, with the CIA-backed CAT from

Taiwan establishing itself in Vientiane with supreme contempt for local sensitivities or sovereignty. Such was the United States influence and dominance in Laos that the CAT organization became Air America, and proceeded to operate a host of different aircraft, part-civil, part-military, part-secret and unidentified, in a widespread support operation of vital importance to the United States presence in southeast Asia.

On 23 July 1958, Prince Souvanna Phouma was forced out of office. In August, the 'Great Laos Fraud' was perpetrated, with exaggerated reports of a North Vietnam invasion intended to escalate the war. Such escalation was to come later, and the main effect was to create utter confusion in Laos, with communist-allied Souvanna Phouma vying with the CIA's General Phoumi Nosavan for sovereignty. In May 1961 the US (Kennedy) administration agreed to a cease-fire between the two factions and in June a coalition Laotian Government was formed between the US-backed Phoumi, Souvanna Phouma (who now seemed to vacillate in his political leanings), and the openly communist Pathet Lao. The old Air Laos ceased to exist and its equipment was taken over by a new company, Royal Air Lao.

Royal Air Lao

The Douglas DC-3s resumed service on domestic routes in 1961 but no other equipment was available until two years later, when a Douglas DC-4 was purchased, and the aerial connection was made once again with the outside world, to Bangkok and to Saïgon. Extension to Hong Kong did not come smoothly, although re-activated briefly in 1964. Cathay Pacific Airways apparently had problems with Laos and the Hong Kong authorities did not allow the Laotian link to be confirmed until operated in pool between the two airlines. By 1965, an understanding had been reached, by which Royal Air Lao operated flights under its own name, but on behalf of Cathay Pacific. The delicacies of airline-to-airline agreements, intertwined with government regulatory uncertainties and vacillation, against a background of political and military conflict, left Air Lao as an almost ghost-like operation, with only a pretence of a scheduled service, even of a vague identity. In fact, with the United States Air Force transferring its northern Vietnam operational base to Vientiane in 1968, the little airline could only with difficulty make its presence felt at all.

A Royal Air Lao Lockheed L-188 Electra.

245

A Lao Aviation Antonov An-24RV. The red, dark blue, red livery duplicates the colours of the Laos flag.

RDPL-34116 is a Lao Aviation Chinese Yun Y-12.

This leased Boeing 737 in Lao colours bears the Icelandic registration TF-ABH.

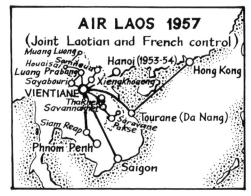

AIRLINES
IN
LAOS

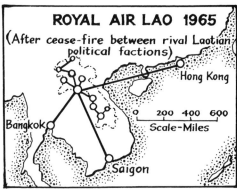

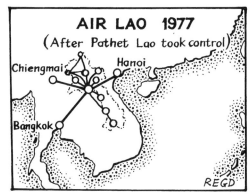

Maps 21. Airlines in Laos
Laos was never more than the poorest of the provinces of the former French Indo-China. And although theoretically a constitutional monarchy from 1949, it was always at the mercy of conflicting military and quasi-military influences from neighbouring states, particularly North Vietnam and South Vietnam when they were at war. This map series shows the limited scope of its small airline, before, during, and after the devastating civil war beyond its borders.

Eventually, with the Second Vietnam War raging to the east, and with the Vietcong turning the length of Laos into the Ho Chi Minh Trail as a supply route for the North Vietnamese guerilla fighters, the Cease-Fire Agreement of 21 February 1973 brought at long last the opportunity for Royal Air Lao to act like an airline. The CIA's Air America began a phased withdrawal; and the other US airline based in Vientiane, Continental Air Services, also packed up its oil-drums. But the survival of the company, brave show that it tried to make, was short-lived. It obtained a Caravelle on lease from Air France and started to fly to Bangkok and Canton; but when the Laotian Government changed a year later it was returned to Air France. The French national flag-carrier used it for special diplomatic flights from Bangkok to Ho Chi Minh City (formerly Saïgon) until a hijacker blew himself up in the cockpit in August 1976.

Left Turn

Sharing in seemingly endless internecine fighting in southeast Asia, Laos finally entered an era of relative serenity when, in May 1975, with the conflict in Vietnam thankfully coming to an end, Prince Souvanna Phouma ordered his government troops to cease fighting, and the Pathet Lao took control. On 3 December of the same year, the Lao People's Democratic Republic was proclaimed, and Air Lao provided the international cross-border link with Thailand, with DC-3s inherited from Royal Air Lao, flying on schedule to both Chiangmai and Bangkok. Consolidating this resumption of comparative normality, an Air Agreement was signed with Thailand on 12 December 1977, thus permitting fuel supplies to be made to a deprived, and commercially isolated, Laos. Shortly thereafter, now with a new fleet of three Antonov An-24s, the Bangkok route was strengthened with a closer association with Thai Airways, and a new route opened, twice a week, to Hanoi. Domestic services were also resumed to seven communities and towns.

Imperial Airways linked the United Kingdom with Hong Kong by a branch line (originally from Penang) from the main trunk route to Australia. The first service was flown by the de Havilland 86 *Dorado* which is seen here at Kai Tak, Hong Kong, in March 1936. (*Courtesy John Stroud*)

CHAPTER TWENTY-TWO

Airlines of Hong Kong (and Macao)

Outpost of Empire

When the idea developed of providing swift communications and mail services by air to distant Colonies and Dominions, the European empire powers of the 1930s provided only limited contact with eastern Asia, the notable exception being KLM's splendid air artery to the Netherlands East Indies. Britain's Imperial Airways' main destination was India, and onwards in due course to Australia, so that Malaya and Singapore, being en route, were fortunately on the priority list; but Hong Kong was only a branch line from the main line to Sydney.

Hong Kong's first scheduled air services, in fact, were by the United States airline Pan American Airways, through, at first, its affiliated Chinese company, China National Airways Corporation (CNAC), in which it held a 45 per cent shareholding. On 8 October 1930, CNAC opened a flying-boat service from Shanghai, via Chinese coastal ports, using Sikorsky S-38s, succeeded later by Douglas Dolphins, and eventually by Douglas DC-3s.

Imperial Airways began service, as a branch line of the Australian route at Penang, on 24 March 1936. De Havilland D.H.86 G-ACWD *Dorado* picked up passengers and mail from an Armstrong Whitworth Atatlanta, and flew via Saïgon and Tourane (now Da Nang) in French Indo-China. The following month, Pan American made the direct connection with its trans-Pacific route, by opening a Manila–Hong Service with the 38-seat Sikorsky S-42B *Hong Kong Clipper*. The contrast between this standard of passenger comfort with that of the D.H.86 biplane was marked, and commented upon by Juan Trippe, Pan Am's president, when he flew westwards around the world to attend a conference in London. Imperial Airways re-routed its D.H.86 from Bangkok via Udorn, Hanoi and Fort Bayard on 19 December 1937, this last point being a small French enclave in China, west of Hong Kong. Air France began to serve the British Colony on 4 August 1938, with an extension of its Indo-China service from Hanoi, also via Fort Bayard, using a Dewoitine D.338.

On 2 September 1938, Hong Kong was included in the Empire Air Mail Scheme, by which all letters were carried by Imperial Airways without surcharge, but this admirable public service was suspended on 15 October 1940, when European hostilities led to the severe curtailment of civil air activities. Pan American's service was also abruptly terminated on 12 July 1941, when its S-42B was destroyed by Japanese bombing, only five days after the surprise attack on Pearl Harbor, Honolulu.

Hong Kong was occupied by Japan for the duration of the Second World War. When, at last, it emerged from the conflict, Imperial Airways had merged with British Airways to become BOAC (the official date was 1 April 1940, so that the last prewar service had been under the flag of the merged airline), and the Empire air routes were being served by a fleet of fine flying-boats, operating from Poole Harbour, in Dorset. Hong Kong rejoined the network on 24 August 1946, when a Short Hythe (S-25 converted Sunderland), G-AGLA *Hunter*, arrived, having connected with another Hythe, G-AGIA *Haslemere* at Karachi. The Hythes gave way to Plymouths (S-25 Sandringham) on 23 June 1947; and, as the flying-boat era came to a close, Canadair DC-4M Argonaut landplanes took over on 23 August 1949.

By this time, Hong Kong was beginning to stand on its own airline wheels. It had always been a great entrepot of the shipping trade, and its merchants, British and Chinese alike, were among the most enterprising in the world. The Chinese mainland was still politically unsettled, and the establishment of local air service demanded, perhaps, a special breed of aviator entrepreneurs. When the moment came, these cavalier airmen came not from Britain, but from the United States and Australia.

Creation of a Hong Kong Airline

Many great airlines have been formed by enthusiastic and dedicated pilots with an intense belief in aviation and the use of the commercial aeroplane to carry people and goods, and to make a good living for its operators. Most of these well-intentioned enterprises lasted for only a short while, before being engulfed by subsidized and/or supported flag carriers; or they closed down in the face of larger and better capitalized competitors. Cathay Pacific Airways was an example of one of these cavalier, swashbuckling outfits that, starting as a buccaneer charter company, prepared to chase the often illegal traffic where it could find it, then grew in stature and respectability, to the stage where, with the injection of substantial private capital, it achieved the status of one of the world's most respected international scheduled trunk airlines.

Cathay Pacific was conceived, if not yet born, in Miami, Florida, the springboard origin point of thousands of aircraft that were ferried from the USA to the eastern hemisphere during the Second World War; and where, towards the end of 1945, many demobilized pilots sought out war-surplus aircraft with which they felt they could make a living with non-scheduled charter operations. Among these was a group of Americans, Roy Farrell, Millard Nasholds, Bob Russell and Bill Geddes-Brown, together with an Australian, Sydney de Kantzow. They pooled their resources and bought what Charlie Eather described in his autobiographical *Syd's Pirates* as 'an oil-stained, unsalubrious, deceivingly-camouflaged scow of a DC-3 of questionable antecedents and dubious age.' It was Cathay's first aircraft and they still have it today, albeit laid to rest in Hong Kong's transport museum.

Roy Farrell and Syd de Kantzow quickly emerged as the natural leaders of the group of DC-3 investors, Farrell as the organizing businessman – he came from an entrepreneurial family in Texas; while de Kantzow was the operational specialist, with many years of flying experience that included Ansett in Australia, Great Western and Southern Air Lines in Britain, with the Royal Air Force, Pan American, and the last-named's subsidiary in China, CNAC. All of them had been involved with CNAC, and they now foresaw excellent marketing prospects between China and Australia, as the Far East recovered from the ravages and deprivations of war.

In October 1945, the DC-3 – actually a C-47-2-DL with military serial 41-18385 and then US registration NC58093, and which had cost $30,000 from the Liquidation Commission – was flown to Shanghai via Recife, Dakar, Karachi, Calcutta, Kunming and Kweilin, the latter part of the journey following the route of the famous 'Hump' supply route from India to China, which was familiar territory to the group. Beginning in the manner in which they intended to carry on, they had loaded the aircraft with western clothing, to be sold at a profit on arrival in Shanghai; but learned a quick lesson when they discovered that little of the consignment was left, having been pilfered by ground staff en route. Arriving in Hong Kong, the venerable DC-3 was re-registered VR-HDB.

Cathay Pacific Airways' first aeroplane, the Douglas C-47 VR-HDB.

At first, the embryo company concentrated on the Hong Kong–Australian traffic, and the sole DC-3, now named *Betsy*, began its first trip on 4 February 1946. Five weeks later, on 11 March, the Roy Farrell Export-Import Company was registered in Sydney. Then in September of the same year, the group met in what was then the Cathay Hotel in Shanghai, to decide their future course of action. They decided to form a legitimate airline, based in Hong Kong, and, after some discussion, chose the name Cathay Pacific Airways. It was formally registered on 24 September 1946, with an authorized capital of HK$5,000,000.

The new airline started its first scheduled service on 10 December, to Singapore, via Bangkok, once a week; but its main business was still in charters, picking up business when and where it could be found, often at short notice. During this period, the countries of southeast Asia were in a state of political unrest, even turmoil, and aircraft were in demand for all kinds of purposes. Almost as a parting gesture, in March 1945, the Japanese had interned French citizens in Indo-China, and declared the creation of Vietnam. When the Emperor Bao Dai signed an agreement with the French aboard a cruiser off the coast at Haiphong, a Cathay Pacific Catalina flying-boat supplied the transport service. Cathay and Bao Dai were old friends: the fledgling airline had evacuated him from Tourane in September 1946 on one of its earliest and unusual charter assignments.

During 1947 and 1948 most of Cathay's activities extended from India to the Philippines, and south to Indonesia, both on scheduled routes and on charters, but sorties were made elsewhere if a good business opportunity arose. Thus, while, by 1948, regular services were established to Manila and Rangoon, as well as to Bangkok and Singapore, the DC-3s – now numbering seven – ventured on charter flights as far as the United Kingdom, Sydney, and to Greece, this last to carry immigrants to Australia. In 1947, Cathay was also involved in assisting the Indonesian DC-3 IRI in running the Dutch blockade on flights from Burma to southern Sumatra.

Cathay's Consolidated PBY-5A Catalina *Miss Macao* which was hijacked and destroyed on a scheduled Hong Kong—Macao flight.

Nearer to home, Farrell had always realized that a healthy trade between Hong Kong and the nearby Portuguese Colony of Macao was there for the pickings. Macao did not possess an airstrip, and so Cathay acquired three Consolidated Catalinas, which began to ply between the two colonies twice a day and often more frequently, on demand. On 1 July 1948, these aircraft were transferred to Macao Air Transport Company (MATCO), presumably as a matter of financial, rather than operational convenience. Unfortunately, only two weeks later, on 16 July, *Miss Macao* was hijacked soon after take-off from Macao; the hijacker shot the pilot, and the Catalina crashed. Twenty-six passengers and the three crew perished, but one passenger survived. The scheduled service from Hong Kong to Macao was then suspended.

Cathay Pacific Reorganizes

In another venture, Cathay had acquired, in November 1947, two Avro Ansons, with which they proceeded to carry fish to Malaya and Burma. One of these crashed in Burma on 9 February 1948, and possibly because Cathay was beginning to attract attention from the Hong Kong authorities on the grounds of safety – two crashes within six months – or because some of its activities seemed to be fishy in more ways than one, the company was reorganized, under pressure from both official and business interests in Hong Kong. Also the British State-owned airline, BOAC, had established, on 4 March 1947, a subsidiary, Hong Kong Airways, and had furnished it with four DC-3s, with which it started to build up services to the Chinese mainland. Clearly, Hong Kong was no longer an outpost of Empire, as in prewar days, but developing into a commercial community in its own right; and because of its relative isolation from overland trade routes, airlines were obviously destined to play an important part in the local business world. Accordingly, the business world took steps to associate themselves with the airline operations.

The legendary trading company, Jardine, Matheson, was founded early in the nineteenth century.. It had built its fortune at least partly on the opium trade, and its historical presence is still marked today by the firing of the 'Jardine Gun' at mid-day from Hong Kong. Jardines were closely associated with BOAC from the outset, and the Gun may have been metaphorically aimed at its traditional rival trading company, Butterfield and Swire, founded in 1867. For on 18 October 1948, complying with Hong Kong legislation that required local participation (Cathay's owners were either American or Australian) Cathay Pacific Airways was completely reorganized.

This had followed a period of several months of negotiation, in which the driving force was the Swire organization in London, and represented throughout by John K Swire. A British airline, Skyways, and the shipping firm Far Eastern Navigation Company, dropped out, and the final participation in Cathay Pacific Airways (1948) Limited was: China Navigation Company (a Swire-owned shipping company) 35 per cent, Australian National Airways (ANA) 35 per cent, John Swire & Sons 10 per cent, de Kantzow 10 per cent and Cathay Pacific Holdings, representing the original founders, 10 per cent. The company then began to settle down to what might be described as fully legitimate operations, in contrast to the previous activities that had been viewed by the authorities with a certain amount of apprehension, especially the non-scheduled flights that some unkind critics characterized as aerial piracy.

Hong Kong Airways

Hong Kong Airways received designated route authority from His Majesty's Government on 22 October 1947. This covered particularly the Chinese mainland, and also to Manila. The airline's mission was to extend and to help protect British commercial interests in China, in the face of substantial inroads made by Pan American Airways, through its Chinese subsidiary, China National Airways Corporation (CNAC). Pan Am had penetrated China back in the 1930s, with a policy that was both commercially aggressive and technically competent. Through

One of Hong Kong Airways' Douglas DC-3s. This view gives a good impression of the proximity of high ground. (*BOAC*).

its Hong Kong subsidiary, BOAC hoped to redress the balance, in spite of the aging DC-3 fleet and in spite of an official restriction to offering more than 50 seats a day on any single route.

Hong Kong Airways started its first scheduled service on 2 December 1947, to Shanghai, and followed this shortly afterwards, on 10 January 1948, to Canton (now Guangzhou). This latter connection with China's biggest southern city was so popular that the twice daily initial frequency was increased to four daily on 22 March 1948. Later in the year, service opened to Manila, a route that it shared with Cathay.

Had political conditions stabilized in China, the BOAC-Hong Kong Airways connections would undoubtedly have gained the British flag carrier a vital entree into China. but the conditions were far from stable. Expanding from its stronghold in Yenan, Shensi Province, Mao Tse-tung's Communist forces gradually occupied the whole of northern China by the summer of 1948 and the whole of the country by the end of 1949. Chiang Kai-shek's Nationalist Government, based in Chungking, and latterly in Chengdu, migrated to the island of Taiwan (Formosa), where it remains today as an independent state. BOAC's enterprise was therefore almost stillborn, as the new Chinese government promptly cut all its ties with the West, and apart from an ill-fated decade of liaison with the Soviet Union, effectively remained in isolation from the rest of the world for a quarter of a century.

But for this development, Hong Kong Airways might have prospered, as on 13 May 1949, the Government ordained a division of the spoils in terms of designated routes, whose ultimate authority came from London. All routes to the north of Hong Kong became the exclusive catchment area for Hong Kong Airways (and this would have included the whole of China as well as Japan and the other emerging country, Korea); while all routes to the south were allocated to Cathay Pacific. The route to Manila, to the southeast, was shared between both airlines and was the geographical dividing line between the two spheres of interest.

In the event, after the Communists took over China, BOAC sold the whole of its shareholding in Hong Kong Airways to Jardine, Matheson on 30 November 1949. The DC-3 fleet was sold, and thereafter the airline confined its activities

Passengers board a Hong Kong Airways' DC-3 at Kai Tak, with cloud obscuring some of the high ground. (*BOAC*)

almost entirely to flights to Taiwan, with aircraft chartered from Northwest Airlines, the US trans-Pacific company.

Cathay Consolidates

Far away from aircraft manufacturing and major airline sources of maintenance support and of spares supply, either in Europe or the United States, the Hong Kong airlines realized that they had to establish a solid technical base right at home, at Kai Tak Airport. The Swire Group established the Pacific Maintenance and Supply Co Ltd (PAMAS) on 4 November 1948, while Jardines formed the Jardine Aircraft Maintenance Co Ltd (JAMCO) about a year later. Realising that this was an area that lent itself to broad-based co-operation, the two companies merged PAMAS and JAMCO on 23 November 1950 to form the Hong Kong Aircraft Engineering Company (HAECO), which became one of the best-known technical support installations in the whole of Asia, and whose reputation for efficiency spread world-wide.

With China now erased from the commercial aviation scene, Cathay's main route to Bangkok and Singapore was Hong Kong's main air route, apart from the intercontinental flights that passed through, mainly BOAC's and Pan American's. (Japan was still recovering from the industrial devastation of the War, and its miracle of prosperity and growth had not yet begun). On 23 September 1949, the Douglas DC-4 entered Cathay service on this important southeast Asian inter-city link, and although the DC-3 fleet was now reduced to five (one had crashed on 29 February 1949) and the Catalinas had been retired, new services were opened to what was then still called Indo-China, to Saïgon, on 2 November 1949, and to Haiphong and Hanoi on 12 November. The British North Borneo (now Sabah, Malaysia) points of Sandakan, Jesselton and Labuan, were added on 5 January 1950; so that when the official route licences were finally signed and sealed on 22 March of that year, Cathay Pacific Airways had a respectable route map that also included Rangoon and Calcutta.

Sydney de Kantzow then sold some of his shares, in April 1950, retaining only 5 per cent, with Cathay Holdings, representing the other founders, still with 10 per cent. The remainder, almost 75 per cent, was divided equally between the

255

Cathay Pacific introduced a Douglas DC-4 in September 1949. It was shot down by a Chinese fighter.

Australian ANA and China Navigation, i.e. the Swire interests. In a further reshuffle, in April 1951, de Kantzow pulled out altogether, as did the other founders, and Cathay Pacific became a key element of the Swire organization, nominally 37 per cent with China Navigation, 23 per cent with Swire Holdings and 40 per cent with ANA. De Kantzow retired to Australia, but sadly, was killed in a car crash on 21 November 1957.

Cathay Pacific Airways maintained its scheduled route network during the early 1950s, although these were still fraught with uncertainties, even though the cavalier charter operations were now a thing of the past. Tensions between the communist regimes of east Asia and the western powers intensified, and in April 1954, Cathay pulled out of northern Vietnam, suspending service to Haiphong and Hanoi. This was none too soon, as the '17th Parallel Agreement' further alienated relations as Vietnam was split into two irreconcilable halves. Such were the political sensitivities that, on 23 July 1954, Cathay's flagship, its sole DC-4, was shot down by a Chinese fighter aircraft. The incident took place off the southeastern tip of Hainan Island. Many of the passengers and some cabin crew were killed by the gunfire, but Captain Cedric Carlton managed to ditch the DC-4 so that the survivors could clamber on board an inflatable dinghy. After being spotted by some RAF patrol aircraft, they were eventually rescued by a Grumman Albatross, commanded by Captain Jack Thompson, from the United States Clarke Air Force Base, north of Manila, who performed a daring and technically brilliant feat of airmanship in alighting on the high seas.

The DC-4 was replaced almost immediately by one purchased from Canadian Pacific Airlines, going into service on 12 August; but the disruption coincided with the withdrawal of service from North Borneo. This was rectified when the Borneo Company purchased a 4 per cent share in Cathay Pacific in 1956. By this time, in April 1955, the fleet had been augmented by a Douglas DC-6, purchased from PANAGRA, and two years later, on 22 June 1958, by a DC-6B. This latter represented a new departure for Cathay Pacific Airways, as the aircraft was obtained directly from Douglas, brand new, and cost HK$6,750,000.

The Merger

The DC-6B was Cathay's first pressurized aircraft. It might have been shamed into this improvement in passenger comfort, because of the resurgence of the old Hong Kong Airways, which, in October 1954, took on a new lease of life by ordering

A Douglas DC-6B was introduced by Cathay in 1958.

(through BOAC, which had bought back its 50 per cent interest) two Vickers Viscount V.760Ds, HKA had managed to struggle on with a single DC-4 during the early 1950s, but now it upgraded the standards of the locally-based Hong Kong airlines. The Viscount went into service on a route to Seoul, Korea, on 25 February 1957, and extended to Manila in March, and Taipei and Tokyo in April and May of that year. Suddenly, Hong Kong Airways had become a force to be reckoned with.

There were, however, some problems with the Japanese authorities, which presumably regarded the HKA link with Tokyo as a thinly-disguised device by the British to gain the ascendancy with a dual-designation service into the Japanese

One of the Vickers-Armstrongs Viscount 760Ds which went into service with Hong Kong Airways in February 1957. (*Vickers*)

257

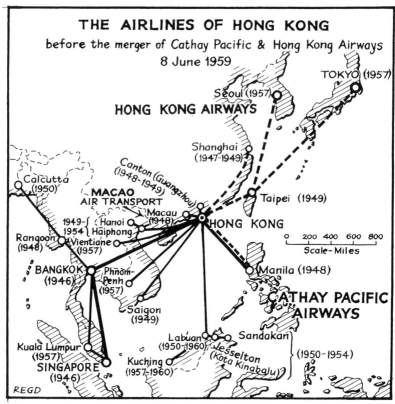

Map 22a. The Airlines of Hong Kong, before the merger of Cathay Pacific and Hong Kong Airways

Before the Second World War, Hong Kong was the terminus of two airlines, Imperial Airways from Great Britain, and Pan American Airways from the United States. With the cessation of hostilities, an indigenous airline industry came to life, one company, Hong Kong Airways, established by British Overseas Airways Corporation (BOAC) as an operating associate, and one by local commercial interests in the trading and banking community. Hong Kong's sphere of influence was to the north, Cathay Pacific's to the south. The two airlines merged in June 1959, and became a powerful component in the competitive air transport arena of the Western Pacific Rim.

capital, now beginning to take its place in the world of commerce and trade. Soon after the new runway was opened at Kai Tak Airport, heralding a new era for Hong Kong commercial aviation, and emphasizing its importance as a strategic point in the airline networks of the Far East, the two companies, Cathay Pacific and Hong Kong Airways, rationalized the situation and came together.

In December 1958, a new company, Cathay Pacific Holdings, was formed by Cathay Pacific Airways, in conjunction with BOAC, which bought out Jardine, Matheson's shareholding in Hong Kong Airways. On 1 February 1959, Cathay took over the management of HKA, and on 8 June 1959, the two companies were officially merged to form the new Cathay Pacific Airways. Jardines had been offered a shareholding, but did not take it up. Butterfield and Swire held the majority and controlling interest, either directly or through the China Navigation Company; BOAC held 15 per cent, and the Australian Ansett Airways, which had taken over Australian National Airways (ANA), retained 12 per cent of the newly capitalized airline. The HKA Viscounts were transferred to Malaysian Airways, another of BOAC's Associated Companies, so that, of the original Cathay fleet, the new company had four Douglas aircraft, a DC-3, a DC-4, a DC-6, and a DC-6B. Operationally, the merger took place on 1 July 1959.

Electras to Australia

The new solidified airline was off to a fine start. In September 1957, Cathay had ordered two Lockheed L-188 Electras, no doubt reacting to Hong Kong Airways' introduction of the Vickers Viscount. The first of the Lockheeds went into service to Manila, Bangkok and Singapore on 24 April 1959 and when the second aircraft arrived, Cathay took a big step, not only extending turbine service to Saïgon, but also to Sydney, with a stop at Darwin, to expand the Hong Kong airline's sphere of direct interest beyond the Asiatic continent.

The first Cathay Pacific Lockheed Electra entered service in April 1959.

Before the merger, the route network had remained quite stable, with only minor changes, these being the result of local conflicts or crises over which Cathay Pacific played the role – as airlines so often do – of a neutral communications supplier, with political indifference. Thus, the routes to North Borneo and to North Vietnam were temporarily suspended in 1954, but partially reinstated, with different destination points, three years later. Also, in 1957, Pnom-Penh, Cambodia, and Vientiane, Laos, were substituted for the Vietnam points; and Kuching, Sarawak, for the points in North Borneo. Kuala Lumpur, the capital of the newly-formed state of Malaysia, was added in the same year, and service to Brunei was inaugurated on 25 February 1960, replacing service to Labuan, suspended a week earlier, and making redundant the Kuching route, dropped on 15 December that year. During the same period, Cathay Pacific also had the privilege of opening the first international air service to Osaka, Japan's second city, and the air gateway to Kyoto, with the Douglas DC-6B.

Cathay's accelerated route expansion received an abrupt set-back when the Lockheed Electra suffered a series of crashes in the United States in 1960, and came close to being grounded by the FAA. The problem had been caused by cyclic vibration in the engine-propeller linkage, causing airframe (wing) fractures, and the FAA

259

a

b

c

d

Some of the men who built air transport in
Hong Kong – *a* J A Swire; *b* J H Bremridge;
c H J C Browne; *d* D R Y Bluck;
e H M P Miles

e

allowed the aircraft to continue flying only on condition that every Electra in service was withdrawn and structurally modified. Lockheed mounted an impressive programme to complete the modifications in the minimum amount of time, and with the minimum inconvenience to the operators, who were financially compensated.

Cathay was lucky. The Electras were out of service from 4 December 1960 to 4 February 1961; but because of its connections with BOAC, the Hong Kong airline was able to lease a Bristol Britannia 102, whose performance was, if anything, better than the Electra's.

Moving onward, with the Electra problems behind it, Cathay reinstated Seoul as a destination in December 1960 (it had been dropped at the time of the merger), and Djakarta was added on 7 September 1961, to bring the new nation of Indonesia closer by air to Hong Kong. Jesselton (soon to be renamed Kota Kinabalu) was also reinstated, but – keeping strictly to the demands of good book-keeping, rather than the desire to retain an impressive line on the map – Sydney was dropped, not to be resumed until twelve years later.

While the propeller-turbine airliners had a place in history, their role in the front line was relatively brief, except in circumstances where certain local conditions favoured them over the jets. In most cases, however, jet airliners swept into service in great numbers in the early 1960s, following Pan American's dominating introductory fleet of Boeing 707s, and the competitive battle between Boeing and Douglas for commercial airline jet supremacy. With Pan American, BOAC, and other jet airlines gracing the runways at Kai Tak (the Comet of the early 1950s had not been able to serve Hong Kong, because of the inadequacy of the old shorter runways), Cathay Pacific had to follow suit.

Cathay Enters the Jet Age

Demonstrating an independence that was to characterize its policies in the future, Cathay Pacific did not order either the Boeing 707 nor the Douglas DC-8, choosing instead the Convair 880. Third in the list of four-engined first-generation jets, the 880 was smaller then either the Boeing or the Douglas, and was claimed to be marginally faster, although it did not have genuinely trans-ocean range. Cathay did not need the longer range, but it could make promotional use of the speed, and its pilots inherited a tradition of competitive flying that harmonized with the technical virtuosity. In the hands of a Cathay crew, the approach into Hong Kong in a Convair 880, whether over the rooftops of Kowloon before coming in sight of the

Cathay Pacific chose the Convair 880 as its first jet equipment.

261

checkerboard on the mountainside and making the most dramatic curved ILS approach in the world, or coming in under radar and steering between the islands off Hong Kong, was an experience to remember; and Cathay thrived on the sheer excitement of flying an aircraft that was as responsive as a fighter.

Once again, with the new addition to its fleet, Cathay consolidated its position as one of the leading airlines of the Far East. It started Convair 880 service on 8 April 1962, and firmly established its 'grandfather' rights on the Hong Kong–Bangkok–Singapore traffic triangle by signing pool agreements with Thai International and Malaysian Airways on 1 August 1963 and 9 January 1963, respectively. It carried its millionth passenger on 20 October 1964. The figure does not seem to be extraordinary today, but this was achieved by an airline that had obtained its first pressurized aircraft less than a decade previously.

With its eyes on the now prospering Japan, and recognizing that this once-defeated country was on its way to becoming the industrial powerhouse of the Pacific, Cathay moved accordingly. From 15 February 1965, the Osaka/Tokyo services were flown only by Convair 880s. On 2 September of that year, service opened to Fukuoka, followed by Nagoya on 10 January 1966, the latter another 'first international' for Cathay. Okinawa, which would later return to Japanese sovereignty, came on line on 1 October 1967, effectively giving Cathay five gateways into Japan. The Hong Kong airline was showing its mettle by increasing its Convair 880 fleet to five, and – almost as a tacit recognition of its growing stature – signed a pool agreement with Japan Air Lines, which by this time was beginning to take its place as one of the world's leading intercontinental airlines.

The early 1970s witnessed mixed fortunes for Cathay as it settled down to its jet operations. Of its nine Convair 880s, two were lost, one previously on 5 November 1967, when it failed to take off and crashed in Kowloon Bay, fortunately without loss of life; and another on 15 June 1972, over Vietnam, after a bomb had been planted on board in Bangkok, by a police lieutenant wishing to collect insurance money. But on the whole, the Convairs did well, and established Cathay's reputation in the entire eastern Asia region for good service undertaken with élan and flair.

A Qantas Boeing 707 on final approach to Hong Kong's runway 13. The pilot is negotiating the final right turn (on the curved approach), having checked his position by the infamous 'checkerboard' on the mountainside. (*Qantas*)

262

It was able to inaugurate service to Perth, Western Australia, via Kuala Lumpur and Jakarta, on 1 April 1970, thus providing direct service from that fast-growing city to Asia (and onwards to Europe) for the first time. A brief experiment with flights to Siem Reap, close to the ancient ruins of Cambodia's Angkor Wat, was unsuccessful; and connections to Pnom Penh and Calcutta were suspended.

Changes were made in the corporate structure, as the airline gained strength. It had already indicated this in October 1968, when it purchased a controlling interest in Bahamas Airways, a long way from home, but in an area that was strategically situated for long-term future planning in the North American vacation market. On 14 April 1971, the powerful Hong Kong & Shanghai Banking Corporation bought a 25 per cent shareholding in Cathay, for $21,000,000, the remaining interests mostly split between Swire interests, at 48 per cent, and BOAC with 15 per cent. Shortly afterwards, on 15 June, Swire increased its holdings by purchasing the 12 per cent still held by Ansett Transport Industries, thus severing the last Australian connection. In little more than twenty years, Cathay Pacific Airways had developed from a small airline run by a group of cavalier pilots to one of Hong Kong's most prominent business ventures, and taking its place alongside the other units of Swire Group's shipping, warehousing, and trading interests.

Cathay Turns to Boeing

While the Convair 880 had performed well, it lacked the necessary range for Cathay to extend and expand its network with nonstop service to the more distant points; and the traffic was growing to a level that demanded a larger aircraft type. The airline bought a fleet of twelve Boeing 707-320Bs from Northwest Airlines, and the first one went into service on 24 August 1971. This event coincided with the installation of Cathay's first computer reservations system, CPARS, which went on line on 1 July.

The romantic resort destination of Denpasar, Bali, received Cathay Pacific service on 17 September 1971, but ran into difficulties with the Indonesian authorities, when its national airline protested that all traffic to Bali should be routed

In 1971 Cathay Pacific bought twelve Boeing 707-320Bs from Northwest Airlines.

through Jakarta. Compensating for this irritant, Kagoshima became the fifth Japanese destination on 17 August 1972, and, after a new runway had been completed at Brunei, Convair 880s reinstated service to the sultanate, via Kota Kinabalu on 27 January 1973, after an absence of six years.

Cathay's growth was gathering further momentum in 1973. On 14 March it carried its 5 millionth passenger; on 3 July it bought four more 707s for HK$120,000,000, the largest order ever in Hong Kong aviation history; and on 21 October, now with the necessary range to dispense with intermediate stops, service to Sydney was resumed.

Possibly testing the competitive climate, as it were, of the long-haul airways to Europe, Cathay had entered into an agreement with British Caledonian Airways in November 1972, breaking the history of involvement and integration with BOAC. The two airlines combined to introduce a low-priced Australia–Europe fare, at US$408 from Perth, and US$472 one-way. The fare included accommodation at hotels in stop-over points in Singapore and/or Jakarta. Not only did the fare undercut the QANTAS US$500 fare, but it offered the convenience of a break in the 12,000-mile, 30-hour journey to London (not to mention the duty-free shops in Singapore); and British Caledonian offered a more generous baggage allowance.

Regional Sparring

By the mid-1970s Cathay Pacific Airways was beginning to flex its muscles and to test its own strength. On 2 January 1974, Butterfield and Swire was renamed John Swire & Sons, recognizing that the Butterfield name was an archaic survival, and in an internal regrouping in May 1975, Swire Pacific acquired the China Navigation's and John Swire and Sons (HK)'s holdings. As the designated British airline linking Hong Kong with Japan, Swires now took on Japan Air Lines, working through the government bilateral negotiating channels. In March 1974, Japan Air Lines was obliged to omit Hong Kong from its Tokyo–Sydney service, in retaliation for Japanese restrictions on Cathay at Osaka. On 15 September, further restrictions were imposed on JAL at Hong Kong, affecting its privileges in picking up and setting down Hong Kong–Singapore (fifth freedom) traffic. With Hong Kong's geographical and commercial strategic position, Cathay and the British negotiators had a strong card to play, and on 1 November, full air services were resumed by both airlines after final agreement by all parties concerned.

One factor that played an important role in commercial aviation affairs in east Asia was the fact that few of the major airlines were members of the International Air Transport Association (IATA) the international agency that was widely viewed – against vigorous but unconvincing potests from the member airlines – as a price-fixing cartel. Japan Air Lines was almost alone among the leading airlines of the region as an IATA member, but (and this was before All Nippon Airways was permitted to fly international routes) it was the dominant carrier, with reported traffic figures greater than those of most European companies. As a defensive measure – or perhaps as a challenging one – JAL's competitors formed, in April 1974, a joint committee of non-IATA airlines. It was named CTMS, after the initials of its members, Cathay, Thai, Malaysian, and Singapore; and it became CCTMS in November when China Airlines joined the group.

No problems of a serious nature had ever existed with the Philippines, but to the south, Indonesia was different. The squabble with Garuda Indonesian Airways dragged on for many years, especially over the rights to fly direct to Bali; but by 1 April 1978, the difficulties had been resolved, and the daily service to Jakarta

Part of the approach lighting at Hong Kong airport (*GEC*)

via Singapore, even allowed fifth freedom rights on the busy Singapore–Jakarta segment, which was, by this time, approaching the status of a high-frequency air shuttle operation, shared between Garuda and Singapore Airlines.

The TriStar Story

The traffic levels on Cathay's main route network demanded larger, wide-bodied aircraft; but as yet the volumes did not appear to justify investment in the very big Boeing 747, whose 360 seats, even in a generous mixed-class layout, was more than double that of the Boeing 707-320 series that it was to replace. The choice was between the Douglas DC-10-30 (or -40) with General Electric (or Pratt & Whitney) engines; or the Lockheed L-1011 TriStar, with Rolls-Royce engines. The European twin-engined Airbus A300 was out of the running because the versions available thus far did not have the range for all of Cathay Pacific's regional routes. On the other hand, while not requiring intercontinental capability, nonstop service

The wide-bodied Lockheed L-1011 TriStar, introduced in September 1975 gave outstanding service to Cathay Pacific.

to Sydney was essential, and a competitive battle ensued between Douglas and Lockheed.

The Lockheed L-1011 TriStar won, and on 18 March 1974, Cathay ordered two 'long-range' versions, the -100 series, and was first on the list of the airlines that opted for this variant. The decision was believed at first to be influenced by Rolls-Royce (whose engines powered the Lockheed) and the inclination to 'Buy British', a perfectly legitimate reason, even if this transcended performance and economics-operational considerations. The TriStar was charged with being able to fly with full payload in all conditions either way nonstop between Hong Kong and Sydney. The Douglas DC-10 could do this with ease, but the L-1011 was only marginally capable. The astonishing sequel to this episode is that, on 10 February 1976, Captain Bernard Smith, Cathay's Director of Flight Operations, admitted that he had received US$80,000 from Lockheed to promote the L-1011, and promptly resigned.

But the deed was done. The TriStars went into service on 15 September 1975, on the Taipei–Tokyo route. It was subsequently deployed everywhere on Cathay's route network, and gave a good account of itself; and though the nonstop Sydney route was not achieved with complete regularity, this was not a serious embarrassment to the operations as a whole.

In an interesting development, following the bilateral agreement negotiations between the British and United States Governments in what became known as 'Bermuda II', Cathay Pacific Airways was designated as the British airline for 'Route 7' from Hong Kong to San Francisco, by the traditional route across the central Pacific originally pioneered by Pan American Airways in 1935. BOAC had entered the trans-Pacific airline fraternity with a Britannia 312 service on 22 August 1959, after protracted and unfraternal protests from Northwest Airlines. But BOAC and its successor, British Airways, found that the route was unproductive and, like other airlines that have aspired to round-the-world services, lost interest and suspended it.

But Cathay was beginning to reach out in other directions. On 16 November 1976, the TriStars began to serve Bahrain, in the Persian Gulf, which also

A Cathay Pacific TriStar on finals to runway 13 at Hong Kong. (*Ray Cranbourne*)

happened to be the eastern terminus of British Airways' prestigious supersonic Concorde service from London. Melbourne was added as the third major Australian Cathay city – Darwin's role was mainly as a technical stop, and service ceased entirely in August 1979. Although the addition of Dubai on 2 November 1977 brought the number of Cathay's stations to twenty, Penang having been added as an en route stop to Singapore on 3 April of that year, the number was less important than the service frequency. On 1 November, with the opening of nonstop daily services to both Tokyo and Osaka, the total of Hong Kong–Japan flights reached 41 a week. On 1 April 1978, Cathay was operating seventeen times a week to Manila and eight a week to Australia; while on 18 December of that year, frequency to Bangkok rose to twenty-two, including those that continued to Persian Gulf points, in pool with Thai International. Also during 1978, Kaohsiung, the important industrial city in southern Taiwan, and Nagoya came on line on 1 November, the latter reinstated after the already mentioned bilateral problems with Japan. Three days later, Port Moresby, the capital of Niugini, received Boeing 707 service, and on 1 February 1980, with improving relations with the People's Republic, service began to mainland China, to Shanghai, the city that, in bygone days, had shared with Hong Kong the leadership in east Asia in British overseas commercial enterprise and trading establishments.

The London Route

Until the late 1970s, Cathay Pacific was always regarded by London as a large regional airline. Possibly, until fundamental changes of government policy in Great Britain were made in parallel with the spirit of 'Bermuda II', the new bilateral agreement with the United States that considerably widened opportunities for new routes and new gateway cities, Cathay's own perspectives and horizons were not much wider. All this changed when, in November 1979, the Hong Kong Air Transport Licensing Authority (ATLA) granted a licence to Cathay Pacific to operate three scheduled services a week from Hong Kong to London, via Dubai and Bahrain. At the same time, British Caledonian Airways, Britain's Second Force airline, was granted four services a week, with a choice of four points in the Persian Gulf. The ATLA's powers were limited in that they did not carry with them full operating authority; but the effect was considerable, as this seemed to be the open door for competition at last on the peculiarly British domestic route (note that, contrary to some references, London–Hong Kong is not cabotage, in the ICAO-defined sense of the term). The peculiarity was that, though a domestic route, it could not be operated without technical or operational stops en route in foreign, albeit friendly, countries, including those of the Commonwealth. British Airways, incidentally, the incumbent, and hitherto enjoying a monopoly, was exempted from the requirement to hold an ATLA licence.

Cathay cause for celebration was as yet, however, premature. Between 13 and 20 December 1979 and 25 January and 8 February 1980, the British Civil Aviation Authority (CAA), in protracted hearings, approved the British Caledonian submission only, and moreover placed no restrictions on either frequency or the number of stopping points. This may well have reflected a true interpretation of the recommendations of the Edwards Report, published on 1 April 1969, which was the inspiration of the Second Force concept and the emergence of British Caledonian as that second force. The CAA rejected Sir Freddie Laker's application for a service similar to his Skytrain trans-Atlantic route.

The battle lines were drawn and the spoils of war, the enormous potential of the Hong Kong route, felt by many to have been poorly served by British Airways (which had been formed on 1 April 1972, by a merger of BOAC and BEA), ensured that no quarter was asked nor given. After much in-fighting in London, and after direct appeals to Prime Minister Margaret Thatcher, the UK Secretary of State, on 17 June 1980, directed that licences should be granted to all three applicants, Cathay, British Caledonian and Laker, and all of them without frequency restrictions. The floodgates were ready to open.

British Airways did not exactly take all this lying down. On 10 July 1980, one week before Cathay Pacific Airways started its thrice-weekly Boeing 747 service, it reduced its first class fares by 10 per cent (from £1,125 one way) and its one-way APEX (Advanced Purchase Economy) fares by 15 per cent to 25 per cent, depending on the direction. Cathay's inauguration on 17 July 1980, an historic date for this hitherto Pacific-rimmed airline, was followed promptly by British Caledonian's inaugural on 1 August. In three weeks, the monopoly route had suddenly become a three-ring circus.

British Caledonian offered four McDonnell-Douglas DC-10-30s a week, and in a dramatic innovation, introduced a £99 stand-by fare. An apocryphal report claimed that this was a mistake, having been approved at top level by ministerial folk who had mistaken a badly-written abbreviation for Houston (HOU) for Hong Kong. In any event, British Airways was forced to match this with its Budget and Firecracker Fares. The whole tariff situation became very confused, and for the first time the travellers between London and Hong Kong had a real choice; and they enjoyed it.

As the year drew on, the situation was somewhat rationalised. Laker continued to press for inclusion among the privileged, requesting service with only one stop, at Sharjah, and continued to campaign for the route. Normally a master of publicity, public affairs and promotion for his cause, Freddie Laker's judgement may

The Boeing 747 made it possible for Cathay Pacific to operate a Hong Kong—London nonstop service.

have strayed in this case. The Hong Kong ATLA, an agency of the Hong Kong Colonial administration, had seldom had to deal with issues of world-wide significance, and it had never had to face a controversial, even confrontational case such as multi-designation on the route to London. The body of men had been composed mainly of senior citizens of Hong Kong, for whom the duties at the ATLA was, in truth, a spare time job. Laker made a tactical error of regarding the ATLA with an attitude of patronage, and chance remarks reached the ears of the distinguished members. And the hitherto almost dormant worm turned. On 20 October 1980, it again refused Laker's application, and simultaneously relaxed its previous frequency restrictions to a maximum of seven a week by each airline. With twenty-one round trips, all with wide-bodied aircraft, fully authorized, Laker's case, which had to be based on the need for adequate capacity, collapsed – to the great relief of the incumbents.

During the next three years, the Hong Kong–London route went through a complete metamorphosis, and if ever there was a case for airline competition on a major city pair, this was it. Before July 1980, the British Airways first class round trip Boeing 747 fare was £2,250. British Caledonian's DC-10 fare in the summer of 1982 was £1,177. Both British Airways and British Caledonian offered Lower Club class round trip fares of £495, while Cathay's higher standard of on-board service, the Marco Polo class, was £545. On 5 February 1982 the Midland Bank forced Laker into receivership, although he had never failed to honour any progress payments on short- or long-term debt, with all payments made on time. Most airlines fail through financial insolvency, including bankruptcy. Laker's was probably the only case in history in which a flourishing airline, and a popular one at that, was put out of business. Years later, after agonizing litigation, the IATA airlines, against whom Laker brought a law-suit, settled out of court, paying Laker several millions in settlement, and also paying about £300 million in outstanding Laker debt.

All this did not affect Cathay, which went from strength to strength. By July 1981, it was operating a daily service to London. By March 1982, its market share exceeded that of British Airways, whose participation on the route went back to Imperial Airways in 1936. And on 2 July 1983 Cathay Pacific Airways introduced a once-weekly nonstop Boeing 747 service on the London route, reducing the journey time from 15 to 13 hours. This 7,225-mile flight was made possible by the introduction of a variant of the Boeing 747-200 series, equipped with Rolls-

269

Royce RB211–524D4 engines. Cathay was the launch customer for this version, and at the time this was the longest airline route in the world to be operated nonstop.

One residual effect of the London route development was that British Airways took the logical step of selling its 15 per cent shareholding in Cathay Pacific, which was now its competitor. As a result, Swire Pacific's holdings increased to more than 70 per cent and the Hong Kong & Shanghai Banking Corporation's to almost 30 per cent. Cathay was now owned entirely by Hong Kong interests.

Cathay Pacific World-wide

The Hong Kong airline now had the bit between its teeth, and proceeded to make its mark across the globe. It began an all-freighter service to Frankfurt, one of Europe's biggest commercial hubs, on 1 October 1981. It reinstated service to India, after twelve years of absence, by adding Bombay as a stop on its route to the Persian Gulf points, on 2 January 1982. Later in the same year, Brisbane became the fourth Australian destination on 1 August, and from the same day the service to Perth was operated nonstop. Then, in a three-way partnership with Air New Zealand and Air Niugini, service began direct to Auckland via Port Moresby. In a wholly sensible arrangement, to serve a route over which the sufficiency of traffic was undetermined, and not enough to share with long-range wide-bodied equipment, the three participants took turns in serving it, 'changing the guard' every six months. Air New Zealand, in fact, operated the route at first.

View at last light of Hong Kong's runway 13 stretching into Kowloon Bay. (*GEC*)

Next came the conquest of the Pacific. Cathay's first entry into the North American market was to Vancouver on 1 May 1983, on which day also it took over the Auckland route from Air New Zealand. By July 1986, the American route had been extended to San Francisco, and this included the fifth freedom authority to carry local traffic between Vancouver and the US terminus.

The connections with Europe – in line with the growing sense of community

270

within that continent – were consolidated. Passenger service opened to Frankfurt on 3 March 1984. Hong Kong–London westbound flights were operated nonstop from 5 May 1984 (the nonstop capability had hitherto been in the eastbound direction only). In April 1986, Rome and Paris received Cathay Pacific service, Amsterdam in May, and on 1 June 1988, Zürich too came on line. On 31 October 1989, Manchester became the seventh European city to have direct Cathay service to Hong Kong; and two days previously, a new service, to Mauritius, brought the Indian Ocean firmly within Cathay's horizons.

Interestingly, Cathay Pacific's planning department, working with its operations colleagues, found an unorthodox solution to the problem of continuing flights to comparatively nearby and sometimes smaller destinations, where the operation of Boeing 747 and Lockheed L-1011 TriStar wide-bodies would normally have been considered uneconomic, if not futile. Cathay had already been willing to operate joint services with other airlines, notably with Air New Zealand and Air Niugini, with Malaysian Airline System to Kota Kinabalu, and with Royal Brunei to Bandar Seri Begawan (formerly Brunei City), often, as a matter of convenience, with the partners' aircraft. Now, from 1984 onwards, a deliberate policy of 'misuse' of aircraft such as the 747 was pursued, because, on balance, this was more economical than purchasing and maintaining a separate aircraft type to service the shorter and thinner traffic routes.

The last Boeing 707-320 had been retired on 12 November 1982, so that Cathay's fleet consisted entirely of Boeing 747s and Lockheed TriStars. In the following year, for a fleeting moment, in a nostalgic and sentimental gesture, and with considerable ceremony, as befitting the historic occasion, the now global airline paid its respects to its ancestry. On 23 September 1983, its first DC-3 *Betsy*, was brought home from Australia, where it had spent its last flying days after being retired by Cathay back in the 1950s. It was restored with tender loving care at the HAECO engineering base, and made its last journey, minus wings and tail, across the Bay to Tsimshatsui East, by barge, and then towed – to the astonishment of the nocturnal citizens of Kowloon – to its final resting place at Hong Kong's Science Museum.

The China Connection

As the Second World War ushered in a period of decolonization throughout the former European overseas empires, the thought – and even sometimes, during periods of extreme agitation, the threat – that Hong Kong would return to China, where it rightfully belonged, was never far from political thinking in the Crown Colony. But in due course, as China gained both economic and military strength, the die-hard British colonists had to bow to the inevitable course of history, and during the early 1980s, protracted discussions were held at the highest diplomatic levels. These concentrated on the ways and means and the timetable by which Hong Kong would return to Chinese sovereignty, and during 1984, agreement was reached to the effect that this historic event would occur in 1997, 150 years after the Opium Wars of the 1840s had led to the cessation by China, under humiliating circumstances, of precious privileges – the Treaty Ports – and, in some cases, territory, the jewel of which was Hong Kong.

Happily for Cathay Pacific Airways, Chinese assurances that Hong Kong's future would be 'business as usual' included the survival of the proud airline division of the Swire Group. In fulfilment of the spirit of the understanding, Cathay negotiated the rights to operate charter services to Beijing in July 1985, and these

GROWTH OF CATHAY PACIFIC 1948-1994

CORE NETWORK

EXTENSION TO JAPAN

EXPANSION IN JAPAN AND FIRST SERVICE TO AUSTRALIA

SERVICES TO AUSTRALASIA, THE GULF, AND LONDON

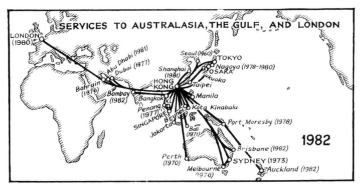

EXPANSION IN EUROPE AND TO NORTH AMERICA

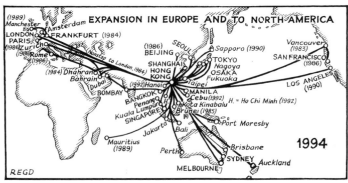

REGD

Maps 22b. Growth of Cathay Pacific, 1948–1994

Founded by a group of true entrepreneurs, American and Australian, Cathay Pacific's first routes were little more than connections on demand. But a scheduled pattern quickly emerged as Hong Kong boomed after the end of the Second World War. It became the flag carrier of the Colony in 1959, and developed a network to several Japanese points, established a permanent route to Australia in 1973, reached London in 1980, and the North American continent in 1983. In 1984, Cathay opened a nonstop service to London, and – once restricted by dependence on London for route authority – established itself as one of the world's leading airlines.

272

were converted into full scheduled status in March 1986, when British Airways withdrew its Hong Kong–Beijing segment.

The operational link with the People's Republic was matched by an administrative one, involving ownership. Already, the Cathay owners, mainly the Swire Group, but also the Hong Kong & Shanghai Bank, had begun to dilute its holdings. On 15 May 1986, they sold 22.5 per cent of the shareholding to local business interests, to the public, and to the staff. The HK$1.5 billion (US$192 million) was the largest stock distribution in the history of the Hong Kong stock exchange. Less than a year later, in January 1987, a further 12.5 per cent was sold, more significantly, to mainland Chinese interests, represented by the China International Trust and Investment Corporation (CITIC) for HK$1.94 billion (US$249 million), two-thirds in newly issued shares. As a result of these transactions, Swire Pacific's shareholding was reduced to a little more than 50 per cent and the Bank's to $16\frac{1}{2}$ per cent.

Entering the last decade of the 20th Century, Cathay's relations were further elaborated by its relationship with a new Hong Kong airline, Dragonair, in which it purchased a stake in February 1990.

Dragonair

From the time it absorbed Hong Kong Airways in 1959, Cathay Pacific Airways was in a unique situation, dictated at least as much by political geography as by commercial or competitive considerations. Hong Kong itself consisted of a few offshore islands, and a small fragment of mainland territory which did not justify air service – the Chinese border was only half an hour's train ride away. So there were no domestic routes. By definition, therefore, all Cathay's routes were international; and following normal bilateral agreement procedures between nations, this effectively meant that, subject to British Airways' sometimes reluctant agreement, Cathay enjoyed a monopoly of UK flag scheduled air services to almost everywhere.

If another company wished to start an air service, it was restricted to those routes that Cathay did not want – and if they were worth operating, then Cathay wanted them; or to charter and non-scheduled work. The aspirant airlines were few and of little significance throughout the 1970s. Hong Kong Air had started helicopter services, with various Bell types, on 15 December 1970, mainly on schedule, from a site near Harcourt Road on Hong Kong (Victoria) Island to Kai Tak Airport. These were supplemented with sightseeing flights, but after some initial success, the little airline faded, its demise precipitated by the construction of the road tunnel from the Island to the mainland. Hong Kong Air also operated to Macao, but Cathay did not mind, as it saw no point in re-establishing a flying-boat service to the Portuguese colony. It did not object either – at least not too vehemently – to some sporadic freight operations by Transmeridian (Hong Kong)'s Canadair CL-44, as an autonomous local operation on behalf of the British independent. The air cargo activity, during the early 1970s also, of Oriental Pearl Airlines, was tolerated with mild indifference.

All this changed at the end of the decade. Hitherto, Cathay had been on the geographical edge of an enormous potential air travel market, as, with the exception of Guangzhou (Canton), all major Chinese cities were far enough away to be able to generate substantial traffic, given a sympathetic political climate. Dormant and aggressively isolated for a quarter-century China began to open its doors to the West towards the end of the 1970s, and suddenly the whole climate of air agreements, operating rights, and competitive privileges changed.

Following the signing of the Air Services Agreement between Hong Kong and China in 1979, which incidentally excluded any commitments on the route to Beijing (Peking), Cathay cautiously entered the Chinese arena with a service to Shanghai in February 1980. It got off to a shaky start but became firmly established by February 1981. The Hong Kong flag carrier did not seem too anxious to expand service to the People's Republic and its attitude could be described as quiet gestation of a new and unprecedented situation.

Then came Dragonair. Formed on 1 April 1985, it was the most vigorous of three candidates for an Air Operator's Certificate (AOC) from the Hong Kong authorities. The only opposition was from Air Hong Kong, a latter-day descendent of Oriental Pearl, and Caledonian Far East Airways, aiming to echo Transmeridian's device of an overseas independent hub. Of these, Dragonair had the inside track, as it had had the foresight to acquire an aircraft, a Boeing 737-200A, from the Irish Guinness-Peat leasing company.

The main backing of Dragonair came from the Hong Kong Macao International Investment (HKMII) company, with substantial mainland Chinese participation, and whose chairman was Chao Kuang-pui, who had built up Novel Enterprises Ltd, one of the largest textile companies in Asia. The fledgling company did not waste time. The Boeing 737 was delivered on 19 June 1985. It obtained its AOC on 24 July, and only two days later operated its first commercial – non-scheduled – flight, from Hong Kong to Kota Kinabalu.

This Dragonair Airbus A320 is white overall with red winglets, tail markings and Chinese characters. The other lettering is black. (*Airbus Industrie*)

At the beginning of October, Dragonair's financial strength and Hong Kong political clout was immeasurably strengthened by the injection of new capital. Sir Yue-Kong Pao, one of Hong Kong's best known – and incidentally one of the richest – businessmen acquired a 35 per cent investment in Dragonair by the addition of fresh capital, and became its chairman. His interests included shipping, banking, land, and hotels; and he was no stranger to the transport industry, owning the Star Ferry (possibly the world's most efficient transport system of any kind), the Hong Kong Tramways (a delightful anachronism that stands a good chance of linking the 19th Century with the 21st), and the Cross Harbour Tunnel. The somewhat colloquial term political clout was not an exaggeration. By this single act, Dragonair was transformed and was galvanized into action.

The airline newcomer now possessed impeccable Chinese connections in the personal sense, and it matched these with Chinese connections in the operational sense. In November 1985 it was granted Air Transport Licensing Authority to operate 'regular charter services' – a euphemism for semi-scheduled flights – to eight points in China. Beijing and Shanghai were excluded from the list, but the eight were important cities, nevertheless. Service started to Xiamen (formerly Amoy), one of the new special development areas, on 30 November, a Red Letter Day in the airline's history. This was quickly followed by service to nearby Guangzhou, on 14 April 1986; to Hangzhou (locale of one of the world's most beautiful gardens, the West Lake) on 26 June; to Guilin (Kweilin), (gateway to the incredible limestone mountains beloved of Chinese artists) on 6 October; and to Nanjing, second city, after Shanghai, of east central China, on 12 December of the same year.

There was no stopping Dragonair now. It willingly and energetically picked up the scraps from Cathay's table as if they were side dishes from a royal banquet. Furthermore, these were, by definition, international routes, and within the stipulations of bilateral agreements. Scheduled service began to the Thai cities of Chiengmai and Phuket, both holiday destinations, on 16 and 18 December 1986, and regular charters began to Kunming, China, on 25 January 1987. Whether this series of route inaugurations could be explained by Cathay's neglect or simply by Dragonair's entrepreneurship is uncertain. But the newcomer had its foot in the airline door and was pushing it wide open.

The pace quickened. On 26 January 1987, the Hong Kong Air Transport Licensing Authority granted scheduled licences to Dragonair to operate to an additional fourteen cities in China, in addition to the eight it already had, with authority to serve four points in Thailand; and also to Guam (USA), Kathmandu (Nepal), and four Japanese cities on the island of Kyushu: Kagoshima, Kumamoto, Oita, and Nagasaki. By March 1987, Dragonair had three Boeing 737s, and on 15 May it demonstrated its confidence in its own future by joining the International Air Transport Association (IATA).

Dragonair was handicapped by an old regulation that denied it the right to operate its charters, regular or otherwise, between the hours of 12.30 and 16.30, but this did not halt the expansion. Also, it was not allowed to advertise its charter flights; but this was easily circumvented by word of mouth – and news travels fast in the streets of Hong Kong. Dragonair scored heavily when it signed a long-term contract with AWR Services Inc, the computer subsidiary of American Airlines, to put it on line with the SABRE reservations system. Services to the Kyushu points began towards the end of 1987 and all were in operation by April 1988. And at this stage of the proceedings, Cathay Pacific Airways, which once virtually dictated policy in Hong Kong's air transport world, called a truce. Dragonair, for its part, was ready to negotiate, as it had lost money by its rapid expansionist policy; and its owners took the pragmatic approach of 'if you can't beat 'em, join 'em.'

Two Can Live As Well As One

On 1 February 1990, Cathay Pacific acquired a substantial shareholding, 35 per cent, in Dragonair; while Chinese (PRC) interests took 38 per cent. Former competitors, all three, Cathay, China, and Dragonair, were now partners.

Dragonair continued its autonomous existence, and was able to lease larger aircraft such as the TriStar from Cathay. The Hong Kong authorities were pleased, as the new amalgamation removed the source of much bickering. Dragonair's 'regular charters' suddenly became scheduled flights. On 1 April 1990, Cathay relinquished the key Chinese routes to Beijing and Shanghai to Dragonair, and furthermore, on 1 July, transferred one of its TriStars to work the route.

While all the negotiating with Dragonair and with China was going on, Cathay Pacific was not neglecting its global network. On 1 July 1990, in a code-sharing agreement with Air Canada, it extended its Vancouver service to Toronto, with the latter airline's Boeing 767s making the connection. On the same day, to increase the number of its North American stations to four, nonstop Boeing 747-400 service began from Hong Kong to Los Angeles, a distance of 7,400 statute miles, even longer than the nonstop route to London. Also on 1 July, in company with several other East Asian airlines (Singapore, Malaysian, Royal Brunei; and Thai was to follow) Cathay Pacific finally joined IATA, three years after Dragonair. Later in the year, service also started to Sapporo, recognizing the northern Japanese city's growing importance, especially as a winter resort centre, and possibly laying the ground work for a future hub/gateway, because of Sapporo's strategic position athwart the North America–East Asia great circle route. And reinforcing its claim to dominance of the London route, on 30 April 1991, it began a daily schedule, with Boeing 747s, into the coveted Heathrow Airport, in addition to the existing services into Gatwick.

The Pearl Becomes A Diamond

The growth of Hong Kong as an airline centre has been truly phenomenal. Once merely a secondary destination for Britain's flag airline, then a postwar regional hub for a locally-based airline, venturing to Australia only in 1959, and reaching London as recently as 1980, it has emerged as one of the world's major airline hubs. With China on its doorstep, it is geographically, as well as politically, the natural gateway to the potential wealth and travel potential of the world's most populous nation. It now ranks alongside long-established metropolises such as London, New York and Tokyo as one of the world's great airline axes around which air transport patterns evolve. Always a Pearl of the Orient, it has now become a glittering diamond.

Another Empire Outpost Lives On

Though a diminutive echo of colonialism, compared with Hong Kong, the Portuguese enclave of Macau traces its history as a European trading outpost to the year 1516, when Portugal had an empire, and more than three centuries were to pass before Hong Kong was even thought of. Its first exposure to commercial aviation affairs was when an attempt to start an airline was made in 1920. On 7 January, Charles de Ricou, a French businessman living in Hong Kong, sailed from New York with three Aeromarine 39B floatplanes. These were for Macau Aerial Transport (MAT) to establish a regular service between Macau and Hong Kong.

The inaugural date was set for 3 June 1920, but objections arose: from Hong Kong, where the authorities worried about possible spying; from China, suspicious that the aircraft might be used to carry illicit goods or help the local warlords in insurrection; and from Macau, where the Portuguese administration insisted that

Air Macau's Airbus A321s have striking blue, white and red tail markings. The registration CS-MAA is believed to be Macau's first. (*Airbus Industrie*)

the company should be Portuguese. But eventually, late in 1922, an agreement was made to sell MAT to the Macau government. But this did not happen.

Much later in 1936, endeavouring to establish a terminus for his trans-Pacific Pan American Airways flying-boat route, Juan Trippe made an ostentatious visit to Macau, implying that, if the British would not concede traffic rights to Pan Am, then he would obtain them from Macau. The little exercise in gamesmanship succeeded; and Macau remained in the aviation shadow of Hong Kong until after the Second World War.

As described earlier in this chapter, Cathay Pacific had a brief flirtation with the Portuguese outpost in 1948, but after an accident, Macau was off the airline map for almost another half-century. Then, following a period of intensified economic inititiative, Air Macau was formed late in 1994. The shareholders were the Macau Aviation Services Company (MASC) (51 per cent), Air Portugal (25 per cent) and other local business interests. In parallel with this intitiative, Macau built a magnificent new airport, and, on the same day when it opened for business, 9 November 1995, Air Macau began daily services to Beijing and Shanghai, using Airbus A321s and an Airbus A320.

The following month, flights began to Kaohsiung, Taiwan, and in January 1996 to Xiamen, China. Interestingly, an agreement has been made between Macau and Taiwan to operate through flights between Taiwan and mainland China, stopping at Macau, and perhaps changing the flight number, to comply with international procedures. This so-called 'Sixth Freedom' arrangement, which enables a country that is geographically situated so as to be able to circumvent the acknowledged 'Fifth Freedom' (the right of an airline to operate between two foreign countries), has been successfully exploited by others, notably the Icelandic airline, Loftleidir. It is not a technical breaking of standard practices or agreements; but it can be seen as a blatant evasion of them; and time alone will tell if this will be tolerated in booming southern China.

One of the minor shareholders in Air Macau, Dr Stanley Ho, in November 1990, started one of the world's smallest airlines, East Asia Airlines, which operates a single Bell 222 twin-engined helicopter from Macau's ferry terminal to Hong Kong's international airport.

CHAPTER TWENTY-THREE

Creation of Philippine Air Lines

A Country Designed for Air Transport

Rather like Indonesia (formerly the Netherlands East Indies), but on a smaller scale, the Philippine islands have always needed a transport system of some kind, to link most of the more important and larger of the archipelago. Of the 7,000 islands, only about 2,500 are large enough to have names, and only 462 of them reach one square mile in area. Nevertheless, eleven of them each cover more than 1,000 square miles, and in a total combined area almost exactly the size of Great Britain and Ireland, many of them are tantalisingly close to each other. Only in recent years has any pair been linked by a bridge. Ferry boats have always plied across the many inland seas, to link the many different peoples, indigenous and colonial, but these have been slow and therefore time-consuming, mostly offering the barest minimum of comfort, and, in a country where typhoons are a regular occurrence, often hazardous.

The potential for air transport, when the use of aeroplanes for such a purpose became recognized after the end of the Great War of 1914–18, was considerable. By this time, the country was under United States administration, having been created as a Commonwealth in 1907 after a brutal uprising by the inhabitants who felt that they should not have been bargaining pawns in the Spanish-American War of 1899. Spain had ruled the Philippines as a Colony since Miguel López de Legazpi had established the first permanent settlement in 1565, forty-four years after Magellan had first set foot there (and had been murdered at Mactan).

The Spanish had, like other colonialists of past centuries, ruled autocratically, with little regard for the welfare of the 45 indigenous peoples. Few in number – they numbered only a few thousand even in the 19th Century – the colonists paid more regard to incursions by Portuguese, Dutch and British rivals. But the seeds of independence were sown in an insurrection in 1872, which led to the foundation of the Liga Filipina by José Rizal in 1891, and the latter's execution in 1896.

The official language had been Spanish, used by the colonial administrators and by the upper class families who comprised the aristocracy – whom the British would describe as the 'landed gentry' – but this was replaced in 1913 by the Americans who, after the bitter strife that was the aftermath of the Spanish-American War, began to rule the country with more consideration for local sensitivities and aspirations. By 1926, 98 per cent of the civil service, almost all of them in Manila, were Filipino; and such was the transition of language use that, with the possible exception of India, the Philippines today, with a population of 65 million, is the third largest English-speaking nation in the world.

Prelude to An Airline Tradition

In a period of what might be described as benevolent colonialism, the Curtiss Aeroplane & Motor Company opened a branch in a suburb of Manila in the autumn of 1919. Two former US Army pilots, Major Joseph Stevenot and Captain Alfred Croft, operated a Curtiss JN-4 Jenny and a Seagull seaplane. Under the name of the Philippine Airways Service, they made a demonstration flight to Cebu and Iloilo, carrying mail, on 29 November 1919. The Director of Posts, José Topacio, was enthusiastic, but could not provide the funds for continued experiments. However, on 7 July 1920 the Council of State, inspired by the emergence of twenty Filipino pilots from the Curtiss Flying School, established the Philippine Air Service, and ordered five seaplanes; but once again, sufficient funds were not forthcoming.

Independently of these efforts, José Tinsay, a young pilot from Iloilo (on the island of Panay, where a prosperous sugar industry was tantalizingly remote by sea from Manila, about 300 miles distant) learned to fly in the United States, bought a Curtiss Oriole, and in 1920 began to operate charter flights across the 27-mile Guimaras Strait that separated Iloilo from the equally prosperous city of Bacolod, on the island of Negros. He was the first to carry a fare-paying passenger in the Philippines. By 1925, he had acquired a Curtiss Junior and an Aeromarine seaplane, and began regular service between the two points, charging a one-way fare of 50 pesos (then equivalent to $25.00), and also offered charter flights to coastal towns on both islands.

In 1933 Tinsay's pioneering operations – they do not appear to have been regular or frequent enough to qualify for the term 'airline' – were replaced by INAEC (*see* later) and no more was heard of him until after the Second World War. He re-appeared as a non-scheduled operator, Philippine Air Express, in

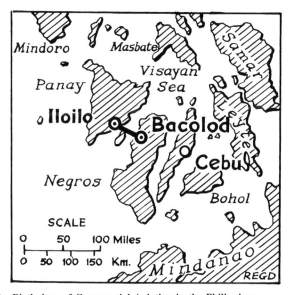

Map 23a. The Birthplace of Commercial Aviation in the Philippines
After earlier charter flights, José Tinsay began the first regular air services in the Philippines, from Iloilo to Bacolod, in 1925. The over-water route, linking two important cities, can be compared in their motivation with the birth of commercial aviation in the United States (St Petersburg—Tampa, and Key West—Havana) and the cross-Channel routes in Europe.

1947, flying a DC-3 on cargo runs between Manila and Iloilo. But tragically, on 22 November of that year, he was killed when the aircraft caught fire and exploded en route.

Andres Soriano and PATCO

Today's Philippine Airlines can trace its heritage back to 1930. On 30 December of that year, the Philippine Aerial Taxi Company (PATCO) was organized by a group of investors, mainly American (including Joseph Stuvenot, from the Curtiss experiments of 1920), but notably including Andres Soriano, president of the San Miguel brewery, which was to become famous first in the Far East, then throughout the Pacific region, then worldwide. Soriano, a man of considerable influence in the Philippines, nevertheless maintained his Spanish citizenship, in common with many of the leading figures of Filipino society.

PATCO was formed to carry bullion, personnel, supplies and equipment to the mines owned by the shareholders, but it began non-scheduled flights for the public on 31 March 1931, and converted the Manila–Baguio service to a regular schedule on 24 December of that year, using a Stinson and a Waco, both single-engined aircraft. On 25 January, the Bureau of Posts awarded a mail contract for the Baguio route – possibly the most lucrative in the country, even though it was on Luzon, the same island as Manila. At an elevation of 5,000 ft, it was the only incorporated city in the Philippines, other than Manila, and was for a time the summer capital, later becoming a summer resort, rather in the style of Simla or Darjeeling in India. In April 1934, three single-engined Bellancas were added to the fleet, and on 14 November a permanent franchise was awarded to PATCO by the Philippine legislature.

This was during a period of important events in Philippine politics and aviation. The Tydings-McDuffie Act of 24 March 1934 paved the way for eventual independence for the Philippines, and on 8 February 1935, a Philippine constitution was adopted, ratified by plebiscite on 14 May, and marked by the election of President Quezon on 15 November. The Act provided for US withdrawal on 4 July 1946, at which time the Philippine Republic would succeed the Commonwealth status.

Ten days after the election, on 25 November 1935, the epoch-making flight of Pan American Airways' *China Clipper* arrived in Manila, carrying the first load of mail across the Pacific Ocean by air. It was greeted by hundreds of thousands of people, and a year later they were to be on hand, albeit in fewer numbers, to welcome the first privileged passengers to pay their way to fly across the world's largest ocean. Interestingly, at this time, Pan Am was able to plan its route without recourse to diplomatic negotiation – although this was to follow as it extended to the mainland of China. The trans-Pacific chain of islands, including the Philippines, was still entirely under US administration.

However, preparations were being made to fulfil the objectives of the 1934 Act. On 1 November 1938, Filipino officers took over the administration of the Bureau of Aeronautics, by which time about 60 airfields, most of them grass or dirt strips, had been built. Following the disappearance of a PATCO aircraft north of Manila on 28 February 1938, and under the direction of Captain Basilio Fernando, the Bureau advised the company that it could not continue operations with single-engined equipment. In September 1939 PATCO went into bankruptcy and operations ceased. During its eight-year existence, it had carried about 25,000 passengers, of whom about 4,000 were to Baguio and 2,000 to Paracale, site of a rich mine owned by the PATCO investors.

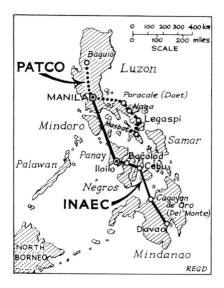

Map 23b. Air Routes in the Philippines, 1935
When Pan American Airways opened its historic trans-Pacific air service with
the *China Clipper* in 1935, the Philippines was still an overseas territory of the
United States, so that Manila was a natural terminus, for both political as well
as geographical reasons. In the early 1930s, Andres Soriano and Eugenio López,
two prominent Filipino businessmen, established PATCO and INAEC, respectively. The latter, interestingly, started on the same route that José Tinsay had
pioneered in 1925.

Eugenio López and INAEC

Geographically located in the centre of the Philippines, the city of Iloilo, separated
by a 27-mile channel from the city of Bacolod, and about 300 miles from Manila,
was the centre of a prosperous suger industry. Back in 1920, the pioneering José
Tinsay had recognized the need for an air service, but had not been able to consolidate one. A decade later – he was said to have been inspired by the Dutch KNILM
in the East Indies – Eugenio López, of the rich sugar-producing and shipping
family of Iloilo, established the Iloilo-Negros Air Express Company (INAEC) in
April 1932. On 3 February 1933 the first flight was made to Manila, and the next
day the first to Bacolod, followed by an inaugural to Cebu on 9 February. On 22
February, using three-engined Stinson SM 6000 Model U aircraft, scheduled
services began to these points, and two years later, these were extended to include
Cagayan de Oro and Davao, in the southern island of Mindanao.

Although one of the Stinsons was lost on 29 May 1936, there were fortunately
no casualties, INAEC was by this time carrying 2,000 passengers a month – or as
many in one year as PATCO carried in its whole period of existence. Such was
its success that, on 22 February 1937, it received its first Sikorsky S-43 amphibian, fitted with 16 seats and providing steward service. By 1939, INAEC was
providing service to all the main cities of the Philippines, with a through route

281

Iloilo-Negros Air Express hangar at Iloilo with the airline's Sikorsky S-43 amphibian, a trimotor Stinson Model U and a single-engine Stinson.

Preparing Iloilo-Negros Air Express Sikorsky S-43 for departure.

from Manila to Davao via Iloilo, Cebu and Cagayan de Oro (location of Del Monte plantations). The frequency was twice weekly, with three extra round trips between Manila and Iloilo, to provide a service on all weekdays.

On 12 February 1941 service was extended to Baguio, the summer resort, but INAEC'S praiseworthy enterprise came to an abrupt end on 18 December of that year, when the total fleet was destroyed by a Japanese air attack at Iloilo. The López family had been evacuated from Manila a week earlier, to wait out the War and to renew their airline interest in 1945.

Establishment of Philippine Air Lines

Late in 1940 Paul Gunn, Andres Soriano's personal pilot, and with memories of PATCO in the 1930s, suggested to his employer that the time was ripe to try again. The López success with INAEC may have provided some incentive to Soriano, in the spirit of commercial rivalry. On 26 February 1941 Philippine Airways was incorporated. Of the 1,000 shares, 225 were held by Soriano, who contributed his personal Beech 18; 495 by Juan Elizalde, who provided a Beech 17 Staggerwing. Other shares were held by members of the Soriano organizations, and Gunn was put in charge of operations.

On 10 March 1941 a contract was signed by the airline with Soriano & Cia for management services, at a monthly fee. This interlocking relationship would continue as a feature of Philippine airline life for many years, under different ownerships, and would later be the subject of investigation by the authorities for blatant abuse; but at this stage of early development, it seemed to be a sensible solution. On 13 March the name had to be changed to Philippine Air Lines, because of a previous registration by a company of the Airways name in 1937, but which had not operated. But two days later, Paul Gunn piloted the first PAL flight, with a Beech 18, from Manila's Nielson Airport to Baguio. On 17 March Elizalde's Staggerwing began service to Legaspi, and with the delivery of a second Beech 18, on 9 April the route network was expanded to include Daet, Naga, Masbate, Tacloban and Cebu. Fares were set at PP0.20 per mile, and gold bullion was flown into Manila from both Baguio and Paracale.

Under the terms of Commonwealth Act No. 643 PAL purchased the old PATCO franchise for a nominal PP500.00 on 22 July 1941. With the approval of President Quezon, the Philippine Government invested in the airline, through the National Development Corporation, whose 34 per cent investment increased the capital to PP1,000,000. With this funding, Soriano ordered two Lockheed Lodestars, and he intended to compete with INAEC, which was still the leading airline in the Philippines. But such plans, which included an overseas route to Hong Kong, came to nothing, as the Japanese joined in the Second World War on 8 December (local time) with its attack on Pearl Harbor and the spectacular over-running of the whole of southeast Asia.

Philippine Air Lines' Beeches and other assorted aeroplanes, including PATCO's old Bellanca and Waco, were part of the famous 'Bamboo Fleet' that evacuated US pilots to Australia and brought back medical supplies. Many heroic missions were made, including one by Gunn himself who, after a crash landing in Mindanao, after an encounter with a Japanese Zero fighter, managed to repair and fly a B-17 bomber to Australia.

As for Soriano, he had applied for Filipino citizenship in June 1941, and this was granted on 11 December 1942. During the 1930s, he had made various political connections, including a friendship with President Quezon, whose military adviser was General Douglas MacArthur. He had visited the United States, flying by the Pan American Clippers, and although, as a Spanish citizen, he had declared in support of General Franco and provided some funds to the Falangist cause, the US recognition of Franco silenced the critics.

Immediately at the outbreak of hostilities with Japan, he had joined the Philippine Army, was commissioned as a captain, assigned to Quezon's staff, and decorated for bravery at the seige of Bataan, before that fortress fell on 9 April 1942. Evacuated by submarine and PT boat to the south, thence by B-17 to Australia in March, he was appointed Secretary of Finance in exile. During 1943 and 1944 he discussed with Jack Frye of TWA the idea of assistance in rehabilitating PAL after the War – and this may have been linked with more far-reaching ambitions by Frye, who had aspirations to challenge Pan American as a globe-circling airline.

Serving as a colonel on General MacArthur's staff, Soriano went ashore with the General at Leyte on 20 October 1944, in fulfilment of the famous 'we shall return' promise, and with such a record was able to apply successfully for US citizenship in 1945, making this move because of his indignation at being denounced in his own country as a fascist, because, as a Spaniard, he had supported Franco – a charge that was not entirely groundless.

Map 23c. Philippine Air Lines (PAL) 1941
Founded in 1941 as Philippine Airways (but hastily renamed because of a previous name registration) this was the successor to Andres Soriano's PATCO of the early 1930s. INAEC was still the leading airline of the Philippines, but both were engulfed by the Japanese invasion at the end of 1941. Nevertheless, this modest network became the nucleus of the nation's flag carrier after the end of the Second World War.

Meanwhile, in October 1942, the Japanese had created a Philippine Republic, with José Laurel as the president, and in April 1943 began direct airline service, under wartime conditions, with Mitsubishi 96s of Dai Nippon Koku (Greater Japan Air Lines) between Tokyo and Manila. Kawanishi H8K Emily flying-boats also represented the Japanese Navy's contribution to a far-flung communications network that had switched the Philippines' overseas air connections from the USA and China, via Pan American, to the conqueror from the north.

Postwar Manoeuvres

On 6 January 1945 General MacArthur landed at the Lingayan Gulf, in northern Luzon, and on 3 February entered Manila in triumph, occupying Malacanang Palace, liberating the prisons, and – with a nice sense of priorities – seizing the San Miguel Brewery. The Japanese surrendered on 15 August. By this time, on 11 August, the former Philippine Air Lines stockholders had already met at the Soriano building in Manila, where Soriano's plans for revival, with TWA assistance, were presented. On 10 January 1946, the capital was increased to PP2,000,000, of which 40 per cent was allotted to TWA, with the National Development Corporation retaining its 34 per cent. Five Douglas C-47s, quickly converted for commercial use, were acquired from the US Foreign Liquidation Commission, and operations were resumed from Nielson Field in Manila on 14 February, to Legaspi and Cebu. By the end of 1946 PAL was serving more than thirty points throughout the Philippines.

But by this time, Soriano's family rivals, the Lópezes from Iloilo, had stolen a march. In November 1945, sensing the parochial image of the Iloilo-Negros association, Eugenio López had changed the name of INAEC to the Far Eastern Air Transport Inc (FEATI) and had resumed operations, on 15 November, between Manila (Grace Park Airport) and Iloilo. He had a fleet of more than a dozen ex-C-47s, and in May 1946 had inaugurated an international route to Hong Kong and Bangkok. On 1 August, demonstrating a strongly competitive stance, FEATI cut its fares to PP0.18 per mile, compared to PAL's PP0.20, and on 20 August began four-engined Douglas DC-4 (ex C-54) services from Manila to Cebu, Iloilo, Hong Kong and Shanghai. PAL still operated only DC-3s.

Philippine Air Lines was a major user of Douglas DC-3s, for which a level grass field was a luxury.

Although the Philippine Civil Aeronautics Board declined FEATI's application for a permanent scheduled trans-Pacific route, López did begin non-scheduled service to Oakland, California, on 15 December 1946. But this show of confidence was rudely shaken when, following a DC-3 crash on 13 December, in which 13 people were killed, a DC-4 was forced to alight in the sea off Laoag, on a flight from Shanghai. Six people were drowned, the FEATI fleet was grounded, and the door was open for Soriano to profit from his competitor's misfortunes.

The old campaigner, Soriano, had not been idle. The two airlines had gone head to head in manoeuvring for position with the air transport authorities; and although PAL did not possess any four-engined equipment, it took steps to begin operations with leased aircraft. In the election campaign, Soriano backed Senator Roxas, but López backed President Sergio Osmena, who had been elected on 9 June 1945. Roxas won, on 28 May 1946, in good time to celebrate Philippine Independence on 4 July 1946, the United States having honoured the terms of the Tydings-McDuffie Act of 1934. Both airlines were operating converted C-47s, fitted with military-style bucket seats, primitive lavatories, no ventilation or soundproofing, and with food service consisting of sandwiches and vacuum-flasked coffee. Maintenance was in the open air and PAL's spare parts store was in the basement of a house near the airport.

Because of some smart and prompt negotiation, Soriano and PAL were able to begin trans-Pacific operations, non-scheduled, but fairly frequently, as early as 31 July 1946. DC-4s, fitted with 40 seats, were leased from Transocean Airlines, the innovative and opportunist non-scheduled US airline based at Oakland, and headed by the inspirational Orvis Nelson, who recognized the opportunities offered by a US west coast shipping strike. The 41-hour trip was routed via Guam, Kwajalein and Honolulu, and was the first trans-Pacific service by any Asian airline. Flown by a Transocean crew, the cabin staff were Filipino who had to cook meals, clean the lavatory, and fend off the amorous advances of the passengers. The service improved to the status of a scheduled trans-Pacific route on 3 December 1946. Pan American Airways, incidentally, did not begin its trans-Pacific postwar service until 20 January 1947, also with DC-4s, the standard equipment until the Constellations and the DC-6s came along.

The Merger

While Soriano and López were no doubt prepared to fight it out in the competitive arena, with, in the Philippine manner, no holds barred, they were overcome by political events beyond their control, but which favoured Soriano's PAL. On 30 July 1946 the Philippines Civil Aeronautics Commission (CAC) had been created, modelled on the CAA of the United States. Existing franchise rights were terminated and duplicate services were authorized and operated by both PAL and FEATI. Both wished to ply the Pacific and were so designated by the CAC. The United States, however, designated both Pan American, the incumbent, and Northwest Airlines from its side, and would grant to FEATI only non-scheduled authority into the USA. This apparent discrimination was to be the bone of contention for many years, but it made no difference to the outcome at the time in the Philippines. The air treaty was signed on 14 November 1946 and accordingly both airlines opened service, as already described, PAL upgraded to scheduled, FEATI still non-scheduled.

To balance two weekly services to Manila by the Chinese flag carrier, CNAC, permission was granted to both PAL and FEATI to operate to China. PAL started DC-3 service to both Hong Kong and Shanghai on 5 September 1946. By the end of the year Soriano was in a strong position, having backed the right candidate for the presidency. Although three of his DC-3s had crashed, there had fortunately been no casualties. By the end of the year PAL had sixteen DC-3s, three Beech 18s and five DC-4s, three of them on lease from Transocean, the other two purchased from the same company. In March 1947 Transocean acquired a minority shareholding in exchange for the two DC-4s. Soriano persuaded President Roxas to agree to the purchase of pressurized Douglas DC-6s, and the capital was increased to PP 5,000,000, of which Soriano himself held 22.5 per cent.

After the immediate postwar boom was over, the Philippine Government made it clear that it would support only one airline, and invited the two competitors to work things out – although the scales were heavily weighted on Soriano's side. Facing the inevitable, Eugenio López sold FEATI to PAL for PP 3,400,000, and PAL promptly increased its capital to PP10,000,000. The date of this critical merger was 3 May 1947, a doubly historic occasion, for on the same day, Philippine Air Lines now carrying the flag of the infant nation, inaugurated service to Europe. The aircraft was a Transocean DC-4, again with Transocean flight crew and Filipino cabin staff, and was routed to Madrid, with overnight stops at Calcutta, Karachi and Cairo. The journey took three days to complete, unpressurized, one way.

To cap a successful year, and under a final bilateral agreement signed by President Truman on 5 June, the Philippine Government transferred the international mail contract from Pan American to PAL in August. This compensated for the somewhat inequitable terms of the agreement, as Pan American was granted

Fifth Freedom rights beyond Manila to all points in Asia and beyond, while Northwest had Fifth Freedom rights between Manila and Tokyo on its Great Circle route to the Orient from Seattle. PAL did not have these reciprocal rights, but, in 1947, was in no position to challenge the international airline dominance of the United States.

But within its own sovereignty, in a land that cried out for air service to link the many island communities that were otherwise days away by sea, PAL was now the master of all it surveyed. Its fleet of DC-3s now numbered more than thirty, and they were perfect for the grass and dirt strips which, though not exactly unprepared, always lacked proper maintenance, as the Government left it to the airline and the local communities to provide the care and attention.

Other than FEATI, there had been little threat from other potential competitors. One could have been presented by Commercial Air Lines Inc (CALI) which, early in 1946, had been established by a group of former US Army pilots, and backed by Alfonso SyCip, a millionaire of Chinese ancestry. It began non-scheduled flights to the south, as far as Davao and Jolo, with a couple of C-47s, and was issued a scheduled permit on 22 July 1947. It was soon operating to Amoy (now Xiamen) (where most of the Filipino-Chinese immigrants had come from), Shanghai and Hong Kong, and by the spring of 1948 had a fleet of twelve C-47s, a C-54 and nine sturdy C-64 Noorduyn Norsemen. Early in 1947, President Roxas had refused permission for CALI to sell out to PAL – a curious reversal from his position regarding FEATI – but, after a Norseman had crashed on a sight-seeing flight at Mati, near Davao, killing twelve passengers, including nine children; and

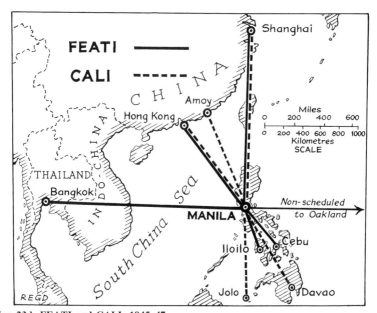

Map 23d. FEATI and CALI, 1945–47
After the end of the Second World War, the pre-war INAEC changed its name to Far Eastern Air Transport, Inc (FEATI) and Commercial Air Lines, Inc (CALI) was a new airline founded by a local millionaire and some former US Army pilots. The two companies were absorbed by Philippine Air Lines (PAL) in 1947 and 1948 respectively.

Roxas having died on 15 April, the way was clear for PAL to acquire CALI, which it did on 1 September 1948, and thus augmented its DC-3 fleet to more than forty.

Other small airlines or air services had been relatively insignificant. Trans-Asiatic Airlines (TAALI) had been formed in 1946 by another group of ex-US Army pilots, to fly to points on the Asiatic mainland. At first, it chartered aircraft from Insular Airways Company (INACO) which had been formed by Victor Osias, who flew PBY amphibians and Norsemen, helping Indonesian nationalists in arms supplies against the Dutch. But INACO lasted only a few months and ceased operations when the Dutch caught its last PBY. TAALI meanwhile had obtained half a dozen C-47s in March 1948, but suspended operations two years later 'after political disturbances and competitive difficulties' – a reported explanation that could have covered a world of sins – and probably did.

The only other companies were José Tinsay's Philippine Air Express, referred to at the beginning of this chapter, and the Pacific Airways Corporation, but their contribution to the postwar airline scene was negligible. So, with the domestic scene completely under its control, PAL concentrated on providing the Philippines with an intercontinental air service.

PAL Spans the World

Early in 1948 PAL began to move its operation from Nielson Field to Nichols Field (at both of which the Japanese had built good runways). Nichols was destined to become Manila International Airport. On 23 May of that year the first Douglas DC-6 arrived, and was put into trans-Pacific service six days later. The aircraft, named *Bataan*, was dubbed *Pacific Pacemaker* and it cut the time across the ocean from 41 to 30 hours, stopping at Wake Island instead of Kwajalein. The aircraft had 52 seats, alternatively 26 bunks, a feature of PAL trans-Pacific flights that has survived to this day. The second DC-6, *Leyte*, was put into service on 26 May, to Shanghai – a short-lived route on the map, as the disruption of daily affairs in China, because of the struggle for power between the warring factions, led to discontinuance on 1 September.

But the loss of service to China was compensated for by additional service to Europe. Rome was added as an intermediate stop and an extension was made from

Philippine Air Lines began operating Douglas DC-6s in May 1948. They visited Amsterdam regularly for inspection and overhaul by KLM. (*Schiphol Airport*)

Map 23e. Philippine Air Lines International Services, 1946–1954
After the end of the Second World War, the Philippine flag carrier showed remarkable initiative in fashioning a network that linked Manila with points in Europe to the west, and across the Pacific to San Francisco to the east. One of the earliest of the post-war challengers to Pan American Airways on the Pacific route, PAL's route stretched two-thirds of the way around the world, before financial stringency forced it to curtail its services. (Philippine Airlines uses its name with Airlines both as one and two words.)

Madrid to London. Bangkok was also included in the route. As already narrated, the purchase of CALI gave PAL a substantial fleet of DC-3s to take care of domestic requirements, and many of these were converted to Super-DC-3s with better engines, refinements to the airframes, and improvements of the interiors, dispensing with the bucket seats. The five DC-4s were sold and additional DC-6s ordered. Of the corporation's shareholding, 70 per cent was Filipino, 53 per cent Government, 17 per cent Soriano interests; and 30 per cent American, seven per cent TWA and eight per cent Transocean.

On 26 January 1949 PAL opened a service to Tokyo, with the DC-6 *Manila*. The following month, after two 60-seat DC-4s had been delivered, it opened the first coach-class service in Asia, both to Tokyo and to Hong Kong. Things were going well. Soriano announced a good profit and continued to waive the management fees of his own company. In June the capital was increased further to PP12,000,000, and Soriano acquired some of the American shares, from Transocean, to become the dominant stockholder. The fourth DC-6, *Mindoro*, was delivered on 25 October 1949 and placed immediately on the European service; but in spite of an apparently brave front, PAL's financial position was deteriorating, partly in the face of considerable activity by European airlines in providing service to the Far East.

289

Megellan's Cross, one of PAL's Douglas DC-6Bs, seen at London-Heathrow in July 1952.
(*John Stroud*)

During 1950 measures were taken to restore the finances. Soriano had proposed that the Government should nationalize the airline, but the offer was declined. Instead, it waived various charges on the company, and increased the level of mail payments. Soriano imposed economy measures within the airline and increaed his own investment. The debt to the Government was converted to a 54 per cent shareholding, reducing Soriano's to 22 per cent. On 27 May the Board approved the sale of the DC-6s, to be replaced by the improved DC-6Bs, two of which were ordered on 21 December. In May 1951 Soriano actually offered his resignation to President Quirino (who had been elected in November 1949) but received assurances of trust that would keep him firmly at the helm of the airline that he had founded and nurtured.

Such was Philippine Air Lines' stature that, in July 1951, in a strange twist of historical fate, it sent a delegation, led by the treasurer, Rafael (Ralph) Igoa, with assistance from Transocean, and a DC-3, to Japan to assist that country in rejuvenating its airline industry. PAL and Transocean helped to train the Japanese technicians and specialists in starting up the postwar Japan Air Lines, and the PAL DC-3 was the first civil aircraft to operate a passenger service in Japan as it rose from the ashes of defeat.

Soriano Consolidates

Marking the beginning of service to Taipei, Taiwan – the 'other' China – on 16 November 1951, Soriano ordered, on the next day, six Convair 340s, at a cost of PP1,110,000 each. Filipinos had begun to replace expatriate foreigners in top management positions and on the flight decks; and although there was a spate of DC-3 accidents between 1949 and 1952, these were not blamed on the airline or the crews. One, for instance, was caused by a bomb, planted in the aircraft because of a family feud; one hit a carabao (Philippine ox) which had no business to be on the airfield at Bacolod; and others were blamed on poor airfields and the lack of proper navigations aids. Another DC-3 was hijacked to China.

On 4 July 1952 the first Douglas DC-6B, *Magellan's Cross* was delivered, and on 30 July introduced PAL service to two more European destinations, Zürich and Frankfurt. The international pattern had settled down to a twice-weekly service on

290

all three main routes, European, trans-Pacific and to Tokyo via Okinawa. Hamburg was added on 1 April 1953, and on 15 November of that year, Beirut became the seventeenth international station on the Philippine network.

There might have been more, had Soriano been able to achieve his cherished ambition of completing a round-the-world service, involving only Spanish-speaking nations. On 24 October 1952 he signed an agreement with the Mexican airline, Aeronaves de Mexico, that would permit PAL to extend its San Francisco (Oakland) service to Mexico City. On 8 June 1953 President Truman approved a US CAB permit for such an extension. But on the eve of the inaugural flight – the DC-6B was all set to leave Manila – Pan American Airways' subsidiary company, Compañía Mexicana de Aviación, secured a court injunction over a technicality and this was upheld by the Mexican courts. Soriano's 'Operation Dream' had been a bold and visionary attempt to create a global network, and it deserved a better fate. But in those days, the influence of Pan American Airways was more powerful than that of governments, and its president, Juan Trippe, objected strongly to any incursion into Pan Am's world; which, in the 1950s, was most of the globe.

The dilapidation and neglect, amounting in some cases to decay, at Philippine airports, at which even the ubiquitous and forgiving DC-3 sometimes had problems, was emphasized in 1953 when, on 4 April, the first Convair 340 was delivered. Only three airports in the Philippines could accept it, and this led to a squabble between PAL and the authorities – to no avail. Consequently, the Convairs, which had been intended partly to improve domestic service, were deployed instead to Hong Kong, on 16 June, and to Taipei, on 23 June. The former service was extended to Bangkok on 27 October. Eventually, on 1 December, the 340 started a 'De Luxe' service from Manila to Cagayan de Oro.

Other domestic service innovations followed. In December 1953 three Hiller H-12 helicopters were put into service, in an attempt to launch a few connecting links to communities which lacked even primitive airports. But this attempt failed, partly because it was very expensive financially, partly because it was very expensive operationally – two of the Hillers crashed, one on 5 June 1954, the second on 27 September of the same year.

The other innovation was longer lived. On 5 January 1954 PAL inaugurated the *El Economico* service, at first to the Ilocos provinces in the north of Luzon. Exchanging comfort standards for cheap fares, 40-seat Douglas DC-3s operated at a fare structure of PP 0.13 per mile. On 15 June of the same year this service was extended to fifteen points in the Visayas (the islands in the central Philippines) and the Ilocos route extended to Taipei. But such developments, which were the forerunner of various attempts to satisfy the requirements of an impatient provincial clientèle, were overcome by events of a far more serious nature.

Collapse of the Global Network

Andres Soriano had made a determined attempt to fashion a world-wide network for Philippine Air Lines, to carry the flag of the newly-created Republic all over the world, and especially to the Spanish-speaking world. His abortive effort to reach Latin America had been foiled by the ever-watchful Pan American, jealously guarding its territory. Had PAL possessed aircraft of sufficient range, it could have closed the global loop with a nonstop (or with a non-traffic technical stop) route from San Francisco to London or Madrid. This would certainly have gained the attention of the intercontinental airline world, accustomed to regarding transocean flying as the exclusive prerogative of European and North American airlines. But while Soriano contemplated the acquisition of long-range Douglas DC-7s, which might have done the job (Pan American permitting!) the Philippine airline, far from expanding its horizons, had to curtail its international services – and quite severely at that.

On 30 March 1954 Soriano presented a wide-ranging plan to modernize PAL; but the new President Magsaysay and his Government would not approve the PP10,000,000 additional investment needed to purchase four Douglas DC-7s and to re-align its existing fleet. It preferred instead to re-direct the development emphasis towards the improvement of airline service to all the rural areas of the Philippines. This was a laudable goal, parallelling somewhat the creation of the Local Service Airlines in the United States; but the government policy – and its financial resources – did not permit expansion on both fronts, international and domestic; and it chose the latter.

Soriano's reaction was immediate. On the next day, 31 March, he suspended all the long-range services to Europe and to the United States. Regional services to Hong Kong, Taipei and Bangkok were retained but these were operated only by the Convair 340s. Even the Bangkok service was withdrawn in April, and the Taipei link maintained by DC-3s. The fleet of Douglas DC-6Bs was offered for sale. Delivery of the balance of the Convair 340 order, three additional aircraft, was postponed indefinitely, and early in 1955, two of the existing fleet were sold also. The situation was almost a case of 'the higher they climb, the harder they fall'. It was a sad end to Soriano's and PAL's praiseworthy ambitions, frustrated perhaps by extenuating circumstances. Less publicized, however, and every bit as praiseworthy, were the airline's efforts to undertake the directives of the Government to bring the privilege of air travel to every corner, however remote, of the disconnected islands of the Philippines.

The Rural Air Service

The Philippine Government could claim to have assisted PAL by restoring law and order in some of the more unsettled areas. On 17 May 1954 the communist Huk

The Philippine's Rural Air Service started in June 1955 using the very reliable de Havilland Canada Otter single-engine monoplane with STOL ability. (*de Havilland Canada*)

Typical Otter country with two PAL Otters present. (*de Havilland Canada*)

leader, Luis Taruc, surrendered, so that the *El Economico* DC-3s were in less danger of being shot at when they landed at remote airstrips. In other directions, however, the Government was not much help. It could not, or would not, take steps to improve airports at the small communities; the Bureau of Posts reduced air mail services, thus reducing some of PAL's indirect subsidy; and the CAB, under the direction of Oscar Ledesma, allowed a new generation of non-scheduled airlines to enter the field and the fray.

Left to its own devices, Soriano's airline took firm steps to adjust to the new situation. All its four-engined aircraft were sold; a thousand employees were laid off, in parallel with the severe reduction of services; the capital was reduced from PP 12.5 to PP 8 million. Among the senior personnal, the Filipino-American Ralph Igoa resigned, but was later made a vice-president in San Francisco – somewhat of a sinecure, as PAL no longer served the USA – but nevertheless keeping the airline's identity alive there. More significant, on 31 December 1954, Soriano promoted two Filipinos to important managerial positions, the first Filipino nationals to be given that honour. Renato Barretto took over traffic and sales and Roberto Lim presided over operations. Together, Rene and Bobby were, in their own ways, to play important roles in the expansion, modernization, and economic stabilization of Philippine Air Lines.

The Rural Air Service was launched on 15 June 1955, with a fleet of five single-engined de Havilland Canada DHC-3 Otters. These versatile aircraft had STOL capabilities, which, in the Filipino context, meant the ability to land on a grass strip about half the length of a football field, and a field, moreover, on which footballers would play only at their own risk. The Otters could carry ten passengers and required only one pilot, who combined the duties of piloting with those of navigating, radio-operating, en route maintenance, baggage-handling, and ticket price negotiation. He was not expected to serve lunch. To ensure that the major southern island of Mindanao (where much of the sometimes religion-inspired insurrection occurred) was not neglected, one Otter was based at Davao and one at Cotabato. On 9 July 1955 a third Otter was based at Cebu, to serve the Visayas.

Less spectacular than the much-publicized events that were marking the arduous beginning of the Jet Age – the first Comets entered service in 1952 and the Tupolev Tu-104 in 1956 – Phillipine Air Lines was pioneering a new and much-needed category of air transport, opening up remote areas with a means of communication and travel hitherto unavailable. In their diminutive way, PAL's little Otters made a significant contribution to the Filipino nation as an element of

Vickers-Armstrongs Viscount 770Ds were acquired by PAL and introduced in June 1957.
(*Vickers*)

unification, thereby spreading harmony and understanding among the many diverse peoples. The same might be said of the de Havilland Dragon Rapides in the Western Isles of Scotland (while BOAC was pioneering jet service to Johannesburg and Tokyo) and of the Antonov An-2s of Aeroflot (while the Tu-104s suddenly brought Vladivostok and Tashkent within a few hours of Moscow).

By the summer of 1956 when the *El Economico* service was extended into the Bicol region of southeast Luzon, the number of domestic points served rose to 52 – and the number would eventually grow to more than seventy. PAL passengers came to know the crews and the stewardesses by their first names. The DC-3s and Otters were truly an aerial bus service. Philippine Air Lines was a model to others as the best community-oriented air service in the world.

Enter the Propeller-Turbines

Despite the setback of losing his global network, and the problems of installing the Rural Air Service, Soriano did not neglect the 'bread-and-butter' operations, the links between the Manila metropolis and the main provincial cities, Cebu, Bacolod, Cagayan de Oro, Davao and Iloilo. On 24 October 1956 the southernmost of these, Davao, gained a nonstop DC-3 service, putting it only $3\frac{1}{2}$ hours away from the capital, not too remarkable, by some international standards,but in the severely restricted circumstances of Philippine commercial aviation at the time, an admirable achievement. For its part, the Government at last stirred into action on the airport front, initiating a programme of improvements at Cebu, Bacolod, Cagayan de Oro and Davao. For of all these places, the Convair 340 could use only Cagayan, and there only marginally. Although the matter was academic, from PAL's viewpoint at this juncture, President Magsaysay was killed in an air force accident at Cebu on 17 March 1957, to be succeeded by Vice-President Carlos Garcia. And the following month, the Mexican Government lifted its injunction against the San Francisco–Mexico City proposed extension. No doubt Pan American felt that, by this time, it had nothing to fear from the Philippines.

Recognizing the inevitable, the Government had finally gone into the airport improvement business when it was faced with international scorn, had it not done so. Otherwise, the Philippines would have been restricted to piston-engined operations, with obsolete aircraft, while the rest of the world was merrily entering the turbine-engined era. Soriano matched the gesture by ordering, on 27 March 1956,

PAL's Viscount services were supplemented in 1960 by 40/44-seat Fokker F.27 Friendships. (*Fokker*)

two Vickers Viscount V-770Ds, ostensibly to upgrade domestic service as well as that to east Asia regional points. In the event, the Viscount's first service was to Hong Kong, on 1 June 1957, as no domestic airport was adequate; but it opened a new era for Cebu, with Rolls-Royce service, on 10 March 1958, following this with Davao (with President Garcia on board) on 15 August. On 12 December the Viscount even started to Zamboanga, the picturesque city at the western tip of Mindanao; but – as if to emphasize the problem – this had to be withdrawn because of the airport inadequacy.

Philippine Air Lines was picking itself up by its boostraps. In addition to the Viscount introduction, it ordered two twin-engined Fokker Friendships in July 1957 – a neat choice, as both types were powered by Rolls-Royce Darts; and in September 1958 Rene Barretto and his team chose the Douglas DC-8 as PAL's first jet, and ordered two of the -50 series. Barretto was gradually rising in stature in the airline, whose Filipino element was augmented by the addition of Silvano Quimbo as operations manager. Soriano still shared about 46 per cent of the shareholding with Pan American; but the Government held 54 per cent, and therefore had a considerable stake in PAL's fortunes. On 29 February 1959 the Secretary of Foreign Affairs, Felix Serrano, served notice on the US Ambassador, Charles Bohlen, of the abrogation of the US-Filipino bilateral air agreement, effective one year hence, the main issue to be the re-negotiation of traffic rights via Tokyo.

The Viscount services were supplemented in 1960 by the introduction of the Fokker Friendships, the first of which arrived on 9 March, and full service began with the arrival of the second on 25 March. Fitted with 40 seats (later 44), its services were also named *Rolls-Royce* and premium fares, at PP0.21 per mile, were charged. Viscount service to Cebu was now running at three round trips a day, and beginning to approach the status of airbus standards, in the eyes of the regular patrons. Hot meals and beer were served en route. The Friendships were radar-equipped. Things were looking up.

To Catch a Falling Star

In March 1959 Rene Barretto and Bobby Lim had been promoted to vice-presidential status, and their elevation in the hierarchy was marked by another

In March 1960 twin-engined Scottish Aviation Twin Pioneers began taking over PAL routes previously worked by the Otters.

innovation, to try to expand and improve domestic air service. On 1 April 1959 Douglas DC-3 *Star* flights were introduced, at fares even lower than the *El Economico's*, PP0.10 versus PP0.13 per mile. This was possible because the *Star* flights were during the night, and were operated by aircraft that would otherwise have been on the ground, and cost calculations could be made on a marginal, rather than a total variable basis. On 15 August the *Southern Star* to Davao, and, on 1 October, the *Bicol Star* to Legaspi, added an extra touch of style to this form of basic air transport, at least for the more impressionable passengers. But the pilots had to cope with a new operational abbreviation, applicable to provincial airfields: CAOWW, or Closed to Aircraft Operations When Wet.

On 15 March 1960 the first of the new Scottish Aviation Twin Pioneers went into service to fifteen points previously served by the DHC-3 Otters. The aircraft were not necessarily any better, but they were twin-engined, which allowed a degree of confidence. On the other hand, there were some difficulties during the training programme, resulting from Filipino misunderstandings with the Scottish accent of the training pilot sent over by Scottish Aviation. The latter, on a training approach, said 'all right, old chap' but the pilot thought he said 'all right, all chop'. Familiar with the American slang term, meaning cut the engines, he dutifully followed instructions. The aircraft fell like a stone. Fortunately, no-one was injured.

Far more serious, and potentially devastating, were two DC-3 crashes at the end of 1960, an emergency landing having already been made in shallow water at Bais, Negros Oriental, on 14 July. On 23 November, 33 people were killed when a DC-3 crashed into Mount Baco, Mindoro, and on 22 December, another DC-3 hit a hill at Talamban, Mindanao. Both flights were on *Star* services, and, amid widespread criticism, Andres Soriano ordered that all the night-time *Star* services be suspended immediately. This was a blow to the airline, as by now it was serving no less than 72 points in the Philippines, almost as a national institution, as much a part of Filipino daily life as the postal or telephone service.

End of a Reign

These tragedies led to a crisis of some magnitude, and, under the chairmanship of a prominent lawyer, Lorenzo Tañada, a Senate Committee on Transportation and Public Service began its hearings on 3 January 1961. Soriano was subjected to intensive cross-questioning during the first week of February, and had to defend a barrage of complaints against the DC-3's longevity and against PAL's maintenance procedures. The press had not been kind – it seldom is in the Philippines where the coveted Freedom of the Press knows no bounds. The López-controlled *Manila Chronicle* had many a field day. Much was made of Soriano's control over the airline, amounting at this time to about 34 per cent, as he voted the Pan American shareholding in addition to his own. A Soriano company, Anscor, was the purchasing agent for PAL; another was the advertising agency; still another was the insurance agency. PAL, in fact, was one part of a Soriano Empire.

Following debates in and out of the Committee, sometimes aggressively confrontational, accompanied by the occasional shouting match, Andres Soriano had had enough. On 11 February 1961 he informed the Government-appointed PAL chairman, Eduardo Romualdez, that he intended to resign; and announced his decision to the press the next day. Neither the PAL management, nor the staff, who felt they might be jumping out of the frying pan into the fire, could persuade him to change his mind. He presented his last report to the shareholders on 23 March and his resignation became effective on the last day of the month. Several PAL executives resigned in sympathy and support. Romualdez took over the presidency, in addition to being chairman, and president of the Philippine Trust Company bank. Ra h Igoa, who had returned to the PAL fold, resigned, and Bobby Lim became the executive vice-president, so that now the entire management was Filipino.

On 18 May 1961 the Tañada Committee published its findings. It praised PAL's safety record, no doubt taking into account the lack of modern air traffic control procedures and installations that the Government should have provided; and it upheld PAL's monopoly position as the only solution for a sound commercial aviation development policy for the Philippines, thus offsetting agitation from some quarters for the establishment of competitive airlines. The 163-page report did, however, criticize Soriano's methods of control, which it described as dictatorial; and it made much of the profits made by PAL's associated companies, all Soriano-controlled.

Some of the criticism was no doubt justified, although some account should have been taken of the way business was conducted in the Philippines during the early decades that followed Independence. The questionable business practices were echoed in many a fledgling republic throughout the world; and Soriano was not the last to perpetrate them in the Philippines. Indeed, the interlocking associations would be repeated in later PAL administrations, and more flagrantly abused. By fair means or foul, for good or for bad, Andres Soriano had created a national airline for the Philippines, just as he had established San Miguel as one of the best-known beverages among connoisseurs of good beer the world over. During PAL's turbulent history, he was to be succeeded by lesser men.

CHAPTER TWENTY-FOUR

A New Era and New Challenges for PAL

The Show Must Go On

Philippine Air Lines did not come to a halt because a Senate Committee was examining its consitutional health. Capable adminsitrators maintained the operations while Andres Soriano stepped aside. On 9 January 1961 Friendship service had begun to Baguio; on 28 June, a *Night Mercury* Viscount service started to Bacolod; and in July the Twin Pioneers, twin-engined though they were, were retired, and the single-engined Otters continued to maintain the Rural Air Service.

In the field of industrial relations, an employee strike, lasting for two weeks at the end of the summer, resulted in the non-strikers being rewarded. The longest strike in PAL history, it was to be followed by many more in subsequent years, during a period when management and staff, salaried and wage-earning, were seldom in harmony, and often in conflict.

There were signs of improvement on the ground. Work had started at the end of 1959 on a new airport for Cebu, second city of the Philippines, on the nearby island of Mactan, and a causeway was under construction to link the airport with the city. On 22 September 1961 the first finger of the new Manila International Airport (MIA) was inaugurated. The stage was set for a new advance.

PAL Enters the Jet Age

This came in the form of the introduction of jet service on the international routes. On 11 December 1961, to compete with the efficient and forceful Cathay Pacific Airways, with its Lockheed Electras, PAL replaced its Viscount service with Boeing 707s. These were leased from Pan American Airways, which found it convenient to allocate residual hours on its trans-Pacific Boeings, in a mutually advantageous arrangement, with memories of Mexican sculduggery and trans-Pacific quarrelling temporarily forgotten.

Then, on 15 June 1962, the first Douglas DC-8-50, *Sampaguita* (PI-C801) was delivered to Manila by KLM, under an agreement with the Dutch airline, under which PAL lease-purchased it; that is, lease payments were made to KLM and after a limited time, these could be converted into purchase payments, by mutual agreement. A tri-coloured paint scheme, inspired by Bobby Lim, was introduced, and curiously, was applied to one side of the aircraft only, causing no little confusion at some ports of call en route. The DC-8 opened service to Hong Kong, replacing Pan Am's 707, on 18 June, and then, on a day that did much for the morale of Philippine Air Lines, service was restored across the Pacific to San Francisco, reached in 15 hours, via Honolulu, sometimes with stops at either Guam or Wake Island. By the end of the year, after Captain Oscar Ramos had become the first Filipino jet commander, a second trans-Pacific frequency had been added, and all the KLM pilots had been replaced.

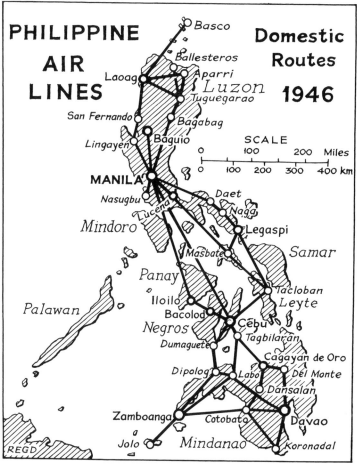

Map 24a. Philippine Air Lines, Domestic Routes, 1946
Immediately after the cessation of hostilities after the Second World War, a national airline
for the Philippines emerged. The nucleus was the old PATCO, founded by Andres Soriano
in the early 1930s, and which had absorbed the other airlines, including Eugenio López's
FEATI, formerly INAEC. Within a few months, with the exception of the island of Palawan,
the new PAL was serving every part of the Philippine island archipelago.

The jet service to Hong Kong had to be suspended. PAL had introduced a
Manila–Hong Kong–Bangkok service on 24 June 1962; but the British
Government, jealously guarding access to Hong Kong, the rights to which were
regarded in London as if it were a local point in Great Britain (and by international air law, legitimately so), objected, on the grounds that Manila was serving
as a subterfuge for KLM to gain access to the Crown Colony. PAL resumed
service with Viscounts.

In June 1962 PAL received its first Douglas DC-8 under a lease-purchase agreement with KLM.

Renato Barretto's Short Spell at the Helm

In the Philippines, important appointments such as airline presidencies have often gone hand in hand with changes of government, much in the same way as they do in other countries, including the United States. When the new administration, under the Presidency of Ramón Macapagal, took over on 19 January 1962, Eduardo Romualdez was obliged to resign. His tenure of office as president of PAL had been short, less than a year, but he had exerted a fair hand and a firm one, and he could look back on his months as head of the airline with satisfaction, having presided during its entry into the jet age.

Renato (Rene) Barretto became the new PAL president, and a young business-man, Benigno ('Benny') Toda Jr, became a member of the board of directors. Barretto faced an immediate problem when, on 21 January, Macapagal decon-trolled the value of the US dollar, and the Philippine peso's value dropped from 2 to 3.9 to the dollar. This affected the price of all those commodities that PAL had to buy from overseas, including aircraft and fuel.

But this was the least of Rene's problems. On 29 March 1962, Benny Toda was elected chairman of the board, and Manuel Marquez, friend and colleague, vice-chairman, and several officers who had resigned with Soriano, returned. In November the airline's capital, severely reduced in 1954, following the curtail-ment of international services, was substantially increased from PP6 million to PP25 million. In July 1963 Toda increased his involvement with PAL, demon-strating his interest by heading a new mission to the United States to seek more equitable traffic rights. He was unsuccessful; but the writing was on the wall.

Barretto had been actively trying to play his part as a caring president. He toured the domestic network, to confirm that the headquarters staff in Manila had not forgotten the problems in the Provinces, and did his best to establish goodwill among all the staff, at all levels. He campaigned for PAL at a time when there was much agitation to introduce competition, spurred on by reports of unheard-of low fares and better service by aspirant newcomers. His argument was not defen-sive. He stressed that, if a rival airline were allowed to start scheduled flights, then it should serve all the routes, and not simply those to the main provincial cities such as Cebu, Davao or Zamboanga, thereby 'skimming off the cream'.

Unhappily, Barretto did not see eye to eye with Benny Toda, who was now firmly in command of PAL affairs, and gaining stature as the real power behind policy decisions. Rene resigned on 5 August 1963 and Toda asked Ralph Igoa to take over the presidency, at least temporarily, until a full reorganization could take place. In November, Benny Toda did his reputation no harm by being elected to the IATA (International Air Transport Association) executive committee; and when Ralph Igoa left on 19 March 1964, Toda's star was in the ascendant. His financial interest in Philippine Air Lines was also in the ascendant. Whether by coincidence or by collusion, events seemed to play into his hands. On 1 July the Supreme Court declared that PAL was controlled by the Government, which would therefore have to compensate all employees for work exceeding 40 hours a week, at an estimated aggregate cost of $6 million. On 24 August the Government Service Insurance System (GSIS) announced the sale of shares to Toda, but widespread protests forced President Macapagal to modify this to a public auction. Thus 5 per cent of PAL was purchased by Anselmo Trinidad, of the Manila Stock Exchange, on 2 September, thus reducing the Government shareholding to 49 per cent.

On 18 January 1965 Benigno Toda Jr, acquired majority control of Philippine Air Lines. He was able to do this because the Philippine Government waived its right to buy new shares, and a new offer was promptly taken up by Rubicon Inc, one of Toda's own companies. He became chairman, with majority control – the first time in PAL history by the private sector – with the GSIS share now reduced to 24 per cent. Pan American still had 20 per cent, and TWA still retained a small minority holding. On 30 March 1965 Philippine Air Lines signed a management contract with Rubicon Inc. In its corporate affairs, PAL's history was beginning to repeat itself.

The First Scent of Competition

While the battles were being waged in the boardrooms, Rene Barretto (until his show-down with Toda in August 1963), Bobby Lim, and Silvano Quimbo had some battles to wage in the fields. The spirit of free, even unfettered, enterpise is strong among Filipinos. The Manila streets teem with thousands of jeepneys – the incomparable passenger version of the army jeep, developed ingeniously and artistically by Filipinos – which are operated by hundreds of individual concerns in a spirit of uninhibited competition. That such a system, which undoubtedly brought the cost of travel down to rock-bottom levels, should be applied to air transport as well as to road transport, seemed logical to many and found sympathy with some members of the administration.

Philippine Air Lines, with it majority shareholding resting with the Government until Benny Toda's coup, enjoyed an airline monopoly status, having absorbed in one way or another the earlier airlines that had tried their luck in the postwar years. In 1950 Paul Gunn, who had played a vital role in re-establishing PAL after the war, but who had resigned over differences with Andres Soriano, formed Philippine Aviation Development, but only as a charter operation, with small single-engined types. In 1954, he was permitted to operate in parallel with PAL with twin-engined Beech 18s, but flights were sporadic and hardly constituted competition. Gunn's potential threat was, in any case, short-lived, as he was killed in a Beech accident at Tanauan, Batangas, on 11 October 1957. His sons sold the fleet. One other name, Philippine Air Transport Service, flitted briefly across the scene in 1950, but its transport service was insignificant.

More serious – and certainly more colourful, both in character of the operation and the appearance of the fleet – was the irritant activities of James Fleming, an American and former CALI pilot, who formed Fleming Airways Systems Transport (FAST) in October 1957, and applied for permission to operate low-fare flights with Douglas DC-3s. He began these on 5 March 1958, under a temporary permit. On 22 March, the sole DC-3 crashed on take-off at Bacolod and burned out. Fleming salvaged another ex-USAAF DC-3, and resumed operations in parallel with PAL to Cebu, second city of the Philippines and the main source of domestic air traffic. Although technically a non-scheduled operation, the definition was difficult to apply. During some periods, there may not have been a published timetable, but everyone knew that a FAST flight would take off from Manila at breakfast-time; and some cynics asserted that PAL's allegedly scheduled operations did not.

The situation became more serious when, on 5 March 1961, Fleming introduced a four-engined Douglas DC-4 on the route to Cebu, transferring the DC-3 to serve Bacolod. The DC-4 had been purchased from KLM, and still retained the vivid light-and-dark blue 'barber's pole' paint scheme on its tail. The FAST aircraft attracted the eye as well as some of PAL's traffic – and the cause-and-effect pattern may have been applicable in this case. Elsewhere, Fleming was not above taking on some dubious work. In April 1962 he flew one Milton Spielman, under investigation for fraud, to Jolo, in the southern Philippines. Spielman boarded a boat, hoping to reach North Borneo, but was murdered by the boat crew.

By 1963 Fleming's FAST air service was sufficiently competitive, scheduled or otherwise, to draw attention from PAL. On 16 March 1964 the latter introduced its own DC-4 *Maya* service, using the same equipment – DC-4s, purchased from Japan Air Lines; operating in the same manner – non-scheduled; and at the same low fares – around PP0.10 per mile (and many a bargain was struck at the departure gates). When, in August 1964, PAL added a second DC-4 on its *Maya* service, it had won the battle, even though Fleming countered with extra 'non-scheduled' frequencies himself. From then on, FAST decelerated rapidly. In December 1964, the DC-4s (and a DC-7C, also ex-KLM) were grounded 'for lack of spare parts'. On 21 December a DC-3 crashed in northern Panay, and on 16 May 1965, another DC-3, the last one, crashed at Cotabato. A lone C-64 Norseman was also written off. Fleming left the country, and FAST closed down on 6 July 1965.

Philippine Air Lines terminated the non-scheduled *Maya* service on 25 February 1966. The four DC-4s had held their own against the efforts of FAST. But for all his melodramatic *modus operandi* James Fleming had left his mark. During a PAL strike in April 1963, his aircraft had flown with full loads to Cebu, Bacolod, Davao, and elsewhere, so that the Filipino air travelling public became aware of the possibilities of an alternative airline, in short, the freedom of choice. Fleming had been a thorn in Rene Barretto's side, and may have contributed to his discomfiture at PAL. By 1966 other independent airlines were emerging, energetically competing with PAL and the withdrawal of the *Maya* service was because one of these, Filipinas Orient, had petitioned the CAB to make it a scheduled service, so that the competition would be fair. The very idea of competition, fair or foul, had, until a few years previously, been unknown along the Philippine airways.

Two other small companies tried their hands in the early 1960s. On 3 May 1962 José Cruz obtained approval to operate three DC-3s, non-scheduled, as Cruz Airways, or Cruzaire. He ordered two Handley Page Dart Heralds in December, but never took delivery, and was bankrupt by the summer of 1963. Later, Southern Airlines, based in Davao, and owned by Jacob Lim, also started DC-3 services to Cotabato, Cebu and Manila; but early in 1966 had to cease operations because one of his aircraft was caught carrying contraband.

More serious competition was to follow, of greater significance to Philippine Air Lines; but meanwhile the flag carrier had other things to attend to; for it faced vigorous competition from overseas as well as at home.

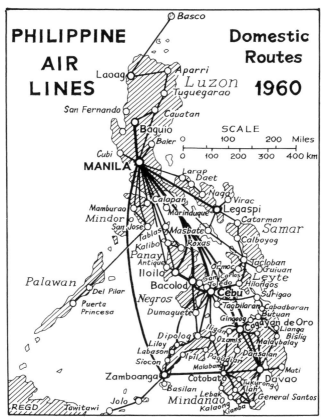

Map 24b. Philippine Air Lines, Domestic Routes, 1960
While going through many vicissitudes of political and industrial strife, PAL nevertheless managed to fulfil its responsibilities, in its role as the national airline charged with linking Manila and the main provincial cities and every small community. For a nation of islands, many of them extremely mountainous, PAL was a communications lifeline that served no fewer than seventy points, many of them in remote mountainous areas without even good roads for surface transport.

Toda Expands His Empire

At the time when Toda's Philippine Air Lines signed a management contract with Toda's Rubicon Inc, the aircraft fleet was beginning to appear well balanced. By the end of 1965 its own Douglas DC-8s were replacing the two on lease from KLM, the old DC-4s were about to be retired, seven Friendships and four Viscounts (with seven more Friendships on order) provided main-line 'Rolls-Royce' domestic service, and 26 faithful old DC-3s did the rest. The search for a 'DC-3 Replacement' was as unrewarding then as it would be today, even though a team from de Havilland searched for a combination of size, economy, and field performance that could cope with the challenges of Philippine rural airfields. If the twin-jet D.H.126/HS 136 project could have operated into places like

303

PAL began BAC One-Eleven services on 1 May 1966 – between Manila and Hong Kong.

Malaybalay in Mindanao, or Tacloban (where a cemetery was conveniently located at the end of the runway) it would have been a world-beater.

Having re-opened the trans-Pacific route in June 1962, PAL attempted to improve its competitive position and a US delegation visited Manila in August 1965 to resolve the dispute over frequencies and routeing. But the talks broke down. PAL was beginning to show its mettle, and was the first trans-Pacific airline to show in-flight films, which it introduced on 27 March 1965. PAL's second DC-8, *Mabuhay*, arrived on 20 September of that year, and was put into service to Sydney on 6 October. Viscount service had been re-opened to Taipei on 15 July 1965 (with the First Lady, Mrs Evangelina Macapagal, as guest); and on 1 November DC-8s began to serve Singapore. The first BAC One-Eleven, ordered in November 1964, went into service on 1 May 1966 as a *PALjet* to Hong Kong. Fitted with 72 seats, the PALjets also began domestic flights three days later, to Cebu, Bacolod and Davao. The 'Rolls-Royce' fare was set at PP0.21 per mile, plus a fixed surcharge of PP10.

These improvements were made against a background of increasing dominance by the Toda interests. Benny Toda was beginning to wave an almost dictatorial wand over PAL's affairs. On 22 April 1964 the airline had purchased a site for its new headquarters on Ayala Avenue, Makati (a modern new suburb of Manila), for PP1,200,000. The seller was Toda, who had purchased it for PP600,000, an astute piece of speculation. In March 1966 Philippine Air Lines increased its capital from PP25 million to PP100 million. Toda and his own company, Rubicon, now held 51.5 per cent of the shares; Rubicon was on a management contract, another Toda firm, Aeroben, was the purchasing agent, and yet another Toda enterprise, Cibeles, acted as insurers. Altogether, Toda's degree of control eclipsed that of the former Soriano regime; and in due course, in March 1968, Benny was able to announce that Rubicon had bought Pan American's 20 per cent share and TWA's 2 per cent, to bring his total up to 74 per cent. For the next decade, Philippine Air Lines would be a dominion of a commercial empire, and Benigno Toda was its emperor.

Stiffer Competition

Encouraged, perhaps, by Fleming's demonstrated ability to compete with Philippine Air Lines, even though his accident-prone and questionable business practices defied the laws of probable survival, other entrepreneurs decided that the way was open, given the right Government attitude, and with a viable operation equipped with a good fleet and staff, to challenge the Toda dominion. The Philippine Government's reduction of its shareholding in PAL in 1964–65 seemed to indicate a more laissez-faire attitude, and this was confirmed by sympathetic ears at the CAB when approaches were made for airline operating certificates. Such an environment developed under Macapagal's presidency, and was continued, even encouraged, after Ferdinand Marcos, former Senate leader, was elected as President of the Philippines on 9 November 1965.

Two new airlines vied for the honour of being the first to offer legitimate scheduled services in direct competition with the national airline, PAL. Fairways was first off the mark. It was organized by the disenchanted former PAL president, Renato Barretto, and by other former colleagues, and during the next few months they proceeded to tempt other experienced staff away from Toda's company, with offers of higher salaries and a rosy future. Under a temporary certificate, Fairways began flying on 6 January 1965 to Bacolod, Cebu, Davao and other points, with a fleet of eight DC-3s and two DC-6Bs. Barretto's knowledge of the domestic route system was a great asset, as he knew where the best traffic was to be had, and had even, when wearing his PAL hat, protested against skimming the cream off the top. Now he was happy to do so.

Even though marred by a DC-3 crash in eastern Luzon on 8 March 1965, Fairways got into top gear in fine style, beginning scheduled service two days later. On 30 March, a 91-seat DC-6B inaugurated a Manila–Cebu *Orchid Service*. Barretto had obtained a P2.7 million loan from the Philippine National Bank and so was financially secure, at least for a time, and was able to intensify the competition with PAL. Fairways duplicated PAL service on five of the seven trunk routes, ten of the 22 secondary routes, but only on two of the 30 or more feeder services. Fairways' DC-3s operated at PP0.07 per mile, against PAL's PP0.10; while the *Orchid* flights were priced at PP0.15 against PAL's 'Rolls-Royce' PP0.22. Fairways, which was renamed Filipinas Orient Airways (FOA) in November 1965, after operations had been suspended for 45 days, following a DC-3 crash near Bacolod on 11 September, finished up the year satisfactorily, having carried 195,000 passengers during the year. PAL had carried 1,540,000, but it was not a bad start. The change of name had coincided with the introduction of twin-turbine Nihon YS-11s, one of which was 'blessed' by the First Lady, Imelda Marcos – which could have done FOA no harm at the time. The airline was now under new management, Barretto having parted company in May.

Simultaneously with the establishment of Fairways, another independent airline of some substance entered the fray. On 14 February 1960 Air Manila was founded by a group of businessmen and retired Philippine Air Force officers, and led by the former ambassador to the United States, Amelito Mutuc. On 27 August it received an operating permit from the CAB, and, equipped with twelve DC-3s, ex-Frontier Airlines, made its first non-scheduled revenue flight on 2 January 1965, to Iloilo. Approval for scheduled operations having been received on 22 February 1965, Air Manila opened these with both DC-3s and a DC-6B (matching Fairways and PAL) on 30 March 1965. Parallelling Fairways' incursions into PAL's domestic system, it served six of the seven trunk routes, twelve of the secondary, but only three of the many feeders. Like Fairways/FOA, it was moderately successful, carrying 135,000 passengers in 1965. In November of that year, Air Manila ordered two Handley Page Dart Herald Series 200s.

The mid-1960s were reasonably satisfactory for both Filipinas Orient and Air

In November 1965 Air Manila ordered two Handley Page Dart Herald 200s.

Manila. Their equipment featured, in the former's case, Nihon YS-11s, and in the latter's, Handley Page Heralds and Fairchild-Hiller F-27s. These well matched PAL's Fokkers, although Toda had put the BAC One-Eleven twin-jets on the main routes in 1966. Curiously, PAL supplemented its Friendships with Hawker Siddeley 748s at the end of 1967 so that, for an airliner connoisseur, all four (or five) of the twin-Dart-engined propeller-turbine types could be photographed on the same day at Manila at that time. Although Air Manila's operations were interrupted by a pilots' strike and financial difficulties in 1968, it had carried 265,000 passengers in 1967. Filipinas had done even better, its YS-11s helping it to mark up 376,000, against PAL's 1.5 million. During the next few years, in fact, while Air Manila's fortunes declined, and with a typhoon destroying seven of its aircraft, Filipinas's passenger boardings rose to 453,000 in 1968, and remained close to that level annually. PAL had had its problems too. A serious DC-3 crash, killing 26 people, on 29 June 1966, had been followed by three Fokker crashes in 1967, in which a total of 41 more fatalities occurred. Thus, although Air Manila suffered a DC-3 crash on 8 March 1968, killing 14, the question of safety became a factor, and generally in the independents' favour.

The same could not be said for the airline finances. In spite of good traffic results, all the airlines lost money, because of the almost cut-throat competition in a continuous price war, in the desperate efforts to obtain higher market shares at any cost.

The Irreplaceable DC-3

While in airline circles, the veteran and venerable Douglas DC-3 was respected for its versatility and the ability to be able to use airstrips that only much smaller aircraft could normally tolerate, the public did not take the same view. The DC-3 looked old-fashioned, as indeed it was, compared to the pressurized post-war-designed nosewheel aircraft such as the Fokker F.27 Friendship that had been introduced in March 1960. Unfortunately, its very versatility tended to put it at risk, because operations departments in the dozens of airlines around the world that depended on the old 'Gooney Bird' – and Philippine Air Lines was no exception – became so confident in it as the 'forgiving' aeroplane that they despatched it to places where no self-respecting transport vehicle ought to go; and often the pilots themselves would become over-confident and tend not to fly 'by the book'. The result was that, exacerbated by the fact that PAL had more DC-3s than any other aircraft type, the statistical laws of probability ordained that most of the accidents were by DC-3s.

At the very time when Fairways/Filipinas and Air Manila were snapping at PAL's heels during the mid-1960s, PAL had a run of them, one in February 1964, in Mindanao, one in Manila in October 1965, and another in June 1966 in Mindoro. The mood in the airline was to modernize the fleet, especially in the face of propeller-turbine competition from its two rivals. The Friendship certainly went some way to alleviating the problem of supplementing the aging DC-3 fleet, but the Dutch aircraft was more particular in its operational requirements, and could only use some of the fields on the domestic network, those with well cared-for runways of 4,500 feet or more, preferably with approach patterns that were unobstructed by mountains almost within a stone's throw of the station buildings.

Such a situation led to a world-wide competition to build the so-called 'DC-3 Replacement'. Many were called, and many thrust themselves forward; but in the final analysis, none were chosen. There never was, and there never will be, a completely satisfactory replacement for the DC-3; for the main reason for its success and presence everywhere was that it was cheap. Almost every postwar DC-3 – of which there may have been as many as 5,000 in operation in the late 1940s – had been purchased as war surplus for the proverbial song. While manufacturers could have matched the DC-3 technically, the prices at which they could achieve operational parity were, in the 1960s, outrageous. Studies made even to start up a new DC-3 production line revealed that the price tag per delivered aircraft would have approached $3,000,000.

One of the aircraft that came very close to matching the DC-3's versatility was the Avro 748, later designated the HS 748, when Hawker Siddeley effected its

PAL began replacing DC-3s with Hawker Siddeley 748s in November 1967.

307

amalgamation of several of the traditionally-named British aircraft manufacturers. The same size as the Friendship, and with the same Rolls-Royce Dart engines, it was a low-wing, rather than a high-wing feeder-liner. The passengers did not have such a good view but the performance at the rough airfields was impressive. It was claimed to be able to land on a ploughed field, and one journalist in Argentina, on a local 748 flight, claimed that he had 'seen unprepared strips before, but these were taken by surprise'.

On 25 February 1967 the HS 748 demonstrator arrived in Manila. On 28 February a PAL Friendship crashed at Mactan, Cebu, killing eleven people. On 10 April 1967, while the comparisons were being made of the various contenders to supplant the DC-3 were being made, the last Viscount flight arrived in Manila from Bacolod – one of the domestic points that could provide both the airfield and the traffic volume to justify an aircraft of this size, and which was being replaced by the BAC One-Eleven. Two weeks later, a Friendship Series 200 arrived, on loan from Indonesia, for demonstration at 'DC-3 airports'. On 27 April 1967, it crashed at Malaybalay, Mindanao, where the airstrip was less than 1,000 metres (about 3,000 ft) long, and where the mountainous terrain was formidable. All nineteen officials and crew were killed.

This did no good for the Fokker challenge to Hawker Siddeley. Then, when another Friendship crashed in Negros Occidental on 6 July 1967, with 21 deaths, the competition was over. Two days later, Benny Toda ordered six HS 748s, and the first one went into service from Manila to Puerto Princesa on 15 November of the same year.

As if to confirm that this was the answer to the DC-3 Replacement problem, all the Douglas veterans were retired on 14 March 1968. The last scheduled flight was by PI-C439, Flight 716, from Virac and Naga into Manila. Even so, the HS 748s could not replace the DC-3s at every point, and ten communities lost airline service as a result of this 'modernization' process.

Such was the importance of this decision to the local communities that were directly affected, being deprived of their major means of transport, that strong protests were made from far and wide, and such were the political reverberations that President Marcos himself directed that DC-3 service should be resumed to those places with the greatest need. Consequently, on 27 May, only two months after the grounding, DC-3 service was resumed to four airports: Jolo, Hilongos, Mamburao and Calapan.

It was a classic case of 'he's dead but he won't lie down'. Partly because the HS 748 was not immune to problems itself, the Douglas DC-3 kept on flying in Philippine Air Lines' colours for another ten years, and was finally retired on 7 April 1978. The episode was significant in the history of Philippine air transport. The airlines, especially PAL, invariably had to provide their own installations, even to maintain their own airfields, throughout the island nation. Unlike the situation in most other countries, the Philippine Government was reluctant to provide much help, and did so only when there was a military or political benefit to be realized. President Marcos took action only when a nationwide protest jeopardized his popularity and political reputation. Twenty years later, he was less inclined to take notice of the mood of the Philippine people.

PAL Spans The World Again

While PAL faced difficulties on the home front, and had to accept some setbacks, things were looking up in the international arena. The map had grown in 1965, with a new route to Sydney. On 4 April 1968, service was resumed to Tokyo, and with the third DC-8, *Champaca*, delivered, a fifth trans-Pacific frequency demonstrated a growing maturity and presence in that important market. A year later, on 3 April 1969, amid much satisfaction to the PAL old hands, service was resumed to Europe, with a weekly DC-8 flight to Amsterdam (reflecting the KLM connection) via Bangkok, Karachi and Rome. In east Asia, a BAC One-Eleven service started to Saïgon, where a number of Filipino workers were employed at US Air bases, on 1 November 1968. The One-Elevens also started flying to Bali on 19 March 1968, but problems with the Indonesian traffic rights led to this route being terminated on 25 November 1969.

By 1 April 1970 the trans-Pacific service had been increased to a daily frequency, with the Tokyo and European trunk lines at two per week. Frankfurt was added to the European list of destinations on 1 April 1971, and Melbourne became a second Australian terminus on 9 September of that year. To counteract the threat of wide-bodied competition, but to cope with steadily growing international traffic, Toda had announced, on 28 February 1968, an order for two DC-8 Series 63s – Douglas's 'stretched' version of the line, and said by some airline economists to be the nearest thing to printing your own money. The value of the order, PP52 million, was almsot equal to the annual budget for the city of Manila. In the event, PAL never did own a 'Stretched Eight' but it did lease one from KLM on 4 May 1942, to stem the tidal wave of Boeing 747s that Pan American Airways and Northwest Orient was deploying across the Pacific Ocean. Pan Am was indirectly aided by President Marcos's declaration, early in January 1970, of an Open Skies policy, relinquishing Philippine restrictions and limitations on foreign airline use of Manila operating rights.

Domestic Agitation

The DC-3 Replacement problem was not the only bone of contention within the Philippine skies. Back in 1961 the Viscount services to Bacolod had been augmented, on 28 June, with a *Night Mercury* flight, an innovation that was extended to other cities during the next few years. This was one of the operational advantages that PAL retained when Fairways and Air Manila were permitted to compete directly on the main routes; and with the Government favouring competition, PAL had to cancel the *Night Mercurys* on 21 April 1967. Toda countered with a Night Jet Manila–Cebu service on 26 June, charging PP0.18 per mile; but had to increase this to PP0.21 after protests by the other airlines. Businessmen in Cebu became exasperated with the constant sparring and manoeuvring, and suggested that there should be comparable fares for comparable types of aircraft with no capacity restrictions. Nevertheless, the *Night Mercurys* were so popular that they were extended in the summer of 1968 to six more points. Predictably, Filipinas Orient (formerly Fairways) and Air Manila protested, but popular opinion was so strongly in favour of the service that President Marcos over-ruled the CAB and retained them. In due course, however, after a Fokker Friendship accident at Iligan, and complaints about poor airfields, the *Night Mercury* services were cancelled.

Special Problems

The continuous vulnerability to the depradations caused by poor airfields was only one of Philippine Air Lines' many problems, some of which were not too common, if they existed at all, in other countries. This is not to say that they did not affect other airlines; but as the predominant commercial air carrier, Toda's airline suffered the most from criminal acts and Acts of God. At least, by the 1960s, local farmers had been trained to graze their cattle at times when PAL aircraft were not expected, but there were other human factors of a more sinister nature that had a habit of recurring from time to time.

Every few years, an accident, often ending in tragedy, would be the result of circumstances that, with the disciplines of the times, were beyond the airline's control. Long before the spate of incidents, culminating in the infamous Pan American Lockerbie holocaust, that led to intense passenger boarding inspection processes at the world's major airports, the Philippines had been well ahead of the Middle Eastern-stimulated count of hijackings and bombings. On 7 May 1949 a DC-3 fatal bombing had been the result of a family feud. On 5 September 1960, an HS 748 was badly damaged by a bomb set off by a passenger, who climbed out of the resultant hole in the roof and fell to his death. Fortunately, the pilots landed the aircraft safely. Less fortunate were 36 people on board another 748 when, on 21 April 1970, a time-bomb, suspected to have been planted on board by rebel factions, exploded in flight.

Back in 1952 a DC-3 had been hijacked by a Chinese fugitive, who, on take-off from Laoag, directed the pilot to fly to the mainland. He shot the pilot and the purser, but the co-pilot, with considerable aplomb, not to mention heroism, managed to land the aircraft in Chinese Nationalist territory, and saved many lives by his sharp-wittedness. Hijacking seemed to go out of fashion for a couple of decades, only to return in the 1970s. On 30 March 1971 six Maoist youths took over a BAC One-Eleven, directing it first to Hong Kong, then to Canton; but the aircraft was returned and no one was hurt. On 13 October 1973 another BAC One-Eleven was diverted by hijackers from a Manila– Davao flight, once again to Hong Kong. In a dramatic piece of public relations, Benny Toda offered himself as a hostage, in exchange for the 52 passengers, on condition that he be returned to Manila safely and with Presidential amnesty for the culprits. Marcos agreed but PAL had to employ the hijackers!

There were two hijackings of PAL aircraft in 1976. On 7 April, yet another One-Eleven was forced to fly from Cagayan de Oro to Manila. This time it was Ralph Igoa's turn. He and others were exchanged and the aircraft was flown to Bangkok, via Kota Kinabalu and Kuala Lumpur. PAL then had to supply a DC-8 to take the hijackers to Libya. At Bangkok, in a bizarre incident, the Filipino security men, disguised as stewards, were refused entry by the Thai immigration authorities because they had omitted to bring their passports. Only six weeks later, on 21 May, Muslim youths at Zamboanga took over a One-Eleven – the type seemed to be favoured by the Hijackers Union – and kept it on the ground during negotiations. These were terminated abruptly by an explosion which triggered a battle with soldiers, resulting in the deaths of ten passengers, three hijackers, and the total loss of the aircraft.

As if these tribulations were not enough, PAL suffered depradations from the weather, specifically the frequent incidence of typhoons of an extremely destructive nature. Mention has already been made of Typhoon Dading, in which, on 29 June 1964, ground crew saved part of the DC-3 fleet by 'flying' them into the teeth of the wind, while still lashed to the ground. Typhoon Yoling, of 19 November 1970, was not so considerate. One DC-3 became airborne, then fell on its back. Two other DC-3s were completely wrecked, and several of the twin turbine types were badly damaged. On 18 July 1972 Typhoon Gloring caused

At the end of 1972 Filipinas leased two Sud-Aviation Caravelles from Sterling Airways.

heavy flooding, but even against top-level directives, PAL continued to serve many places, in relief efforts, the aircraft tending to reach terra firma by aquaplaning techniques.

PAL Wins a Battle

During the latter 1960s and early 1970s Philippine Air Lines (or Philippine Airlines, as it became in 1968) continued to face competition from Filipinas Orient and Air Manila. But the two independents were on shaky financial foundations, mainly because the cut-throat fares competition reduced yields to levels that did not cover the operational costs; and the slender margins did not leave room for investment in better equipment. Filipinas leased two Caravelles from the Danish Sterling Airways at the end of 1972, and late in 1971, Air Manila had tried to introduce two ex-Eastern Air Lines Lockheed L-188 Electras, but was unable to keep them flying, for lack of spares and because of damage by heavy landings.

Much wheeling and dealing went on behind the scenes in the labyrinth of Philippine politics, especially in the case of Air Manila. Early in 1972, with an injection of fresh capital from the Delta Air Corporation, a local air taxi service, it acquired two Boeing 707s, while the Philippine National Bank converted its loan to a 48 per cent equity. In May 1972 Air Manila also purchased an ex-Pan American 707 formerly owned by no less than Robert Vesco, the financier of dubious credentials who had been obliged to exile himself from the USA. This aircraft had a sauna, an exercise room, a study, a bedroom and a dance floor. It cost $750,000 and was apparently intended for the use of President Marcos and the First Lady. In October 1972 having adopted the more impressive name of Air Manila International (AMI) Air Manila opened an international route from Davao to Menado, in the north of the island of Sulawesi, Indonesia. But this did not last long. The first 707 arrived in Manila on 1 January 1973 and was then leased to Egyptair.

The independents had had their chance. In February 1971 the CAB had authorized PAL to suspend service at 18 points, and 13 of these were allocated to Filipinas and Air Manila. But the latter either could not, or would not, operate to the small communities, where traffic was light and pockets were often empty. This did not rest too well with Filipinos everywhere. They were not too happy

311

with the Marcos regime anyway and there was much talk of insurrection and actual disturbances in the mainly Moslem island of Mindanao. Benny Toda was prepared to play a hard game, and, with labour problems and strikes of his own to contend with, had no compunction about terminating airline service if it suited him.

Interestingly, during the period when airline service was at its lowest level, in the early 1970s, the Philippine Air Force tried to supplement the commercial carriers with its Air Maharlika service, using DHC-2 Beavers acquired from the USAF in Vietnam. But it found that providing a regular and reliable series of flights was quite different from its normal routine, and was no threat to PAL.

Amid mounting disaffection with the entire system, on 23 September 1972, President Marcos signed Proclamation No. 1081, declaring martial law. The Philippine Air Force was given the task of supervising the airlines, one of its main objectives being to subdue the insurgents in Mindanao. Earlier in the same month, the control of air fares had reached almost farcical proportions, with the CAB authorizing increases, the Supreme Court, or Marcos himself, countermanding them, and then the High Tribunal revoking the Court and the President.

His patience running out, and recognizing a real crisis, President Marcos directed, on 31 March 1973, that all three airlines should merge, with Philippine Airlines as the surviving company. Toda took what he wanted and no more: three of Filipinas's Nihon YS-11As, which were put into service on 28 February 1974; and two of Air Manila's F.27s, to add to its own. PAL's fleet was in need of reinforcement. Only six of its thirteen HS 748s were serviceable.

On 1 January 1974 PAL became the sole scheduled airline of the Philippines and the designated flag carrier. A Letter of Instruction (LOI), No. 151, to the Secretary of National Defence enabled the Philippine National Bank to take over the assets of Filipinas Orient and Air Manila. LOI No. 151A confirmed the foreclosure of both airlines and instructed PAL to expand its route system from 32 to 49 points.

The experiment in airline competition had been a complete failure. It accomplished little except to increase the cost of air service and to depress the quality of the service rendered, not to mention the deprivation of air service at many points. This was the opposite effect from the advantages that were claimed. The theoretical benefits from competition do not apply when there is clearly an upper limit to the market demand, and one that can be forecast to remain so with reasonable confidence.

The Wide-Bodied Era Begins

Having wrestled with a finance problem of considerable complexity, Benny Toda finally managed to place an order for two 269-seat McDonnell Douglas DC-10-30 tri-jet wide-bodied airliners. Backed by the Development Bank of the Philippines, loans were obtained from KLM and a Dutch lender, accounting for 40.5 per cent of the $49,284,000 order. Forty-five per cent came from US sources, 4.5 per cent from McDonnell Douglas, and only 10 per cent in cash from the airline itself. The order was placed on 14 June 1973, and the first DC-10 went into service on 17 July 1974, providing four of the five trans-Pacific frequencies.

The introduction was not without its special problems. When the first aircraft arrived at San Francisco, the US CAB had already disapproved the schedule submitted by PAL, and it was met by a US marshal and impounded, complete with the 156 passengers. The Philippine authorities hastily agreed to increase the sched-

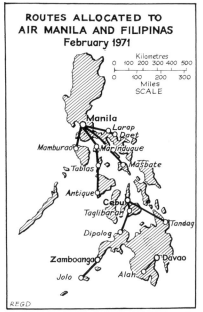

Maps 24c. Philippine Rural Air Routes in the 1970s
During the 1960s, PAL had struggled to satisfy both the public and the politicians with adequate service to every community in the Philippine islands, yet at the same time to try to make ends meet. The rural routes were always operated at a loss, and in the 1970s, attempts were made by the administration to ease PAL's burden. The two leading independent challengers to PAL were asked to operate some rural routes, as well as simply taking the cream off the top of the domestic services. But Air Manila and Filipinas Orient never met these obligations. Later on, PAL established a subsidiary, PATI, to operate rural routes as a semi-autonomous centre; but this too lasted only a few years.

ules permitted to US airlines into and through Manila, and PAL had to post a $200,000 bond as security.

Such irritations apart, however, there was much reason for optimism in the international field of operations. Service was resumed to Bali in November 1974, in co-operation with the Indonesian Merpati Nusantara, but this was again short-lived and on a charter basis. The DC-10s started on the European services on 1 November 1976, releasing the DC-8s to expand the network on the Pacific Rim, to Kuala Lumpur and Jakarta on 7 April 1977, and to Port Moresby, Niugini, on 1 September of that year.

The Emperor's Clothes

By 1968, with his acquisition of additional shares to command 74 per cent of the PAL total, Benigno Toda Jr, had reason to believe that he was in charge of an organization that was his private property and that he could do what he liked with it. On 8 January 1969 he brought back Ralph Igoa as his right-hand man, to be elected executive vice-president on 29 March. Igoa's contract was generous, for ten years, with an option to purchase 100,000 shares, and with

313

a house whose redecoration cost PAL PP375,000.

Although the Secretary of Commerce and Chairman of the CAB had some misgivings about Toda's absolute control of PAL, this did not seem to worry Benny, who was acting like a rich absentee landlord. He spent as much of his time out of the country as in it. When he was back in the Philippines, he was usually to be found at his private island, Hermana Mayor, for which journeys PAL substituted special charter flights instead of some scheduled ones. Toda left Ralph Igoa to run the airline, along with a number of non-Filipinos appointed to senior positions. Igoa's management style was not popular, and it occurred during a period when, with two domestic competitors, PAL was cutting back its operations. On 12 December 1970, after a work stoppage by major unions in October, about two-thirds of the pilots resigned. Service to 23 domestic points was suspended and international services had to be reduced. PAL maintained a skeleton operation with non-union and management staff. The autocratic Igoa was non-negotiable. Recalling Marie Antoinette, perhaps, his reaction was 'Let them crawl back'. After the allocation of routes to the rivals in February 1971, 530 PAL employees were laid off, with much alleged favouritism.

Meanwhile, the company posted a P29 million loss in 1970, the first loss for many years. Suffering from a cash shortage, PAL sold the nine remaining Friendships to the Philippine Air Force, and the PAL Building on Ayala Avenue, to Toda's own insurance company, Cibeles, for P24 million. The offices were moved partly to a former super-market at the airport and partly to a building on Roxas Boulevard. In the early 1970s, even as PAL introduced wide-bodied DC-10 service and became the sole scheduled airline in the Philippines, there were rumours that Toda was losing his grip on affairs. On one of her many commandeered flights to overseas destinations (often for little more than shopping trips) the First Lady, on a special diplomatic mission to Beijing, advised Benny Toda, who was also along for the trip, of the President's dissatisfaction with the way PAL was being managed. One commentator observed 'At the close of 1975, PAL would impress anyone as a textbook example of a monopoly so endowed with power and influence that it could increase its fares and inflict inefficiency on its customers with impunity. After three years of martial law, it remained in the control of one man as the majority stockholder; and after nearly thirty years of existence, it was still run largely by foreigners'.

In July 1976 PAL was ordered by the Government to 'cut excessive expenses in payments to leech companies, to increase its capital, and to get rid of foreigners'. Some months later, on 19 April 1977, another report revealed that, during 1975, PP55 million had been paid by PAL to Toda companies, and an equal amount paid in mysterious write-offs and other 'expenses'. The financial details were, by any measure, extraordinary and astonishing. Most of the bad debts were to a fictitious Alfa Manufacturing Company.

A few months earlier, a press report had revealed that Benny Toda had billed the President for PP2,400,000 for aircraft chartered by the First Lady. Just for once, the expenses could probably have been accounted for; but this was hardly the time to irritate a President who was not noted for tolerating opposition.

The end was near. On 19 October Toda offered his shares to the Government, and on 17 November 1977 it obliged and took over the Rubicon 74 per cent. The balance was already held by the Government Service Insurance System (GSIS) so that PAL became a State-owned corporation. All contracts with Toda companies, Rubicon, Aeroben, and Cibeles, were terminated, and the share capital immediately increased from PP25 to PP250 million, to be used mainly to finance the purchase of three Boeing 747s, which were ordered on 12 August 1978. Reportedly, Benny Toda received nothing for his shares, because of the feud with the President and the First Lady, it being alleged that he had acquired contol of the airline only through political favours made to the former President. In Philippine politics, there were no Queensberry Rules.

CHAPTER TWENTY-FIVE

The Philippine National Airline Reaches Maturity

Cruz Steadies the Ship

The day after the take over of Philippine Airlines on 17 November 1977, Marcos asked Ramón A Cruz to assume the Presidency of Philippine Airlines. Cruz had formerly been the manager of the Government Service Insurance System (GSIS) which had held 25 per cent of the shares of PAL. He set about his task with commendable vigour, and in complete contrast to the attitude to the staff conducted by the previous owner. Almost immediately, he visited the maintenance department, and addressed the workers, speaking in Tagalog – a symbolic indication that the era of foreign direction was to give way to a Filipino one.

Recognizing the dire need to bring the aircraft fleet up to a better standard of serviceability, he ordered half the fleet to be grounded, for complete overhaul; and this led to some routes being transferred to Philippine Aero Transport (PATI). He revitalized the catering department and insisted on the need to offer better service on board. He was determined, he said, to kill the popular interpretation of the PAL abbreviation: Plane Always Late, or, in Tagalog, Palaging Atrasado Lamang.

Internationally, the airline took on a new momentum, deriving strength from a strong and fair leadership, and now with adequate capital with which to improve and to invest. In April 1978, one of the DC-10 trans-Pacific flights began to extend to Singapore, thus taking advantage of Manila's geographically advantageous position to exploit the so-called Sixth Freedom traffic. In June of the same year, the US CAB extended PAL's special low-fare Balikbayan deal for home-coming Filipinos, in spite of opposition from Pan American Airways. On 15 November, Cruz (who had been elected president of IATA) ordered two A300B-4 Airbuses, costing $89 million. Fitted with 246 seats, they were intended to serve the regional routes of east Asia. To wind up a year of reorganization, in December, PAL took over the rural air services of PATI, thus regaining domestic ground that it had lost during the past five years.

PATI

Reference has already been made to the difficulties faced by Philippine Airlines in trying to continue flying to outlying communities for whom air service was essential but whose resources were not up to providing the ground installations, nor even the airstrips, to provide it. Such services are invariably money-losers, as insufficient traffic, at inadequate yields, cannot cover the high operating costs. PAL had done its best, back in the 1950s, by introducing the Rural Air Service, with DHC-3 Otters; but, without any Government support, was forced to discontinue it in 1964. When, during the heat of the competitive manoeuvring during the 1970s, the two independent airlines had been offered a substantial slice of the rural air service cake, they had ignored such plain fare, preferring the main inter-city domestic routes – the icing on the top of the cake.

Possibly believing that neither Philippine Air Lines nor any of the independents could provide a proper rural service, officialdom took a hand. On 24 May 1975 the Government-owned Philippine Aerospace Development Corporation started service with the Philippine Aero Transport Inc (PATI) which it had established as a subsidiary, to serve those routes discarded by PAL. Its fleet consisted of twelve 10-seat Britten-Norman BN-2 Islanders, and the grand plan was to operate to 41 points in the Visayas, Mindanao and Luzon – in fact all over the Philippines.

Beginning cautiously, by December 1975, it had opened a hub at Cebu, taking over additional segments from PAL and connecting the Philippines' second city with 18 points throughout the Visayas (the name given to the group of islands lying between Luzon and Mindanao). Some indication that history was about to repeat itself was soon forthcoming. An Islander crashed at Mactan, with two fatalities. The sturdy single-engined Otters and the maid-of-all-work DC-3s had not been able to cope; now the little British bush aircraft, built for the job, was equally vulnerable.

PATI pressed on, however, and by September 1976 was serving 23 points, of which 19 connected directly at points served by PAL. Operationally, this was an entirely sensible system, and might have succeeded; but the convoluted politics of the Philippines thwarted the best intentions. In December 1978 PAL was ordered to take over the PATI services, including the ten BN-2s still operating with their 27 pilots. The PATI aircraft and schedules were continued under its own name, but the inspiration for autonomy, and the elements necessary to feed such inspiration (such as with Loganair in Scotland) seemed to be lacking. PATI faded away. On 15 September 1979, ten points were suspended, seven being transferred to PAL, and three losing service altogether. All PATI flights ended on 1 February 1980, and the Islander fleet was sold soon afterwards.

Philippine Airlines World-wide

No doubt, the management of the country's national airline and flag carrier felt it had more important things to think about than a rural air service which, over the years, it had done its best to create, had faced innumerable and often insuperable difficulties, and had received no thanks for the effort. Completely nationalized (Igoa had sold his 100,000 shares for PP5,747,000 on 31 January 1979) Philippine Airlines had a mandate to represent its country overseas, and in literally showing the flag, to act as an ambassador as well as a travel service wherever it went.

Ramón Cruz soon found that events were often beyond the control of the best-laid plans. Because of the dramatic and tragic American Airlines DC-10 accident at Chicago, PAL's mainline fleet was totally grounded from 25 May until 23 June 1979, while the Federal Aviation Administration in the United States investigated the accident. The DC-8s maintained trans-Pacific service in the interim; but were no match for the other airlines, which had Boeing 747s as well as the grounded tri-jet. Two 140-seat Boeing 727s were also leased from Hughes Airwest, to take care of some of the regional and mainline domestic services.

Triumphing, as it were, over this temporary adversity, PAL bounced back. For a hectic six months following the return to service of the DC-10s, there was never a dull moment. The morale of the troops must have been uplifted by an announcement on 14 July 1979 (Bastille Day) by the prestigious Les Chaînes de Rotissiers, which made Philippine Airlines the first airline ever to be a member of that ancient and exclusive order of gourmets. Ramón Cruz's plea for improvements in catering must have fallen on receptive ears. On 25 July Athens and Bahrain were added

Leased PAL Boeing 727s opened routes to China in 1979.

At the end of 1979 PAL introduced its first Airbus A300B-4 on services to Singapore.
(*GIFAS*)

as intermediate stops on the European routes. The first Boeing 727 inaugurated two new routes on 1 August – both to the People's Republic of China, to Beijing and Guangzhou (formerly Peking and Canton, respectively). PAL thus became the first airline in east Asia to be permitted to fly both to China and to Taiwan. The second 727 arrived on 10 September and was immediately put to work on the two main domestic routes to Cebu and Davao.

More good news was to come. On 4 December the first Airbus A300 entered the ranks, first destination Singapore. Then, to cap this, on 4 January 1980, the first Boeing 747 replaced the DC-10s on the trans-Pacific routes. PAL's service was something special. It featured full-size Skybeds in the Cloud Nine upper deck, and PAL was authorized by the US FAA (not noted for giving favours to foreigners) to permit sleeping passengers to remain undisturbed during the stop at Honolulu. No other airline provided such a standard of luxury. In a neat balancing act, the same aircraft carried Jambolilit passengers at budget ticket prices to make up the loads of the 360-seat aircraft. On 31 March 1980 the 747 took over the service to London, and the European network increased to four frequencies a week. On 28 August the *Mabuhay* super-business class was introduced. A new air agreement with the United States was more liberal than any previous bilateral, opening new gateways, to Guam, Palau and Saipan; granting unlimited cargo service; and, at long last, routes to the USA via Tokyo, provided the Japanese agreed. Delivery of the fourth 747 on 14 December permitted a new trans-Pacific service, to Los Angeles, to be opened three days later, so that PAL was now operating ten trans-Pacific flights a week, and was an established carrier in this major

PAL's first Boeing 747 was delivered at the end of 1979 and introduced on trans-Pacific services on 4 January 1980. (*Boeing*)

world market. As if to mark the maturity of a new era, the last Douglas DC-8 was retired on 26 March 1981.

On the domestic front, the continued fascination with overnight flights to the main provincial cities, offering cheap fares because of a marginal costing system of accounting, was renewed. On 12 May 1980 Bululit jet fares on night flights were introduced, at 40 per cent lower levels than the daytime ones. They applied to all flights from Manila to Cebu, Davao and Zamboanga (Iloilo was added on 6 June) that departed between sunset and sunrise. The YS-11As continued to serve the Visayas, where many airfields could still not take the BAC One-Elevens, of which PAL now had a round dozen, including some of the -500 series.

The year 1981 was mainly one of consolidation, after the impact of the introduction of two new wide-bodied aircraft types in 1980. On 17 March political tension was slightly alleviated when President Marcos lifted martial law. Astutely, he timed this to occur three days before President Reagan was inaugurated as President of the United States, and one month before the visit of Pope John Paul II, who might have had something to say about Human Rights. Philippine Air Lines was designated to carry His Holiness on a tour of the Philippines. The aircraft was one of the 727s, which unfortunately still bore the inscription *Hooray for Hollywood*. At Cebu, where the citizens have a fine sense of what is right, the inscription was changed to *Viva Il Papa*.

In a top level managerial reshuffle, on 7 May 1982, Eduardo Romualdez – the same who had steadied the ship back in 1961, when Andres Soriano resigned without warning – was again appointed chairman, while Cruz continued at the helm as president. PAL now had good leadership, and a good team of directors, including Martin Bonoan, a fine man, who was sadly to die within a few years, while relatively young. On 22 May 1982, he survived a remarkable incident at Cebu, when a disgruntled war veteran hijacked a BAC One-Eleven (always a One-Eleven!) and threatened to blow it up with a hand-grenade. He demanded ransom, which was given. A scuffle followed, the hijacker was subdued, but Martin Bonoan received a bite wound on his chest. As already observed, there was seldom a dull moment in PAL.

Such weird incidents apart, Philippine Air Lines maintained its momentum of growth. The international network was augmented considerably during a period of expansion, of less than a year, between the summer of 1982 and the spring of 1983. Brisbane was added to the Australian service on 5 June 1982, Dubai

319

included as a Middle East destination on 7 August, and Paris and Zürich became the sixth and seventh European destinations on 4 November. A weekly DC-10 service to Seoul began on 2 March 1983, but had to be suspended on 6 May the following year, because of a Filipino-Korean dispute over the reciprocal carriage of guest workers to the Middle East, in which lucrative traffic both PAL and Korean Air Lines were active participants. To round off this flurry of route inaugurations, a weekly Boeing 727 started flights to Kota Kinabalu and Bandar Seri Bagawan, in East Malaysia and Brunei, respectively. Even more important, perhaps, than adding a new place on the map was the signing of an air agreement with Japan on 21 April 1983, giving Philippine Airlines, at long last, the coveted Fifth Freedom rights to San Francisco via Tokyo. The service via the Number One Pacific Rim gateway began on 2 August 1983.

There were times when PAL may have regretted its expansion in Europe. The First Lady, Imelda Marcos, tended to regard the Philippine national airline, now nationalized and therefore subject to Presidential requirements, if necessary, as her personal executive fleet. Aircraft were known to be taken out of service to be placed at her disposal, and to await her pleasure at the airports in foreign parts until she had finished her shopping and socializing.

Such bizarre occurrences were a manifestation of a deteriorating political situation in the Philippines. The First Lady's whims aside, her husband devalued the currency on 23 June 1983 (to PP11.00 to the US $) as the Philippines overseas debt reached the record level of $343 million. Domestic costs and fares rose accordingly. This severely affected PAL's fortunes, just when it had been incurring hard currency expense with its overseas expansion; and at home the Muslim insurgence in the south was a disincentive to air travel.

Even so – and with another disincentive of a far more serious nature – Ramón Cruz and his administration maintained a policy of optimism, reflected in positive marketing decisions and actions, possibly aided by the final retirement of Ralph Igoa, symbol of foreign influence, on 23 December. The trans-Pacific service was upgraded to match the standards of the best airlines on this highly competitive route. On 2 January 1984 the frequency to Los Angeles was increased to a daily service. First-class seating was reduced from 24 to 20, but there were Skybeds upstairs for 14. The *Mabuhay* business section was reduced from 48 to 34, and Cruz was buoyant enough to state that 'we are within hailing distance of survival' – although, in the circumstances, he might have reflected that a stranded rock-climber can hover between survival and death, yet still be within hailing distance.

But PAL was certainly keeping faith with its mandate to represent its country overseas and to serve it at home. The last Boeing 727 was retired on 31 May 1984, and the last Nihon YS-11 on 20 November, signifying an appreciable upgrading of the domestic and local regional scene. With the delivery of the fourth Airbus on 31 August, the second city of the Philippines, Cebu, began to enjoy widebodied service three times a week; and such was its success and popularity that on 1 December, the A300s were operating three times a day on some days of the week. On 16 October, Manila–Cebu passengers were able to enjoy the *Mabuhay* business-class comfort as well as the economy class, which was also upgraded to international standards.

Overseas, Xiamen (formerly Amoy) replaced Guangzhou (Canton) on 1 April 1985 as the Chinese staging point to Beijing, partly to accommodate increasing numbers of provincial immigrants. The trans-Pacific service was extended to Chicago on 17 November; and service to Ho Chi Minh (Saïgon) began on 25 November, the reciprocal flights by Hang Khong Vietnam having started on 10

September. The A300 service to Dubai was extended to Cairo on 3 December.

Cruz and PAL were putting on a brave show of 'business as usual' while the country moved inexorably towards a political crisis and a political revolution that was unprecedented in history. Cruz could, in retrospect, be identified as the type of man who kept his head while all around him were losing theirs – because he was unaware of the true state of affairs. But this would be over-cynical. As the nation's flag carrier, right or wrong, PAL maintained the creed of all airlines across the world, and kept on flying until wisdom and good judgement took precedence over courage and fortitude.

Revolution

Between the closing weeks of 1985 and the end of February 1986, Philippine Air Lines could have crashed several aircraft and sustained half a dozen hijackings, and nobody would have noticed, such was the dramatic turn of events on the political scene in the Philippine Republic. The seeds of discontent had been fertilized on 21 August 1983, when former Senator Benigno Aquino, of the opposition party to the ruling Marcos faction, returned from self-exile to the United States, possibly feeling that the level of violence, always smouldering subliminally in Filipino political circles, had diminished. He was wrong. On arrival at Manila International Airport, he was assassinated in a fusillade of gunfire. Ramón Cruz, a Marcos man, was incensed at the pro-Aquino mood within PAL.

Throughout 1984 – at the very time when, under Cruz's direction, the national airline was putting its once-tottering house in order – the situation deteriorated sharply. In May, the opposition party gained many seats in the local Manila elections; in July, demonstrations in the streets were put down with tear gas; in October, strong rumours circulated that the Aquino murder had been the result of a Marocs-initiated conspiracy, and the news reverberated around the whole world. Tension reached a new level early in 1985 when, after much legal confrontation, the trial of General Ver and 25 other army officers got under way. The charge was double murder. Benigno's widow, Corzaon Aquino, became the rallying figure of a ground swell of popular anti-Marcos opinion throughout the land. In August, Mrs Aquino called for a non-violent struggle for justice and 51 members of parliament voted to impeach the President. The head of the Catholic church, the strangely-named Cardinal Sin, provided strong moral support. Such was the disdainful attitude of the Presidency that, within two weeks of the ending of the trial, and while a final decision was awaited, the First Lady requisitioned yet another PAL aircraft for a shopping expedition overseas.

This was the last such flight she would take. On 2 December, against overwhelming evidence that should have resulted in a far different verdict, all the 26 officers, including General Ver, were acquitted. President Marcos had already announced that elections were to be held on 7 February 1986. Corazon Aquino declared her candidacy. Ramón Cruz actively campaigned for Marcos. Then followed one of the most dramatic overthrows of a government that has occurred during this century, short of the result of war.

On 15 February, the Batasang Pambasa, overseers of the election, proclaimed Marcos the winner, amid strong protests on all sides. The United States Senate, now completely alerted to the dangers of a bloody uprising in an area of importance to American interests, noted that there was such widespread fraud in the election that it could not be considered to be a fair reflection of the people's will. Mrs Aquino launched a truly remarkable movement which she called 'People

Power'. The Filipino population, quite literally and en masse, took to the streets. On 22 February, the Minister of National Defence, Juan Enrile, and Lieut Fidel Ramos, Vice-Chief of Staff, swung their support over to Aquino. A huge crowd, tens of thousands of Aquino supporters, assembled at Camp Crane in Manila, demonstrating against Marcos. When the pro-Marcos armed forces approached the Camp, intent on dispersing the crowds with a show of potential gunfire from tanks and armoured cars, the crowds stood in their way, defying them to shoot. The People Power forces won.

On this historic day, 23 February 1986, and overlooked during the sheer drama of what was happening in the streets of Manila, a group of 105 soldiers commandeered a PAL One-Eleven (again!) at Cotabato, and ordered the crew to take them to Manila – where they were promptly arrested. Later, PAL asked them to reimburse the company for the fares, which they did. The balance of justice takes strange turns in the Philippines.

On 24 February Ramón Cruz resigned and Martin Bonoan assumed the presidency, prudently cancelling all international flights, and the next day suspending all domestic operations too. That evening, as the Philippine people marched on the Presidential Palace at Malacanang (to discover, among much other loot, the astonishing collections of shoes and garments and other possessions resulting from the First Lady's shopping trips) the Marcoses prepared to leave. Their exit, early next morning, was anything but dignified or ceremonial. Helicopters of the United States Air Force whisked them from Malacanang to Clark Air Force Base – still an important piece of American property north of Manila – and thence they were taken into exile to Hawaii. Ferdinand Marcos died there. Several years were to pass before Aquino permitted his body to be returned to his birthplace in northern Luzon; and the event passed with a notable lack of public interest.

Cruz had been an excellent administrator, whatever his politics. He had modernized the national airline and stifled corruption. He gave the entire staff a new spirit. The many international flights commandeered by the First Lady and lavishly financed by the public purse were characteristic of a corporation regarded by its dictatorial ruler as a mere chattel. On the other hand, Cruz was not entirely blameless. As head of Philippine Air Lines, he was a servant of the dictatorial system, and complied with its wishes. But he was in a difficult situation, as a loyal supporter of the Marcoses, and was powerless to make any overt move that could be construed as opposition, even if he had wished to. But his legacy was that he had transformed an autocracy into a democracy.

A Brand New Look

Philippine Air Lines' fortunes during the next few months were subordinated entirely to the momentous political upheaval that was to change the course of Philippine politics for ever. On a rare occasion in world history, Filipinos had demonstrated that the will of the people, in peaceful protest against a ruler who was so contemptuous of the rule of law that he came close to being a tyrant, could overcome even guns and tanks.

The king is dead, long live the king! The moment that the Marcoses fled the country, PAL was back in business, resuming full service on 27 February 1986. On 6 April José Antonio Gonzales was appointed chairman, albeit on a temporary basis; Dante G Santos president; and Martin Bonoan executive vice-president and chief operating officer. Gonzales was a businessman who had openly defied Marcos; Santos was an engineer and former president of the Philippine Chamber

On 1 July 1986 PAL adopted a new aircraft livery with all-white fuselages and a sunburst scheme on the vertical tail surfaces. The word 'Philippines' replaced the airline's name. The new livery is seen here on the first of the Short 360s acquired for the inter-island network.

of Commerce; the experienced Bonoan needed no credentials.

Now it could be told. An accounting audit revealed that the obligatory trips made by the Marcoses, often at short notice, and invariably at the expense of some scheduled flights, still stood in the debit column to the tune of PP10 million. This, at least, was one unnecessary expense, that, at long last, would be non-recurring.

On 1 July 1986, to symbolize the proverbial turning over of a new leaf, PAL adopted a new livery, adding a sunburst to the 25-year-old tricolour design, with an all-white fuselage and the country's name boldly – and, with some reason, proudly – displayed in place of the airline's.

On 15 October a commission of enquiry into PAL's finances revealed several questionable, though not devastating shortcomings, including what were described as the irregular purchases of two of the Airbuses, high salaries for the senior officials, and 'anomolous' disbursements, as well as the losses from the Marcos jaunts. Ramón Cruz observed that the world's airline industry was on the decline, not just that of the Philippines; and recognizing the real problems that had confronted him, Santos supported Cruz.

As it had done in the past, PAL still had to cope with unrest, for Corazon Aquino was still meeting opposition, and the aftermath of the revolutionary crisis included incidents of violence, even bloodshed. Thus, quite apart from the age-old problems of challenging terrain and inadequate fields, the next generation of feeder aircraft, introduced to maintain service to relatively isolated and ill-equipped communities, had to risk the dangers of insurgency, especially in Mindanao. Fortunately, the introduction of the Shorts SD 360–300 36-seat propeller-turbine aircraft went comparatively smoothly, even though the clientèle expected its new Sunriser SD 360s to provide the same standard of comfort as the A300s, which, on 21 May 1987, provided an exclusively wide-bodied service between Manila and Cebu.

Safety in Perspective

In spite of nationalization, revolution (of a peaceful kind), considerable expansion both internationally and on the home front, the occasional heavy landing or hijacking, even Mrs Marcos's shopping, Philippine Air Lines had operated safely for twelve years, before an HS 748 struck a mountain peak near Baguio on 26 June 1987, killing all 50 on board. An A300 overshot the runway at Manila in September, and on 13 December, one of the new SD 360s also hit a mountain, this time near Ilagan, in Mindanao. But to put these tragedies into horrifying perspective, and as a reminder that other forms of transport can be at least as dangerous, and often more so, than aviation, PAL's losses paled into insignificance, compared with those of the ferry boats.

On 20 December 1987, the MV *Doña Paz* collided with a tanker between Mindoro and Marinduque – almost the same place where the *Don Juan* had sunk in April 1980. Only 24 passengers and two crewmen were saved in this, the worst shipping disaster in Philippine history, and one of the worst in the world in the post-Second World War era. The boat was licenced to carry 1,492 passengers and 50 crew; but with an overload because of the imminent Christmas holidays, the death toll was said to have been as high as 3,000, including 1,000 children. To compound the maritime tragedy, on 24 October 1988, Typhoon Unsang caught the *Doña Marilyn*, bound for Tacloban. Again, about a thousand lives were lost, most of them children.

While PAL did not count its losses of life in the hundreds, much less the thousands (and its international service, if not immaculate, had been excellent, without a fatality since 1954) there was still much concern. This was given fresh impetus on 21 May 1988, when Bobby Lim, who had served Philippine Air Lines faithfully and well for many years in the past, filed charges against PAL, claiming \$2 million in damages, and another £20 million (P400 million) to establish a better organisation to act as a watchdog on air operations within the Republic. Lim had always been a shrewd executive, and now he did a real service for his country in synthesizing and defining a problem that had awaited such initiative for far too long. As a direct result of Lim's advocacy, the Philippine Air Safety Foundation was established on 28 February 1989, formally founded on 27 June of that year, and with a fine sense of picking the right man, Lim was made the first chairman. Bobby had brought the action because his wife had been killed in the HS 748 crash at Baguio in 1987; and his success in making real progress out of adversity was an achievement of which his father, a hero of the Japanese occupation, would have been proud.

Business as Unusual

As has been observed already in this chapter, life in the Philippines – and aviation life is no exception – has been full of incident, with seldom a dull moment. Even with the stability of government and the removal of abuses and excesses that the Aquino regime ensured, Philippine Air Lines could not sit back and rest on its laurels.

As always there was the problem of upgrading the domestic fleet, now beginning to show signs of wear. Both the 748s and the One-Elevens had, by the time of the introduction of the SD 360s in 1987 at the lower echelons of service, put in a couple of decades of work; and with the airfields, the terrain, the weather, the hijackings, and the revolution, this had been hard work too. With the short average distances and flight times, the domestic aircraft in the Philippines made as many landings and take offs in a year as the average US aircraft would make in two.

Both veteran types were replaced or supplemented in the late 1980s. After an evaluation of candidate types, the Fokker 50, an improved development of the long-lived F.27 Friendship, started to replace HS 748s on 25 September 1988. Such was the speed of retirement of the old 'Avros' that the last scheduled flight was made, from General Santos, in southern Mindanao, to Cebu on 31 May 1989. During twenty-two years of service, PAL had operated, coincidentally, the same

Fokker 50s began replacing PAL's HS 748s in September 1988. (*Fokker*)

number of the type, since its introduction in November 1967.

Because of its proven record, and earlier delivery, the Boeing 737-300 was selected over the Fokker 100, to replace the BAC One-Eleven. Survivor of countless hijackings and other incidents, the seemingly accident-prone (by Fate, not by design) aircraft seemed to confirm the need for its being laid to rest. On 21 July 1989, only three weeks before the first 737 was delivered, a One-Eleven overshot the runway an Manila, crossed the super-highway, struck four vehicles, and blocked the railway tracks. In a few seconds, it had brought three modes of transport to a standstill, a feat that might qualify it for the *Guiness Book of Records*. There were no airline casualties, but eight people were killed in the melée on the road. As if to put a stop to all this, the Boeing 737-300 entered service on 28 August 1989, and PAL took the opportunity to raise the fares. With the A300s on the trunk routes, 737s on the secondary and Fokker 50s on the third level, Philippine Air Lines had a modern fleet to take it into the 21st Century.

Another Whiff of Competition

Astutely PAL made a good deal with the One-Elevens. To continue to back up the new fleet, ten of them remained in service, under an arrangement with the Irish Guinness-Peat Leasing company. PAL sold the fleet for $26,000,000 and then leased them back again.

Once again, they were in need of all the help they could get; because President Aquino re-introduced the element of domestic airline competition in August 1988 by revoking LOI 151/151A of December 1983, under the terms of which Ferdinand Marcos had nationalized Philippine Air Lines. This opened the way for the formation of new independent airlines. To supplement this move towards wider commercial freedom in the Philippine skies, a Government task force decided, on 16 December 1988, that the Government shareholding in PAL would be substantially reduced, perhaps to as little as 30 per cent.

Aquino needed to attend to other aspects of airline operations. Nowhere in the world is the saying (originally coined by Clement Keys in 1929 in the United States) 'Ninety percent of Aviation is on the Ground' more true than in the Philippines. And nowhere in the world has a succession of governments, of whatever shade of political persuasion, done less to support its national airline, which has been the essential communications link that binds the disparate elements of the country together.

Generation after generation of aircraft types have had to cope with poor airfields and frightening weather. Generation after generation of aircrews have had to cope with inadequate air traffic control, poor airfield lighting, and problem passengers.

On 30 October 1988, however, after years of complaints against the airline by the clientèle, these latter finally realized that the problems were not all PAL's fault. The standards of air traffic control, airfield lighting, and other installations at many of the provincial airports had become so bad that groups of PAL passengers staged 'sit-ins' on some flights, refusing to move from their seats in a non-violent protest against Government apathy and inertia.

PAL's president, Dante Santos, also had a taste of the more extreme displays of discontent. There had, for many years, been a running battle between the good citizens of Cebu, second city of the Republic, and the seat of power in Manila. Like many such situations, provincial cities often feel that they are not receiving a fair share of the national cake, the largest slices always being allocated to the capital. Much of the mood for the creation of independent airlines could be traced to Cebu. Apparently frustrated by endless discussions which led nowhere, Senator Osmena, from Cebu, had a confrontation with Santos on 4 May 1989, and to demonstrate his disgust, and that of his constituency, he had the lights turned out at Mactan Airport just as an A300, with 225 passengers on board, was coming in to land. It had to return to Manila. In Philippine politics, no holds are barred.

Following the Aquino decision of August 1988, by Executive Order No. 333, airminded businessmen sought ways to enter the fray. One company, Airlift, was already operating two DHC-6 Twin Otters, among other small types, flying tourists to Baracay Island, off the northern tip of the island of Panay. In September 1988, it announced an increase in capital, to PP6 million, and planned to acquire a new Beech 1900. A local Cebu Beech dealer, Miguel Campos, acquired a 30 per cent interest, and more aircraft were ordered.

On 24 December 1988, Airlift service began between Cebu and Manila, the first to offer scheduled competition to Philippine Air Lines since the enforced demise of Air Manila and Filipinas Orient in 1974. The former had been authorized on 4 April 1974 to continue operations, strictly as a non-scheduled charter carrier, and its president, Ricardo Silverio, had actually obtained trans-Pacific charter rights from the US, carrying more than 30;000 passengers on affinity tours in 1975. By

Early in 1996 Philippine Air Lines had no less than forty Airbus aircraft in service or on order. This is a computer-generated image showing an Airbus A330-300 in Philippines livery. (*Airbus Industrie*)

There are quite large numbers of light transports operating in the Philippines outside the PAL network. This Manila Airways Volpar Beech 18 was photographed at Manila in 1988.

the following year, having added 'International' to its original name, it boasted a fleet of two Boeing 707s, three Lockheed Electras and three Fokker F.27s. But Air Manila's ambitions came to an end when, on 4 June 1976, an Electra crashed on take-off at Guam, killing 45 on the aircraft and the driver of a passing car. One of the Electra's propellers had been feathered and the flaps were inoperative. The Philippines CAB grounded Air Manila; and that was the last of any competition, scheduled or otherwise, that PAL had to contend with until Airlift.

The Beech 1900 that showed its colours on a scheduled run on the Christmas Eve of 1988 recalled a bygone age, that of the DC-3. For at Cebu, it operated into the old Luhag airport, quite close to the city centre, and in many ways more convenient than Mactan, out on the island of that name and reached by a longer road over a causeway. The same situation can be observed all over the world, where an old airfield, deserted by the front-line prima donna airlines in favour of the new giant airport, secures a new lease of life through the initiative of opportunist companies. Southwest Airlines, based at Love Field, close to the downtown area of Dallas, Texas, owes its success, at least much of it, to this convenience for the Dallas travelling public, who hesitate to make the journey, which takes at least an hour, to the Greater Dallas-Fort Worth International airport. Incidentally, Cebu could now claim Mactan as its own international gateway, as, on 7 February 1988, direct A300 service had started to Tokyo.

On 10 August 1989, Airlift received CAB authority to serve 24 domestic points from Manila. Additional competition was already imminent from its own town, as early in 1988, a group of concerned citizens of Cebu had, through its Representative, Raul del Mar, obtained the support of 189 congressmen for an airline franchise, and the same Raul was one of the signatories of a letter to President Aquino, calling for the dismissal of PAL chairman Dante Santos.

CHAPTER TWENTY-SIX

Colonial Airlines in Prewar China

The Game of Political Monopoly

China has never appeared on the map as a Colony, Protectorate, or Dominion of any foreign power. Yet for most of the second half of the 19th Century and the first two decades of the 20th, it was subject to foreign dominance and control more than many territories that were nominally subject to foreign rule. More important than the shade of colour on the map was the extent of foreign control of the economy and commerce that constituted the exploitable wealth of China; and the five major spheres of influence in this vast land of (in the 1920s) some 500 million people were overseas territories of foreign powers in everything but name.

They played with Chinese sovereignty much as monopoly game players move their pieces on the board. Although some tidbits of land were acquired, such as Hong Kong by the British, Kwangchow by the French, Tsingtao by the Germans, and Port Arthur alternately by the Russians and Japanese, the huge area of China was mainly divided by the great powers into 'spheres of interest'. Thus, Russia controlled Mongolia and most of Manchuria (until Japan made its expansionist moves in the 1930s); Japan had acquired Korea and Formosa (Taiwan) as part of its empire; Germany controlled the province of Shantung from its foothold at Tsingtao; the British controlled all the rest, except the provinces of Yunnan and Kwangsi, in the far south, adjacent to French Indo-China, and economically linked to the French Colony. The great powers nibbled away at the edges, and China was left like a turtle deprived of its shell.

Channels of Trade

Until the end of the 19th Century, almost all trading and commercial activity was by sea and waterways. Land transport of any kind was almost non-existent. The foreign powers, especially Great Britain, seized every opportunity to obtain special privileges, and the 1842 Treaty of Nanking (which gave the British the island of Hong Kong), the 1858 Treaty of Tientsin (which extended the number of Treaty Ports, over which China had little control), and the sequel to the latter which, in 1860, gave Vladivostok to Russia, were only the more prominent of the many Unequal Treaties (as they were eventually to become known) that conferred successive indignities upon the nominal Chinese rulers. The Emperor and his government in Peking did not help themselves. Corruption and gross inefficiency abounded. The armed forces, upon which, before a more enlightened world tried diplomatic negotiation as a substitute for naked aggression, all countries depended, was even more corrupt and inefficient than its rulers, and furthermore was fragmented, and spent more time fighting among itself than in providing any cohesive strength. The navy was, to all practical purposes, non-existent.

Because they could not rely upon Chinese organizations or agencies to do the job properly, the foreign powers took charge of all the channels of communication, almost all of which they built or provided, mainly for their own use. The customs administration at the ports, both sea-going, such as the great entrepots of trade, Shanghai and Hong Kong, and at the Treaty Ports up the great Yangtse River and along the coast of southern China: these were mostly in the hands of foreigners. The postal and telegraph systems were also established and operated by the foreigners; and the same situation applied to the fragmented railway system, which consisted of a series of lines which connected with each other at only a few points, and did not even serve some of the most prosperous and productive parts of China, such as Szechwan. The first railway line in China was built only a decade before the first flight of the Wright brothers. When the first airlines were established in the late 1920s, China had only 7,500 miles of line. In British India, in striking contrast, there were 39,000.

The First Attempts at Airline Operation

With the awareness of air transport as a practical use for the aeroplane heightened as a result of its widespread use during the Great War of 1914–18, China joined a host of other countries all over the world in exploring the possibilities of an airline system. And this transport- and communications-starved land was an ideal proving ground. As early as 1918, the Peking Government, which had joined the Allies by declaring war on Germany on 14 August 1917, established a Bureau of Planning of Aeronautical Affairs, as a department of the Ministry of Communications, and headed by General Ting Shih-yuan. Plans were drawn up to connect the capital with Hankow and Shanghai. On 24 February 1919, Ting signed a contract with T A Barson, of the Peking Syndicate, representing the British Handley Page company, which had ended the war by producing the H.P. O/400 heavy bomber. In Britain these machines were converted into passenger-carrying aircraft, and Mr Barson's contract was for six of them, at £10,540 each, or about US $45,000 at the rate of exchange at the time.

A rival faction in the Chinese Government was then permitted to set up its own aviation agency, the Aeronautics Department, which then signed a contract with the British Vickers company, which had also built a large bomber and which was also converting the design for transport use. The type was the Vimy, which achieved lasting fame by being the first aircraft to fly across the Atlantic without stopping at the Azores or without en route support from naval vessels, and it was also the first aircraft to fly from England to Australia. Both feats of airmanship were achieved in 1919, and the Chinese Aeronautics Department must have been mightily impressed. For its contract with Vickers was for no less than 95 Vimy Commercials. The deal was financed by a loan of £1,803,200 (about $7,500,000), backed by the issue of Chinese Treasury notes at 8 percent, to mature in 1925–29. Lloyd's Bank, with British Government approval, sold the notes on the London market at £98 each.

In October 1919, Colonel F V Holt, of the Royal Air Force, was appointed to the position of air advisor to the Chinese Government, and the next two years were to be the busiest and most eventful in his life. But for the unsettled – and that is a mild term to describe the situation – circumstances in China in the early 1920s, Holt might have made his name as a pioneer of air transport in the Orient.

Losing no time, the first Handley Page aircraft arrived in November, and on 6 December 1919 the first successful test flight was accomplished, at the Nanyuang flying field, near Peking, which had been established by the French in 1913. Preparations were made for a point-to-point flight, and a trial one was made to

This Handley Page O/7 version of the O/400 bomber was the first of six shipped to China in 1919. It may have been the aircraft which, on 6 December 1919, flew from Peking to Tientsin with mail and newspapers – the first air mail flight in China. (*Handley Page*)

Tientsin (Tianjin), the important city and port 80 miles to the east. The second trial flight was accompanied by a certain amount of commercial promotion. Commanded by RAF Captains Mackenzie and Jones, the H.P. O/400 left Peking at 9.40 a.m. and arrived at Tientsin at 11.00 a.m. It carried 35 letters and 40 copies of the *North China Daily Mail*. On the return flight, which arrived in Peking at 6 p.m. on the same day, it carried 195 letters and 100 newspapers. This was the first air mail flight in China, and except for the historic series of flights in India in 1911, the first in Asia.

Immediately after this notable event, open warfare erupted in northern China. General Ting commandeered all the aircraft belonging to the embryo airline, but all British subjects were excluded, for their own safety, if for no other reason. One of the Handley Pages, possibly the very one that had carried the mail to and from Tientsin, was engaged in a single bombing mission. It was flown by a Swiss mechanic, reported to have had little flying experience, and to have been drunk at the time.

Colonel Holt appears to have transferred his allegiance and his expertise to the Vickers enterprise. During the winter of 1920–21, he established a commercial flying training school at Nanyuan, and ambitiously planned a commercial air service between Peking and Shanghai, China's great port and largest city, with intermediate stops at Tientsin, Tsinan, Suchow, and Nanking. The airline fleet would consist of 40 Vickers Vimy Commercials. No record exists of what happened to the 95* that were sent to China, but one report later suggested that many of them were never taken out of their crates after being off-loaded from the ship; and they simply disintegrated with age, or were looted for various purposes.

On 1 July 1921, Holt's first Vimy left Peking, flying south. It never reached Shanghai, and turned around at Tsinan, because the authorities in southern and central China feared that the air service would be a step towards further political dominance of the country by Peking. The mail completed its journey to Shanghai by train. In retrospect, this was an extraordinary development, mirroring the divisive nature of Chinese politics. If the quasi-colonials had divided China into five or more spheres of interest, the Chinese themselves were in the process of dividing the country into at least that many provincial domains, presided over by local

*Some reports give the figure as 70

The Chinese Aeronautics Department ordered 95 Vickers Vimy Commercials. A few were used for short periods but it is believed that many were never uncrated. The number ordered has also been quoted as 70 with 40 for airline use. (*Vickers*)

dominant leaders, sometimes called strong men, and remembered by historians as war-lords. Far from welcoming an air service as an element of unification and improved progress and production, they opposed it as a threat to their own local areas of overlordship.

Facing insuperable difficulties of this kind, Holt had to suspend the service on 10 July, after barely a week of endeavour. He started again on 18 July but had to stop again four weeks later, on 15 August. The Peking—Tsinan air service of 1921 had made a brave attempt; and its permanent suspension was not because of insurgency but for a reason which is still familiar today: the costs of operation far outweighed the revenue from the mail, in this case by a factor of about one hundred.

In one last effort to try to popularize air transport – for the Chinese were reluctant to take to the air, in spite of their long tradition with experiments with flight with kites and balloons – a service was offered during August and September of 1921 from Peking to Peitaiho, a summer resort on the coast of the Gulf of Chihli. The distance was 225 miles from the summer heat of Peking, but was not operated for long.

In 1922, the spread of civil war and banditry (the two terms were almost synonymous in China at the time) prevented the resumption of the Peking—Shanghai line, even as far as Tsinan. Colonel Holt, no doubt disillusioned by the whole affair, left China. Flights were reported to have taken place in 1923 between Peking and Tientsin, but there is no record, official or otherwise, of such activity. For the period of the next five years, which could be described as China's Dark Years, was one of strife and conflict, in which, except for in the larger cities such as Peking, Shanghai and Canton, life in China was almost on a wartime footing, with little social or commercial activity to relieve the constant presence of civil war.

Establishment of the First Chinese Airlines

During this troubled period, during which the machinery of a centralized government in Peking ceased to exist, little progress was made in the furtherance of air transport, or, for that matter, of any form of transport. The only known indication of any interest came from Germany, in 1925, when a Captain Walter, who was to become a director of Eurasia in the future, made some overtures in the Chinese capital, inviting China to participate in what, in modern times, is known as a joint venture. He offered German equipment, personnel, and training, in exchange for Chinese capital investment, together with its own personnel, even local manufacture. The approaches must have gained strength when, on 30 August 1926, two Junkers-G 24s, in an expedition led by Dr Robert Knauss, arrived in Peking, having flown from Berlin in five weeks, including a delay at Kurgan, in Soviet Siberia, while an airstrip was built, and nine days delay at the Chinese frontier, awaiting diplomatic clearance.

The struggle for power in China was, meanwhile, beginning to resolve itself. The Kuomintang Party, now under the leadership of Chiang Kai-shek, augmenting the idealistic manifesto of its founder, Sun Yat-sen, with some more pragmatic clauses of his own, gained the ascendancy. Having been isolated in Canton in the early 1920s, Chiang had moved his headquarters north to Hankow, and in 1926 was able to advance to Peking and overcome the Anfu faction there. By 1928, Chiang controlled most of China, although the provinces on the periphery tended to go their own way, especially in the southwest, where the Kuomintang never completely held sway until the years of the Second World War, backed by a strong United States presence. In the north, in Manchuria especially, Chiang was powerless. In 1928, reflecting perhaps an intuitive sense of a power base in the geographical centre, Chiang moved the capital of China from Peking, which he now renamed Peiping (northern capital) to Nanking (southern capital), a major city 200 miles west of Shanghai, and on the banks of the Yangtse where the main railway lines met, but would have to wait three more decades and a revolution before a bridge would link the two sides.

New approaches were now made by foreign countries to Chiang Kai-shek's Nationalist Government. Wilhelm Schmidt, of Deutsche Luft Hansa, following up Walter's initial contact, went to Nanking, where he was supported by the German ambassador. He met Li Ching Tung, of the Foreign Ministry, who presented the proposals to Chiang's cabinet on 7 November 1928. These amounted to founding a DLH-affiliated company in China, and one that might eventually provide the infrastructure for the terminus of a trans-Asiatic DLH trunk line to Peking and Shanghai. Such empire-building methods were similar to those employed by the Germans in setting up subsidiaries and affiliates in South America, in preparation for a trans-ocean route across the South Atlantic. Schmidt was able to amplify the proposals later in the month, but on 23 November, the Army Minister Feng Yu Liang made enough objections to thwart the plans, and on 19 December they were abandoned. On 27 April 1929, Li made fresh presentations, and Feng resigned.

The idea that a foreign organisation, albeit with nominal Chinese representation, should control China's commercial airways was a matter of the highest importance, and little wonder that high-level confrontations and ministerial resignations occurred, not to mention the amount of 'consultancy fees' that might accompany the establishment and operation of air routes throughout the country. Strangely, in the light of the first efforts of Colonel Holt in 1920–22, the British remained aloof, even though they were the dominant force in overseas commerce, to the extent that Shanghai and much of the Yangtse River hinterland might well have been a British colony. But the other big English-speaking country, the United States of America, leaped into the Chinese aviation arena with both feet.

One of these feet was the big Curtiss-Wright Corporation, headed by Clement Keys (the man who first said that 90 percent of aviation is on the ground) and who established, in 1928, Intercontinent Aviation Inc, in partnership with an investment banker, Clarence Dillon. Ten million dollars were allocated to develop airlines and aviation in foreign countries, and a subsidiary company, Aviation Exploration Inc, was set up to make preliminary surveys. In December 1928 R O Hayward, representing Keys, arrived in China for discussions with Sun Fo, son of Sun Yat-sen, and now Minister of Railways. Hayward offered Curtiss-Wright investment in exchange for an air mail and air passenger monopoly. On 8 January 1929, Keys requested the support of the US Secretary of State, Frank Kellogg, but received little encouragement. Nevertheless, by mid-February, Major William B Robertson, former aeroplane manufacturer and airline operator and now representing Curtiss-Wright, arrived in Shanghai.

During March and April, demonstration and survey flights were made, and proposals made under the China Trade Act to establish a corporation, with 60 percent US ownership and 40 percent Chinese. The airline, China National Aviation Corporation (CNAC) was created by the Chinese Government on 12 April 1929, and its first objectives were to link Shanghai with Hankow, Peking, and Canton by air.

On 20 April 1929, Sun Fo, the new CNAC president, signed contracts with Robertson, giving the Aviation Exploration Inc exclusive rights on the three routes designated, for ten years, with a commitment to fly one round trip daily on each. The Chinese would construct airports and emergency fields. Payments would range from $1.50 to $4.50 a mile, dependent on aircraft capacity. But the payments would be made up to the total balance by promissory notes.

This action precipitated a crisis in Nanking. The president of the Chinese National Aeronautics Association, General Chang Ching-yu, made a strong protest, alleging the encroachment of Chinese sovereignty. The Minister of War supported Chang, and denied the use of airfields to CNAC; and the Minister of Communications, Wang Po-chun, lined up with the War Minister, against Sun Fo and CNAC. To emphasize the degree of opposition, this same Ministry of Communications signed an agreement in May with the Stinson company, also from the United States, and imported four Stinson Detroiter single-engined high-wing monoplanes, able to carry four passengers. Two pilots and a mechanic came along with the shipment, and Wang Po-chun must have derived considerable satisfaction by claiming the honour of starting the first sustained passenger and mail air service in China. It was called the Shanghai—Chengtu Air Mail Line, and although the inaugural flight, on 8 July 1929, went only as far as Nanking, this was an achievement of some magnitude, bearing in mind the political environment of the times. The line never did reach beyond Nanking; but, linking as it did the great port and business centre of Shanghai with the new Chinese capital, it made an important

The Stinson Detroiter was used on the Shanghai—Chengtu Air Mail Line and also by the later CNAC.

contribution to the commercial fraternity, carrying 354 passengers during its first year of service.

Because of the Minister of War's ban on the use of airfields, Sun Fo obtained a loan agreement with Curtiss-Wright to circumvent the opposition by building its own fields. Clement Keys reacted promptly. He appointed Harry G Smith, an aviation man of some experience, to manage CNAC. Smith immediately recommended the use of amphibious aircraft, thus circumventing the restrictions on airfield use. On 27 July 1929, a team of pilots, mechanics, and radio technicians left Seattle to support the operation of five six-seat Loening Air Yachts, which were crated and shipped to Shanghai.

On 26 August, China Airways Federal Inc was incorporated as a wholly-owned subsidiary of Intercontinent Aviation (i.e. Curtiss-Wright) under the provisions of the China Trade Act of 1922. Price, formerly of the US Foreign Service, and an 'old China hand', was appointed as the first president. He had to contend with problems that would not normally arise with an enterprise that was trying to establish a public service that would benefit the nation. It had to use, as its en route stations, on the route to Hankow, a mooring buoy in the river at Nanking, and a lake at Kiukiang, some way from the city. At Hankow, it was permitted to use the military field, but not allowed to erect a hangar. Worst of all, at Shanghai, base of the operations, it was able to use only a small piece of land by the Whangpoo River, and this was sometimes flooded. Unable to build a hangar, as no contractor was allowed, or did not dare, to supply materials or labour, the infant airline demonstrated a resourcefulness that was to be its normal routine throughout its history. While hardly qualifying as a hangar, it built a shelter for the Loenings out of the packing cases in which they had been shipped from Seattle.

The first trial flights up the Yangtse took place on 12–13 October 1929, and scheduled service began on 21 October. The 525-mile route to Hankow, via Nanking, Anking and Kiukiang, carried one pound of mail and two passengers: Mr and Mrs Sun Fo. But at least, this was an air route that made an impact by the time-saving. Even with the handicaps imposed by the Minister of War, the Loenings could complete the journey in a day, sometimes in about six or seven

CNAC employed Loening Air Yacht amphibians because of the unavailability of land aerodromes. Later the wheels were removed to save weight.

A Loening Air Yacht being lowered onto the water. This view shows to advantage its unusual configuration.

hours. The steamboat could take as long as nine days. In contrast, the Ministry of Communications' line, while able to fly from Shanghai to Nanking in about two hours, was in competition with the trains that could make the journey in about eight hours, at a much cheaper price.

The rivalry between Sun Fo and Wang Po-chun reached a flash point when, on 15 November, Ernest B Price, representing Curtiss, tried to obtain payment, as contracted, from the Chinese Government, but met with procrastination and evasion. Sun Fo resigned as president of CNAC and the Minister of Communications, the very man who had been a thorn in the Curtiss-Wright side, was appointed in his place. Meanwhile, China Airways Federal stopped service when, on 15 December, still unpaid, Price approached the Minister of Finance, T V Soong (whose sister married Chiang Kai-shek), claiming violation of contract. Within hours, the payment was made, and two days later, China Airways Federal resumed service, on behalf of CNAC, which still had to get itself organized.

The next round went to Wang, who by now would not even speak to Price. On 31 January 1930, China Airways Federal's contract was cancelled, by a petition from Wang; but Price's protests received widespread publicity and led to pressure from US diplomatic channels. On 7 February, the State Council voted to cancel the cancellation order; but possibly because of Wang going directly to Curtiss-Wright, Price achieved a hollow victory, as he was dismissed. A few weeks later, Max S Polin arrived in Shanghai to renegotiate a new contract, which, in traditional Chinese fashion, took four months of bargaining. Freely translated, the Chinese popular name for the airline activity had been the Topside Rickshas of the Middle Kingdom Space Machine Family. This was a fair reflection of the level of maturity shown so far by the Chinese authorities; and the time had come to start putting things in proper order.

Eurasia Makes a Start

German perseverance had its reward. The spade work done by Walter and Schmidt paid dividends, when, on 21 February 1930, the Chinesisch-Deutsche

Eurasia Aviation Corporation began operation with Junkers-F 13s. Instead of registrations the aircraft bore the word 'Eurasia' followed by a Roman numeral. (*DLH*)

Luftverkehrsgesellschaft was organized. Always known as the Eurasia Aviation Corporation, under which name it traded, this joint venture was nominally controlled by the Chinese two-thirds ownership, but Deutsche Luft Hansa owned the other third, and provided aircraft, technical assistance, and advised on route policy. The first fleet consisted of two Junkers-F 13s and two Junkers-W 33s, sturdy metal-built landplanes that could withstand the rigours of Chinese operating conditions, if anything could.

Final negotiations for complete ratification dragged on until the autumn of 1930; but eventually the first service was inaugurated on 1 June 1931. Although the original intention for Eurasia's existence had been to forge a link with Germany across western China and the central Asian portion of the USSR, this could not be accomplished at first, because of the delay in setting up the necessary installations over a long route. Instead, a connection was made northwards from Peking to the border station of the Trans-Siberian Railway at Manchouli, in northern Manchuria.

336

Quite apart from the hazards of the dangerous terrain and the need to navigate not only without adequate radio but also without adequate or even accurate maps, the route had its own special shortcomings. On 31 July 1931, pilot Johannes Rathje and radio operator/flight engineer Otto Kolber had landed at the mid-point, Linse, to refuel. Fighting high winds, they were then driven off course and over the Mongolian frontier. The W 33 was, almost literally, shot down, as a bullet hit Kolber in the leg, and Rathje had to make a forced landing. They escaped being shot as spies only by diplomatic intervention, and the two were released – Kolber with an amputated leg, the operation performed under primitive conditions – to return to Peking on 15 September.

The Manchouli line had had its southern terminal at Shanghai, and had been able to deliver the mails, and perhaps a few intrepid passengers, to the Trans-Siberian Railway for onward transmission to Europe. But this service did not last long. The risks of flying had been vividly illustrated by Rathje's adventure; and furthermore the area of northern China was subject to much flooding by the Hwang Ho River – 'China's Sorrow' as it was known, because of the hundreds of thousands of people who were killed because of its eccentric flow patterns and the deposits of yellow earth (Hwang Ho means Yellow River) which accumulate. In 1852, in fact, such unpredictability had led to a change of course in its lower reaches from an eastern direction into the Yellow Sea to a northeasterly one into the Gulf of Chihli, north of the Shantung Peninsula. Eurasia had to suspend service in eastern China because of this natural hazard, river flooding, one that only in recent years, as the result of extensive and scientifically planned waterway control, has China been able to overcome.

Junkers-W 33s were among the original Eurasia fleet. Here one is taking off from the Lanchow aerodrome at an elevation of about 2,000 metres. (*Lufthansa*)

The New CNAC

At long last, on 8 July 1930, the various bickering factions seeking a place in the sun of Chinese air transport in the central and southern, and most productive areas of the country, finally made their peace. A new company, also named the China National Aviation Company (CNAC) was incorporated, with an authorized capital of ten million yuan, or $3.3 million. The Ministry of Communications held 55 percent and China Federal 45 percent. The new company amalgamated the previous entities, China Airways Federal (Shanghai—Hankow), the Ministry of Communications' Shanghai—Chengtu line (Shanghai—Nanking), and the old

In July 1930 a new CNAC was formed. Like the earlier airline with the same initials it operated a fleet of Stinson Detroiters.

CNAC, which had never operated. The fleet consisted of five Stinson Detroiters, ex-Shanghai—Nanking, and five Loening amphibians, ex-China Airways Federal. Exclusive mail rights were conferred for the three trunk routes radiating from Shanghai: to Peking in the north; to Chungking, up the Yangtse to the west; and to Canton in the south. Contracts were signed for a ten-year duration, and the State Council ratified the contract on 26 July 1930.

So that regular flying could be planned for this, the first Chinese airline that stood a chance of fulfilling a role in helping to unify the country by better communications, agreements had to be made with the local 'war-lords', whose rule over their local areas amounted to unofficial autonomy. Agreements were made with Hopei, where General Chang Hsueh-Liang, the 'Young Marshal', held sway; with the Province of Shantung; with the local authorities in Peiping; and with General Liu Hsiang, who controlled Szechwan.

Local political sensitivities having been settled, General Neih Kai-I, CNAC's vice-president of operations, made a trail-blazing survey flight to Chungking on 12 September 1930, making the round trip in four days; and one to Peiping on 4 March 1931, in three days. On 15 March, two Stinsons made the journey to the northern capital nonstop in seven hours. On Christmas Day 1930 Captain George Westervelt, specially despatched by Clement Keys to decide CNAC's future, had arrived in Shanghai. Probably on his recommendation, Keys then sent out William Langhorn Bond to take over the whole operation. His title was a modest operations manager, but effectively he proceeded, without much demur, to act as president and chief executive officer – to use a familiar title in today's usage.

Bond arrived in Shanghai on 17 March 1931. Within seven months he was able to oversee the fulfilment of two of the three main route objectives in the CNAC charter. Exactly two weeks after his arrival, the Yangtse service was extended to Ichang, with stops at Wuhu and Shasi, using the Loenings, which were now converted to flying-boats, i.e. without the ability to land at airports, thus saving the weight of the undercarriage, an improvement made possible by the meeting of the minds when the new CNAC was formed. On 15 April, the Stinsons extended the Shanghai—Nanking line northward to Peking, via Suchow, Tsinan and Tientsin; but service was suspended from 8 June until 12 September while the Stinsons were fitted with better engines. But problems remained. One of the Stinsons crashed on Taishan Mountain in Shantung on 18 November, and shortly afterwards, two more crash-landed near Peiping, leading to another service suspension. Hitherto, only mail had been carried on this northern route. Passengers still went by train; and under the circumstances, who could blame them?

On 31 October 1931, the Yangtse River route was finally extended to Chungking, with a stop at Wahsien, with the Loenings, General Liu Hsiang of Szechwan having finally accepted the march of progress. It had been an eventful year, and CNAC seemed at last to be getting under way. Then, on 28 January 1932, Japanese troops attacked Shanghai, causing CNAC to halt all services. But Bill Bond refused to keep his fleet on the ground for long, and resumed flying on 9 February, in spite of Japanese protests to the United States consul. Such was the growing influence and infiltration of Japan into China, even in the early Thirties, that it expected to have its voice heard. And in the north it did more than that.

On 12 January 1933, service on the northern route to Peiping was resumed on a permanent basis by Captain E M Allison. The Stinsons flew the mail twice a week, this time routed via Haichow, Tsingtao and Tientsin; and on 1 February CNAC began passenger service from Shanghai to Peiping.

Northwest Passage

While Bond and Allison and CNAC were moving ahead in the centre, the German-sponsored Eurasia was changing direction in the north, in the fulfilment, at least partially, of fashioning a link with Europe via the USSR. Having abandoned the route to Manchouli and, in any case, with the Japanese moving in, Eurasia began service in December 1932 as far as Tsukhutsak (or Chuguchak – the precise spelling is uncertain) in far off Sinkiang, on the frontier with Soviet Kazakhstan. The main base was at Lanchow, chief city of Kansu, and the line split at Loyang to provide access to both Peiping and Shanghai, via Nanking. By this time more Junkers-W 33s had arrived, but in July 1933, the 'Sinkiang Incident' prevented the continuation of air service west of Lanchow. Still, it was a visionary enterprise, over a route that, even today, since a railway has been built along the whole length, the journey is long and arduous. Eurasia's pioneering would come in useful in an unexpected way several years later.

Southwest Passage

Chiang Kai-shek and the Kuomintang may have ruled the eastern and central parts of China in the early 1930s, but the southwestern provinces of Kwangtung and Kwangsi were a law unto themselves. The Canton Aviation Bureau had been formed on 1 December 1930 by the military governors of the two provinces, ostensibly under the authority of Nanking; and some flights were made between Canton and Wuchow, on the Hsi Chang River, and proposals made to open routes to Pakhoi, on the coast of the Gulf of Tonkin, and to Hoihow, on the island of Hainan.

But, as with CNAC's problems in Szechwan, and Eurasia's problems in Sinkiang, and for the same reason, this venture came to nothing, as Wen Chen Chi Tang – yet another 'strong man' – this time of Kwangtung, rebelled against the Kuomintang, and commandeered all the Cantonese aircraft. Interestingly, had this embryo airline kept going, its flagships would probably have been Ryan Broughams, quite a few of which were imported into China, following a wave of enthusiasm for the Ryans after Charles Lindbergh's epic flight of May 1927 across the North Atlantic. General Chang Wei-Chang had made a long-distance flight in a Ryan, covering 3,500 miles from Canton to Mukden (now Guangzhou to Shenyang). But although the Wuhan (Hankow) Civil Aviation Association also purchased a fleet of five Broughams, Ryan never made its presence felt, either in the Yangtse basin or in the southwest.

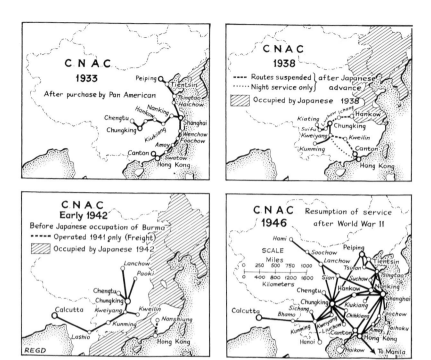

Maps 26a. CNAC 1933–1946

For thirteen eventful years, the most important airline in China was the one first established by the Curtiss Airplane Corporation and taken over by Pan American Airways in 1933. After the Japanese invasion in 1937, its headquarters moved westwards from Shanghai to Chungking, with a short stop in Hankow. After the Pearl Harbor attack, and Japanese armed forces occupied the whole of southeast Asia, CNAC helped to maintain a vital air supply route, the 'Hump', from India to the besieged nation. After the war ended, it enjoyed a brief spell of prosperity, establishing a nationwide network of air routes.

Pan American Airways Moves In

The turning point in the advancement of civil air transport in China came on 31 March 1933, when Pan American Airways purchased China Airways Federal, which owned 45 percent of the stock of CNAC. The actual transaction was the payment of $282,258 by Pan Am to Intercontinent Aviation, the Curtiss-Wright subsidiary that owned China Federal, even though the latter had paid $561,943 for the shareholding less than three years previously. Apart from the route franchises and limited ground installations, Pan Am received the five Loening 'boats and the five Stinsons. Only one of the latter was still airworthy. There were seven pilots, six of whom were American, one German. And there was William Langhorn Bond.

Pan American was skilled in setting up subsidiaries in foreign lands as an extension to its growing network which, until now, had been confined to the Americas south of the Rio Grande. Its visionary leader, Juan Trippe, however, had his sights set on encircling the globe with Pan Am routes, and the two great oceans, the Atlantic and the Pacific, were the first formidable challenges. Frustrated on the Atlantic by political difficulties, especially with the British, he concentrated at first

340

on conquering the Pacific. Systematically, he prepared for this mighty task, first by surveying the Great Circle route to the Orient via Alaska, through the agency of Charles Lindbergh and his wife, who flew their Lockheed Sirius to China, via Nome, the Kamchatka Peninsula and Japan, to Nanking in the summer of 1931. He then established firm footholds at each end of what would have been the preferred route, had not Soviet recalcitrance and the emergence of long-range flying-boats altered the route plans. In Alaska, Pan American purchased two local airlines to form Pacific Alaska Airways, for the western foothold; in China, it purchased the Curtiss-Wright interest for the eastern one.

As it had always done, Pan Am immediately upgraded the flying equipment. It always demanded the best, and such insistence was to play no little part in the technical development world-wide of the commercial aeroplane in the decades to come. Thus, in June 1933, two Sikorsky S-38 eight-seat amphibians were delivered to CNAC. The entire purpose was to forge a coastal route from Shanghai to Canton, to complete the third main route radiating from the Chinese port, and make Pan American lord of the Chinese skies. On 3 October, Trippe's representative, Harold Bixby, signed an agreement with the Chinese authorities for this operation, through a subsidiary, Pacific American Airways; but this identity had to be concealed, to give the impression of Chinese sovereignty, thus preventing the Japanese from claiming equal privileges. At this time, Japan ruled over Formosa (Taiwan) and it regarded the nearby province of Fukien as its sphere of influence on the mainland of southern China. CNAC provided the concealment.

In June 1933 CNAC acquired two Sikorsky S-38 flying-boats. This one, with US registration NC 16V, is seen at Shanghai in that year.

A proving flight having been made on 8 July, air mail service began on 24 October, from Shanghai to Canton, via Wenchow, Foochow, Amoy and Swatow. As yet, Trippe had not negotiated successfully with the British to call at Hong Kong. The S-38s began to carry passengers on 24 November, but Pan American was soon to learn that operations in China were not always plain sailing, or flying. Late in 1933, one of the Sikorskys crashed in Hangchow Bay; and on 10 April 1934, the other one came to grief, also in the Bay. Service on the coastal route was not restored until the arrival of two Douglas Dolphin amphibians, which began carrying the mails on 1 November of that year.

The ageing Stinsons, or what was left of the fleet, were transferred to Chungking, where they opened an extension of the Yangtse River route from Chungking to Chengtu. At last, the original intention of the Shanghai—Chengtu Air Mail Line of 1929 had been fulfilled. The final segment, linking the two big cities of Szechwan, took about two hours of flying time, a substantial improvement over a ten- to fifteen-day journey by sedan-chair – presumably the equivalent of travelling first class – or by wheelbarrow. In the 1930s there were few roads in the fertile Red Basin of Szechwan; and the humble Stinsons were the first to suggest that the old Chinese saying – that it was easier to reach heaven than Szechwan – might now be disproved.

In April 1935 CNAC began operation of Ford Tri-Motors.

Early in 1935, two Ford Tri-Motors, formerly used on Pan Am's route to Mexico, arrived, and after making a survey flight to Kunming on 25 March, began service as far as Kweiyang in April, and a weekly service to the Yunnan capital early in July. Almost according to time-honoured tradition, however, like the Loenings, Stinsons, and Sikorskys before, a Ford was written off en route and the Kunming service temporarily suspended.

Possibly realizing that it might be losing face, and, more important, the vital franchise in China, Pan American broke the practice of delivering aircraft that were cast off from other parts of its system. Early in 1935, the first of four 14-seat Douglas DC-2 airliners arrived in Shanghai. Equipped with comfortable seating, heating, a coffee machine, and other amenities, these were representative of a new class of commercial aeroplane. Previously there had been transport aircraft, now the DC-2 brought airliner comfort to China, matching the standards that KLM was bringing to Asia on its trunk route to Batavia. CNAC's DC-2s were the first to operate domestic routes at this level in the whole of Asia.

Early in 1935 the first of four CNAC Douglas DC-2s arrived at Shanghai. All four are seen here on the apron at Shanghai. (*Pan American Airways*)

A CNAC Douglas DC-2 over the densely packed city of Shanghai.

Primitive refuelling of a CNAC Douglas DC-2.

In 1936 Pan American and CNAC finally gained access to the great British commercial centre of Hong Kong. Negotiations had started in March 1934, when, because of the switch from the Great Circle to the direct trans-Pacific itinerary for Pan Am's trans-ocean route, Juan Trippe needed a southern Chinese gateway. The British were not forthcoming, and not until Trippe threatened to use Macao, the

CNAC's passenger terminal at Shanghai during the early 1930s.

tiny Portuguese enclave nearby, did London relent. On 5 November, Hong Kong became a stop on the Shanghai—Canton route; on 19 January 1937, Harold Bixby signed an air mail contract for the trans-Pacific route; and on 16 April of that year, the Douglas Dolphins were scheduled to make direct connections with the Sikorsky S-42 flying-boats which, in turn, made the connection with the Martin 130 *China Clipper* class at Manila in the Philippines.

Eurasia Expands

Having tried the north, and then the west, Eurasia, the German-partnered airline based at Lanchow, now moved south. On 1 May 1934, under pressure from the Chinese Government, it started a route from Peiping to Canton, via Hankow. The network now was in the shape of a cross, with the Lanchow—Shanghai route crossing the Peiping—Canton route at Changchow which – to stretch the currently fashionable term somewhat – could be regarded as Eurasia's central hub. In November of the same year, a branch line was opened from Lanchow to Ninshia and Paotow. To support this growing network, a steady flow of aircraft arrived from Germany, Junkers-W 33s and W 34s by ship, and Junkers-Ju 52/3ms flown in by the southern Asia route through India. Eurasia was encouraged to start yet another connection, first a branch from Sian to Chengtu, in 1935, thus connecting with CNAC; and then extending this to Kunming. But the German experience in trying to 'keep 'em flying' was, if anything, worse than Pan Am's affiliate's. Four of the six W 33s had crashed and only one F 13 was left by the beginning of 1933, and four of six W 34s crashed during a period of seven months in 1935. Eurasia was writing off aircraft almost as quickly as they were being delivered.

345

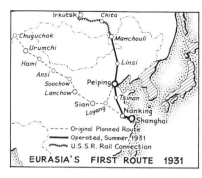

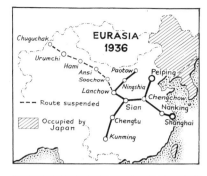

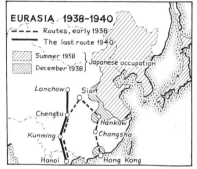

Maps 26b. Eurasia, 1931–1940
Enterprising German aviation interests, handicapped by the lack of territorial sovereignty, tried to gain a foothold in East Asia by founding Eurasia, an airline in China, with plans to link it with a Deutsche Luft Hansa trunk route across the continent. Although this ambitious goal was never achieved, Eurasia did establish a presence in China during the latter 1930s, with a network that challenged the Pan American-sponsored CNAC in its influence. With conflicting loyalties because of the Second World War, its end came with the last of its Junkers aircraft helping the Chinese cause against Germany's Axis partner, Japan.

China's First International Route

The two main airlines of China, both sponsored from powerful overseas interests, concentrated on providing a network of internal services, connecting the main cities of China; and in this, with certain reservations as to regularity and punctuality, they succeeded, in all but the far northeast, where Japan had seized Manchuria in 1932. Peiping, Tientsin, Shanghai, Sian, Chengtu, Chungking, Hankow and Canton: all were connected by air, thanks partly to the Kuomintang's gradual ascendancy over its rivals.

Even in the southwest, the rebels had been neutralized, and by October 1933, the local military governments of Kwangtung, Kwangsi and Unnan were able to establish a regional airline, the South-Western Aviation Corporation. The capital of two million yuan was subscribed partly from military agencies, partly from the civil administration, and partly from Cantonese merchants. On 25 January 1935, the Chinese Executive Council approved an application to start air services, and these were duly begun on 1 May. A small fleet of Stinson Reliants opened the first route, from Canton to Lungchow, via Wuchow and Nanning. Later in the year, a second route opened to Hoihow (Kingchow) on Hainan Island, via Maoming.

346

To meet its growing traffic needs Eurasia added Junkers-Ju 52/3ms to its fleet.

Then, on 10 July 1936, the Lungchow route was extended to Hanoi, in French Indo-China, the focal point of French influence in the whole region, including the Chinese southwestern provinces, to which the French had already built connecting railways. Thus, the honour of opening China's first international air service went, not to one of the major airlines, but to the diminutive South-Western, which also consolidated the connection with a parallel route, via the coastal points, on 4 April 1937.

South-Western Aviation Corporation was operating Stinson Reliants from Canton in the mid-1930s.

South-Western's waiting room at Canton in 1935.

In the spring of 1937 CNAC still had two Douglas Dolphin amphibians in its fleet.

Lull Before the Storm

Whether Chiang Kai-shek expected the Japanese to attack China with such ferocity in 1937 will probably never be known. Subsequently, with a certain logic, Chinese historians would claim that the Shanghai 'Incident' of August 1937 marked the real beginning of the Second World War. At the time, however, life seemed to go on as usual, and the airlines seemed to be booming. In 1936, in fact, one of CNAC's Chinese pilots, Captain Moon Chin, surveyed a route from China to India, and, in the light of subsequent events, it was well that he did so.

In the spring of 1937 CNAC's fleet consisted of thirteen aircraft, including one

Sikorsky S-38, two Fords, two Loenings, two Stinsons, and two Dolphins – all well-worn veterans—plus four flagship Douglas DC-2s. Eurasia had four single-engined Junkers types and six of the Ju 52/3m trimotors, slow but reliable. And South-Western had three Stinsons. Such was the apparent air of calm that – rather as Nero fiddled while Rome burned—CNAC actually provided a service, early in 1937, from Shanghai and Nanking to Kiukiang, for those who wished to visit the summer resort at Kuling.

In less than eight years, starting from scratch, China had laboriously fashioned a domestic airline system. The path had not exactly been strewn with flowers. There had been many obstacles, some of them erected by the very people who should have cleared the way. For those who had overcome all the difficulties, it had been a life of adventure, even, at times, excitement, and occasionally, danger. Now, in the summer of 1937, all these conditions would be combined into a struggle for survival itself.

CHAPTER TWENTY-SEVEN

Airlines to the Defence of China

The Struggle Begins

Hitherto, the story of CNAC had been quite an adventure, filled with incident, perhaps undergoing more trials and tribulations than most airlines in their infancy and adolescence, but nevertheless until 1937 it was simply a commercial enterprise providing a service to the community. During the mid-1930s, the Kuomintang Party under Chiang Kai-shek had unified, often against opposition, and always under suffrance, the whole of China that was not already occupied by Japan, namely, the province of Jehol and the four provinces that constituted Manchuria, now renamed Manchukuo by the Japanese. The Kuomintang had transferred its capital from Peking to Nanking, partly, perhaps, to put more distance between itself and the Japanese. It also appeared to be more concerned with battling with its communist rivals, and in 1936, Chiang Kai-shek had suffered the indignity of being captured by them, and was released only by the intervention of Chou En-lai, acting, as later, as a great statesman.

But any illusions of a peaceful co-existence with Japan came abruptly to an end in July and August 1937. There was a clash near Peking, in the infamous 'Marco Polo Bridge Incident', blown out of proportion by the aggressive Japanese; and this was followed by another 'incident' in Shanghai on 9 August. Five days later, Japanese aircraft bombed Shanghai, and CNAC had its first taste of real war. Two of its Douglas Dolphins were destroyed as they lay at anchor on the Whangpoo River, at CNAC's base.

On 22 August CNAC suspended service, its aircraft and its personnel having been mobilized for the emergency. All United States personnel were withdrawn, and the Chinese regarded this as desertion – although the men involved, as US citizens, had little choice. William Bond, however, not only an Old China Hand by now, but regarding himself – and was so regarded by others – as the soul of CNAC, resigned from Pan American and took over the management of the airline as an employee of the Chinese Government, which owned 55 percent of the share-holding, and thus control.

During the next few months, amid much slaughter both of Chinese soldiers and civilians, and rape, pillage and torture on a scale unknown since the days of Genghiz Khan, the Japanese advanced on two fronts: southwards from its northern foothold, occupying Peiping and Tientsin in July; and westwards from Shanghai, where Japan was in full control by November. Nanking fell on 13 December 1937, and Chiang Kai-shek moved his capital to Hankow.

CNAC, however, with some foresight, moved its headquarters further west, to Chungking, remembering perhaps the old proverb about the difficulty of getting into Szechwan, compared with the ease of reaching heaven. Certainly, progress of an army, even an all-conquering Japanese one, would not be easy up the almost impenetrable Yangtse River Gorge, compared with the advance across the flat plains of eastern China.

In December 1937 the contract with Pan American was renewed, as the Chinese found that the American expertise and technical support was essential. But Bond and others remained as Chinese Government employees. Before the year was out CNAC opened its first precarious route after the suspension, from Chungking to Kweilin, and soon afterwards extended this to Canton and Hong Kong.

A new route structure was developed, based at Chungking. The airport was on an island – little more than a large sand-bar, which flooded when the Yangtse was running high, and at the best of times the runway was only about 2,000 ft long. Even so CNAC kept the link going with the Kuomintang temporary capital at Hankow, with an extension to Changsha; and opened new lines, in May 1938 to the Szechwan cities of Luchow, Suifu, and Kiating (Loshan); and in August to Kweiyang and Kunming; and to Kweilin and Hong Kong. The air route to Kunming, which would figure so largely on the air map during the next few years, had hitherto been a whole month away from Chungking by surface transport. Now the DC-2s took four hours.

In The Front Line

Many airlines, in times of war in the service of their countries, have provided essential supply lines and logistic support to the armed forces. But no airline, not even the US carriers that were heavily involved in the Vietnam War, was ever thrust into the fray as intensively as CNAC from the time the Japanese invaded eastern China. It even had to pay for the privilege. At Hankow, in 1938, the contractors who repaired the runways at the airfield, where Japanese bombing raids stopped operations, charged $2.50 Mex for each crater on the military field, $3.00 on the commercial airport. The former was given wholesale rates, based on a greater volume of business. At Chungking, where the airport flooded all too frequently, the local contractor undertook to pave the field with tombstones, charging $11.00 Mex per fong (100 sq ft) in 1938, and, with galloping inflation, $1,260.00 per fong by 1942.

Some repair jobs were more costly, both in labour and in lives. On 24 August 1938, Captain Woods, flying the DC-2 *Kweilin*, was attacked by Japanese fighters north of Hong Kong. Forced down on the banks of the Pearl River, the CNAC DC-2 was then strafed, and 14 people were killed. The aircraft was salvaged, and subsequently, the airline flew the route between Chungking and Hong Kong only at night or in weather that was so foul that the Japanese Nakajimas could not or would not venture into the air.

On 21 October 1938 Canton fell to the Japanese, who had also taken the main coastal cities between Shanghai and that city. Hankow was also under siege. Between 22 and 25 October, two CNAC DC-2s evacuated 296 government officials, including Mme Chiang. Oil lamps were used to light the field for night flying, and the take-offs and landings were made in the knowledge that the runway had been mined. Interestingly, two other aircraft took part, honourably, in the Hankow evacuation. These were Consolidated Commodores, which had started their service lives with the New York, Rio, and Buenos Aires Line in 1929, were taken over by Pan American, and then transferred to China. They made a total of fifteen refugee flights, taking Chiang Kai-shek himself to Hengyang. The last flight was to Shasi, on the Yangtse west of Hankow, and the veteran Captain Moon alighted with the help of a hand-torch.

One of the New York, Rio and Buenos Aires Line's Consolidated Commodores which passed to CNAC and took part in refugee flights.

Eurasia Closes Down

South-Western Aviation's success in opening China's first international air service was short-lived. As Chiang Kai-shek's Kuomintang troops retreated from the Japanese, who, as related, occupied Canton on 21 October 1938. They soon exerted military control over the whole of southwestern China, and put an end to local enterprises that might relate to defence considerations; and South-Western ceased operations.

Eurasia lasted a little longer. It too had suffered at the hands of the Japanese. Its last single-engined F 13 and W 33 were both destroyed when the invaders bombed Shanghai's airfield, and a Junkers-Ju 52/3m was destroyed at Hanchung in 1939. Such fine distinctions as Germany's interests in Eurasia cut no ice with the Japanese pilots. Any aircraft, civil or military, with Chinese markings on it was fair game to them. But the airline soldiered on – and that was the operative term – with a depleted fleet of only four airworthy aircraft: one W 34 and three Ju 52s.

Already, in 1937, there had been criticism from Chinese interests of Eurasia's conduct, for example paying high salaries to expatriates (a common habit with the quasi-colonial foreign joint ventures) and low wages to the local staff; slow indiginization; operation of old equipment (though, to be fair, the Ju 52/3m was still the main workhorse of Deutsche Lufthansa in Europe at the time); and no development of local industry. Such criticism had led to the formation of the Chinische Fluggevate AG (Chiflag), but this never became an active entity and the war with Japan curtailed all efforts to take it beyond the stage of a hopeful project.

On 21 February, the ten-year agreement that had established Eurasia expired, but an extension clause allowed one more year's operation; but such an arrangement became moot when, on 2 July 1941, the Kuomintang broke diplomatic relations with Berlin. On 1 August the Ministry of Transport took over the operations, and the seal was set on the exclusion of all German participation when, on 9 December, China declared war on Germany, Italy and Japan.

The Magnificent Salvage

Before folding its wings, the Eurasia aircrews and ground-crews had valiantly tried to keep the operation going at all costs. Such were the many hazards that almost weekly disasters of some kind became the rule rather than the exception. One such incident was truly remarkable, not just for the determination, ingenuity, and resourcefulness demonstrated, but because it was unique in the annals of air transport history.

On 13 April 1939, a Junkers-Ju 52/3m, piloted by Captain Rathje – the same who had been captured by the Mongolians in 1931 – crash-landed on a mountain slope just north of the Indo-Chinese frontier in southwestern China, having been strafed and bombed by Japanese fighters. Rathje was carried on a stretcher through the jungle for five days before reaching help in Indo-China on the railway that linked Kunming with Hanoi.

Any transport aircraft was such a priceless asset to China at the time that a decision was made to salvage the Junkers. It could not be moved down the mountain, as almost certainly it would have been wrecked beyond possible repair. In fact, except for the undercarriage and one wingtip, the damage was not severe, and so, in a real-life case of the Mountain Coming to Mahomet, the aircraft was repaired *in situ*, and a runway was prepared so that it could take off under its own power. Under the supervision of Ing Schneider, Eurasia's master mechanic, 33 pack animals, loaded with spare parts and equipment, were sent to the crash site. Then, quite amazingly, about 1,000 workers methodically dug out a runway on the steep mountain slope. It was a masterpiece of ingenuity and improvisation. On 15 October, six months after the crash, and with only four feet to spare on each side of the 900 ft-long mud-surfaced strip, Eurasia aircraft Eu XIX flew to Kunming, to resume its much-needed supporting role for the defence of China.

Hamiata

Though many books have been written and many archives have been compiled about the efforts to supply China, under acute and stringent siege from 1937 to 1944, by the southwestern route from India and Burma, at first by tortuous roads and later by an armada of aircraft flying over the Hump, little attention has been paid to the other supply route to China, from the northwest, from the Soviet Union. Unlike the fiendish construction problems of the Burma Road, because of the precipitous mountain ranges that had to be surmounted with endless hairpin bends – often a dozen or more just to climb one mountainside – the road from Soviet Central Asia, though difficult, was not only across relatively easy terrain; it was also out of the range of Japanese aircraft. By 1938, the road had been completed by about 100,000 labourers, guarded by soldiers, and the supply line through Sinkiang, where Governor Sheng Shih-tsai was vigorously anti-colonialist and friendly with both the Soviet Union and Mao Tse-tung, the Chinese communist enemy of Chiang Kai-shek. In a complicated political situation, the Kansu—Sinkiang Highway was nevertheless opened to traffic, on a route from the Soviet frontier east of Alma Ata, through Urumchi, Lanchow, Sian, Hanchung and Chengtu, to reach Chungking, a distance of 3,278 miles (5,274 km).

From Eurasia's point of view, the situation was bizarre, as its joint owners could not have been sure as to whose side they were on from one day to another. The airline is believed to have made a trial flight westwards from Lanchow, through Hami and Urumchi, to reach Alma Ata, Kazakhstan, on 24 March 1939; and to have started regular service on 2 April. But no sooner had this begun when, on 23 August 1939, the USSR-Germany Non-Aggression Pact was signed by Ribbentrop and Molotov. On 9 September, the Sino-Soviet Aviation Company was formed, with a capital of $1 million, split exactly in half between the USSR and

China, each of whom provided three directors. The President was Chinese, the Vice-President was of Soviet citizenship. The flying personnel was Soviet and the equipment was probably Soviet also, although the details are not known for certain.

The whole idea was to provide a through route from Moscow to Chungking. The Soviet airline, Aeroflot, was responsible for the Moscow—Alma Ata segment; Eurasia linked Lanchow with Chungking, and also extended westwards as far as the small community of Hami, a kind of way-station on the traditional camel caravan route to Sinkiang, or, as it was familiarly known at the time, Chinese Turkestan. In the middle, linking Hami with Alma Ata, was the Sino-Soviet company. For the sake of simplicity, the line became known as Hamiata, reflecting the names of the two termini. The German-Italian-Japanese Tripartite Pact was signed in September 1940, and thus, as described earlier, all German interest in Eurasia was terminated. Although little, if any, official records are available, Hamiata appears to have operated, on a wartime footing, throughout the Second World War, and it emerged from the conflict as a viable operation.

A CNAC Douglas DC-3 with, in the background, two of the Curtiss Condors.

Eurasia, on the other hand, ceased to exist. On 3 March 1943, the Chinese Ministry of Communications established the Central Air Transport Corporation (CATC or CATCO), wholly-owned by the Government. On 1 June 1943 Eurasia was dissolved, and for a while, pending delivery of American transport aircraft, CATC took over the few Junkers aircraft that were still flyable.

Flight of the Condors

The United States supported airline of the south, CNAC, was just as deprived of aircraft as was Eurasia in the north. On paper, and in peacetime, 1939 should have been a great year, as on 25 January, China and the United Kingdom signed an agreement to open a route to Rangoon, Burma, then part of British India. After the route from Chungking to Kunming was extended on 15 March to Hanoi (CNAC's first foreign route, following in South-Western's footsteps), this was extended further, to Rangoon, on 30 October. But to maintain the service, with such a depleted fleet, was a struggle. The DC-2 *Kweilin* was, for the second time, forced to land by Japanese military aircraft and again strafed. Of the 14 on board, nine were killed and two wounded. On 20 January 1940, the sole remaining Ford crashed in Kiangsi province; and in February 1941, a DC-2 crashed in Hunan province. CNAC had only one or two flyable Douglases, and only a skeleton service was possible by the spring of 1941, with the route to Hanoi suspended in November 1940.

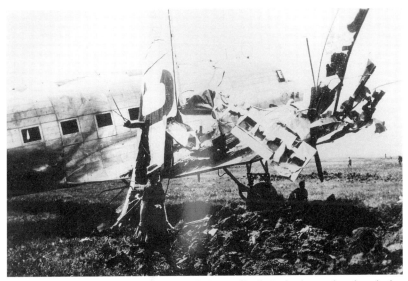

Although of very poor quality this photograph shows effectively the damaged starboard wing of the CNAC DC-3 attacked by the Japanese at Suifu west of Chungking.

In desperation, CNAC contracted with a US aircraft dealer, the Babb Corporation, for the purchase of six venerable, though hardly venerated, Curtiss Condor biplanes. Long retired from scheduled service in the United States, where they had been the last of the biplanes to grace the air routes, they had originally been intended for the Republican forces in the Spanish Civil War, and were awaiting shipment at the port of Veracruz in Mexico. They were taken to Los Angeles, and rebuilt and overhauled, with new fabric. The collector rings on the engines, it was reported, were fixed by a volunteer Chinese welder. CNAC paid $25,000 each for them, and they were intended for the Kunming—Hanoi route. But when the Japanese occupied Hanoi, they could no longer fly westwards, because of the terrain.

Known as the DC-2½, this is the CNAC DC-3 which was so badly damaged at Suifu after its starboard wing was replaced by one from the smaller DC-2. There was 10ft difference in the span of the two types.

Necessity is the mother of invention. From March until July 1941, the Condors were put into service on a temporary route from Hong Kong to Nanshiung (Namyang), in the north of Kwangtung Province, and the site of a tungsten ore mine. The episode was a valiant epilogue to the life of a once-famous airliner of yesteryear.

The DC-2½

One of the best-known stories of strange improvizations ingeniously fashioned to 'keep 'em flying' is an incident that occurred during CNAC's hectic months of 1941. In May, a Douglas DC-3, of which type the airline had only two or three at the time, was grounded on a piece of rough ground at Suifu, west of Chungking, and where the now regular Japanese strafing had irrevocably damaged one wing. No spare DC-3 wing was available anywhere in China. But a spare DC-2 wing was available at Hong Kong. With nothing to lose, this wing was flown to Suifu, lashed to the side of the fuselage of another DC-2, itself a hardy survivor of similar narrow escapes. The DC-2 wing was fitted on to the DC-3, and the aircraft made a successful escape to safety, where, in due course, its original silhouette was restored.

Surveying the Hump

Captain Moon Chin had already surveyed the 'Hump' route across the cordillera of precipitous mountains that lay athwart the direct air route between China and

356

This picture was taken at Likiang near the Tibetan border on 23 November 1941 after the first flight over the 'Hump'. Unfortunately it has only been possible to identify four people and only by surnames. Front from left – Young, C.L. Sharp (pilot) and W. Langhorn Bond. Second from right – Nieh (CNAC assistant operations manager).

the safe haven of India. On 22 May 1941 William Bond submitted proposals to Lauchlin Currie, an aide to President Roosevelt, for the supply of additional Douglas C-47 (military DC-3) aircraft, so as to create a vital supply route for the beleaguered armed forces of China. Roosevelt acted swiftly and authorized the much-needed reinforcements. And not before time ...

On 8 December 1941 (7 December, US time), the Japanese Navy attacked Pearl Harbor and Japan simultaneously declared war on the United States and the Allied nations. Great Britain's outposts of empire, inadequately defended, were easy prey for the Japanese military, which advanced with remarkable speed to occupy the whole of southeast Asia within a few months. Hong Kong was immediately besieged. Kai Tak airport was bombed, destroying two of CNAC's DC-2s, and three of its Condors, as well as sinking one of Pan American's Sikorsky S-42 flying-boats in the harbour. Two DC-3s and one DC-2 survived, and these were evacuated to Namyung about 200 miles to the north. Such scanty regular flying that the airline was trying to maintain was promptly discontinued, and during the two days following the outbreak of total war, CNAC evacuated 275 people from Hong Kong on special evacuation flights. Among the evacuees were Mme Sun Yat Sen, widow of the founder of the Kuomintang, Mme Chiang Kai-shek, and H H Kung, a leading Chinese industrialist.

Whistling Willie

Not content with the DC-2$\frac{1}{2}$ story to put into the record books, CNAC's incident-filled diary of December 1941 contained another strange story. One of the DC-3s that had flown to Namyung had been shot up by Japanese fighters. Being shot up by the Japanese was almost part of the flying routine by this time. The crew had drained off the fuel and oil, and so the fierce strafing did not result in an aircraft bonfire. But the engines and propellers were damaged and the airframe was esti-

357

mated to have been hit by 3,000 bullets, affecting – to use a mild description of the damage – instruments, tyres, control lines, undercarriage and fuel tanks. Engines were flown in from Chungking, and somehow or other, the aircraft was patched up, flown to Kunming, and patched up even more.

Patch was the operative word. The necessary metal-working machines and parts not being available, the holes were covered with fabric patches, with attachment adhesives of varying quality and chemical content. When Captain Sharp took off and flew the wounded DC-3 to Lashio, in Burma, the patches gradually came off in the airstream, most of them because the adhesive was not water-resistant. The bullet holes, thus exposed, acted like the stops in a musical instrument, and like a hundred flutes all out of tune, gave forth a noise that earned the DC-3 the nickname of Whistling Willie, or to some, the Banshee of Burma. Flute music or not, the aircraft was still airworthy, and Sharp flew it to Calcutta with a load of passengers, mail, and freight, without incident.

The day after Whistling Willie left Hong Kong, on 12 December 1941, the mainland side of the Hong Kong colony, Kowloon, where Kai Tak Airport was situated, fell to the Japanese; and CNAC lost a precious base and source of supply. By the time Hong Kong fell to the Japanese completely, on Christmas Day, Bond and his men had curtailed the airline service to a short line to Chengtu, and a new route to India, flying to Lashio three times a week, with one flight a week continuing on to Calcutta. With this tenuous link, the Chinese airline managed to keep going, even though a cartographer would have been hard pressed to keep up with the changes on the map, and a schedule compiler would have been driven to distraction.

Burmese Interlude

As already mentioned, Japan over-ran southeast Asia in an amazingly short time. Singapore, last bastion of the British in the Malay peninsula, fell on 15 February 1942, and Rangoon shortly thereafter. Such links that CNAC had been able to keep with the latter city were broken. The Japanese now began to advance northwards from Rangoon into central Burma, and once again, the airline became an escape channel for refugees. During the last week of February CNAC made 70 flights between Shwebo, near Mandalay, and Chittagong, in southern Bengal (now Bangladesh). The last DC-2 of the once-proud fleet of four crashed at Kunming on 14 March 1942, but fortunately, reinforcements were at last on the way, as Pan American Airways transferred a DC-3 from Alaska, and aircraft began to arrive in India from the west.

With the Japanese threat in northern Burma at crisis point, and with the British troops under Wavell and the Americans under Stilwell with their backs to the wall, CNAC continued to play its part as a civilian arm of a military transport and supply operation. On 8 April 1942, it began a service – if a series of flights operated with constant urgency and as frequently as possibly could be described in such everyday terms – from Myitkyina (pronounced Mitch-ee-naw), in northern Burma, to Dinjan airfield, near Dibrugarh, in northern Assam, India. Myitkyina, like Lashio, was the terminus of a railway line; and Dinjan was a Royal Air Force aerodrome of respectable standard, and respectably far enough away from the Japanese Army. During this operation, which lasted about a month, CNAC carried 16 tons of supplies every day to Stilwell's forces; and on the return flights, evacuated 2,400 people and 50 tons of freight.

Record Flight

On 5 May 1942 a CNAC DC-3 had left Chungking on a flight across the Hump, as it was soon to be called, and had landed at Myitkyina, delivering six passengers. The load on its onward journey was somewhat different. Designed to carry 21 passengers in normal prewar seating accommodation, and extended to 28 in a four-abreast layout, Captain Paul Kessler carved his place in history by loading up his aircraft so as to take 78 people to Calcutta. This, of course, broke all the regulations, but Kessler's excuse (which, by all accounts, was accepted) was that There Was A War On.

The Hump

Whole books, dozens of reports, and probably scores of personal memoirs have been written about the Hump operation between China and India that lasted for three years from the summer of 1942 to the summer of 1945. Aircraft began to arrive from the production lines in the United States, via the trans-African route that had been established, on President Roosevelt's request to Juan Trippe, by Pan American Airways during the summer of 1941, primarily to supply material to the British 8th Army in Egypt, but which quickly added a branch line through southern Arabia and India to channel aircraft and supplies to the China theatre.

Massive reinforcements began to arrive in April 1943, but until then CNAC bore the brunt of the burden of the India-China aerial lifeline. It began full service, in an 'all-in-a-day's-work' attitude, on 1 July 1942, on a route from Kunming to Calcutta, via Dinjan, with ten C-47s supplied under Lend-Lease arrangements. At last Bond had a sizeable fleet. The connection to Chiang Kai-shek's capital in Chungking was flown from Kunming as a regular route, and in August, a new route extended northwards from Chungking to Lanchow, connecting with what was left of Eurasia. There was also a route to Kweilin, where the US Air Force had a forward base for harassing the Japanese.

Kunming became the hub of the Hump operations. At an altitude of 6,000 ft, heavily-laden – and often over-loaded – aircraft on the westbound flights could be vulnerable to the dangers of an operational ceiling that was lower than the crests of the several mountain ranges that decorated the route. One technique was to take off, circle a few times, climbing all the while, and if the aircraft was still gaining height on the third circuit, then it was cleared to head for Dinjan.

Aircraft would crash fairly frequently. This was no route for the faint-hearted. With so much at stake aircrew and ground-staff alike became inured to the risks and the dangers, becoming philosophical, even fatalistic; retaining, however, a sense of disciplined responsibility and a true measure of priorities. On one occasion, the wife of the British consul in Chungking was hitching a ride to Calcutta for a little rest and recuperation. She asked the despatch officer what she should do if the aircraft came to grief. Eyeing the brief-case and sensing that this may have been the secondary reason for the official trip, he thought for a moment, produced a box of matches, and said 'burn the documents'.

A Proud Record

Flying across the formidable Hump became routine – routine, that is, if losses through enemy action or by misadventure over the mountains every few weeks could be called routine. The Japanese were on the watch at the eastern segment, and from October 1943 the aircraft used Suifu as their base rather than Chungking. If a DC-3 lost an engine in certain parts of the route, where the Mekong and Salween Rivers carved chasms through mountains higher than the Rockies or the Alps, failure to maintain altitude meant inevitable disaster. Many aircraft, of CNAC and of the US Air Forces, still remain there, their disintegrated remnants undiscovered and undiscoverable.

During 1943 the base of the whole operation was moved to Calcutta as a precautionary measure should Kunming fall (fortunately it did not). Night flying was introduced, partly to thwart the Japanese, whose fighters could not find the air supply aircraft in the dark. In China, where air raids were frequent, CNAC timed its departures '15 minutes before the second raid, 30 minutes before the third.' But at least, in spite of losses, General Stilwell guaranteed that the Chinese airline should always have three DC-3s allocated to it under the Lend-Lease programme.

The year 1944 saw CNAC reaping the benefit of its hard-won front-line experience. During the twelve-month period, it flew approximately 9,000 round trips over the Hump, after the Burma Road fell to the Japanese. It carried 35,000 tons of Lend-Lease materials, and ranked second only to the US Air Transport Command in the delivery of strategic air cargoes on world routes during the year – 38 percent against the ATC's 57 percent.

Rice-Kicking Duty

At the end of the summer of 1944 the famous Burma Road supply line, that had once been an invaluable, if ponderous, supply route, and which had been blocked by the Japanese since 1940, was no longer under direct military threat. The tide of the war was turning, and the decision was made to re-open the road. Thousands of labourers were impressed into what, in British criminal parlance, would have been described as Six Months Hard Labour. Isolated in the mountains from normal surface supply routes, they were sustained by a special service provided by CNAC.

Official records show that, between 22 October 1944 and 21 January 1945, the airline made 523 flights to Paoshan, the eastern staging point on the road at the Chinese end, and to Myitkyina, the Burmese point at the western segment, past the mountains. During this operation CNAC carried more than 900 tons of rice to the gangs of workmen, and the sacks were quite literally kicked out of the cargo doors of the C-47s by men recruited for the job. 224 trips were also made, carrying almost 300 tons of equipment and 736 people.

Rather as an anti-climax, the Ledo Road, as it came to be called, after its terminus at the railhead in Assam, was never to contribute substantially to the war effort; by the time it was ready for heavy traffic, early in 1945, the supply of transport aircraft from the American manufacturing arsenal was in full swing, including large numbers of Curtiss C-46s, able to carry twice the load of a C-47, and to which most of the honours should go as the US Air Force's most valuable asset for the Hump airlift.

On 28 March 1945 CNAC extended its Lanchow route to Hami, making the direct link with Hamiata and thus extending its sphere of influence over a wider geographical area. In May, 45 aircraft were delivered as part of the Lend-Lease programme, mostly C-46s. In June CNAC bought six C-47s and three C-53s (both military versions of the DC-3) from the Army-Navy Liquidation Commission and Surplus Property Commission.

On 6 August 1945 an atomic bomb dropped on the Japanese city of Hiroshima, effectively destroying it. On 9 August, a second bomb did the same to Nagasaki. On 2 September Japan capitulated. The Second World War mercifully came to an end. Strengthened by the absence of attacking aircraft and the reinforcement of substantial numbers of aircraft, CNAC prepared to serve China in peacetime, and declared its intentions by resuming flights to Shanghai in September.

The term Magnificent Men in Their Flying Machines has been applied to a fictional account of early aviation; but such a description could truly apply to CNAC's record during the Second World War. Had the airline been mobilized and militarily administered, its staff would have collected chestfulls of medals. In the event, their memory is marked mainly by the respect of their colleagues and by tributes to their dedication and valour by historians, of which the author of this book is one.

CHAPTER TWENTY-EIGHT

Airline Transfer to an Offshore Island

CATC

As recorded in the previous chapter, the German-sponsored airline Eurasia was dissolved in 1943, to be replaced by the Central Air Transport Corporation (CATC or CATCO), a wholly-owned Chinese corporation under the jurisdiction of the Ministry of Communications. It had hoped to receive aircraft from the United States but these did not materialize and it had to make do with what was left of Eurasia's fleet, which, at the nadir of its and CATC's fortunes, consisted of one Junkers-Ju 52/3m, plus, remarkably, a Japanese Nakajima A.T, captured somewhere in the north. So bereft was it of aircraft that, on 28 March 1945, the US-associated airline CNAC opened a service to Hami to connect with the Soviet supply route via Hamiata, thus encroaching into territory that was, *de facto* if not *de jure*, in CATC's area of responsibility.

But when the Second World War came to a merciful end in the late summer of 1945, CATC was able to secure a loan from a private banker to purchase twelve Douglas C-47s from the United States Army Air Force in India, where they were no longer needed for the Hump and other vital supply missions to China. With these, it participated, along with CNAC, in an airlift for the Kuomintang Government to transfer government personnel and freight from the temporary capital in Chungking to the former capital, Nanking, and to the coastal cities, particularly Shanghai.

In July 1946 CATC purchased about 100 war-surplus aircraft, largely from the US armed forces, for a bargain price – as well it should have been, for most of the aircraft were fit, at best, for marginally safe operation; and at worst, for cannibalizing for spare parts. Nevertheless, these were sufficient to establish a network of routes, mostly in northern China. At the end of 1947 the airline invested in five passenger-carrying DC-3s (the same basic type as the military C-47 cargo- and troop-carrier) and was able to offer regular service over 27 routes, from Shanghai to Sinkiang in the far northwest.

Commercially, if not politically, the prospects seemed good for the new airline as, even in an uncertain environment, at least it could fly without the immediate danger of being attacked by Japanese aircraft. Such was CATC's confidence that, on 15 July 1947 it signed a contract to purchase six new Convair 240s, with which it planned to reinforce its main routes and to begin service on some overseas and trans-border routes to neighbouring countries. The first Convair-Liner entered service early in 1949, and, for a few short months, was the pride of its – and China's – civil air fleet. But pride came before a fall, and both airline and aircraft suffered different fates: the former to become part of a new airline, Civil Air Transport (CAT) which evacuated to Taiwan, after the ignominious defeat of the Kuomintang at the hands of the Communist forces in a bitter civil war; the latter to become part of the fleet of the new airline that was quickly formed after Mao Tse-Tung proudly announced the formation of the People's Republic of China on 1 October 1949.

The Twilight Years of CNAC

The exploits of CNAC during the Second World War in transporting supplies and personnel across the notorious Hump between India and China had become legendary. In the allocation of aircraft, it had had to take second priority; the larger C-46s and the C-54s went first to the US Army transport units, and CNAC had to make do for most of the time with the older C-47s. During an estimated 80,000 flights across the aerial No Man's Land, CNAC lost 46 aircraft either completely so in the mountains or damaged beyond repair elsewhere. Twenty-five crews were killed, perhaps a record for any airline, anywhere in the world, at any time.

On 20 December 1945 the China National Aviation Corporation (CNAC) was completely re-organized – once again, for it had done this before, in 1930. The Chinese Government, through the Ministry of Communications, held 80 percent of the stock. Pan American Airways sold its former 45 percent for $5.1 million, then re-purchased 20 percent of the new company for $1.55 million.

At the end of 1945, the base was moved back from Calcutta, where CNAC had sought a safe haven during the worst days of the War, to Shanghai, which had been its original base before it had evacuated, first to Hankow, then to Chungking, and with short stays in Hong Kong and Kunming. Rather like CATC's, its prospects seemed good. Its fleet numbered about fifty C-47s and C-46s from the Army/Navy Liquidation Commission, and were probably almost all intact – unlike the northern rival's. CNAC also bought six Douglas C-54s, and early in 1946, began to operate a network of routes throughout China.

Two of the many Curtiss C-46s that were supplied to Chinese airlines just after the war.

But 1946 was not a good year. The airline suffered from almost all the problems that can beset any airline; and it suffered them all at the same time. It had put 25 aircraft into service the length and breadth of China, except for the peripheral provinces beyond what may be termed as the Chinese equivalent of The Pale. But the airline's staff, including the aircrew, went on strike, protesting against the continued inequities of the remuneration and conditions of employment in which foreign-hired pilots, for example, were paid more than twice as much for the same work, and with more fringe benefits. On 18 June 1946 the Chinese Air Force took over CNAC's operations, and proceeded to fly the routes with the standards of military requirements. Between December 1946 and January 1947 six CNAC aircraft crashed, killing 156 passengers and crew. It was worse than the Hump.

If this was not bad enough from the operations side, the situation was becoming impossible in the marketing and commercial branches. Galloping inflation had taken a vice-like grip on the Chinese economy. In December 1946 the exchange rate was 6,500 Chinese dollars to one US dollar. By August 1947, it was 45,000 to one, and still rising. In a situation reminiscent of the German crisis of 1923, when it was cheaper to paper a wall with money than to buy the wallpaper, there were many reports of shoppers carrying their 'wallet' in a wheelbarrow.

But there was a silver lining. In 1947 the Chinese Government granted permission to CNAC to operate a number of international services. In addition to those to eastern Asian destinations such as Calcutta, Manila, Bangkok and Hong Kong, there was also a pearl: a trans-Pacific route from Shanghai to San Francisco. This was inaugurated on 10 June 1947, with the DC-4s, with en route stops at Guam, Wake Island and Honolulu.

But yet again, CNAC's destiny was to move. Its files should have been kept in mobile offices. First, in December 1948, it went to Hong Kong, and in January 1950, when the Kuomintang, headed by Chiang Kai-shek and all his retinue, made its undignified flight to Taiwan, all the assets of this once-great airline – or what was left of them, which was not much – were taken over by CAT, the upstart airline which usurped the heritage of pioneers like William Langhorn Bond, Capt E M Allison, and Capt Moon Chin.

Some of CNAC's aircraft, together with some of CATC's were flown from Hong Kong to Tientsin, by crews who believed that they should be retained in China, by the Chinese, of whatever political persuasion. For the legal record, Pan American sold its 20 percent interest to the Chinese Government, the new one, in Taipei, on 31 December 1949. And so ended the story of an airline whose incident-punctuated life was truly stranger and more exciting than fiction.

A Rose By Any Other Name

The official records show that CNRRA Air Transport was organized as an airline in Shanghai by Major-General Claire Chennault and Whiting Willauer, together with a Chinese businessman, Dr Wang Wen-san, probably representing T V Soong, Chiang's multi-millionaire ambassador to the United States. Chennault had gained fame as leader of the Flying Tigers, the US flying corps who had valiantly fought off the Japanese Air Force in the defence of China, and to whom Chiang Kai-shek probably owed his reputation, if not his life. Willauer had been the Far Eastern Director of the US Foreign Economic Administration, charged with providing aid to allied nations and sympathetic organizations. There was another player in the game, a character of dubious reputation who may have been the first influence-peddler to have established strong links in Washington between politicians and businessmen for their mutual benefit.

Thomas G Corcoran, who Franklin Roosevelt called Tommy the Cork, had wheeled and dealed in Washington for many years before and during the Second World War. During the War, Corcoran had served FDR as an unofficial head of Lend-Lease to China, and as a result was able to become involved in various business ventures that sprang up on the cessation of hostilities. In the summer of 1946 he persuaded Fiorello LaGuardia (former Mayor of New York, and after whom the airport is named), in his capacity as director general of the United Nations Relief and Rehabilitation Administration (UNRRA), to help form an airline. UNRRA would put up $2 million to purchase surplus cargo aircraft, fuel and supplies so as to ferry relief supplies to war-devastated China. This airline would be charged with delivering all the loads that UNRRA demanded, after which it would be free to carry revenue-earning traffic.

It was a sweet deal. Often the UNRRA loads would be supplemented by cash-yielding loads, in proportions that perhaps LaGuardia had not foreseen. But the airline did fulfil its mission, and a few of its pilots and ground crews from the former Flying Tigers. CNRRA Air Transport made its first flight, from Shanghai to Canton, on 31 January 1947, and full operations on a regular schedule began three days later. Within a short time, its aircraft were to be seen all over China, as far north as Mukden (Shenyang). During the year, it flew seven million ton-miles of cargo, making it the biggest air freight carrier in the world at the time.

The CAT Adventure

On 31 December 1947 as some degree of normality was appearing to return to China – although this was mainly wishful thinking by the Kuomintang who seemed either to be unaware of, or chose to ignore, the growing popularity and therefore widespread strength of the Communists – CNRRA was liquidated. On 2 January 1948 a new contract was negotiated with the Chinese Government, and Chennault and Willauer formed a new airline, with the same fleet and the same personnel, under the name of Civil Air Transport (CAT). It continued the good work. In the first five months of 1948, it flew more ton-miles of freight than in the record-breaking year of 1947, and 200 million passenger-miles as well.

On 20 February 1948 its tentacles were spread far to the northwest, to Tihwa (Urumchi) in Sinkiang, on the route to the USSR; and on 24 September it opened its first international route, from Canton to Haiphong, in French Indo-China, and the port for Hanoi. But this was the lull before the storm. In a classic case of history repeating itself, the Kuomintang Government ceased to retain a grip on the country; and as the Communists advanced, it retreated westwards and southwards, and CAT went with it, performing some heroic missions. It carried 7,000 people out of Mukden, which was probably a world's record for evacuation of any city by air. In a reverse action, it carried supplies into Taiyuan, in a textbook exercise later undertaken in the Berlin Airlift, that enabled the local commander, the anti-communist Marshal Yen Hsieh-shan, to hold out for several months against the encircling forces. In June 1949 it began an airlift from the important tin-mines in Yunnan Province to Haiphong, and on 11 October (by which time Mao Tse-Tung had already proclaimed the formation of the People's Republic) evacuated personnel from Canton to the safety of British Hong Kong.

But all to no avail. At the end of 1949, the Nationalist (Kuomintang) Government moved lock, stock and barrel, with hoards of gold bullion and half the treasures of Chinese art and culture, to Taiwan. CAT moved with it, and on 15 January 1950, with tacit support from the CIA, acquired both the Central Air Transport Corporation and the China National Aviation Corporation. This time, however, the move was complicated by the British courts in Hong Kong, which impounded the aircraft that comprised a substantial part of the fleet.

The Nine Points of the Law

Possession is, as the axiom goes, nine points of the law; but who is the possessor? This was the problem that faced the British authorities in Hong Kong, where, at Kai Tak Airport, a large number of Chinese aircraft, formerly of CATC and CNAC and now claimed by CAT were parked, awaiting a decision as to the rightful owners. One problem was that, as yet, Britain did not recognize the Chinese Nationalists as the rightful government of China – and was not to do so in the foreseeable future. And although the situation regarding recognition of the PRC was

One of the six Convair CV-240s purchased by Central Air Transport Corporation (CATC) and put into service for a short time in 1949. (*Consolidated Vultee*)

still obscure and awaiting much diplomatic manoeuvring, the harsh truth of the matter was that the Communists under Mao ruled over all the territory of China, every single province except one – the offshore island that had only recently been recovered from the Japanese.

The total number of aircraft has been variously reported, but appears to have consisted almost entirely of about sixty DC-3s and C-46s, five Convair 240s, and four DC-4s. Late in 1950 the Lower Court in Hong Kong, representing the British Government, awarded the whole fleet to Peking, based on the fact that the effective government of China was located there. In fact some of the grounded fleet had already been neatly ungrounded, and flown to Tientsin, near Peking, loaded to the bulkheads with about $3 million's worth of spare parts. The United States, possibly backing Taipei and the Nationalists, appealed against the decision, and the British Privy Council, passing down a kind of Solomon's Judgement, ordered the remaining fleet of aircraft still in Hong Kong to be returned to the United States, that is, neither to Peking nor Taipei. The fleet, or what was left of it, was taken back to Santa Barbara by a US aircraft carrier in 1951, by which time very little of it was still flyable or even repairable. The CV-240s were sold, at a good price.

CAT's Douglas DC4 B-1014 at Hong Kong Airport (Kai Tak) in 1969. (*Douglas*)

366

Starting Over

On 20 April 1950 CAT began a weekly round trip DC-4 service that provided a through service from Singapore, Bangkok and Hong Kong through to Tokyo, via Taipei, taking advantage of the geographical position of Taiwan to exercise the so-called Sixth Freedom rights – not recognized by IATA carriers, but exercised all the same by airlines that chose to do so. Internal services were also developed in Taiwan (the Chinese name of the island was adopted in preference to Formosa); and on 30 March 1952, flights began to Pusan, South Korea, and on 26 June 1952, to Manila. The Pusan service was extended to Seoul on 9 September 1954.

By this time, the Korean War, which started on 25 June 1950, had ended with the partition of the country on 27 July 1953; and the CAT service was perceived as an important link between the emerging new nation of South Korea and nations of eastern Asia sympathetic to its political leaning, which was fairly heavily to the right and vehemently anti-Communist, as might be imagined. Both had fought against the Chinese Red Army, so there was a natural affinity between the two countries. CAT acted as a communications channel for businessmen, politicians, military 'advisors', and clandestine agents.

Originally founded as an opportunist piece of entrepreneurship, with more than a touch of chicanery in its roots, CAT's early years in its new Taiwan base were often cavalier in its commercial posture, though its operations were carried out with strict adherence to correct procedures of maintenance and safety. But by the mid-1950s, the swashbuckling approach was giving way to orthodoxy. In 1954 the Nationalist Government acquired a minority shareholding, which turned CAT into the flag carrier of Taiwan, at that time struggling to gain legitimacy in the eyes of the world. On 27 July 1958, General Claire Chennault died in New Orleans – where he had been living since Tommy the Cork had first put him up to the idea of CNRRA – and things were never quite the same again. The legend of mysterious clandestine activity faded and CAT took its place among the airlines of the Orient as they started to emerge from infancy to precocious adolescence.

On 15 October 1958, a CAT Douglas DC-6B opened the *Mandarin* service, to link Taipei with the capital cities of the region with superb on-board service by Chinese stewardesses whose slit-skirted chong sams quickly became as legendary as the airline itself. While using a fleet of C-46s and DC-3s to perform the many duties required of it, overtly or covertly, by the authorities, CAT's shop-window was its *Mandarin* service, which it managed to maintain with only one DC-6B. Three years later, having been named by Madame Chiang herself on the previous day, the first and only Convair 880 introduced the *Mandarin Jet* service on 12 July 1961. Two weeks later, the last of the veteran DC-4s was retired.

Gradually, almost imperceptibly, and in spite of the obvious prestige value of CAT to Taiwan, the airline seemed to be suffering from an unseen infection beyond its control. First it lost its domestic routes. The service to Taitung was transferred to a small company, Foshing Airlines, on 18 January 1964; that to the offshore island of Makung was suspended on 18 July; and the Taipei—Hualien connection went to China Air Lines on 31 December of the same year. Its reputation was not helped when a C-46 crashed near Taichung on 20 June, killing 52 passengers and five crew. The crash, serious enough in itself, attracted much attention throughout east Asia because one of those killed was Loke Wan Tho, the Hong Kong movie magnate, reputed to be the richest man in Asia. Sabotage was suspected but never proved.

Further inundations took place in 1964. Air America, with direct links to CAT

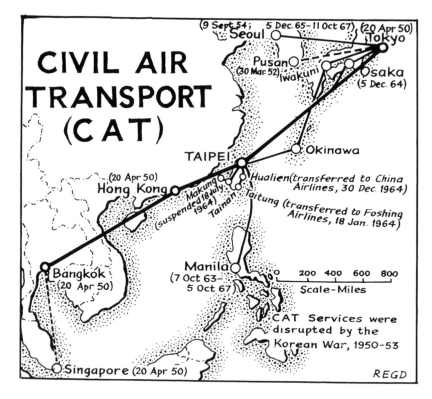

Map 28a. Civil Air Transport (CAT)
The airline that emerged from the confusion that reigned after the Kuomintang set up a government in Taiwan had more to do with politics than commercial enterprise. CAT was an extraordinary airline that, while operating scheduled routes, linking the most important traffic hubs in east Asia, it also served as a vital communications arm of the United States armed and security organizations, including the CIA. Nevertheless, its wide-ranging activities, which included logistics support in both the Korean and Vietnamese wars, generated a great *esprit de corps* among its employees. It ceased operations in 1968, after a widely-publicized Boeing 727 crash.

in the top hierarchy, and whose direct ownership by the US Central Intelligence Agency (CIA) was one of the worst-kept secrets of international espionage of the period, took over the route to Okinawa and operated the routes to the Ryukyu Islands until 30 June 1967, using a couple of C-46s and three Beech 18s. By this time, 60 percent of the ownership of CAT had been, since the 1950s, controlled by the Pacific Corporation, a Delaware corporation that also owned Air Asia and Air America, i.e. covert operations of the CIA.

CAT's main route was now curtailed. Under Republic of China (Taiwan) Government edict, services to Manila and Seoul were suspended on 5 October and 11 October respectively. On 10 January 1968, the Convair 880 was sold, in all its finery, to Cathay Pacific Airways of Hong Kong, to be replaced by a Boeing 727. The death knell came soon afterwards, when the 727 crashed on 16 February, near Taipei, killing eighteen passengers and three crew. If certain interests in Taiwan

368

wanted an excuse to shut down CAT, here it was. On 17 February 1968, all international passenger services were suspended by order of the Government; and on 29 May, the few remaining domestic services were terminated. CAT ended as it began, shrouded in strange circumstances, and behind a curtain of stealth, murkily.

China Airlines

On 10 December 1959 a group of retired Chinese Air Force officers founded China Airlines in Taipei. It began modestly, with a staff of only 26 and a fleet of two PBY-5A Catalinas, with which it performed military charters to the offshore islands near the Chinese mainland, and still claimed by the Nationalist Chinese in Taiwan. By 1961, permission had been obtained to operate domestic services to Hualien, Taitung, Kaohsiung and Makung, with a typical assembly of cast-off DC-3s and C-46s. By October 1962 a scheduled service started to Taitung, and by the following year, China Airlines (CAL) was operating a round-the-island route. Later this would be withdrawn as Far Eastern Air Transport (FAT) would acquire virtual monopoly rights.

For some time China Airlines used Sud-Aviation Caravelles on mainline domestic and the shorter regional routes.

CAL had wider ambitions, as it watched the status of Civil Air Transport (CAT) erode, and no doubt actively lobbied the Taipei Government to encourage such erosion. In October 1966, it bought a Lockheed Super Constellation from the US Flying Tiger Line and, only eight weeks later opened its first international route, from Taipei to Saigon, on 1 December 1966. Meanwhile, it had purchased two Boeing 727s, and with these was able to start service to Osaka and Tokyo, to cater for Japanese tourists, eager to enjoy the pleasures of free-wheeling Taipei, and also to Hong Kong. In October, it replaced CAT on the routes to Seoul and Manila; and in January 1968, those to Bangkok, Kuala Lumpur and Singapore. Claire Chennault's airline was wound up on 29 May, and China Airlines became the flag carrier of Taiwan. It now had 32 aircraft and more than 2,000 staff. It took over the route to Okinawa on 1 January 1969, and on 22 January gained international recognition and legitimacy by becoming a member of the International Air Transport Association (IATA).

CAL now began to expand rapidly. It acquired aircraft to suit the various levels of its operations: Japanese YS-11 propeller-turbine twins for the short domestic services, where traffic was booming, because of the congestion on the rail links between north and south Taiwan; French Caravelles for the main domestic city pairs, especially to the industrial and port city of Kaohsiung; and most important,

China Airlines opened a trans-Pacific service to San Francisco on 2 February 1970 with Boeing 707-320s. (*Boeing*)

Boeing 707-320Cs, with which it opened a trans-Pacific service to San Francisco on 2 February 1970. This was routed via Tokyo and Anchorage, but once again the traffic grew quickly, as on other routes, and on 26 April 1971 a second trans-Pacific itinerary included Honolulu in a more remunerative, if not more direct routing. By this time, CAL was maintaining a daily trans-Pacific service, and its credentials in the airline, if not the political world, were well established.

But in the Republic of China's (or ROC's) case, the political and the commercial worlds were inextricably interwoven, because of the visceral debate about which government was the true one, Peking's or Taipei's. Common sense would have suggested that, with Peking ruling over one billion people in 28 Provinces, and the ROC ruling over about 16 million in one Province, there was no argument. But this did not deter the fanatically anti-communist exiles – there were two million of them – in Taiwan, who, sometimes inspired by dreams of a US-supported invasion of mainland China, cherished the hope that one day they would prevail.

The dream was shattered beyond recall when, on 25 October 1971, the People's Republic of China replaced the Nationalist Government of Taiwan as the officially recognized member of the United Nations. Taiwan was automatically expelled from the International Civil Aviation Organization (ICAO) and with President Nixon's historic visit to Peking, now renamed Beijing, to conform with a new phonetic transliteration, during the last week of February 1972, CAL's status in the international airline community became precarious.

The Malaysian Government, for example, suspended CAL's traffic rights at Kuala Lumpur in November 1972. But far more serious was the termination of the Japan-China Air Agreement on 20 April 1974. Japan took the view that the flag of the ROC was only a trade mark, and not that of a Sovereign State, an attitude that cannot have been viewed kindly in Taipei. Japanese aircraft en route to Hong Kong had to make a wide detour around the island of Taiwan.

Undeterred, CAL started an all-cargo service to the United States on 1 June 1974. A Boeing 707 was converted to carry 65,000 lb of cargo (or perhaps 2,000 television sets, one of the many 'high-tech' items being manufactured in the highly productive factories of Taiwan by the industrious Chinese, determined to make their way in the world through hard work) and began a Taipei—Los Angeles service, calling at Kaohsiung for fill-up loads.

On 15 September 1974, China Airlines withdrew from IATA, ostensibly for economic reasons, but stated that it would continue to abide by the international agency's regulations and practices, which meant that it would not indulge in ruthless price wars. In this case, it was in good company; for many of the airlines of eastern Asia, notably Cathay Pacific, All Nippon, and Thai International, all highly regarded by their peers in the airline business, were not IATA members. (Oddly, for many years, this circumstance clouded the awareness of the growing strength of the oriental airlines as a group; for the IATA statistics, accepted as the standard reference worldwide, did not include those of the non-IATA members, whose combined output was larger than that of the 'legitimate' carriers in the region.)

But the effect of the political isolation, with Taiwan playing the role of an outcast, was severe. Recognition of the People's Republic of China by Japan was a body-blow. Not only was the lucrative route to Japan terminated, and much high-yield traffic lost but access to South Korea was effectively cut, because of the infringement of Japanese airspace. To make matters worse, the collapse of South Vietnam ended the Saïgon route, and Taiwan's relations with Thailand and the Philippines hit a new low. The fuel crisis hit CAL as badly as any other airline; and its trans-Pacific route could no longer be routed through Tokyo.

Down But Not Out

But such was the resilience and determination of the Taiwanese business community to rise above political adversity that CAL was able to ride on a wave of economic prosperity which could hardly be called a recovery, because in spite of all the commercial hurdles that had to be overcome, the demand for Taiwanese goods, from high-quality electronic instruments to illicitly-printed *Encyclopaedia Britannicas*, had continued unabated. The reason was simple. Taiwanese-made

China Airlines was an operator of both the Boeing 727 and 737, the latter being used, in part to replace Caravelles.

371

goods were cheap. Trade, they say, follows the flag. In this case, the roles were reversed. The sheer momentum of Taiwan's export trade helped to put the country back on the map and into the international halls of respectability.

Echoing this movement, China Airlines leased a Boeing 747 in June 1975, and put it on the trans-Pacific route, with standards of service that matched those of pace-setters such as Japan Air Lines. In October of that year, an agreement was signed, significantly by non-government negotiators, to resume flights between Japan and Taiwan. The crisis with Japan had cost CAL dearly, conservatively $10 million in lost revenues, but it now hastened to recover, adding Fukuoka as a third Japanese point in July 1976, and resuming service to Seoul, Korea, via Fukuoka, almost directly en route. So as to avoid confrontations with the Chinese airline from Beijing, CAL operated into Tokyo's Haneda Airport, instead of the new Narita; but this was no bad thing, as Haneda was much more convenient to down-town Tokyo and the satellite cities of Yokohama and Kawasaki.

The commerce and the political leanings of Taiwan were always to the east, across the Pacific, to the ever-friendly United States. Relations with Europe ranged from cautious acceptance to frigid hostility. In 1975, however, CAL began to feel its way westwards. On 3 January of that year, Taiwan and Jordan signed a provisional air transport agreement for the benefit of both countries. The airlines of the two countries met at Bangkok, where passengers, mail, and freight could change aircraft for a through route between Taipei and Amman. But little came of this, and Jordan it was that changed, setting up an alliance with Air Siam. More concrete was the agreement with Saudi Arabia, signed on 27 February 1976, which allowed through flights by both CAL and Saudia, via Hong Kong, Singapore, and a point in India, between Taipei and Jeddah. During the same month, Chang Lin-teh took over the presidency of the airline from Ben Chow, who had guided its fortunes through thick and thin since its entry into commercial air service. The thick had been very thick: an 80 percent growth in the two years 1972–73; but the thin had been equally emphatic: almost 40 percent decline in 1974–75. Chang came in at a good time. The figures for 1976 showed a 65 percent increase over those of 1975, and China Airlines was back on the road to full recovery.

In April 1977 China Airlines began nonstop Tokyo—San Francisco services with a Boeing 747SP. (*Boeing*)

372

In July 1978 China Airlines ordered four Airbus A300B4-200s, the last being delivered in July 1983. (*Airbus*)

In April 1977 it put one long-haul Boeing 747SP on to the trans-Pacific route, nonstop from Tokyo to San Francisco, on a twice-weekly frequency that originated in Hong Kong, and one frequency that terminated in Los Angeles. Three Boeing 737s had been added for the mainline domestic and the shorter regional routes, and the YS-11s and Caravelles were being retired. On 28 July 1978 CAL signed a Letter of Intent to buy four Airbus A300B4-200 wide-bodied twin-jets from the European consortium, and there was some suspicion that this choice may have been connected with the offer of European traffic rights. Simultaneously an agreement was signed with Luxembourg to allow flights by Luxair and Cargolux to Taipei, to cope with the ever-increasing volume of air cargo destined for Europe. With such progress, with increasing security over its own destiny, CAL was able to shrug off the news that, on 15 December 1978, the United States finally recognized the PRC as the Government of China.

China Airlines Around the World

In 1980 China Airlines suffered its first financial loss in its 21-year history. Although not affecting the total balance sheet very much, this was the year when surface transport in Taiwan made a substantial improvement. Most of the island's population was concentrated on the coastal strip along the western side, along which a succession of industrial cities accounted for the nation's wealth. Through this near-megalopolis, the railway was electrified and considerably improved, and a new express highway built to relieve the traffic congestion – and to decrease the need for local air transport. The financial figures were of no consequence, in the light of CAL's future potential, both in passenger and freight traffic; and in spite of the problems imposed by the political intransigence in Taipei, it expanded its world-wide network. During 1980, it extended its all-cargo service to the United States with a route to Los Angeles, via Fairbanks, Alaska; service to Okinawa was resumed; and some Jeddah flights were re-routed via Singapore. In January 1981 the cargo service was extended to New York, and with Anchorage replacing Fairbanks in August of that year, the demand for Taiwanese products was such that many extra sections were flown.

On 10 May 1982 CAL achieved its goal of opening a service to Europe, to show

China Airlines operated two leased Airbus A320s. (*Airbus Industrie*)

the flag of the Republic of China (ROC) in that continent, albeit in one of the smallest countries, Luxembourg. The all-cargo route stopped at Singapore and Dubai westbound, and Jeddah and Dubai eastbound. Then, on 12 April 1984, the New York route was extended to Amsterdam, to complete a round-the-world service for passengers, mail and freight; and special stamps were issued in Taipei to mark the occasion.China Airlines has always been severely handicapped by the political estrangement of Taiwan from the community of nations throughout the world. When the People's Republic was admitted to the United Nations in 1971, the Republic of China, i.e. Taiwan, was actually expelled, which was the international equivalent of expelling an unruly child from school. During the mid-1980s, when the airlines of the Orient were galloping along, and trying to keep pace with the burgeoning economies of all the countries from Korea to Indonesia, CAL was unable to benefit from the normal freedoms, not least because any nation signing up through bilateral air agreements for mutual flights or services stood the danger of the PRC's displeasure, and possible ostracism. At the height of a travel boom, in 1987, only seventeen nations in the world recognized the ROC, and many of these were not exactly large traffic generators.

Potentially, the biggest single market for air travel was just across the Taiwan Straits to the mainland of China, where the two million emigrant refugees of 1949 still had relatives to visit and ancestors' graves to tend. As the confrontational mood between the two Chinas mellowed into a gentler form of peaceful coexistence, travel opportunities increased. In 1988, 200,000 Taiwanese visited the mainland; but unfortunately this helped China Airlines only in a limited manner. For it could not fly direct to China, only to connecting points such as Hong Kong or Tokyo, whence they were carried to Guangzhou, Xiamen, Fuzhou, Shanghai or Beijing by other airlines.

Even the Tiananmen Square student riots and the ruthless suppression by the police and the armed forces on 3–4 June 1989 did not stop the flow of Taiwanese visitors back to their roots. By 1990 an estimated 750,000 were making the trip, a travel bonanza that must have been frustrating in the extreme to China Airlines, whose network of world routes was flimsy by comparison with those of its neighbours. Considering all the circumstances, with so many deterrents that would not normally affect an airline's policy, China Airlines deserves much credit for surviving in an inhospitable environment; and its management – sometimes, in the past,

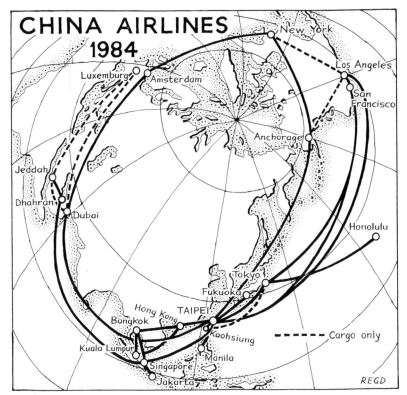

Map 28b. China Airlines, 1984
Although founded in 1959, China Airlines did not flex its muscles until the demise of CAT in 1968, by which time it had begun regional services in parallel with its rival. it began trans-Pacific service in 1970, but promptly ran into difficulties because of China's admission to the United Nations in 1971, and Taiwan's insistence that it was also the true China resulted in political and commercial problems everywhere. Nevertheless, by astute negotiation, China Airlines fashioned a network that, by 1984, achieved round-the-world status – one of the few airlines in history to have achieved that distinction.

referred to as the Retired Generals' Club – has performed well, never resorting to desperate measures such as self-destructive fare-cutting, and maintaining its dignity through the years. It has also maintained an excellent standard of service, as anyone who has enjoyed the luxury of its *Dynasty Class*, introduced on 1 April 1984, can testify.

Taiwan Shuttle Service

The opportunities for domestic air transport on the island of Taiwan would not, at first glance at the map, appear to be extensive. The oval-shaped land is less than 250 miles long from north to south; two-thirds of the area consists of barren or forested mountains; and the eastern, or Pacific, coast is only sparsely inhabited. Along the western side, the coastal plain accounts for almost all the population,

375

which has been served by a railway since the beginning of the century, after the Japanese acquisition. With the great influx of Chinese immigrants in 1949, the swelling numbers needed good surface communications; and these were put on the priority list by the Kuomintang government-in-exile as an essential step towards self-reliance in a modern industrial society. Even with improvements in the track and the rolling stock, including electrification, of the railway, however, plus the construction of high-speed express roads, the pressures were so great that the airline business thrived. A discerning public preferred the comparative serenity of the airliner to the crowded trains and the congested freeways. Also, for all the improvements, the journey time between Taipei, the capital in the north, and Kaohsiung, the southern port and industrial city that had grown with great speed after 1949, was too long and too uncomfortable, five hours by train.

On the other hand, the Taipei—Kaohsiung inter-city route, at only 200 miles, was close to the minimum distance at which an airline can reasonably hope to break even; so that although the traffic potential was considerable, an airline would be hard pressed to sustain the operation and keep its accounts out of the red. And, of the several city pairs – and the coastal plain contains four other urban concentrations of about a million inhabitants each – Taipei–Kaohsiung is the longest. Consequently, the competition to operate the routes has never gone through the fierce stages that have sometimes characterized inter-city air routes. While China Airlines was happy to take over the routes when CAT fell into political disfavour, it did not cling on to them with the determined zeal that might normally have been expected. In fact, it concentrated on the more remunerative international routes, and did not complain too much when another airline campaigned for, and was granted permission to operate in parallel within Taiwan.

In August 1957 a rich businessman, T C Hwoo, founded Far Eastern Air Transport (FAT), together with K T Siao and two brothers in the Chinese Air Force. Operations had already begun on an ad hoc basis, with Beech 18s, between Taipei and the southern cities, in October 1955. FAT concentrated on the Taipei—Kaohsiung route, and by 1960 was operating Douglas DC-3s. A fleet of seven were acquired, and these were used also for cargo, and some were leased to Air Vietnam. Later, as they were superseded by propeller-turbine types, they were used almost entirely for delivering early-morning newspapers.

With surface transport still awaiting improvements in the 1960s, the traffic grew healthily. Fifty-seat Handley Page Dart Heralds were put into service on 21 February 1966, and 80-seat Douglas DC-6Bs, purchased from Ansett in Australia, for cash, soon followed, on 12 March 1967. Then, in April 1970, the first of a fleet of nine Viscount 800 Series, mostly bought, once again, from Australia, replaced the DC-6Bs and the DC-3s, which were chartered to Air Vietnam for military support in the war that was being waged there. The Dart Heralds, however, remained in service, on the east coast route, where the demand was lower. In April 1974, FAT introduced Caravelles, but quickly found that these too had to be replaced in favour of larger aircraft, and the first Boeing 737, with 128 seats, went into service in June 1976. In less than twenty years, the Taipei—Kaohsiung route had grown from an eight-seat Beech 18 to an aircraft fifteen times larger.

In addition to obtaining aircraft from Australia, T C Hwoo may have gleaned the idea of controlled, rather than cut-throat competition. For he and China Airlines appeared to have agreed to share the spoils – and presumably the operating costs – of the domestic routes. The record was marred in August 1981, when a 737 crashed into the sea with the loss of 105 lives; but by 1982 FAT was oper-

Far Eastern Air Transport introduced 128-passenger Boeing 737s in June 1976.

ating an all-jet fleet, just the one type, the Boeing 737s. It shared the busy route between the north and south metropolises with China Airlines, each company operating seven round trips a day. T C Hwoo died in 1987, and left no will. The Government appointed H I Chiang as the administrator of FAT, pending a legal settlement, and by this time Taiwan's 'second force' airline was carrying two million passengers every year – and this in a country smaller than Switzerland, and just as mountainous.

Taiwan Third Level

Two other small airlines deserve recognition for their community service, both in the social aspects of that term, in providing communication with outlying and remote areas, and in the more popular aspects – that of carrying holiday traffic. In January 1966 Yung Shing (literally, Forever Prosperous) Airlines was founded by U T Wei, at first equipped with helicopters, for agricultural crop-spraying, but also with one Britten-Norman Islander. Ten years later, he was able to take advantage of more liberal local regulations to use this Islander to start a scheduled service, from Taichung, Taiwan's third largest city, to Makung, in the Pescadores

FAT was also a user of the Fokker F.27 Friendship.

377

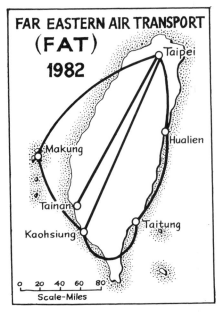

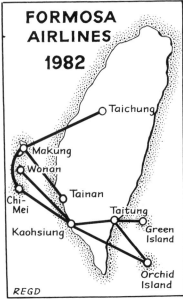

Maps 28c. The Feeder Airlines of Taiwan

Although only a small island – less than half the size of Ireland – Taiwan's teeming population of 20 million, almost all of it crammed along the western coastline, has demanded an efficient air transport system. Thus, in addition to the trunk international flag carriers (first CAT, then China Airlines), Taiwan has had a second-line carrier, FAT, which has connected the larger cities; together with third-level companies that have served the smaller offshore islands. Formosa Airlines, portrayed in this map, is one of several in the latter category.

Islands, some 30 miles offshore, in the Taiwan Straits. Business declined, however, after the initial response, even after a second route was added from Tainan.

On 15 July 1978 Y L Wang, a former banker, took over the airline, and began to rebuild it, renaming it Formosa Airlines, recalling the name given to the island by the early Spanish explorers. He bought another Islander and three Cessna 404s, small single-engined aircraft normally used for executive flying, but the right size for this local need. Service was expanded to Makung from Kaohsiung, and the other Pescadores islands, Chi-Mei and Wonan, were also connected to the southern city. Additionally, routes were opened from Taitung, on the southeast coast, to Green Island and Orchid Island, thirty or forty miles offshore. The latter island was inhabited by a non-Chinese race speaking a language more akin to dialects spoken in the Philippines, and their customs and life-style, together with the natural beauty of Orchid Island, attracted many visitors from the Taiwan 'mainland'. Formosa Airlines seemed to thrive, for it introduced a 19-seat Dornier 228 on 11 February 1983, and later built up the fleet with a Shorts 360 and 37-seat SAAB 340s. By 1990 it was operating the largest commuter network in Taiwan, on 16 of the 22 domestic routes, but was running into financial troubles, sufficient to precipitate an employee strike – rare in this part of the world.

378

Formosa Airlines' fleet included Saab 340s (illustrated) and Short 360s.

Formosa's main competitor at the lowest stratum of air routes in Taiwan was one that identified itself closely with its locale. Taiwan Airlines was founded on 1 April 1966 by Tu Fuan Lan, mainly as an agent for foreign airlines, but it also owned a DC-3, which it used for charter flights. On 26 June 1970, it began scheduled flights from Taitung to Orchid Island, using a Cessna 206, so that it preceded Formosa on this interesting route, and was given the authority to do so at the Government's request, as a social service to the Yamis, an aboriginal people of Buddhist faith. Service expanded, to Green Island, and from Kaohsiung as well as Taitung; and with Britten-Norman Islanders and Trislanders, duplicated the routes of Formosa Airlines to the Pescadores. Originally the Taiwan Airlines Aviation Company, it shortened its name in 1973, and was known as TAC; and after some years of local 'third level' competition with Formosa, biding its time, it began to prepare for an explosive expansion.

Poised for a Reunion

As Taiwan entered the 1990s, all the elements for continued airline growth were present. The economy and export trade flourished; the Government was following the world-wide trend, sparked off in 1978 in the United States, to deregulate the airlines, and so the competition would further stimulate airline activity; domestic travel, even, would still be a factor, as the busy railway could not provide adequate service, in comfort, convenience, or speed. These were good cards in the airlines' hands; and now another one seemed to rise to the top of the pack, awaiting the draw.

There were signs that further easing of controls and a softening of the political climate between mainland China and offshore Taiwan might reach the stage whereby direct air service would be permitted to start. For China Airlines, this would reduce the demand for capacity to Hong Kong and Tokyo; but would be handsomely compensated for by an unprecedented order book for tickets to a dozen places in China. For the other airlines of Taiwan, with few limitations on their freedom of access to the potential market, blue skies lay ahead.

The incumbent domestic operators recognized that, if not actually directed to operate to designated destinations, the bulk of the market would go to China Airlines. The international flag carrier had the equipment, the experience, and the political clout to ensure that the routes to the major cities on the mainland, Shanghai, Beijing and Guangzhou, would be added to its route map immediately the barrier was raised. But there were many other Chinese destinations where the pickings would be substantial. The cities of Fuzhou and Xiamen (Amoy), in Fujian Province, with the latter point declared a special duty-free economic zone by Beijing, were only 200 miles away across the Taiwan Straits. And a dozen other cities, such as Chungking and Chengdu, in Szechwan, Wuhan in Hubei, and Changsha in Hunan, awaited direct airline service both for business links and to reunite families.

A Different Kind of Flag

The term flag carrier has come into general use to denote the airline that, whether totally or partially owned by a State or nation, or chosen by such a State or nation to represent its interests, is identified as an instrument of the political policy of that State. Thus, the late great Pan American Airways, though always privately-owned (in a country that regarded State ownership as worse than sacrilege) was nevertheless the acknowledged flag-carrier of the United States, which accepted the synonymous term 'chosen instrument'. While such recognition sometimes caused political controversy within the home country that adopted such a policy, it usually made little difference to a destination country, whose main concern was simply that any airline, State-owned or private, should follow the regulations and requirements as requested.

Taiwan was different. Divorced from mainland China after a bitter civil war, and the refuge of a political party and its followers who had evacuated from their homeland in 1949, the island that was formerly Chinese and, during most of the 20th Century, a territory of Japan, was once again nominally liberated. But the Communists under Mao Tse-tung had never set foot on it, as the remnants of the Kuomintang under Chiang Kai-shek had stubbornly established themselves to such an extent that it became a *de facto* government, to such an extent that, during the early years of the 1950s and 1960s, it defiantly declared itself to be the seat of government of the whole of China. As time went on, however, the very idea of the 20 million or so inhabitants of Taiwan (not all of whom were Kuomintang anyway) gaining control of the thousand million people on the mainland wore thin. Beijing and Taipei could never come to terms with each other, and for decades were not on speaking terms. But one thing they did agree on: Taiwan was a Province of China. The problem was: which capital was the home of the flag carrier, or the chosen instrument, of China?

Taipei and Beijing still agree to disagree over this issue, one that will prevail until the two Governments ever resolve their differences, an outcome that seems unlikely in the foreseeable future. The State-owned CAAC had always been the representative of Beijing, and until recently virtually an arm of the Government itself; the jointly-owned China Airlines, with the Taiwan Government holding a stake and private investors heavily involved, represented Taiwan overseas.

The Beijing Government has always taken a tough stand on the representation issue. Any country that permitted its official airline – flag carrier, chosen instrument, whatever – to serve Taipei automatically forfeited its right to serve any point on the Chinese mainland. Countries that wished to establish close commercial relations with the People's Republic had to be very careful about their relations with Taiwan. The delicacy of the air transport situation was not much of an issue until the 'bamboo curtain' that isolated mainland China from the rest of the world was lifted towards the end of the 1970s; and then special solutions had to be found.

In the case of Japan, in a masterly example of commercial tight-rope walking, the dominant airline of Asia, Japan Air Lines, found the answer. In 1975 (*see* Chapter 35) it founded Japan Asia Airways as a subsidiary whose sole objective was to provide an air link between Tokyo and Taipei, and whose aircraft would never corrupt the soil of the mainland by daring to touch down in Beijing.

Fifteen years later, the same set of circumstances presented itself in Taiwan, where China Airlines was unable to expand its services overseas because too many nations were faced with the choice of serving either Beijing (or other points in the PRC) *or* Taipei (or other points in Taiwan) but not both. Invariably they chose Beijing and the enormous potential of an emergent China to such an extent that, for all its energetic and wholly commendable drive and initiative, Taiwan was becoming an outcast in the world of airlines.

Things came to a head in the late 1980s, and almost reached crisis point by 1990. Clearly the surging economy generated by the industrious Taiwanese Chinese justified considerable expansion of the overseas air network. Furthermore, the relaxation of Government travel restrictions released a pent-up traffic demand that had to be reconciled with available capacity. In 1990 the number of passengers travelling to the United States alone increased to 257,000, and unprecedented 63 percent increase over the previous year's figure.

The Taiwanese solution was not quite parallel to that of Japan. The new airline that was created to plug the many international gaps in the air map had nothing to do with China Airlines. It was formed by the Evergreen marine and investment company, one of the largest sea freight container shipping lines in the world, and owned by the Chang Yung-fa family. With vast financial resources, this shipping conglomerate founded Eva Airways, to trade as Eva Air, at the end of 1990; and to show that it was jumping into the arena with both feet, it placed orders for fourteen McDonnell Douglas MD-11s and eight Boeing 747-400s for its long-haul routes, and four Boeing 767-300ERs for its regional routes.

Eva Air began service with a flourish on 1 July 1991, with the four 767s, plus two more leased from Great Britain, from Taipei to six east Asian cities: Jakarta, Bangkok, Penang, Seoul, Kuala Lumpur and Singapore. Almost overnight, Eva Air had established a presence along the whole of the Pacific Rim, one that was augmented within a few months by routes to Manila, Vientiane, Ho Chi Minh City and Malé (Maldives), and the opening of a second Taiwan gateway at Kaohsiung.

On 12 December 1992 the Evergreen house flag flew at Los Angeles, when Eva opened service with Boeing 747-400s, the latest of that great line of wide-bodied airliners, and in this case including a 142-seat 'economy deluxe' cabin, a contradiction in terms that did not worry the clientele who could enjoy more generous seat pitch and width than those of the other trans-Pacific competitors.

The rules of the People's Republic of China (PRC) v Republic of China (ROC), i.e. Taiwan, had been bent a little in the case of the United States, where the mutual understanding was that the two flag-carriers did not serve the same destination. There were many gateways into the USA, several of which were of special interest to the Chinese, of whatever origin, because of large emigrant enclaves in the so-called Chinatowns in various cities. Thus China Airlines of Taipei served San Francisco, and CAAC, now Air China, served New York. But Taiwan was poorly represented in Europe, and had never had an air service to the biggest

One of TransAsia Airways Airbus A320s. The red, gold and black stripes on the top of the fuselage are unusual and repeat the tail markings. (*Airbus Industrie*)

international hub, London, entirely because the British Government had been one of the first to recognize the legitimacy of Peking (Beijing) in 1957, which automatically made Taipei ineligible for a place on the British Airways map.

Now at last, Eva Air was able to circumvent the hitherto essential transfer from one airline to another at Hong Kong, for all travellers wishing to go to the United Kingdom. On 29 March it began service, direct from Taipei to London via Bangkok, which it already served, and Vienna, with a Boeing 767-300ER (Extended Range). In a reciprocal move, British Asia Airways, a British Airways subsidiary, began London—Taipei service via Hong Kong, the next day. This transparent evasion of political realities drew no protest from Beijing.

Soon afterwards, Eva showed its flag, following delivery of its third Boeing 747-400, in Seattle and New York, starting service on 8 June 1993. Evergreen was spreading its wings, and spreading its corporate insignia to some of the key points on the world's air network: Los Angeles, London, New York; and there was more to come. In so doing, it was transforming Taiwan's stature in the world of airline nations from that of an outcast to become one of the international fraternity.

The success of Eva Air in entering the commercial airline fray must have encouraged others. For a small company, Foshing Airlines, which for many years had hovered within the status of irregular non-scheduled operations (and was sometimes apparently dormant), suddenly emerged in 1992, renamed TransAsia Airlines, as a jet operator. With Airbus A320s, it began a shuttle service – eight a day – between Taipei and Tainan, with three a day between Taipei and Kinmen; and offered charter flights to Manila, Cebu (Philippines) and to Phnom Penh (Cambodia).

CHAPTER TWENTY-NINE

Airline of a Revolution

A New Start

The fortunes of China's airlines at the end of the Second World War have been described in the previous two chapters. The German-sponsored Eurasia had ceased to exist; the US-supported CNAC and the Chinese CATC fled with the Kuomintang to Taiwan at the end of 1949; only Hamiata, the Sino-Soviet airline that maintained a flimsy air link across northwest China, through Sinkiang, to Alma Ata, survived the revolution that, on 1 October 1949, saw the People's Republic of China (PRC) proclaimed in Peking. On 2 November, the new administration established an airline to fill the void in southern China. The China Civil Aviation Administration (CCAC) quickly started services – though these must have been operated on an ad hoc basis – on twelve routes, linking Peking with the southern cities of Hankow, Chungking, Kunming and Canton. The equipment was an improvised collection of aircraft left behind by the departing airlines – but most of this had been flown to Hong Kong, and placed in the care of the British.

The legal complications that led eventually to most of the Hong Kong refugee aircraft finally ending up in the United States are described in Chapter 28, and mention was made of some of the grounded aircraft being flown back to China. The subsequent fate of this small squadron of commercial air transports is interesting, almost an adventure story. Many of the crew members of CNAC were not particularly politically minded, and many were prepared to take their chances with the Communists as much as with the Nationalists. They were disenchanted with the rampant corruption at all levels, and they were dissatisfied with the unfairly low pay scales. The all-Chinese CATC paid four times the rate as the US-controlled CNAC. A group of these aircrew decided that, politics and civil war apart, they were Chinese, and so were the aircraft, and the capital of China was Peking.

On 9 November 1949, therefore, eight C-47s, three C-46s, and one Convair 240, pride of the CATC fleet, were surreptitiously fuelled up, and, led by Pan Guaoding, flown to Tientsin, the port city for Peking. Later on, no less than 2,800 crew and technicians followed, bringing with them valuable spare parts, maintenance manuals, and other items to support the aircraft, which had already been loaded up with as much equipment as they could carry.

Somewhat apprehensive as to the reception they would receive, the little civil armada actually arrived in triumph. Chinese Premier Chou En-lai welcomed the group and hosted a great banquet at the Peking Hotel (then still called the Grand Hotel du Pekin des Wagon Lits), and the next month, Chou ordered the formation of an airline for the People's Republic. The lone Convair 240 became the flagship of the line, and was named *Beijing*, with Chairman Mao himself writing the stylized calligraphy for the aircraft's paint scheme.

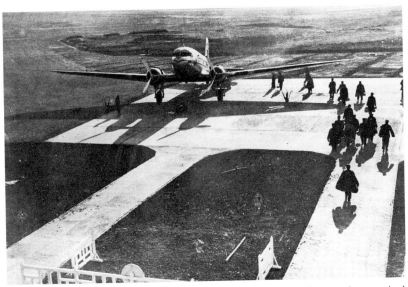

When the People's Republic of China began airline operations its fleet mostly comprised Douglas DC-3s and Curtiss C-46s. Passengers are seen embarking on a DC-3, most likely at Peking (Beijing).

SKOAGA

With Soviet help, the Civil Aviation Bureau was first established at the beginning of 1950. Nominally under the Ministry of Communications (which had always played a part in airline development since 1927) it was in practice controlled by a high-level military committee. Having just won a civil war, the PRC had no illusions about the Kuomintang's efforts to win the support of the United States to mount an invasion of the southeastern coast; and it rightly regarded aviation as a whole, commercial and military, as a complementary arm of the defence forces.

On 27 March 1950 the operating airline came into being. The Chinese name was Ren Ming Hong Kong Kun Sze, but it was more commonly known by the Russian acronym, SKOAGA (sometimes shortened to SKOGA) which, in Russian, stood for Sovietsko-Kitaysko Aktsioneren Obschestvo Grazhdanskoi Aviatsii. The English translation was the Sino-Soviet Joint Stock Company. The stock was held in equal amounts, 50 percent each. It took over Hamiata, the similarly-owned joint airline that had been founded as a wartime expedient, and Hamiata's fleet of Lisunov Li-2s, the Soviet-built ubiquitous DC-3 'Gooney Birds', passed to SKOAGA. The Soviet airline, Aeroflot, provided technical assistance for its new-found fellow-communist airline that now operated around the southern perimeter of its own Siberian network.

Rather as in the past, when Eurasia had tended to serve northern China, and CNAC had served the central and the south, the same spheres-of-influence arrangement prevailed. SKOAGA took care of the north, CCAC spread its wings in the south. In the north, SKOAGA regained the airways of Manchuria, and by reaching across the border, established a foreign route to Chita, a staging point on

384

Maintenance in progress on one of the Curtiss C-46 fleet of the PRC airline in its early period.

Aeroflot's trans-Siberian network, and thus a direct air connection between Peking and Moscow. To the northwest, the old Hamiata route was maintained to Alma Ata. In the south, CCAC began a service on 1 August 1950 northwards from Canton to Hankow (which, with Wuchang and Henyang, became the tri-city of Wuhan); and on to Tientsin; then, from this strategic point on the Yangtse River, a link to Szechwan, at Chungking and Chengtu. There seems to have been some manoeuvring during the early 1950s, as the formation of a China People's Aviation Company was announced on 17 July 1952. SKOAGA was gradually maturing, to provide essential links with what, at the time, was China's Big Brother; and extended its route to Siberia so as to terminate at the important city of Irkutsk, starting in December 1952. A few months later, it reached out to China's far west, by extending a branch from the old Hamiata route at Urumchi (Tihwa) to Kashgar (Kashi). This was quite a branch. The distance of the extension alone is about 1,200 miles, or half the width of the United States.

Minhaiduy

Then, in March 1954, an important merger took place. SKOAGA and CCAC merged to form, under the general jurisdiction of the China Civil Aviation Bureau, the Zhongua Ming Hong Jui (which appears to have been transliterated briefly as Minhaiduy). There were six major regional bureaux, at Peking, Shanghai, Guangzhou, Shenyang, Si'an and Wuhan, with sub-bureaux at Chungking and Lanchow. The fleet was almost entirely composed of a mixture of US-built

DC-3s and Soviet-built DC-3s, the latter being the Lisunov Li-2s. Soon afterwards, the first Ilyushin Il-12s and Il-14s began to arrive from Moscow. The new national airline was placed under the command of Kuang Jen-nung, who had been a Lieut-General in the Korean War, flying MiG-15s.

Cautiously the new airline began to feel its way as the national flag carrier, but its freedom was closely restricted to friendly neighbours, of communist or near-communist persuasion. Otherwise, it was a hostile world. On 11 April 1956, the first trans-border route (other than to the USSR) was opened, from Kunming to Rangoon, via Mandalay, with an Ilyushin 14. Curiously, this was closely parallel to the first trans-border route made by its prewar predecessor, CNAC, but in entirely different circumstances. On 29 May 1956, a second route, from Guangzhou (Canton) to Hanoi, via Nanning, found another friendly destination; and on 3 April 1959, the third route, from Beijing to Pyongyang, North Korea, via Shenyang, completed China's air links with its political allies.

By the late 1950s CAAC had no less than fifty-eight Ilyushin Il-14s, many built in China.

Interestingly, both of the last-named routes were opened with the Lisunov Li-2, a design that went back to 1935, so that, at this time, the People's Republic was not giving top priority to showing the flag overseas. It had more important things to do. One of Chairman Mao's main objectives on assuming power was to unify the country, which, since the domination of the Manchus, had steadily fallen apart. The colonists (*see* Chapter 26) had effectively divided up the land into spheres of exploitable interest; the war lords had followed suit during the 1920s, and even Chiang Kai-shek's Kuomintang had never gained complete control over more than about a quarter of China, mainly in the coastal areas and along the Yangtse River. Mao realized that the key to unification was good communication, and he allocated the highest priority to a massive programme of railway construction. By feats of engineering that may have been matched, but never surpassed, in the whole world, hundreds of thousands of construction gangs laid thousands of miles of track, year after year. Szechwan (Sichuan) was finally linked with the outside world (other than by riverboat down the Yangtse Gorge or by air) when, in 1956, the Si'an—Chengtu rail link was completed; and in a time span of only two decades, every provincial capital and major city were linked with Peking (Beijing) and with each other. Only Lhasa, in the almost impenetrable remoteness of the high plateau of Tibet, and almost 12,000 ft above sea level, was denied the privilege of cheap rail travel to the rest of China.

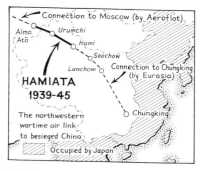

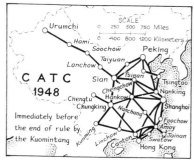

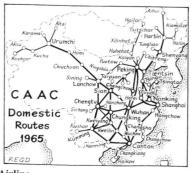

Maps 29a Emergence of a Chinese National Airline
A little-known contribution to the Chinese cause during the Second World War was by the
airline formed jointly by Chinese and Soviet interests. Hamiata, as it was generally known,
operated from Alma Ata, in Kazakhstan, to Hami, in Northwest China, whence it connected
with surface routes and with the German-sponsored Eurasia. After the war, under the
Kuomintang regime, the Chinese airline, CATC, operated in parallel and in competition with
the US-sponsored CNAC, but both were terminated by the Communist victory in 1949 the
first two state airlines, SKOGA and CCAC, served the People's Republic (the PRC) but
these merged into a single State airline, CAAC (the Civil Aviation Administration of China)
in 1954.

With such emphasis being given to railway construction, the Civil Aviation
Bureau had to play second fiddle, including its place in the budget appropriations
pecking order. Another of Mao's priorities was to build up China's military
strength, including that of the Air Force; and in the pursuance of this goal, and
with technical help from the Soviets, aircraft factories were built and aircraft
production initiated, almost entirely in the construction of Soviet designs, under
Soviet licence agreements. At least the airline benefitted from the aviation
programme, so that, by the late 1950s, it had a fleet of twenty-eight Lisunov
Li-2s, most of them built in China; five Ilyushin Il-12s from the USSR; fifty-eight
Ilyushin Il-14s, many of them Chinese-built; and no less than 300 Antonov An-2s,
that sturdy little maid-of-all-work single-engined biplane, and of which about two-
thirds were built in China. Also, some Czech Aero 45s, and Soviet Yakovlev
Yak-12s and Yak-18s completed the fleet for training and communications work.

With this adequate but old-fashioned fleet, Minhaiduy built up a network of
routes that served the whole country; but the service provided bore little compar-

ison with an air service in the West. While a route map and a timetable existed, most flights were made according to local demand, and this was restricted, almost by definition, to administrators, Communist dignitaries, and bureaucrats. Air traffic control was rudimentary, and flights were cancelled at the slightest indication of bad weather; for navigational aids were all but non-existent. The same applied to reservations and ticketing, which was a ponderous, almost primitive system. The Civil Aviation Bureau was coy about publishing information or statistics, merely reporting, in 1958, that the network had doubled in length in five years to 26,000 km (16,000 miles); the number of routes to 29; and the number of cities served to 42. Interestingly, two of the new points served were Fuyang, from Hofei; and Sining, from Lanchow, both with the diminutive An-2, which came into service at the end of 1955. Of one aspect of airline operation, however, it could be well satisfied: it had a 100 percent safety record, at least reportedly so.

One of the large CAAC fleet of Il-14s, seen at Guangzhou. (*Gordon S Williams*)

Changing Friendships

By now almost entirely dependent upon Soviet aircraft, either imported or built under licence, China's airline suffered a setback during the early 1960s as relations between Peking and Moscow deteriorated. This was an ideological conflict, and concerned differing views of the application of communist political theory, especially in what China's Marxist fundamentalists viewed as betrayal, if not party treason, when the Soviet Union, under Khrushchev, steered away from the strict orthodoxy of Stalinist principles. Such was the vehemence of the opposing sides that the Soviet Union withdrew thousands of people who had been sent to China

A Yun-5 (An-2) at Xi'an in 1985 after being retired by CAAC from scheduled service.
(*R E G Davies*)

as advisers, and these included a large number of aircraft industry technicians.The Chinese, under Russian tutelage, had been learning how to install and to operate heavy industry and manufacturing, but it still had a long way to go. By 1960, however, it was able to build its own jet fighters and bombers, but apart from basic types such as the DC-3/Li-2, its progress in the production of commercial aircraft had been limited to the little Antonov An-2 and a few Antonov An-14s. Fortunately, the ties with the Soviet Union had not been shattered completely, as, pragmatically, China was still able to import some four-engined Ilyushin Il-18s, a couple of Antonov An-24s, two Tupolev Tu-124 jets and five of the large Mil Mi-6 helicopters. But this came later, and meanwhile, the airline had to do something to avoid the charge that its equipment was beginning to look positively mediaeval.

Trading with what was then considered to be the capitalist arch-enemy, the United States, was out of the question. But fortuitously, relations with Great Britain were improving, even though the Chinese history books still emphasized strongly the injustices and the inequities of the Opium Wars and the Unequal Treaties. For in 1957, Britain had initiated the first cautious moves towards loosening trade embargoes with China; and, in lieu of an Embassy or Consulate, China was able to find a presence in London in the form of a Commercial and Cultural Office. In 1961, after much behind-closed-doors negotiation, the China Civil Aviation Bureau ordered six Vickers Viscount Series 843s. With these four-engined propeller-turbine airliners, China could, at last, move into a new age of technology.

CAAC Begins to Regain Lost Ground

In April 1962 the Civil Aviation Bureau became the Civil Aviation Administration of China (CAAC), under which name it was to operate during the next thirty years. During the next decade great strides were made both at home and abroad. Within China, services were improved when, in 1965, twenty Ilyushin Il-18s were acquired to supplement the six Viscounts that had entered service in 1963. These 100-seat aircraft became, as they had already done in the Soviet Union, the main-

389

Capital Airport, Beijing, during the latter part of the 1950s. On the apron are a Lisunov Li-2 (DC-3) and two Il-14s of CAAC and in the foreground is an Aeroflot Tupolev Tu-104.

line workhorses of the fleet, flying the vital routes between all the big cities. One of the Il-18s was selected and modified as Chou En-lai's personal aircraft, to be used for diplomatic missions overseas. These journeys were not too frequent as China still did not have too many friends, although it was beginning to strike up some non-belligerent acquaintanceships. One of these was with Cambodia (Kampuchea) where Prince Norodom Sihanouk attempted a neutral position in the involved squabbles in Indo-China, and a direct air link was opened between Canton and Phnom Penh, in 1964.

Cambodia's Royal Air Cambodge was preceded as a foreign airline entrant into China only by Aeroflot and the North Korean airline, both friendly neighbours. In that same year, however, a far more important airline was to show its flag in Peking. On 29 April, Pakistan International Airlines (PIA) opened a service from Karachi, via the East Wing of Pakistan at Dacca, and Canton (Guangzhou) to Shanghai. Not only was this the first foreign airline from the West. It was a jet operator and the PIA Boeing 707s were the first western jet aircraft to be seen at

A much changed Beijing Airport, in 1981. (*Gordon S Williams*)

390

Six Vickers-Armstrongs Viscount 843s delivered to CAAC in the winter of 1963–4 were among the last nine Viscounts built. (*R E G Davies*).

Twenty Ilyushin Il-18s were imported for CAAC in 1965, one is seen at Beijing in 1981. (*Gordon S Williams*)

The staff of CAAC at Xi'an were very proud of Ilyushin Il-18 B-208 because it was always used by Chou En-lai. (*R E G Davies*)

a Chinese airport. (Later on, in 1971, when East Pakistan broke free to create Bangladesh, PIA had to re-route its aircraft via Colombo, Sri Lanka). Some reports suggested that Pakistan had achieved this airline scoop because it had agreed to purchase some Chinese-built MiG fighter aircraft, and there may have been some substance to this.

At the beginning of 1964, France recognized the People's Republic of China and established diplomatic relations. In a cause-and-effect relationship, Air France opened a Boeing 707 Paris—Shanghai service, via Athens, Cairo, Karachi and Phnom Penh, on 20 September 1966. At last, China had a direct air link with Europe; but many years were to pass before its own airline was able to reciprocate.

Five Ilyushin Il-62s were ordered for CAAC in 1970.

CAAC Enters The Jet Age

The Chinese airline had much more ground to make up, other than by introducing propeller-turbine aircraft on its domestic routes, and being able to observe the first jet airliners close at hand. But it made a start, still reluctant, however, to go to the production lines of the United States for its aircraft purchases. It ordered five Ilyushin Il-62 four-engined jets from Moscow in 1970, and simultaneously struck a deal with Pakistan to buy PIA's four Hawker Siddeley Trident 1Es, which had been operating out of Karachi for several years. This was almost certainly a straight swop for a squadron of Chinese MiG-19s for the Pakistan Air Force. In 1970 also, CAAC introduced the Antonov An-24 for its secondary routes, and these were to perform solidly for the next twenty years.

On 13 May 1971 the first Ilyushin Il-62 made its first revenue passenger flight, on a nonstop Peking—Canton (Beijing—Guangzhou) routeing, thus dispensing with the almost mandatory stop at Wuhan (formerly Hankow) which had become a crossing point and way-station for all of the mainline inter-city links in the domestic heartland of China. On 24 August 1971, apparently satisfied with the ex-PIA aircraft's performance, and with both airframe and engine product support forthcoming from the British, CAAC ordered six Trident 2Es, fitted with 140 seats, at a price of £20 million ($48 million). The record was marred slightly during the year, when a Trident (one of PIA's) crashed in September 1971 in Inner Mongolia, north of Peking, on a special flight. It was carrying the Defence Minister, Lin Piao, who had fallen out of favour with the strictly orthodox Chinese politicians; and the cause of the crash was strongly rumoured to have been sabotage.

CAAC introduced twin-propeller-turbine Antonov An-24s in 1970. This one, B-454, is seen at Beijing in 1981. (*Gordon S Williams*)

However, on a much broader front, the hitherto reticent flag carrier of China was beginning to emerge from its shell; and its Government helped by joining the International Civil Aviation Organization (ICAO) in November 1971 as an observer, preparatory to full membership.

China and CAAC Break Out

On 21 February 1972, President Nixon arrived in Beijing on his historic visit that at last broke the ice that had characterized the frigid relationship between mainland China, the People's Republic, and the United States, between which two countries, only a sporting event involving table tennis – in which the Chinese excel – had gone close to easing the tension, and that only a few months previously. But the deed was done, and the sustained trans-Pacific confrontation gave way to a new era in which overtures were made on all fronts, including the idea of industrial partnerships that would assist China in releasing itself from the harsh restrictions imposed by a regime that, for a decade, had shunned all aspects of culture, education, and advanced thinking in what was curiously called the Cultural Revolution. Ruthlessly monitored by young gangs of Red Guards, China

After buying Pakistan International Airlines' four Hawker Siddeley Trident 1Es, China ordered six Trident 2Es. Another twenty Tridents were ordered later. (*Hawker Siddeley*)

393

had turned its back on progress. Teachers were condemned to working in the rice fields, libraries of books were burned, laboratory apparatus and machines were destroyed. Capping Chairman Mao's Great Leap Forward – which was only a little leap in any case – the Cultural Revolution had put China backwards by at least a decade.

Yet CAAC in a manner that seemed to be the hallmark of airlines the world over, somehow showed a resilience to this chaotic state of affairs, and moved forward, even with confidence. During 1972 there was a flurry of orders for new aircraft, beginning, spectacularly, with one on 24 July for two Anglo-French supersonic Concorde airliners, priced at $34 million each; and a third aircraft was ordered a few weeks later, and the plan was to operate a route from Peking to Paris, via Karachi, Teheran and Bucharest, all points where China's political relations had been friendly enough to permit serious discussions on the establishment of air services. Like many other supersonic aspirants, however, CAAC abandoned the Concorde order for many other reasons: operational problems and financial difficulties, not the least of which were the impossibility of flying over land areas because of the sonic boom; and the even more remote possibility of being able to cover the operating costs with enough revenue from passengers who would pay fares at a level higher than the first-class rates.

Far more practical was the order, confirmed on 11 September, for ten Boeing 707s, for a total of $120 million, plus 40 spare Pratt & Whitney JT3D engines for $26 million, and a Redifon Boeing 707/Trident simulator for $4.8 million. That China was now getting serious about entering the jet age was demonstrated not only by the report that the delegation visiting Seattle had paid in cash; but that the simulator covered the Trident as well. This was because, early in August, six more Trident 2Es (making twelve) had been ordered, for $56 million; and on 13 November the Trident order was raised to twenty, for a further $59 million. Two of the Tridents were the Series 3B version, with a longer fuselage and a passenger capacity of up to 180.

The spending spree did not quite stop there; for in 1973, thirty more Antonov An-24s were ordered from the Soviet Union, so as to provide a good second-tier domestic airline support for the Tridents, intended for the mainline routes; and on 4 December of that year, the Trident order was once again raised, to a total of thirty-five. The fifteen additional tri-jets cost about $100 million, and this time there was a new element in the transaction: China's reserves of foreign currency had almost been exhausted, and the sum had to be raised by loans from western banks. Less prominent in this flurry of activity in the order books was the purchase, during the same year, of fifteen Australian GAF Nomad 15-seaters, for the Chinese equivalent of bush services.

The spring of 1973 also marked the beginning of a new era for CAAC as it came to grips with the jet age other than by signatures on contracts. Tridents began domestic services on 15 March, the first route between the two largest cities, Beijing and Shanghai. The first route to Europe was inaugurated on 18 April, with an Ilyushin Il-62 flying once a week from Beijing to Tirana, Albania, via Teheran and Bucharest. Albania seemed a curious destination for an intercontinental route; but the tiny Balkan country had been China's staunchest friend throughout its quarter-century of isolation, and had sponsored its membership of the United Nations, and perhaps this was Beijing's way of acknowledging a debt. Far more pragmatic was the service, opened on 27 October 1974, from Beijing to Paris, with only one stop, at Karachi, with the new Boeing 707s. Trial runs had been made with the Boeings on the Tirana route from August 1973, and they had also

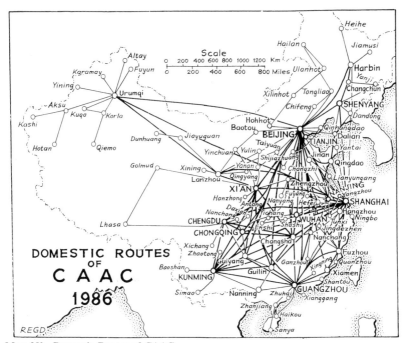

Map 29b. Domestic Routes of CAAC
Slowly at first, but gathering momentum after complete dependence on Soviet technology and support was abandoned in the early 1970s, the State airline of the People's Republic built up an extensive network of trunk, secondary, and third-level routes. Concentrating on the inter-city routes of eastern and central China, CAAC also provided the air links to the far corners of the land, from northeast Manchuria to the far western reaches of Sinkiang and Tibet.

opened the all-important link with nearby Tokyo on 29 September 1974, to provide an air connection across the Pacific as well as to Europe. The Ilyushin Il-62s opened a direct service to Moscow on 30 January 1974 and the 707s replaced the Il-62s permanently on the route to Bucharest on 29 November, the symbolic Tirana terminus having been quietly dropped. As if to confirm its re-entry into the international airline community, China joined ICAO as a full member in October 1974.

In reciprocal moves, more foreign airlines opened services into China. On 22 February 1973 Ethiopian Airlines, representing its new left-wing government, opened a Boeing 707 service from Addis Ababa to Shanghai, via Bombay, the first new foreign entrant since Air France in 1966. In November 1974 Iranair matched CAAC's flights from Teheran; and on 21 December, the Romanian TAROM started flying to Beijing with Ilyushin Il-62s. To round off the additional links with the West, Swissair started service from Zürich to Beijing on 7 April 1975.

The next few years were ones of consolidation as CAAC digested the change-over from propeller-driven aircraft to jets. As the services increased, more in frequencies on existing routes and in the upgrading of aircraft types than the addition of new city pairs, the airline began to adjust to a new level of operational

In October 1974 CAAC began one-stop Boeing 707 services between Beijing and Paris.
(*Boeing*)

efficiency. Its reservation system was, by western standards, still almost archaic; its infrastructure of navigational aids and air traffic control were ponderous, even primitive, so that the aircraft utilization was extremely low – only a few hours on average per day. It experienced the first serious fatal accident, when an Antonov An-24 crashed en route from Guangzhou to Shanghai, killing 40 people. But by 1977, the old DC-3/Li-2s had been retired from scheduled service; the Boeing 707s and Ilyushin Il-62s were taking care of the international routes; while the Tridents, Ilyushin Il-18s, Viscounts and a few Ilyushin Il-14s, in descending order of network strata, provided a comprehensive web of domestic connections throughout China.

New Goals

Early in 1978 Shen Tu became the Director General of CAAC and until his retirement in April 1985, he was to preside over the most important period of development in the airline's history. Enormous challenges lay ahead if China was to take its place in the world of air transport as an equal with the flag carriers of the industrial nations of the west, and even with the airline representatives of what were becoming known as nations of the Third World. And China's leaders did not wish to be classified as among these latter because its airliners – symbolic ambassadors abroad – were of an obsolescent generation. Yet these were the hard facts. China's Ilyushin Il-62s and Boeing 707s had gone into service a full decade and a half after the Pan American trans-Atlantic inaugural of 1958. When he took office, Shen had been conscious of the fact that Pan American's very large Boeing 747s had been in service already for eight years. So, on 16 December 1978, CAAC signed a contract with Boeing for three 747SPs, the shorter version which had a longer range than that of the standard 747, and able to fly from Shanghai nonstop to New York. All the trans-Pacific airlines were flying wide-bodied jets, and China was not intending to be a humiliated exception.

Before beginning this new era, however, some consolidation occurred, both in strengthening CAAC's network, and in allowing more airlines to open service into China from overseas. On 1 April 1978 a new route to a new continent was opened, when CAAC paralleled Ethiopian Airlines to Addis Ababa, via Karachi. On 4 May of the same year, also with 707s, it matched Swissair on a route to Zürich, with a technical stop at Urumchi and a traffic stop at Belgrade. On 3 May 1979

At the end of 1978 CAAC ordered three Boeing 747SPs, capable of flying nonstop from Shanghai to New York. (*Boeing*)

Ilyushin Il-62s began flying to Frankfurt, via Teheran and Bucharest. In this last case, at least, CAAC was ahead of the game; Lufthansa's DC-10s did not start until 7 April 1980. A direct connection to the Middle East was made on 28 July of the same year, to Sharjah and Baghdad.

Closer links were also made with the neighbouring countries in east Asia. Osaka had already been added as the second Japanese destination in 1976, and Nagasaki became the third, on 1 November 1979, not long after the route to Manila opened, on 4 September. Bangkok was added on 29 August 1980. Withdrawing from the previous policy of serving allied nations for purely political reasons, the service to Phnom Penh, begun on 23 January 1976, was terminated in February 1979, as the confused and destructive conflict in Cambodia seemed to show no end; and all flights to Tirana, occasionally served as extensions to the Bucharest service, ended at about the same time.

The most significant regional expansion, however, was right on the doorstep. Still under foreign control, but with the easing of diplomatic and trading barriers, increasingly playing an important part in the business world of China as a whole, Hong Kong had, since 1949, been strictly off limits. On 12 October 1978, the airway door was opened and CAAC Tridents began a connecting link with nearby Guangzhou, thus complementing a rail journey that took about four hours, including the customs and immigration formalities at the frontier. The Hong Kong links were forged even more strongly on 21 June 1980, when, after much negotiation, a pooled service opened from Shanghai, on a daily frequency, that comprised five CAAC Tridents and two Boeing 707s of Cathay Pacific Airways.

The first Boeing 747SP was delivered to Beijing on 27 February 1980, and was introduced on the route to Paris on 1 April 1980, Air France matching the service with its own 747s five days later. Always cautious in its route development, and now especially so as much prestige was at stake, CAAC made its first flights to the United States in October 1980; but these were on a special charter for General Motors, and six flights were made from Seattle (where good support was available, if needed) to China. This paved the way for a major entry into the English-speaking world, aside from the British colony of Hong Kong. On 15 November 1980, the Frankfurt service was extended to London; and on 7 January 1981, on what must have been a Red Letter Day in CAAC's calendar, a Boeing 747SP began service from Beijing and Shanghai to San Francisco and New York.

397

On 3 November 1981, direct Trident service to Kunming saved Hong Kong businessmen and tourists the change of aircraft or train at Guangzhou. On 12 April 1982, a new trans-Pacific service terminated at Los Angeles. In the eyes of the ever-critical airline world, CAAC seemed to have won its spurs and to have come of age, albeit with still many lessons to learn in the universally-accepted standards and procedures expected of the even more critical fraternity of airline passengers.

A Bold Joint Venture

The first foreign airline to fly to China from the Western world (Pakistan International in 1964) had used a Boeing aircraft; President Nixon had arrived in 1972 in a Boeing; and China and CAAC felt that these indications, followed by other western airline visitors' apparent preference for Boeings, was a strong recommendation for the best available equipment. McDonnell Douglas had to do something about this and they did.

In 1978 overtures were made to enter into an unprecedented and innovative programme of manufacturing co-operation which led to one of the most intensive and complete examples of an industrial joint venture ever attempted. The ultimate objective was, quite simply, that if CAAC would order Douglas DC-9s, then in progressive stages, McDonnell Douglas would enter into an agreement under which the Shanghai Aircraft Factory would be permitted to build the DC-9 or its developments, under a licensing agreement. Douglas had a long history of such sub-contracting on a grand scale. Before the Second World War, the Soviet Union and Japan had been given the rights to build DC-3s; more recently, parts of the Douglas jets were built under sub-contract in foreign countries. But now, once again, as with the 1937 agreement with the Soviet American Trading Organization (AMTORG), serious discussions began with the China National Machinery Import and Export Corporation (CATIC), the trading agency responsible for importing and exporting aviation equipment of all kinds.

Exchange visits were made by delegations from both sides, both on technical

One of CAAC's Airbus A310s at Shanghai in August 1985. (*R E G Davies*)

398

matters and on commercial and financial aspects, not only for aircraft manufacture but also for airline operation. China's record of manufacture was mixed. It had been able to build military aircraft with precision and skill. When the Soviet Union withdrew all its technical support when the idealogical rift occurred in the late 1950s, it was reported that it took back to Moscow all the technical drawings too; and that the Chinese literally dismantled an aircraft down to the last rivet and made new drawings from the tens of thousands of components. Anyone familiar with Chinese artistry and building skills would have few doubts about the ability to match those of any other country. What it lacked was the organizational experience to produce commercial aircraft, and the depth of hard-won knowledge in research into the structural, aerodynamic, and systems that had been accumulated in the West, but which had been ruthlessly destroyed in the Cultural Revolution in China.

Feeling its way carefully, Douglas gave the Shanghai factory a test, asking it to build a set of nose-wheel doors, and send it to Long Beach for inspection. By March 1981 the test piece was sent to California, where it passed with flying colours, and serious negotiations then began. McDonnell Douglas set up a corporation based in Hong Kong, headed up by a Chinese-American, Gareth Chang, who combined the business acumen of the West with an instinctive appreciation of the bargaining abilities and endless patience of the East. On 9 December 1983 two McDonnell Douglas MD-80s arrived in Shanghai, as demonstrator aircraft, but with the presumption of a sale if they were satisfactory. The Shanghai region of CAAC put them into intermittent service. The Chinese were now testing Douglas.

They had good reason to do so, for Boeing had not sat still in the quest to collar the big short- and medium-haul markets in this big under-equipped land. In 1981, while the delegations were going back and forth between Shanghai and Long Beach, Boeing sent a Boeing 737-200 demonstrator to tour CAAC's routes. The six-day itinerary included Lhasa, Tibet, at an elevation of 11,600 ft and ringed with even higher mountains, where the twin-engined competitor to the Douglas series performed well. In mid-November 1982 CAAC ordered ten of the Boeing twins, and significantly made the deal directly with Boeing, rather than through the purchasing agency, CATIC. By 1984, the 737s were coming into service and McDonnell Douglas's Chang had his work cut out to keep up the momentum of the negotiations for the joint venture.

Eventually, the patience and the integrity of the product had its reward. On 12 April 1985 the final agreement was signed in China for the purchase of 26 McDonnell Douglas MD-80s, with formal approval from the Chinese Government.

Ten Boeing 737s were ordered by CAAC in November 1982. (*Boeing*)

The negotiations had taken six years. Twenty-five of the aircraft would be assembled in Shanghai, from sub-assemblies delivered from Douglas at Long Beach, starting in January 1986. The exact type variant was the MD-82, with 147 seats. The Pratt & Whitney JT8D-217A engines were rated at 20,000 lb (9,072 kg) thrust, and the aircraft had a range of 2,360 miles. The value of the contract was more than $800 million, with future growth possibilities.

Instead of delegations, hundreds of technicians and engineers now began to travel back and forth across the Pacific. It was a great learning experience for both sides. The first Shanghai-built MD-82 entered service on 4 August 1987, from Shenyang. As time went on, the Shanghai factory was able to undertake more work, and be less dependent upon Long Beach for detail manufacture; and such was the success of the co-operative effort that, in June 1992, a further agreement was reached for continued production beyond the 28 MD-82s originally contracted for. Forty more aircraft were ordered for the joint programme, of which 17 would be of the first type, but the remainder would be the stretched version, the MD-90. These latter would be modified with a new main undercarriage, with four wheels on each leg, so as to distribute the load. In China this was still important, as at many of its airfields, the isolated single wheel load (ISWL) characteristics were inadequate for heavy aircraft such as the MD-90.

Time For A Change

As CAAC gradually probed the waters of the capitalistic world, it found them to be rougher than expected. Long accustomed to the privileges of protectionism, and without competition, it now faced the harsh realities of meeting a market demand. In the old days, the airline called the tune. If the flight was cancelled, for any reason (and the slightest indication of bad weather was usually sufficient) the passengers simply had to wait, without complaint. Undoubtedly, this was a factor in the achievement of a good safety record, for no risks were ever taken. Standards of service, both on the ground and in the air, were poor, and quite unacceptable by western standards – and that was the arena into which the carrier of the Chinese flag was now plunging. And this was not only on the international routes. With the easing of travel restrictions for foreigners, tour groups began to invade China to see the wonders of the Forbidden City, the Great Wall, the incredible 6,000 terracotta soldiers at Xi'an, and the grandeur of the Yangtse River Gorge. And the tourists expected seat belts, catering, and efficient service, all the way from one hotel to the next, including the air journey.

The transition from the old ways, when everything was forgiven if the indiscretion was by a government agency, to the new ways, when nothing was forgiven by a discerning and often critical public, was painful. CAAC now had a big responsibility in presenting the face of China to the world. Meeting as it had to the increasing demands of stricter scheduling, higher service standards, and improved equipment quality, both to fly and to maintain, was not easy. As the national flag carrier, it attracted stricter scrutiny in Beijing.

CAAC's reputation was not helped by an increase in the number of fatal accidents, which, as the airline was under examination on all sides, tended to be publicized extensively. After its first-ever accident in 1976 – and there may have been some that were never publicly reported – there were more. A Trident crashed on take-off at Beijing on 14 March 1979, killing 44 people; another crashed en route from Guangzhou to the holiday resort of Guilin (Kweilin) on 27 April 1982, killing 112; an Ilyushin Il-18 burst into flames on landing at Guangzhou on 24

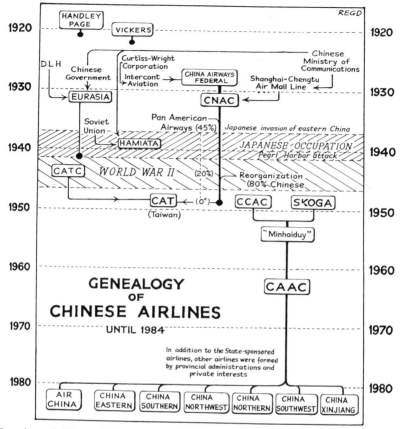

Genealogy of Chinese Airlines until 1984
This chart illustrates the changing fortunes of the early airlines in China, as foreign interests extended their influence; followed by the hazards of wartime power struggles, and the emergence, after the Second World War and the revolution that brought the Communists to rule all China, of a single Chinese and Chinese-owned airline.

December 1982, killing 23 and injuring 28 (a passenger was said to be smoking in the lavatory); and yet another Trident collided with a military aircraft at Guilin on 14 September 1983, killing all on board, fortunately only eleven. The accidents, which seemed to be occurring at a rate of about one a year, exacerbated the criticism, and pressure was brought to bear at the highest levels of government in Beijing, to re-organize the entire civil aviation system, whose destiny had hitherto been controlled by bureaucrats, by delegating more authority and control to the regions, so that the airline services could be directed by those who were intimately involved with the operations. As late as 1980, and although selected numbers of aircraft were deployed at regional bases such as Urumchi, Shenyang and Xi'an, the local managements could hardly sharpen a pencil without permission from Beijing.

The result of all this dissatisfaction, from all sides, even including the Chinese

B-3601, the first of eight Short 360s ordered for CAAC.

travelling public itself, which was now beginning to include businessmen who were quickly adapting to western ways, was what amounted to an administrative revolution in the airline structure of China; and after September 1984, as will be described in the next chapter, things were never the same again.

CHAPTER THIRTY

Airlines of the New China

Decentralization

The first hint that the long-rumoured changes in the structure and administration of CAAC were at last about to happen came in September 1984, when Gu Mu, a member of the State Council in charge of the country's modernization programme, announced the formation of four regional airlines to serve domestic routes, the separation of CAAC's international routes as an autonomous unit, and the removal of the national airline as the nominal and organizational administrator of what, in western terms, is called aerial work – survey, exploration, fire patrol and agricultural activities – which were henceforth to come under the aegis of the China General Aviation Company.

The policy decision having been made, the practical matters were left in the hands of Shen Tu, who had presided over the affairs of China's State airline monopoly since 1978. The four domestic regional airlines were to be based at Shanghai – recognizing the importance of China's main commercial entrepôt of trade; Guangzhou – equally recognizing the importance of the south of China, and the nearby presence of Hong Kong; Chengdu – as the capital of Sichuan, the most populous province, and far inland; and Urumchi – capital of Xinchiang, the autonomous and geographically the most remote province in China's far west. The international division was to be renamed Air China. At first the four regionals were named, respectively, Eastern, Southern, Southwestern, and Northwestern, but these quickly acquired the prefix China, and approval was soon forthcoming from the State Council in December 1984.

While all the new airlines were still part of the CAAC Beijing-based controlling arm of the Chinese Government, they were aimed to satisfy local sensibilities and especially to remove the impression that the operational departments would be directed by a bureaucratic office in the capital, even though ultimate power still rested in Beijing, which would continue to be responsible for regulatory functions, particularly those affecting airline infrastructure: airways, airports, navigational aids, international bilateral agreements and other aspects that were of a national, rather than a regional importance. The whole re-structuring initiative was aimed to end the inertia which had seemed to overcome CAAC, partly because of the obsessive centralization and of the reluctance to invest in new equipment. The Xinhua news agency put the situation succinctly: the new aviation enterprises, it said, would be owned by the whole people, and would 'mobilize all positive factors, various regions, departments, and enterprises, who would be encouraged to invest in the development of civil air service, at various levels, so that a new situation will be created in which the mainstay aviation enterprises co-exist and develop together with local and small aviation enterprises'.

All this was in line with the drive towards modernization that was sweeping across the land, in harmony with an opening up of the country to freer trade and commercial expansion with the outside world, and in the promotion of which several special economic zones had been created along China's coastline, in which foreign investment was invited to match an unprecedented effort by China itself to develop industry and compete on equal terms with western countries.

Almost like captive songbirds released from a cage, the new airlines seized the new freedom and wasted little time in trying to recover the years of lost opportunities as CAAC had run out of steam. By the end of 1984, the original four regionals, China Eastern (Shanghai), China Southern (Guangzhou), China Southwestern (Chengdu), and China Northwestern (Urumchi) had been joined by two others: China Northern (Dalian, later Shenyang) and one based at Xi'an, which became China Northwestern; while the Urumchi-based regional group appears to have claimed an even greater autonomy as China Xinjiang Airlines.

As envisaged in this almost revolutionary move towards the Market Economy (as Capitalism is now fashionably known) the Provinces were not only permitted, they were encouraged to establish their own local airlines, even though this would often result in direct competition with the CAAC – affiliated domestic 'chosen instruments'. At a national civil aviation conference, convened in the early spring of 1985, the special economic zone of Xiamen, in China's southeastern Fujian Province (and the one closest to Taiwan) was almost directed to improve air service to Shanghai and Guangzhou; while the authorities at Urumchi were similarly urged to improve service from the far west to the main cities of the eastern seaboard. Additionally, preparations were announced to set up the Capital Helicopter Company of China, to operate special services for local authorities and departments. But as if to remind the new lusty escapees from Beijing discipline and centralized direction, the conference also disclosed that it would inspect the airlines periodically to ensure that they were maintaining proper standards to comply with the provisions of their licences to operate, and that those who did not comply would have their operations suspended, unless they 'shaped up' within a set time.

Having steered CAAC through a truly remarkable period of international expansion during a five-year period which included the opening of new routes to western Europe, including Frankfurt and London; and trans-Pacific routes to New York and Los Angeles; the ordering of wide-bodied Boeing 747SPs and 737 twin-jets; and coping with the adverse publicity of aircraft crashes (most of which were, to be fair, not entirely CAAC's fault); Shen Tu retired in April 1985. His place was taken by Hu Yizhao, who now faced head-on the formidable problem of somehow enabling China's outmoded airline to undergo a metamorphosis of organization, and at the same time to expand in almost spectacular fashion to keep pace with the demands of a nation that was embracing western technology, commerce and business, not to mention tourism, with almost fanatical zeal. As a measure of the problem, China's airline traffic in 1984 was 40 percent more than in 1983; and in the first quarter of 1985, just before Hu took over, traffic jumped by 60 percent.

Hu's background was far different from the orthodox career, within the Communist system, of Shen. He had actually worked for CNAC as an aircraft engineer, but when that airline transferred to Taiwan along with the Kuomintang in 1949, he was one of the group who hijacked some of the fleet and flew them to Beijing. He is believed to have been a victim of the notorious (and mis-named) Cultural Revolution, and was sent to a farm to work as a labourer. But he survived such an ordeal, as did Jiang Tong, an executive of the Export-Import Corporation, CATIC, who philosophically reflected (to this author) that those years in the rice-paddies were among the best in his life; healthy outdoor invigorating work, with no mental stress or responsibility. As for Hu, he brought into CAAC a vigorous attitude to work and combined this with practical experience, both in the maintenance shops and in the field – literally.

Spending Spree

Even before he took over, CAAC had at last begun to put on new clothes, especially to upgrade its domestic services, for which no mainline aircraft had been added since the mid-1970s – and these were Trident 3Bs, the last of a line which itself was moribund. As previously mentioned in Chapter 29, the first McDonnell Douglas MD-80s had arrived at the end of 1983 and had gone into service in the Shanghai region. In January 1985 CAAC ordered eight Shorts 360 regional airliners and these were delivered in short order, to be deployed for service in the Shanghai region in July, and in the Wuhan region in August of that year. While this was a modest enough beginning, it was the harbinger of greater things to come. In April 1985, through the China Aviation Supplies Corporation, it ordered three Airbus A310-200s, each with 218 seats, of which 18 were first-class – a term that was now permitted in a once classless society, where, on the trains, the more comfortable seating was called 'soft-class'. The first two Airbuses went into service in June.

Showing impartiality in its supply sources, CAAC also ordered ten Tupolev Tu-154s, intended for the Xinjiang Division; signed a letter of intent for ten British Aerospace BAe 146-100s; and on 23 May 1985, Hu himself signed a contract for eight Boeing airliners, one 747–200 Combi, two 767s and five 737-200s, at a total cost of $350 million. Such contractual activity seems to have been undertaken as an emergency measure to ensure that no time was lost in trying to match the burgeoning traffic demand with enough aircraft to cope with it. While much local autonomy had been granted to such potentially powerful regional airlines as China Eastern or China Southern, the administrative machinery was not yet organized at the sub-divisional level to permit high-level contractual negotiations, and international ones at that, by willing, but inexperienced, executives. This direct ordering procedure was to come later. Meanwhile CAAC kept a watchful eye on the critical developments that were changing the face of China's airline community in a manner that could not have been contemplated only half a decade earlier.

Fragmentation of CAAC

During the first two years of the new-found autonomy, the new airlines of China began to organize themselves. Control over scheduling became more disciplined, and reservations systems were at last improved to a reasonable standard of efficiency, with computerized equipment. Gone were the days when a passenger could not book the return journey until he or she arrived at the destination. Equally the utilization of aircraft was improved. Until the 1980s the idea of circulating aircraft around the route network, so as to derive higher aircraft productivity in terms of hours flown per day, was given little, if any, attention. A Trident would fly from Beijing to Guangzhou, and that was its day's work. Now, with western forms of accountancy replacing a system in which almost every aspect of airline life was subordinated to the needs and demands of a bureaucracy dominated by political motives; and with the threat of independent airlines being formed to provide competition – a word equivalent to sacrilege in bygone days – CAAC's new subdivisions plunged themselves into the deep end of the pool of market economy.

For the travelling public, this revolution was welcomed. Hitherto, on-board service standards had, by western criteria, been appalling; and the service at the airports was even worse. The demands of dictatorial authority were such that the concept of service to the passenger, in a personal sense, was almost unknown. The passenger was treated no better than a piece of freight, a consignment that had to be conveyed from one place to another. The CAAC employees were poorly paid, even by Chinese standards, and could not be expected to show much enthusiasm for the job. Only in the late 1970s, when China began to open its doors to tourists, and, if only to save face, and to demonstrate that the country was not completely unfeeling to its guests, did the national airline do more than the military arm of an air force might have done through its transport division. Now, with the fragmentation of the omnipotent autocracy, a new spirit in attitudes, both internally within the operators, and externally, in their relations with the public, began to reveal itself.

Part of the new approach was spurred by the awareness that, for the first time in the history of the airlines in China, the air traveller had a choice. Under the new system, regional pride was at last permitted to assert itself in an overt, rather than a covert manner. Anything that China Eastern could do, in its service between Guanzhou and Shanghai, for example, then China Southern would do better; for now the revenues from ticket sales did not disappear into some mysterious State coffer in Beijing; they went to the regional airline, to balance against its expenditures, not least the costs of acquiring, staffing and maintaining its aircraft fleet, a function that had previously been regarded with no thought towards financial viability.

Such an all-embracing revolution, from State-controlled monopoly, to regionally directed oligopoly, could have been doomed from the start, had the reins of authority been unconditionally released, and unrestricted competition been allowed to flourish, unburdened by regulations controlling route franchises. But the transition was made with commendable restraint, partly because the regions themselves took a little time to adjust to the new circumstances of airline life, partly because Beijing, through the CAAC, which now adopted the role of a presiding government agency (rather on the lines of the former Civil Aeronautics Board of the United States) ensured that the new-found freedom did not go to the regional heads, and that the recipients of that freedom did not take leave of their senses. Thus, if two airlines both wished to open a new city-pair segment, authority to do so had to be obtained from and agreed to with CAAC which – rather in the manner of the former US CAB – made the ultimate judgement, based largely

China Northwest Airlines employs several Airbus A300-600s in its fleet of about fifty aircraft. (*K Murai*)

on the level and potential of traffic demand, and whether such demand could support one, or more than one, airline.

The franchises varied in scope, but were eminently sensible and put into effect with a logic that would doubtless have met with the approval of any western airline consultant, or even the critical eye of the *Wall Street Journal*. The intercontinental route responsibility was clearly Air China's and centralized on the capital, Beijing. This airline automatically became the nation's flag-carrier, and simply took over the long-haul fleet of the former CAAC. It provided the main air link with Asia's industrial giant, Japan, and provided capacity on the main inter-city domestic routes between the main centres of population in China. Of the regionally-based airlines, China Eastern and China Southern, based in two major provincial cities, Shanghai and Guangzhou, respectively, were also permitted to operate certain international routes. Recognizing the traditional importance of Shanghai's heritage as one of the world's commercial trading hubs, China Eastern was permitted to fly both to the United States and to Europe, albeit on a restricted basis; and China Southern was able to expand its network throughout southeast Asia, and to provide direct routes to Singapore, for instance, from the new economic-zone cities of Shenzhen and Xiamen.

The China Southern Airlines fleet of more than one hundred aircraft includes twelve Boeing 737-500s. (*Boeing*)

Both China Southern and China Eastern became, within a very few years, major airlines, though not yet ranking among the world's top twenty or so. Constantly observing the headlong prosperity of neighbouring Hong Kong, and the success of its airline, Cathay Pacific, China Southern's text-book was almost next door. It also echoed another example of unparalleled free enterprise, the Hong Kong Aircraft Engineering Corporation (HAECO) by converting the former CAAC maintenance base to a progressive – and even aggressively competitive, because of its low labour rates – high-technology maintenance facility, the Guangzhou Aircraft Maintenance Company (GAMECO). Such developments were typical of the new age in China's airline industry, the most important being the new attitude towards international co-operation. Back in the late 1970s, when McDonnell Douglas made its first overtures towards a joint-venture production programme to

407

One of the Airbus A300-600R fleet of China Eastern Airlines. (*Airbus Industrie*)

build the MD-80, the early discussions might well have been with people who, while of equal intelligence and ability, could have come from another planet. Now, GAMECO was established as a joint venture, with Lockheed Aircraft Service International and Hong Kong's Hutchison China Trade Holdings, with few communication problems.

In other directions, training centres were started up, to replace the former on-the-job methods. Technical assistance and support was welcomed, instead of regarded with deep suspicion. Work that had formerly been contracted out, even to the extent of allowing foreign firms such as Rolls-Royce to provide overhaul and maintenance installations within China, was now replaced or supplemented by foreign joint ventures. As early as 1985 CAAC had co-operated with Lufthansa to set up a technical base in Beijing. In May 1988 Air China converted this into a joint corporation, Ameco Beijing, with Lufthansa holding 40 percent of the capital. Also, modelled on Pakistan International's fine establishment in Karachi, Beijing Air Catering was founded to improve the catering standards on Air China's and other airlines' aircraft serving the capital. The provision of a full Chinese menu on board, complete with Peking Duck, should be a valuable, if indefinable asset to the objective of improving market shares on international routes.

While Air China, China Southern, and China Eastern were the most prominent of the new CAAC-sponsored airlines, because they were the regional flag-carriers of China's main foreign-trading cities, the other sibling enterprises played their parts in special ways. China Northern, based in the industrial centre of Shenyang, in the area formerly known as Manchuria, was responsible for domestic service in

Two of China Eastern's McDonnell Douglas MD-82s. (*McDonnell Douglas*)

China Northern Airlines operates several Airbus A300-600Rs. (*Airbus Industrie*)

China Northern has no less than twenty-five McDonnell Douglas MD-82s. Seven of the airline's MD-82s are seen here at Shenyang. (*McDonnell Douglas*)

a region throbbing with manufacturing activity. The three Manchurian Provinces of Liaoning, Jilin and Heilongjiang have no less than nine cities with more than a million inhabitants each; and with the growing prosperity of the nation as a whole, the airline's potential for growth is considerable. Its trans-border routes include those to Siberia and Far Eastern Russia, which surrounds the area on three sides, to neighbouring Korea, North and South, and to Japan.

China Southwestern's catchment area includes not only the fertile Red Basin of Sichuan, with its 120-million people also involved in industry in a cluster of cities around Chengdu and Chungking; it is responsible for providing the essential air link with Tibet. The goal of linking every one of China's Provincial capitals by a modern railway system, the main priority in Chairman Mao's policy, was an outstanding success, transforming a disjointed and partly antiquated system into a

A Boeing 757-200 of China Southwest Airlines. As the following illustration shows not all of the airline's fleet carry the airline name in English. (*Rob Finlayson*)

powerful unifying agency. But it fell short of its formidable target only in failing to reach Tibet's capital, Lhasa, only half a century removed from almost total inaccessibility from the outside world. China's railway builders had created what must be one of the engineering Wonders of the World, with its Chengdu-Kunming line, which wanders from precipice to precipice through the Daxue Shan mountains of southern Sichuan; but in Tibet, the peerless engineers had reached only as far as Golmud, in the autonomous northwestern Province of Qinghai, and both the finance and manpower ran out by the late 1970s, together with the weakening of the political incentive to strengthen Lhasa's links with Beijing, as much for military logistic reasons as for any other. China Southwestern, therefore, became China's main connection with Tibet, except for the long and tortuous route by roads that rival the notorious wartime Burma Road in challenging gradients and fiendish successions of hairpin bends.

The equipment used by the new airlines varied considerably, and in the wave of

One of China Southwest's Boeing 737-300s. (*Rob Finlayson*)

410

enthusiasm to match the demand, and even to stimulate it, almost every manufacturer world-wide was received in an atmosphere of expectations of sales. And in most cases these were duly made. Boeing was the main benefactor, building on the established success of its CAAC-operated fleets of successive generations since the first Boeing 707; but also making a considerable impression by demonstrating the airfield performance of the Boeing 737 twin-jet at Lhasa (*see* also Chapter 29). McDonnell Douglas's MD-82s were allocated to China Eastern and China Northern, and the former airline also put the new MD-11 intercontinental tri-jet into service in 1992, as well as consolidating its domestic routes with Airbus A300s and A310s.

For feeder routes, all except one of the CAAC group operated the Yun 7, the Chinese-built Antonov An-24, a sturdy twin propeller-turbine type of which more than a thousand were put into service by Aeroflot Soviet Airlines, and whose general design, similar to that of the Fokker Friendship, has stood the test of time, both in technical merit and in economic survival. The exception was China Xinjiang, based in Urumchi, whose proximity to and community of interest with the formerly Soviet Kazakhstan, now an independent nation, and with Uzbekistan, of the same recent history, recalled memories of an era when the whole region was known as Turkestan (Singkiang, or Xinjiang, was termed Chinese Turkestan). The common denominators are its ethnicity – the inhabitants are mostly Uygurs, a Turkic race, quite alien to the Han Chinese; and religion – they are predominantly Moslem. Possibly because of this circumstance, China Xinjiang still turned to the former Soviet manufacturers, and, by a leasing agreement with Uzbekistan Airways, operated a small fleet of Tupolev Tu-154s and even a couple of wide-bodied Ilyushin Il-86s. The Tu-154 was still also used by China Northern, China Southwestern, and China Northwest, all of whom were within relatively close distance from sources of maintenance, overhaul and spares; while China Southern, with its mini-traffic explosion in Guangdong, also sub-leased the 350-seat Il-86.

The New Independents

The transition from centralized to dispersed authority took place, as stated earlier, over a period of a few exploratory years. The official date of Air China's forma-

At the end of 1995 China Xinjiang Airlines was operating two Boeing 737-300s in its mixed fleet of Canadian, Chinese, Russian and United States aircraft. (*Boeing*)

411

Air China's fleet includes three versions of the Boeing 747, the -400 (illustrated), the -200F freighter and -200 Combi. (*Boeing*)

One of Air China's Boeing 767-300s. (*Boeing*)

tion is 1 July 1988, and the other airlines appear to have received their official statutory franchises on that date. In practical terms, the process of transfer of powers at different levels, the allocation of aircraft and staff, and a myriad of other details, had been going on since the end of 1984. But by the close of the 1980s, the new airline fleets were resplendent in their new colour schemes and proudly displaying their new insignias. It was a brave new world.

The original directive of the State Council had recognized the intensity and emotional depth of the spirit of independence to the extent that, in addition to splitting CAAC asunder, it provided also for the establishment of completely independent airlines. It was once said that in every Chinese heart lurks a merchant, and the speed with which the trading instincts of the urban Chinese rose to the surface, with Deng Ziao Ping's more liberal policies replacing the sternness of the Communist hierarchy of 35 years, was quite remarkable. Chinese entrepreneurs were now able to indulge in trading at all levels, from selling their wares on the streets to setting up corporations, including airlines. Notably, for the first time, this was possible without the former almost mandatory initiative of foreign interests; for the great British trading companies such as Jardine Matheson and the foreign banks such as the Hong Kong and Shanghai, while happy to participate in

412

China General Aviation's fleet consists of some fifty aircraft of about ten types. Included are a number of Yakovlev Yak-42Ds.

investment and finance, were no longer effectively in charge of business affairs. For the first time ever, duty-free shops were to be found at the main airports, and the entire airline environment turned its back on the rigidity of the past and enthusiastically welcomed the opportunities provided as China itself accepted the inevitability of the market economy.

With some exceptions, the independent airlines, i.e., the ones that were completely new, and not hived off from the former CAAC, were local in their scope, often representing a single Province. Once again, there was some similarity with the former structure of the airline industry in the United States, where the trunk airlines were complemented by the local service, or regional, companies. During the late 1980s and early 1990s, they seemed to spring up everywhere. The first appears to have been, somewhat unexpectedly, founded at a medium-sized city in northern Henan, in July 1985. Anyang Airlines, with a motto of 'good service and absolute safety,' began service to Beijing in the north and Shenzhen in the south, with the objective, in the words of the vice-chairman of the local committee of the National People's Congress, of 'developing local aviation to boost the people's prosperity.'

Subsequently, other airlines were formed, and these are summarized in Table 1. The first company, other than the small Anyang, to be established with substantial capital and with front-line aircraft, was Xiamen Airlines, which was affiliated with China Southern, in Guangzhou, which owned 50 percent of the shares, and

Shanghai Airlines mainly uses Boeing 757s. They have a striking red, black, and white livery. (*Boeing*)

413

One of Xiamen Airlines' Boeing 737-500s at Hong Kong in November 1992. (*Rob Finlayson*)

which started operations with three Boeing 737-200s. Even more impressive was the founding of Shanghai Airlines, with the full backing of the municipality, and which ordered a fleet of Boeing's best short-medium-haul airliners, the 757 and 767. The city of Shanghai, once the commercial nucleus of China, had long anguished under the shadow of Beijing, from which power centre it had received little help during the decades of centralized Communist rule. When, as early as May 1984, Premier Zhao Ziyang called for an end of State monopolies, the Mayor of Shanghai responded immediately, and made it clear that Shanghai's own airline

Shenzhen Airlines fleet at the end of 1995 consisted of five Boeing 737-300s. (*Boeing*)

414

would be a model for others to follow, and would operate at standards matching those of the West, and would replace the mismanagement, poor service and poor safety record of CAAC with a level of efficiency that would help to bring back the pride of a great city. By 1990 its first three 757s were carrying 400,000 passengers in the year, and, with China's airline business climbing at a dizzy rate, Shanghai Airlines' annual growth was averaging about 30 percent. As China's leading independent airline, it will play its part in putting its parent city back to the top of the world's entrepôts of trade.

Pitfalls along the Way

At first, after the dramatic *volte-face* of political direction in 1984, the derogatory presumptions about CAAC seemed to be fully justified, in particular in the suspicions about poor safety standards. On 18 January 1985 an Antonov An-24 feederliner crashed at Jinan, killing 38 passengers and crew; and on 31 August of the same year – the year in which the new airlines were girding their loins for the fray – a Trident crash-landed at Hong Kong. Both aircraft were still flying in CAAC's colours, and in the latter case, the fact that the accident occurred at Hong Kong was to guarantee that the maximum publicity was given. Such was the stress and emphasis placed on safety that the new airlines made statements on the subject, thereby breaking an unwritten rule among the world's airlines, (in which superstition plays a part) that, except when applied to a specific tragedy, it is never discussed. The statistically safest airline in the world never uses its wholly creditable achievement for promotional purposes. The airlines of China were to learn that they were not immune from the hazards that beset the best of them.

A mixture of Boeing 737-300s and 737-400s form the main fleet of Hainan Airlines. (*Boeing*)

Meanwhile, a setback of an entirely different kind affected the headlong course of traffic growth, one that was tragically to cast a cloud over all aspects of life in China for several years. Voltaire once observed that, paradoxically, revolutions occur when conditions are improving, not when they are getting worse; and many

One of Wuhan Airlines' red, white, and blue Boeing 737-300s. (*Pemco Aeroplex*)

historical events bear witness to this axiom. And so it was as the far-reaching economic reforms in China opened up new vistas of the future for a hitherto oppressed people. On 4 May 1989 about 100,000 students and workers staged a march in Beijing to demand even more liberal reforms, and the movement gathered strength to the stage that, when, in the following week, the Soviet leader Mikhail Gorbachev made the first State visit to the Chinese capital for thirty years, the centre of Beijing was thronged by more than a million protesters. The movement spread to other cities, and martial law was imposed on 20 May.

The protests continued, and in a desperate move, the Chinese Army moved into Beijing. On 3–4 June the protestors were ruthlessly dispersed by soldiers, backed by tanks, and in the now historic agonized drama of what has become known as the Tiananmen Square Massacre, an estimated 5,000 people were killed, and perhaps double that number wounded. The effect on the airline business was instantaneous, especially on the foreign airlines that were sharing in the traffic boom that was sweeping across China in line with its commercial revolution. Aircraft which had been flying almost invariably full up, now flew almost empty, as the reverberations of the tragedy of Tiananmen Square ground everything to a halt.

At first there were fears that the main source of supply of new aircraft, Boeing, would be cut off, as the United States might remove China from its list of 'most-favoured nations (MFNs)' and thus handicap trade relations for a long time; and that the joint-venture programme involving the construction of McDonnell Douglas MD-82s in the Shanghai Aircraft Factory would be similarly affected. Fortunately for all concerned, the United States did not take this shattering step, no doubt pragmatically noticing that, with the aircraft manufacturing industry showing the only bright spot on an otherwise dismal balance-of-trade reckoning, there was no point in cutting off the American nose to save its face.

Gradually, the new airline industry began to collect itself and settled into the task of adapting to the new capitalist ways, that is to say, to have to keep strict accounts of expenditures and to guard against wasteful practices, because all costs would now have to be paid for from earned revenues, and not be met from

416

At the end of 1995 Air Great Wall was operating two Tupolev Tu-154Ms. (*Rob Finlayson*)

One of China Xinhua's Boeing 737-300s at Shenzhen. (*Boeing*)

Government funds voted by a politically-motivated agency. They adapted well, and aided by low labour rates, were able to demonstrate financial viability and stability. But they were to learn that airline life was not always a bed of roses, and that some aspects of airline life applied to them as to any other.

One of these was the ever-present danger of hijacking. The Chinese were more vulnerable than most because the progress made in the air had not been matched on the ground, where airport installations, amenities and practices were unable to keep pace. In the more obviously visible sense, airport buildings could not be expanded at 30 percent a year, although in the big hubs at the larger metropolises such as Guangzhou, massive construction was undertaken. In the less visible sense, the procedures were still lax, for while a more positive attitude towards the clientèle was commendable, to inflict strict baggage- and personal-searching for boarding passengers should have been accepted as a safety measure, whereas it

417

seemed to reflect the old regime, and was neglected. The danger of hijacking was exacerbated by the proximity of the dissident island of Taiwan, seen as a refuge for all revolutionary fanatics who were desperate to escape from mainland China. The classic 'take me to Cuba' phrase of the paperback writer was translated into 'take me to Taiwan'.

This was no fiction. On 2 October 1990 a hijacker took command of a Xiamen Airlines Boeing 737, and, with explosives strapped to his body, forced the pilot to land on his own at Guangzhou. Without full support from his crew, and possibly trying heroically to resist, the pilot crash-landed, hit two other aircraft, and as a result a total of 130 passengers in two aircraft were killed. The hijacker had gained access to the flight deck on the pretext that he wished to present a bouquet of flowers to the crew to celebrate the Chinese National Day holiday.

A Shandong Airlines Boeing 737-300 at Seattle before delivery. (*Boeing*).

Two years later, the efficiencies of old-fashioned and inadequate airports were thrown into dramatic relief when a China Southern Airlines Boeing 737-300 crashed into high ground on approaching Guilin (formerly Kweilin), the beautifully situated tourist destination in the Guangzhi Province of southwestern China. The 'sugarloaf' mountains beloved of Chinese artists consisted of limestone peaks scattered all around the Guilin airport, which was the sixth busiest in China, and were an ever-present hazard. The 133 deaths from the 737 on 24 November 1992 highlighted the deficiencies of the airline infrastructure.

There was an outbreak of hijacking in 1993 when, in the first week of November, there were three of them. One, a China Northern MD-82, was returned safely from Taiwan with no loss of life. Fortunately, this was the case also with a Xiamen Airlines 737 and a Zhejiang Airlines de Havilland Canada Dash 8, the last incident characterized by the alleged explosive turning out to be a bar of soap.

China Takes Its Place in the Airline World

In less than a decade, the Chinese Government has reconstructed its ailing airline industry to become one of the driving forces of the new market-oriented economic structure of the nation. It has transformed a creaking monopoly of an anachronis-

One of Sichuan Airlines Airbus A320s. Markings are mainly red with black lettering. (*Airbus Industrie*)

tic era into a systematic group of companies that, while Beijing retains ultimate State control, enjoy substantial freedom in the decision-making process, and by all accounts, have taken to their new-found environment like ducks to water.

Astonishingly, from a nation that had been parsimonious in its dealings, so that it appeared to invest in new equipment only at the very last resort, it had become eager to be in the van of progress. In 1993 China was Boeing's best customer, and Boeing at this time represented about two-thirds of the world's production capacity of mainline commercial airliners. Collectively, the seven State-sponsored and a dozen or two independent companies operate more than 250 modern front-line aircraft, and these are complemented by about 100 more regional types. By the end of the century, with traffic growth bounding upwards at a pace that is the envy of the rest of the world, the fleet could well reach 500 or more. These airlines are listed in the tables.

Once an outcast in the world of nations – by its own choosing, let it be said – China is now an integral part of the world's trading and merchandizing industry, exporting in considerable volumes products of every kind, agricultural and industrial.

No mistaking the operator – a Zhongyuan Airlines Boeing 737-300. (*Boeing*).

419

China Yunnan Airlines has an all-Boeing fleet. At the end of 1995 this comprised seven Boeing 737-300s with three 737s and three 767-300s on order. (*Boeing*)

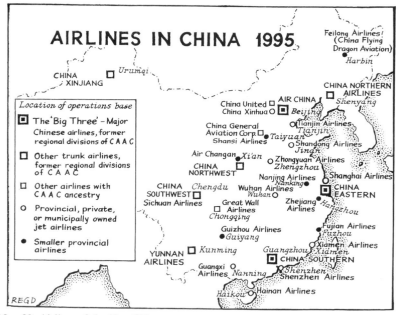

Map 30. Airlines of the New China

The 'Made in China' emblem is to be found everywhere, on textiles, stationery, clothing, furniture and electronic instruments. The potential for growth is enormous. Its thousand million-strong population were formerly subsistence farmers, with the exception of a privileged few. The changes that have occurred in the recent decades, drawing strength from huge national programmes under the Communist regime, such as the fashioning of the railway network, the harnessing of the rivers to eliminate disastrous flooding and consequent famine, and urban rehousing, must have evoked thoughts of ancient times when the Chinese called themselves the Middle Kingdom, meaning the centre of the world. As the biggest nation on earth, with a quarter of its population, China will move into the 21st Century with confidence; and if current indications are a guide, the Chinese airlines will be the standard-bearers of a vigorous born-again nation.

TABLE 1

Chinese Provincial, Private, or Municipally owned airlines, 1995

Airline and Base	Route Network	Aircraft Fleet	Remarks
Shanghai Airlines (Shanghai)	Domestic routes to major cities of China, and to Hong Kong	Boeing 757, 767	Formed late in 1985 by the Shanghai municipality and local investors. Largest of the Chinese new independent airlines
Xiamen Airlines (Xiamen)	Domestic routes in southeast China, radiating from Xiamen, and linking Shanghai and Hong Kong	Boeing 737-200, Boeing 757	First independent airline to be established under the new liberal policy. Close association with China Southern, which acquired 50% shareholding
Shenzhen Airlines (Shenzhen)	Routes mainly to southern China, providing air links with Shenzhen special economic zone	Boeing 737	Started operations, 15 October 1993
Hainan Airlines (Haikou)	Routes form Hainan island, developing as vacation destination, to Chinese mainland cities	Boeing 737	Started operations, 1 April 1993 – first route to Shenzhen
Wuhan Airlines (Wuhan)	Domestic routes radiating from Wuhan	Boeing 737, Yun-7	Wuhan is strategically situated at the hub of main north-south and east-west trunk routes
China Great Wall Corp. Chongqing	Domestic services mainly in Sichuan	Tupolev Tu-154 Boeing 737-200 Yun-7	Also known as Air Great Wall Founded 21 July 1992 by Civil Aviation Flying Institute of China
China Xinhau (Beijing)	Domestic services based in Beijing	Boeing 737-300	Founded August 1992 by Beijing Municipal Govt and private investors
Fujian Airlines (Fuzhou)	Local services in Fujian province	Yun-7	Founded 8 August 1993 by China Southern
Guangxi Airlines (Nanning)	Local services in Guangxi autonomous region, and to Guangzhou	Boeing 737-500	Founded in 1994 by Guangxi local government
Guizhou Airlines (Guiyang)	Local services in Guizhou province	Yun-7, Yun-12	Founded by Guizhou Government in 1991
Nanjing Airlines (Nanjing)	Local services in Anhui province and to Shanghai	Yun-7	Founded in 1994 by Nanjing local government in collaboration with China Northwest

Airline and Base	Route Network	Aircraft Fleet	Remarks
Shandong Airlines (Jinan)	Domestic routes mainly in eastern China	Boeing 757-300 Yun-7	Founded November 1994 by Shandong provincial government
Shanxi Airlines (Taiyuan)	Domestic routes linking Taiyuan with main cities of China	Yun-7 (replaced Ilyushin Il-14)	Possibly the first independent airline to be established under the new liberal policy, but only (at first) as a Charter company, in 1984. Accident in 1988 led to temporary suspension of service
Sichuan Airlines (Chengdu)	Domestic services, linking main cities of Sichuan with other large cities of China	Tupolev Tu-154 Airbus A320 Yun-7	Founded in 1986 as the provincial airline of Sichuan Government. First service July 1988
Tianjin Airlines (Tianjin)	Domestic services	Boeing 737-300	
Zhejiang Airlines (Hangzhou)	Local services, connecting mainly Hangzhou with Shanghai	Tupolev Tu-154 DHC Dash 8-300	Founded 7 September 1990 by Zhejiang provincial government and China Eastern
Zhongyuam Airlines (Zhengzhou)	Local services, connect-Henan cities with main cities of eastern China	Boeing 737-300 Yun-7	Founded 17 May 1986 as the Henan provincial airline
China Flying Dragon Aviation (Harbin)	Operates local services in northeastern (Manchurian) provinces, but also performs general aviation work, forestry protection, etc.	Yun-12, 11, 9 Eurocopter Ecureuil	Founded in 1981 by Harbin Aircraft Manufacturing and Ministry of Geological-Mineral Resources. Limited airline service as Feilong Airlines
Air Changan (Xian)	Local services in Shaanxi province	Yun-7	Formed in 1991 as a joint venture between Xi'an municipal government and the Shaanxi and Xi'an aircraft manufacturing companies

TABLE 2

Airlines descended from, or affiliated to, the former CAAC – 1995

Airline and Base	Route Network	Aircraft Fleet	Remarks
Air China (Beijing)	Intercontinental, international, and mainline domestic routes. Main link with Japan	Boeing 747SP, -200/400, 767, 707, 737-200/300	Took over CAAC's international network, 1 July 1988
China Southern (Guangzhou)	Extensive international route network, mainline domestic routes. Main link with Hong Kong. Trans-Pacific routes	Boeing 737-200/300/ 500, 757, 767, 777, Airbus A340, Yun-7/ An-24. Shorts 360	Took over CAAC's operations February 1991, but had been operating since 1989. Formed GAMECO maintenance/ overhaul base. Invested in Xiamen Airlines. Largest of 'Big Three' Chinese airlines, with 120 aircraft, 160 routes, 8 million passengers in 1992
China Eastern (Shanghai)	International and mainline domestic routes. Trans-Pacific and European intercontinental services	MD-11, MD-82/ 90, Airbus A300/ 310/330, BAe 146, Fokker 100, Yun-7, Yun-8, Shorts 360	Established December 1987, took over CAAC's operations May 1988. Main link Shanghai-Hong Kong. One of China's 'Big Three'
China Northern (Shenyang))	Domestic routes to major Chinese cities, and throughout the provinces of Manchuria. International routes to Russian Far East, Korea and Japan	MD 82/90, Yun-7, Airbus A300, Tupolev Tu-154	Founded in 1988. Leased Ilyushin Il-86 from Uzbekistan in 1996
China Southwest (Chengdu)	Mainline and feeder routes from points in Sichuan. Main link with Lhasa, Tibet	Boeing 737-300, 707, 757-300, Tupolev Tu-154M, Yun-7, Yun-12	Founded October 1987 from CAAC regional directorate, and attained full autonomy in 1989. Airport at Lhasa is 3,540m (11,600 ft) amsl
China Northwest (Xi'an)	Domestic services in northwestern provinces of Shaanxi and Gansu	Airbus A300-600, A 310, Tupolev Tu-154, BAe 146, An-24, Yun-7	Former CAAC regional directorate, attained local autonomy December 1989
China Xinjiang (Urumchi)	Domestic routes, mainly in Xinjiang autonomous region	Boeing 737-300 Ilyushin Il-86, Tupolev Tu-154 DHC-6	Founded in 1985. Aircraft leasing arrangements with Uzbekistan Airlines
Yunnan Airlines (Kunming)	Domestic routes, mainly in Yunnan province. International route to Hanoi	Boeing 737-400	Began operations in 1993, at first with aircraft leased from Malaysian Airlines

China United (Nanyuan)	Contract work for Chinese Government	Ilyushin Il-76, Tupolev Tu-154, Boeing 737, Trident	Transport Division of Chinese Air Force, but also operates commercially. Founded 25 December 1986
China General Aviation (Taiyuan)	Only large general aviation operator in China, but operates a few scheduled and charter services	Antonov An-30. Ilyushin Il-14, Yakovlev Yak-42 DHC-6, Yun-7, 12, various helicopters	Established July 1989

CHAPTER THIRTY-ONE

Early Airline Growth in Prewar Japan

An Emergent Industrial Power

Until the arrival of Commodore Matthew Calbraith Perry, of the United States Navy, on 14 July 1853, Japan was so isolated from the rest of the world that it might almost have been on another planet. No Japanese was ever allowed to go abroad, and no foreigner, except for a limited number of Dutch traders, was allowed to visit. The country was ruled under a strict feudal system and its history was one of complex internecine warfare and struggle for supremacy by local feudal lords. Nevertheless, as a people, the Japanese had demonstrated considerable resilience to invasion. Mongol threats in the 13th Century had been repulsed, when Kublai Khan's navy was fortuitously destroyed by a typhoon, subsequently revered as The Divine Wind (Kamikaze), in 1281. Commercial and missionary, as opposed to military invasions, had been barely tolerated. Portuguese Jesuits, in 1549; Spanish Franciscans in 1593, and Dutch traders in 1605: all had suffered repression, indignity, and sometimes slaughter. In 1673 the English sent a ship, under the flag of the East India Company, to Nagasaki, to try to start trading on a limited scale, like the Dutch. The ship was called the *Return* and was appropriately named. It was sent on its way and the seclusion of Japan was complete.

Perry's intervention was a turning point. In July 1859, the Treaty of Kanagawa established diplomatic and commercial relations with the United States, opening up the port of Yokohama. The British, in August; and the French, in October of the same year, concluded similar treaties. The Japanese sent foreign envoys to Washington in 1860, and to all the great European powers in 1862. Internal disruption continued, as the local warlords vied for supremacy, but the feudal system was at an end. Many reforms were introduced. Japanese citizens could travel abroad, and foreigners, especially those who could advise on modern construction and development, were welcomed. Oppressive methods were reduced, such as torture and the insistence of *hara kiri*, and Christianity was permitted. Steamships were built, telegraph lines laid down, and the first railway was opened, from Tokyo to Yokohama, in 1872. The Emperor opened the House of Peers and the House of Representatives, in November 1890, to give Japan a parliamentary constitution.

Much of the industrial and commercial progress had been stimulated by the accession of the Meiji Emperor, who, in 1868, had overthrown the power of the feudal barons, the Shoguns, and assumed the full power of an Emperor, and decreed that 'intercourse with foreign countries shall in future be carried on in accordance with the public laws of the whole world'. This generalization apparently included participation in foreign military exploits. The war with China, in 1894–5, alliance with European nations in the Boxer Rebellion in Peking in 1900, and the outstanding triumph over the Russian fleet in 1904–5 gave notice that Japan was no colonial or quasi-colonial vassal. In an age when naval supremacy was the key to political dominance, Japan quickly built a modern navy, based on

British traditions and discipline, and by the turn of the century had eight battleships and four heavy cruisers.

With such military mobility and flexibility, Japan began to establish territorial sovereignty over neighbouring islands and on the Asiatic mainland. The war with China gave Formosa to Japan, in 1895; and the Pacific Bonin and Kurile Islands were annexed; southern Sakhalin (Karafuto) and the port of Dairen (Port Arthur) were ceded by Russia in 1905, after the naval victory, and perhaps as significantly, much of Manchuria fell into the sphere of Japanese commercial influence. The Peace of Shimonoseki of 1895 had given Japan wide control of Formosa (Taiwan) and this was translated into complete annexation in 1910. But, with the Peace of Portsmouth, which settled the Russo-Japanese War, Japan was already firmly in charge of the northwestern rim of the Pacific Ocean.

Japan joined the Allies against Germany in the First World War, taking over the German Colony at Kiao-Chiao in the Chinese Shantung Peninsula. This included Tsingtao, an important port and site of a famous brewery, from which the current excellent Japanese beers may well have been derived. After its wartime co-operation with the Royal Navy, Japan retained a postwar League of Nations mandate over the formerly German Marshall, Pelew, Mariana and Marshall Islands (now known collectively as Micronesia). The Japanese Navy escorted 788 Allied ships through the Mediterranean. And the Japanese Army joined in the anti-Bolshevik encirclement, reaching Chita and Omsk in support of Admiral Kolchak, in 1920. Altogether, by the end of the First World War, and with the beginning of the awareness of the aeroplane as an instrument of transport in the 1920s, Japan was technically and psychologically ready to advance in step with Europe and America.

Birth of an Airline Industry

Almost alone among the countries of Asia, Japan created an airline industry, by a combination of interests from commercial enterprises, individual initiative, and government sponsorship. The only other country of Asia to start airline service in the early 1920s was Thailand, then called Siam. That these two were the only independent nations east of Afghanistan was no coincidence.

Most of Asia consisted of colonial or partially self-governing territories of European colonial powers and, in the case of the Philippines, of the United States. None of the colonialists were particularly interested, it seemed, in developing air routes within the colonies; but all of them, for purely nationalistic reasons, were keenly devoted to the idea of operating an air service to and from the homeland, or 'mother country' as the contemporary imperialists liked to call it. Thus, the British priority was to establish an air route to India, the French to Indo-China (now Vietnam, Laos, and Cambodia), and the Dutch to the East Indies (now Indonesia). The Russians had the same ambitions in the north, while the Americans, frustrated for more than a decade by the vast expanses of the Pacific Ocean, had Manila as their goal for intercontinental expansion to the East.

As for China, the British abandoned hope as that country entered the chaotic period of civil wars during the early and middle Twenties, and only at the end of the decade did German and American interests grasp a foothold. But once again, the objective was not to serve the Chinese; but to dig foundations for ultimate inter-continental expansion later on, by securing operational bases at the farthest termini from Berlin and San Francisco respectively.

With Imperial-Airways seeking only to link London with Delhi and Calcutta; Air Orient (merging into Air France in 1933) to link Paris with Saïgon; and KLM doing the same – with conspicuous success – from Amsterdam to Batavia (now Jakarta): the field in eastern Asia was relatively clear for Japanese airline expansion.

The distances, however, linking Japan with its overseas possessions, were formidable for the somewhat primitive air transport machines of the early Twenties. Even the 80 miles separating Shiminoseki, at the southwestern end of Honshu, with Pusan, at the southern end of Japan's mainland vassal, Korea, could be faced only with apprehension, if not trepidation.

As for domestic routes, the demographic justification for air routes between Japan's major cities, such as Tokyo—Osaka via Nagoya and Kyoto, or from Osaka to Fukuoka via Hiroshima and Shiminoseki and the industrial northern Kyushu, seemed obvious. Elsewhere in Japan, the mountainous terrain provided tremendous challenges to airmanship, equalling the difficulties faced by the pioneer airlines in the USA in crossing the Allegheny Mountains – and these were not so high as the Japanese Alps. Also, along the whole distance from Tokyo to Nagasaki, embracing perhaps 70 percent of the population, and 80 percent of the industrial activity of Japan, a good railway system served everyone's needs. The metre-gauge system was not especially fast or spectacular, did not establish any speed records; but it was efficient, coping with the growing volumes of passenger and freight traffic as Japan's population and industry expanded after the end of the First World War.

Japan's Pioneer Airline

As a consequence, the fact that Japan's first airline enterprise was across a stretch of water, where the surface competition was much slower than that of the railways, was a logical outcome. By the initiative of Mr Choichi Inouye, of the Itoh Flying School, the Nippon Koku Yuso Kenkyujo (NKYK), or the Japan Air Transport Research Institute (JATRI) was founded on 4 June 1922. Its base was on the beach at Sakai City, a contiguous city-suburb of Osaka, and in the vicinity of the site of the new international airport constructed on land reclaimed from Osaka Bay. With a capital of 500,000 yen, Inouye bought ten Yokosho floatplanes, at a bargain price from the Japanese Navy. These had been built by the Yokosuka Kaigun Kosho (later the Yokosuka Koku Kosho) – the Yokosuka Naval Air Arsenal.

On 15 November 1922, Inouye's NKYK began the first regular air service in Japan. The route was from Sakai (for Osaka) to Tokushima, across Osaka Bay on the island of Shikoku, via Wakayama on Honshu, south of Sakai, and closest to the other island. The fare was a reasonable 5 yen, worth perhaps about US $10 or $12 today. But Inouye could not persuade the cautious Japanese to take to the skies, and certainly not over water. Thus, he had to ask a local girl who ran a small saki bar to accompany him, free of charge. This story has been elaborated to suggest that he took his favourite geisha girl, but this is most probably apocryphal.

In 1923 the route was extended along the northern coast of Shikoku, through the serenely beautiful Inland Sea, to a coastal town, the equally serene and beautiful Imabari. Routed via Takamatsu, the frequency was once a week; but the $1\frac{1}{2}$-hour flight was in good contrast to the six hours required by ship, and the demand was sufficient to increase the frequency to three a week. By the end of the first year, however, NKYK had carried only 27 passengers and 1,107 kg of cargo, happily supported by a government subsidy of 8,000 yen, or about $20,000 in today's values.

One of the Aichi AB-4s used on NKYK's routes from Osaka.

More than in almost any other country of the world, the transport systems of Japan have had to cope with hazards that are not the result of human negligence or accident, but because of the forces of Nature, or Acts of God, as the insurance companies call them. The Great Earthquake of September 1923, that devastated the Kanto area around Tokyo (about which more later) did not directly affect Inouye. But on 13 March 1925, a great tornado succeeded in overturning the hangars at Sakai City. Nevertheless, on 20 May of the same year, the Osaka—Imabari service was increased to a daily frequency, and a year later extended to Oita, close to Beppu, on the island of Kyushu, and a resort destination.

Inter-City Service

The Inouye operation, commendable though it was, and taking pride of place in being Japan's first, was not providing much more than what a specialized commuter airline would be doing today: carrying vacationers to their holiday destinations; in other words a specialized operation for privileged people. In contrast, the second airline aimed to connect Japan's two largest cities. On 11 January 1923 the Tozai Teiki Koku-Kai (TTKK) (the East and West Scheduled Air Transport Society) was founded at Tachigawa airfield, near Tokyo (and later to expand to become a large US Air Force Base after the Second World War). With the co-operation of the Itoh and the Shirato Flying Schools, TTKK began a scheduled service from Tokyo to Osaka, via Hamamatsu, in July 1923. For the first two years, only mail was carried in the Nakajima Type V aircraft.

This was not surprising, as, shortly after opening the service, the Great Earthquake shook Japan – and the term is absolute in both the literal and the metaphorical sense. It was not the most destructive or the most lethal earthquake in history; but located as it was in Sagami Bay, Tokyo, its effect was devastating. Most of the brick and stone buildings were destroyed when the earth shook on 1 September 1923, and more wooden buildings were razed in the fires that raged for several days throughout the cities of Tokyo and Yokohama. Almost 100,000 people were killed, 104,000 people were injured, many severely, and about 44,000 people were listed as missing. With such a disaster to cope with, Japan had more things on its mind than the development of civil aviation. Indeed, the repercussions following the criticism of the lack of resolve by the Government led to political recriminations and changes in political power.

From the outset, the driving force behind the Tozai Teiki Koku-Kai was the *Asahi Shimbun*, largest newspaper in Japan and one of the largest in the world. The two flying schools, founded by Otojiro Itoh and Einosuke Shirato, had designed and built two-seat biplanes, one each, with the aid of their students. With six Nakajima biplanes, TTKK thus had a fleet of eight aircraft. The newspaper actually took over the management of the company in August 1924, and offered passenger accommodation on its flights. But, unlike Inouye, who had to take unorthodox steps at first to persuade people to ride with him, the Asahi's reason for not charging a fare was for self-interest – it was apprehensive of the possible adverse publicity if anything went wrong.

The aircraft, incidentally, were based at each end of the route, Tokyo and Osaka, and met halfway, at Hamamatsu, where they turned around and returned to their own bases. Towards the end of 1924, a commercial certificate was granted to begin passenger service, and the Tokyo—Osaka fare was set at 35 yen, or perhaps about US $100.00 in today's currency values. By March 1925, 384 flights were reported to have been completed, indicating a steady and reliable operation. In 1926, a new route was opened northwards from Tokyo, to Sendai, but not sustained for more than a year or so. The two 'home-builts' were retired, and replaced by three Dornier Komets, built under licence by Kawasaki.

The German export initiative was one of the reasons for getting the Japanese airlines into their stride. The Komets enabled TTKK to start full passenger service between Tokyo and Osaka on 27 August 1927. Not to be outdone, Choichi Inouye's NKYK introduced two Junkers-F 13 floatplanes in January 1928 and began full passenger service – other than flights especially for the resorts presumably – in July of that year. During the 1930s Inouye also had ten Hansa Brandenburgs, an Avro, a Supermarine Southampton, a Savoia Marchetti S.62, and other Japanese types, all of them floatplanes.

Indications of further initiatives, under official auspices, were evident in the early Twenties, when, in April 1923, the Nihon Koku Kabushiki Kaisha (NKKK) was founded in Osaka by Ryuzo Kawanishi, who proceeded to build an air base at the mouth of the Kitsu River at Osaka. Translated, NKKK means the Japan Air

NKYK had among its fleet a Supermarine Southampton. It was used on the Osaka—Beppu services and was almost certainly the only passenger-configured Southampton. It had accommodation for sixteen passengers.

Lines Co Ltd and its subsequent destiny suggested that it was well named. Its first route was from Osaka to Beppu via the small island of Shohdo-Shima in the Inland Sea. Paralleling Inouye's route, it also used Yokosho (Naval Arsenal) floatplanes at first, graduating later to Dornier Wals, constructed by Kawasaki. By this time, NKKK had started a service to the important Kyushu city of Fukuoka, and significantly this was done under the specific direction of the Ministry of Posts and Telecommunications.

Late Extra!

By the time the Tozai Teiki Koku-Kai had introduced its Dornier Komets into passenger service from Tokyo to Osaka in 1927, the *Asahi Shimbun* newspaper chain had already decided to isolate its interests in commercial aviation, directing them more specifically towards it specialized needs. In February 1927, it formed the Asahi Teiki Koku-Kai (ATKK) (The Asahi Periodical Air Navigation Society) to carry mail and periodicals during the summer months, on the routes from Tokyo to Niigata and from Osaka to Niigata, via Toyama. These routes were to cities on the Sea of Japan, on the western coast of Honshu, and across the mountain chain that presents a formidable barrier to swift surface transport. Undoubtedly, the Asahi management was possessed of visionary initiative in realising the value of the aeroplane in disseminating its products – this was before wireless (radio) reached ordinary homes.

TTKK replaced its early aircraft with three Dornier Komets.

When the TTKK and the NKKK merged in 1928 (*see* Chapter 32), the ATKK, very much a family business, remained independent, concentrating on carrying newspapers. It also sought to use aircraft for sending its reporters or photographers on missions for the *Asahi Shimbun,* to obtain the so-called scoops, cherished by all good newspapermen as epitomizing their vocation. Much credit must go to the Chief Editor, Masuichi Midoro, who was also Head of the Air Transport Department, assisted by the deputy director, Katsuyoshi Nakano. These two promoted the use of aviation within the Asahi organization, and in April 1937, with considerable verve, despatched an aeroplane that did more than achieve a newspaper scoop. Pilots Masaaki Iinuma and Kenji Tsukagasaki, flying a Mitsubishi Karigane I, the *Kamikaze-gou,* or *Divine Wind*, made a world record-breaking long-range flight from Tokyo to London, to photograph the Coronation

430

Ceremony of King George VI. The flight to London took 94 hr 18 min, with an actual flying time of 51 hr 19 min. Until this time, little was known in Europe of Japanese aviation activity; but much in the same way as Chkalov's and Gromov's trans-polar flights from Moscow to the United States served notice that Soviet aviation was on the move, so too did the *Divine Wind* suggest that something was stirring in the Orient.

Maintaining their spirit of independence in the postwar years, Mr Midoro and Mr Nakano were, in December 1952, to establish Nippeli – the Japan Helicopter and Aeroplane Transport Company, and when this company merged with Far Eastern Airlines in 1958, Midoro-san was its first president.

Other First Steps

Before moving to the main stream of Japanese commercial airline development before the Second World War, mention should be made of three small companies that operated quasi-scheduled flights, mainly during the summer, and then only sporadically. In September 1928, the Tokyo Koku Kabushiki-Kaisha (TKKK) was formed to operate seaplane services to the resorts to the south and west of Tokyo, as far as Shimizu. These included the popular seaside towns of Atami and Ito, and the island of Oshima – broadly the Japanese equivalent of the English Southend or the American Atlantic City, with perhaps a little more refinement. TKKK's Nakajima 90s and Aichi AB-1 flying-boats also did good work in locating schools of fish – staple diet of the Japanese more then even than now.

TKKK operated seaplane services from Tokyo to holiday resorts. Its fleet included Aichi AB-1s on twin floats.

Somewhat in the same manner, in Osaka, in July 1931, the Nihon-Kai Koku Kabushiki-Kaisa (NKKKK) (Japan Sea Air Transport Company) was formed, as its name implies, to provide a service to that coastline. Using Mitsubishi TC 1 seaplanes, it linked Osaka with Saigo, on Dogo Island, via Kinosaki, Tottori and Matsui.

These two companies were very small, but by comparison, another was a midget, albeit a sporting one. As early as January 1920, Koozo Ando had established a flying school near Nagoya, the Ando Hikoki Kenkyujo (Ando Flying Institute); and in about 1931 began a once weekly summer service to the seaside towns of Gamagori and Futami. Koozo Ando was a pilot who was also a sports flyer who sometimes took passengers. He was also a member of the Japanese

JAPAN'S PIONEER AIRLINES

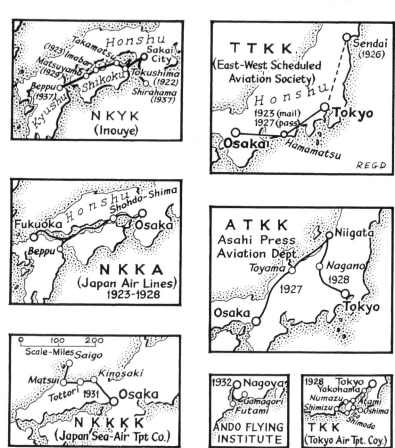

Maps 31. Japan's Pioneer Airlines

Vying with Siam (Thailand) for the claim to have started the first airline in Asia, Japan had several pioneering air transport enterprises during the 1920s. Mr Inouye deserves great credit for having been the first, and his floatplane route through the enchanting Inland Sea must have been a revelation in travel at the time. The powerful Asahi publishing group established a service that was partly to deliver its newspapers to places where surface communication was slow. The East-West and Japan Air Lines companies combined to establish the national airline that was to provide air services to Japan's growing empire during the 1930s.

An early Japanese air transport scene. The nearest two air taxi aeroplanes are Tokyo Koku Kaisha's Aiba Tubames.

Parliament and his air service seems to have been a prerequisite offered to influential friends rather than a public utility.

Diminutive though the operation was, Ando shared with the other early operators a characteristic that seemed to be almost a common denominator: they seemed to convey holiday-makers to seaside places, almost entirely in seaplanes. Each with its local operating sphere of influence, they were parochial in their geographical range, and apparently in their aspirations for growth. Exceptionally, two of the early operators were marked out for a greater future, and were to form the nucleus of a Japanese national airline and flag carrier.

CHAPTER THIRTY-TWO

A National Trunk Airline For Japan

Prospects for an Empire Route

On 20 October 1928 the Nihon Koku Yuso Kabushiki Kaisha (NKYKK) or the Japan Air Transport Company, was incorporated with a capital of 10 million yen. It was formed under the direct jurisdiction not only of the civil authorities but of the military departments of the Japanese Government as well. It was intended to be the 'chosen instrument' of an embryo airline industry, and its main objectives were clearly linked with Japanese political expansionism in the Far East.

Early in 1929, it took over two of the pioneer airlines. One was the Tozai Teiki Koku Kai (TTKK), founded in 1923 and which had received a commercial certificate from Japanese authorities late in 1924. The other was the Nihon Koku Kabushiki Kaisha (NKKK) (Japan Air Lines Company), also founded early in 1923, and which was already carrying air mail for the Ministry of Posts and Communications. TTKK translated as the East and West Scheduled Air Transport Society and linked the Kanto and Kansai regions, that is Tokyo and Osaka; while NKKK flew from Osaka to Fukuoka.

The new chosen instrument immediately set to work. On 1 April 1929, using a military Salmson 2-A.2 single-engined biplane, it started a through service from Tokyo to Fukuoka via Osaka. Used at first only to carry mail and to train pilots over the route, it provided expedited communication between almost all the main cities of Japan. NKYKK had taken over eighteen of the Salmson biplanes from the military authorities, and significantly, it also started a route in Korea, from Pusan to Seoul and Pyongyang, and onwards to Dairen, the Japanese enclave-port in Manchuria, still at that time Chinese, though plainly vulnerable because of the

NKYKK acquired eighteen Salmson 2-A.2s from the military authorities and began a Tokyo—Osaka—Fukuoka service with them on 1 April 1929. (*Courtesy John Stroud*)

435

chaotic conditions in China as the warlords struggled for power.

Japan regarded Korea as a Colony and Chosen, as it was called by the Japanese (the name is Chinese in origin) had been under direct Japanese occupation and administration since the early part of the 20th Century. Korea had suffered from Japanese interference since the 16th Century, when, after much piracy, Japan invaded Korea in 1592. The country was a battlefield for Japanese and Chinese armies and although Japan withdrew from direct sovereignty, its influence was thereafter always strong. After a long stormy history of foreign interference, with punitive expeditions from European nations and even the United States as well as Russia, Japan eventually asserted its authority after its great victory over Russia in the war of 1904–5. A treaty confirmed Japan's control over foreign affairs, and Korea soon lost all semblance of independence. On 29 August 1910 the Emperor of Korea formally surrendered his country and crown, and Japan's annexation was complete.

This transfer of power was accompanied by a ruthless extermination of all things Korean, including its language, its culture and its wealth. Koreans were deprived of all privileges, lost their private land holdings, and were altogether reduced to the status of second-class citizens, and in some areas their condition was close to slavery. Under a harsh military rule, however, much material progress was made. Railways and roads were built, public buildings constructed, agriculture and industry improved, sanitation and living conditions – at least for the Japanese – improved. Communications, formerly slow and almost primitive, were vastly reorganized; and the introduction of NKYKK's air services was a logical part of the modernization process.

Fokker Universals played an important part in developing Japanese air transport. This group were operated by Nihon Koku Kabushiki Kaisha (Japan Airlines Company).

The First Overseas Sortie

At the beginning, the crossing of the Korea Strait, from Fukuoka to Pusan, was made by ship, as the old military biplanes did not have sufficient range, certainly not with any payload. But on 21 June 1929 – wasting no time – the first overwater flight was made, after special pilot training. Ten Fokker Super Universal passenger aircraft were delivered from the United States and quickly assembled. On 1 July an experimental flight was made from Osaka to Fukuoka and on to Shanghai, although, as yet, this had no commercial objective. Far more important was the route inaugurated on 15 July 1929, from Tokyo to Fukuoka, via Osaka, with the Fokker Universals. Each one was fitted with six seats, and was publicly available. While sporadic services, on a seasonal basis, and with uncertain frequency, had previously been made by the small companies, this was the first scheduled passenger service, by the definition of the term as we know it today, to be opened in Japan.

Expansion thereafter was prompt and effective, as shown in the map series on page 443. On 10 September 1929 the service for passengers was extended to Seoul and Dairen, and such was the acceptance of the Fokkers in Japanese aviation circles that the Nakajima company began to produce the Super Universal under licence. Additionally, Fokker F.VIIb/3m tri-motors, imported from the Netherlands, were added to the fleet; and Kawasaki began to build Dornier Wal flying-boats, again under licence from the manufacturer. One of these made a trial flight from Fukuoka to Shanghai on 7 March 1930. Japan was spreading its commercial aviation wings, and there was little hiding the fact that such activity was an adjunct to imperialist ambitions.

Fokker F.VIIb/3ms later supplemented the Fokker Universals and Super Universals. This F.VII belonged to Japan Air Transport.

Japan had made no secret of its intention to force its way to a position of both military and commercial dominance of east Asia, taking advantage of the confusion in China and the decline of Russian influence, which had never recovered from the disastrous defeat of 1904–5 and had been handicapped by its own relative stagnation as it put itself together again after the near-dismemberment following the 1917 Revolution. One of the sequels to the Russo-Japanese War, and confirmed by post-First World War negotiation, was Japan's control over the South Manchurian Railway (SMR) connecting Mukden (now Shenyang), the biggest city of Manchuria, with the Kwantung Peninsula, with its strategically vital ports of Dairen and Port Arthur. On the night of 18 September 1931, using as an excuse the alleged provocation by Chinese forces blowing up a part of the SMR near Mukden, the Japanese Army occupied all the territory adjacent to the railway, and quickly extended this to a large area of southern Manchuria. Dutifully fulfilling its chosen instrument role, NKYKK followed the army only three months later, and extended a branch of its Dairen route to Mukden on 28 December 1931, and made its subsequent intentions quite clear by opening a branch line northwards from Mukden to Changchun and Harbin.

Back at home, the Japanese aviation authorities had been methodically persevering with improving its inter-city air services, and with making itself less dependent on foreign supplies of aircraft and of expertise. On 1 November 1933 a daily night air mail service began between Tokyo and Osaka, using Nakajima P.1 mailplanes. With commendable enterprise, sixteen aerial lighthouses were put into operation on the route, rather in the manner of the Lighted Airway pioneered in the USA during the 1920s. Unfortunately, this initiative did not meet with success. For all its ambitions and determination, Japan was still at the lower end

In November 1933 night air mail services were begun between Tokyo and Osaka, using Nakajima P.1s.

of the learning curve. There were several crashes, and the service was suspended after a few months of operation.

Such a setback was unimportant, compared with the overseas developments. On 1 March 1934 Pu Yi, who had been the titular Emperor of China in 1912 when the Manchu dynasty abdicated its control and China became a republic, formally announced his ascendancy to the throne of what was called the 'Empire of the Manchu', to provide some kind of historical legitimacy. Pu Yi was simply a puppet for the Japanese, but he was able to live in comfort at Changchun (Hsinking) where the semblance of a new capital city was created. Changchun was on the direct NKYKK route to Harbin.

Modernizing the Fleet

Meanwhile technical progress was being made as the airline modernized its fleet. In December 1934 the first Douglas DC-2 was imported, and the emergent Japanese aircraft manufacturing industry lost no time in capitalizing on the opportunity to catch up with the rest of the world in airframe technology. The Nakajima firm started immediately to build DC-2s under licence, and the first one was completed almost within the year.

Daily air mail service began from Tokyo to Darien and to Changchun (the 'capital' of Manchuria) on 1 April 1935. The night air mail flights between Tokyo and Osaka resumed, and the passenger flight frequency to Darien was increased from the previous thrice weekly to daily. Nakajima-built Douglas DC-2s became standard equipment, superseding the Fokkers; and British-built Airspeed Envoys were also introduced. But these latter did not last long, and were retired in 1936. For the record, Nakajima built six DC-2s, of which one crashed and five were, in due course, chartered by the Army, and most of these were damaged on the ground or crashed. Nevertheless, Japan had, by the agency of NKYKK, firmly established a trunk air route to its newly acquired overseas territory, one that was of enormous potential wealth, agriculturally and industrially, able to provide the

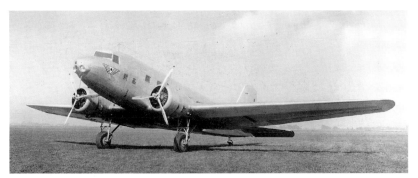

Nakajima-built Douglas DC-2s mainly replaced Fokkers on Japan's air routes. This one was one of Japan Air Transport's fleet.

1930s scene at Fukuoka with a Douglas DC-2, Fokker Super Universal and an Airspeed Envoy.

foundations of an overseas empire. Such was its importance that it had its own airline, completely financed and developed by Japanese interests, and important enough in its own right to justify a separate chapter in this book.

Quite apart from its territorial expansion in Manchuria (called Manchukuo by the Japanese and given *de facto* acceptance by the world during the latter 1930s) Japan did not neglect the other arm of its Pacific Rim empire, the island of Formosa or Taiwan, which had been annexed in 1910. On 8 October 1935 scheduled service began from Fukuoka to Taipei, via Naha (Okinawa), using Fokker F.VIIb/3ms, released from other duties as the faster Airspeed Envoys were introduced on the trunk route to Korea and Manchuria.

For a time Japan used a number of Airspeed Envoys. Some were supplied from the United Kingdom while others were built in Japan by Mitsubishi and given the name Hina-Zuru (Young Crane).

Well into the decade of the 1930s, the Nakajima-Douglas DC-2s supplemented the Fokkers and the Envoys, and Nakajima also began production of its own design, the Type AT-2. Thirty-three of these were built, both for NKYKK and MKK, the Manchurian airline, but were not used extensively, as the DC-2s were themselves being supplemented by Nakajima-built DC-3s. The first prototype AT-2 was delivered to MKK on 12 September 1936, and was deployed throughout the NKYKK system, internationally and domestically.

Thirty-three Nakajima AT-2s were built for NKYKK and the Manchurian airline MKK. The example illustrated belonged to Japan Air Transport.

With DC-2s responsible for the mainline service, AT-2s were able to inaugurate feeder routes within Japan on 1 October 1936. These radiated from Tokyo and Osaka to the northern coast of the island of Honshu, bordering the Sea of Japan, to cities such as Niigata, Toyama, Tottori and Matsue. The first air route to the

440

island of Shikoku opened, with an Osaka—Tokushima—Kochi connection; while in Taiwan, domestic routes were opened from Tapei along the west coast to Kaiochung at the southern tip of the island, and also to Hualien on the east coast. With the opening of a service to Sapporo via Sendai and Aomori on 1 April 1937, all four of Japan's main islands were now connected by NKYKK.

Aggressive Expansion

The Nakajima AT enjoyed an hour of glory on 1 June 1937, when it made an express flight from Tokyo to Changchun (Hsinking), and subsequently developed fast flights to the Manchurian cities and to Dairen. By this time, the Japanese Army was aggressively moving forward on the Asiatic mainland, and NKYKK was right behind it.

Almost in a repetition of the 'Manchurian Incident' of 18 September 1931, the Japanese instigated another such episode on 7 July 1937, when Chinese soldiers were alleged to have fired upon Japanese soldiers at the Marco Polo Bridge in Peking. By the time the Chinese defenders had been driven out of Shanghai in November of that year, NKYKK had already opened a military support route to

Map 32a. Hui Tung Kung Sze 1941
This was the airline set up in China in 1941 to provide transport service in the areas occupied by Japan. These were confined mainly in the north and along the coast, but a route was also started along the Yangtse River as far as Hankow, replacing that of CNAC, the Kuomintang-Pan American airline that had retreated westwards. Connections were made, as indicated on the map, both to industrial Manchukuo and to Japan itself.

441

Haneda Airport, Tokyo. The prewar terminal.

that great port city on 2 October. Now firmly in control of the northern Chinese Provinces, Japan was able to complete its air network with a direct route from Fukuoka to Peking, across the China Sea via Tsingtao, where Japan had superseded Germany as commercial controller of that foreign enclave on the Shantung Peninsula. When Chiang Kai-shek's Nationalist Chinese capital of Nanking fell to the Japanese occupying forces on 13 December 1937, NKYKK's Shanghai route was extended accordingly in the following March. By this time, for all its main overseas routes, the Lockheed Model 14 became the fleet flagship, going on to the trunk line from Tokyo to Changchun (Hsinking) on 1 August 1938. On the same date, in a mountainous country where, like Japan, only a narrow coastal strip could be developed, the island of Taiwan was encircled by an NKYKK route.

The Lockheed 14 became the Japan Air Transport flagship in the years just before the war.

442

N K Y K K Follows the Flag

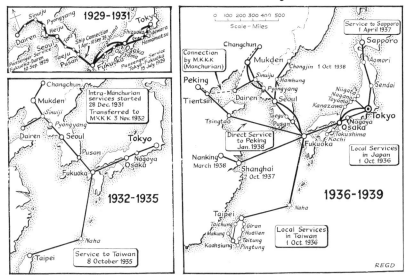

Maps 32b. NKYKK Follows the Flag
The initials translate as the Japan Air Transport Company, which was both the national airline and a supporting arm of the military establishment during Japan's expansionist era of the 1930s. The first important step was the development of the trunk line to Korea, then under Japanese rule, and then this line was extended into Manchuria, which was occupied by military force from China in 1931. Further overseas routes began in 1935, to Taiwan, then Japanese territory, and, when Japan invaded China in 1937, NKYKK followed the armed forces to provide the vital transport link with the homeland.

Japanese Air Routes in China

Following the rapid and successful invasion of the Chinese mainland by Japanese forces in 1937, the occupation was completed of the northern and coastal Provinces as far south as Shanghai, and as far inland as Hankow, as well as the seizure of key ports in the south such as Wenchow, Amoy and Swatow. Without delay, Japan established, in 1938, its own airline in China. Named the Hui Tung Kung Sze (China Air Transport) it served as a surrogate for NKYKK for a few short years during a period of precarious peace – though this latter term must be regarded with reservations. Although Japan was in firm command of the cities, the Chinese were, to all intents and purposes, in firm command of the countryside. Japanese patrols penetrated the rice paddies with the same peril that Chinese patriots infiltrated the cities.

Using a few of the handed-down Nakajima-Douglas DC-2s and the obsolescent Fokker F.VII/3ms, and even the odd de Havilland Puss Moth or two, Hui Tung operated as an affiliate of NKYKK and for a while its services also paralleled those of the former parent company. By the latter part of 1941, it had quite an extensive network (*see* map) but, with the onset of Japan's direct, rather than indirect involvement in the Second World War, all civil air services in China, except for priority military-associated activities, came to an end.

Chinese historians will assert, with a certain amount of logic, that the Second World War really began with the Marco Polo Bridge incident on 7 July 1937, not

443

on 3 September 1939, when Britain and France declared war on Germany, nor on 7 December 1941, when the Japanese Navy attacked and almost destroyed the United States fleet on anchor in Pearl Harbor, Hawaii. This was certainly another 'incident' but unlike the previous two, the consequences were far different. However, at least in the first few years, Japan's colonial and occupational territorial expansion continued; and the airline was there to support the air communication and airborne logistics requirements. But by 1941 NKYKK had lost its identity, as it was engulfed into a larger organization that, in Japanese eyes, more closely matched the ideals of its self-styled East Asian Co-Prosperity Sphere. Effectively, NKYKK became Dai Nippon Koku (DNK) on 28 November 1938.

Greater Japan Airlines

Preoccupied as they were with political developments of dire consequence much nearer home, the European, nations watching Nazi Germany's conquests in Europe, were inclined to ignore, or at least to pass over lightly, news of Japanese commercial expansion in the Far East. They would have been wise to have studied them more closely; for just as the development of the Japanese airline network had gone hand-in-hand with the military conquest of Manchuria and China, so did the expansion of the reinforced national airline prove to be the harbinger of imperialistic ambitions. Almost unnoticed in the West, the Japanese airline had, by 1938, grown to rank among the top ten airlines of the world, measured by total passenger-miles flown. By 1939 it ranked seventh, and in 1940, still growing apace, and with Europe in turmoil, it was fourth, surpassed only by the United States, the Soviet Union, and – by a small margin – Australia.

On 28 November 1938 Dai Nippon Koku (DNK) or the International Air Transportation Company, was formed in Tokyo, as a privately-owned corporation. It was a merger of the old NKYKK and the Kokusai Koku KK which had been formed in Changchun, nominal capital of Manchuria, in August 1937, under the sponsorship of the Japanese Army, and which had undergone some extraordinary adventures during its embryo months.

On 4 April 1939, to give notice, so to speak, of its future plans, Dai Nippon made a survey flight from Yokohama to Saipan and Palau, using a Kawanishi flying-boat. In the same month, DNK made another survey flight to Teheran, using a Mitsubishi Type 96, in connection with the Prince of Iran's wedding. Had it been consolidated as a regular service, it would have connected with Deutsche Lufthansa's direct service to Berlin, thus providing an airline connection between two far-flung members of the Axis Powers. The same aircraft type, incidentally, later made another such long-distance flight, in December 1939, to Rome, to pay its respects to the third Axis Power, which at the time had not entered the war.

On 31 August 1939 DNK was reorganized as a joint stock company, with the Japanese Government holding 37.3 percent of the total capital of 100 million yen. The fleet consisted of a number of 20-seat Douglas DC-3s, 10-seat Mitsubishi MC-20s, 16-seat Kawanishi Type 97 flying-boats and some passenger versions of the Mitsubishi G3M Nell bombers. On 1 October of the same year, DNK became the sole airline of Japan, taking over all the other domestic airlines, or their routes, in addition to being the nation's flag carrier. The Asahi newspaper's operation ceased, as did those of the three small companies, TKY, AHK (Ando) and NKKKK, and that of NKYK, the one started by Choichi Inouye in 1922 (*see* Chapter 31).

Thus ended the airline involvement of Japan's first pioneer. Formerly a non-commissioned officer in the Japanese Navy, and in its adolescent flying corps,

Inouye was remembered as a far-sighted individual, dynamic and straightforward in all his dealings. He had remained defiantly independent, and when DNK took over, he was still operating his service west of Osaka through the Inland Sea, and had extended it to Beppu in 1937, and had even opened a small branch line to Shirahama, on the Kii-Hanto Peninsula.

Supporting the Greater Co-Prosperity Sphere

With the full weight of the Government behind it, and with the benefits and amenities that this brought in its recognition as the State airline, Dai Nippon lost no time in pursuing its goals of route expansion. In March 1940 Kawanishi Type 97s began regular flights from Yokohama to Saipan and Palau, only a year after the exploratory sortie of 1939. The established route from Tokyo through Fukuoka to Taipei was extended to Canton (today's Guangzhou), by this time also under Japanese control, and on to Bangkok, a weekly service starting on 10 June 1940, using Mitsubishi Type 96s. Then the Saipan service was extended to Dili in Portuguese Timor, an outpost of the once great empire, now an anachronistic enclave in the Netherlands East Indies. Local services were started, as a semi-military operation, with naval assistance, between islands of the Caroline group, officially governed as a League of Nations mandate, an artifice that no-one believed, or at the time, seemed to care about. But the move was clearly part of the preparations for the invasion of Indonesia.

Mitsubishi MC-20s went into service on the Tokyo—Seoul—Changchun (Hsinking) route on 17 March 1941; and with permission from a friendly Vichy French Government, the Bangkok service included stops at Hanoi, Tourane (Da Nang), and Saïgon (Ho Chi Minh) from 1 April. The Seoul—Dairen flights were extended direct to Peking, and at the request of the Japanese Navy, an alternate stop was also made at Haikou on the island of Hainan, on the southern route.

Japanese Gooney Bird

Reference has already been made to Nakajima's Douglas DC-2 production during the mid-1930s. The Japanese also obtained, in 1939, a production licence to build DC-3s, and the task was entrusted to a new factory, Government owned, named Showa, after the reigning dynasty. Concerned that his new manufacturing venture might lack the necessary experience to build good aeroplanes, the Japanese Navy successfully negotiated the construction of the first Japanese DC-3 prototype by Nakajima. Beginning in 1940, Nakajima produced seventy-one DC-3s for the Navy. Meanwhile, Showa built 416 of the versatile aircraft, thus making a Japanese total of 487. Dai Nippon used between thirty and forty of these, with a maximum fleet of perhaps twenty or so in 1943.

And so Japan plunged into the Second World War, as war was declared on 7 December 1941. At that time, Dai Nippon was operating 30,600 km of routes, of which 17,850 were domestic. Within the span of a single decade, Japan's airline industry had grown from an infant quasi-military support route, with only a couple of years' experience in carrying passengers on a regular basis, into an international carrier of considerable substance. Throughout the ensuing worldwide conflict DNK continued to provide military air transport support throughout East Asia; and to Manila, Hong Kong and Singapore, together with Batavia and other points throughout the scattered territory of the Netherlands East Indies: all these places, in the Co-Prosperity Sphere, were to have the privilege – if that is the correct term – of a direct air service to Tokyo.

The Airline of Manchukuo

Foundation of MKKK

On 18 September 1931 Japanese Army units stationed at Mukden (now Shenyang) fabricated a pretext to open fire on Chinese forces under the command of Chang Hsueh-Liang. They were alleged to have blown up part of the track of the South Manchurian Railway, then under Japanese control as the result of prolonged negotiations as to the dispersal of foreign assets in China after the end of the First World War. Chang was the *de facto* ruler of northeastern China, as the various warring factions in that unsettled country vied for power and supremacy. Japan benefitted from the internal unrest (in 1936 Chang kidnapped Chiang Kai-shek in an effort to come to terms with the Chinese communists) and in the coveted area of Manchuria, the events served as an excellent case history of 'divide and conquer' – with the ironic twist that the conquerors did not need to do the dividing.

By the time Japan had created Manchuria as a puppet protectorate, renaming it Manchukuo on 18 February 1932, the newly-formed Japanese 'chosen instrument' airline, NKYKK, had already extended its overseas route, hitherto terminating at Seoul, Korea (Chosen, in Japan). On 28 December 1931, its three-engined Fokkers started to fly to Dairen, Mukden and Harbin. Between Mukden and Harbin, the aircraft stopped at Changchun (Hsinking), designated by the Japanese as the new capital of its protectorate.

Manshu Koko Kabushiki Kaisha (MKKK), known familiarly as Manko, was established on 26 September 1932. Freely translated as the Manchurian Air Transport Company Ltd or the Manchurian Aviation Corporation, it was organized by the South Manchurian Railway Company, the Sumitomo Syndicate, and the Manchurian Government. It received 'guidance and protection' from the Japanese Military Air Force, which in exchange received all the logistics and passenger transport services it required. Throughout its existence, MKKK was always a quasi-military organization. But its subsequent record of operating a network of air routes throughout Manchukuo, introducing modern aircraft types, and even building its own aircraft, is an often-forgotten slice of air transport history.

Quick Consolidation

Reflecting the pace of Japanese expansionist activity during this period, the new airline set to work immediately. On 3 November 1932 it opened the first routes, from Mukden, the largest city of Manchukuo, to Changchun (Hsinking) and Harbin, the hub of rail, road and river traffic in the northern Province of Heilunjiang; from Harbin to Tsitsihar, an important city on the Chinese Eastern Railway, that important link from the Russian Soviet frontier and the Trans-Siberian Railway near Chita to Vladivostok; and from Mukden to Sinuiju, on the Korean border, connecting with the NKYKK service to Tokyo. The inaugural flight was made by a Fokker Super Universal, leased from NKYKK, which had left Osaka at 07.25 hr and covered the 2,660 km to Harbin in what was then rapid time, arriving at 13.35 hr the next day.

In June 1933 new services were added to Dairen, supplementing the NKYKK trunk line from Tokyo to that city; a branch line was opened from Hsinking to Kirin and Chongchin, in northern Korea; and the line from Harbin to Tsitsihar was extended to Hailar and Manchuli, on the Soviet frontier and border junction for the Chinese Eastern Railway and the Trans-Siberian. Japan now had a direct air link, with serviceable airfields and ground support staff, all the way from Tokyo to a strategic communications point connecting the Soviet port of Vladivostok with the rest of the USSR. The all-Russian Trans-Sib route was circuitous and time-consuming, so that whoever controlled the Chinese Eastern could severely handicap Soviet contacts with its Far Eastern province. The advantages of swift air transport were being put to good use by the Japanese. The point was not lost in the Kremlin. Later, in 1936, when the Soviet pilot Chkalov and his crew flew nonstop from Moscow to the Far East in an ANT-25, Stalin was heard to remark that his demonstration of air capability was 'worth two armies'.

Manchurian Air Transport (MKKK) opened its first route on 3 November 1932, from Mukden to Changchun and Harbin, using a Fokker Super Universal leased from NKYKK in Japan.

MKKK was well equipped. It imported aircraft and it built them. The first two Super Universals were completed at the workshops in Mukden on 2 October 1933, and were known as the Manko Type 1. These Fokker-designed aircraft were originally produced by the United States branch of the Dutch company (they were never built in Europe), and were being built under licence from the US by Nakajima in Japan. Nakajima sublicenced them to Manko for local manufacture. They were modified for the operating conditions in Manchukuo, and fitted with 460 hp Kotobuki engines, licence-built Jupiters from the British Bristol Engine Company. Whether either Fokker in Amsterdam, or Bristol at Bristol, knew what was going on with their products in Mukden, Manchukuo, is an interesting speculation.

Manko also imported two Fokker F.VII/3ms but is not believed to have built any of them. These were probably designated Manko Type 2s. But it did build de Havilland Puss Moths, or Manko Type 3s. In 1933 the MKKK fleet totalled thirty aircraft: sixteen Super Universals, two F.VII/3ms, and twelve Puss Moths. During that year the Japanese Army, blatantly expressing Japan's predatory intentions towards China, advanced to capture the province of Jehol, and MKKK in its role of air support and communication, opened up routes to Chengte, Jehol's chief city, one from Mukden and one from Hsinking.

The technical and engineering departments of MKKK were very active during the mid-1930s, testing different aircraft types and experimenting with them, as well as building more than forty Super Universals and fifteen Puss Moths. In November 1933, a Photographic Division was established, with some of the Super Universals modified with a window in the underside of the fuselage for photography. The Photographic Division also used Northrop Gammas, a Fairchild FC-2, a Mitsubishi Type 97 and a Kawasaki Type 98. MKKK seemed to be prepared to try anything that came its way or was available.

It even had one of the rare Clark G.A.43s, obtained through the Mitsui Corporation. Constructed at a time when General Motors, the giant car manufacturer of Detroit, was exploring the idea of entering the aircraft business, through its subsidiary, General Aviation, the Clark was visualized as a possible competitor to the Douglas DC-2, and a modern design to supersede the ponderous 100 mph aircraft of the Fokker-Ford Tri-Motor generation. But it was never a success, and MKKK's experience was not a happy one. Registered as J-BAEP, it crashed on its first flight, in Tokyo on 10 February 1934. Then, as M-701, it took off en route to Mukden on 18 May, but it crashed again. The Manchurian airline received a Puss Moth from Mitsui, in compensation for the loss.

Speeding Up The Service

On 1 April 1935 a formal agreement was signed between MKKK and the Japanese flag carrier airline, NKYKK. Route extensions and other forms of interchanges, including aircraft, were permitted in each other's spheres of influence, especially in the border regions of Manchukuo and Korea (Chosen). The first Nakajima AT-2 flew to Mukden on 12 September 1936, for route testing and evaluation, and operated until December. MKKK was apparently satisfied with its performance, as it ordered five more, and it entered service on the trunk route from Mukden to Harbin in May 1937. Interestingly, the first stewardesses were hired at this time, five of them joining MKKK to take care of the clientèle on the long route from the main cities of Manchukuo back to the home country, to Fukuoka, Osaka and Tokyo.

MKKK and NKYKK started joint service on this trunk route on 1 June 1937. The journey time from Hsinking, the Manchukuo capital (where the puppet emperor, Pu Yi, had been installed on 1 March 1934) and Tokyo, over a distance of 2,270 km, had been reduced to ten hours. The interchange between the two airlines took place at Seoul in Korea, and the end-to-end timing had thus been reduced by two-thirds in less than five years.

At the same time when the Nakajima AT-2 speeded up the connection from Manchukuo to Japan, the MKKK workshops at Mukden introduced its own indigenous aircraft type. It made its debut in April 1937, and was designated the Manko Transport No. 1, or MT1, and was also referred to as the Manko Type Kayabusa (Falcon). It went into service on the main trunk route in Manchukuo in May of the same year.

The German Connection

In November 1936, Germany and Japan signed the Anti-Comintern Pact, designed as a move to co-ordinate its mutual interests – plainly politico-military – against a common political opponent and potential common enemy (or target): the Soviet Union. In January 1937 Italy joined the Pact, following the creation of the Berlin-

Rome Axis in October 1936. After the end of its civil war, Spain joined the Pact in March 1939, and not long after the outbreak of the Second World War in Europe, on 3 September 1939, the three founder nations, Germany, Italy and Japan, signed the Three-Power Pact in 1940. Ultimately, the satellite nations of Axis countries in Europe, together with Japan's acting government in China, became signatories to the Pact; and after the Japanese attack on Pearl Harbor on 7 December 1941, Germany, Italy and Japan dotted the i's, so to speak, by a formal military alliance.

The writing had been on the wall for many years. Japan had made no secret of its imperial aims in systematically achieving domination over the whole of East Asia. It had already established permanent sovereignty over the southern half of Sakhalin and the Kurile Islands, the whole of Korea, Taiwan (Formosa) and the Ryukyu Islands; and it had been allocated a League of Nations mandate over several island groups covering a large area of the western Pacific. It started to expand its territory during the 1930s, starting with an incursion – invasion would be equally correct – into Manchuria, and methodically continued its advance across the northern frontiers of China. Formerly, in the years following the First World War, assuming a conciliatory approach in its dealing with China and the USSR, and ostensibly abandoning the policy of force, the entire Japanese policy underwent a *volte face* in 1927 when the prime minister, General Tanaka, published his notorious Memorandum, clearly stating an expansionist policy, one that was enthusiastically and cynically exploited by the military departments of government. The signing of the Anti-Comintern Pact in 1936 provided new opportunities for making preparations for further aggression.

One of the initiatives prompted by the Pact was an agreement signed between the German airline, Deutsche Lufthansa, and MKKK on 18 December 1936. Its objective was to establish an air route between Berlin and Tokyo, via Afghanistan, Mongolia and Manchukuo. The trials and tribulations of this amazing episode in air transport endeavour are separately chronicled later; but the German co-operation extended into MKKK itself, in strengthening its domestic network.

In 1938 a barter agreement was signed between Germany and Manchukuo. Germany would supply Junkers-Ju 86 airliners to Manchukuo; the latter, in return, would supply the equivalent value in soya beans – although there is little record of shiploads of that nourishing commodity ever having reached Germany. But the Ju 86s did reach Manchukuo. The first one arrived in October 1938 and began its trials. On 1 January 1939 it made its inaugural scheduled flight from Dairen to Chiamussu (Jiamusi today), in the northeast, via Mukden, Hsinking and Harbin, by now the main air artery of Manchukuo.

Like many other large transport aircraft being built in Germany during the 1930s, the Junkers-Ju 86 was designed to be adaptable for both commercial and military use. The ones delivered to Mukden were clearly regarded as potential bombers in case of emergency, much in the same way as those delivered to Bolivia were used in support of the Chaco War with Paraguay. Those at Mukden were soon put on the alert.

In yet another 'incident,' on 11 May 1939, Manchurian-Japanese troops set fire to a large area of prairie-type grass in northern Manchukuo, imperilling a contingent of Soviet troops. Fortunately not inflating to a full-scale conflict, eight Manko Type 1 aircraft were despatched to the scene of the 'Nomonhan Incident' and six Ju 86s were ordered to Hsinking in June. These soon returned to normal service, presumably exercising a quick-change routine of seats-for-bomb-racks, and were soon plying the main routes, including the 'homeland' connection at Seoul, and a

MKKK began operation of the first of its Junkers-Ju 86s on the first day of 1939. The Manchurian Ju 86s were reported as being supplied in return for soya beans.

service to Peking, via Chinchow and Tientsin. These latter cities had been added to the Japanese-occupied territory in China after the Sino-Japanese Marco Polo Bridge Incident of 7 July 1937, and MKKK started service from the Manchukou capital to Peking in February 1939.

The zenith of German technical support for MKKK came when, towards the end of 1940, a Heinkel He 116 four-engined airliner reported for duty at Mukden. On 3 December it made a nonstop survey flight directly from the nominal capital of Manchukuo, Hsinking (Changchun) to Tokyo. Crossing the northern part of Korea, it flew straight across the Sea of Japan, halving the ten-hour journey by the circuitous route via Seoul and Fukuoka. Unlike previous such survey flights, however, this was not the harbinger of a new express air service, at least not by Heinkel He 116s. Using radio navigation for the first time in the area, its deployment in the Far East was at least as much for military preparations as it was for commercial enterprise.

Indeed, when a nonstop route was opened on 1 April 1941 – only eight months before Japan was at war with the USA – the aircraft selected was the Mitsubishi MC-20. The journey time was $4\frac{1}{2}$ hours. Unfortunately, one of these Mitsubishis crashed in the Sea of Japan on 21 June, shortly after the inauguration, and 16 passengers were killed.

Wartime Dispersal of a Commercial Fleet

While MKKK was partially founded to provide an efficient and fast transport service in an important territory of Japan's fast-growing empire in East Asia, its mission was at least as much directed to provide reserve aircraft for logistics support as the military ambitions of the Greater East Asia Co-Prosperity Sphere gathered momentum. The Manchurian airline, in fact, was a valuable additional source of transport aircraft whenever they were called for by the Japanese Army or Navy. And the frequency of such requests increased as Japan successively over-ran the countries of southeast Asia.

The first 'call to arms' came in the autumn of 1938, when Japanese forces had advanced up the Yangtse River, westwards from Shanghai, in pursuit of Chiang Kai-shek's Kuomintang Chinese Army. Chiang had transferred his headquarters from Nanking to Hankow when the Kuomintang capital fell on 13 December 1937. He was there only eight months and had to evacuate to Chungking in October 1938. MKKK sent aircraft to Hankow in support of the Japanese Army. This was not an extensive operation, but it served as a trial run for more extensive missions three years later.

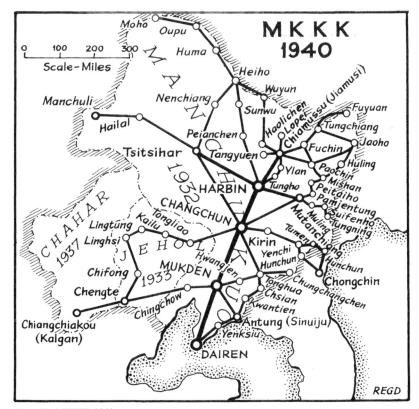

Map 33. MKKK 1940
Having occupied Manchuria by force in 1931, and renaming the territory Manchukuo, Japan proceeded to develop that country's natural resources, especially its mineral wealth, and establishing heavy industries. Partly, no doubt, to help prepare for further expansion, an efficient airline system was founded, as a regional extension of Japan Air Transport. By 1940, when the penetration into China was extensive, MKKK extended its service into the former provinces of Jehol and Chahar.

In October 1941 twelve Nakajima AT-2s were deployed in French Indo-China (now Vietnam) for transport support service in the Saïgon area; and further aircraft reinforcements were despatched in December. The fleet of Mitsubishi MC-20s was sent southwards in 1943, as, after initial success in penetrating the central and southwestern Pacific, Japanese forces went on to the defensive after American naval victories, after the Battle of the Coral Sea (7–8 May 1942), the Battle of Midway (3–7 June 1942) and the gradual reconquest by Allied troops in the second half of 1943 of the Solomon Islands and the Bismarck Archipelago.

For the Mitsubishi MC-20s, this was a far cry from the 4½-hour prestige flights from Hsinking to Tokyo during the last months of comparative peace in April 1941. When they were flown to Rabaul, the important Japanese base in New Britain, in March 1943, this was to be their ultimate resting place, and their fate is unknown. One MC-20 was used for photographic-reconnaissance of the

Philippines from December 1943, from bases in Japan; and it too disappeared from the records.

End of an Airline

The first atomic bomb fell on Hiroshima on 6 August 1945, the second one on Nagasaki on 9 August, and Japan capitulated on 2 September, although all fighting and resistance had terminated on 15 August. The USSR, which enigmatically had held back from declaring war on Japan throughout the Second World War, did so on 8 August. It occupied Sakhalin and the Kuriles – settling an old score – and proceeded to send forces across the borders of Korea and Manchukuo.

On 19 August the Emperor of Manchukuo, the puppet Pu Yi, was actually on his way to escape to Japan. He was at the airfield at Mukden, ready to board a Mitsubishi MC-20, when a Soviet parachute contingent arrived and re-directed him to Siberia, whence he was re-located to Peking, eventually to be re-educated and to undergo penance in the Chinese manner.

In September the assets of MKKK were distributed between the airlines or the military transport units of the occupying troops, those of the Soviet Union and the emergent communist Chinese airline. Little is known of the fate of the fleet, but thirteen of the Fokker Super Universals are believed to have been flown to Ulan Bator, captial of Mongolia. These aircraft were probably the last of the early Fokkers to remain in any kind of transport service.

Intercontinental Adventure

The agreement signed between MKKK and Deutsche Lufthansa on 18 December 1936, already referred to, had been inspired by an imaginative idea put forward by Saburo Nagabuchi, a senior staff member of the Manchurian airline. An ex-army pilot, he associated his commercial airline experience with his military instincts and came up with a suggestion that was daring, ambitious, and inventive. He recognized that, even in peacetime, and certainly in times of war, the traditional air route between Germany and Japan would be difficult to maintain, if not impossible. Instead of developing a route through the Middle East and the Indian Sub-continent, therefore, he proposed a route that would skirt the northern fastnesses of the Chinese Empire, and link up with Lufthansa's route to Afghanistan. This would avoid territory to the south controlled by the British and French; and would ingeniously avoid Soviet territory to the north.

For its part, the German airline was no less adventurous. Recognizing this geographically-inspired opportunity, DLH's Captain Drechsel surveyed the forbidding Pamir mountains and the Hindu Kush in Afghanistan in a Junkers-Ju 52/3m in the summer of 1936. Drawing from Drechsel's reports, one of most famous of Germany's peacetime pilots, Karl August Freiherr von Gablenz, partnered by Drechsel himself in a second aircraft, steered two Ju 52/3ms through the 16,000-ft elevation Wakhan Pass, the narrow corridor between Soviet Tadjikistan and British India (now Pakistan), leaving Kabul on 24 and 26 August 1937. Both aircraft reached Si'an, northern China, one of DLH's overseas satellite airline bases (*see* Chapter 15). Von Gablenz was held hostage for several weeks after a forced landing in Sinkiang on the return journey. Undaunted, DLH extended its eastern service from Teheran to Kabul on 15 April 1938.

The Manchukuo airline was no less short of inspiration and initiative. With the sponsorship of the Japanese Army, it formed the Kokusai Koku Kabushiki

Kaisha (KKKK) or the International Air Transport Company. (Incidentally, it seems to have achieved the last permutation of confusing initials resulting from free translations from Japanese). Its objective was simple: to establish a regular air route from Hsinking to Kabul, via Mongolia, one that could be termed a northern 'Silk Route' – a term recalling the traditional road used by traders between Asia and Europe in centuries gone by and immortalized in the diaries of Marco Polo.

Planning a New Silk Route

A week after Deutsche Lufthansa opened its route to Kabul, two Heinkel He 116 four-engined long-range aircraft left Berlin on 23 April 1938. Registered as J-BAKD and J-EAKF, and named *Nogi* and *Tokyo* respectively, they arrived in Tokyo on 29 April. Japanese crews were trained in Germany. These fine aircraft might have gone into service, dramatically plying the New Air Silk Road, had it ever started. The enterprise came to a sticky end, but this was not through any technical deficiency or lack of effort. At least one He 116 was subsequently used sporadically by MKKK.

In January 1936, the Nakajima aircraft factory completed its first Type LB2, designed as a long-range bomber. Having gained experience in metal aircraft construction by its licence to build the Douglas DC-2, the LB2 looked promising. Like all new aircraft, however, it did have some problems. The undercarriage did not always retract or extend properly, and when flying at maximum speed, the fuselage was reported to 'twist to a dangerous extent and was inclined to disintegrate in the air'.

Meanwhile (possibly subconsciously recalling Clement Keys' famous and visionary axiom that 'ninety percent of aviation is on the ground') MKK and the Japanese Army began to prepare emergency landing strips and supplies of fuel at selected points along the fringe of the Gobi Desert, starting at Chengte, provincial capital of the Chinese Jehol, which had been over-run by Japan in 1933, and with the next stop at Kalgan (Chengchiakou), provincial capital of Chahar, over-run in 1937. Then came the difficult bit.

Suitable sites for emergency strips were located at remote spots in Inner Mongolia (now an autonomous region of China) at a point in the Ala-shan Desert; and at Tingyuanying (Bayenhot), now in the Ningxhia autonomous region. Neither was exactly an hospitable place. The first was hundreds of arid miles from the nearest railway, and even the second, Tingyuanying, was close to the edge of the waterless sandy desert. Apart from the formidable nature of the terrain, the only human inhabitants of the Ala-shan were the Torgod Mongols. Their very name did not suggest a warm welcome.

End of a Dream

As the Japanese often demonstrated during the Second World War, they were nothing if not determined and resourceful, when faced with a challenge. Today, under happier conditions, this is shown by their courageous – and successful – attempts to climb the highest peaks of the Himalayas. In the Gobi Desert, specifically in the Ala-Shan, the driest part, in 1937, they fashioned airstrips and transported fuel to them. Railways came nowhere near the area; and roads were non-existent. And so camel caravans were organized, 350 camels in each caravan, with each camel carrying four 18-litre cans.

When a Nakajima LB2, named *Akatsuki (Dawn)* made a successful proving flight on 26 June 1937, it did not, fortunately, have to make an emergency landing at any of these points; and so the suitability of the strips was never tested. The *Akatsuki* flew 3,000 km from Hsinking to a point in western Mongolia, north of Urumchi, in faraway Sinkiang. It must have returned safely, for two LB2s were then delivered to KKKK.

Alas for this extraordinary enterprise and for the Japanese equivalent of 'the difficult we do immediately, but miracles take a little time', the Gobi Desert pioneers were forestalled by events. On 7 July, less than two weeks after the daring venture by the LB2, the Sino-Japanese Incident at the Marco Polo Bridge in Peking precipitated Japan and China into a full-scale war, rather than a series of disjointed incidents. While the Chinese were invariably on the receiving end of a superior onslaught by better trained soldiers and better equipped air forces, there was one incident in which the Japanese came off worse. One of the KKKK fuel supply caravans was massacred by Chinese troops, and the entire enterprise had to be abandoned.

On 28 November 1938 the Kokusai Koku Kabushiki Kaisha ceased to exist as a corporate entity. It merged with NKYKK to establish Dai Nippon Koku (DNK) (*see* Chapter 32). Its Heinkel He 116s were transferred to MKKK. It had been a brave try.

CHAPTER THIRTY-FOUR

Japanese Air Transport in the Second World War

Making the Adjustment

During times of war, even during periods of emergency that are considered a serious threat to security in times of peace, the involved countries invariably look to their national airlines for logistics support to the armed forces. During the Second World War BOAC provided essential air services throughout the British Commonwealth, devising, among other feats of improvization, the 'Horseshoe' route from South Africa to Australia via the Indian Sub-content, to avoid the conflicts and barriers to communication in the Middle East. Deutsche Lufthansa did the same throughout Europe as the Third Reich extended its frontiers and conquests. DLH was there to provide swift transport and travel for essential personnel, either military or civil, in pursuit of the war effort. In the United States, all the privately-owned airlines pitched in as at least half their fleets were requisitioned for vast logistics challenges across the nation and across the oceans. On the Pacific Rim, in the area that quickly fell under Japanese occupation – the coveted East Asia Co-Prosperity Sphere, Dai Nippon Koku (DNK) (Greater Japan Air Lines) was ready to do the same after the Pearl Harbor attack on 7 December 1941.

As described in Chapter 32, it was already operating from the Japanese homeland to the overseas Provinces of Korea, Taiwan, and Manchukuo, and had opened routes to China, Indo-China, and Siam (Thailand). Landplane services provided direct flights to Hsinking and Mukden, Tientsin and Peking, Shanghai and Nanking, Hanoi and Saïgon. A Mitsubishi 96 express service linked Tokyo directly with Bangkok, via Fukuoka, Taipei, Canton and Hanoi, in less than a day. Kawanishi flying-boats went to Saipan, Palau and other more distant points in the Carolines. The network and the infrastructure were in place, as Japan began to wage war.

Widening the Bridgeheads

In the aftershock of Pearl Harbor, the amazing rapidity of the Japanese advances in southeast Asia has, if not overlooked, often been cast in a subordinate role. Consider the timetable: Guam fell on 10 December, Hong Kong on Christmas Day. The Japanese seized Manila on 2 January 1942 and proceeded to over-run the Philippines, with the final surrender of the Corregidor bastion on 6 May. Demonstrating a hitherto unknown, or at least a hitherto considerably under-estimated level of air power, Japanese dive-bombers sank the *Repulse* and the *Prince of Wales*, proud flagships of the Royal Navy, off the east coast of Malaya, on 12 December 1941; and by 15 February 1942 had raised the Rising Sun flag in Singapore. Simultaneously, the inexorable conquest of the Netherlands East Indies was undertaken with ruthless efficiency, starting on 11 January, with the Dutch capitulating on 8 March. By April 1942, Japanese troops had occupied Rangoon.

Dai Nippon Koku (Greater Japan Air Lines) operated a large fleet including Mitsubishi MC-20s.

Behind this astonishing oriental blitzkrieg came the logistics support of Japanese air transport resources, as well as from the Navy, the Army, and the merchant shipping. Dai Nippon Koku's Mitsubishi MC-20s and 96s, together with Japanese-built DC-3s, followed closely behind the Army and the Navy. Saïgon became a southeast Asian air hub, with DNK routes radiating to Bangkok, Moulmein and Rangoon to the northwest; to Alor Star and Singapore, and on to Batavia (Jakarta) and Sourabaya to the southwest; and to Kuching and Tarakan, in Borneo, to the southeast. In the Philippines, local services in collaboration with the Japanese Army, linked Manila with all the main cities as far as Davão.

This expansion enabled military and naval leaders to sit side by side with Japanese businessmen and economic specialists who sought to exploit the riches of the area, and to achieve the objectives of the Co-Prosperity Sphere. At the time, with a population of about 450 million, the whole region produced vital resources to feed the engines of war in the factories of Japan. Malaya, especially, produced about 90 percent of the world's natural rubber, and 70 percent of the world's tin. In Dutch Borneo (now Indonesian Kalimantan), Royal Dutch Shell produced high-grade oil at Tarakan, as well as in the British Protectorate of Brunei and in Sarawak. Food supplies were plentiful, not least the production of about three-quarters of the world's rice.

The map of DNK's routes in 1942, and the distribution of these commodities, tells the story (*see* page 458).

The Army Lends a Hand

Dai Nippon Koku, in its role as the flag carrier and 'chosen instrument' of Japan's commercial air transport industry, was obliged to make itself readily available to the armed forces. During the incredible four months from December 1941 to the end of March 1942 during which Japan replaced three European nations and the United States as resident colonists of southeast Asia, DNK co-operated with the Army in maintaining services throughout the island-studded region. Aircraft of DNK and the Army, some of them merely different versions of the same basic

456

Dai Nippon used Douglas DC-3s as well as numerous Japanese types.

type such as the Mitsubishi 96, operated interchangeably; and the ubiquitous DC-3 no doubt proved to be almost as indispensable as an all-purpose transport as it did with the Allied forces.

There seems to be some evidence that the administration of DNK and the High Command of the Japanese Army did not always see eye to eye. At all events, the Army gradually took over, and by the end of 1942 the far-flung network of long-haul routes, from Sapporo in the north to Jakarta in the south, were under Army control. The transfer of authority was arguably necessary, simply because the focus of the whole operation was concentrated in the south, and the organization of supplies of men and material, and provisions of all kinds, was more conveniently undertaken where the problems occurred.

Accordingly, on 10 July 1942, the Japanese Imperial Army formed Nanpo Koku Yusobu (NKY) (Southern Air Transport Division). The headquarters were in Singapore, and there were seven regional branch offices, in Surabaya, Saïgon, Bangkok, Rangoon, Manila, Kuching and Taipei. This was no transient or superficial bureaucratic pretence. NKY had a total staff of 2,200. At the training centre in Batavia, 250 aircrew were continuously under instruction. Full maintenance and repair shops were set up at Singapore, where only a few months earlier, the Royal Air Force had been in charge.

The turnover of the fleet of Mitsubishi MC-20s, Mitsubishi 96s and 97s, Nakajima-built DC-3s and Nakajima AT-2s, was high. The peak in fleet numbers, reached in 1944, was about 150, which, by any standards of the time, was a considerable array of aerial logistics capability. Many aircraft were lost, because of strafing and bombing of the airfields, and the grand total of transport aircraft estimated to have served the Southern Air Transport Division probably exceeded 400.

The organization drew from Dai Nippon Koku's experience. Indeed, there were grounds to assume that, in many respects, Dai Nippon had served as a training ground for the Imperial Army even during the uneasy and precarious peace during 1940 and 1941, when, with the determined occupation of much of mainland China, the intentions of territorial expansion were hardly disguised. As time went on, Dai Nippon's role changed from an advisory and supportive position to one of supplier. Its aircraft and crews were completely absorbed by the Army, and the aircraft were re-registered from their commercial nomenclature to military markings. Right at the end of the war, however, such administrative requirements became confused and irrelevant, as aircraft, men, training, and maintenance were gradually reduced to the status of permanent emergency and improvization. Such

JAPANESE ARMY WARTIME SCHEDULED SERVICES

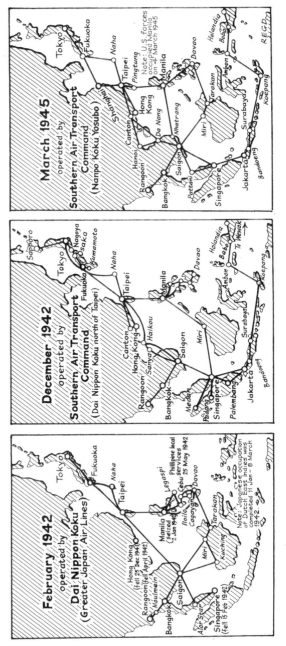

Maps 34a. Japanese Army Wartime Scheduled Services

After Japan entered the Second World War, by its surprise attack on Pearl Harbor, Hawaii, on 7 December 1941, it quickly deployed its forces throughout southeast Asia, over which it reigned supreme for the next three years. While Greater Japan Air Lines (Dai Nippon Koku) at first provided the military transport support service, a secondary unit, the Southern Air Transport Command (Nanpo Koku Yosubo) was also established in Singapore, as a geographically and strategically situated base. Regular services were maintained throughout the period of occupation, throughout southeast Asia and connecting to Japan, largely in association with Dai Nippon, which provided technical advice and shared in the administration, as well as supplying experienced air crews.

subservience by Dai Nippon to the Army was not, however, repeated in its relations with the Japanese Navy.

The Navy Plays Its Part

Unlike the Nanpo Koku Yusobu of the Japanese Imperial Army, the Navy co-operated with Dai Nippon Koku to form a special transport unit, still operating under Dai Nippon's colours; under commercial, not military registrations; and with crews and maintenance staff still under Dai Nippon's administration and on its payroll. Ultimate direction and control rested, of course, with the Navy. For its part Dai Nippon was able to operate as an autonomous unit, because the Navy recognized that the airline understood the problems of long-range regular operations best and that it would do a better job if left alone.

The operation was not as intensive as that of the Army, although, over the main trunk route from Japan through the southeast Asian countries as far as Singapore and Jakarta, both Army and Navy routes and services duplicated each other. In one respect, the Navy's operation was far different. Although the fleet was composed of the same Mitsubishi types, DC-3s, and the Kawanishi 97, the Naval

Naval operations of Dai Nippon included long-range over-water flights using Kawanishi H6K3 and H8K2 four-engined flying-boats. One of the former is illustrated.

operations of Dai Nippon were remarkable in that they included some long-range over-water flights by the Kawanishi H8K Emily four-engined flying-boats. These fine aircraft, regarded by some analysts and air industry specialists as the finest flying-boat ever built, had a gross weight of 72,000 lb, could carry 64 passengers (troops or naval personnel), and had a range of up to about 3,000 miles. Though probably unable to carry its full payload to that extreme distance, it was at least as good a load-carrier as the more famous Boeing 314, the type that pioneered Pan American's trans-Atlantic route in 1939. First launched in 1943, a total of 167 H8Ks were built, of which perhaps half a dozen or so were allocated to Dai Nippon for its Naval support services.

459

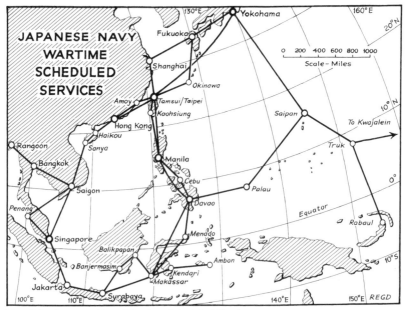

Map 34b. Japanese Navy Wartime Scheduled Services
While the Japanese Army provided landplane service through southeast Asia during the Second World War, the Japanese Navy insisted on – and indeed was justified in so doing – its own air service. Its trunk route to Java was via the Philippines and Celebes, but it also parallelled the Army routes on the Asian mainland to Singapore. More important, it was able to supply Japanese occuping forces on the isolated islands in the western Pacific, throughout Micronesia, and even as far as Kwajalein, using, among other aircraft, the fine Kawanishi H8K2 Navy 2 (Emily) long-range flying boat.

These were most impressive, as the map shows. Not only did they maintain service throughout the countries of southeast Asia; they also provided an air support link throughout the islands of what is now termed Micronesia. From Saipan, one route reached Davão, in Mindanao, southern Philippines, and stopping at Palau. The other route turned southeastwards to Truk and Ponape, in the Caroline Islands; and as far east as Kwajalein, in the Marshall Islands. From Truk, yet another branch headed due south to Rabaul, in New Britain, chief city of the Bismarck Archipelago, and the main base for Japanese operations in the central Pacific, from which strategic region they posed a threat to Australia.

Collapse of an Empire

By the summer of 1945 the tide had turned. The Rising Sun, proud emblem of Japanese supremacy and domination over the western Pacific, was setting, as Allied forces converged from all sides. The turning point had been the great naval battles in 1942, when, in the Coral Sea on 7–8 May, and even more emphatically, at Midway Island on 3–7 June, the United States Navy defeated the Japanese. Starting with the landing of the US Marines at Guadacanal, Solomon Islands, on 7 August, 1942, the island-hopping occupation by the Allies led in due course to

460

the defeat of the Japanese in the Philippines by the end of February 1945.
Meanwhile Burma had been liberated by British, US and Chinese troops, and in
an historic moment, the Stars and Stripes were raised on the island of Okinawa,
Ryukyu Islands, on 19 February. Territory was regained in parts of the
Netherlands East Indies, particularly in northern New Guinea; Chinese forces
reoccupied the fringes of Japanese domains in their country.

The Japanese forces grimly resisted with fearless, often suicidal, defence of
their hard-won territory, their pride, and their Emperor. Speculation on how long
they could hold out was ruthlessly ended on 6 August 1945. On that day, one that
will stay in the history books for all time as one of the great turning points of
Mankind, the Boeing B-29 bomber *Enola Gay* dropped the first atomic bomb on
the Japanese city of Hiroshima, turning the name of that medium-sized urban
community into a household word, and a symbol of the devastating power of
human ingenuity when directed to the goal of indiscriminate destruction. While the
Japanese tried to come to grips with this overpowering blow, and while even the
fanatical military dictatorship was flinching, the second bomb was dropped on the
port city of Nagasaki on 9 August.

On 24 August all civil flying was banned; but this was a mere administrative
formality. The country was still stunned by the unbelievable reality of seeing two
large cities utterly destroyed by two single bombs. Even earlier, a fire-bombing
air raid on Tokyo had resulted in an estimated more than 80,000 deaths, more than
either of the atomic holocausts. The Emperor Hirohito emerged from his sancti-

This damaged Tachikawa Ki-54c Army Type 1 Transport Model C is an example of the
Japanese aircraft used throughout the Pacific War.

fied historical and traditional seclusion and publicly told the Japanese people that his country had surrendered. The Second World War was mercifully at an end, with the official capitulation on 2 September.

The Green Cross

With the country in a state of chaos, all transport services were directed to the relief of suffering and hardship, with the emphasis on the transport of food and medical supplies, as well as the people responsible for humanitarian work. As part of this relief effort, Dai Nippon Koku resumed domestic services within Japan on 14 September 1945, in co-operation with both the Army and the Navy. This was possibly the first time that the Army and the Navy had broken tradition and co-operated on anytyhing, as throughout the war, the inability of the two forces to co-ordinate aviation policy had become legendary. With a fleet of twenty-seven assorted aircraft, mostly DC-3s and Mitsubishi MC-20s, but with even a few Shiragiku six-seat trainers, 'Green Cross' services were operated between all the major cities of Japan, from Fukuoka on Kyushu, Takamatsu on Shikoku, in the south, and the metropolises of Osaka, Nagoya and Tokyo on Honshu, to Sendai and Sapporo in the north. A branch line also linked the west coast on the Sea of Japan.

The Green Cross – exactly that, a green cross on a white background – replaced the rising sun emblem of Japan, as a symbolic declaration of peace and mercy replacing that of aggression and war. The co-operative effort seems to have been primarily a naval operation, if the personnel numbers were an indication: about 50 from DNK, 50 from the Army, but as many as 250 from the Navy.

These efforts, altruistic in their objectives though they may have been, ceased on 9 October 1945, by order of the Supreme Commander of the Allied Powers, General Douglas MacArthur. The last flight was from Sapporo to Matsudo, in Chiba Province, an airfield on the northeastern edge of Tokyo. All civil flying ceased on this date, and on 31 October Dai Nippon Koku was liquidated. On that date it had 4,400 employees – which may have made it one of the largest, if not the largest airline in the world at the time – who worked at 50 different branch offices. It still had more than 100 aircraft, of which 89 were still in Japan, and of which 21 were in flying condition.

The Dark Age of Japanese Commercial Aviation

The victorious Allied forces were in no mood to forgive and forget. The war had been harsh. No quarter had been asked for nor given. There had been atrocities, massacres and mass suicides. The occupation administration in Japan, as in Germany and Austria, controlled all commercial activity, at least for a few years, if only to ensure that the ability to recuperate for warlike purposes would not re-emerge. Aviation activities of any kind, associated as they were technically and operationally with the ability to make some kind of reactionary act of revenge, were suppressed. On 23 November 1945 the Supreme Commander for the Allied Powers imposed a complete prohibition on civil aviation. This directive, SCAPIN 301, was quite specific. It terminated all civil, commercial, institutional, or club flying, and this of course included any transport enterprise. It prohibited any flight, acquisition, study, experiment, or aircraft maintenance activity; and this applied also to any teaching, analysis, or experiment in aircraft, aerodynamics, even balloons.

General MacArthur would later be remembered as a fair-minded and compassionate, if not benevolent administrator of occupied Japan. But in the beginning, there was no compromise. Japan would have to do as it was told. And SCAPIN 301, in all its uncompromising absolutism, remained in force for five years of the reconstruction period.

CHAPTER THIRTY-FIVE

Japan Rejoins The World

Preliminary Sparring

During the late 1940s and the early 1950s Japan embarked on the long and painful process of recovery from a devastating war and on the equally demanding challenge of redefining its role in the postwar world. The United States military government of occupation undertook the task of all victors over defeated enemies: how to deal with the finances and materials of reparations, and the trial of war criminals. It also supervised the resettlement of people from Japan's former colonial empire, i.e. Manchuria, Korea, Sakhalin and the islands of the west Pacific; the redistribution of property; and the transformation of the government from a military dictatorship to a parliamentary democracy.

Eventually, on 4 September 1951, the Peace Treaty of San Francisco set the seal on the re-establishment of normal political and commercial relations between Japan and the United States, by now the most powerful industrial and military nation in the world. Undoubtedly, Japan benefited from the changing balance of world power, with the United States especially fearing the spread of communism with a 'domino effect' that saw, during the late 1940s, active and successful communist regimes emerging in China, Korea and Vietnam. Japan was seen as a potential bulwark against the threat of the USSR and its allies taking over the entire Pacific Rim from Kamchatka to Java.

Concurrently with the gradual move towards normalization, the air transport industry had begun to show signs of a reincarnation. The total ban on aviation of any kind, imposed by the instruction SCAPIN 301 of the Supreme Commander for the Allied Powers (SCAP) (General MacArthur) was, after five years of hiatus, replaced by a modified measure designed to restore some form of domestic airline network. On 26 June 1950 SCAPIN 2106 authorized the creation of an internal Japanese airline. Permission was given to the foreign airlines that had operated to Japan between 1945 and 1950 to organize a jointly-owned company to operate domestic services. The airlines qualifying for this privilege were Pan American, Northwest, BOAC, Canadian Pacific, Philippine Air Lines, QANTAS and Civil Air Transport (Taiwan). These airlines, with the exception of BOAC and QANTAS, which remained aloof, organized the Japan Domestic Air Corporation (JDAC). This was no more, however, than a study group – what is sometimes known as a 'paper' airline; but it was influential in the subsequent organization of a Japanese airline.

The idea presented certain difficulties. First, the foreign airlines were not too enthusiastic. Whether this derived from mutual suspicion, or the inability to agree on shareholdings or control, or from the presumption that this could, at best, be only a temporary measure, will never be known. In any event, on 27 January 1951 an important corollary was added to SCAPIN 2106. This permitted the creation of a Japanese airline, to be financed with Japanese capital. Aircraft were to be leased from the JDAC and pilots would be supplied by Northwest Orient Airlines.

Maintenance would be supplied by Transocean Airlines (TAL or TALOA), a non-scheduled contract airline organization started by Orvis Nelson, an ex-United Air Lines pilot, after the Second World War, and with considerable experience of trans-Pacific operations.

Formation of Japan Air Lines

On 22 May 1951 the Minister of Transport gave his approval for the start of a Japanese airline; and on 1 August, the Japanese Air Lines Company (JAL) was formed as a private concern, with a capital of 100 million yen – at that time worth about \$280,000. The San Francisco Peace Treaty having been signed on 4 September the way was clear; and on 25 October, at 7.43 hr, the first aircraft, a Martin 2-0-2, took off from Haneda Airport in Tokyo bound for Osaka and Fukuoka, followed shortly afterwards by another flight from Tokyo to Sapporo.

Japan Air Lines' first operations office at Haneda Airport, Tokyo. It was known as the Kennel and bore the words 'Temporary Office'.

JAL had five of the Martin twin-engined airliners. Three of these had been sold by Northwest Orient Airlines to Transocean on 15 August, the remaining two coming from Pioneer Airlines, from Texas, early in 1952. As yet, no Japanese airman was allowed to pilot the JAL aircraft. Also, a Douglas DC-4 was acquired from Transocean (all the JAL fleet was leased) in November 1951. Sadly, one of the Martins crashed at Oshima on 9 April 1952, and one of the country's most prominent businessmen was among the 37 people killed. This was not a good start, but the new airline's personnel, busy taking refresher courses, were ready for bigger things when, on 20 September 1952, a full domestic air traffic licence was handed down from the Transport Ministry.

Exactly a year after its first nominal service, JAL began services with its own aircraft on 25 October 1952, this time with an ex-Northwest DC-4. The Martins were returned to Transocean. By the end of the year six DC-4s were in service,

Japan Air Lines began operations on 25 October 1951, the first service being from Tokyo to Osaka. The initial fleet was five Martin 2-0-2s. Foreign pilots had to be used.

and three Beech AT-11s were on constant call for flying training. This array of equipment may not have been too impressive in an age when the non-pressurized DC-4 had beeen superseded by pressurized DC-6s and Constellations in most countries. But the infant Japanese airline gave some indication of its future plans and of its perceived stature by ordering two de Havilland Comet Series 2 jet airliners on 18 November 1952. The British pacesetter was to undergo an agonizing reappraisal when it had to be withdrawn from service early in 1954 because of a structural fault; but in 1952 JAL was already having to face the reality of international competition. BOAC had opened Comet services to Tokyo on 3 April 1953.

JAL air hostesses by one of the airline's Douglas DC-3s.

JAL began service with its own aircraft in October 1952. This was an ex-Northwest Airlines' Douglas DC-4.

Just like its prewar namesake, JAL was accepted as the 'Chosen instrument' of Japanese air transport overseas, and on 1 August 1953, a law was passed in the Diet making it the sole international airline of Japan. Consolidating its position, JAL was reorganized on 1 October 1953. The new Japan Air Lines Company Ltd (JAL) (Nihon Koku Kabashiki Kaisha) (NKKK) was capitalized at $5,500,000, of which the Japanese Government held half. Traffic rights were quickly obtained from the United States and three Douglas DC-6As were acquired, two from the Flying Tiger Line, one from Slick Airways, both all-cargo airlines from the United States. The aircraft were modified to DC-6Bs, and the first one went into service on the Tokyo—Sapporo route on 2 October, the day after the formal registration of the reorganized company.

Across the Pacific

Four months later, on an historic occasion for the rejuvenated Japanese airline fraternity, Japan Air Lines inaugurated trans-Pacific service, when, on 2 February 1954, the DC-6B *City of Tokyo* flew from Tokyo to San Francisco, via Wake Island and Honolulu. To be precise, the aircraft landed at Oakland, because of local weather problems on the western side of the Bay, after a 23-hour journey. While this flight made no great strides in technical or operational innovations, it was notable for the introduction of a new embellishment to the standards of cabin

Douglas DC-6Bs were introduced by JAL in October 1953. This one was named *City of Nagoya*.

467

Douglas DC-7Cs began trans-Pacific operation for JAL on 15 February 1958. *City of San Francisco* (illustrated) worked the first service, replacing DC-6Bs.

service. Japan Air Lines offered the traditional courtesy of the *oshibori* hot towel service to all its patrons. The refreshing custom was much appreciated by both national and international travellers, and the idea was quickly taken up by its competitors. Today, JAL alone serves about 30 million *oshibori* every year.

Progress in establishing an intercontinental route network was subsequently made with almost mechanical regularity and efficiency. If anyone outside Japan ever doubted the vanquished nation's ability to recover from its depths of despair in 1945, then a review of Japan Air Lines' steady and unspectacular expansion should have removed all scepticism. First, the route to southeast Asia was laid down, with service openings to Okinawa on 5 February 1954, to Hong Kong on 4 February 1955, to Bangkok on 7 October 1956, and to Singapore on 8 May 1958. Douglas DC-7C Seven Seas airliners augmented the DC-6B fleet on 15 February 1958, when the *City of San Francisco* entered the trans-Pacific traffic arena, enabling the frequency to San Francisco to be increased to daily on 15 April of that year. Trans-ocean services were intensified when, on 28 May 1959, one-stop Tokyo—Los Angeles flights began, calling only at Honolulu; and a third route to the USA was flown to Seattle, by the Great Circle route (this was later withdrawn) in April 1961.

Of a less routine nature, other unobtrusive but key developments were also worthy of note during the latter 1950s. By September 1955 all JAL domestic flights were flown by Japanese crews; and although foreign pilots and aircrew still took care of most of the international services, Japanese colleagues increased as a proportion of the total. In November 1954 and March 1955 two flights were made to Brazil, to join the celebrations for that country's 400th Anniversary. While ceremonial in nature, they also served to provide an introduction for JAL to a possible new destination. In the State of São Paulo more than half a million people were of Japanese descent, most of them still retained a fellow feeling for the land of their ancestors; and an airline link seemed to be a distinctly good prospect. But bilateral negotiations with Brazil, and the tricky question of en route traffic rights in the USA and elsewhere, were long protracted; and Japan Air Lines did not achieve this goal until 1978.

Domestic services were rationalized. Service to smaller cities, Aomori, Nagoya and Iwakuni (for Hiroshima) were suspended; so that JAL flew from Tokyo only to Osaka, Fukuoka, Sapporo and Okinawa. These were shrewd choices. Today the first three rank as the three busiest air routes in the world (Tokyo—Sapporo is No.1) and the route to Okinawa ranks tenth. On 10 October 1959 a pooling arrangement was signed with All Nippon Airways, the other strongly-based domestic airline, and although this agreement had a chequered history, the two airlines both managed to maintain superb air service between Japan's big cities, on a basis of unfettered competition.

Underpinning this dynamic expansion during the zenith of the piston-engined era of commercial airliner development, Japan Air Lines expanded its financial foundations. Literally every few months during the late 1950s and throughout the 1960s, public stock issues raised the necessary funds to buy new aircraft and to stock and to staff the growing chain of JAL offices throughout the world. The investors were not disappointed. Not until 1975, when Japan was severely affected by the Middle East fuel crisis, did the airline fail to make a profit in its annual trading. The Japanese Government, incidentally, was no bystander. By 1960 it was holding 75 percent of JAL stock, soon reduced to 50 per cent, and later still to 35.5 percent.

The Jet Age

The initial re-entry of a Japanese airline into the world of commercial air transport, after the profound readjustments following the Second World War, had been swift. In less than a decade after the collapse of Dai Nippon Koku in 1945, the new Japan Air Lines was spanning the Pacific Ocean, with full airline service to the United States. Intercontinental expansion thereafter, however, was not as rapid, and seven more years were to elapse before JAL's aircraft were to be seen in Europe. Interestingly, the leisurely pace of further expansion, dictated partly by prolonged negotiations for traffic and transit rights (a complicated process, compared with flying to the USA which involved only one nation) meant that when the time arrived for the European connection, JAL was able to do it with jet aircraft.

As early as 15 December 1955, JAL had quickly followed Pan American's globe-shattering order for 45 big commercial jet airliners. Pan Am had hinted at a preference for the Douglas DC-8 – 25 of the 45 were for the Eight, 20 for the Boeing 707 – and Japan Air Lines ordered four. During the first jet era, before the arrival of the wide-bodied jets, JAL spread its favours: it had aircraft from all three of the major manufacturers, Douglas, Convair and Boeing. It never operated a Boeing 707, but, on 12 August 1960, it opened a co-operative route to Paris, using Air France's 707s on the latter's Polar route. This was a matter of mutual convenience: Air France was able to consolidate its service to the Far East, and by the device of a shared published timetable, if not shared ownership of the aircraft, Japan Air Lines at last had its foot in the European door.

For its part, the European airline industry was aware of the growing industrial and commercial strength of Japan, and recognized that service to Tokyo was an essential cornerstone of future intercontinental planning. There were severe problems in establishing service, however, partly geographical, because the traditional route via the Middle East and India was circuitous, and therefore somewhat time-consuming and costly; and the direct route, by the shortest distance, was across the USSR, which in the 1950s and 1960s was reluctant to permit foreign airlines even to provide air service to Moscow, much less allow flights across its territory.

The Scandinavian airline, SAS, had devised an ingenious and operationally innovative solution to the dilemma. On 15 November 1954 – not long after JAL's

JAL began jet operation with Douglas DC-8s. This one was named *Fuji*.

trans-Pacific inaugural – it had launched its Polar service from Copenhagen to California. Though not a truly polar service, in that it traversed Greenland, not the North Pole, it was nevertheless a bright idea, and set a precedent that was followed by others. SAS was again the pioneer of a second Polar route, when it started a direct service from Copenhagen to Tokyo on 14 February 1957. This time, the aircraft went much closer to, if not actually over the Pole, and stopped at Anchorage, Alaska. Air France was the second airline to fly 'across the Pole' to Tokyo, with Lockheed Model 1649As on 10 April 1958.

Japan Air Lines began jet service, with considerable oriental elegance, on the trans-Pacific route to San Francisco, on 12 August 1960. Not only with the *oshibori*, but with additional amenities such as happi-coats for first-class patrons, and a new standard of tasteful provisions in the toilets, including toothbrush sets and disposable razors, Japan's national airline was beginning to be the subject of praise from customers and competitors alike. For long journeys, the special attention to passenger comfort was much appreciated, and especially so when JAL started its own Polar Service, on 6–7 June 1961, to London via Anchorage. The aircraft was the Douglas DC-8. The new president, Shizuma Matsuo, who had taken over from Seijiro Yanagita on 19 January, had good reason to be pleased with JAL's progress.

On 4 October 1962 Japan Air Lines began its new *Silk Road* service to Europe, routed via Hong Kong, Bangkok, Calcutta, Karachi, Kuwait, Cairo, Rome and Frankfurt. With this event, it introduced the Convair 880 jets, slightly smaller but marginally faster than the DC-8s or the 707s, to its international clientèle, having at first put it to work on the busy Tokyo—Sapporo route on 25 September 1961. Once again, JAL's onboard service made an impact on the wide variety of travellers who enjoyed the gracious concern of the kimono-clad flight attendants who, in the long traditions of Japanese hospitality, made the passengers feel that they were honoured guests. Other airlines were forced to take notice; and several of them instituted new hiring practices that ensured oriental-style cabin service east of Calcutta.

High Flying Flirtations

Other developments varied from the routine to the dramatic. During the flurry of new intercontinental service introduction, the opening of an all-cargo trans-Pacific service, cautiously only once a week at first, on 2 May 1959, had gone almost unnoticed. Taipei was included as a stop on the Hong Kong route on 30 July of the same year; and Osaka was also added as an alternate Japanese gateway to Hong Kong on 3 June 1960, to recognize the importance of the Kansai city, with its proximity to the ancient and beautiful capital, Kyoto. The Indonesian capital, Jakarta, received JAL Convair 880 service from 16 June 1962, while Seoul was added to the network on 15 April 1964.

The boardroom at Japan Air Lines' headquarters was, however, during the mid-1980s, preoccupied with concerns which it felt were of greater long-term consequence than mere route expansion. That was taking care of itself, as the airline grew in popularity everywhere it flew. The burning issue of the commercial aviation world at the time was the supersonic airliner. The race was on. The Anglo-French Concorde, the United States SST, and the Soviet Tupolev Tu-144: all were contenders for a market that was, at first, thought to be the natural successor to the jets of subsonic performance. This was before the scientists and the engineers from the manufacturing side had to admit that the sonic boom was technically insuperable; and before the airlines – the customers – looked closely at the figures, and decided that economic operations were outside the realm of reality. Nevertheless, such was the almost fanatical obsession with supersonics during the 1960s that no airline aspiring to be considered among the world's leaders could afford to ignore the even distant possibility that it might be operating faster than the speed of sound from continent to continent.

Accordingly, on 15 November 1963, Japan Air Lines placed a deposit on five American SSTs (delivery positions 19, 23, 30, 46, and 57), even though as yet this was only a US nationally-sponsored programme, supervised by the Federal Aviation Agency. Hedging its bets, JAL reserved three delivery positions for the Concorde on 30 September 1965. In the event, the United States Senate wisely rejected all further funding by the US taxpayer on the SST (now a Boeing design) on 3 December 1970; and JAL itself made a final decision to recover all deposits on the Concorde in June 1973.

Down-to-Earth Competition

Japan had moved out of its isolation in 1853, built its first railway in 1872, and slowly but surely modernized its social and industrial structure, including its mobility, by improvements in transport beyond that of the animal-drawn cart or the man-carried sedan chair. By the turn of the 20th Century, there were about 5,000 miles of railways. With a surge of construction during the 1920s and early 1930s, this mileage had grown to 18,000 by the beginning of the Second World War. The track gauge, however, was one metre, not the 4ft $8\frac{1}{2}$in that was standard in most countries of the world, or the 5ft gauge adopted in some others, notably Russia. This narrower track width inhibited the train performance, at least in speed, if not mechanical realiability, an aspect of operation on which the Japanese concentrated with dedication and discipline.

Service standards in the postwar era were excellent. Stewardesses brought refreshments through the coaches; the seats were comfortable; and on the main-line trains, telephones were introduced by 1960. But the speed of the trains was limited by the frequent deceleration needed to negotiate the too-often winding tracks that varied from the circuitous to the almost labyrinthine. Japan National Railway (JNR) made a decision in the latter 1950s that was to change the face of transport in Japan. Not only that, it astonished the world, and brought railway engineers hotfoot to Japan to examine the astonishing new development in steel-wheel on steel-rail technology.

JNR surveyed a route and began construction of a brand-new line, to link Tokyo and Osaka. The two metropolitan areas had a combined population of more than 30 million people (Tokyo about 20, Osaka about 10); while the densely-populated regions of Kanto and Kansai, in which Tokyo and Osaka were situated, respectively, together with other coastal areas in between, accounted for close to half of the population of Japan as a whole. The travel market potential was enormous, and the JNR solution to the problem was visionary and imaginative.

The Shin Kansen – freely translated as the New High-Speed Line, and later to be called the Bullet Trains – was built to the internationally standard gauge of 4ft $8\frac{1}{2}$ in and more important was built as nearly to a continuous straight and level direction and contour as possible. And almost everything was possible. The minimum curvature was set at a five-mile radius; the maximum gradient at 1:250. Very little of the 305-mile line from Tokyo to Osaka was on level ground. Most of it was on viaducts or bridges, or through tunnels. The track was laid with strength and precision: strength to accept 16-car trains (to accommodate the enormous passenger demand); precision to ensure speed and safety (the track is closed down every night from midnight to 06.00hr for meticulous inspection).

The new line opened in August 1964, with *Hikari* trains every half hour, stopping only at Nagoya and Kyoto, and *Kodama* trains stopping more often, at intermediate cities such as Yokohama, Shizuoka and Hamamatsu. On 1 October 1965, the *Tokkaido* trains – so named because the route was almost identical with the ancient itinerary followed since time immemorial – went on to a new schedule, with the *Hikari* trains covering the 305 miles in 3 hr 10 min. The train drivers were rumoured to be subject to a fine if they ran a minute late or a minute early.

This was more than another simple increment in the chronology of train speed records. As early as 1904 the British *City of Truro* had attained a speed, going downhill with five mailvans, of about 100 mph. During the 1930s many British and other steam trains recorded speeds with passenger loads that comfortably exceeded 100 mph, but these were not average speeds between termini. These rarely exceeded 60 mph because of curvature of lines, restrictions over bridge sections, and time lost on acceleration and deceleration. After the Second World War, widespread use of diesel-electric power and electrification permitted some improvements, to perhaps 80 mph in isolated instances. But the Shin Kansen was both a revelation and a revolution. The trains cruised at 125 mph and *averaged* close to 100 mph. This was not just a new improved railway. It was effectively a new form of transport.

This was an intriguing situation in which the two main Japanese airlines, JAL and All Nippon Airways (*see* Chapter 36) could actually welcome the impact of surface competition. Tens of millions of people travel annually between the two huge metropolitan concentrations of Japan, and the two airlines alone could never possibly have handled the loads. Nevertheless, while the dramatic and sudden improvement in city-centre travel time in 1964 brought about the transfer of some traffic from air to train, the two airlines continued to provide frequent services on their inter-city routes. On 1 August 1965 JAL introduced the Boeing 727 on the routes from Tokyo to Osaka and Fukuoka, and both airlines each operated fifteen flights a day in both directions. As the 727s came in, the DC-7Cs went out, but the old workhorse 'thoroughbred' DC-6B was not finally retired until 30 March 1969.

Boeing 727s began working JAL's services to Osaka and Fukuoka in August 1965.

Global Strategies

While coping with the challenges on the home front, Japan Air Lines continued to seek ways of widening its marketing opportunities abroad. It made modest additions to its existing route structure, with the Polar flights re-routed via Hamburg on 2 May 1965 and the *Silk Road* including Paris and Delhi on one of the weekly frequencies. A new Polar service to Amsterdam began on 2 April 1966; two days later Teheran was added to the *Silk Road*; and on 12 November 1966, the trans-Pacific service was extended to New York, by which time the total frequencies across the ocean amounted to twenty.

Finally turning its back on supersonic speculation, JAL attended to more practical matters. Firmly subsonic, it ordered three Boeing 747 wide-bodied jet airliners on 16 June, and followed this with five Douglas DC-8-62 stretched versions of the basic type on 29 September.

On 1 April 1965, consolidating its *Silk Road* routes to Europe via southern Asia, JAL had signed a four-airline pool agreement with three European airlines: Air

Japan Air Lines added Douglas DC-8-62s to its jet fleet.

473

France, Alitalia and Lufthansa. This gave Japan a firm foothold in three of the busiest airports in continental Europe, as well as securing maintenance facilities with those airlines, which were later to pool their technical resources under an arrangement known as the ATLAS Group. With such support, Japan Air Lines was encouraged to begin what it felt to be a prestigious Round-the-World service, on 6 March 1967. This was a combination of the trans-Pacific service, now extended as far as New York, and the various *Silk Road* services to Europe. On this date, JAL simply forged the last link in the chain, from New York to London.

JAL's girdle round the earth was not the first. Pan American Airways had started a service as early as 17 June 1947, from New York to San Francisco the long way round, but had been denied permission to make the US transcontinental connection by the Civil Aeronautics Board. The first genuinely round-the-world service was claimed by the Australian airline QANTAS, which started on 14 January 1948; and BOAC followed suit on 22 August 1959, after some bitter negotiations with the US over trans-Pacific rights. Air France and TAI, the French independent airline, combined in a delightful routeing via New Caledonia and Tahiti, from 6 May 1960. Like the others, however, JAL discovered that, while embellishing its promotional literature, the route did not embellish the figures in the profit-and-loss account. People just did not fly around the world, and the load factor (percentage of seats filled) was woefully low on the San Francisco—New York and the New York—London segments. Both were withdrawn on 7 December 1972.

Even the Round-the-World service was eclipsed as a talking point in the air transport world, for within a month of its inauguration, another service began, on 17 April 1967, that was to be historic in its own right, and a harbinger of greater things to come. A year earlier, the civil aviation authorities of the USSR had responded to Japan's persistent efforts to try to find a shorter way to western Europe than via the North Pole or the Indian Ocean. On 20 January 1967 they granted to Japan Air Lines the right to fly to various points via Moscow. This permission was conditional upon the use of Soviet aircraft, and the use of Soviet

On 17 April 1967 JAL began a service to the West via Moscow. JAL had to use Soviet aircraft and flight crews and this resulted in joint operation of the largest propeller-turbine aircraft, the Tupolev Tu-114. The Tu-114s carried JAL's name on the forward fuselage and the airline's tsuru (crane) crest. The photograph shows a Tu-114 arriving at Tokyo, probably on the first service.

crews, at least on the flight deck. The result of this intriguing arrangement was that the service began with Tupolev Tu-114s, the largest propeller-turbine airliner ever to go into service anywhere in the world. Japan Air Lines supplied cabin staff and shared the revenues with the Soviet airline Aeroflot, and the aircraft had dual Aeroflot and JAL markings. By this time, incidentally, the Japanese airline had adopted the elegant *tsuru* – crane – as its symbol, and this was to be seen also on the Ilyushin Il-62s which succeeded the Tu-114s on 3 June 1969. Japan Air Lines is the only non-Soviet airline to have operated the Tupolev Tu-114, and is believed also to have been the only one to have operated the Ilyushin Il-62 outside the Communist world.

After three years of apparently harmonious co-operation, both Aeroflot and Japan Air Lines began to operate their own services with their own aircraft, Aeroflot with the Ilyushin Il-62, Japan Air Lines with the Douglas DC-8-62. On 28 March 1970 JAL opened a one-stop service to Paris via Moscow, in an elapsed journey time of 14 hr 40 min. On 2 June a second service opened to London. Both Paris and London were served twice weekly. It was the first trans-Siberian route to be operated by any airline other than Aeroflot.

Encouraged perhaps by its success in drawing a new line on its map, Japan Air Lines moved to forge a closer link with the USSR, helping indirectly to heel the wounds of wartime antagonism in years past. On 28 May 1971 a Boeing 727 started service from Tokyo to Khabarovsk, the capital of the Russian Far Eastern Province. Aeroflot used the Tupolev Tu-134. This pair of inaugurals were cargo flights and both sides were right to be sceptical of passenger demand. When seats were offered on 2 June, JAL carried six people and Aeroflot carried five. But, if only for political and cultural reasons, both airlines persevered and the route is still operating today, with the Japanese terminal transferred to Niigata, on the Sea of Japan, since 15 June 1973.

Japan Air Lines appears in full to the right of the passenger steps, while the tsuru is partly obscured by the steps. Beneath the flight deck windows of the Tu-114 is the Tupolev logo – it reads 'Tu'.

Relations with the Soviet Union on the Moscow services were so cordial that in January 1973, an agreement was signed that allowed Japan Air Lines to operate to six European destinations via the Soviet capital. Services to Paris and London had been the first, in 1970; Copenhagen was added on 3 April 1972 and Frankfurt on 5 April 1974.

Surmounting the Great Wall

Japan Air Lines was now carrying its country's flag to all the countries of east and southeast Asia, except for those under communist governments, notably the People's Republic of China, with which near-neighbour Japan was anxious to resume commercial relations. This was an extremely delicate matter, as Japan had recognized the Nationalist Government of China, which ruled over the island province of Taiwan (formerly Formosa). Under the isolationist policies decreed by Chairman Mao Tse-tung, contact and communication with the Chinese Government in Peking (Beijing) was almost non-existent. Very few people from the outside world had ever visited mainland China since the Communist victory of 1948–49; but now, after almost a quarter of a century, the ice was showing signs of a thaw.

During 1971, the Japanese parliament wrestled with the apparent impasse caused by the diplomatic situation resulting from the existence of two governments, both of which called themselves China. On the initiative of the transport minister, Kyoshiro Niwa, preliminary enquiries were made to ascertain whether air services were possible between Japan and China (the PRC), even though diplomatic relations did not yet exist. For its part, Japan Air Lines President Shizuo Asada asked the Japan-China Friendship Association to intercede on its behalf during a goodwill visit to Peking.

By 1972 Japan had signed a technical co-operation agreement with the PRC, and in March 1972, a former JAL board member, and former foreign minister, Eiichiro Fujiyama, was able to discuss the idea of an air service with the great Chinese statesman, Chou En-lai. Nothing came of this immediately. In the Orient, such far-reaching decisions are not made hastily; and the circumstances underlying these were sensitive in the extreme.

Ultimately, however, on 20 April 1974, Japan and China signed a bilateral air agreement. This allowed for JAL to operate twice weekly from Tokyo to Peking (Beijing), with one flight stopping at Osaka and Shanghai. JAL would use Douglas DC-8s, CAAC, the Chinese airline, would use either Boeing 707s or Hawker Siddeley Tridents. JAL would have onward rights (though these were never taken up) but there was one important clause in the agreement that reverberated throughout the airline world of east Asia. The Japanese flag-carrier would not be allowed to operate both to mainland China (the PRC) and to Taiwan.

Japan Air Lines wasted no time, and proceeded to implement the terms of the agreement with un-oriental speed. Service to Taipei was suspended the day after the agreement, and the first DC-8 flew into Beijing on 29 September. To compensate the Taiwan Republic of China (ROC) for the loss, JAL founded a wholly-owned subsidiary on 9 August 1975, and the new airline, Japan Asia Airways (JAA) started service from Tokyo to Taipei on 15 September of that year.

The Wide-Bodied Era

Japan Air Lines' momentum grew apace during the 1960s, as the Japanese economy made its astonishing recovery from the nadir of 1945. By 1965 its crude steel production exceeded 40 million tons a year; the shipyards of Nagasaki, Sasebo and other ports rocketed Japan into first place among the shipbuilding nations, not least in the construction of giant oil tankers. With the invention of the underwater bulbous bow Japanese hydronamicists discovered a means of increasing speed and reducing the bow-wave effect. Japan's car builders were unable to keep up with the demand for top-quality vehicles at bargain prices. Japanese radios, televisions and cameras, as well as countless other products, swept the world and bolstered prosperity at home. The resultant improved standards of living put a great deal of money in Japanese pockets, and a growing percentage of the new wealth was spent on travel, including air travel abroad. Japanese tourists were to be seen in all the capitals and tourist destinations of the world, and many of them were carried by Japan Air Lines, mostly through its Creative Tours organization, set up on 4 April 1969, and marketed as JALPAK.

There were plenty of places to go to. In 1967 the network in east Asia had been reinforced by additional frequencies and by new destinations: Kuala Lumpur on 8 May, and Manila on 20 November. Later on, from 1 October 1970, the island of Guam received direct service from Tokyo – under much happier circumstances than when the last Japanese airline had flown there, in support of wartime military operations. Possibly because of long and sad memories, service to nearby Saipan did not start until 1 October 1977. On 11 September 1968, Vancouver was included on some frequencies to San Francisco; and perhaps even more important, another country of the British Commonwealth, Australia, was added to the map when the Hong Kong service was extended to Sydney on 30 September 1969, re-routed via Manila on 24 May 1970.

These additions and extensions had been undertaken by the faithful Douglas DC-8s. But these flagships had to give way to the new generation of wide-bodied – *i.e.* up to 10-abreast seating, with two aisles – aircraft. The standard-bearer of these truly giant aircraft was the Boeing 747, a project that was launched on 13 April 1966 by Boeing, working closely in conjunction with Pan American Airways, at that time master of the intercontinental skies. The 747 could carry about 360 passengers in a generous mixed-class configuration, and with Japan's steady climb up the international air traffic charts, an order from JAL was only a matter of time. This came on 16 June 1966 and the first one went into service on the Tokyo—Honolulu—Los Angeles route on 1 July 1970.

During its closing years as Japan Air Lines' flagships, the DC-8s had their ups and downs, metaphorically as well as literally. On 16 June 1968 a DC-8-62 started a nonstop trans-Pacific service directly from Tokyo to San Francisco, and the stretched DC-8-61 entered the busy southeast Asia route system on 1 April 1969. Even after the drama of the trans-Pacific wide-bodied boom – 747 frequency was up to daily – the DC-8 was still in the picture. On the same day when the 747 went on to the Polar route, on 3 April 1972, DC-8 service to Vancouver was extended to Mexico City, to put Japan Air Lines into Latin America for the first time. A DC-8-62 later had the honour of opening the first service to São Paulo and Rio de Janeiro, on 20 June 1977, and it also inaugurated service to Fiji and Auckland, New Zealand, on 4 July 1980.

The successes were marred, however, by a series of accidents. On 14 June 1972, a DC-8 crashed at Delhi, killing 83 people, after what was described as 'a high rate of descent' and the Indian Court of Enquiry blamed an inexperienced crew. Then, on 28 November of the same year, another DC-8 crashed immediately after taking off from Moscow's Sheremetyevo Airport. Of the 76 on board, 60 were killed; and once again the experience of the crew was questioned. Japan

JAL became a major operator of Boeing 747s, some with as many as 563 seats!

Air Lines was alarmed. On 7 December it began intensified training and sharpened up its maintenance procedures. A fine reputation was at stake, The measures were strictly enforced and were effective.

During the 1970s, when world air passenger traffic quadrupled in a decade, Japan Air Lines' growth was statistically on a tear. This applied not only to the world-wide international network, but also to the intensive domestic trunk arteries that linked Japan's major cities. In spite of the incursions of the Shin Kan-sen high-speed Bullet Trains, the traffic still grew, and both JAL and All Nippon were hard pressed to keep up with the demand for seats, which seemed almost insatiable.

After a protracted evaluation, in which the McDonnell Douglas DC-10 and the Lockheed L-1011 TriStar were given serious consideration, Japan Air Lines placed an order on 30 October 1972 for four Boeing 747SR (Short-Range) wide-bodied airliners. These mighty load-carriers, fitted with 498 seats each, went into service on the Tokyo—Okinawa route on 7 October 1973 and on internal domestic service to Fukuoka and Sapporo on 1 April 1974. Service to Osaka with these huge aircraft had to wait until 17 May 1977, when the airport at Japan's second city was extended and strengthened, and the terminal buildings improved to allow the onrush of the passenger mobs. On 14 February 1980 the seating capacity on the SRs was increased to 550. And if this was not enough, on 26 March 1986, JAL introduced into service a special SR version of the Boeing 747-300SUD (Stretched Upper Deck), with 563 seats. Fortunately, the Japanese are, in general, small people; and they are also very polite.

Against the *Guinness Book of Records* performance (and another sadder one was to be added) Japan Air Lines sought also to supplement the wide-bodied 747 fleet with a smaller type, to hedge its bets, as it were, against the problem of deploying 498-seaters on some routes that could not generate enough traffic to provide a break-even number of passengers on every flight, on every route, year-round. For this insurance against what was referred to by some airline economists as the downside risk, JAL ordered six McDonnell Douglas DC-10-40s on 28 December 1973. Although the standard DC-10s had General Electric CF6 engines, JAL was one of only two airlines (the other was Northwest) that specified Pratt & Whitneys. For international services, the DC-10s had 277 seats, for domestic routes, they had 327.

On 17 March 1976 the DC-10 went into service to all the main cities on the domestic network. Soon afterwards, there was much speculation as to how Japan Air Lines would react to Pan American's introduction of another special version of the 747, the SP (Special Performance). This was a shortened verison of the standard 747 (irreverently described by the folks at Long Beach as the Fat Albert) and seats were traded off for extra fuel, enabling the SP to fly from almost any point on the Pacific Rim to almost any point in the United States. The specification, in fact, hinged on its ability to carry the full payload of 233 passengers nonstop over the 6,754 statute miles between Tokyo and New York. Pan American put this remarkable aircraft into service on that route on 25 April 1976. Surprisingly, Japan Air Lines did not react in a manner that many analysts expected, that is, by matching the service with its own SPs. Instead, it continued to operate with stops at Anchorage, and the DC-10 went into service on that route on 1 April 1977. JAL had decided that the total traffic potential on this, one of the few routes that was beyond the normal range of either the standard 747 or the DC-10 but which generated sufficient demand, was not enough to justify the investment; and it was prepared to lose some of its market share, if necessary, rather than lose its shirt on the rather uneconomical 747SP. Subsequent experience suggests that this was a wise decision. The SP was never a great success, and only about thirty were built. Eventually, improvements in the standard 747, especially in greater fuel efficiency in the engines, gave JAL all the range it needed, by which time the traffic levels had grown to fill the aircraft.

The DC-10-40s did nothing especially spectacular for Japan Air Lines. But it was a versatile airliner, able to fly (except for the extreme 200 miles or so) on any route normally allocated to the 747. It filled a useful gap between the obsolescent DC-8s, the last of which was retired on 31 December 1987 after 27 years of service, and the larger 747s. It replaced the Eights, for example, on the New Zealand route, on 2 April 1982, but as the popularity of the line grew, because of the tourist attractions at both ends, the DC-10 itself gave way to the 747s on 2 November 1987. Mainly, it became a familiar sight at the busy airports throughout east and southeast Asia.

Japan Air Lines' progress during the late 1970s and the 1980s was, on the whole, unremarkable. New points were added in the Middle East, as that oil-rich area began to attract more air traffic. In 1978 Abu Dhabi and Baghdad became *Silk Road* stations on 2 June and 1 November respectively; and in 1981 Kuwait replaced Teheran on 11 February and Jeddah came on line on 28 December; and Bahrain received service on 3 April 1984. As previously noted, JAL's world had embraced Brazil, in 1978, and New Zealand by 1980. In Europe, Zürich (1 April 1979), Madrid (7 July 1980) and Düsseldorf (3 June 1985) made JAL's comprehensive service to that continent almost complete.

Such steady enrichment of the operational structure might easily have led to complacency, as memories of the DC-8 crashes of 1972 had receded, and the one on 9 February 1982, when another DC-8 came in short of the runway at Haneda Airport and flew straight into Tokyo Bay, had, like the others, been blamed on the crew's lack of sufficient experience. JAL was still employing as many as 200 foreign pilots, partly because the country as a whole had lost so many during the war, and had never been able really to catch up with the shortfall. The general public, and the investment community, unfortunately tends to judge an airline as much by its safety record as by any other criterion; so that Japan Air Lines was dealt almost a mortal blow when, on 12 August 1985, a fully-loaded Boeing 747SR crashed into a mountain 70 miles northwest of Tokyo. The number of passengers killed, 520, was a bitter world's record for a single airliner disaster. Miraculously, there were four survivors. After exhaustive investigation, when most of the vertical tail surfaces were found to have come off, it was discovered that the rear

JA8123 was one of JAL's cargo Boeing 747s. (*Boeing*)

pressure bulkhead had been improperly repaired by Boeing, after the aircraft had made a hard landing – on its tail – in 1978. But while, as with many an air crash, the fault could not be laid entirely at the door of Japan Air Lines, the repurcussions went much further than the realms of air safety.

Privatization

In a dignified and compassionate statement distributed to the entire staff, the President of Japan Air Lines expressed his sympathy to the victims of the crash, and expressed his gratitude to all those members of JAL who had worked so assiduously to mitigate the anguish of the families. Instinctively recognizing that this was also a turning point in the airline's history and a time for a measured review of the company's position as a business entity and of its role in Japanese commerce, he went on to outline some problems and some proposed action to solve them.

While the tragic incident of the 747 crash polarized opinions, fundamental changes were already occurring in the body politic of Japanese commercial air transport. It had started almost as the biblical Cloud No Bigger Than a Man's Hand. On 21 September 1978 a new airline, Nippon Air Cargo Airlines, had been formed with the approval of the Japanese Government. The company was owned by an alliance of shipping companies, freight forwarders and JAL's rival airline All Nippon Airways. After much delay, the Ministry of Transport let it be known that it was fashioning a new airline policy, that would come into effect in the 1990s. The Ministry would be overcome by events, unwittingly of its own making.

Nippon Cargo Airlines soon gave notice that its horizons were not confined to Japan nor to east Asia. It applied for a licence to operate to the United States, starting on 1 April 1985. This, to put no finer point on it, put a cat among the pigeons, unleashing a flurry of activity that, in retrospect, was the turning point in Japanese airline history.

Believing that such approval would receive almost automatic consideration by the US authorities, because freight airlines had not traditionally been instruments of foreign air policy, the Japanese were taken aback, if not stunned, when the Americans started to bargain. After negotiation, NCA obtained its licence, but only after Japan had conceded the rights of three new US airlines to operate from Japan to the USA. In return, Japan was permitted to designate two new airlines of its own to operate to the USA. Whether this had been a carefully-disguised plan by All Nippon Airways, hitherto restricted to domestic routes, except for charters,

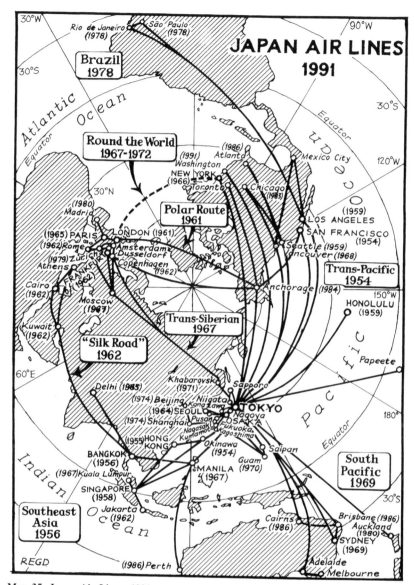

Map 35. Japan Air Lines, 1991
After making a new start in 1951, the new Japan Air Lines (loosely a descendant of the pre-war airline, but only in the re-employment of personnel and the preservation of a tradition, not as a corporate entity) quickly built up a world-wide route network, echoing Japan's almost miraculous emergence as a world power in industry, commerce, and economic prosperity. Trans-Pacific service began in 1954, followed by routes to southeast Asia by the end of the decade. The first routes to Europe started in the early 1960s, both by the Polar route and by the traditional 'Silk Road'; and subsequently Japan's flag carrier spread its wings to Australasia and South America.

481

will never be known. But if it had not – and there is no evidence that it was – the outcome could not have been better for JAL's rival.

JAL itself recognized the new political realities, and decided that it must be free of the provisions of the Japan Air Lines Law (abbreviated in Japanese to Nikko-Ho), created as far back as 1953, when the original corporation structure of JAL was established. Its policies and progress had been little affected when, in 1970, a Cabinet Agreement, followed in 1972 by a Transport Ministry Directive, had laid down provisions to prevent excessive and self-defeating competition among the Japanese airlines to stabilize the industry without inhibiting growth. One result of this new policy had been the creation of Toa Domestic Airlines (TDA) by merging Toa with Japan Domestic Airlines (JDA) in May 1971 (*see* Chapter 36). JAL was restricted to the five biggest domestic cities, but enjoyed a monopoly of foreign routes. All Nippon, in exchange, was allowed complete freedom to operate both trunk and feeder routes throughout Japan. Toa Domestic was at first restricted to feeder routes, but with the understanding that it could operate trunk routes at a later date.

Like all best-laid plans, these had been modified, when the crisis arose in 1975 with the problem of the two Chinas and Japan Asia Airways was formed as a device to skate neatly around international law. But both All Nippon and TDA had been frustrated in their own hope that the special political situation might have opened an international door for them.

On 1 April 1981, the Japan Air Lines Company Law was revised to provide greater commercial flexibility. Then, on 10 September 1985, the Minister of Transport formally asked an advisory committee to study the whole problem of competition, both at home and abroad, to study the roles of all the Japanese airlines, and to consider privatization. All this might never have happened, if All Nippon Airways had not put its foot firmly in the air cargo door. In December 1985, the committee issued its preliminary findings: that there should be multiple designation of Japanese airlines abroad, and that there should be more competition at home, both in route certification and in fares policy.

The immediate results were that the Japanese Government scrapped the 1970/72 policy on 17 December 1985. This was perhaps pre-ordained. It was the same day of the year when the Wright brothers made their historic first flight in 1903; and when the Douglas DC-3 made its first flgiht in 1935. All three events were to change the course of aviation in some way or other.

In March 1986, like a greyhound released from the traps, All Nippon Airways (ANA) started scheduled service to Guam, where its aircraft had been familiar visitors with loads of charter groups. Then, in July 1986, it started service to Washington, DC, the very seat of power that had precipitated this new course of Japanese air transport. On the other hand, JAL opened its first new domestic route for thirty years, with a direct Tokyo–Kagoshima connection on 20 July, and this was followed by Tokyo—Komatsu on 1 October, and Nagoya—Fukuoka on 20 October. The bonds of long tradition and regulation had been broken; and there was much more to come.

The original timetable for the transition of Japan Air Lines into private ownership had called for completion by 1988; but the shattering effect of the 1985 Boeing 747 crash hastened the process. On 20 August 1987 the Diet's Lower House passed a bill to abolish the Japan Air Lines Law, as a first stage towards formally privatizing the airline. The Upper House gave its blessing on 4 September, and on 18 November 1987, Japan Air Lines became a private company. On 15 December, the Government's 34.5 percent shareholding was sold for 664.5 billion yen, or about 4 billion US dollars. About half of this went to financial institutions, the remainder to private individual investors, who number about 400,000.

The outward, visible changes were predictable. All the staff were issued with new uniforms, coming into use on 1 January 1988. A new corporate insignia was adopted, emphasizing the JAL abbreviation, but still retaining the *tsuru* on the tail fin; and Japan Air Lines became Japan Airlines: these latter changes coming into effect on 17 May 1989. Internally, there had been disagreements and a changing of the guard was observed at the top levels of management. Susumu Yamaji had taken over as president on 18 December 1985, after Yasimoto Takagi had resigned as a matter of honour after the dreadful 747 crash. He was replaced by Junji Ito on 27 May 1986, but he too resigned on 31 March 1987. Fumio Watanabe became the first chairman of the new reconstituted Japan Airlines, on 11 January 1988.

While, as part of the free market economy, the airline would no longer qualify for low-interest government loans, there were many advantages to being privately owned. The often protracted debates and endless conferences needed to decide on investments and purchases, the appointment of board members, the framing of business plans, decisions to increase capital; all these critical actions would henceforth be free of the inevitable procrastination that seems to accompany measures taken by joint-stock companies. Japan Airlines would be able to react quickly to competitive challenges.

One important feature of the privatization was that JAL could participate in fields of commerce and transport that were not necessarily directly related to air transport. Thus, within a few months of starting its new life, JAL was a partner in the City Air Link, a helicopter service, operating Bell 412s, that started flights between Tokyo's two airports, Narita and Haneda, on 20 June 1988. Confident of its new freedom, JAL had already formed the company, in association with a helicopter business, Asahi Koyo, on 24 February 1987. In other fields, it founded the JAL Foundation, a non-profit organization to promote cultural activities, on 16 April 1990; and renamed its 26-year-old Japan Creative Tours and its package operator JALPAK to JALPAK and I'll respectively on 9 January 1991. On 1 April 1991, the JAL Flight Academy formed a small commuter airline, J-Air, and began flying across the Inland Sea from Hiroshima to Matsuyama and Oita.

But perhaps the most important and far-reaching of all the new JAL associations, were the steps taken to co-operate with surface transport. For many years the Japanese airlines and the Tokyo authorities had wrestled with the problem of how to take people to and from the airport. Tokyo is the most congested city in the world, one that is notorious for employing 'people-pushers' to squash passengers into the underground trains during busy rush-hours. During the 1970s, a monorail line had been built from Haneda, using the German ALWEG system, but this was not especially fast, and it terminated at Hamamatsucho, which was two stations distant from the business district. Possibly arguing that as it 'floated' on air, a magnetic-levitation vehicle could be termed an aircraft, Japan Air Lines, had, as early as 1975, dabbled in experimentation with a high-speed solution. On 22 December, it demonstrated, for the first time, its HSST (High Speed Surface Transport), and little more than two years later, on 14 February 1978, an HSST prototype reached a speed of 190 mph (308 km/h). A new company, HSST Company Ltd, was formed on 25 November 1985, demonstrations were made at EXPO 86 at Vancouver, in May 1986, and later in the year, plans were announced to develop HSST commercially.

So far nothing has come of this revolutionary invention, as the engineers strug-

A prototype of the HSST high-speed vehicle (190 mph).

gle with the technical problems of levitated traction and powerful magnetic forces. More practical is the attempt to shorten the time taken to move from Narita Airport, about 35 miles from central Tokyo, into the city. The high-speed buses were too often helpless in the grid-locked traffic of the congested elevated expressways. Journey times of three hours from the Narita bus-platforms to the Okura Hotel, for example, were not uncommon. In a service improvement that, in terms of passenger convenience and comfort, was as great an advance as the Shin Kansen's historic break-through of 1964, the Narita Express or N'EX trains of the East Japan Railway Company started a new line on 22 March 1991. Boarding from escalator connections straight from the arrival hall at Narita, passengers were whisked to Tokyo's Central Station in 58 minutes.

Southwest/Japan Transocean

The almost clandestine Air America operation known as Scheduled Air Service Ryukyu (SASR) (see page 368) was replaced on 1 July 1967 by Southwest Airlines, 51 per cent of which was owned by Japan Air Lines, and operated under contract for the United States Civil Administration on Okinawa. At first, its route network was confined to the Ryukyu Islands, and was served by a small fleet of Convair 240s and a Beech 18. These were later superseded by a small fleet of NAMCO YS-11s.

When the Ryukyus returned to Japanese jurisdiction in May 1973, Southwest (SWAL) became Japan's fourth scheduled airline, and was permitted to expand its routes to the Japanese mainland islands, particularly to points in Kyushu.

In 1993, it was renamed Japan Transocean Airlines, and, having already supplemented the YS-11s with DHC-6 Twin Otters, moved into pure jet operations with Boeing 737-400s in the summer of 1994. Based in Okinawa, it is regarded today as an essential element of the economy of the Ryukus, and Japan's southernmost province.

CHAPTER THIRTY-SIX

Japan's Second Force Airline

The Kominsha

In Chapter 31, in the chronology of the early years of Japanese commercial aviation, the Asahi newspaper group was shown to be one of prime movers in the formation of the pioneer airlines. Two key members of the Asahi organization during the 1930s were to play an important part in the rejuvenation of Japanese airlines after the end of the Second World War.

The elder statesman of the two was Masuichi Midoro, born in 1886 in Okayama. He joined the *Asahi News* in 1908 and was eventually to become vice-president and chief editor in 1943. The younger man was Katsuyoshi Nakano, born in 1904, and who joined the Aviation Department of the *Asahi News* in 1930. Nakano was immediately involved in promoting aeronautics in Japan, as the newspaper was one of the sponsors of the Japan Student Aviation Federation. It promoted that group's glider championship in 1936, and Nakano himself helped to plan the Kamikaze-gou flight to London, to bring back pictures of the British Coronation.

In the autumn of 1945, when Japan was still recoiling in the aftermath of the atomic bombs, the surrender to the Allied forces, and the humility of defeat, Nakano and Midoro had a key meeting, to renew their mutual interest in the restoration of commercial aviation. This led to the formation, in December, of the kominsha (literally, the re-establishment or revival) movement. Another member of the kominsha was Kaheita Okazaki, also from Okayama, born in 1897, a banker who, in 1938, had joined the Kakou Commercial Bank in Shanghai when Japan occupied that Chinese city. Other participants were Ryuichi Fukumoto and Seiji Torii.

One of the praiseworthy objectives of the kominsha was to preserve a nucleus of avation people during a period when all aviation in Japan was banned to Japanese citizens. Many of them were able to work in other businesses, such as trucking fruit to the big cities, and in many ways experienced aviation staff were protected from poverty. Some of them, as time went on and the bitter memories of war receded, were able to obtain some training in maintenance and engineering as a courtesy from the USAAF's Far East Asia Maintenance Command (FEAMCOM).

Meanwhile, Kaheita Okazaki had been active. He became president of Ikegai Steel and began to play a leading role in the long process of postwar reconciliation with China. He instigated the formation of the International Trade Promotion Institute, the Japan-China Trade Committee, and the Japan-China Economic Committee. That Okazaki was able to do this reflected well on his character. Most former Japanese, who had been part of the occupying administration during the 1937–1945 seizure of the eastern provinces of China, were personae non grata; but Okazaki was apparently a notable exception.

By the time the San Francisco Peace Treaty was signed on 4 September 1951, the door was already open for the re-establishment of airline services in Japan. As narrated in Chapter 35, the movement was initiated to create a national airline with the help of foreign airlines, leading to the creation of Japan Air Lines as a joint-stock corporation on 1 August 1953, and the simultaneous passing of the Japan Air Lines Law. While recognizing JAL as a 'chosen instrument', however, the Government took a liberal view of commercial aviation affairs; and unlike the course of events in many other countries, the possibility of other airlines entering the scheduled airlines business was not ruled out.

The foresight and initiative of the kominsha now began to reap some dividends. On 18 January 1950 the founding committee of Japan Helicopter and Aeroplane Transport (JHAT) was established, and Ryuichi Fukumoto, one of the founder members of the kominsha, was the chairman. The main task was to be ready to form an airline as soon as they were legally entitled to do so.

Nippeli

On the day that the Civil Aviation Law was announced, on 15 July 1952, the law that permitted the start of domestic air transport and the importation of aircraft, the Japan Helicopter and Aeroplane Transport Company applied for operating licences. The Japanese name was Nihon Herikoputa Yuso Kabushiki Kaisha (NHYKK), also known familiarly as 'Nippeli', and in this reconstruction period in the aftermath of the war, with Japan vigorously trying to re-assert itself internationally, the English name was the better known and the most widely used. This was a tacit recognition that English was the international language of the air transport world, and a sensible coming to terms with realities.

From the start Nippeli sought capital from all sources in Japan, from every type of company or corporation, even those in competition with each other, and these included some of the largest corporations in Japan (and a couple of decades later, so ranked in the world) such as Mitsui, Mitsubishi, Sumitomo and C Itoh, as well as some of the private railways. Midoro and Nakano shrewdly realised that if their little company could eventually become a national one, their independence would be sacrificed if one single investor had enough of the capital to exercise control. Midoro even refused a handsome offer from the Tokyu Den Detsu (Tokyo Kyoko Express railway company) to subscribe all the required capital to put Nippeli on its feet. Tokyu later acquired control of Toa Domestic Airlines. Even today, the biggest single shareholder of Nippeli's descendant, All Nippon Airways, holds only five percent of the total shares.

And so JHAT, or NHYKK, or Nippeli, was registered in Tokyo, on 27 December 1952. Masuichi Midoro was the president, Kaheira Okazaki his deputy, Katsuyoshi Nakano and Ryuichi Fukumoto were senior vice-presidents and Seiji Torii was a vice-president. They could have called the company Kominsha Airlines. The capital was set at 150 million yen (about $450,000). There were twelve board members, sixteen employees and 673 stockholders, a somewhat unusual ratio. Only two days previously, Nippeli had taken delivery of its first aircraft, two Bell 47D-1 helicopters.

When, on 15 July, Nippeli had applied for operating licences, these had been in three categories: 'aircraft projects' – sometimes called aerial work; charter flights; and regular air transport. The fledgling airline had to take these one by one, and was able to start on 20 February 1953 with contract work for the helicopters. Permission to operate charter flights was granted on 26 May of that year, and soon started with a de Havilland D.H.104 Dove. By the time it received its full air

Japan Helicopter and Aeroplane Transport (NHYKK) at one time had three de Havilland Heron 1Bs. (*de Havilland*)

transport licence for regular scheduled service, the Japan Helicopter and Aeroplane Transport Company boasted a fleet of four Bell 47s and two Doves.

Far Eastern Airlines

Shortly after the promulgation of the Civil Aviation Law, and trailing Nippeli by a month, Far Eastern Airlines (Kyokuto Koku) applied to the Ministry of Transport for an operating licence. Like Nippeli, the best it could do was to obtain, on 21 October 1952, an 'aircraft project licence' (Kokuki Shyo Gigyo) for aerial work. Unlike the helicopter company, however, it proposed to do its contract work with fixed-wing aircraft, and on 15 November purchased two Auster Autocars. This must have been the most modest beginning made by any postwar airline that was ultimately to develop into one of the world's top-ranking industry leaders.

But while Far Eastern was not quite so well capitalized as JHAT, its 50 million yen (about $150,000) was ample to start a small airline. Registered in Osaka on 26 December 1952 (a day before JHAT), Far Eastern's president was Tomoo Kondo, representing a number of prominent investors in the Kansei area of Japan around Osaka; and the vice-president was none other than Choichi Inouye, the founder of Japan's very first airline in 1922 (*see* Chapter 31).

Far Eastern Airlines received permission to operate domestic charter flights on 26 May 1953, the same day as Nippeli; and the licence to operate regular scheduled services was granted on 15 October 1953, also the same day as Nippeli. For this task, Far Eastern had ordered two Handley Page Marathons from the British company on 18 March and had purchased two D.H. Doves from Nippeli at the end of that month. Already there were signs that the two airlines were ready to co-operate.

Early Feeder Routes

Of the two apparently friendly rivals, JHAT, or Nippeli, was first off the mark. It began cargo flights between Tokyo and Osaka on 15 December 1953, with a D.H. Dove. This flight was remarkable for two reasons: very few Doves were ever used for cargo operations, and this was not in de Havilland's mind when it

Far Eastern Airlines was among the few operators of Miles (Handley Page) Marathons.

was designed; but it was the first flight to be piloted by a Japanese national since the end of the Second World War. A Dove also launched Far Eastern into scheduled operation, on the same route on 20 January 1954, between Japan's two largest cities, but carrying mail, not freight. Then on 1 February, Nippeli started full passenger service on the same route, and Far Eastern started its passenger service exactly a month later. In the latter case, however, this was a service from Osaka to Iwakuni, on the island of Honshu west of Hiroshima on the Inland Sea of Japan, and the location of the flying-boat base that had been used by the British airline BOAC, when it started flying-boat services from Great Britain to Japan in 1947. But while both airlines had actually given the diminutive eight-seat de Havilland Dove its claim to fame in operating between Tokyo and Osaka in the two inaugurals, the main direction of Nippeli and Far Eastern, at the start, was to develop a system of feeder routes and to establish a comprehensive route network the length and breadth of Japan, to serve all the cities of medium size and larger, and to provide some services to holiday resort destinations.

The development patterns are shown on the map on page 491; and while the Tokyo—Osaka link was common to both, clearly there was an understanding that the two airlines would be complementary to one another, and not competitive. Japan Air Lines was providing all the competition on the inter-city routes that was needed; and within two years of starting service, both airlines were thinking about, if not actually discussing, a merger. It all made sense. Nippeli's routes to western Honshu, Shikoku and Kyushu Islands would tie in neatly with Far Eastern's routes in central and northern Honshu, and to Hokkaido in the far north.

Both airlines began to pick up some hard-earned experience from day-to-day operations. On 15 November 1955, for example, Nippeli put its first Douglas DC-3 into service, a leased aeroplane, on the Tokyo—Nagoya—Osaka route. Yoko Kitano, the airline's first stewardess, remembers it well. An evening flight, in the dark, it was made at an altitude of 6,000 ft – half the height of Mount Fuji, almost directly en route – and encountered a severe thunderstorm. She did her best to serve green tea, candy, and to interest the passengers in magazines. But for all of them, it was their first flight and half of them were sick.

As for Far Eastern, it was having technical problems with its aircraft. Little more than a year after introducing the Handley Page Marathon on a route from Osaka to Kochi on 1 October 1955, the 20-seat feederliner had to be withdrawn from service, on 4 October 1955. The rivets had started to pop, and new wing mountings required 5,000 hours of work. Although permission to resume flying was forthcoming on 27 October, this was the end of a not very long Marathon run.

One of them was to be seen on the roof of a building at Nagoya's airport for many years as a silent and salutory warning against unwise aircraft procurement. And Far Eastern also had to endure the sadness of a crash, only a minor one (an Auster Autocar crashed into the Sea near Osaka on 1 August 1957, killing the only passenger and the two crew), but nevertheless a sharp reminder that an airline's destiny is one of constant vigilance and rigid discipline.

All Nippon Airways is Born

On 1 March 1958 the merger of Nippeli and Far Eastern, to form All Nippon Airways, was completed. The first discussions towards this logical fusion were held during the autumn of 1956 and the change of name was announced on 1 December 1957. While described as a merger, the Japan Helicopter and Aeroplane Transport Company – Nippeli – was clearly the stronger partner. All the higher officers of All Nippon, quickly abbreviated to ANA (a convenience that fortunately almost coincided with the demise of Australian National Airways a year earlier) were from Nippeli; and the insignia of the merged airline continued to be the symbolic reproduction of Leonardo da Vinci's historic helicopter design.

The new airline did not have an auspicious start. It had hardly got used to the new name when, on 12 August 1958, a DC-3 crashed en route from Tokyo to Nagoya, and all the 30 passengers and two crew were killed. The DC-3s were promptly removed from service, a severe humiliation for this consistently reliable and 'forgiving' veteran airliner. The problem was traced to procedures by which repairs were too often made by the cannibalization process, by which parts are borrowed from grounded or derelict aircraft, to save buying replacements. After the accident, this custom was eliminated, and the Government assisted ANA with a loan to purchase spare parts, especially for the engines. The Japanese traveller is very sensitive to accidents, and ANA felt the chill of customer scepticism for a while. A modest financial loss of 400,000 yen in 1957 was followed by one of 200 million yen in 1958. Japanese memories are also, from bitter experience, short.

All Nippon Airways, though shaken, shrugged off the blow of the accident, and went about its work to upgrade itself from the status of a feeder airline whose fleet still had DC-3s as its flagships, supplemented with a few Doves and Herons. It began trunk-line operations on 1 April 1959, with two DC-3s scheduled twice daily between Tokyo and Osaka, omitting the stop at Nagoya. On 27 April the capital was raised to 600 million yen (about $2 million) and the first Convair 440 pressurized twin-engined airliners started to arrive. Before they could go into service, however, they were requisitioned by the Government in a time of national emergency: a tremendous typhoon had hit Nagoya on 26 September, resulting in more than 5,000 deaths. ANA's pilots were not yet qualified on the type, but the instructors were and helped in the relief operations.

The airline introduced three new types of modern airliner during a period of less than two years. The Convair 440 went into service, to provide pressurized comfort for the first time, on 10 October 1959, on the trunk routes from Tokyo to Osaka, Sapporo and Nagoya; and the Sendai route was extended to Misawa, an important US Air Force base. During 1959, the important cities of Nagasaki, Hakodate and Kumamoto were all added to the network.

All Nippon Airways put propeller-turbine aircraft into service soon afterwards. On 1 August 1960, the four-engined Viscount (Type 744) went into service on the direct Tokyo-Sapporo route. On the same day that the Convair 440s had elevated ANA's status, it had signed a pooling agreement with Japan Air Lines on fares on

All Nippon Airways replaced its Douglas DC-3s with Dart-powered Fokker F.27 Friendships
(*Fokker*)

the trunk routes, but this did not inhibit its competitive spirit. Passengers were invited to look out of the Viscount's windows 'to see the competition as we go by', this latter being JAL's DC-4s and DC-6Bs.

Not to neglect the feeder services, the Fokker F.27 Friendship was added on 10 July 1961, based at Osaka, and charged with operating flights to all the main towns and cities to the west, including Okayama and Fukuyama, as well as replacing the DC-3s as soon as reinforcements of F.27s arrived from Amsterdam. This programme was so successful that the last DC-3 was retired on 15 March 1964.

The Beam Routes

During the 1960s, and especially during the first half of the decade, All Nippon Airways maintained an almost unbelievable rate of traffic growth. For the years 1960–1964, inclusive, the *average annual* growth rate for passengers was 53 percent, and that for cargo was 46 percent. This was a reflection of the equally astonishing rate of growth of Japan's economy as a whole. Industry and commerce were bursting at the seams as the latent energy, discipline, and innovative talents of the Japanese were unleashed by the lifting of trade restrictions. In 1960 the Prime Minister, Mr Ikeda, called for the doubling of the gross national product, and the consequent doubling of national wealth, spread among the population, in the time span of ten years. Japan achieved the target in five.

Such augmentation of the wealth, with a corresponding increase in discretionary income, i.e. money for spending on non-essentials, was a tremendous stimulant to the airlines, as the Japanese public began to spend freely on consumer goods, including airline tickets. And air travel was becoming cheaper. The actual ticket prices remained the same but the prices of other commodities was rising steadily, if not at a dangerously inflationary pace. Thus the relative price of air travel went down, at the same time that Japan's aerodromes were improved and the airlines found minimum bureaucratic obstruction as they applied for permission to operate more routes. The population itself was increasing – the 1960s witnessed the 'baby boom' in Japan as elsewhere; and furthermore this population was becoming more urbanized as Japan revolutionized its entire way of life from what, before the Second World War, had been a primarily agrarian society, into an emphatically industrial one. And as if to put the icing on this tasty multi-layer cake, the 1964

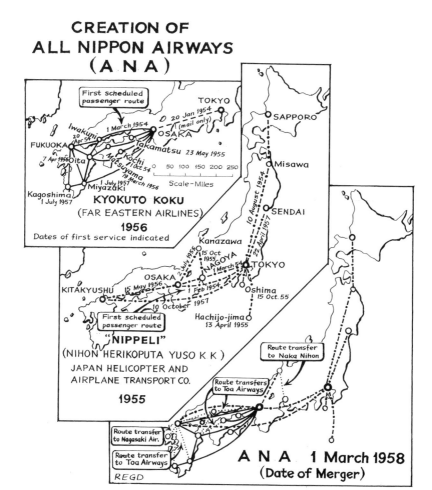

CREATION OF
ALL NIPPON AIRWAYS
(A N A)

Maps 36a. Creation of All Nippon Airways (ANA)

Japan's 'Second Force' airline had relatively modest beginnings. At first, Kyokuto Koku (Far Eastern Airlines) and 'Nippeli:' (Japan Helicopter and Aeroplane Transport Company) were two of several small airlines created when the ban on commercial airline activity was lifted in 1951. Far Eastern, oddly, concentrated on routes to the west of Osaka, especially to the island of Kyushu, while Nippeli served the length of Honshu, reaching Kitakyushu in the southwest and Sapporo, on Hokkaido in the north. With the merger of the two airlines in 1958, ANA became a force to be reckoned with.

Tokyo Olympic Games stimulated all kinds of supporting infrastructual activities, including the improvement of access roads, airports, and the organization of travel, especially in groups.

All these factors stimulated All Nippon Airways to explore to the full the opportunities for expansion in its designated sphere of air transport development: the feeder routes of Japan, that is, other than the trunk line artery that ran from north to south, from Sapporo to Fukuoka via Tokyo, Nagoya and Osaka. Already a

491

group of routes radiated westwards from Osaka – All Nippon had worked out its hub-and-spoke system long before the term became fashionable in the United States – and now it proceeded to duplicate these from Tokyo as well as Osaka, and to add more routes and more destinations in the process. Soon the map of Japan was strewn with ANA routes, in a system that the airline called its 'beam' routes, a term perhaps derived from the idea of the rays of the sun – reminiscent of the former flag of Japan? – or sunbeams, and possibly moonbeams for the night flights.

Fujita Air Lines was another Japanese operator of Fokker Friendships. Fujita was acquired by All Nippon Airways. (*Fokker*)

One interesting exception to the concentration of routes arcing from Tokyo and Osaka was that opened on 23 September 1961, from Kagoshima, southernmost city of Japan's mainland group of islands, to Naha, Okinawa. At that time, Okinawa was still occupied by the United States, on behalf of the United Nations, and was not returned to Japan until May 1972. Stretching the definition a little, therefore, All Nippon Airways was able to claim the opening of an international route.

Riding on the crest of the economic wave, quite a number of small enterprises entered the aviation business, and by the early 1960s, there were about thirty companies that operated commercial aircraft for hire and reward. Most of these were occupied with what is often loosely described as aerial work: surveying, sightseeing, and advertising, and such activity. Some of these obtained licences to operate passenger charters, and a few went even further and indulged in the luxury of becoming small scheduled airlines. (Most of these are reviewed in Chapter 37.)

All Nippon Airways quickly recognized that these small airlines could usefully co-operate with the larger airlines such as itself, in a manner that was strikingly similar to the obsession that possessed the airlines of the United States in the 1980s when the trunk airlines struck up computer reservations code-sharing partnerships with the commuter airlines. On 22 August 1962 ANA signed a letter of intent with Toa Airways, an airline based at Hiroshima, and which specialized in routes in Kyushu and to the Ryukyu Islands to the southwest. On 15 and 17 September ANA signed similar letters with Naka Nihon Koku (Central Japan Airlines) of Nagoya, and with Nagasaki Airlines, respectively.

In pursuance of both the idea of co-operation, and with the objective of being able to concentrate on the beam routes out of the major cities of Tokyo, Osaka and Nagoya, All Nippon transferred some of its lesser routes on the fringes of its pattern, to Toa. On 11 February 1963 Toa acquired some from Hiroshima, on 16 October of the same year some from Fukuoka, and on 15 June 1964 some from Osaka. All these strengthened Toa's network, at the same time relieving ANA of smaller routes so that it could concentrate on the burgeoning traffic demand elsewhere. At the time, the idea of a complete merger was a distinct possibility, but preliminary discussions fell through; and Toa was able to seek other fields to conquer.

All Nippon did, however, purchase another airline, Naka Nihon Koku, on 25 January 1965, to strengthen its position in Nagoya. Mainly a helicopter operator, founded on 4 May 1953, it had also operated a scheduled route from 15 July 1962 with Grumman Goose amphibians to the resorts of Shima and Kashimoto on the Kii Peninsula, and had also made connections to the Sea of Japan coast at Kanagawa. ANA had already bought Fujita Airlines, which specialized in carrying holiday-makers and weekenders mainly from Tokyo, but also from Osaka and Nagoya, to the popular islands of Oshima, from 15 May 1958, and later on to Hachijo-jima, the latter lying some 200 miles to the south of Tokyo. Fujita had had a complicated ancestry, considering its small size, tracing back to Aoki Airlines, founded in 26 April 1952, and Nihon Yuran Hiko (Japan Sightseeing Flying), founded in September 1952. The name was changed to Fujita on 11 June 1961, and the 'merger' with All Nippon enabled it to replace the small de Havilland Doves and Herons with 40-seat Fokker F.27s. The effective date of this acquisition by All Nippon was 31 August 1963.

A Nagasaki Airways de Havilland Dove at Kagoshima in 1962 with the always-smoking Sakura-jima in the background. (*R E G Davies*)

Completing its sweep of small airlines within its sphere of influence, All Nippon took over Nagasaki Airways on 1 December 1967. This tiny company had been founded on 12 June 1961 and operated from Nagasaki to the nearby resort island of Fukue, later adding another over-water link from Fukuoka to Iki Island. And finally, on 5 October 1970, Yokohama Airlines, operating a similar vacation ferry service from Tokyo to Nii-jima Island, came under ANA's wing.

While these co-operative agreements undoubtedly served to All Nippon Airways' advantage, the process of merger and acquisition was encouraged by the Japanese civil aviation authorities, which not only felt that there were too many small airlines, making supervision and regulation inconvenient if not inefficient;

but it had also been disturbed by the frequency of small accidents and incidents that had occurred during the early 1960s. Most of these were not spectacular, some were on training, and some were without casualties. But in two years, from February 1962 to February 1964, 53 people had been killed in five crashes or crash-landings, all by aircraft of the small airlines. Much pressure was exerted from the administration, therefore, to effect a more rational arrangement of the disparate group of what would have been called Local Service or Regional airlines in the United States.

The Sweet Smell of Success

Events in the unfolding story of All Nippon Airways' headlong rise to prominence seemed to come in threes. In the banner year of 1960 it had introduced three new aircraft types, the Convair 440, the Viscount 744 and the Fokker F.27. Now, in 1964, three more events occurred to set ANA's course towards the future. These involved a nationwide airline merger, upgrading to jet service, and competition from an inspired new railway.

First of this trio was the formation, on 15 April, of Japan Domestic Airlines (JDA). This resulted partly from the concerns outlined above, with the Government favouring two regional airlines of substance, rather than a large number of small airlines of questionable viability. JDA was the merger of Kita Nihon Koku (North Japan Airlines), Nitto Airlines, and Fuji Airlines (*see* Chapter 37) and was supported technically and financially by Japan Air Lines. The other regional airline was intended to be a marriage of All Nippon and Toa, but for various reasons, this never happened.

As previously noted, ANA and Toa had already been co-operating, to the extent that route transfers had taken place, to the two airlines' mutual convenience and advantage. Toa's finances had not been in good shape, which must have been a disappointment to the biggest stockholder, the Daihatsu car manufacturer. But problems arose in such matters as who should be represented on the board, and in short what exactly should be the balance of power between the two airlines. The discussions dragged on, and as they did so, Toa's finances improved, as it too shared in the great boom of the early 1960s. By 1969 the plan had fallen through, but later the people at All Nippon were heard to observe ruefully that Toa never returned the transferred routes.

But in any case, the issue was almost irrelevant as ANA took a major step forward. On 25 May 1964, using an aircraft leased from Boeing, it started jet service with a single Boeing 727-100 on the Tokyo—Sapporo route. Such was the demand that an all-reservation system had to be introduced. During the first two months of service, 320 flights suffered only two cancellations and thirteen delays, all weather-related.

The excitement of entering the jet age offset any concern for the competitive effect of JDA. Also, because of the upgrading of equipment, coupled with the continuing boom in traffic, the opening of the high-speed rail service, the Shin Kan-sen, from Tokyo to Osaka, did not make severe inroads to ANA's traffic as a whole. The performance and the influence of the Bullet trains has been discussed in Chapter 35. Because its primary role in Japan's domestic airline system had been to serve the secondary routes to medium-sized cities, All Nippon was not affected by the new trains so much as Japan Air Lines, whose main domestic system, indeed, its only one, parallelled the Shin Kan-sen.

ANA's whole network was growing at a furious pace, and its fleet planning

ANA began jet services, between Tokyo and Sapporo, on 25 May 1964 using a Boeing 727 leased from Boeing. (*Boeing*)

department was hard pressed to keep up. On 30 November, the last Convair 440 (of only four) was retired, as the Viscount demonstrated all-round superiority in that size class, with the 'stretched' Viscount 828 coming on line in March 1965. ANA's propeller-turbines were everywhere. On 8 December 1964 the 25th Fokker F.27 Friendship was delivered, making this the largest fleet of its type anywhere in the world. Then on 20 September 1965, the twin-engined NAMCO YS-11 60-seater entered service on the Osaka—Kochi route.

The YS-11 takes its name from the Yusoki Sekei Kenkyu Kyokai – the Transport Machinery Drafting and Study Institute. NAMCO is simply the acronym for the Nihon Aircraft Manufacturing Corporation, a production and sales organization set up by six prominent manufacturing companies, including Mitsubishi and Kawasaki, to market this first postwar product of the Japanese aircraft building industry. At first thought to be the sign that Japan was about to make its mark in the aviation field, as in motor-bikes, cars, cameras, radios and televisions, the YS-11 was a disappointment, not because it was a bad aircraft – some were even sold to a US regional airline, Piedmont – but it suffered from management problems.

The YS-11 had had its hour of glory. On 9 September 1964, a year before it entered commercial service, a prototype, hand-painted with loving care, had carried the Olympic flame from Naha, Okinawa, en route from Athens to the site of the 1964 Olympics, Tokyo. It had called at several All Nippon stations, and because of this association, ANA's YS-11s were called Olympias.

Japan has always seemed to be a land in which all things are polarized. The successes are outstanding, yet some of the failures are disastrous. Japan Air Lines, for example, has the biggest fleet of the biggest airliner in the world; but it also suffered the biggest tragedy. With Mount Fuji, Japan possesses one of Nature's most beautiful handiwork; but that fickle entity also condemns Japan to some of worst natural disasters in history, with typhoons and earthquakes. Even All Nippon Airways has had its share of these ups and downs.

Going full swing in the mid-1960s with its growing propeller-turbine fleet and its elevation to jet status – the Tokyo—Osaka route was an all-727 route by 1 October 1965 – All Nippon Airways sustained the awful reality of two bad fatal crashes in the same year. On 4 February 1966, a 727 crashed in Tokyo Harbour,

ANA began operating Japanese aircraft when on 20 September 1965 it introduced the NAMCO YS-11 on the Osaka—Kochi route.

killing all 133 on board; and on 13 November, a YS-11 crashed at Matsuyama, killing 50 people. Reacting to the double tragedy, the Japanese air travelling public lost its enthusiasm for All Nippon for a while, and the airline suffered a serious decrease in traffic in 1966. But the memories faded, and it bounced back in 1967, and averaged a 26 percent annual passenger growth rate during the next five years.

Because of the dramatic crashes, the president of All Nippon Airways, Kaheita Okazaki, as a matter of honour, resigned on 22 April 1967. He had been in China, negotiating for the terms of the trade agreement, when the second crash occurred, and was criticized for not concentrating on the airline affairs and having the clairvoyance to be at his desk at the Tokyo head office. Only a few years previously ANA had lost another of its pioneer founders, when Katsuyoshi Nakano, had been killed in the crash of an Auster Autocar in Hokkaido on 16 November 1960. The names of Okazaki, Nakano and Midoro (who died in 1973) are not well known in the world outside Japan; but they were the founders of what is today one of the biggest passenger-carrying airlines; and they deserve places in aviation's hall of fame, along with the other world airline legendary leaders.

Further Fields to Conquer

All Nippon Airways' growth continued inexorably during the 1970s. Although not many new routes were left to add, one or two new points had appeared on the map, notably some of the smaller cities on the northern coastal area of Honshu, such as Yonago (1 August 1964), Fukui (1 July 1966) and Tottori (1 August 1967). But all the existing routes were showing regular increments in the traffic statistics, and ANA intensified the service both in frequencies and by adding more and larger aircraft. The first Boeing 737 went into service on 20 June 1969, and the first 'stretched' Boeing 727-200 on 1 October of that year. With the 60-seat YS-11s replacing the 40-seat F.27s on many of the feeder routes, the summer traffic especially reached record high levels. On 27 August 1972, the millionth passenger was carried during that same month. The last Boeing 727-100 was retired on 9 May 1974, after only ten years of service on the trunk routes, for which it was now too small. On 6 September 1976 ANA reported its 100 millionth passenger since its inaugural flight, less than a quarter of a century previously.

Perhaps one of the reasons for its success was that, in contrast to Japan Air

Lines, which flew only on international and domestic trunk routes, All Nippon Airways was known to all the people of Japan, not only those who lived in the four largest cities. It was well known to the holiday-makers who flocked to the islands near Tokyo, and appreciated the new service to Miyake-jima, started on 4 March 1966; and those near Nagoya, who could fly to Shirahama, from 1 March 1969. Fukuoka (and nearby residents of the industrial chain of cities amalgamated to form Kitakyushu (North Kyushu)), could escape from the urban scene to Tsushima Island after 10 October 1975. And these operations were not flown by small commuter aircraft. They were always with F.27s or YS-11s. Indeed, no new route, in ANA's apparent search to complete its permutation of city pairs within Japan, was ever begun with less than a daily service; and in the case of the one to Tsushima, with two. Ever resourceful, on 20 July 1975, in conjunction with the Okinawa Marine Expo, All Nippon started YS-11 service to two small neighbouring islands, Amami-O-Shima and Ie-Shima, to ensure that the local people, as well as the jet-setters from foreign parts, could see the show.

With such concentrated activity, this Japanese domestic airline, never seen outside the confines of its native land, nevertheless began to acquire stature among its peers in the corridors of aviation business, even though it was not a member of the influential International Air Transport Association (IATA). It did not qualify for membership, and therefore its enormous output of passengers carried and freight hauled was little known around the airline world generally. The impressive statistics did not appear in the IATA rankings, published annually, and outside Japan, only the statisticians and aficionados, and the companies that did good business in selling aircraft to All Nippon, were aware of the sheer size of the operation. And All Nippon Airways, it could be said, was bursting at the seams.

Interest in overseas adventures and possible expansion therein therefore seemed inevitable. Growth or demise being the only accepted alternatives of progress in the airline industry worldwide, this appeared to be All Nippon's only choice, as domestic growth was close to impossible because of the almost saturated state of the market. The first glimmer of hope came on 4 June 1970, when an Aviation Committee of the Ministry of Transport announced its Principles of Air Transport Policy, and stated that 'ANA should be given permission to operate short-range international routes in the future.' ANA was given permission to operate two round-trip charter flights to Pusan, South Korea, and two YS-11s accordingly took off from Fukuoka on 15 and 31 July. A glance at the map confirms the emphasis on short range. Except for an unlikely service to Korea from Tsushima, this was the shortest one possible.

But All Nippon Airways has never been criticized for lack of energy or resourcefulness. After the Air Transport Policy had received cabinet approval in November 1970, it took full advantage of the provisions of the new policy that permitted Affinity Group Charters, following the highly successful practice in Europe where, once launched, intra-European non-scheduled air traffic – almost all of it group charters – had exceeded the volume of scheduled traffic by the early 1970s.

The first affinity charter group, no doubt assembled from a club or group that must have been delighted at the new opportunities afforded by the device, flew from Tokyo to Hong Kong on 21 February 1971. Then, on 3 August 1971, the first one took off to Bangkok, this time from Nagoya; and another first was chalked up to the Thai capital from Kumamoto on 31 March 1972. As shown on the accompanying map, the All Nippon affinity groups were soon to be seen everywhere in southeast Asia during the 1970s. Sixty round trips were made to Hong

497

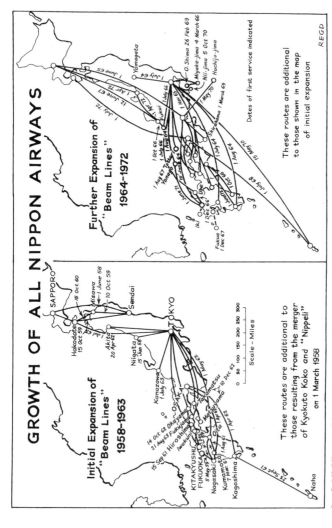

GROWTH OF ALL NIPPON AIRWAYS

Initial Expansion of "Beam Lines" 1958-1963

These routes are additional to those resulting from the merger of Kyokuto Koko and "Nippeli" on 1 March 1958

Scale - Miles
0 50 100 150 200 250 300

SAPPORO

Hakodate 15 Oct 59
Misawa 15 Oct 60
1 June 58
Akita 20 Apr 61
Sendai 10 Oct 59

Niigata 15 Jun 58
Kanazawa 1 July 63
1 May 61
OSAKA
14 Oct 62 Okayama
21 Aug 63 Fukuyama Tokushima
15 Sep 61 Hiroshima Matsuyama 10 Dec 62
Iwakuni Kochi
KITAKYUSHU 5 May 59
FUKUOKA 1 Aug 60
Nagasaki 1 Apr 61
Kumamoto 7 Mar
Kagoshima

Naha 22 Sept 61

TOKYO

Further Expansion of "Beam Lines" 1964-1972

Yamagata
1 July 65
1 July 64

O.Shima 26 Feb 69
Miyake-jima 4 March 66
Nii-jima 5 Oct 70
Hachijo-jima

12 June 67
1 July 72
1 Apr 72

1 Aug 67
Yonago 1 July 67
1 June 67
Ube

1 Oct 66
1 Aug 64
Fukui 1 July 64
1 July 66
1 Nov 69
1 May 70
Shizuoka 1 March 69

1 July 64
1 Aug 64

15 May 70
Iki
Fukue 1 Dec 67
1 Dec 67

1 July 68

Dates of first service indicated

These routes are additional to those shown in the map of initial expansion

REGD

Maps 36b. Growth of All Nippon Airways

After the merger that created All Nippon Airways, and with a Civil Aviation Directorate that encouraged development, the airline moved ahead with determination, skill, and ambition. It concentrated on providing service – nonstop service – to the many cities along the southern coastline of Honshu, and to Hokkaido. The programme of expansion was familiarly known as the 'Beam Lines' and collectively served, by the dynamic increase in traffic everywhere, to project All Nippon Airways to rank, by the 1970s, as one of the world's leading airlines, measured by the number of passengers boarded annually.

Kong and Bangkok alone in 1971. By the mid-1970s flights were leaving almost every day. From 1971 to 1978, when the artificial pretence of the Affinity Groups gave way to a more straightforward Inclusive Tour Charter (ITC) system, All Nippon Airways carried more than half a million Japanese tourists to more than half a dozen destinations. And these were anything but short-range flights. Tokyo to Singapore is almost exactly the same distance as London to New York. Needless to state, this was very good business for ANA and in line with the more liberal regulations, it founded ANA World Tours on 29 September 1978. Only a week previously, it had also founded Nippon Cargo Airlines. Both decisions were critical steps towards a transformation of the entire structure of Japanese commercial aviation: what has been described in Chapter 35 as the Turning Point, and which will be reviewed later on in this chapter.

ANA was a user of the twin-jet Boeing 737. (*Boeing*)

The TriStar Story

The recurrent theme throughout All Nippon Airways' history is its consistent high rate of growth and expansion. With All Nippon, aircraft types came and went, in whole generations, while other airlines were making up their minds. Omitting the infant steps of the predecessor Nippeli and Far Eastern Airlines' diminutive Doves and Herons, the size of All Nippon's front-line aircraft had increased from 32-seat DC-3s in the late 1950s to 120-seat 727-100s in the mid-1960s and 178-seat 727-200s in the late 1960s. The high demand produced load factors that, in the summer months, consistently reached 90 percent or more. The two major airports, Tokyo's Haneda and Osaka's Itami, were completely saturated and improvement plans for additional airport capacity, either by extension or by new airport construction, were many years' distant prospects. To buy larger aircraft was the only feasible solution.

After intensive competition for the selection of a wide-bodied tri-jet for the trunk routes, All Nippon Airways announced its selection of the Lockheed L-1011 TriStar on 30 October 1972. The details of the order were not precisely revealed at the time, but were confirmed on 11 January 1973 to be for six aircraft, with an option on fifteen more. There were strong rumours that political interests had influenced the decision, and that ANA's arm had been twisted, either willingly or reluctantly – this will never be known.

499

Until a few weeks before the announcement, the choice had apparently been made in favour of McDonnell Douglas's DC-10. Six aircraft were on the production line at the Douglas plant in Long Beach, and four of these were advanced enough to the stage where no changes to optional systems could be made. A letter of intent is believed to have been lodged with Douglas by the Mitsui Bank, acting on All Nippon's behalf. Then, in June, both Lockheed and Douglas were requested to demonstrate their products. A TriStar complied on 23 June, and a DC-10 on 26 June. This was perplexing for Douglas, whose engineers from the product support department had been going to work each day at All Nippon's maintenance base at Haneda in preparation for the DC-10's introduction. Then one day in September, they were suddenly refused admission. Something was clearly strange about this *volte face* by All Nippon.

The political influence could have stemmed from a top-level meeting in Honolulu, not long before the startling decision, between Japanese Prime Minister Tanaka and US President Nixon, accompanied by Henry Kissinger. Lockheed, one of the biggest US defence contractors, needed to cover a $250 million bank loan that had been guaranteed by the US Treasury; and it desperately needed orders in an international wide-bodied tri-jet competition that it was losing. The US Government may well have been trying to protect its loan. Certainly, ANA's quoted reasons for its choice: better safety, passenger appeal, maintenance system, noise level, and other trivial elements: these were not convincing.

While Douglas swallowed the blow, Lockheed's Palmdale plant went ahead and was able to start delivery of the Rolls-Royce-powered TriStars early in 1974. The 326-seat airliner made its Japanese scheduled service debut on 10 March 1974, on the medium-range route from Tokyo to Okinawa, and on 1 April was deployed on the trunk routes to Sapporo and Fukuoka. It subsequently became the familiar flagship at all Japan's big cities, and even to others. As early as 20 July, the TriStar went on to the Tokyo—Kagoshima route. Kagoshima had received its first service in July 1957 with an eight-seat de Havilland Dove; and this was only from Osaka. That within less than two decades the direct route from Tokyo justified a wide-bodied 326-seat aircraft is a vivid illustration of All Nippon's explosive growth and the way in which it affected the lives of Japanese people everywhere.

The Lockheed TriStar was a good aircraft. Except in the matter of long range, in which the DC-10 was superior, there was little to choose between the two rivals, judged by ANA's own stated criteria. But the satisfaction that, technically, its choice was justified, was marred when, in 1976, more rumours started. These culminated in the public – and widely publicized – revelation on 4 February 1976 that the whole affair had been the result of corruption on an enormous scale, bribery no less.

The repercussions were staggering. A prominent Japanese businessman, acting as an intermediary betwen all the subversive parties involved, committed suicide – not by the traditional hara kiri; he jumped off a high building. The prime minister of Japan, Kakuei Tanaka, was actually arrested on 27 July 1976, and of course resigned. The chairman of Lockheed, Carl Kochian, revealed the sordid details, at least most of them, before the US Securities and Exchange Commission. The entire affair was investigated by the Multi-National Enterprise Committee of the US Senate. Even such illustrious figures as Prince Bernhard of the Netherlands were involved in a global scandal of which ANA's selection was only a part.

But the die was cast. All Nippon Airways emerged from the investigations comparatively unharmed, and the accusatory fingers surprisingly did not point too sternly at the airline itself. With a whole fleet of TriStars working hard since 1974, there was no going back. In any case, there were more important issues at stake.

The Turning Point

The course of Japanese commercial aviation, like the Hand of God, often moves in mysterious ways. The way in which All Nippon Airways eventually achieved its foothold in the international door was as extraordinary as it was protracted over a period of more than a quarter of a century. The movement started as early as 1959, and curiously not in the passenger business, but what some optimists used to call the Sleeping Giant of air transport. The sleeper often turned over and grunted now and again, but never quite awoke. But in All Nippon's case, this sleeper, the air freight business, was the smouldering ember that, in the fullness of time, was to burst into flame.

Japan Air Lines had given thought to the idea of a separate air cargo airline back in 1959, only a year after All Nippon Airways was born from the merger of two tiny companies. It had held discussions with some of the biggest shipping lines of Japan, including Mitsui-OSK, Nihon Yusen Kaisha (NYK), and the Osaka Shosen. These became involved in 1964, under government pressure, in one of the mightiest merger movements in history. Eighty-eight shipping companies, owning 658 ships, aggregating almost ten million deadweight tons, were amalgamated into six groups. Of these, Mitsui-OSK and Nihon Yusen emerged as the second and third largest shippers in the world, ranking only just below the British P & O Line.

All Nippon Airways did not get into this air cargo picture until 1970, when it too became associated with some shipping lines. These were not quite as big as the JAL-affiliated giants, but they were big enough. Kawasaki was fifth and the Yamashita-Shinnihon was tenth-ranked in the world. Also, a leading trucking company, Nihon Tuun, was in the ANA group that began to study the idea of an air cargo company.

In 1971 the Mitsui-NYK group submitted a plan to the Ministry of Transport. By this time Japan Air Lines had apparently lost interest, pursuing its own plans, and had withdrawn from that group. The next year, ANA's group agreed to establish a company provisionally named Japan International Cargo Transport; and the year after that, the Mitsui-NYK re-submitted its revised proposals. Once again, in an annual alternating march through the Ministry's revolving door, ANA's consortium of air, sea and land freighting interests, tried again, in 1974. Perhaps the Ministry lent a hand in knocking a few heads together. For, after a few more years, the next approach was made, on 29 June 1978, by a merged group of both contenders. All Nippon Airways found itself in elevated company; in Mitsui, Nihon Yusen, Kawasaki and Yamashita, it was in partnership with four of the largest shipping companies in the world. On 21 September of that year, showing that it meant business, the group founded Nippon Air Cargo Lines, and on 16 November, applied for a licence to operate scheduled air cargo services.

Meanwhile, All Nippon Airways' flourishing charter business was becoming too flourishing for Japan Air Lines' peace of mind. There were times when ANA aircraft were seen more frequently at some airports in southeast Asia than were those of JAL. The latter may have drawn the attention of the Minister of Transport to the original wording of the Air Transport Policy Committee of 1970 which gave ANA permission for 'short-range international' routes. In the event, the Minister ordained, in June 1979, that this could be defined as those within the range of a

From small beginnings ANA grew to become a major airline numbering Boeing 747s in its fleet. (*Boeing*)

Boeing 727. This immediately put Singapore, Jakarta and Bangkok out of range, and even Hong Kong, 2,000 miles from Tokyo, was a little marginal with a full load and a strong headwind. ANA was banned from these points for two years, no doubt to the benefit of Japan Air Lines' load factors, but with a change at the Ministry, order was restored in April 1981; and a year later the Japan—USA air agreement opened up Guam and Saipan to ANA charter flights.

The tide was now flowing strongly in the direction of All Nippon Airways, both commercially, where it was operating with smooth efficiency, and politically, where it was winning friends. In Japan there exists a very powerful group called the Keidandren, a Confederation of Economic Associations, consisting of representatives at the high levels of shipping companies, bankers and other pillars of Japanese industry. It is a kind of industrial freemasonry, conducted from the top floors of some of the richest and most powerful corporations on earth. And the Keidandren appears to have backed All Nippon's case for a better place in the sun.

Early in 1984 Nippon Air Cargo Lines changed its name to the shorter Nippon Cargo Airlines (NCA) and displayed its intentions by applying for a licence to operate to the United States, and backed this by ordering two Boeing 747 -200F freighters, each capable of flying loads of up to 100 tons nonstop from Tokyo to San Francisco. Then new problems arose, as the United States, pursuing a policy of deregulation for the airlines, ostensibly an 'Open Skies' approach, suddenly found itself confronted with some strong lobbying pressure from its own airlines, particularly the Flying Tiger Line, one of whose board members was ex-president Gerald Ford.

The case was fraught with complications, from both sides. The Japanese had felt for many years that the US had been obstructionist in allowing only one Japanese airline to operate to the USA, while the Americans had several operating into Japan. On the shipping side, the flow of traffic was highly directional – 2:1 eastbound in volume, 2:1 westbound in value; but the shipping lanes were dominated by Japanese vessels, including specialized ships that were designed to carry nothing else except motor cars. The Americans were also concerned about the ownership of NCA. The shipping comapnies controlled 51 percent of the shares, 33 banks had 16 percent, two large insurance companies held 11 percent. Interestingly, All Nippon only held 10 percent. But to American eyes, this looked suspiciously like Japan Incorporated, dba (doing business as) Nippon Cargo Airlines.

In spite of vigorous representations by Flying Tiger and other protective interests, but with other pressures from airlines such as Delta, that wished to take advantage of the more liberal Open Skies air agreements that were being forged worldwide, the affair was finally settled, and an agreement signed on 1 May 1985, exactly one month after NCA had wished to start operations, with All Nippon Airways crews and maintenance. The two Boeing 747 freighters had been parked at Narita and NCA had to write off an estimated $4 million for the delay; but it was able to inaugurate service to San Francisco and New York on 8 May 1985. This was the first time a Japanese airline, other than Japan Air Lines, had ever touched down on the United States mainland. Because of the wave of liberalization that was sweeping around the world, the United States, which had started the whole thing back in 1978, discovered that it could not eat its deregulated cake and have it too. Perhaps the deregulators, who had brought the Airline Deregulation Bill to President Carter for signature on 24 October 1978, had not noticed that NCA had been founded just a month previously. At any rate, Flying Tiger now had one by the tail; and for All Nippon Airways, this was the thin end of a wedge that it proceeded to push further in the door.

Breaking Out

After much haggling, the Japan—US Air Agreement was signed on 30 April 1985 (1 May in the USA). Concessions were made on both sides, in both cases resulting in the liberalization from existing restrictions in a mutually creative manner. The long-term effect of this agreement could be as far-reaching as the historic US—UK agreement of 1946 – the so-called Bermuda Agreement.

One clause of the agreement finally put an end to the squabbling between Flying Tiger and the Japanese, and between Japan Air Lines and the shipping companies. Nippon Cargo Airlines was forthwith permitted to start. Another clause authorized two airlines from each country to fly to the Micronesian Islands, including Guam and Saipan. But these items, though important, were parenthetical compared with the main issues that were resolved.

Effective from 1 April 1986, three new routes to the United States were authorized – these would be termed gateways from the US point of view. These designated cities were Washington, DC, Atlanta and Los Angeles. Further, each country could certificate up to three new airlines to operate across the Pacific Ocean. Already, the USA had United (which had bought Pan American's entire Pacific network and the allocated aircraft for a bargain price), Northwest, Flying Tiger and Continental/Air Micronesia. Now it would add Delta, American, and Federal Express, the highly successful air express package operator which then proceeded to purchase an ailing Flying Tiger. On the Japanese side, Japan Air Lines not only had to give up its fight against Nippon Cargo, but it also had to face a formidable new competitor in All Nippon Airways, the third nomination on the Japanese side.

All Nippon Airways had been going about its business while all this critical negotiation was going on. It had already, in 1974 formed a small airline to take care of some of the feeder services. Nihon Kinkyori Airlines (NKA) provided Twin Otter operations to small communities in Hokkaido, Kyushu and some of the more sparsely-travelled routes. Its main domestic operations were doing well, and the new Boeing 767 had gone into service on 21 June 1983. As for the charter routes, these were going well too.

After founding its ANA World Tours in 1978, it expanded the scope of that segment of its charter activity. Flights were made to Beijing in August and October 1979, from Sendai, Oita and Kagoshima – All Nippon spread its favours widely. Other destinations included Shanghai, Penang, Guam, Saipan, Honolulu and Palau. Not long after the Japan-US Air Agreement, the first charter visited Australia, when a flight linked Nagoya with Perth. On 24 August 1984 ANA recorded its millionth charter passenger – and this was in spite of a decision made on 4 June 1982 concerning flights to US-controlled points. Of an allocation for Japanese airlines of 300 flights to Guam and Saipan, Japan Air Lines received 240 and All Nippon only 60.

But all these developments, the NKA formation, the Boeing 767s, the charter business: successful though they were, paled into insignificance compared with the excitement of entering, at long last, the international scheduled passenger market. It had tried for 25 years, and the turning point of 1978 had been followed by favourable political influences. Undoubtedly, the change of government in October 1982, when Yasukiro Nakasone took over as prime minister, was a great help. The new administration had observed the effects of US air deregulation policy that was spreading all around the world, in such countries as the United Kingdom and Australia; and many politicians abandoned the old conservative policy that favoured the idea of a government-controlled 'chosen instrument'. And the severe US trade deficit with Japan had led to a great deal of embarrassing 'Japan-bashing'. Liberalization of the national airlines on overseas routes was politically a good thing to do.

All Nippon needed no more help after the 1985 Agreement. It was off and running. On 3 March 1986 it opened the first scheduled international route in its history (the one to Okinawa on 23 September 1961 was 'international' only on a temporary basis as a legacy of the Second World War). To the people in Guam and the Japanese visitors, this must have seemed like no big deal. All Nippon charter flights had been regular events for several years, with increasing frequency. For the airline, the route must have been like a trial run, a preparation for the big breakout.

This came as a double event on July 16 and 26, when new routes were opened from Tokyo to Los Angeles and Washington, DC. The first was in parallel with Japan Air Lines and other US carriers that had been operating for many years. The second was an innovation. It was the first capital-to-capital nonstop scheduled flight between Japan and the United States, and a landmark event. Like Japan Air Lines on its flights to New York, which could take 12–14 hours, ANA offered superb comfort and amenities for the arduous journey.

During the next four years, and including the three already mentioned, All Nippon Airways opened twenty new routes, almost all of them flown by 315-seat Boeing 747ERs. The progress clearly indicates the dedication and energy that the airline put into the programme. This was going to make its mark in Montreal, where the IATA statisticians would add an important new name to its listings. All Nippon Airways joined the International Air Transport Association on 1 January 1989.

The current leaders at the helm of ANA have never made any secret about their ambitions, any more than did their predecessors. As recently as 1989, the chairman, Tokuji Wakasa, and the president, Akio Kondo, were saying with one voice 'ANA intends to be a world-class airline.' They were at first concerned that they were unknown in the world's capitals because their airline was seldom seen outside east Asia. They need not have worried on either score.

CHAPTER THIRTY-SEVEN

Japan's Airline-by-Merger

The First Feeder Airlines

To paraphrase a philosophical observation about people, some airlines (like Japan Air Lines) were born great, because they were either state or 'chosen instrument' corporations; some (like All Nippon Airways) became great, because of wise investment, economic and political influences, and perhaps a little luck; while others, like the present-day Japan Air System, seem to have had greatness thrust upon them. In the case of JAS, its corporate structure and operating mandate were established in 1971, with the formation of Toa Domestic Airlines. Yet less than twenty years previously, this airline, now equipped with a hundred aircraft, of which twenty-nine are wide-bodied mainliners, was a collection of a handful of small companies independent from each other, and operating aircraft such as the de Havilland Doves and Herons, Grumman Mallard amphibians, even Beech 18s and single-engined Cessnas and Pipers. Like Topsy, Japan Air System just growed.

When the gates were opened for the start-up of Japanese postwar commercial aviation on 22 May 1951, with the Minister of Transport authorizing the establishment of Japan Air Lines, the smaller companies were not far behind. The spirit of reconstruction through free enterprise was afoot, and with Japan breaking out of its Allied-occupation strait-jacket, many entrepreneurs tried their hands at running small airlines, much in the same way as they might start a small bus company or a taxi hire service.

Of the ancestral components of JAS, first off the mark was Nitto Air Lines (NA) founded on 4 July 1952 in Osaka by Tadashi Fujimoto, a small aviation company, backed by the Sankei newspaper of Osaka. The initial fleet consisted of ten-seat Grumman Mallards and five-seat Grumman Widgeons. These were amphibians and, in December 1954, they began scheduled services from Osaka's Itami Airport to an anchorage at Shirahama, a resort on the shores of the Kii Peninsula, where, like the British going to Brighton and the Californians going to Catalina Island, the city dwellers of Japan's second city sought to escape from the urban bustle for a while. Nitto concentrated on this kind of holiday traffic, extending to points on the Inland Sea in the late 1950s and, in June 1960, extending its first route to Kushimoto and Shima, the latter resort also being connected to Japan's third city, Nagoya.

The second airline of the group that was to be part of a significant merger was Fuji Airlines, founded in Tokyo on 13 September 1952. If Nitto's amphibians were modest, Fuji's beginning was self-effacing. Its initial fleet was two single-engined Cessna 170s. But these were sufficient for the sightseeing or surveying jobs under contract, which was the kind of aerial work that enabled the first fledgling airlines to gain experience in the air. By the time Fuji opened scheduled service, in March 1958, from Kagoshima to the island of Tanega-Shima – serving it as a resort as well as providing a much-needed amenity for the islanders – it had upgraded (if

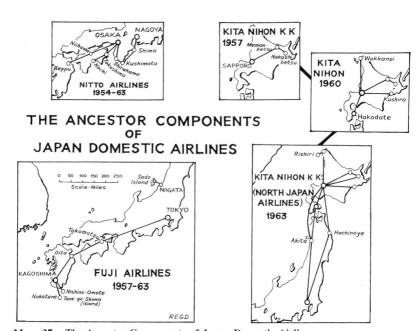

Maps 37a. The Ancestor Components of Japan Domestic Airlines
Just as the merger that created All Nippon Airways had reduced the number of small independent airlines that launched Japan's post-war revival in the 1950s, so did another group work in parallel to increase efficiency by a logical merger. Led by Kita Nihon KK (North Japan Airlines) which had established a presence in Hokkaido and northern Honshu, Japan Domestic Airlines (JDA) was formed by joining up with Nitto Airlines (which operated flying-boats to Shikoku Island, in a distant echo of the pioneer Inouye) and Fuji Airlines, which could forge the link between the other two.

that is the term at such a lowly level of the aircraft strata) its equipment to a four-seat Piper Apache and a seven-seat Beech 18. Enterprisingly, it found another outlet for the use of aircraft for ferrying people to and from offshore islands, this time from Niigata, on the Sea of Japan, to the neighbouring Sado Island, with seventeen-seat de Havilland Herons, starting on 1 August 1959.

Last of the trio that was to merge into Japan Domestic Airlines (JDA) was Kita Nihon Kabushiki Kaisha (KNKK) (North Japan Air Lines), founded in Sapporo on 30 June 1953. This was a company of a slightly different stature to that of Nitto and Fuji. It was founded by the Hokkaido local government and Hokkaido investors, who brought with them a mood of independence that has long been traditional in Japan's big northern island. Thus, it started up like the others with small 'craft, Cessna single-engined machines; but when it began scheduled service from Sapporo to Memanbetsu and Nakashibetsu, in July 1957, it did so with Douglas DC-3s, fitted with 32 seats. In June 1959, it added a new route, from Sapporo to Wakkanai, Japan's northernmost city. These routes in Hokkaido, where the weather can be like that of the Canadian north or the Orkneys and Shetlands during the fierce winters, were operated seasonally for many years.

Pressurized Interlude

When the smaller airlines of Japan got under way during the 1950s, one of the problems was the dearth of aircrew. The death toll of air force and naval pilots during the Second World War had been appalling. Quite apart from those lost in orthodox combat – if that term may be permitted in this context – the suicides by the *kamikaze* pilots, whose mission was to self-destruct by turning themselves into human bombs for their Emperor, amounted to more than 1,500. All the good surviving pilots went to Japan Air Lines or All Nippon. The small airlines were therefore issued, as a rule, with non-scheduled certificates, so that their pilots did not have to possess ATR (Air Transport Rating). They could operate on a more casual basis, with fewer pressures to maintain exacting schedules, on what were called Senior Business Class, and, a little lower down the scale, Business Class flying licences, both of which were more stringent than the Private Licence. It was a good device to help the small airlines.

The time came when this lower echelon of Japan's infant airline industry felt it appropriate that they should move up in the ranks, so to speak, and operate modern aircraft, specifically, pressurized Convair 240s, seventeen of which had been imported by the Sikiya Trading Company. Kita Nihon put them into service on the Sapporo—Hakodate route on 1 August 1960. The route to Hokkaido's second city was less than 100 miles but the surface journey was very circuitous, because of the unusual indentations of the coastline of the Oshima Peninsula. The air traffic, therefore, was good, and of all the smaller airlines of Japan, Kita Nihon seemed to be headed in the right direction. It followed this with a route to Kushiro, to the east of Hokkaido, and then made the bold move with a route to Akita on the Honshu mainland on 1 April 1962. By the summer of 1963 Kita Nihon was providing service to Tokyo, both via Hakodate and Akita, and alternatively via Hachinoye, a coastal city in northeast Honshu.

Possibly encouraged by this northern success, Fuji Airlines tried to match this in the south and started Convair 240 service from Tokyo to Kagoshima via Takamatsu and Oita in July 1963. Nitto Air Lines also began to prepare for Convair 240 operations, from Nagoya and Osaka to Kochi, on Shikoku Island, and beyond. Unfortunately, the whole question of upgrading the role of the small

Fuji Airlines used this Sikorsky S-62 helicopter. The registration was JA9000. (*Sikorsky*)

feeder airlines was suddenly put on hold. In February 1964 a Fuji Airlines Convair crash-landed at Oita, killing 20 people. Meanwhile, Nitto had sustained two relatively minor, but nevertheless disturbing incidents. A de Havilland (Canada) Otter had crashed at Awaji-Oshima in May 1963, killing nine; and a Mallard crash-landed at Osaka, and two people died, also in February 1964. Three creashes by the small airlines, two of them in the same month, set the alarm bells ringing in the Ministry of Transport, and it acted swiftly, clearly believing that the feeder routes of Japan could not be left to develop by themselves, by fragmented units. It took quick action to rationalize the whole domestic airline system.

Japan Domestic Airlines

The regulatory authorities felt that the problem had an obvious solution. There were six small airlines: Fujita, Naka Nihon (*see* Chapter 36), Toa (of which more later), Nitto, Fuji and Kita Nihon. There were also two major carriers: Japan Air Lines and All Nippon Airways. These latter two could take the others under their wing, forming them into two groups and acting as chaperones, advising in technical, commercial and administrative matters. In fact, All Nippon had already set the ball rolling by purchasing Naka Nihon in 1963.

Kita Nihon KK had shown signs of stability and maturity beyond the level of the others, and one of the groups was formed around it. On 15 April 1964 Nitto and Fuji were amalgamated with Kita Nihon to form Japan Domestic Airlines (JDA), with a fleet of nine Convair 240s, drawn from all three (Nitto never put one into service, although one was painted in its colour scheme). Japan Air Lines acted as the caretaker, and no doubt assumed that, in due course JDA would become a subsidiary company.

The objectives of the rationalization worked well in JDA's case. The three components had not competed with each other for routes, so that the fusion of the three small networks was constructive and logical. Steps were taken to strengthen the grid, by an east coast route to the north, via Toyama and Niigata, to link Osaka with Hokkaido without stopping at Tokyo; and several northern Honshu cities were incorporated into the route system. By March 1965, during the period when the explosion of Japanese air passenger traffic as a whole was defying all the airlines to provide enough capacity, JDA was operating some of the frequencies on the trunk routes from Tokyo to Sapporo and from Tokyo to Fukuoka. After unsuccessfully attempting to operate two of Japan Air Lines' Convair 880s in 1965

Japan Domestic Airlines was formed by a merger of Fuji Airlines, North Japan Airlines and Nitto Airlines. It included Boeing 727s in its fleet. (*Boeing*)

(they were subsequently used by JAL for training) Japan Domestic Airlines started sustained jet services on 15 March 1966 with Boeing 727-100s, also ex-JAL.

Taking its plan towards a logical conclusion, the Ministry had, on 20 May 1966, obtained cabinet agreement for the complete merger of JDA with Japan Air Lines, and a similar one of Toa Airways with All Nippon Airways. The results would have been a neat division of the airline spoils into two strong corporations. But things did not work out quite as the bureaucrats had imagined.

The Road to the Isles

Some of the small airlines carved out special niches for themselves, and while they provided a welcome air service for city-dwellers escaping to the serenity of the many tiny islands and islets around Japan's coasts, they also created a social service for the islanders themselves, for whom a journey to the four mainland islands had hitherto been something of an adventure. Even those who lived in the northern half of the Ryukyu Island chain (Nansei-shoto), such as Amami-o-shima, were as far from Kagoshima, southernmost city of Japan, as Osaka is from Tokyo. It was a long boat trip to go shopping at the department stores in the big cities.

In the early 1950s, therefore, the advent of a scheduled air service in the islands was an historic occasion. The arrival of the first Convair 240 of Toa Airways at Kikai-shima on 5 August 1959 is remembered today as an event that changed the lives of the community. Toa – its full name was Toa Kotan Ltd, and was sometimes known as TAW – was founded on 30 November 1953, at Hiroshima, by the Daihatsu car manufacturer. At first, like the other small airlines, it could offer only non-scheduled flights, with de Havilland Doves and Herons, to the nearer Osumi-Shoto group, immediately south of Kagoshima, but among the islanders, Toa became an institution.

Toa had had its troubles too. In February 1962, a Heron had crashed southwest of Hiroshima, just as it extended its service, on 15 February, from Kagoshima to Kumamoto and Kokura (Kitakyushu) in northern Kyushu. Not long afterwards, Toa a signed a letter of intent with All Nippon Airways. This was on 22 August 1962, and seemed to suggest that the two airlines saw eye to eye with the plans of the Ministry of Transport. As if to match words with deeds, Toa strengthened its route network considerably by the transfer of a number of routes, in three instalments, from All Nippon from July 1963 to June 1964. This last included a vital link from Hiroshima to the metropolis of Osaka. For the little Toa, it was like being promoted to the big leagues.

Toa Domestic Airlines

The owners of Toa Airways must have thought that, if they could maintain corporate viability, there was no need to merge with anybody, even a co-operative partner like All Nippon Airways. For however cordial and co-operative, All Nippon Airways would have emerged as the dominant shareholder and firmly in control, simply because of its size. At the time of the discussions in 1964, ANA was already operating Vickers Viscounts and Fokker F.27 Friendships, together with its first Boeing 727 jets. Toa, on the other hand, only had piston-engined Convair-Liners, although YS-11s were on their way. No doubt Toa felt that it would rather be a respectably-sized, if not a big fish, in a small sea, rather than end up as a small, and perhaps forgotten fish in a big sea.

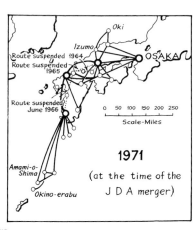

EARLY GROWTH
OF
TOA AIRWAYS

before merger with J D. A
to form TOA DOMESTIC AIRLINES

1962

Kokura
Kumamoto
Kagoshima
Nishi-no-Omote
Nakatane
Kikai-jima
Tokunoshima

1963

Transfer from
All Nippon,
11 Feb 1963
Yonago
Kokura
FUKUOKA
HIROSHIMA
Matsuyama
Oomura
Oita
Hofu
Kochi
Transfer from
All Nippon
16 Oct 1964
Miyazaki
Yaku-jima
REGD

1971
(at the time of the J D A merger)

Oki
Izumo
Route suspended 1964
Route suspended 1965
OSAKA
Route suspended
June 1966
Amami-o-Shima
Okino-erabu

0 50 100 150 200 250
Scale-Miles

Maps 37b. Early Growth of Toa Airways
While, throughout the highly-industrialized areas of Japan, All Nippon Airways and Japan
Domestic Airlines vied for the burgeoning inter-city traffic between the metropolises of Tokyo
and Osaka, and to Kitakyushu/Fukuoka in Kyushu and Sapporo in Hokkaido, one of the postwar start-up airlines pursued a different objective. It specialized in providing service to the
Ryukyu Islands, the chain of island outposts that Japan was still able to retain (although many
years were to pass before Okinawa was returned) along the eastern fringe of the South China
Sea. Unlike its other contemporaries, Toa provided a genuine social service, and its name is
held with affection by the islanders even to this day.

And this is how things turned out. For in a revision of the rationalization policy,
the idea of two big airlines, each with its own feeder-route affiliate, was superseded by a plan to create a third airline, to operate all domestic routes, both trunk
and feeder. In a way, history was repeating itself, for All Nippon Airwyas started
in much the same way in 1958. Now, only thirteen years later, Toa Domestic
Airlines (TDA) was formed by the merger of Toa Airways and Japan Domestic
Airlines on 15 May 1971. The main shareholder was the Tokyo Electric Express
Railway, with 26 percent; Toa held about 11 percent; and Japan Air Lines had
about 9 percent. Other railways and investment groups held the remainder.

The new airline did not start well. On 3 July, only seven weeks after the merger,
a YS-11 crashed on Mt Yokutso near Hakodate. The cause of the crash was judged
to be pilot error – it was an error of navigation, certainly – but, in time-honoured
custom, the new president, Goro Tominaga, resigned, accepting responsibility. A
full fleet of YS-11s is still in service in the 1990s, incidentally, having already
chalked up a quarter-century of continuous and fairly intensive operations.

510

In spite of this setback Toa Domestic soon began to spread its wings. The merging of the two route networks enabled it to introduce several connecting routes between cities large and small; and to add jet equipment to many of the existing ones. In December 1973 the McDonnell Douglas DC-9-41 appeared on a direct service from Tokyo to Kushiro, Hokkaido; and by May 1975 this twin-engined jet was deployed on the trunk routes from Tokyo to Sapporo and to Fukuoka. Though only with five-abreast seating, compared to the six-abreast of the Boeing 727s, the Nines were fitted with what became known as a wide-body interior, with well-designed fittings, especially in the treatment of the overhead racks, that mitigated the tube-like effect of the long fuselage. Toa, incidentally, was the only airline other than the Scandinavian SAS to have the -40 series.

Imitation, perhaps, being the sincerest form of flattery, TDA began to develop its route map in much the same manner as had All Nippon Airways before it. Just as ANA had fashioned its system of 'beam' routes from the big cities along the densely-populated coastal corridor from Tokyo to Kobe and beyond, so now did Toa Domestic during the latter 1970s. With deliveries of the DC-9s adding to the YS-11 fleet, it was able to 'double-track' All Nippon Airways on many growing routes, such as Tokyo—Kagoshima, Kumamoto and Hakodate, and to add what might be termed 'beamlets' to complement ANA's beams.

If there were any doubts about Toa Domestic Airlines' ability to survive in the big leagues of Japan's highly competitive domestic transport world, these should have been dispelled when, in March 1981, it introduced two new aircraft types. And these were not feeder types. The 281-seat Airbus A300 made its debut on the Tokyo—Kagoshima route; while the 163-seat McDonnell Douglas DC-9 Super 80 went on to the Tokyo—Oita and Tokyo—Misawa routes. As if to underline its senior stature, TDA established, on 1 July 1981, its own feeder-route subsidiary, Japan Air Commuter, based at Kagoshima, and charged with operating the small routes to the islands that had been the inspiration for Toa's own heritage. Respecting the needs of the islanders, TDA also ordered new aircraft, with STOL (Short Take Off and Landing) performance, so that the sometimes limited strips on the islands would not be a handicap. The 19-seat Dornier 228-200 entered service on 10 December 1983.

The Third Force

Throughout the 1980s Toa Domestic Airlines prospered. On 30 March 1988, the first McDonnell Douglas DC-10-30 was delivered, and TDA marked the event by changing its names to Japan Air System (JAS), effective on the next day, 1 April. Shortly afterwards, it operated its first international scheduled route, Tokyo–Seoul (Korea), on the same day that All Nippon Airways opened its service as well. Then, on 3 June 1991, in an act of route expansion that should confirm JAS's basis of equality with the other two big airlines, it opened scheduled service from Tokyo to Honolulu, a destination that for many years had been regarded as a paradise for Japanese holiday-makers, and whose desire to flock there in large numbers had at first been inhibited by the memories of Pearl Harbor, but had been dissipated as the bitter memories faded.

Today Japan Air System boasts a fleet of 27 wide-bodied twin-engined Airbuses, of which the latest version, and the largest, with 308 seats, was delivery on 25 April 1991. of the Douglases, it has, in addition to the two DC-10 tri-jets, 48 of the twins, the DC-9s and the MD-80s, and is selling off 12 of the early DC-9-40s. The faithful YS-11 – 25 of them – continue to serve dozens of small communities and smaller cities in Japan.

In March 1981 Toa Domestic Airlines introduced two new types of aircraft, the 163-passenger McDonnell Douglas MD-81 (illustrated) and the 281-passenger Airbus A300B-4.

Toa Domestic's other March 1981 introduction – the Airbus A300B-4. Both the MD-81 and Airbus illustrations are after the airline name change to Japan Air System on 1 April 1988.

JAS's first McDonnell Douglas DC-10-30 was delivered on 30 March 1988.

Almost astonishingly – or not so astonishingly to those who have kept a close watch on the spectacular progress made by the Japanese airline industry as a whole in the 40 years since the postwar reconstruction process began in 1951 – JAS has ordered four Boeing 747-400s (with two more on lease), able to fly across the Pacific Ocean or to Europe nonstop with consummate ease, with a full load of passengers that could number up to more than 400; or if deployed on high-density domestic routes, up to 563 (Japan Air Lines' current layout).

Japan Air System, that only four decades ago, consisted of a motley collection of diminutive companies that were little known, even in Japan, is now threatening

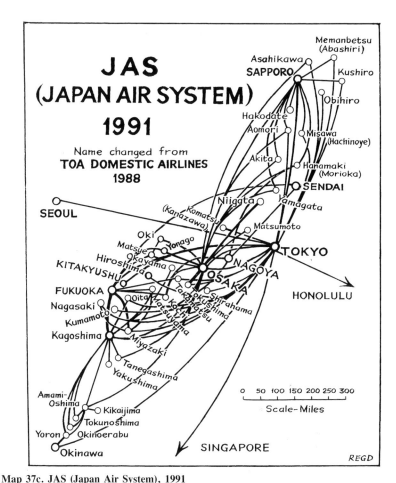

Map 37c. JAS (Japan Air System), 1991
Following along the path taken by many other prominent airline countries, including the
United States, Great Britain, Brazil, and India, the Japanese air transport industry moved
towards an oligopolistic system. While All Nippon Airways and Japan Air Lines competed
vigorously for the dense traffic on the inter-city trunk routes, Toa and Japan Domestic
Airlines (JDA) competed for the secondary and regional traffic. Eventually, they too merged,
to form Toa Domestic Airlines which, in 1988, changed its name to Japan Air System.

to become an international force. Once again, history seems to be repeating itself.
Only a few years ago All Nippon Airways was unknown to most of the world; but
is certainly making its presence known today, as its intercontinental scheduled
route tentacles reach out to the United States, Europe and Australia. At the
moment, Japan Air System is very little known outside Japan. And here, it seems,
is where we came in.

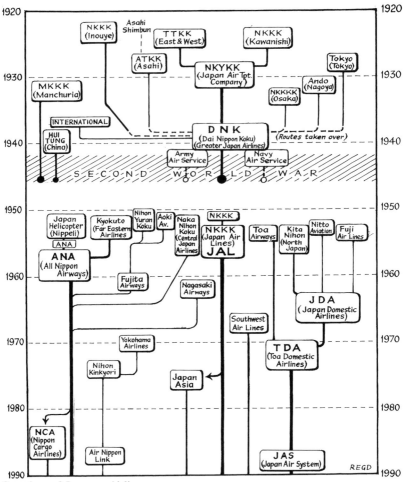

Genealogy of Japanese Airlines

This chart synthesizes the complex relationships and mergers that have characterized the progress of Japanese commercial aviation, both during the inter-war years (and including the wartime expedients from 1941 to 1945) and since the resurgence of Japanese airlines in the early 1950s. Within little more than a decade, ten airlines merged to become only five; and three of these comprise the oligopoly of today that forms one of the most powerful air transport systems in the world.

CHAPTER THIRTY-EIGHT

Airlines of South Korea

A History of Suppression

To some extent, the long history of Korea is parallel to that of Poland, except Korea's plight through the ages has been longer in time, and no less brutal than that of its European counterpart. Both countries have been through an agonizing succession of wars, invasions, occupations and partitions. Both can look back to periods when each was the seat of a powerful nation. Both have re-emerged as nations only in the 20th Century, Poland as a result of the Peace Treaties following the Great War of 1914–18, Korea as the result of the Potsdam Agreement following the Second World War.

Ancient records of Korea go back for 3,000 years and it was united as a kingdom in 668 AD, almost exactly at the time when Alfred the Great was uniting England under Saxon rule. In subsequent centuries, it was under increasing pressure from China, its great neighbour to the west, and came under the latter's sovereignty in 1392, with limited autonomy in later years, but with Chinese patronage. In 1592 Japan invaded Korea with an army of 300,000, and although China came to the rescue, Korea itself was devastated. By 1790 the Japanese were firmly in control, although China did not recognize such rule. But with the declining influence of China under the Manchus, and with the steadily strengthening military and naval power of Japan, Korea's fate was settled in 1905, when the Russian fleet was all but destroyed in the Tsushima Straits (between Korea and Japan) in the Russo-Japanese War.

Japan proceeded to colonize Korea and annexed the country by formal treaty on 1 October 1910. The succeeding years were humiliating for Koreans, who were treated as second class citizens, with no privileges of any kind, and no individual freedom. In 1919 peaceful protests against the degrading social conditions were suppressed ruthlessly and cruelly, and for the next quarter of a century, Korea was simply a vassal state and part of the Japanese empire. Material progress, however, was made, with the establishment of industries and the exploitation of mineral wealth, and railways were constructed. Also, during the inter-war years, as narrated in Chapter 32, the former Japan Air Transport Company established a trunk air route in the territory, as a vital link with its expanding ambitions in Manchuria, its naval base at Dairen, and ultimately the planned conquest of China. Passenger service was opened to Seoul and Dairen on 10 September 1929 with Fokker Super Universals.

Emergence of a Divided Nation

After dominating eastern Asia for a decade, Japan itself was subjected to an humiliation no less devastating than that which it had inflicted on others – and the suffering, as always, as much on innocent people as on the militarists, was as great. Already having seen its capital reduced to an inferno by fire-bombing (the casualties in Tokyo were the worst of any attack), an atomic bomb was dropped on Hiroshima on 6 August and another on Nagasaki on 9 August 1945. Japan surrendered unconditionally on 15 August. Already in July, the Potsdam Accord had recognized the division of Korea into, at first, spheres of influence by occupying powers, dividing the country into two at the 38th parallel of latitude. Russian troops entered Korea on 10 August 1945, American troops entered on 8 September. In May 1948, two separate governments were formed, the Republic of Korea in the south, and the Democratic People's Republic of Korea in the north.

North Korea is slightly larger in area than South Korea, both being about the same size as an average mid-western state in the USA. Two-thirds of the total population, however, live in the south, which is also highly industrialized, as the Korean people seized their opportunities with tremendous energy, once the ending of the World War had given them their freedom. Many Koreans emigrated, especially to the USA, to seek a new life; but most remained, to create a new Korea that was to become a potent force in the world's economy.

The First Airline

The new nation, the Republic of Korea (sometimes abbreviated in the East to ROK) gradually began to organize itself into a modern apparatus of government. This was no easy task, for under various periods of foreign domination, either from Japan or China, it had not enjoyed the notion of independence for several centuries. Nevertheless, things began to take shape after a few years, and as part of the effort to provide good communications, the Ministry of Transport organized Korean National Airlines (KNA) in 1949. Equipped modestly with a fleet of three Stinson Voyagers, this little airline, which had first been launched as a semi-scheduled operation in 1945 by Captain Yong Wook Shinn (who owned 86.5 percent of the stock), provided service to four coastal points that were, at the time, several hours distant from Seoul by train or by road (*see* Map on page 518).

In April 1950 the ubiquitous Douglas C-47/DC-3 replaced the Stinsons but the airline had hardly had time to check the tyres when, on 25 June of that year, 60,000 North Korean troops crossed the 38th parallel in an invasion that was transparently an attempt to over-run the whole of Korea, so that the entire mainland coastline of Asia, from north Vietnam to the Bering Straits, would fall under Communist rule. Acutely conscious of the so-called 'domino theory' of the spread of Communism, the United States, under the aegis of the United Nations, reacted immediately, from its stronghold military bases in occupied Japan. President

Korean National Airlines began operation with three single-engine light aeroplanes but soon replaced them with Douglas DC-3s.

516

Truman ordered troops into Korea on 27 June; air strikes began on 30 June; and that was the end of KNA, for the time being, as the Ministry of Defence immediately commandeered all available aircraft.

In a highly volatile situation, US forces landed at Inchon, the main port of Seoul, on 15 September. They reached the frontier of China, at the Yalu River, having crossed North Korea, on 20 November 1950. The US Supreme Commander of the forces, General MacArthur, threatened to invade China, and was summarily dismissed by Truman for insubordination, as this was against US policy, and certainly against the principles of the United Nations. This was on 11 April 1951, and the world seemed to be on the brink of the Third World War, when 200,000 Chinese troops crossed the Yalu River, southward bound. Thankfully for the whole world, common sense prevailed and a ceasefire was agreed in July; and although the armistice agreement was not signed until 27 July 1953, South Korea began to go back to normal.

Early in 1952 KNA resumed regular commercial services, with DC-3s of course, from Seoul to Pusan, Korea's second city and main port; and to Kunsan and Kwangju, both cities in the southwestern area, and off-line from the main surface trunk artery between Seoul and Pusan via Taejon and Taegu. Later in 1952, under an agreement with Civil Air Transport (CAT) in Taiwan (and which had strong connections with US military and intelligence agencies – *see* Chapter 28), KNA started an international route, with aircraft chartered from Taipei, from Seoul to Iwakuni and Tokyo, to establish the first international air route under the Korean flag.

Soon after the armistice was signed, Korean National Airlines acquired its own Douglas DC-4 four-engined airliner, from the Air Carrier Service Corporation, and planned, ambitiously, to operate a trans-Pacific service to the USA; but this did not materialize – neither the States nor Korea was yet ready for direct liaison by air – and the DC-4 was used regionally, starting service in 1954 to Taipei and Hong Kong. But while Japan was gearing up for its miraculous economic revival that astonished the world in the 1960s and thereafter, Korea was also girding its loins, confident that, though starting with a collection of handicaps: the inexperience of nationhood, the lack of an industrial infrastructure, and the disruption of a civil war; it could follow in Japan's footsteps. And so, KNA bided its time, as the Republic of Korea moved from infancy into adolescence.

In July 1959, having won a US foreign air carrier permit to fly to Seattle, KNA ordered a Lockheed Model 049 Constellation, also from the Air Carrier Service Corporation, but almost simultaneously received a setback when it had to suspend the Hong Kong service because of a dispute with Cathay Pacific Airways, the Hong Kong chosen instrument, in a familiar disagreement involving frequencies, capacities and traffic rights. The connection with the Crown Colony was not resumed until 4 July 1960, but was operated nonstop from Seoul, an indication that South Korea was inching its way towards recognition as a nation in its own right, and not simply an occupied territory and a residual of previous military conflicts.

The Constellation was duly purchased, but KNA appears to have run into political and operational troubles, combining to create a financial crisis, and the airline was close to bankruptcy. The Korean Government considered whether to abandon KNA and start a new airline, completely independent. In this direction, it may have been influenced by the increasing visibility of the Hanjin Transportation Company, headed by Choong Hoon Cho, which had established Air Korea, quite separately from KNA, to operate domestic routes. In the event, the management

KOREAN NATIONAL AIRLINES

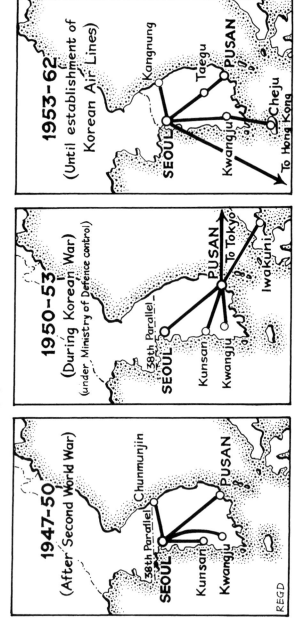

Maps 38a. Korean National Airlines

Korea gained its independence from Japan after the end of the Second World War, but, as with Germany and Austria, was divided into two political spheres of influence, the north under the strong influence of China and the Soviet Union, the south as a free nation, determined to join the ranks of the world's industrial nations. Its first airline was Korean National, based at first in the capital, Seoul, then moving to Pusan, because of the dangers of the Korean War. During the conflict, it provided air service to nearby Japan, before moving back to Seoul when the war was over. The airline ceased operations in 1962, having started a route to Hong Kong which, in the event, was almost still-born.

518

of KNA, and effective control, was transferred from the previous administration, which was part of the bureaucracy, to a new team, late in 1962.

Korean Air Lines Lays the Foundations

Korean Air Lines (KAL) was founded on 3 March 1962, under the provisions of Corporation Law No. 1041, to take over Korean National Airlines and its routes. On 30 April Shin You-hyop was named president and Lee Kak-sun his vice-president. The Government subscribed 60 percent of the 250 million won capital, the remainder was by private investors. On 2 December, equipped with one Douglas DC-4 and two DC-3s, domestic services were resumed from Seoul to the cities of Pusan, Taegu and Kwangju in the south, to Kangnung and Samchok on the east coast, and to the island of Cheju off the southern tip of the mainland, and beginning to become a vacation resort.

On 12 February 1964, Korea finally began to emerge from the piston-engined used aircraft market, and began domestic flights with twin-propeller-turbine Fokker F.27s, and with these same aircraft established international service to Japan shortly thereafter, to Osaka on 12 March, Tokyo on 15 April, and Fukuoka on 1 September. To be able to show the Korean flag at the three main Japanese airports, and to open ticket offices in such prominent commercial cities in the land of a former ruler must have given great satisfaction to the new generation that was throwing off the yoke of serfdom.

As the new Republic began to flex its adolescent muscles, the airline kept pace. On 26 April 1966 it began charter flights in east Asia with a Constellation leased from Flying Tigers, and to gain respectability and status among its peer airlines in the region, it became a member of the Orient Airlines Association (OAA) on 30 September of that year. Additional F.27s (actually FH-227s, from Fairchild) were added in the spring of 1967, and service started to Hong Kong via Taipei. Then, to demonstrate to the airline world that Korea was going to keep up with the oriental Joneses, KAL introduced Douglas DC-9 twin-jets to Osaka on 9 August 1967, and to Hong Kong five days later.

Alas, while the national airline was bravely showing the flag abroad, all was not well back in the Seoul boardroom. Shin You-hyop resigned on 27 September, to be succeeded by Chang Sung-hwan, who had the thankless task of taking over the captaincy of a ship that, if not sinking, was certainly foundering, because of

Korean Air Lines, founded in March 1962, took over KNA and its routes and in 1964 began using Fokker F.27 Friendships on domestic routes.

KAL introduced Douglas DC-9s on services to Osaka on 9 August 1967 and to Hong Kong five days later.

managerial inexperience in the highly demanding airline business. On 18 November all flights to southeast Asia were suspended, and in a general retrenchment, the offices in Taipei and Hong Kong were closed. The DC-9s did, however, continue flying to Japan, and on 25 July 1968, such was the traffic demand between the two capital cities, the Seoul—Tokyo service was increased to six a week, or close to a daily service. Nevertheless, the finances and the reputation of KAL were at a new low point; and, with some recriminations against the idea of government control over an essentially commercial enterprise, the airline was turned over to private hands.

Hanjin Takes Over

There have been many precedents for corporations involved in the transport business, in railways, shipping, even bus lines, to become interested enough in the airline industry to invest in it, even to initiate it. The pioneer airlines of Germany in the 1920s were backed by shipping interests; railways and bus companies developed the internal air routes of the British Isles during the inter-war years; powerful railways in the USA pioneered the main air routes, including the transcontinental lines, before the Air Mail Scandals of 1934 led to legislation that forced them out. Korea had no overseas empire, nor did it have aspirations for any political influence outside its own frontiers; but it did have powerful commercial motives as, in the postwar years (interrupted though they were by the civil war) the energy, ingenuity and commercial acumen of the Korean people began to make itself felt.

Much as the Cunard or P & O shipping lines were almost household names in Britain; Mitsui and Mitsubishi the epitome of big business in Japan; or Krupp and IG Farben representative of heavy industry and chemicals, respectively, in Germany; the Hanjin Group of Korea was a force to be reckoned with. The parent company, Hanjin Transportation, had been founded by Choong Hoon Cho in 1945, and it was to become the largest integrated air-land-sea service organization in Korea, and perhaps the biggest in the whole of east Asia and the Pacific Rim – comparing, perhaps, to the Ansett Group in Australia. In 1965 it had already formed the Korea Airport Service Company, mainly to provide fuelling service to airlines at all Korean airports; and in 1968 it had added to the growing empire the Korean Air Terminal Service, to provide ground handling too. During the same year, the Hanil Development Company was also established, to build large constructions such as hotels, airports, ports, roads and offices, both in Korea and overseas. As previously mentioned, a famous spokesman for the air industry in the USA once declared that 'ninety percent of aviation is on the ground'; in Korea,

Japanese NAMC YS-11s went into service with KAL in 1969.

that ninety percent was one hundred percent Hanjin.

In an historic decision, on 1 March 1969, Korean Air Lines was turned over to the Hanjin Group. Choong Hoon Cho automatically became chairman, and his brother, Choong Kun Cho – known to one and all, genially, as Charlie – was named vice-president. Together, the Cho brothers set about the task of putting KAL's house in order, and they did so in a systematic manner that earned them the respect, sometimes amounting to a grudging awe, from their fellow airline chiefs in the neighbourhood, that is, from Tokyo to Singapore and everywhere in between; and in an amazingly short time, this reputation spread across the oceans as the revitalized airline moved quickly from failure to success.

The Cho brothers had a free hand, as the Government abolished Corporation Law 1041 on 4 August 1969, less than half a year after Hanjin took over. By this time, things had started to happen. On 28 April, the first of three 60-seat Nihon YS-11s went into service and these were soon augmented by two Boeing 720s, the first four-engined jets in Korea. On 2 October these latter re-opened the southeast Asia connection to Taipei and Hong Kong, and extended the route to Saïgon and Bangkok. On 7 October, to support the growing resort business at Cheju, a direct flight linked Osaka with that holiday island, via Pusan. And although the Cho brothers were welcomed to the world of airlines with a high-jacking of a YS-11 to North Korea on 11 December, a direct service from Seoul to Hong Kong began on 22 December. Korean Air Lines was on the move.

While there were one or two minor setbacks in the smooth running of the regional routes, because of temporary disputes with bilateral airline partners, the year 1970 was one of consolidation, with the acquisition of more F.27s and YS-11s, to build a fleet of a dozen aircraft, all with Rolls-Royce Dart propeller-turbines. Then, on 26 April 1971, KAL began to spread its wings, opening a Boeing 707-320C all-cargo service to Los Angeles. This reflected the importance of the growing manufacturing industry in Korea, including the specialization in electronic goods, and a determination to match Japan in its economic miracle, especially in exporting such items as television sets and stereo radio-gramophone-speaker assemblies. The Hanjin Transportation Group and Korean Air Lines were part of the systematic rebirth of national pride through the demonstrated achievements of its hard-working people.

Korean Air Lines (Airlines as one word on this aircraft) used the Boeing 707-320C on both passenger and cargo services. (*Boeing*)

Explosive Growth

The nineteenth of April 1972 was a Red Letter Day for KAL and the Cho brothers, who had picked up an ailing airline by its bootstraps only three years previously. For on that day the Korean flag carrier opened full trans-Pacific passenger service from Seoul to Los Angeles via Tokyo and Honolulu. The equipment was the Boeing 707-320C, and the frequency was twice weekly. Such was the pent-up demand for travel, even though Korean nationals were as yet not allowed to go abroad as tourists, that a year later, after successive increases during 1972, the frequency was up to six a week; and on 16 May 1973 the 707s were replaced by Boeing 747s. The capacity had increased from 340 to 2,240 seats each way per week in only thirteen months. And to consolidate the establishment of the KAL name across this highly competitive air artery, on 10 September 1974, the trans-Pacific all-cargo service, opened in 1971 with 707s, was also replaced by 747Fs. This was the first all-cargo wide-bodied trans-Pacific air service; and that it was inaugurated by the most recent entrant to the route was a strong indication that Korean Air Lines was going to challenge the market leaders such as Pan American, Northwest Airlines and Japan Air Lines. To augment the predominantly Boeing capacity, three McDonnell Douglas DC-8-63s were also leased from the manufacturer, the first entering service on 11 December 1972.

Though less spectacular, progress was also being made nearer home. Korean Air Lines became involved in the intra-east Asian air traffic that was booming even more than the trans-Pacific route. Japan was at the time far and away the dominant industrial and commercial power in an area that was beginning to be called the Pacific

In May 1973 KAL replaced Boeing 707s with Boeing 747s on trans-Pacific services.

GROWTH OF KOREAN AIR LINES
INTERNATIONAL ROUTES

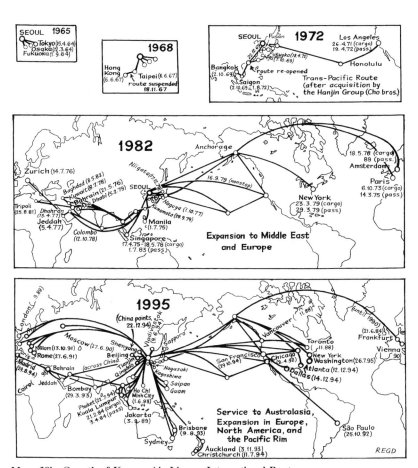

Maps 38b. Growth of Korean Air Lines – International Routes
One of the fastest-growing airlines in the world, Korean Air Lines enjoyed phenomenal success within a period of only two decades, partly by aggressive marketing and competitive fares. After inaugurating the trans-Pacific route in 1972, it never looked back, reaching Europe in 1973, and expanding substantially to points in the Middle East, where it served the needs of many thousands of Korean guest workers. By 1995, Korean reached all the world's continents.

Rim; but another group of emerging nations was beginning to provide a flourishing 'second level' and Korean, in company with Hong Kong and Taiwan especially, and with the Philippines, Thailand, Malaysia, Singapore, and Indonesia not far behind, was a leader of the rivals to Japan. Air traffic was jealously sought after and equally jealously guarded; and many were the disputes, ranging from delicate negotiations to irate squabbles, that characterized the bilateral negotiations.

On 18 April 1972, for example, the Chos were able to include Tokyo as an extension beyond Seoul of its route from southeast Asia, originating in Bangkok, and calling at Hong Kong and Taipei. Carriage of traffic from these latter points to Tokyo or Osaka, for example, was legitimized by the so-called Sixth Freedom rights, that were open to a country that was conveniently situated geographically in between two other countries, which it could serve simply by bringing passengers or freight to the mid-point – in this case Seoul, which was not too far off track – and then, on a different flight, if necessary, carrying the traffic to the onward destination. While legitimate in the strict interpretation of the terms of the Five Freedoms of the Air, the other carriers did not like it, partly because KAL was taking advantage of the situation very aggressively.

Korean had obtained Japanese compliance with the Sixth Freedom routeing by trading rights to serve Pusan and Cheju Island; and it further strengthened its footholds in Japan by signing a contract in July 1972 with Kokusai Kohyo Ltd, a Japanese corporation that operated buses, taxis, hotels and restaurants, thus providing a good infrastructure for development, complementing this by augmenting, at the same time, the short-medium-haul fleet by the lease of three Boeing 727-200s from Japan Air Lines.

In July 1972 KAL started operating Boeing 727s.

The next goal was a service to Europe. The selected destination was Paris; and following a precedent that suggested a careful, but not necessarily cautious approach, the first KAL service was, once again, for cargo only. Operating at the modest frequency of once a week, and jointly with Air France, it flew by the Polar Route, stopping only at Anchorage, starting on 6 October 1973. A year later, on 14 September 1974, Paris was also connected via the traditional southern route, still only for cargo; but on 14 March 1975, another Red Letter Day, full passenger service, using Boeing 707-320Cs, began over the Pole. The journey time was 17 hours, including the Anchorage stop, beating all other routes between Seoul and Paris by eight hours.

Expanding the European base, service to Zürich started on 14 July 1976, but several years were to pass before further inroads were made on that continent; and KAL also had to be content with United States service only to the west coast for a few more years. Happily for the Cho brothers, they were able to ride on the crest of a new wave of traffic that was one of the phenomena of the changing postwar world.

Long Range Commuting

The custom of employing labour from overseas on a large scale was practised during the 19th Century by the large merchant shipping companies, especially those of Great Britain, which employed men from the Indian Sub-continent and neighbouring areas to become part of ships' crews, at the lowest level, performing menial tasks. These lascars, as they were called, spent much of their working lives away from their homes, going wherever the ships took them. Such exploitation of human effort has all but disappeared; but a new variation of the general idea of cutting costs, whether in the manufacturing, mining, or service industries, by importing cheap labour, has continued; and indeed, since the Second World War, revived to such an extent that in many countries the overseas ethnic groups have become a significant element of the population and social structure.

In the more advanced industrial societies of Europe, a wave of such overseas workers gathered momentum in the postwar years, the majority of them descending on Germany, which eagerly welcomed Turks, Jugoslavs and other migrants from the poorer countries of the Mediterranean region to man its car factories, chemical plants and other industrial enterprises. These people could not be called emigrants, at least most of them; for they were hired only on a temporary basis, and even though the period of employment could be several years, they were not absorbed as nationals of the host country. But one characteristic of their way of life was that they returned home at intervals to visit their families; and conversely their families came to visit them. And in the modern postwar world, much of such travel was done by air, to such an extent that it could be classified as a different form of travel, distinct from accepted categories such as business, cultural, leisure, or VFR (Visiting Friends and Relations).

These contracted workers from overseas or across the borders became known as guest workers, even though this was stretching the definition of the word guest. Germany was the prime recipient, to the extent that cynics would claim that the Mercedes cars should be classified as Turkish-built. France too received hundreds of thousands of immigrant workers from Algeria and other former French territories in North Africa; and many of them, like the Indians, Pakistanis and Bengalis in Britain, managed to obtain permanent residential qualifications, and were absorbed into the community.

The essential factors that created this cosmopolitan mélange were, first, the intensive demand for labour from the host country; and second, the ready availability of cheap labour from overseas. The European demand was based on the manufacturing industries. Then, in the 1970s, a new variant on the theme emerged in the Middle East, where the booming oil industry had produced hitherto unimaginable wealth for the oil-producing countries. A substantial percentage of this enormous wealth was poured into welfare programmes, urban development and public works. Small fishing towns – difficult to find on almost any map – along the Persian Gulf coast of the Arabian Peninsula became the centres for commercial enterprise, and began to grow, first into small cities, and then into large ones. Today, several of these Gulf cities each have more than 250,000 inhabitants; Abu Dhabi has 750,000. In Saudi Arabia, the capital city, Riyadh, which in 1945 had about 20,000 people, is now a metropolis with more than 3,000,000 and connected with the port city of Dammam by a railway. The Saudi port of Jeddah, on the Red Sea coast, has grown from the indignity of not even rating an entry in the prewar edition of the *Encyclopaedia Britannica* to a thriving entrepot of 2,500,000 people. In a country where there was only one metalled road (from Jeddah to Mecca) before the war, a network of roads link every community and multi-lane motor-ways connect the main cities.

Such extraordinary statistics are mentioned only to offer some idea of the unprecedented efforts that have been made in the construction business throughout the Middle East and especially in the Arabian Peninsula. To build the cities, the airports, the roads, the infrastructure, the desalinization plants, the hotels, the ports and a myriad of other edifices, technicians came from Europe and America – and some from the Pacific Rim; and to undertake the vast modernization and expansion plans, hundreds of thousands of guest workers poured in from the Orient: from Pakistan, India, Sri Lanka, Malaysia, the Philippines and Korea.

The transport of these armies of workers presented a traffic demand for the airlines which was, in fact, a mixed blessing; for, like the annual Haj, much of the demand was uni-directional, and the problem was how to fill the aircraft on the return loads. But as the deployment of the workers increased to the level where there were entire colonies of overseas residents, the airlines welcomed the new form of traffic base, and overcame the difficulties of scheduling and loading. In the case of Korea, the influx was not confined to unskilled labour. Accompanying Japan on its way towards its own economic miracle, Korea had a surplus of workers who were white-collar as well as blue-collar; technicians who could bid for large construction contracts, administrators of the projects when the bids were successful, and a supply of labourers to do the work. All of these could be carried to the Middle East by air, and Korean Air Lines was happy to oblige, especially as one of its sister companies, the Hanil Development Company, was one of the contractors. The Cho brothers were able to supply the transport as well as the construction troops.

McDonnell Douglas DC-10s began a scheduled service between Korea and Bahrain in May 1976.

Charter flights had begun in the mid-1970s, and the first scheduled service from Korea, on a twice-weekly frequency, started on 21 May 1976, to Bahrain, using McDonnell Douglas DC-10s. The following year, this route was extended to Jeddah on 5 April, and a new direct service to the Saudi Arabian capital, Riyadh, began on 13 April. Hanil was the main contractor for building the magnificent new airport there. Kuwait was added on 8 July 1978 and Abu Dhabi on 5 February 1979; and after three more years, Baghdad became KAL's sixth destination in the Middle East on 8 May 1982. By this time the flow of Korean nationals, at all strata of business activity, from company presidents to concrete pourers, had reached a level of almost a quarter of a million annually, and yielding 23 percent of the airline's revenues.

Korea's economic miracle drew some of its strength and momentum from this heavy involvement with the Middle East. Korean oil tankers of mammoth size vied with the Japanese giants carrying Gulf oil. The Korean workforce contributed to the earnings of Korean families. And KAL and its sister companies reaped the benefits all round in a classic case of eating one's cake and having it too.

The Rocky Road of Success

The traffic boom of the Middle East would have accounted for an even larger segment of the airline's productivity, had the remainder of the network not forged ahead at a healthy clip. To cope with the east Asian regional traffic, KAL ordered a fleet of Airbuses, twin-engined wide-bodied aircraft that could carry up to 260 passengers each. In August 1975 these entered service on the Seoul—Taipei—Hong Kong—Bangkok trunk route, as well as on routes to Japan, and to the newly-opened station in Manila. To meet the ever-increasing demand, much investment was needed, and the capital was doubled in the mid-1970s, to almost 12 billion won by the end of 1976; and then almost doubled again, to 23 billion won by the end of 1978. Direct service from Tsegu, Korea's third city, to Cheju Island began on 1 March 1976; but services to Chinju, Yosu and Kangnung were suspended as new expressways improved surface connections with these smaller cities, and relieved KAL of the need to operate over routes that were seldom profitable because of low traffic volume and short stage length.

A constant stream of Korean Air Line aircraft flew backwards and forwards across the Tsushima Straits, once the scene of the 1905 naval battle between Russia and Japan that had sealed Korea's fate as an oppressed territory of Japan for the next forty years until liberation in 1945. Now a grid pattern of routes, flown proudly by the distinctive light blue KAL airliners, suggested that the two nations were working as one in the furtherance of improving their community of interest. Nagoya appeared on the map on 1 October 1977, and in 1979, Kumamoto and Niigata became the fifth and sixth Japanese cities on KAL's list; Sapporo was added in 1989, and by 1990 Nagasaki and Kagoshima too completed a network from Japan's far north to its far south. And the grid was not concentrated solely on Seoul. Tokyo—Pusan service started on 1 July 1979, and Osaka—Cheju on 28 February 1981.

Important though these regional network additions were, their contribution to Korean Air Lines' growing stature was overshadowed by important additions to the intercontinental route map. On 23 March 1979 a direct cargo service started to New York, augmented by full passenger service six days later; and on 16 September of the same year, the connection with Los Angeles, hitherto either via Honolulu or Anchorage, was supplemented by a direct nonstop service. Ever since its first entry on to the airline scene, KAL had placed as much emphasis on cargo as on passengers, and this was now emphasized by the construction of a new cargo terminal at Los Angeles International Airport. Opened on 3 December 1981, it was the largest on the west coast of North America, and one of the largest on the whole continent.

While these were positive steps, there were some clouds which cast a shadow over Korean's bright horizons. One of these was its growing reputation for offering fares that were below the levels agreed by the International Air Transport Association (IATA), to which most of the leading airlines of the world, and all the leading trans-Pacific operators belonged. This did not worry the Cho brothers too much, even though the criticism sometimes led to questions being asked in high quarters; for the travelling public did not mind. Korean Air Lines on-board service was as good as that of any other; and even if it was not, passengers were always willing to trade off a third choice of vegetables for savings in the price of a ticket that could run into hundreds of dollars. In today's deregulated airline world, the idea of cutting fares in an environment of free competition is regarded not as a sin, as it was in IATA-dominated days, but as a virtue; and KAL was able to weather this storm with equanimity.

Much more serious was its reputation for safety, not because its pilots were less competent, nor that its maintenance was suspect – the base at Seoul's Kimpo International Airport was as good as any other airline's. But, quite simply, KAL flights seemed to have the habit of running into trouble of an improbable nature. On 20 April 1978 a Boeing 707, bound from Paris to Seoul by the polar route via Anchorage, managed to veer off course so violently that instead of heading west, it turned east, then southeast, and, after flying over the headquarters of the Soviet Northern Russian Naval Fleet at Severomorsk, near Murmansk, it was shot down by Sukhoi Su-15 fighters. Making a forced crash-landing at Kem, some 280 miles south of Murmansk, all on board were safe, except for two fatalities and thirteen injuries caused by the shrapnel from the Sukhois' missiles. The airliner was 1,000 miles off course, and the drama of the occasion almost caused a diplomatic incident.

On 19 November 1980 a Boeing 747 crash-landed in fog at Anchorage, and caught fire when the undercarriage collapsed. Thirteen of the flight deck and cabin crew were killed, but the 213 passengers were able to escape down the emergency chutes. KAL's reputation was not shattered by this incident; but it was certainly tarnished, even allowing for the notorious freak weather in Alaska.

Far worse – and this did cause a diplomatic incident – was the loss of Boeing 747 Flight 007, shot down by Sukhois yet again, this time over the Sea of Okhotsk, at the opposite end of the Soviet Union, eleven time zones away, but coincidentally close to the Pacific naval bases. Flight 007 deviated from its normal course on 1 September 1983 to such an extent that it flew over Soviet military and naval installations at Petropavlovsk on the Kamchatka Peninsula, and then headed directly for similarly top-secret establishments at the southern end of Sakhalin Island. It was also heading directly for Vladivostok, headquarters of the Soviet Pacific Fleet. On this occasion, 269 people were killed. Allegations of aerial piracy were muted somewhat by suspicions that to be 365 miles off course in a highly protected danger area was no accident; and that 007 was co-operating in an exercise in international espionage. And the indignation from the United States was further muted when its own navy shot down an Iranair Airbus over the Persian Gulf on 3 July 1988. In both cases there were similarities in the claims and counter-claims: both defending countries claimed that many warnings had previously been made to the victim airliners; and both were denied. And again in both cases the acts of aggression were defended on the grounds that military aeroplanes are often indistinguishable from their civilian variants, even with the most modern detection devices.

Korean's calendar of disasters was not yet ended. On 29 November 1987 a Boeing 707 exploded off the Malayan coast, en route from Baghdad to Seoul, and was almost certainly caused by a bomb, planted by a beautiful lady in Bahrain. On 27 July 1989 a DC-10 landed short of the runway at Tripoli. The casualties were again high, 115 in the 707, 73 in the DC-10. The accidents emphasized only too clearly the narrow margin that always lies between safety and disaster, between serenity and holocaust. Paradoxically, in the midst of the adverse publicity that inevitably accompanies the headlined crashes, Korean Air Lines was, in 1989, commended by the Airbus manufacturer as its leader in despatch reliability, and was similarly honoured by General Electric, the engine manufacturer for the Airbuses and DC-10s, for outstanding reliability. Korean's, in fact, was 99.7 percent, which is commendable by any standards.

World Status

Not all the news in the mid-1980s was bad. Brushing off the adverse publicity of the Flight 007 incident, Korean Air Lines went about its business, consolidating its coverage of southeast Asia by passenger service to Singapore start-up on 1 July 1983, and onward to Kuala Lumpur on 3 April 1984. Service to Frankfurt began on 21 June 1984 and on 30 March 1985, the demand on the New York route had increased to a level that justified a daily nonstop service with Boeing 747SPs.

Traffic between Korea and New York justified a daily nonstop service with Boeing 747SPs.
(*Boeing*)

The year 1985 was marked also by the addition of the new Boeing 747-300, sometimes known as the 747-SUD (Stretched Upper Deck) and the announcement of an order for McDonnell-Douglas MD-82s – also stretched airliners, derived from the original Douglas DC-9, and now able to carry twice as many passengers in its extended fuselage length. But overshadowing these news items was the welcome confirmation on 9 September 1985 that Korean Air Lines had been nominated as the official airline for the 1988 Olympic Games which were to be held in Seoul, and for which lavish preparations and construction was undertaken to ensure their success.

In a less publicized move, on 8 March 1986, KAL started helicopter services from Cheju City to Sogwipo, on the other side of Cheju Island, following a coastal route to avoid the towering Mount Hallasan; and also from Pusan to Kojedo, another city on a nearby offshore island.

Partly in readiness for the Games and partly to keep pace with its burgeoning traffic growth, Korean announced an order for McDonnell Douglas MD-11s – once again a considerably improved and stretched version of the Douglas DC-10 – on 26 February 1987, to put it among the first airlines in the world to put its name down,

One of Korean Air's fleet of McDonnell Douglas MD-82s. The upper half of the fuselage, tail and engine nacelles are light blue. (*McDonnell Douglas*)

and thus give notice to the airline world that it was now among the global leaders of that fraternity. During the same year that Korea hosted the Games, KAL started services to two important countries of the English-speaking world: to London, and to Vancouver and Toronto in Canada. By adding London to Paris and Frankfurt, Korean Air Lines now served the three main air hubs and traffic generators in Europe.

An unprecedented boost to traffic came on New Year's Day in 1989, when, for the first time, restrictions on overseas air travel was lifted for Korean nationals. The pent-up demand was so great that advance bookings interfered with the needs of the business travellers who tended to buy tickets with a short lead time. Quite apart from Korea's own population of 42 million – almost as big and almost as affluent as, say, England, France, or Italy – there were perhaps four million overseas Koreans, of whom two million were in northern China (formerly Manchuria), one million in the United States, almost that number in Japan, and half a million in Uzbekistan. And this did not include the contingents of guest workers in the Middle East. As if to celebrate this new dimension of air travel, KAL joined IATA in the same year; and nothing was said about its fares policy.

The Cho brothers led their airline into the end of the 20th Century as an established world carrier. Amsterdam and Vienna were added as additional points in Europe; service began to Moscow, en route to those points, on 27 June 1990; Bombay became the first Indian city on the KAL map on 29 March 1993; an A300–600 made KAL one of the first foreign airlines to resume service to Ho Chi Minh City on 1 June of that year; and on 3 November, service to Auckland in New Zealand, added another continent to the network.

Korean Air Lines' fleet in 1993 comprised 29 Boeing 747s, 27 Airbuses, 16 Douglases and 16 other aircraft, for a total of 88. Measured in either passengers or passenger-miles, it ranked among the top twenty airlines of the world, and with its fleet of ten 747-200Fs and two A300BFs, was the fifth largest air cargo carrier in the world. All this was achieved in three decades, starting in 1962, with two borrowed aircraft. And having taken over the leadership of the corporation in 1969, the Cho brothers' stewardship over a quarter of a century may be regarded as one of greatest airline success stories in history.

530

In 1993 KAL had 27 Airbuses in its fleet. This one is an A300B-4. (*GIFAS*)

The Strong Breath of Competition

The traffic explosion that followed inevitably after the lifting of travel restrictions on 1 January 1989 no doubt influenced the Korean Government's decision to allow airline competition to replace the policy of a single chosen instrument. This trend had been evident in many countries that had emerged from Third World status, at which time an airline was effectively just an agency to serve national interests, to a stage when growing affluence created a consumer market; and one of the outlets for consumer spending was air travel. Public pressures for competition gradually prevailed over protected monopoly, and there were precedents for the trend all over the world, including east Asia. To keep pace with contemporary thought in this direction in Korea, the Kum Ho Business Group, one of the largest in the country, formed Asiana Airlines in February 1988.

Kum Ho had started as a taxi company in 1946, and later on started a bus line, then moving on to other activities, including aviation. The Chairman of the new airline was Seong-Hwang Park, a former transport minister, and he was able to launch the new venture with a capital of $36.5 million, of which 35 percent was held by the Korean Development Bank.

Services began on 23 December 1988 – just before the travel restrictions were lifted – on a domestic route pattern centred on Seoul and Cheju, as north and south hubs, respectively, with intermediate points. Unlike its competitor, KAL which had started humbly with two well-used aircraft, 26 years previously, Asiana was equipped with six modern Boeing 737-300s, 153-seaters, leased from the GPA group in Ireland. Displaying confidence and strong competitiveness, Asiana ordered five more 737s, of the -400 series, plus an array of letters of intent for more, and for 767s and 747s, within a few months of starting up, on 11 April 1989. Although the demand for seats was fierce, right from the start, the airline adopted a policy of service quality, rather than cheap fares and high density. This was rewarded by high loads and high demand, to the extent that, by April 1990, Asiana had carried three million passengers in only 16 months of operation. It had begun service to four cities in Japan: Tokyo, Nagoya, Sendai and Fukuoka.

While its policy of high service quality was commendable, this was a case of making a virtue out of necessity, as domestic fares within Korea were already so low that cost-cutting by fare war would have been financially disastrous. Even so, Asiana, like most new airlines, did not move into profitability immediately, and clearly, the Kum Ho venture into air transport was a long-term investment. But it

531

served notice that it was not going to tread cautiously in its development programme, and was prepared to challenge the Cho brothers head-on. To do otherwise would have killed the initiative and played into KAL's hands. And so, on 1 September 1990, less than two years after it started, Asiana announced a six-billion dollar order package with Boeing: 27 aircraft, of which nine were 747-400s, ten 767-300s, and eight 737-400s; and these numbers were accompanied by 24 more options.

Early in 1991 the Boeing 767 was flying Asiana's colours into Taipei, Hong Kong, Bangkok and Singapore, to embrace the most important cities of east and southeast Asian commerce, other than those of Korea and Japan. Then, to trump its own route expansion ace, on 15 November 1991, Asiana inaugurated Seoul—Los Angeles nonstop service, with a Boeing 747-400 Combi, fitted out with 279 passenger seats and cargo capacity for 34 tons in the lower deck. Delivery of a second 747 in January permitted an increase of frequency to and from Los Angeles to daily, an astonishing market break-in, even taking into account the potential of the large Korean community in southern California. Flushed with success, Asiana added service to San Francisco and New York, by separate routes, on 9 December of the same year. That a brand-new airline from a foreign country should be so bold as to serve three of the four biggest US air gateways, only three years after its first flight, epitomises the New Deal that has swept the airline world since the United States paved the way with the Airline Deregulation Act of 1978. Asiana's penetration of the US market would have been quite impossible under the late Civil Aeronautics Board rules and practices; and no doubt several of the old Members are turning in their graves.

Asiana rested on its laurels for a while before further route expansion, but on 1 July 1993, it started Boeing 767-300 service to Ho Chi Minh City, only one month after Korean Air Lines, strongly suggesting that, as a nation, Korea will play a big part in the restoration and modernization of that war-torn land.

In the same month, on 20 July, a direct service, with the same aircraft, opened to Honolulu, but Asiana experienced the other side of the coin of airline fortune when, six days later, it sustained its first crash, when a 737 hit a mountainside near Mokpo, on Korea's southern coast. But this was brushed off as in October, the New York service increased to a daily frequency, and on 1 November this new – some would say upstart – airline became the launch customer for a new version of the Boeing 767, the -38E freighter, possibly to celebrate the flight of its 20 millionth passenger, less than five years after it first began.

CHAPTER THIRTY-NINE

North Korean Airline

A Political Offspring

Much in the same way as Germans and Austrians were divided into factions in the aftermath of the Second World War, with the armies of foreign powers influencing political and social thoughts and aspirations in their different ways, so it was with Korea. The Potsdam Agreement had split the Korean nation, which had not known independence for several centuries, into two politically divided parts. The southern half (approximately) was occupied by Allied troops, almost entirely United States, displacing the Japanese colonial rulers; the northern half by Russians and Chinese, who seized the opportunity to indoctrinate their zone with communist thought, word and deed. The Potsdam decision to fix the dividing line at the 38th parallel of latitude was made on 10 August 1945, and for three years an uneasy period of settling in gave way to complete Russian dominance in the north. On 1 May 1948, the Democratic People's Republic of Korea was founded; and its opposition to the government of the southern half of the country was undisguised.

Under Japanese rule, the north had been a source of mineral wealth, with less emphasis on manufacturing and production than either across the border in Manchukuo or in southern Korea. Now the people were subjected to a centralized communist rule that was more harshly imposed than in many other states of Marxist leanings, and such was the discipline that, along with Cuba, North Korea is likely to move into the 21st Century with only the veneer of a market-oriented economy to relieve the strict standardization forced upon a nation by an authoritarian bureaucracy whose definition of democracy, as implied by its name, was contrary to most definitions in most dictionaries.

One of Air Koryo's Antonov An-24s, at Beijing in November 1992. (*R Finlayson*)

Even so, North Korea did what every embryo nation does, almost as soon as it designs its flag: it started an airline. Just as it had done in eastern Europe, the Soviet Union established a joint venture with the North Koreans, and in the early months of 1950, organized SOKAO, which is the acronym in Korean for Soviet-North Korean Airline. Its first mission was to provide regular air links with neighbouring Russian cities, first to Vladivostok, then to Peking and Chita, the latter via Mukden, Harbin, Tsitsihar and Hailar, all cities in Manchuria. It also operated a few domestic routes, mainly to Chongjin, in the northeast, en route to Vladivostok, and all services were operated by the versatile Lisunov Li-2, the Douglas DC-3 built under licence in Tashkent, strikingly similar to the ex-C-47s in use just across the border to the south.

No sooner had SOKAO made its first few flights when hostilities began on the 38th parallel; and the ensuing civil war between North and South Korea, both supported by sympathetic and allied forces, came close to starting a Third World War. Operations were resumed in 1953, with emphasis on the route to Moscow by the air link with Chita, key point on both the railway and the air services across Siberia.

Air Koryo's Ilyushin Il-62M P-881. (*Matthias Winkler*)

North Korea then proceeded to cut itself off from most of the world, and even its relations with its Big Brother were not always harmonious. The self-imposed exile was accompanied by a reign of information silence, compared with which the KGB's files were public domain. Except for the constant irritations of a military nature at the border with South Korea, the North withdrew into its shell. Aeroflot provided technical and material assistance to SOKAO in every way, but the joint venture came to an end in 1954, when the Ministry of Communications took over the airline in its entirety, renaming it UKAMPS – another acronym of unpronounceable derivation, which, in turn, during the 1970s, was replaced by CAAK (parallelling the Chinese model, CAAC) which at least was a straightforward Civil Aviation Administration of Korea, or, in Korean, Choson Minhang.

During the forty years since the truce was signed, the North Korean airline built up its fleet with all the Soviet airliners that were readily available from Moscow: Ilyushin Il-14s for the domestic and local regional routes, to replace the Li-2s; four-engined propeller-turbine powered Ilyushin Il–18s and Il-62 four-engined jets for the long-hauls to Irkutsk and Moscow, started in the 1960s. Antonov An-24s (similar to the Fokker Friendship or F.27) succeeded the Il-14s, and first Tupolev Tu-134s, then Tu-154 tri-jets replaced the Il-18s. And of course the ubiquitous Antonov An-2 provided the bush services into the small strips, mainly in the northeastern area, where none of the other aircraft could

Tupolev Tu-154B-2 P-552 of Air Koryo. (*K. Murai*)

land. This single-engined biplane with non-retractable undercarriage seems an anachronism in the world of modern jets; but it still does its job of carrying the essentials of life to remote communities, in this case, to the Hamgyong-sanmack mountains.

North Korea's withdrawal symptoms seem finally to be easing slightly, and communications with the outside world are slowly being forged. There is even talk about an eventual agreement for trading and cultural relations between North and South; and there is little doubt that any improvement in cross-border traffic would be of inestimable benefit to the North. Recognizing this, and the inevitable onward march of mild capitalism, CAAK changed its name and its image in 1993 to become Air Koryo (Air Korea), even venturing to advertise the natural and cultural beauty of the land. In spite of the intense regimentation of the more than 21 million North Koreans, there is much hope that the concentration on the production of nuclear weapons will give way to something far more mundane and of real everyday use. At least, Air Koryo appears to be showing the way, at a modest level, with once-weekly flights to Bangkok and Khabarovsk.

The good will of the world is waiting to be tapped. While South Korea gained enormous prestige by hosting the 1988 Olympic Games, North Korea once had its hour of glory. In 1966, its football (soccer) team knocked the fancied Italians out

An Ilyushin Il-76 of Air Koryo. (*K Murai*)

535

of the World Cup, and became overnight heroes in the sporting world. Who knows, little Air Koryo may be the vanguard of the lifting of the Bamboo Curtain and help to carry its native land to a new destiny, and recall the memory of a rare and dramatic claim to fame.

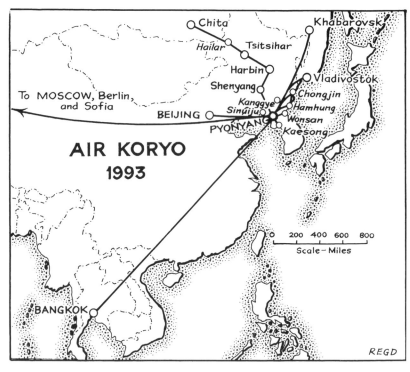

Map 39. Air Koryo 1993
Beginning in 1950 as SOKAO, the acronym for the Soviet-North Korean Airline, it was renamed UKAMPS in 1954, and then CAAK in the 1970s. In 1993, it changed its image from a rather introspective politically-dominated organization to a more outgoing enterprise, and adopting the less ponderous trading name of Air Koryo. Previously operating internationally only to nearby Communist states, it recently stepped out with a service to Bangkok, possibly a harbinger of wider horizons in the future.

536

CHAPTER FORTY

Wings Over the Gobi Desert

The Russian Connection

From time immemorial Mongolia has been regarded as one of the most inaccessible and one of the most inhospitable countries on earth: inaccessible because the formidable Gobi Desert – not a true sandy desert, but arid enough all the same – separated it from China; and inhospitable because the memory of the ravages of the Mongols in the 13th Century has never completely faded. Crossing the Gobi has been, until recent times, an adventure to be undertaken only with great fortitude. Until the 20th Century, there was no road, only caravan routes. Even in the 1920s, to take motor vehicles into Mongolia required a carefully planned expedition. Not until the 1950s, when the Soviet Union and China were forging close political, cultural, and commercial partnerships, was a railway built to connect Ulan Bator (formerly Urga), Mongolia's capital, with Peking.

The Russians had been one of the many nations and peoples of the Eurasian continent to have been victims of brutal conquest, massacre, and pillage, when Genghis Khan's warriors drove westwards, to reach the Donetz River in AD 1221, Moscow in 1239, and Poland and Hungary in 1241. The Mongols had ruled a territory from Korea to the Persian Gulf, even after withdrawing from Europe, until 1609, when the Manchus gained sovereignty, and who ruled Mongolia as part of China until the Republican Revolution of 1911. With Russian support, Mongolia declared its independence on 11 July 1921, after the world settled down after the First Great War, and signed a treaty with the embryonic Soviet Union, still Russia at the time, on 5 November of that year. This formally recognized China's sovereignty but at the same time gave Russia unlimited and unrestricted trading and communication rights, to such an extent that Mongolia was close to becoming a Soviet Republic, even then.

This Mongolian Antonov An-2, with 'Mongol-024' on its fuselage, was photographed in Moscow. (*Colin Ballantine*)

Mongolian Airlines Antonov An-24 5HMAY-3009. The aircraft illustrated in this chapter each have a different form of registration. (*Colin Ballantine*)

This relationship was consolidated in 1924 when the theocratic nominal Mongolian ruler, the so-called Living Buddha, and the last, died; and the Mongolian People's Republic was born. Ever since, it has been a faithful satellite of the Soviet Union, and a Soviet Republic in all but name.

The first air service in Mongolia was thus to be developed not only from political initiative – and the Russians were not backward in this facet of communications – but also because Urga, as it was then called, was relatively close to the trans-Siberian route, only about 450 km (280 miles) away, and moreover along a river route rather than across a desert to the south. Not only that, there was no railway and so an air service seemed to be an obvious solution.

Before the various airlines in the Soviet Union amalgamated to form what became known as Aeroflot, the Russian carrier was Dobrolet, which began to operate on 1 May 1924. Its mission at first was clearly political, to show the flag to the central Asian recruits to the Soviet family, in the newly-created republics of Uzbekistan, Turkmenistan, Tadjikistan, Kazakhstan and Kirghizia, actually still in the process of definition and identification. Then, on 20 July 1926, Dobrolet opened its first international service, not to a neighbouring country in Europe, but to Mongolia.

This unusual distinction was achieved with a small fleet of Junkers-Ju 13s (Russian-built Junkers-F 13s), built in Moscow, and assembled in Verkne Udinsk (now Ulan Ude, and still a big aircraft manufacturing centre). Floatplane versions were produced for operations down the Lena River to Yakutsk; and landplanes forged the link with Urga, via the frontier station of Altan Bulak. At the same time, the Russians sent some small aircraft to Urga, but these were not used for regular air service. The vital connection from the Mongolian capital to the outside world was maintained, however, by Aeroflot, continuously, and the old Junkers veterans gave way to more modern aircraft only after the end of the Second World War, and these replacements were modest enough – Polikarpov general-purpose Po-2 biplanes. But the ever-faithful Lisunov Li-2, the Soviet-built DC-3, came on to the Ulan Ude—Ulan Bator route by the early 1950s.

Mongolian Airlines Tupolev Tu-154 MPR-85644. (*Colin Ballantine*)

Mongolia's Own Airline

While closely affiliated to the Soviet Union, Mongolia did not subscribe to the idea of its being completely identified with Moscow, and the spirit of independence gradually emerged, as the previously mainly nomadic people began to settle into the framework of society more akin to the modern age, with roads replacing the caravan tracks, the construction of a railway across the Gobi Desert to link Ulan Bator with Peking as well as with the Trans-Siberian Railway, and with additional freight rail lines in the far east of the country to exploit mineral deposits. With this departure from its isolation, Mongolia did what all aspiring new nations do: it formed its own airline.

Air Mongol

Still with assistance and material support from Aeroflot, Mongolian Airlines was founded on 7 July 1956. Its full name was Mongolyn Irgeniy Agaaryn Teever (MIAT). Its fleet consisted of 32-seat Ilyushin Il-14s, 12-seat Antonov An-2s and four-seat Yakovlev Yak-12s. The Ilyushins were able to show the Mongolian flag at a foreign airport for the first time, with services to Irkutsk and to Beijing. During the 1960s, a network was built up to link the capital with all the outlying communities of the country. This was no mean accomplishment, as installations were virtually non-existent, and airstrips were little more than cleared areas of grassland. The MIAT aircraft were hardly profit-making commercially-oriented vehicles. They provided a social service to villages in a vast sparsely-populated region where an inhabited area of two thousand people was regarded as a metropolis. Mongolia is twice the size of Texas and three times the size of France, yet it has a population of only 2.3 million, a quarter of whom live in Ulan Bator, the capital.

During the 1970s, Antonov An-24s and An-26s, both high-winged twin-engined propeller-turbine 40-seat feederliners, were introduced, to add a measure of reliability and relative comfort for the domestic travellers. But with limited resources, and with recognizably limited airline objectives, progress was slow. Eventually, a modern jet, a Tupolev Tu-154M was leased from Aeroflot in the late 1980s. A

Mongolian Airlines Mil Mi-8 'Mongolia-20409. Stripes are red and yellow and the nose light blue. (*Colin Ballantine*)

few years later, in 1992, by which time the Soviet Union had ceased to exist, and the channels of trade widened beyond the confines of the communist world that surrounded it, Air Mongol (as MIAT had become known) was able to introduce its first western-built aircraft, a Boeing 727-200, donated by Korean Air Lines, and put into service, twice weekly, on a route to Moscow.

Map 40. Air Mongol
Mongolia is a sparsely-populated land, consisting mainly of scrub plains, mountains, and with large areas that are simply desert. The notorious Gobi Desert, in fact, is almost synonymous with the extremes of arid and waterless wastelands. Except for the important railway line that crosses Mongolia from the Trans-Siberian to Beijing, via the national capital, Ulan Bator (formerly Urga) communications throughout the land are poor, with few roads. Air Mongol, therefore, is an essential part of the economy, with vital connections from Ulan Bator to all parts.

540

Bibliography

(Books and Monographs devoted to Asian air transport.)

Allen, Roy. *SIA: Takeoff to Success.* Singapore: Singapore Airlines, 1990.
Anand, R P, et al. eds. *Recent Developments in Civil Aviation in India.* New Delhi: Lancers Books, 1987.
Anwar, Captain Mustafa. *Civil Aviation in India.* Calcutta: Thacher, Spink & Co, 1953.
Ballantine, Colin, and Pamela Tang. *Chinese Airlines—Airline Colours of China.* Shrewsbury: Airlife, 1995.
Dhekney, Malhar R. *Air Transport in India: Growth and Problems.* Bombay: Vohra & Co, 1953
Directorate of Civil Aviation [later Civil Aviation Department], Government of India. *Report on the Progress of Civil Aviation in India.* Delhi: Manager of Publications, 1930-1964, annual; 1967-68, 1970-71, 1973, 1975-83, annual.
Douglas Aircraft Company, Market Research Department. *Research Reports.* Long Beach, CA.
Tokyo-Osaka Air Corridor, August 1971.
Scenic Routes of East Asia, January 1972.
Airlines of Japan, May 1972.
Japanese Domestic Traffic Forecasts and Aircraft Requirements, June 1972.
Trans-Asian Trunk Air Routes, February 1974.
Airlines of Indonesia, January 1977.
Airlines of Southern Asia, January 1978.
Airlines of East Asia, January 1971 and April 1979.
Eather, Charles E. *Syd's Pirates: A Story of an Airline.* Sydney: Durnmount, 1983.
——*We Flew in Burma: A Story of Flying in Burma, with Cathay Pacific Airways and Union of Burma Airways.* Surfer's Paradise, Queensland: Ching Chic Publishers, 1993.
Hamlin, George W, with photography by Mel Lawrence. *Skyliners 3: Journey to Asia.* Sandpoint, ID: Airways International, 1995.
Hutabarat, Arifin. *To Our Beloved Country: The History of Garuda Indonesia.* Jakarta: Ganesia P R, n.d.
Hutton, Peter and Michael Chua. *Wings Over Singapore: The Story of Singapore Changi Airport.* Singapore: MPH Magazines, 1981.
Inzerilli, Florence, *Air Transport in China.* Paris: Institute of Air Transport, 1989.
Jamall, Enver, *I Remember: A Mosaic of My Memories of Civil Aviation on the Sub-Continent 1939-1981.* Karachi: the author, 1989.
Kohri, Katsu, et al. *The Fifty Years of Japanese Aviation.* Tokyo: Kantosha Co., 1961, two volumes.
Leary, William M Jr. *The Dragon's Wings: The China National Aviation*

Corporation and the Development of Commercial Aviation in China. Athens: University of Georgia Press, 1976.

——Perilous Mission: Civil Air Transport and CIA Covert Operations in Asia. Tuscaloosa: University of Alabama Press, 1984.

Lumholdt, Niels and William Warren. Aviation in Thailand. Hong Kong: Travel Publishing Asia Ltd, 1987.

Nagvi, S K Irtiza. Air Transport in India. Allahabad: Kitab-Mahal, 1950.

Nawab, Abdul W. Economic Development of Indian Air Transport. Delhi: National Publishing House, 1967.

Nunn, R R Report on Civil Aviation. Singapore: Government Printing Office, 1935.

Okuda, Akinobu. Asian Airliners. Tokyo: Ikaros Publications, 1996.

Piggott, Peter. Kai Tak: A History of Aviation in Hong Kong. Hong Kong: Government Publications Centre, 1990.

Porch, Harriett, E. Civil Aviation in Communist China Since 1949. Santa Monica, CA: Rand, December 1968.

Schwieterman, Joseph P. Air Cargo and the Opening of China: New Opportunities for Hong Kong. Hong Kong: Chinese University Press, 1993.

Santos, Enrique B. Philippine Wings. Manila: Philippine Airlines, 1969.

——Trails in Philippine Skies. A History of Aviation in the Philippines from 1909 to 1941. Manila: Philippine Airlines, 1980.

Sen, A. Five Golden Decades of Indian Aviation: Tata's Memorable Years. Bombay: Aeronautical Publications of India, 1978.

Singapore Fly-past: A Pictoral Review of Civil Aviation in Singapore, 1911–1981. Singapore: Department of Civil Aviation, Archives and Local History Department, 1982.

Smith, Sydney Bernard. Air Transport in the Pacific Area. New York: Institute of Pacific Relations, 1942.

The Story of an Airline. Bombay: Air India, 1953.

Tata, J R D. The Story of Indian Air Transport. London: Royal Aeronautical Society, 16th British Commonwealth Lecture, 1960.

Wiethoff, Bodo, Luftverkehr in China, 1928–1949. Wiesbaden, Germany: Otto Harrasowitz, 1975 (in German with English summary).

Willing, Martin J. From Betsy to Boeing: The Aircraft of Cathay Pacific Airways 1946–1988. Hong Kong: Arden Publishing, 1988.

——Betsy: The Story of a DC-3. Hong Kong: the author, 1991.

Young, Edward M. Aerial Nationalism: History of Aviation in Thailand. Washington, DC: Smithsonian Institution Press, 1995.

Young, Gavin. Beyond Lion Rock: The Story of Cathay Pacific. London: Hutchinson, 1988.

List of Maps and Charts

Index

All entries are contained in one single index. References to items other than in the main text are dealt with by suffixes as follows: C = Chart (genealogical), M = Map, P = Photograph, T = Table.

Major airline or aircraft references are shown in bold type. Aircraft are normally listed by manufacturer and type only, and referenced under an operating airline only to draw attention to a special aircraft-related event. This also applies to photographs.

548

552

563